THE ROUGH GUIDE TO

Syria

D0508165

There are more than two hundred Rough Guide titles
covering destinations from Alaska to Zimbabwe
and subjects from Acoustic Guitar to Travel Health

Forthcoming travel guides include
Devon & Cornwall • Malta • Tenerife
Thai Beaches and Islands • US Rockies • Vancouver

Forthcoming reference guides include
Cuban Music • 100 Essential Latin CDs • Personal Computers
Pregnancy & Birth • Trumpet & Trombone

Rough Guides Online
www.roughguides.com

ROUGH GUIDE CREDITS

Text editor: Richard Lim
Series editor: Mark Ellingham
Editorial: Martin Dunford, Jonathan Buckley, Jo
Mead, Kate Berens, Amanda Tomlin, Ann-Marie Shaw,
Paul Gray, Helena Smith, Judith Bamber, Orla Duane,
Olivia Eccleshall, Ruth Blackmore, Geoff Howard, Claire
Saunders, Gavin Thomas, Alexander Mark Rogers, Polly
Thomas, Joe Staines, Andrew Tomičić, Duncan Clark,
Peter Buckley, Sam Thorne, Lucy Ratcliffe, Clifton
Wilkinson, David Glen (UK); Andrew Rosenberg, Mary
Beth Maioli, Stephen Timblin, Yuki Takagaki (US)
Production: Susanne Hillen, Andy Hilliard, Link Hall,
Helen Ostick, Julia Bovis, Michelle Draycott, Katie
Pringle, Robert Evers, Mike Hancock, Zoë Nobes

Cartography: Melissa Baker, Maxine Repath, Ed Wright,
Katie Lloyd-Jones
Picture research: Louise Boulton, Sharon Martins
Online: Kelly Cross, Anja Mutić-Blessing, Jennifer Gold,
Audra Epstein, Suzanne Welles (US)
Finance: John Fisher, Gary Singh, Edward Downey,
Mark Hall, Tim Bill
Marketing & Publicity: Richard Trillo, Niki Smith,
David Wearn, Chloë Roberts, Birgit Hartmann, Claire
Southern (UK); Simon Carloss, David Wechsler, Kathleen
Rushforth (US)
Administration: Tania Hummel, Demelza Dallow, Julie
Sanderson

ACKNOWLEDGEMENTS

Joint thanks from the authors to Paul Gray and Richard
Lim for their patient and thorough editorial work on
the first and second editions of this book respectively, and to Martin Dunford and the editorial staff
at Rough Guides for their support during the writing
and research of both editions.

Thanks from **Andrew** to Peter Cheshire for his front-
line research into Aleppo eateries and the curative
properties of arrack during our 1997 visit to Syria;
to Elaine Galloway and EC pupils on the 1997
school cruise, who saw more of Tartous harbour
than they initially bargained for but enjoyed the trip
to the Crac; and to Joan Smith for contributing the
language section in Contexts.

Tim would like give a thank you to all the numerous
people across Syria whose friendliness and hospitality on a daily basis made researching the book so
much pleasure. Thanks in particular go to Mustafa
and Khalid in Tartous; Nader in Deir Ez-Zur; Mustafa
in Raqqa; Randa, Hani and Ismael in Latakia; and
George in Hafeh.

Shukran jazeelan from the editor to Narrell Leffman
and Rich McHugh for additional research, Derek
Wilde for proofreading, Link Hall for typesetting, Ed
Wright for the maps, and John and Chris for miscel-
laneous historical morsels.

PUBLISHING INFORMATION

This second edition published May 2001 by
Rough Guides Ltd, 62–70 Shorts Gardens,
London WC2H 9AH.
Distributed by the Penguin Group:
Penguin Books Ltd, 27 Wrights Lane, London W8 5TZ
Penguin Putnam, Inc., 375 Hudson Street, NY 10014,
USA
Penguin Books Australia Ltd, 487 Maroondah Highway,
PO Box 257, Ringwood, Victoria 3134, Australia
Penguin Books Canada Ltd, 10 Alcorn Avenue, Toronto,
Ontario, Canada M4V 1E4
Penguin Books (NZ) Ltd, 182–190 Wairau Road,
Auckland 10, New Zealand
Typeset in Linotron Univers and Century Old Style to an
original design by Andrew Oliver.
Printed in England by Clays Ltd, St Ives PLC
Illustrations in Part One and Part Three by Edward Briant.

Illustrations on p.1 & p.297 by Link Hall
© Andrew Beattie and Tim Pepper 2001
No part of this book may be reproduced in any form
without permission from the publisher except for the
quotation of brief passages in reviews.
368pp – Includes index
A catalogue record for this book is available from the
British Library.
ISBN 1-85828-718-9

The publishers and authors have done their best to
ensure the accuracy and currency of all the information
in *The Rough Guide to Syria*, however, they can accept
no responsibility for any loss, injury, or inconvenience
sustained by any traveller as a result of information or
advice contained in the guide.

THE ROUGH GUIDE TO

Syria

written and researched by

Andrew Beattie
and Tim Pepper

with an additional contribution by

Joan Smith

ROUGH
GUIDES

We set out to do something different when the first Rough Guide was published in 1982. Mark Ellingham, just out of university, was travelling in Greece. He brought along the popular guides of the day, but found they were all lacking in some way. They were either strong on ruins and museums but went on for pages without mentioning a beach or taverna. Or they were so conscious of the need to save money that they lost sight of Greece's cultural and historical significance. Also, none of the books told him anything about Greece's contemporary life – its politics, its culture, its people, and how they lived.

So with no job in prospect, Mark decided to write his own guidebook, one which aimed to provide practical information that was second to none, detailing the best beaches and the hottest clubs and restaurants, while also giving hard-hitting accounts of every sight, both famous and obscure, and providing up-to-the-minute information on contemporary culture. It was a guide that encouraged independent travellers to find the best of Greece, and was a great success, getting shortlisted for the Thomas Cook travel guide award, and encouraging Mark, along with three friends, to expand the series.

The Rough Guide list grew rapidly and the letters flooded in, indicating a much broader readership than had been anticipated, but one which uniformly appreciated the Rough Guide mix of practical detail and humour, irreverence and enthusiasm. Things haven't changed. The same four friends who began the series are still the caretakers of the Rough Guide mission today: to provide the most reliable, up-to-date and entertaining information to independent-minded travellers of all ages, on all budgets.

We now publish more than 150 titles and have offices in London and New York. The travel guides are written and researched by a dedicated team of more than 100 authors, based in Britain, Europe, the USA and Australia. We have also created a unique series of phrasebooks to accompany the travel series, along with an acclaimed series of music guides, and a best-selling pocket guide to the Internet and World Wide Web. We also publish comprehensive travel information on our Web site:

www.roughguides.com

HELP US UPDATE

We've gone to a lot of effort to ensure that the second edition of *The Rough Guide to Syria* is accurate and up to date. However, things change – places get "discovered", opening hours are notoriously fickle, restaurants and rooms raise prices or lower standards. If you feel we've got it wrong or left something out, we'd like to know, and if you can remember the address, the price, the time, the phone number, so much the better.

We'll credit all contributions, and send a copy of the next edition (or any other Rough Guide if you prefer) for the best letters. Please mark letters "Rough Guide Syria Update" and send to:

Rough Guides, 62–70 Shorts Gardens, London WC2H 9AH, or Rough Guides, 4th Floor, 345 Hudson St, New York, NY 10014.

Or send email to: mail@roughguides.co.uk

Online updates about this book can be found on Rough Guides' Web site at **www.roughguides.com**

THE AUTHORS

Andrew Beattie read geography at Oxford University, specializing in the Middle East, and has travelled widely throughout Asia from Turkey to Borneo, in addition to visiting Switzerland and Eastern Europe where his other books were co-researched; back home in London he works as a teacher at an independent school, writing and directing plays and indulging in frequent bouts of heavy-duty marking.

Tim Pepper studied history at Oxford University and has contributed to guidebooks to a number of different destinations. When not out travelling the world, writing down his thoughts and talking about his feelings, Tim resides in leafy South Buckinghamshire and devotes the majority of his time to providing practical IT solutions to complex waste-management problems.

READERS' LETTERS

Thanks to all the people who wrote in with comments on the previous edition of this guide and suggestions for this edition, in no particular order:
Edward Clay, David Birkner, Kristina Winther Jacobsen, Bill & Carolyn Thomas, Susan Saxton, Kenneth Morton, Julia M. Crockett, Anders W. Frederiksen, Penny Hitchin, Ingrid van Hout & Karin van der Moot, Brenda & Tony Last, Martin Mann, Graham Clapp, John Garratt & Monica Mackaness, Göran Paulson, Maureen Bangston, Sheila Grove, Shahab Ahmed, Scott Berry, Jennifer Wallace and Rob Cowley.

CONTENTS

Introduction x

● CHAPTER 3: THE ORONTES VALLEY 148–173

● CHAPTER 4: THE COAST AND THE MOUNTAINS 174–209

● CHAPTER 5: ALEPPO AND AROUND 210–250

● CHAPTER 6: THE EUPHRATES VALLEY AND THE NORTHEAST 251–275

● CHAPTER 7: PALMYRA AND THE DESERT 276–295

PART THREE CONTEXTS 297

LIST OF MAPS

MAP SYMBOLS

═══	Railway	ⓘ	Tourist office
═══	Road	✉	Post office
- - - -	Path	@	Internet café
────	Waterway	▲	Peak
─ ─ ─	Chapter division boundary	⌃⌃	Mountains
─ ─ · ─	International borders	✈	Airport
⊞⊞⊞	Steps	★	Bus/taxi stop
◆	Point of interest	◉	Accommodation
🕌	Mosque/madrasa	■	Restaurant
♖	Castle	▬	Building
∴	Ruins	⊞	Church/monastery
⊞	Hospital	‡	Church/monastery (regional maps)
⚖	Souk/market	⁺⁺⁺	Cemetery
⊛	Bank/exchange booth	▨	Park
⬗	Swimming pool	░	Beach

INTRODUCTION

Syria is one of the most enticing destinations for travellers in the Middle East. Formerly home to some of the world's earliest civilizations (the cities of Damascus and Aleppo both claim to be the oldest sites of continuous settlement in the world), the country played a pivotal role in the early history of both Christianity and Islam, and boasts a **rich past** which encompasses the architectural and cultural influence of the Romans, the early Arabs, colonial France and imperial Turkey. That so much history and variety can be crammed into one small country is part of its appeal as a destination; still more so, though, is the character of the Syrian people themselves, who are unfailingly courteous and welcoming to foreign visitors.

Politically, modern Syria is a result of boundary drawing by the old colonial masters of the region, France and Britain. The **French** took over Syria in 1920, occupying the political vacuum left by the end of four hundred years of **Ottoman rule** after World War I, and separated their territory from British-administered Transjordan by drawing a ruler-straight line across the desert. During its 26-year rule France did little for the country, governing it without the consent of the people and treating it largely as a barracks. So it was with an understandable lack of confidence that Syria approached its hard-won **independence**: coup followed coup in the early 1950s, and then came the disastrous political union with Egypt, which broke up into a further period of political instability in the 1960s. From 1971 until 2000 the country was ruled by President **Hafez al-Assad**, the leader of the Syrian wing of the Ba'ath (Arab Socialist) party, and a former air-force commander and defence minister. Assad maintained power with unerring shrewdness, never letting his country lapse into the civil war and anarchy that beset neighbouring Lebanon for much of the 1970s and 1980s, and he left a legacy of political stability to his son **Bashar**, who succeeded him in June 2000 without any obvious show of popular discontent.

Despite its myriad attractions, Syria remains one of the least-visited, and least-familiar, countries in the world. Jammed in between the vastly more popular tourist destina-

TRANSLITERATION OF ARABIC WORDS

There's no standard system of transliterating Arabic into English – world-renowned scholars have broken their heads over the task, yet it remains a complete dog's breakfast. Many sounds in Arabic have no equivalent in English and any attempt to render them in English script is bound to be imprecise – you're certain to come across Arabic words and proper names in this book that don't match transliterations elsewhere. Place names are the biggest sources of confusion, varying from map to map and often from sign to sign, so where possible we've used the transliteration that's most common on the spot; in less clear instances, we've stuck to the most frequent national transliteration. Note that the style of transliteration in Syria is, unsurprisingly, French-influenced – therefore the name of the state-run hotel chain, "Cham", is pronounced "Sham" (deriving from the local name for Damascus, Ash-Sham), and "Tartous" is rendered "Tartoos", not "Tartus". In this book, the definite article "al" and its various elisions have been removed from most place names, except where it's common practice to keep it.

The best way to deal with transliteration is just to practise a little lateral thinking: if you want to go to Deir ez-Zur and you see a sign to Deir Aw Zawr, followed by one to Deir ez-Zor, you know you're heading in the right direction. For reference in situations where there is no transliteration – such as when bus destinations are listed in Arabic script only, or when you can't make your destination understood to a minibus driver – we've listed some commonly encountered Syrian place names in Arabic on p.331.

tions of Turkey, Jordan and Israel, for many years it has been considered an unlikely destination by many travellers, who have been scared off by a combination of perceived safety worries, the yards of red tape that a visit required, and Syria's internal-security-obsessed military government. Through much of the 1980s these fears were justified: Syria was cast as a supporter of international terrorism and a number of Western countries broke off diplomatic relations with it, making it virtually impossible for many nationalities (including Britons and Americans) even to set foot there. But after President Assad voiced support for the Allies during the Gulf War and helped to secure the release of Western hostages in Beirut, things started looking up as far as travellers were concerned. A steadily growing stream of Westerners visited the country in the late 1990s, and the smooth accession to power of Bashar al-Assad, coupled with the new president's determination to build on the positive changes in economic and diplomatic outlook of the country which his father had laid the foundation for during the last years of his rule, suggest that the country's tourist fortunes can only develop further in the early years of the new century.

Most Syrians are **Arabs**, though there is some degree of diversity – in Aleppo, for example, you'll find Armenians and Turks. The greatest concentration of non-Arabs, however, is in the northeast, where **Kurdish** is spoken by those who dare – using the language has long been seen as a sign of dissent, particularly in the light of the Kurdish uprising in neighbouring Turkey. Syrians are divided more on religious than ethnic grounds: although the majority are followers of **Sunni Islam**, there is a large **Christian** minority (itself divided into a number of sects), plus a tiny number of Jews. President Bashar al-Assad himself, like his father, is a follower of the **Alawite** religion, a curious offshoot of Islam followed in the mountains of the northwest, with the **Druze** and the **Shiites** making up the remaining minority groups.

Though Syria is a small country (about twice the size of Scotland, or half the size of California), its history of political isolation and continuing high rate of population growth reduce the amount and effectiveness of international aid, and the country is one of the poorest in the region, with huge internal disparities in the levels of prosperity. The rich, Europeanized urban elite of Aleppo and Damascus, most of whom have got where they are through government connections, live largely separate lives from the majority of the people. In the same cities, however, you'll find the familiar trappings of developing-world poverty – shoe-shine boys out in force, begging, prostitution, and hawking of all kinds – while in the countryside agriculture is carried out using age-old techniques of irrigation, planting and harvesting with a proliferation of carts and working animals, and few modern machines. Many of the **Bedouin**, the traditional tent-dwelling nomads of the Middle East, have been forcibly resettled by the government in towns and cities, but some still roam the desert with their herds of goats and sheep, their lifestyle substantially unchanged for centuries.

Where to go

With most road, rail and air routes into Syria leading to **Damascus**, it's not surprising that virtually all visitors to the country spend at least a couple of days in the capital. Much of its rich historical legacy is smothered by almost defiantly ugly urban highways and half-built office blocks, but there's still plenty to see here, and once you get used to the noise, grime and heat of the place you can't fail to be overwhelmed by the fabulous Islamic monuments and the pungent, hectic souks of the Old City. Retreating to the hills around – as Damascenes do – is easy, and forty minutes' journey by road (or three hours by narrow-gauge train) brings you to the clean, cool air of **Bloudane** and **Zabadani**, mountain resorts in the Anti-Lebanon Range to the west of the city.

Beyond Damascus, Syria's landscape is crammed with a bewildering variety of archeological sites, reflecting the value that was placed on the region by a long list of warlike major powers, from Egyptians and Hittites, through Assyrians, Babylonians, Persians,

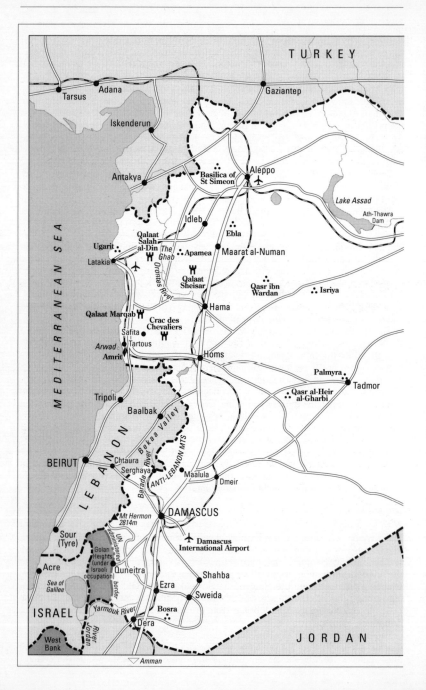

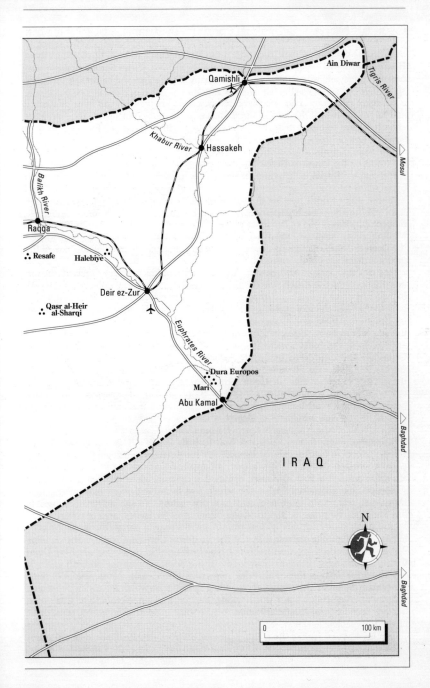

Ain Diwar

Qamishli

Khabur River

Hassakeh

Mosul

Balikh River

Raqqa

Resafe

Halebiye

Deir ez-Zur

Qasr al-Heir
al-Sharqi

Euphrates River

Dura Europos

Mari

Abu Kamal

Baghdad

I R A Q

N

Baghdad

0   100 km

Greeks and Romans, to the medieval Crusaders. The **Hauran**, a tableland of wheat fields and desert scrub between the capital and the Jordanian border, is characterized by outcrops of black volcanic rock which the Romans used to build the trading city of **Bosra**. One of the "big three" archeological sites in Syria, it's an absorbing place, surprisingly intact and with families inhabiting many of the shops and bathhouses that still stand. The centrepiece is the fabulous theatre, its survival guaranteed by conversion to a defensive citadel by Arab occupiers. Many visit Bosra as a day-trip from the capital and forget the rest of the region, but if you've got time on your hands, the Byzantine church at **Ezra** (thought to be the burial place of St George) and the Roman sites near **Sweida**, east of Bosra, would justify a longer foray.

The main highway north from Damascus to Aleppo passes through two very different towns on the **Orontes River**: **Homs** is a busy provincial town that's safe to ignore if you can, but **Hama** is delightful, boasting one of the most attractive town centres in Syria, where you can eat at riverside restaurants and watch the turning *noria*s, restored medieval water wheels now set in manicured gardens. Hama is also the obvious base from which to see nearby **Apamea**, an expansive and fascinating Roman trading settlement which was one of the most westerly caravan halts on the long trek from the Mediterranean coast to China. It's dramatically set on a high desert ridge above the fertile Orontes Valley, though its accessibility from Hama means that it's now one of the most touristed sites in the country.

The two main coastal settlements, **Tartous** and **Latakia**, are very different: the former has an attractive beach-side corniche and an intact medieval quarter, with plenty of evidence of its former occupation by the **Crusaders**, whereas the latter is a larger, busier, wealthier and more cosmopolitan place with some very attractive **beaches** close by. Both towns make good bases for day-trips into the **mountains** that run parallel to the sea, where tiny villages and forested ravines are overlooked by a wealth of lofty ancient sites. Pre-eminent among them is the **Crac des Chevaliers**, built by the Crusaders and considered by T.E. Lawrence to be "the finest medieval castle in the world". Nearby are the attractive mountain resorts of **Mashta al-Helu** and **Safita**, and the ancient Roman temple of **Hosn Suleiman**, the latter located amid rocky, wild mountain scenery. Further north is **Qalaat Salah al-Din**, the spectacular defensive haunt of one of Islam's most famous commanders, and the extensive ruins of the ancient Bronze Age settlement of **Ugarit**, where one of the world's first alphabets was devised, both of which are easily reached from Latakia — as is the very different town of **Qardaha**, where former President Assad's body lies in a huge purpose-built mausoleum. North of Latakia, around **Kassab**, it's the **scenery** which appeals most: long, narrow forested valleys run down from mountain resorts to the sea, and there are attractive beaches at **Ras al-Bassit**, hemmed in right up against the Turkish border.

Aleppo, the second city, is on the whole less hectic and more manageable than Damascus, and proves more appealing to many visitors. It's similarly a storehouse of fine early Islamic remains, and its souks, vaunted as the largest area of covered markets in the Middle East, are no less vibrant, but it's easy to escape the bustle by making for the charming narrow lanes of the medieval Christian quarter. Surrounding Aleppo is the greatest concentration of historical sites in Syria: the so-called **Dead Cities**, Byzantine settlements abandoned to the desert during the seventh century, whose appeal today is their staggering degree of preservation. Most visitors to Syria see **Qalaat Semaan**, the church surrounding the pillar on which the mystic St Simeon sat for forty years, but it's well worth taking time to travel out to other Dead Cities, particularly those around Maarat al-Numan, where some of the best-preserved remains lie in almost complete isolation.

The least-visited part of the country, the northeast, consists of flat semi-arid plains cut through by the green swathe of farmland along the banks of the **Euphrates River**, which has dominated the history and geography of this region. Of the two main riverside towns, **Raqqa** and **Deir ez-Zur**, the latter is much the more appealing, with a laid-back feel, and is the best spot to appreciate the languid river. The major historical sites around here are the remote, largely Roman settlements of **Resafe** and **Halebiye**, and the more ancient strongholds of **Mari** and **Dura Europos**, set on bleak ridges above the Euphrates southeast of Deir. **Qamishli**, the main town in the far northeast, has little to offer travellers except an unusual back-door entry route into Turkey, though it is the jumping-off point for the Arab bridge at **Ain Diwar** on the River Tigris, set amid the most stunning scenery in the whole country.

Last but not least, there's no denying that **Palmyra** is probably Syria's most exciting destination. Although the ancient site has been somewhat blighted by tourism in recent years, the extraordinary spectacles of the 2000-year-old columns and tower-tombs, and of the sun setting over the seventeenth-century Arab castle, will undoubtedly form some of your most vivid memories of Syria. Indeed, only four hours by road from Damascus, it's a good place to see last of all, spending two or three days ambling through the ruins before heading for home; and when travelling to and from Palmyra, you can't fail to be impressed by the **desert** itself – so expansive, empty and harsh as to be almost shocking.

When to go

As Syria receives comparatively few visitors, there is no particular tourist high season, so the weather is the main determinant of when is best to visit the country. With hot, dry summers and wet, cold winters, **spring** and **autumn** are the ideal times to visit; changeable weather characterizes both these seasons, when the days are predominantly warm and sunny (seldom hot), interspersed with grey skies bringing rain or showers.

Summers in Syria can get unbearably hot, particularly in the eastern desert, around Palmyra and Deir ez-Zur; in mid-afternoon in July and August it regularly reaches 40°C here and can climb even higher. However, there's often a stiff breeze to moderate the temperature quite considerably, and the heat is dry rather than humid, which makes things more bearable. Damascus and Aleppo are slightly cooler during these months, but with pollution and the lack of desert breezes, things can get wearying and unpleasant there, too. Summers on the coast and in the mountains are rather different: it's cool and cloudy in the hills, hot and humid on the coast, and it occasionally rains in these areas – usually in the form of short, violent thunderstorms in the early evening or late afternoon. But the majority of the country experiences cloudless skies from June to September, and by early autumn is parched dry.

CLIMATE

	J	F	M	A	M	J	J	A	S	O	N	D
Damascus												
Average minimum temperature (°C)	2	4	6	9	13	16	18	18	16	12	8	4
Average maximum temperature (°C)	12	14	18	24	29	33	36	37	33	27	19	13
Average no. of days with rain	7	6	2	3	1	0	0	0	2	2	5	5
Average monthly rainfall (mm)	43	43	8	13	3	0	0	0	18	10	41	41
	J	**F**	**M**	**A**	**M**	**J**	**J**	**A**	**S**	**O**	**N**	**D**
Aleppo												
Average minimum temperature (°C)	1	3	4	9	13	17	21	21	16	12	7	3
Average maximum temperature (°C)	10	13	18	24	29	34	36	36	33	27	19	12
Average no. of days with rain	11	10	7	4	2	0	0	0	0	4	8	10
Average monthly rainfall (mm)	89	64	38	28	8	3	0	0	0	25	56	84

Winters, on the other hand, can be cold, wet and miserable. From December to February temperatures in Damascus and Aleppo rise little above 10°C, with rain, overcast skies and chilly evenings and nights the norm; very occasionally these cities grind to a halt after heavy snow. In the mountains you can be certain of snow and freezing temperatures during January and February, while biting winds in the east of the country regularly bring night-time temperatures down below zero; winds blowing down from the high mountains of eastern Turkey can even bring a dusty smattering of snow to Palmyra. Tartous and Latakia on the coast can also be dispiritingly cold and wet in midwinter, battered frequently by Mediterranean gales which can occur well into April.

PART ONE

THE

BASICS

GETTING THERE FROM BRITAIN AND IRELAND

The simplest way of getting to Syria from Britain and Ireland is to fly, with two airlines, Syrianair and the British Airways subsidiary British Mediterranean (BMed), operating direct scheduled flights to Syria from London Heathrow. There are no direct flights to Syria from Ireland or from regional cities in the UK, though it's straightforward to catch a connecting flight to an airline hub city in Europe or the Middle East, and catch an onward flight to Syria from there.

It's possible to take in Syria as part of wider travels around the Mediterranean or the Middle East. One way is to pick up an inexpensive **charter flight to** Cyprus, Turkey or Egypt, and continue your journey to Syria by sea or land routes (see p.14); another is to make the relatively straightforward **overland** trip by train or bus across Europe and Turkey (an InterRail ticket can be used right up to the Syrian–Turkish border, within 40km of Aleppo; see p.7). At the other end of the scale, consider hitching up with one of the upmarket **archeological tours** on offer if you find the thought of visiting Syria independently too daunting.

SHOPPING FOR TICKETS

Rather than dealing with the airline direct, it can be slightly cheaper to buy your ticket from a

FLIGHT AGENTS IN BRITAIN

Bridge the World, 47 Chalk Farm Rd, London NW1 8AN (☎020/7911 0900). Specialists in Round-the-World tickets, with good deals aimed at the backpacker market.

Destination Group, 14 Greville Street, London EC1V 8SB (☎020/7400 7000, www.destination -group.com). Good discount fares.

Flightbookers, 177–178 Tottenham Court Rd, London W1P 0LX (☎020/7757 2444, www.ebookers.com). Low fares on an extensive offering of scheduled flights.

London Flight Centre, 131 Earls Court Rd, London SW5 9RH (☎020/7244 6411). Long-established agent dealing in discount flights.

North South Travel, Moulsham Mill Centre, Parkway, Chelmsford, Essex CM2 7PX (☎ & fax 01245/608 291). Friendly, competitive travel agency, offering discounted fares worldwide – profits are used to support projects in the developing world.

Quest Worldwide, 10 Richmond Rd, Kingston, Surrey KT2 5HL (☎020/8547 3322, www.quest-travel.co.uk). Specialists in Round-the-World discount fares.

STA Travel www.statravel.co.uk 86 Old Brompton Rd, London SW7 3LH and branches in many UK cities and on university campuses. Specialists in low-cost flights and tours, with a particular emphasis on students and under-26s.

Trailfinders www.trailfinders.co.uk 42–50 Earls Court Rd, London W8 6FT (☎020/7938 3366); 58 Deansgate, Manchester M3 2FF (☎0161/839 6969) and branches in Birmingham, Bristol and Glasgow. One of the best-informed and most efficient agents for independent travellers.

Travel Bug www.flynow.com 125 Gloucester Rd, London, SW7 4SF (☎020/7835 2000); 597 Cheetham Hill Rd, Manchester M8 5EJ (☎0161/721 4000). Large range of discounted tickets.

Travel Cuts, 295a Regent St, London W1R 7YA (☎020/7255 2082, www.travelcuts.co.uk). Established in Canada in 1974, they specialize in budget, student and youth travel and Round-the-World tickets.

usit CAMPUS ☎0870/240 1010, www.usitcampus. co.uk 52 Grosvenor Gardens, London SW1W 0AG and branches in major UK cities and on university campuses. Student/youth travel specialists.

AIRLINES IN BRITAIN

Air France ☎0845/084 5111, *www.airfrance.com* Flies daily from London and several British regional cities to Paris, connecting with their four weekly flights to Damascus.

Alitalia ☎0870/544 8259, *www.alitalia.it* Flies daily from Heathrow to Milan, with three onward flights a week to Damascus.

Austrian Airlines ☎0845/601 0948, *www.aua.com* Daily connections from London and Manchester to Vienna, from where they fly five times a week to Damascus and twice a week to Aleppo.

British Mediterranean Airways (BMed) A franchise holder of British Airways (☎0845/773 3377, *www.british-airways.com*), which handles all their booking arrangements. BMed flies five times a week from Heathrow to Damascus, stopping off twice a week in Aleppo en route; BA can arrange connecting flights to London from various regional British cities.

British Midland ☎0870/607 0555, *www.britishmidland.com* Flies from Belfast and Dublin to London Heathrow.

Egyptair ☎020/7734 2395, *www.egyptair.com.eg* Flies from Cairo to Damascus (3 weekly) and to Aleppo (1 weekly); daily connections from London to Cairo.

KLM ☎08705/074 074, *www.klm.com* Numerous flights from British regional cities to Amsterdam, with five weekly services from there to Damascus.

Malev Hungarian Airlines ☎020/7439 0577, *www.malev.hu* or c/o Danube Travel ☎020/7724 7577. Flies from London to Damascus via Budapest three times a week.

Syrianair, 27 Albemarle St, London W1X 3HF (☎020/7493 2851). Three nonstop flights a week from London Heathrow to Damascus.

Turkish Airlines ☎020/7766 9300, *www.thy.com* Flies twice a week from London to Damascus, via Istanbul.

discount flight agency. These firms can be found on the Internet – *www.cheapflights.co.uk* and *www.lastminute.com* among them – and advertise in newspapers such as *The Sunday Times*, the Saturday editions of *The Guardian* and *The Independent*, as well as London's *Time Out* or the *Evening Standard* (see also the boxes on p.3 and p.5). **Student/youth travel specialists** such as usit CAMPUS, usit NOW and STA Travel offer seats sold on to them cheap by European airlines, allowing for travel to Damascus with a change of planes in that airline's European hub. You don't have to be a student to obtain tickets through these agencies, but if you are under 26 or can prove that you are studying full-time, there are likely to be further reductions on top of already discounted fares. Bear in mind that these cheap flights may involve inconvenient departure times, or a long wait (possibly overnight) at the airport where you change planes.

FLIGHTS FROM BRITAIN

Syrianair flies to **Damascus** nonstop from **London Heathrow** three times a week; some of their services use comfortable, modern Airbus A320 aircraft, others rather more elderly Boeing 747s (see their published timetables, available direct from the airline, for specific details). Of the

five weekly **BMed** flights to Damascus from Heathrow, three are nonstop, and the other two make a brief stopover at **Aleppo** en route.

Several other airlines (see the box on p.4) can sell you flights to Damascus from Britain, leaving from London and British regional airports and travelling via their home airport (typically Paris, Amsterdam, Vienna or Istanbul). Standards and prices vary considerably, from upmarket options such as Air France and KLM to cheaper airlines such as Malev Hungarian Airlines and Turkish Airlines.

FARES

Return **fares** on Syrianair are very reasonable, at £300 in low season, rising to £340 in high season (July, Aug & Dec 12–24). Fares on British Mediterranean Airways start from around £450 return to Damascus or Aleppo throughout the year, for a stay of between 6 and 45 days.

Turkish Airlines charges some of the cheapest prices going: a London–Damascus return ticket with them, valid for a stay of between 6 and 35 days, costs £260 in the low season, rising to £310 in August and around Christmas, with the attractive possibility of a stopover for a few days in Istanbul if you don't mind paying an extra £10 or so; tickets on their flights from Manchester to Damascus via Istanbul are available at comparable fares. Slightly more expensive are Malev's

FLIGHT AGENTS IN IRELAND

Aran Travel, 58 Dominick St, Galway (☎091/562 595, fax 564 581, *arantvl@iol.ie*).

CIE Tours International, 35 Abbey St Lower, Dublin 1 (☎01/703 1888).

Co-op Travel Care, 35 Belmont Rd, Belfast 4 (☎028/9047 1717, fax 9047 1339).

Fahy Travel, 3 Bridge St, Galway (☎091/563 055).

Joe Walsh Tours, 69 Upper O'Connell St, Dublin 2 (☎01/872 2555); 8–11 Baggot St, Dublin 2 (☎01/676 3053); 117 St Patrick St, Cork (☎021/277 959). General budget fares agent.

Lee Travel, 24 Princes St, Cork (☎021/277 111).

McCarthy Travel, 56 Patrick St, Cork (☎021/270 127).

Silk Road Travel, 64 South William St, Dublin 2 (☎01/677 1029 or 677 1147). Far Eastern and "exotic" destinations.

Student & Group Travel, First Floor, 71 Dame St, Dublin 2 (☎01/677 7834). Student and group specialists, mostly to Europe.

Thomas Cook, 11 Donegall Place, Belfast (☎028/9055 0232/9055 4455); 118 Grafton St, Dublin 2 (☎01/677 0469). Package holiday and flight agent, with occasional discount offers.

Trailfinders, 4–5 Dawson St, Dublin 2 (☎01/677 7888). Competitive fares out of all Irish airports, as well as deals on hotels, insurance, tours and car rental worldwide.

Travel Machine, 39 Dame Street, Dublin (☎01/679 9020).

usit NOW, Fountain Centre, College St, Belfast BT1 6ET (☎028/9032 4073); 19 Aston Quay, Dublin 2 (☎01/602 1700) and branches in other cities in the Republic. Student and youth specialists for flights and trains.

Williames, 18–20 Howard St, Belfast BT1 6FQ (☎028/9023 0714, fax 9043 9637).

World Travel Centre, 35 Pearse St, Dublin 2 (☎01/671 7155).

---

flights to Damascus, via Budapest, which go for between £280 and £340.

FLIGHTS FROM IRELAND

Two airlines, BA/BMed and Air France, offer frequent, convenient through services on their own aircraft between Ireland and Syria (via London and Paris respectively). From **Belfast**, **Dublin**, **Shannon** or **Cork**, the most convenient arrangement is to buy a through BA/BMed ticket to Aleppo or Damascus via London. However, it's cheaper to fly from any of these starting points to London on a relatively inexpensive airline (such as British Midland) and then change onto a flight to Damascus on Syrianair or Turkish Airlines (though this may involve the inconvenience of an airport transfer within London). From Dublin, it's also worth considering Aer Lingus, who sell through tickets from there to Damascus, on which there is a change of plane and airline in a European hub.

FARES

The **cheapest** way to fly to Syria from Ireland is to buy separate tickets for a flight to London (around £70/IR£100/€125 return) and for an

AIRLINES IN IRELAND

Where no Northern Ireland contact details are provided below, see the Airlines in Britain box for details.

Aer Lingus *www.aerlingus.ie* In the Republic ☎01/705 3333; in Northern Ireland ☎0645/737 747. Through tickets from Ireland to Damascus via a European city, the Damascus leg of the journey being with another European carrier.

Air France *www.airfrance.com* In the Republic ☎01/844 5633. Daily Dublin–Paris flights, with four flights a week from Paris to Damascus.

British Airways *www.britishairways.com* In the Republic ☎1-800/626747; in Northern Ireland

☎0845/773 3377. Daily flights to London Heathrow from Belfast, Dublin, Cork and Shannon, connecting with British Mediterranean's flights to Damascus and Aleppo.

British Midland *www.britishmidland.com* In the Republic ☎01/283 8833; in Northern Ireland ☎0870/607 0555. Flies from Belfast and Dublin to London Heathrow.

onward flight to Damascus on an inexpensive carrier such as Syrianair or Turkish Airlines. There's very little difference costwise among those airlines which can through-ticket you to Damascus: BA/BMed charge about £600/IR£750/€950 for their flights from Ireland to Syria, via London, as do Aer Lingus and Air France, flying out of Dublin.

PACKAGES AND TOURS

A number of British specialist travel companies offer **tours** to Syria, often combined with visits to Jordan or Lebanon; look out for their box advertisements in the travel and classified sections of weekend broadsheets, and see the box on below. Most of these packages comprise visits to Damascus and Aleppo and tours of the main archeological sites, led by experienced British or Syrian academics. Such tours to Syria, however, are expensive compared with similar trips to Jordan or Egypt, and the choice on offer is rather limited. No British tour operators seem to be interested in offering sun-seeking holidays to the Syrian Mediterranean, and there is nothing to suggest that they will in the foreseeable future.

OVERLAND ROUTES

Travelling to Syria **overland** through Europe and Turkey only makes sense if you want to take in a number of other countries en route, but it remains an exciting and unusual option, giving you the opportunity of travelling through cities as diverse

as Brussels and Istanbul. If you're not taking your own vehicle, you can travel by bus or train (or more expensively a combination of both), or you might even want to include a ferry trip in the latter stages of the journey, taking advantage of services between Larnaca in Cyprus and Beirut (see p.15). If you're heading out to Syria overland and intend to fly back, buy your single airline ticket back in Damascus or Aleppo rather than before you set out – they're at least a third cheaper, and all Western airline offices in these cities accept major credit cards.

BY TRAIN

The most obvious **train route** from London to Aleppo is via Brussels, Frankfurt, Vienna, Budapest, Bucharest, Sofia and Istanbul; rail links between Turkey and Syria are discussed on p.14. This suggested itinerary purposely avoids the former Yugoslavia, parts of which at the time of writing are still fairly lawless and unpredictable for foreigners, with travellers reportedly being the frequent victims of robbery or assault. If you're British or Irish, the only visas you'll need for this trip are for Romania and Turkey, and you can buy these at the land frontiers of both countries. Another, longer option would take you through Switzerland to Brindisi on the Italian Adriatic, where you can catch a ferry to Patras in Greece and travel to Istanbul via Athens and Thessaloniki. How long your journey takes obvi-

---

SPECIALIST TOUR OPERATORS IN BRITAIN

Bales Tours, Junction Rd, Dorking, Surrey RH4 3HB (☎01306/885991, *www.balesworldwide.com*). Among their tours to the Middle East is an eleven-day visit to Syria costing £1500.

British Museum Tours, 46 Bloomsbury St, London WC1B 3QQ (☎020/7323 8895, *www.britishmuseumtraveller.co.uk*). Thirteen-day tour of Syria for around £1400.

Cox and King's, St James Court, 45 Buckingham Gate, London SW1E 6AF (☎020/7873 5000, *www.coxandkings.co.uk*). Offers an eight-day tour of Syria with guest lecturers; prices start at £1100.

Dragoman, Camp Green, Debenham, Stowmarket IP14 6LA (☎01728/861133, *www.dragoman.co.uk*). Extended overland journeys in purpose-built expedition vehicles through Asia and Africa; they include Syria as part of trips from the UK to Egypt and India.

Hayes & Jarvis, Hayes House, 152 King St, London W6 0QU (☎0870/898 9890, *www.hayes-jarvis.com*). Offers a combined Syria and Jordan tour with prices starting at £1300.

Jasmin Tours, 53–55 Balham Hill, London SW12 9DR (☎020/8675 8886). A variety of tours on offer including some linked with Lebanon or Jordan; their nine-day tour of Syria costs around £1000.

Martin Randall Travel, 10 Barley Mow Passage, London W4 4PH (☎020/8742 3355, fax 8742 7766, *www.martinrandall.com*). Small-group archeological tours to Syria and other Middle Eastern destinations.

Swan Hellenic Cruises, 77 New Oxford St, London WC1A 1DS (☎020/7800 2200, *www.swanhellenic.co.uk*). Some of their cruises stop off at Tartous and/or Latakia, with tours of the Crac des Chevaliers and/or Palmyra on offer.

TRAIN PASS AGENTS

BRITAIN AND IRELAND
Continental Rail Desk, CIE Tours International, 35 Lower Abbey St, Dublin 1 (☎01/703 1888).
Rail Europe, 179 Piccadilly, London W1V 0BA (☎0870/584 8848, *www.raileurope.co.uk*).
usit CAMPUS, 52 Grosvenor Gardens, London SW1W 0AG (☎0870/240 1010, *www.usitcampus.co.uk*).
usit NOW *www.usitnow.com* Fountain Centre, College St, Belfast BT1 6ET (☎028/9032 4073); 19 Aston Quay, Dublin 2 (☎01/602 1777 or 677 8117).

US AND CANADA
Rail Europe, 226 Westchester Ave, White Plains, NY 10604 (%1-800/438-7245 in USA, ☎1-800/361-7245 in Canada; *www.raileurope.com*).

AUSTRALIA AND NEW ZEALAND
Thomas Cook Rail Direct, Level 8, 130 Pitt St, Sydney 2000 (☎1300/361 941); 96 Anzac Ave, Auckland 1 (☎09/263 7260).

ously depends on how long you want to spend in each place, but count on a week as the absolute minimum – and take at least two weeks if you want to make this option worthwhile.

The cheapest way of doing the journey is to buy an **InterRail** pass, which allows the freedom of unlimited train travel in selected European countries for a month. Residence in Europe for at least the preceding six months is required to purchase an InterRail pass; if you don't have a European passport you may be asked to prove to the issuer that you've fulfilled this requirement. Tickets are sold according to which European rail zones you want to travel in; a one-month ticket which gets you from the English Channel to the Turkish–Syrian border and covers all possible zones costs £229 (for those under under 26) and £309 (for those over 26).

In the UK tickets can be **bought** at main train stations or at travel agencies, or from *www.inter -rail.co.uk* (booking online gets you a £10 reduction). Train **schedules** can be looked up in the *Thomas Cook European Timetable,* published every month and available from booksellers, branches of Thomas Cook and in some UK public libraries.

BY BUS

Travelling to Syria **by bus** is possible from Britain, but it's difficult to see any advantages this has over trains. The journey from London to Aleppo can be done in three stages. National Express Coaches (☎0870/580 8080) can sell you a ticket from London to Bucharest (45hr, £135 one-way, with a change of buses in Frankfurt); from there you need to pick up a service to Istanbul (around 36hr), which may involve another change of buses in Sofia. More imaginative, and inevitably more expensive, options between London and Istanbul might take

you via Prague and/or Budapest. Bus links between Istanbul and Aleppo are discussed on p.14.

BY CAR

To **drive** from the UK to Syria, through Eastern Europe and Turkey, takes at least a week and requires drivers to have a *carnet de passage* to prove ownership of the vehicle, an international driving permit, and registration and insurance ("green card") documents to complement the third-party insurance which must be purchased upon driving into Syria. In addition, drivers are required by law in Turkey (and in many other countries en route) to have with them a fire extinguisher, first-aid kit, two warning triangles and headlamp beam converters. For more information on documentation and insurance, contact your motoring organization (such as the AA or RAC) and your insurance company well before your departure date. Advice on breakdowns is given on p.33.

LIFT SHARING

You are very unlikely to be able to arrange a **lift share** which takes you all the way to Damascus, but arranging a lift to Istanbul or another East European city (from where you can continue to Syria by bus or train) is feasible. As there is currently no agency arranging lift shares in the UK, the best option is to consult the notice-boards of specialist travellers' bookshops or put up your own notice; Nomad Books at 781 Fulham Rd, London SW6 5HA (☎020/7736 4000) has a particularly good notice-board downstairs. The travel magazine *Wanderlust* (*www.wanderlust.co.uk*) has a useful "Connections" page worth consulting for possible lift shares/travel companions.

GETTING THERE FROM THE US AND CANADA

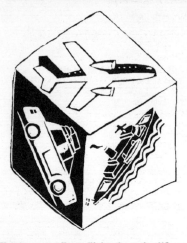

There are no direct flights from the US or Canada to Syria; the US Government currently has an embargo on Syrianair, which might otherwise be your most obvious choice of airline. However, there's no shortage of airlines flying into Syria from North America, with a change of planes in a European city.

Alternatively, flying to **Jordan** or **Turkey** and making your way overland into Syria from there (see p.14–15) can be cheaper than flying into Syria, significantly so in the case of flights to Istanbul. If Syria is just one stop on an extensive itinerary you've planned, you may even want to consider buying a **Round-the-World (RTW)** ticket. For those with a particular interest in archeology, there are a wide range of **specialist tours** to Syria (and surrounding Middle Eastern countries) offered by North American operators, but most of these don't include transatlantic flights in the cost of the package.

SHOPPING FOR TICKETS

Barring special offers, the cheapest of the airlines' published fares is usually an **APEX** ticket, although it carries certain restrictions: you will,

DISCOUNT AGENTS AND CONSOLIDATORS

Air Brokers International, 150 Post St, Suite 620, San Francisco, CA 94108 (☎1-800/883-3273 or 415/397-1383, *www.airbrokers.com*). Consolidator and specialist in RTW tickets.

Council Travel, 205 E 42nd St, New York, NY 10017 (☎1-800/226-8624, *www.counciltravel.com*), and branches in many other US cities. Student/budget travel agency..

High Adventure Travel, 442 Post St, Suite 400, San Francisco, CA 94102 (☎1-800/350-0612 or ☎415/912-5600, *www.airtreks.com*). Their extensive Web site features an interactive database called "Farebuilder" that lets you build your own RTW itinerary.

New Frontiers/Nouvelles Frontières *www.nouvelles-frontiers.com* 12 E 33rd St, New York, NY 10016 (☎1-800/366-6387 or 212/779-0600); 1180 Drummond, Suite 330, Montreal, H3G 2R7 (☎514/871-3060); and other branches in LA, San Francisco and Quebec City. Discount travel firm.

STA Travel *www.sta-travel.com* 10 Downing St, New York, NY 10014 (☎212/627-3111) and branches in many other US cities. Discount travel firm specializing in student/youth fares worldwide; also student IDs, travel insurance, car rental, rail passes, etc.

Travac Tours, 989 6th Ave, 16th Floor, New York NY 10018 (☎1-800/872-8800 or 212/563-3303, *www.thetravelsite.com*). Consolidator.

Travel Avenue, 10 S Riverside Plaza, Suite 1404, Chicago, IL 60606 (☎1-800/333-3335 or ☎312/876-6866, *www.travelavenue.com*). Offers discounts in the form of rebates.

Travel CUTS *www.travelcuts.com* 187 College St, Toronto, ON M5T 1P7 (☎416/979-2406 or in Canada only 1-800/667-2887); with other branches all over Canada. Organization specializing in student fares, IDs and other travel services.

Travelocity *www.travelocity.com* Online consolidator.

UniTravel, 11737 Administration Dr, Suite 120, St Louis, MO 63146 (☎1-800/325-2222 or 314/569-2501, *www.flightsforless.com*). Consolidator.

Worldtek Travel, 111 Water St., New Haven, CT 06511 (☎1-800/243-1723, *www.worldtek.com*). Discount travel agency for worldwide travel.

SPECIALIST TOUR OPERATORS

Note that package-tour prices given below do not include airfares unless otherwise stated.

Abercrombie & Kent (☎1-800/323-7308, www.abercrombiekent.com). They do six-day tours around Syria and thirteen-day Jordan and Syria tours, priced at around US$2600 and US$3400 respectively.

Adventure Center (☎1-800/227-8747, www.adventurecenter.com). Among the tours run by this self-styled "active vacation" specialist are a nine-day "On the Road to Damascus" tour (around US$650) and a sixteen-day tour of Lebanon and Syria (US$1200).

Adventures Abroad (☎1-800/665-3998, www.adventures-abroad.com). A range of tours offering Syria on its own (two weeks from US$2900) or combined with other Middle Eastern destinations.

Archeological Tours (☎212/986-3054). Their sixteen-day tour of Jordan and Syria (with an optional extension to Israel) is led by an archeology professor and local guides. From US$4450 including airfare.

Cox & Kings (☎1-800/999-1758, www.coxandkingsusa.com). Their "Ancient

Civilizations" tour of Syria and Jordan lasts fifteen days and costs around US$3800.

Himalayan Travel (☎1-800/225-2380, www.gorp.com/himtravel). Two packages to Syria: "Syrian Highlights" (nine days from US$1000) and "Journey through Jordan and Syria" (fifteen days from US$1700).

Saga Holidays (☎1-800/343-0273, www.sagaholidays.com). Specializes in group travel for seniors. Their "Syria – The Undiscovered Land" tours, lasting ten days, cost from US$2500 including air fare (US$2900 with an optional three-day Jordan extension).

Wilderness Travel (☎1-800/368-2794, www.wildernesstravel.com). Offers a sixteen-day cultural and archeological adventure tour to Syria and Jordan.

Worldwide Quest Adventures (☎1-800/387-1483, www.worldwidequest.com). They operate a seventeen-day tour to Jordan and Syria (US$2800).

most likely, have to book – and pay – up to 21 days before departure, spend at least seven days abroad (maximum stay three months), and you tend to get penalized if you change your schedule. You can normally cut costs further by going through a specialist flight agent – either a **consolidator**, who buys up blocks of tickets from the airlines and sells them at a discount, or a **discount agent**; the latter, in addition to dealing with discounted flights, may also offer special student and youth fares and a range of other travel-related services such as travel insurance, car rentals, tours and the like. Some agents offer **customized RTW** tickets, which is useful if you want to reach Syria directly, as Damascus isn't on the itineraries of standard RTW trips. If you travel a lot, **discount travel clubs** are yet another option – the annual membership fee may be worth it for benefits like cut-price air tickets and car rental.

Don't automatically assume that tickets purchased through a travel specialist will be cheapest – once you get a quote, check with the airlines and you may turn up an even better deal. Be advised also that the pool of travel companies is swimming with sharks – exercise caution

and never deal with a company that demands cash upfront or refuses to accept payment by credit card.

ROUTES AND FARES

Most airlines which serve Syria fly into **Damascus** only, though British Mediterranean (BMed for short, a subsidiary of British Airways) and Austrian Airways into **Aleppo** also. Flying from the US and Canada, you need to change planes in a Middle Eastern or (more likely) a European city – typically London, Paris, Milan or Vienna – en route to Syria.

Fares vary significantly depending on what time of year you want to fly: during the **high season** for travel to Syria (generally July, Aug and the two weeks leading up to Christmas), fares can increase by forty percent or more over prices charged in the rest of the year. The fares quoted below are for round-trip tickets, travelling mid-week (weekend fares can be twenty percent higher), and exclude taxes (roughly US$75 on flights from the US and CDN$75 from Canada). A customized **RTW** ticket that includes Damascus, where available, starts at around US$2000.

AIRLINES IN THE US AND CANADA

Transatlantic flights are generally overnight, and the days listed below refer to the first leg of the journey; the Europe–Syria leg will be on the following day.

Air Canada www.aircanada.ca In the US ☎1-800/776-3000, in Canada ☎1-800/263-0882. Offers flights to Istanbul in conjunction with Turkish Airlines.

Air France www.airfrance.fr In the US ☎1-800/237-2747; in Canada, ☎1-800/667-2747. Flies four times a week from Paris to Damascus, with connecting flights available from New York and Toronto.

Alitalia (☎1-800/223-5730; in Canada, ☎1-800/361-8336; www.alitalia.com). Three flights a week from Milan to Damascus, with connections available from New York.

Austrian Airlines See United Airlines.

British Airways ☎1-800/247-9297, www.british-airways.com Five flights a week from London to Damascus (two of these stop in Aleppo en route), operated by its subsidiary British Mediterranean. Connections available from major North American cities.

Egyptair ☎1-800/334-6787 or 212/315-0900, www.egyptair.com.eg Flights from New York to Damascus via Cairo.

Northwest/KLM Airlines ☎1-800/447-4747, www.nwa.com Five flights a week to Damascus from Amsterdam, with connections from New York and Toronto.

Royal Jordanian Airlines ☎1-800/223-0470 or 212/949-0050, www.rja.com.jo Flies from New York, Chicago and San Francisco to Amman, from where it's possible to continue to Damascus overland or using one of their connecting flights.

Turkish Airlines ☎1-800/874-8875, www.thy.com Daily flights from North America to Istanbul, with connecting flights to Damascus available.

TWA ☎1-800/892-4141, www.twa.com Two flights a week to Damascus, via Cairo.

United Airlines ☎1-800/241-6522, www.ual.com Serves Syria in conjunction with Austrian Airlines (www.aua.com); United flies daily to Vienna, from where Austrian operates services to Damascus and Aleppo.

FROM THE USA

British Airways, KLM, Air France and United Airlines offer some of the cheaper fares from the US to **Damascus**. A BA/BMed flight there from New York costs around US$850 in low season, rising to US$1450 in high; flying from Chicago or Los Angeles adds around US$100 or US$400 respectively to the cost. Flights to **Aleppo** with BMed (with the London connecting flight furnished by BA) cost about the same in high season, though low-season fares are expensive at around US$1100 from New York.

Northwest/KLM, United and Royal Jordanian all have very reasonable fares from New York to **Amman** (around US$800 in low season, US$1100 high). Cheapest of all are flights to **Istanbul** in Turkey, with prices around US$600 from New York in low season, rising to US$1000 in high.

FROM CANADA

Flights from Toronto or Montreal to **Damascus** cost around CDN$1900/2100 (low/high season), with an additional CDN$300 payable to fly there out of Vancouver. There's no significant saving to be made by flying to Jordan, but it is much cheaper to get to **Istanbul**, with flights there costing just CDN$1200 from Toronto in low season.

BY TRAIN FROM EUROPE

If you intend to travel through Europe to reach Syria, consider buying a **Eurail** pass, which pays for unlimited train travel in Austria, Belgium, Denmark, Finland, France, Germany, Greece, Hungary, the Republic of Ireland, Italy, Luxembourg, Netherlands, Norway, Portugal, Spain, Sweden and Switzerland. It makes sense to travel to Syria via Switzerland, Italy and Greece, as Eastern European countries are not covered by the pass. You can get as far as Istanbul by train (see p.14 for onward routes into Syria); unfortunately, you have to pay for train tickets once you reach the Greek–Turkish border, since Turkey isn't covered by the pass either. Eurail passes should be purchased either before you arrive in Europe, or in London (where you'll need to be able to prove residency outside Europe to buy one) at usit CAMPUS or Rail Europe (see p.7 for addresses).

If you're over 26, you have to buy a first-class pass, available in several durations from fifteen days (US$550) up to three months (US$1550). Under-26s can save money with a **Eurail Youthpass**, valid for second-class travel and available in the same durations as the Eurail pass (a fifteen-day Youthpass costs US$400, a three-month Youthpass US$1100).

If you don't need to travel by train daily throughout your trip, you stand a better chance of getting your money's worth out of a **Eurail**

Flexipass, which is good for ten or fifteen travel days in a two-month period. Ten days cost around US$625/$450 first-class/second-class (the latter for under-26s only); fifteen days, $850/$600. If you're travelling with one to four other companions, the joint **Eurail Saverpass** and **Eurail Saver Flexipass** can knock about fifteen percent off the cost of travelling with individual Eurail passes and Eurail Flexipass respectively.

GETTING THERE FROM AUSTRALIA AND NEW ZEALAND

There are no direct flights from Australia and New Zealand to Syria, so your only option is to fly via Asia or Europe. The Middle Eastern and Asian airlines, plus Olympic and Alitalia, tend to offer the best deals. Gulf Air, Emirates and Egyptair offer some of the most direct routes, going from Sydney and Melbourne to Damascus via Singapore and respectively Bahrain, Dubai or Cairo, while Royal Jordanian and Kuwait Airways both team up with Ansett, Qantas, Malaysia Airlines, Singapore Airlines or Thai Airways to offer regular flights to Damascus from Auckland and major Australian cities.

Given that you have to touch down en route to Syria anyway, it might be worth looking at some of the good-value **stopover deals** on offer with

most of the Asian and Middle Eastern airlines. Alternatively, consider flying to a Mediterranean city outside Syria (Beirut, Istanbul, Amman and Cairo are among the more obvious possibilities) and continuing your journey **overland**; see pp.14–15 for details of reaching Syria from neighbouring countries, and opposite for information on the various **Eurail passes**, which allow unlimited travel on Europe's train network.

Round-the-World (RTW) tickets that take in the Middle East are worth considering, especially if you have the time to make the most of some stopovers. Although few, if any, itineraries take in Damascus specifically, several offer a stop in Cairo or Istanbul, from where you can take a side-trip to Syria (see pp.14–15).

Whatever kind of ticket you're after, you should first call a **discount flight agent** (see the list in the box overleaf), who can fill you in on all the latest fares and any special offers. The best discounts are offered by companies such as Flight Centres, STA and Trailfinders; these can also help with visas, travel insurance and tours. You might also want to have a look on the **Internet**; *www.travel.com.au* offers discounted fares online, as does *www.sydneytravel.com*

ROUTES AND FARES

Fares vary depending on the time of year you want to travel, with high season mid-May to August and December to mid-January, shoulder seasons March to mid-May and September, and low season the rest of the year. If you're flying **from Australia**, the lowest fares to Syria are with Gulf Air and Egyptair from Sydney or Melbourne – around A$1450 in low season,

DISCOUNT FLIGHT AGENTS

Anywhere Travel, 345 Anzac Parade, Kingsford, Sydney (☎02/9663 0411, *anywhere@ozemail. com.au*).

Budget Travel, 16 Fort St, Auckland, plus branches around the city (☎09/366 0061 & 0800/808 040).

Destinations Unlimited, 220 Queen St, Auckland (☎09/373 4033).

Flight Centre In Australia: 82 Elizabeth St, Sydney, plus branches nationwide (☎02/9235 3522, nearest branch ☎13/1600, *www.flightcentre.com.au*); in New Zealand: 350 Queen St, Auckland (☎09/358 4310).

Northern Gateway, 22 Cavenagh St, Darwin ☎08/8941 1394, *oztravel@norgate.com.au*).

STA Travel In Australia: 855 George St, Sydney; 256 Flinders St, Melbourne; other offices in state capitals and major universities (nearest branch ☎13/1776, fastfare telesales ☎1300/360 960; *www.statravel.com.au*). In New Zealand: 10 High St, Auckland (☎09/309 0458, fastfare telesales ☎09/366 6673), plus branches in other cities and at major universities.

Student Uni Travel, 92 Pitt St, Sydney (☎02/9232 8444, *sydney@backpackers.net*) plus branches in Brisbane, Cairns, Darwin, Melbourne and Perth.

Thomas Cook In Australia: 175 Pitt St, Sydney (☎02/9231 2877); 257 Collins St, Melbourne (☎03/ 9282 0222); plus branches in other state capitals (local branch ☎13/1771, Thomas Cook Direct telesales ☎1800/801 002, *www.thomas-cook.com.au*). In New Zealand: 191 Queen St, Auckland (☎09/379 3920).

Trailfinders *www.travel.com.au* 8 Spring St, Sydney (☎02/9247 7666); plus branches in Perth, Brisbane, Melbourne and Cairns.

Travel.com.au, 76–80 Clarence St, Sydney (☎02/9249 5444 & 1800 000 447, *www.travel.com.au*).

usit BEYOND *www.usitbeyond.co.nz* Cnr Shortland St and Jean Batten Place, Auckland (☎09/379 4224 or ☎0800/788 336), plus branches in Christchurch, Wellington and other cities.

A$2200 in high season. Alitalia and Olympic, who also fly from Sydney or Melbourne, cost a little more at A$1600/A$2400; in the same ball park are Royal Jordanian and Kuwait, who operate flights from eastern Australia, Perth and Darwin in conjunction with a number of other airlines. An example **RTW** itinerary is to start out in Sydney, fly to Hong Kong, Singapore, Cairo, and travel

SPECIALIST AGENTS AND TOUR OPERATORS IN AUSTRALIA AND NEW ZEALAND

Abercrombie and Kent In Australia: 90 Bridport St, Albert Park, Melbourne (☎03/9699 9766 or 1800/331429, *contact@aandktravel.com.au*); plus branches in Brisbane and Sydney. In New Zealand: 1/88 Rockfield Rd, Penrose, Auckland (☎09/579 3369). Fully inclusive tours of Syria, including an eight-day "Journey to Mesopotamia" which, despite its name, is a tour of historical Syrian cities, costing A$3600/NZ$4500.

Adventure World In Australia: 73 Walker St, North Sydney (☎02/9956 7766 or 1300/363 055, *www.adventureworld.com.au*), plus branches in Adelaide, Brisbane, Melbourne and Perth. In New Zealand: 101 Great South Rd, Remuera, Auckland (☎09/524 5118). Agents for Explore Worldwide tours.

Australians Studying Abroad, 1/970 High St, Armadale, Melbourne (☎1800/645 755 or

03/9509 1955, *www.asatravinfo.com.au*). All-inclusive twenty-day art and archeological lecture tours of Syria and Jordan.

Intrepid Adventure Travel, 12 Spring St, Fitzroy, Melbourne (☎1300/360 667 or 03/9473 2626, *www.intrepidworld.com.au*). Small-group tours with the emphasis on cross-cultural contact and low-impact tourism. Agents for Imaginative Traveller tours.

Peregrine Adventures, 258 Lonsdale St, Melbourne (☎03/9663 8611, *www.peregrine.net.au*), plus offices in Brisbane, Sydney, Adelaide and Perth. Agents for Exodus' extended overland tours.

Ya'lla Tours, 1st Floor, West Tower, 608 St Kilda Rd, Melbourne (☎03/9510 2844). Five- to eight-day packages in Syria, with customized tours available.

AIRLINES IN AUSTRALIA AND NEW ZEALAND

Alitalia *www.alitalia.it* In Australia ☎02/9244 2400; in New Zealand ☎09/ 302 1452. Several flights a week to Milan from Sydney and Melbourne, with onward connections to Damascus.

Ansett *www.ansett.com.au* In Australia ☎13/1414 or ☎02/9352 6707; in New Zealand ☎09/336 2364. Offers flights to Syria in collaboration with Royal Jordanian and Kuwait Airways.

Egyptair *www.egyptair.com.eg* In Australia ☎02/9267 6979; no NZ office. Two flights a week from Sydney and Melbourne to Damascus, via Cairo.

Emirates *www.emirates.com* In Australia ☎1300/303 777 or ☎02/9290 9700; in New Zealand ☎09/377 6004. Several flights a week to Damascus and Beirut, via Abu Dhabi, from Sydney, Melbourne and Brisbane.

Gulf Air *www.gulfairco.com* In Australia ☎02/9244 2199; in New Zealand ☎09/308 3366. Three flights a week to Damascus from Sydney and Melbourne, via Bahrain.

Kuwait Airways *www.kuwait-airways.com* In Australia ☎02/9264 8277; no NZ office. Several flights a week to Damascus from major Australian and New Zealand cities, operated in conjunction with Ansett, Qantas, Thai, Malaysia or Singapore Airlines.

Malaysia Airlines *www.mas.com.my* In Australia ☎13/2627; in New Zealand ☎09/373 2741 or 0800/657 472. Flies via Kuala Lumpur twice a week to Cairo and three times a week to Beirut from major Australian cities and Auckland; also

offers flights to Syria in conjunction with Royal Jordanian and Kuwait Airways.

Olympic Airways *www.olympic-airways.com* In Australia ☎1800/221 663 or ☎02/9251 2044; no NZ office. Three flights a week to Athens from Sydney, with onward connections to Damascus.

Qantas *www.qantas.com.au* In Australia ☎13/1313; in New Zealand ☎09/357 8900 or ☎0800/808 767. Offers flights to Syria in conjunction with Kuwait Airways, Royal Jordanian or Turkish Airlines.

Royal Jordanian Airlines *www.rja.com.jo* In Australia ☎02/9244 2701; New Zealand ☎03/365 3910. Three flights a week to Damascus, via Amman, from major Australian cities and Auckland, in conjunction with Ansett, Qantas, Thai, Malaysia and Singapore Airlines.

Singapore Airlines *www.singaporeair.com* In Australia ☎13/1011 or 02/9350 0262; in New Zealand ☎09/303 2129 or 0800/808 909. Flies to Cairo and Istanbul from major Australian cities and Auckland; also offers flights to Syria in conjunction with Royal Jordanian and Kuwait Airways.

Thai Airways *www.thaiair.com* In Australia ☎1300/651 960; New Zealand ☎09/377 3886. Offers flights to Syria in collaboration with Royal Jordanian and Kuwait Airways.

Turkish Airlines *www.thy.com* In Australia ☎02/9299 8400; no NZ office. In conjunction with Qantas, operates three flights a week to Istanbul from major Australian and New Zealand cities, via Singapore, with onward connections to Damascus.

---

overland to London, before flying on to Chicago, Denver, Los Angeles and back to Sydney; fares for this route start at A$2300.

The choice of airlines is more limited if you're flying **from New Zealand**. From Auckland, the best deals are with Royal Jordanian and Kuwait; their fares start at NZ$2000, rising to NZ$2800 or more during high season (add around NZ$100–150 for a connection from Christchurch). A possible **RTW** route would be Auckland to Los Angeles, London, Cairo, Singapore and Melbourne, then back to Auckland, with fares starting from NZ$2500.

PACKAGES AND TOURS

Package deals from Australia and New Zealand are pretty flexible, and most specialist agents

(see box opposite) can do anything from booking a few nights' accommodation in Damascus for when you first arrive, to arranging a fully escorted tour. As an example of the former, Adventure World offer two-day city-stays in Syria which include half-board hotel accommodation, transfers (though not flights to the country) and sightseeing tours with an English-speaking guide, for around A$650/NZ$850 per person (twin share).

For escorted **tours**, most companies offer a range of itineraries that take in the major sights (Damascus, Palmyra, Aleppo and Crak des Chevaliers), with the option of spending a few days in Egypt or Jordan as well. As an example, Explore Worldwide's nine-day "On the Road to Damascus" starts from A$1000/NZ$1200 (twin share) and includes all transport and accommodation and some meals, but not flights from Australia. The more adventure-oriented Imaginative Traveller offer small-group escorted tours, ranging from their nine-

day "Syria Highlights" (from A$1350/NZ$1650) to their fifteen-day "A Journey Through Syria and Lebanon" (from A$2050/NZ$2600).

GETTING THERE FROM NEIGHBOURING COUNTRIES

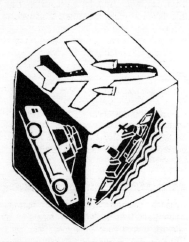

If your travels include Turkey, Lebanon, Jordan, Cyprus or Egypt, moving on to Syria is fairly straightforward; travelling overland from Israel to Syria is virtually impossible, however. Air services to Damascus from nearby Middle Eastern cities are relatively expensive, and with rail services slow and irregular from Turkey and Jordan, you're likely to make all your border crossings by road.

FROM TURKEY

Among a number of **road** crossing points between Turkey and Syria, the one at **Bab al-Hawa** on the Antakya–Aleppo road is the most frequently used, and usually the most crowded. If you're driving, you're probably better off heading for the crossing at **Kassab** on the Antakya–Latakia road, probably the least busy of those along the western portion of the border.

There are many competing **bus** companies on the **Istanbul–Aleppo** route, with some selling through tickets to **Damascus** as well. Most firms

at the huge Aksaray bus station in Istanbul charge around US$25 for the journey to Aleppo (24hr), and US$30 to Damascus (30hr). Agencies in downtown Istanbul often charge US$40 for the same journey, taking a fair cut of this fare themselves. Count yourself very lucky if you don't end up having to change buses at least once, probably in Antakya.

You can also cross by road between **Gaziantep** and Aleppo. There's supposedly a daily bus linking the two cities; as a last resort, however, take a taxi from Gaziantep or **Killis** (the town nearest the border) to the frontier post, and walk along the road across no-man's-land. On the other side you can get a taxi to Aleppo or to Azaz, from where you can continue to Aleppo by bus. Hiring a taxi for the whole Gaziantep–Aleppo journey costs around US$50.

The **trains** in the *Thomas Cook World Timetable* linking Istanbul and Aleppo often seem to exist mainly in the dreams of the timetablers, and don't bear much relation to reality. If you're planning to travel from Istanbul to Syria by train it's probably best to turn up at Haydarpasa Station in Istanbul and see what the current situation is. If you do get a through train, the journey time is a sedate 36 hours (at least). Couchettes are in short supply on these journeys (some trains don't have them at all), and are best booked in advance. If you're on an InterRail pass, staff at Haydarpasa Station in Istanbul will sell you a ticket from the Turkish–Syrian border to Aleppo. If there's no through service to Aleppo, take a train from Istanbul to Adana or Gaziantep in southeastern Turkey, from where you can continue to Aleppo by road via Antakya or Killis respectively.

FROM LEBANON

Frequent buses run from **Beirut** to Damascus (4hr), Tartous (up to 8hr) and Latakia (up to 9hr), and from **Tripoli** to Tartous (up to 4hr) and Latakia (up to 5hr); Karnak, the Syrian state bus company, runs daily services on these routes. It's not possible to obtain a Syrian visa in Lebanon, so you must have obtained one before arriving there if you want to make one of these journeys. You can visit both countries with just a single-entry Syrian visa, though it's worth considering buying a multiple-entry Syrian visa, with which you can then pop in and out of Lebanon as you please (Lebanese visas are available with a minimum of fuss at the border; see pp.114–115).

Syrianair operate one nonstop **flight** per week from Beirut to Damascus, and two flights to Aleppo. There are at present no passenger ferry sailings along the coast between Beirut and Latakia.

FROM JORDAN

There are two **road** crossing points between Syria and Jordan, both of them close to **Dera** (see p.132). Things can get quite congested at the Dera/Ramtha crossing, but if you're on the main Amman–Damascus highway, you use the less busy Nasib/Jaber crossing, which is also used by buses.

The government **bus** companies of Syria and Jordan (Karnak and JETT, respectively) each run a daily service between Amman and Damascus, which takes up to seven hours and costs around US$5. Karnak also offers through tickets between Amman and Aleppo, though a change of bus in Damascus is likely. In Amman, buses depart from the JETT international office 500m up the hill from the Abdali bus and service-taxi (ie shared taxi) station; from the latter you can also pick up faster service taxis to Damascus. Crossing between Irbid (Jordan) and Dera is not difficult: get a bus to Ramtha, from where service taxis run regularly to Dera.

Once a week, an extremely slow **train** (sometimes hauled by hundred-year-old steam locomotives) travels the old **Hedjaz rail line** between Amman and Damascus (US$3), taking nine hours to complete the trip (5hr Amman–Dera). The train finishes up at the old **Hedjaz Station** right in the centre of Damascus, which is the main advantage of entering the country this way.

Flights between Amman and Damascus are expensive, often inconveniently timed, and actually not much quicker than road, once the time taken travelling between airports and city centres

is included. However you leave Jordan, don't forget about the JD4 **exit tax** that needs to be paid when you depart.

FROM EGYPT AND CYPRUS

From **Egypt**, there are daily **air services** between **Cairo** and Damascus; Syrianair also operates services from Cairo to Aleppo (3 weekly) and Latakia (1 weekly). From **Cyprus**, **Larnaca**–Damascus flights operate most days, and there's a regular (currently 1 weekly) **ferry** service from Larnaca to Jounieh, just north of Beirut, from where getting to Damascus or Tartous by road is fairly straightforward.

Unfortunately, ferry services to Latakia from Alexandria (Egypt), Famagusta (Turkish North Cyprus) and Larnaca (Cyprus) are currently in abeyance. However, if you are in any of these ports it might be worth asking around at shipping agencies, as cruise ships operating into Tartous or Latakia occasionally sell off some of their spare space to passengers who only want to travel between two ports.

FROM ELSEWHERE IN THE MIDDLE EAST

Syrianair operates weekly flights between **Kuwait** and **Deir ez-Zur**, which makes for an interesting back-door entry route into Syria. Damascus itself is well served by air routes operated by Syrianair and other Middle Eastern national carriers, with flights on at least a daily basis from Bahrain, Dubai and Tehran, among other cities.

Although it's possible to be in **Israel** and get within sight of the Syrian flag flying above Quneitra (see p.146), the main settlement in the UN-administered Syrian–Israeli border zone, there's no way of crossing the border here – in either direction. Until there's a major leap forward in the peace process, the only viable overland route between Jerusalem and Damascus is via the West Bank and Jordan.

Most crossing points between Syria and **Iraq** have been closed since the early 1980s; however, the summer of 2000 saw the revival of the direct train service linking Aleppo with Mosul in northern Iraq, though it's hard to envisage this becoming popular with travellers in the near future.

VISAS AND RED TAPE

Most Syrian bureaucracy is frustratingly slow, but with a little patience and good humour you should find that obtaining visas (and extensions to visas) is straightforward enough. Syrian officials are usually polite, speak a modicum of English, and are very apologetic about how patient you'll have to be while the formalities are completed. Government business with foreigners is sometimes carried out in French rather than English, so if you have a smattering of the language you might be marginally better off dealing with the paperwork than someone who hasn't.

VISAS

All visitors to Syria must hold a **passport** valid for at least six months beyond the proposed date of entry into the country; virtually all nationalities must also obtain a **tourist visa** to gain entry to Syria. It's best to purchase your visa before leaving home; Syrian visas can in principle be obtained at their embassies in Amman, Ankara or Cairo, but a "letter of recommendation" from your own embassy – costly and time-consuming to obtain – is generally needed in these cities, and so you may face considerable delays to your application. You can't obtain a Syrian visa in Lebanon, so if you're planning to visit Lebanon from Syria you may want to consider obtaining a **multiple-entry** Syrian visa (see also the box on pp.114–115), valid for use within six months of the date of issue; with both single- and multiple-entry visas you need to get a **visa extension** (see opposite) if you stay more than fifteen consecutive days in the country.

Though Syria maintains **embassies** in only a limited number of countries of the world, obtaining visas through the ones listed in the box below is generally unproblematic, whether by post (allow at least two weeks) or in person (in which case your visa will be ready to collect in three days). If you plan to visit the embassy in person, phone ahead beforehand – opening hours are sometimes rather bizarre. With your application, you may be asked to provide a letter from your employer on their headed paper, confirming the nature of your occupation. The application form also asks your religion; if you put "Jewish", you can assume your application will be refused, as it probably will be if you answer "yes" to the question "Have you visited occupied Palestine?" (ie Israel). When returning the form, you need to include a registered or recorded stamped addressed envelope, your passport, the required number of photos, and a postal or money order (not a personal cheque). Apply **well in advance**: the two-week waiting time for postal applications quoted by embassy staff may not be long enough at busy times.

The **cost** depends on the type of visa and your nationality. UK and Irish citizens pay around UK£35/50 (single/multiple entry); Canadians US$55/110; Australians and New Zealanders pay A$35/NZ$45 for a single/multiple entry visa. For

SYRIAN EMBASSIES AND CONSULATES

UK, 8 Belgrave Square, London SW1X 8PH (☎020/7245 9012).

Ireland No embassy; apply to the embassy in London.

USA, 2215 Wyoming Ave NW, Washington DC 20008 (☎202/232-6313).

Canada, Suite 1000, 151 Slater St, Ottawa K1P 5H3 (☎613/569 5556).

Australia, 57 Cardigan St, Carlton, Victoria 3053 (☎03/9347 8445).

New Zealand No embassy; contact the Australian consul for information.

Americans, the cost is US$60 for a single- or double-entry visa (multiple-entry visas being unavailable to Americans).

VISAS AND ISRAEL

Evidence of a visit to **Israel** in your passport automatically disqualifies you from obtaining a Syrian visa, and invalidates any visa you have already obtained. If you want to visit both Syria and Israel on one trip, and are fortunate enough to have two passports, you can keep your Israeli and Syrian documentation in **separate passports**; otherwise head for Syria before going on to Israel. If this isn't possible, ask Israeli immigration officials not to put the entrance and exit stamps in your passport but on a separate slip of paper; bear in mind, however, that Egyptian stamps from border posts at Rafah or Tabah, or Jordanian stamps from the Allenby bridge, are telltale signs that you've been to Israel, and Syrian embassy or border officials are adept at noticing them in your passport.

RED TAPE WITHIN SYRIA

On entering Syria, foreign visitors are given a **yellow immigration card** which must be filled in; this is usually given to air passengers before they land. Look after this card carefully, as it must be presented when leaving the country; losing it results in all sorts of hassle.

Outside your hotel, it's important to keep your passport with you at all times in Syria. Generally you need to show your passport when using any form of public transport between towns, and sometimes also when entering bus or train stations where the police are quite security-conscious; furthermore, **checkpoints** are common on roads in the desert, in border regions, near military zones and in the northeast. Of course you always need your passport to change money, collect your mail at post offices and register at hotels. If you lose your passport, you should immediately report the loss to your embassy or consulate, and to a Syrian passport and immigration office; it's wise to keep a separate photocopy of your passport for this eventuality. You need a special **permit** to visit Quneitra in the Golan Heights (see p.146) but otherwise you're free to travel where you want in the country.

VISA EXTENSIONS

To stay in Syria longer than the fifteen days provided by a tourist visa requires a **visa exten-sion**, lasting up to four weeks, which can only be granted in Syria on the fourteenth or fifteenth day of your visit. When buying an extension, you must state your intended date of departure from Syria; only one extension will be granted per trip – which means that if you've a multiple-entry visa, you can stay a maximum of thirty days at one time before you need to leave the country (though you can subsequently re-enter Syria while your multiple-entry visa remains valid). Extensions must be obtained at passport and immigration offices (usually open daily except Fri 8am–2pm), which can be found in Damascus, Aleppo, Tartous, Latakia, Homs, Hama, Dera, Hassakeh and Deir ez-Zur (their locations are shown on the maps of these towns in this book). Extensions can usually be given on the same day, but sometimes, especially in Damascus, you will be asked to return the next day to complete the procedures and pick up the extension permit.

Arranging the extension involves a great deal of waiting around and filling in forms, and all you end up with at the end of it are a few extra stamps in your passport and a slip of paper which will be removed, along with your yellow card, when you leave the country. At least extensions are cheap, about US$2 for all nationalities, payable either in Syrian currency at the office, or by buying a revenue stamp (used to indicate on paperwork that you have paid for a government service) for the amount from a designated booth outside the immigration office. You also need **passport photographs** (black-and-white or colour are accepted); some passport offices (such as the one in Aleppo) require four photos, while others need fewer. To save trouble, it's best to bring out a number of these photos from home, though photographic shops which can produce the required photos within a few hours are found in most cities; automatic photobooths do not exist.

CUSTOMS AND CURRENCY DECLARATIONS

In contrast to the visa and passport requirements, Syrian **customs** regulations are unlikely to trouble you. Import/export limits are two hundred cigarettes and two bottles of spirits; no vegetable or olive oils, or meat products can be taken out of Syria. There's no need to declare possession of cameras or other equipment, although if you bring your own car into the country you'll probably need to prove that you're the owner. Foreign **currency** up to a value of US$5000 can be brought into Syria or taken out of the country without having to declare it; up to S£2000 can be taken out with you, although there isn't much point to doing so, as Syrian pounds are hard to change outside Syria.

HEALTH

There are no mandatory inoculations required for entry to Syria, but you should have jabs against tetanus, typhoid and hepatitis A, in addition to a polio booster, before you leave home. If you're going to be travelling near the Euphrates in summer you should also take out a supply of anti-malaria pills, as an additional precaution.

Dust and smog might affect your eyes and sinuses, particularly in summer when breezes constantly blow trapped city fumes into your face, and in the desert, where grit can easily get into your eye with each fresh breath of wind; if you want to wear **contact lenses** in Syria, consider bringing eye drops that you can use at the same time (or wearing glasses or sunglasses in the dustier areas). You might want to wear a scarf or similar to protect your **sinuses** which, like the eyes, can be irritated by dust carried in the wind.

WATER

Tap water is in theory safe to drink, being heavily chlorinated and (in restaurants) filtered, but you may prefer to buy **bottled water**, which is cheap and widely available. If you're avoiding tap water, then you'll also want to stay off ice in your drinks, most ice cream as well as salad vegetables. **Milk and cream** should be avoided, as generally the products aren't pasteurized to the standards that your stomach is used to, although boiled milk which is added to Western-style coffee is OK.

You should definitely avoid contact with any **stagnant water** alongside the Euphrates and Orontes rivers. Although the risk is not so great as along the Nile, such water may harbour **bilharzia** (schistosomiasis) and other parasites which can enter your body through the skin (a sign of infection is blood in urine). Don't bathe in irrigation canals or the like, or walk barefoot on mud or grass wet with Orontes or Euphrates water; there's even a slight risk if you decide to go swimming in the main channels of these or other rivers.

If you're planning to head well off the beaten track into the desert, you might want to consider taking a **water purifier** with you. While boiling water for ten minutes kills most micro-organisms, it's not the most convenient method. Sterilization with iodine tablets is effective, but the resulting liquid doesn't taste very pleasant and you'll probably want to filter the water as well. (Iodine is unsafe for pregnant women, babies and people with thyroid complaints.) Portable water purifiers, which sterilize and filter the water, give the most complete treatment; before you travel, consult a camping equipment specialist at home for advice on which water purifiers best suit your needs.

HEAT

Many health problems in Syria are caused by the excessive **heat** experienced during the summer. Ideally, you should aim to start your day early and spend the afternoon resting, particularly in the east of the country where summer daytime temperatures above 40°C are common.

Sweat evaporates very quickly in the dry air, and it's easy to become **dehydrated** without realizing it; you should always maintain your fluid intake (at least three litres per day), and steer clear of too much caffeine or alcohol, which exacerbate dehydration. It does no harm to take a bit of **salt** with your food, as you lose a lot of body salts during perspiration.

To avoid **sunburn**, always try to stay out of direct sunlight, even if the only concession you make is wearing a hat; it's a good idea to bring out a good brand of suncream with you (unavailable in Syria) and keep as much of your skin covered as possible when you're out in the sun.

Try to wear **loose-fitting clothes**, made preferably from cotton rather than synthetic fabrics, which will help to prevent **prickly heat**, an

TRAVEL CLINICS AND INFORMATION FOR TRAVELLERS

BRITAIN

The Department of Health's comprehensive booklet *Health Advice for Travellers* is available free at post offices (or by calling the Health Literature Line on ☎0800/555777); it includes an application for Form E111, which UK residents must obtain to receive free emergency treatment in the European Economic Area – useful if you're travelling to Syria overland. The content of the booklet is constantly updated on pages 460–464 of CEEFAX (or you can consult it on *www.doh.gov.uk/traveladvice*). For more detailed info a **travel clinic** is better; some clinics also sell travel accessories, including mosquito nets and first-aid kits.

British Airways Travel Clinics, 156 Regent St, London W1 (☎020/7439 9584), and at more than twenty other locations around the country (call ☎01276/685040 for the one nearest to you or consult *www.britishairways.com/travelqa/*). They provide vaccinations, tailored advice from their on-line database and a complete range of travel healthcare products.

Hospital for Tropical Diseases, Travel Clinic, 2nd Floor, Mortimer Market Centre, off Capper St, London WC1E 6AU (Mon–Fri 9am–5pm by appointment only; ☎020/7388 9600). The consultation fee is waived if you have your injections here; they also have a recorded Health Line (☎0839/337 733; 50p per min) giving hints on hygiene and illness prevention as well as listing appropriate immunizations.

Malaria Helpline 24hr recorded advice (☎0891/600 350; 60p per min).

MASTA (Medical Advisory Service for Travellers Abroad), London School of Hygiene and Tropical Medicine. Operates a pre-recorded 24-hour Travellers' Health Line (☎0906/822 4100; 60p per min), giving written information tailored to your journey by return of post.

Nomad Pharmacy, 40 Bernard St, London WC1, opposite Russell Square tube station (Mon–Fri 9.30am–6pm; ☎020/7833 4114). They give travel advice free if you go in person, or you can get advice from their telephone helpline (☎0891/633 414, 60p a minute).

Trailfinders, 194 Kensington High St, London W8 7RG (Mon–Fri 9am–5pm, Thurs to 6pm, Sat 9.30am–4pm; ☎020/7938 3999). This branch of the travel agency runs no-appointments-necessary immunization clinics.

IRELAND

Both these places offer medical treatment and pre-trip advice.

Travel Medicine Services, PO Box 254, 16 College St, Belfast 1 (☎028/9031 5200).

Tropical Medical Bureau, Grafton St Medical Centre, 34 Grafton St, Dublin 2 (☎01/671 9200, *www.iol.ie/~tmb/*).

US AND CANADA

Canadian Society for International Health, 1 Nicholas St., Suite 1105, Ottawa, ON K1N 7B7 (☎613/241-5785, *www.csih.org*). Distributes a free pamphlet, *Health Information for Canadian Travellers*, containing an extensive list of travel health centres in Canada.

Centers for Disease Control, 1600 Clifton Rd NE, Atlanta, GA 30333 (☎404/639-3311, *www.cdc.gov*). Publishes disease outbreak warnings, suggested inoculations, health precautions and other background information for travellers. Their Web site is very useful, as is their International Travelers Hotline (☎1/888-232-3228).

International Association for Medical Assistance to Travellers (IAMAT) *www.sentex.net/~iamat* In the US: 417 Center St, Lewiston, NY 14092 (☎716/754-4883); in Canada 40 Regal Rd, Guelph, ON N1K 1B5 (☎519/836-0102). This non-profit organization can provide

lists of English-speaking doctors in many countries, as well as leaflets on various diseases and inoculations.

International SOS Assistance, PO Box 11568, Philadelphia, PA 19116 (☎1-800/523-8930, *www.intsos.com*). Members receive pre-trip medical referral information, as well as overseas emergency services designed to complement travel insurance coverage.

Travel Medicine, 351 Pleasant St, Suite 312, Northampton, MA 01060 (☎1-800/872-8633, *www.travmed.com*). Sells first-aid kits, mosquito netting, water filters and other health-related travel products.

Travelers Medical Center, 31 Washington Square West, New York, NY 10011 (☎212/982-1600). Consultation service on immunizations and treatment of diseases for people travelling to developing countries.

continues overleaf...

TRAVEL CLINICS AND INFORMATION FOR TRAVELLERS cont.

AUSTRALIA AND NEW ZEALAND

Travellers' Medical and Vaccination Centres *www.tmvc.com.au* In Australia: 7/428 George St, Sydney (☎02/9221 7133); in New Zealand: Shop 15, Grand Arcade, 14–16 Willis St, Wellington (☎04/473 0991); plus branches in major Australian and New Zealand cities. Their Web site lists all their branches plus general information on travel health.

itchy rash caused by perspiration trapped within your skin. **Fungal infections** such as athlete's foot or ringworm can result from perspiration trapped within clothes, though it's straightforward to treat them using creams or powder available from pharmacists (and such problems are best avoided by changing your clothes frequently).

More serious are **heat stroke** and **heat exhaustion**, whose symptoms include fatigue, headaches, fever, vomiting or stomach cramps, moving on to an inability to sweat, a flushing of the skin and a rise in body temperature. Serious heat stroke can be fatal. Treatment for both ailments is to stay indoors and stay cool, preferably with wet towels wrapped around you to reduce body temperature. If you arrive in Syria in summer direct from a much cooler area, you should spend the first few days taking things easy to get acclimatized to the heat, and leave it a while before heading out to the desert – which can be like walking into an oven if you're not prepared for the extremes of temperature.

DIGESTIVE INFECTIONS

Most travellers in Syria are unlikely to encounter any problems beyond bouts of **diarrhoea**, brought on through exhaustion or exposure to infected water or food. It's difficult to avoid dodgy food completely in Syria, but you can help yourself by avoiding street food from places that don't look clean, dishes in restaurants which look as though they have been standing around for some time, and undercooked meat and fish. Resting up for a few days, drinking only mineral water, sweetened tea or fruit juice, is the recommended remedy, getting rid of the bacteria by simply denying them sustenance; when you can manage to eat something, bread and plain, boiled white rice are the best things to start off with. If you need to be on the move, however, you should have a supply of an anti-diarrhoea preparation with you (such as Diocalm or the much stronger Lomotil or Imodium), which will block you up for a certain period but won't kill whatever's inside you making you ill. Whatever you do, you should ensure that you keep your fluid intake up to avoid dehydration – particularly dangerous during the summer. You might want to bring out with you a medical **rehydration preparation** to be taken should the need arise.

If symptoms include severe fever, vomiting, stomach cramps, and/or blood present in stools, then you might have **dysentery** or **typhoid**; dysentery comes in two forms – bacillary dysentery can be treated with antibiotics, but amoebic dysentery is harder to cure and may mean flying home. If you experience serious or stubborn food poisoning, seek medical attention immediately.

Hepatitis A is easily picked up from infected food in Syria, so it makes a lot of sense to get inoculated against it before you set out. Symptoms include a darkening of urine and your skin turning yellow. If you've contracted it, you'll need to return home, as it can drag on for months.

ANIMAL HAZARDS

Snakes and **scorpions** often make their home among rocks and ruins, but they're generally nocturnal and will hide if people appear. Any bite from one of these creatures should receive immediate medical attention, and you should try to take note of the animal concerned in order to describe it to a doctor. Thankfully, unwelcome attention from these beasts is very rare, but it makes sense not to turn over stones or poke your hand into dark crevices, for fear of what may be lurking there; likewise, be very careful with shoes and clothes – tempting resting places for little reptiles and insects – if you decide to camp out in the desert.

More likely hazards in the countryside are **dogs**: most Bedouin keep semi-wild, often extremely ferocious animals, which can dampen your appreciation of the Bedouin's famed hospitality, and in Bosra and other ancient sites you'll come across ordinary families living among the ruins, whose pets may not take kindly to you admiring bits of Roman stonework around their home. If you get bitten by a dog then get medical help immediately; first aid includes washing the wound with soap and water, and applying a bandage and antiseptic cream. As soon as possible you should begin a course of **anti-rabies treatment**, available free from Syrian state hospitals: all of them keep a stock of the French drug Verorab, which is given in the arm and not nearly as painful as the old stomach-injected shots. If you are bitten, or suffer an open wound, you might also be at risk from **tetanus** and should ask for a booster jab from a doctor, to supplement the preventative inoculation you should have had before leaving home.

Mosquitoes are present in many places in Syria, so bring mosquito repellent. In summer (May–Oct) around the Euphrates they can carry **malaria**: the risk is slight, but you should bring a course of anti-malarial pills (Chloroquine; available from pharmacies at home, but not in Syria). **Flies** can be a real nuisance out in the desert, particularly around Palmyra. It's difficult to suggest any appropriate remedies for dealing with them beyond continually brushing them away from your skin; insect sprays (available locally) have some effect, but air conditioning is what really gets rid of them.

Bedbugs can be a problem in the cheapest hotels. The usual giveaway is tiny specks of blood on bed linen; treatment includes preparations easily obtainable from pharmacists, but prevention is better than cure – find another hotel. Other unwelcome features of cheap hotels are fleas, mites and giant cockroaches, all of which might result in skin irritation.

MEDICAL TREATMENT AND PHARMACIES

Every city and small town has a **pharmacy** (sometimes labelled just that in English, and called *saydaliyyeh* in Arabic), where you can obtain remedies for minor ailments such as diarrhoea or bites and stings. Many pharmacists are English-speaking; most medicines have details printed on them in English (at least with the barest information about what they're for). Medicines are cheap, and many drugs which would require a prescription back home can be dispensed over the counter here. However, you should **bring with you** a good supply of any medication you might need on a regular basis, as what you require (or its exact equivalent) may not be available in Syria; this advice extends to contact-lens accessories, tampons and contraceptives.

Only in the smallest towns is finding a **doctor** or **dentist** a problem; they advertise their presence using English-language signs above clinic and surgery entrances – and most hotels (or your embassy) can put you in contact with one quickly. Most of Syria's doctors have been trained in Europe, and have a good working knowledge of English. Expect a **consultation fee** of around US$30–40, and remember to pick up a receipt for insurance purposes. If you are given an injection, insist that needles are taken out of the packet in front of you, and discarded afterwards; if you are in any doubt, then ask to buy a new syringe from a pharmacy (syringes are very cheap, but you will need a prescription from a doctor to buy one).

Emergency hospital treatment is free of charge in Syrian state **hospitals**, but if you're able to it's always better to make a doctor, rather than a hospital, your first port of call. The **Shamy Diplomatic Hospital** in Damascus (address on p.111) is the only private hospital in the country, and its services are vastly better than anything offered by the state. If all else fails then most medical insurance policies cover the cost of an emergency flight home.

TRAVELLER'S FIRST-AID KIT

Among items you might want to carry with you are the following:

Antiseptic cream	Paracetamol/aspirin
Insect repellent	Multi-vitamin and mineral tablets
Plasters/band aids	Rehydration sachets
Lint and sealed bandages	Hypodermic needles and sterilized skin wipes (more for the security of knowing you have them, than any fear that a local hospital would fail to observe basic sanitary precautions)
A course of flagyl antibiotics	
Imodium (Lomotil) for emergency diarrhoea treatment	

INSURANCE

It's essential to take out a good **travel insurance policy**, but before doing so, check what levels of cover you may have from other sources. For example, **bank and credit cards** (particularly American Express) often have certain levels of medical or other insurance included, especially if you use them to pay for your trip. Such cover can be quite comprehensive, anticipating anything from lost or stolen baggage and missed connections to charter companies going bankrupt; however, certain policies (notably in North America) only cover medical costs. A good all-risks home insurance policy may even cover your possessions against loss or theft overseas.

UK and **Irish** citizens would do well to take out an insurance policy before travelling to cover against theft, loss and illness or injury, especially since EU health care privileges don't exist in Syria. Many private medical schemes such as BUPA or PPP also offer coverage plans for abroad, including baggage loss, cancellation or curtailment and cash replacement as well as sickness or accident. Travel agents and tour operators are likely to require some sort of insurance when you book a package holiday, though according to UK law they can't make you buy their own.

Americans and **Canadians** should also check that they're not already covered. Canadian provincial health plans usually provide partial cover for medical mishaps overseas. Holders of official student/teacher/youth cards are entitled to meagre accident coverage and hospital in-patient benefits. Students will often find that their student health coverage extends during the vacations and for one term beyond the date of last enrolment. Homeowners' or renters' insurance often covers theft or loss of documents, money and valuables while overseas, though conditions and maximum amounts vary from company to company.

Note that very few insurers will arrange on-the-spot payments in the event of a major expense or loss; you will usually be **reimbursed** only after going home. In all cases of loss or theft of goods, you have to file a report with the local police so that your insurer can process the claim. If you plan to participate in any **sports** your insurer deems hazardous, you have to pay an extra premium to cover you for these activities.

ROUGH GUIDES TRAVEL INSURANCE

Rough Guides now offer their own **travel insurance**, customized for our readers by a leading UK broker and backed by a Lloyds underwriter. It's available for anyone, of any nationality or age, travelling anywhere in the world, and we are convinced that this is the best-value scheme you'll find.

There are two main Rough Guide insurance plans: **Essential**, for effective, no-frills cover, starting at £11.75 for two weeks; and **Premier** – more expensive but with more generous and extensive benefits. Each offers European or Worldwide cover, and can be supplemented with a "Hazardous Activities Premium" if you plan to indulge in sports considered dangerous, such as skiing, scuba-diving or trekking. Unlike many policies, the Rough Guides schemes are calculated by the day, so if you're travelling for 27 days rather than a month, that's all you pay for. Alternatively, you can take out annual **multi-trip insurance**, which covers you for all your travel throughout the year (with a maximum of sixty days for any one trip).

For a **policy quote**, call the Rough Guides Insurance Line on UK freefone ☎0800/015 0906, or US toll-free 1-866/220-5588, or on ☎44/1243 621046 from other countries. Alternatively, you can get a quote and buy your policy online at *www.roughguides.com/insurance*

DISABLED TRAVELLERS

Syria makes little provision for travellers with disabilities. There are no ramps to help you negotiate crossing the road, public transport (particularly buses and microbuses) is not adapted for disabled travellers, and ruins and archeological sites will be very difficult to get around for the most part. There are organized tours and holidays specifically for people with disabilities –

the contacts in the box below can put you in touch with any specialists in trips to Syria.

If you want to be more independent, it's important to become an authority on where you must be self-reliant and where you may expect help, especially regarding transport and accommodation. It is also vital to be honest – with travel agencies, insurance companies and travel companions. Know your limitations and make sure others know

---

ADVICE FOR TRAVELLERS WITH DISABILITIES

UK AND IRELAND

Disability Action Group, 2 Annadale Ave, Belfast BT7 3JH (☎028/9049 1011).

Irish Wheelchair Association, Blackheath Drive, Clontarf, Dublin 3 (☎01/833 8241, fax 833 3873, *iwa@iol.ie*).

RADAR (Royal Association for Disability and Rehabilitation), 12 City Forum, 250 City Rd, London EC1V 8AF (☎020/7250 3222; minicom

☎020/7250 4119). They produce a guide giving advice about long-haul travel.

Tripscope, The Courtyard, Evelyn Rd, London W4 5JL (☎020/8994 9294, fax 8994 3618). Runs a national telephone information service offering free advice on international travel for those with a mobility problem.

US AND CANADA

Access First, 239 Commercial St, Malden, MA 02148 (☎1/800-557-2047 or 781/322-1610). Current information for disabled travellers.

Directions Unlimited, 123 Green Lane, Bedford Hills, NY 10507 (☎1-800/533-5343 or 914/241-1700, *cruisesusa@aol.com*). Tour operator specializing in custom tours, packages and cruises for people with disabilities.

Jewish Rehabilitation Hospital, 3205 Place Alton Goldbloom, Chomedy Laval, Quebec H7V 1RT (☎450/688-9550, ext 226). Guidebooks and travel information.

Mobility International USA, PO Box 10767, Eugene, OR 97440 (☎541/343-1284, *www.miusa.org*). Information and referral services, access guides, tours and exchange programmes. Annual membership $35 (includes quarterly newsletter).

Society for the Advancement of Travel for the Handicapped (SATH), 347 5th Ave, Suite 610, New York, NY 10016 (☎212/447-7284,

www.sath.org). Non-profit travel-industry referral service that passes queries on to its members as appropriate; allow plenty of time for a response.

Travel Information Service Moss Rehabilitation Hospital, 1200 West Tabor Rd, Philadelphia, PA 19141 (☎215/456-9603). Telephone information and referral service.

Twin Peaks Press, Box 129, Vancouver, WA 98666 (☎1-800/637-2256 or ☎360/694-2462, *www.pacifier.com/twinpeak*). Publisher of the *Directory of Travel Agencies for the Disabled*, listing more than 370 agencies worldwide; *Travel for the Disabled*; the *Directory of Accessible Van Rentals* and *Wheelchair Vagabond*, loaded with personal tips.

Wheels Up! (☎1-888/389-4335, *www.wheelsup.com*). Provides discounted airfare, tour and cruise prices for disabled travellers, also publishes a free monthly newsletter and has a comprehensive Web site.

AUSTRALIA AND NEW ZEALAND

ACROD (Australian Council for Rehabilitation of the Disabled), PO Box 60, Curtin, ACT 2605 (☎02/6282 4333, *www.acrod.org.au*).

Disabled Persons Assembly, Level 4, 173–175 Victoria St, Wellington (☎04/801 9100, *www.dpa.org.nz*).

them. If your walking capabilities are limited, remember that you are likely to need to cover greater distances while travelling (often over rougher terrain and in hotter temperatures) than you are used to; if you use a wheelchair, have it serviced before you go and carry a repair kit.

Read your **travel insurance** small print carefully to make sure that people with a pre-existing medical condition are not excluded. And use your travel agent to make your journey simpler: airline or bus companies can cope better if they are expecting you, with a wheelchair provided at air-ports and staff primed to help. A **medical certificate** of your fitness to travel, provided by your doctor, is also extremely useful; some airlines or insurance companies may insist on it. Make sure that you have extra supplies of **medicines** you need – carried with you if you fly – and a pre-scription including the generic name in case of emergency. Carry spares of any clothing or equipment that might be hard to find; if there's an association representing people with your disability, contact them early in the planning process.

COSTS, MONEY AND BANKS

Syria is a remarkably cheap country in which to travel. It's quite possible to exist on under UK£10/US$15 a day if you don't mind roughing it in terms of both food and accommodation – although after a while you may tire of staying in the cheapest hotels and eating nothing but falafels. If you've arrived in Syria from Turkey or (especially) from Jordan, you'll find that your cash stretches much further here than in those countries; public transport, in particular, is dirt-cheap in Syria. There's little geographical variation in prices across the country, although food and accommodation are a little more expensive in Damascus and Aleppo than elsewhere.

CURRENCY

The **currency** used in Syria is the **Syrian pound** (or *lira*), sometimes abbreviated to SP or LS (*Livre*

Syrien), but more often shown as S£, which we have used throughout this guide. There are one hundred piastres, known as *qirsh*, to the pound, although you rarely deal with these as the pound is such a small unit of currency.

Most transactions are conducted using **paper money**; some of the smaller-value notes can be rather ragged and well-used, and you'll have trouble using a note if it's torn in any way. There are notes for 5, 10, 25, 100, 500 and 1000 pounds (their denominations are printed in both English and Arabic), and **coins** for a quarter, half, 1, 5, 10 and 25 pounds. The S£500 notes, which you'll be given wads of if you change a lot of money at one go, are often too large a denomination to be accepted for small purchases such as transport tickets; S£1000 notes are of course even worse in this respect.

Obtaining Syrian currency before you enter the country is difficult, though major travel agents in the UK such as Thomas Cook should be able to sell you Syrian pounds, so long as you give them sufficient notice. Both Damascus and Aleppo **airports** have exchange facilities which are open 24 hours, seven days a week, so there isn't much point in trying to get hold of Syrian currency in advance if you're arriving by air; if you're entering Syria via Jordan or Turkey, you can obtain Syrian pounds in banks (or on the black market) in those countries. Note that it can be difficult to change Syrian pounds into foreign currency within Syria, and since the Syrian pound isn't a hard currency, it's especially sensible to be conservative about changing foreign currency during your visit.

CARRYING YOUR MONEY

Given the time it takes to exchange travellers' cheques (see below), you'll probably want to bring at least some of your money in foreign notes. This should be in the form of **US dollars** (preferably a variety of denominations), which act as the unofficial second currency in Syria. Often stallholders and taxi drivers will ask for payment in dollars, and in all but the cheapest hotels, prices are quoted in, and bills are often expected to be settled in, US dollars (see p.35 for further details). Note that Australian and Canadian dollars, pounds sterling and the major European currencies can also be exchanged at banks in Syria, but that Irish and New Zealand currencies cannot.

CHEQUES AND CREDIT CARDS

American Express seems to be the most recognized brand of **travellers' cheque**, though most brands are acceptable; Eurocheques, however, can't be used in Syria. Thomas Cook and American Express have representatives in Damascus, but they are of little use, being unable to sell or replace travellers' cheques.

Credit cards can only be used in a very limited number of outlets, including some three-star and all four- and five-star hotels, car rental outfits, moderately or expensively priced restaurants, international airline offices and a few souk stalls in Aleppo, Damascus and Palmyra which are used to seeing tourists. In theory it is impossible to get a cash advance in Syria on any type of credit card, although you could try a sympathetic stallholder or hotel owner to see whether they will carry out this transaction for you. If all else fails you could get on a bus to Beirut where there are plenty of banks that will give cash advances.

BANKS AND EXCHANGE

In recent years inflation has been remarkably low, and **exchange rates** have remained very stable: UK£1 is offically worth just over S£60, US$1 just over S£40. However, in December 2000 the Syrian government announced its intention to let the official exchange rate reflect the free-market value of Syrian pounds, which is likely to see a new rate of around S£50 to US$1 (S£70 to UK£1), reflecting that on Syria's foreign currency black market.

BANKS

Accompanying exchange-rate reform is the government's intention to relinquish its hitherto complete control over the banking sector. It was not clear at the time of writing when this would take place, but when it does it should make changing money a lot less time-consuming, and will mean that a lot more places will offer exchange facilities. Until then, there is only one institution in Syria which changes money – the **Commercial Bank of Syria**. It's the only high-street bank (no foreign banks have branches in Syria), and controls exchange booths in city centres and at airports and hotels. The Commercial Bank maintains branches in most large towns, though not all change foreign currency; among those branches that do, some cannot change travellers' cheques. The exchange rate is the same at all their branches – don't bother to shop around. Keep all **exchange receipts** as you may be asked to show that you have changed money legally before making large purchases.

Opening hours vary slightly from branch to branch, but usually they open between 8am and 9am and close for the day at around 2pm. In the cities and some large towns, banks also open up in the early evening, from 5pm to 7pm or 8pm. All banks are closed on Fridays. In large cities **exchange booths** can be found, usually nestling amid the shops in the centre (to spot one, look out for the words "Commercial Bank of Syria" marked on the door); these are usually open long hours, typically 8am to 6pm, seven days a week, but often for the exchange of cash only.

Some banks (ludicrously) ask those who exchange **travellers' cheques** to show the **receipts** given when the cheques were purchased, ignoring the fact that these are not meant to be kept with the cheques themselves. Although persuasion will normally win them round, it may be worth asking banks at home to give two separate receipts which prove the sale of the cheques. It can take an age to exchange travellers' cheques, particularly in out-of-the-way places where you'll need to go from office to office getting signatures on your paperwork, so it's best to change as much as you dare at any one time. If you find an exchange booth that changes cheques, use it – this is the quickest place in town to cash them.

THE BLACK MARKET

Until the official exchange rate reflects the free-market value of the Syrian pound, the active black market in foreign currency will continue, fuelled by the fact that Syrians can use foreign exchange to buy items which are otherwise unobtainable. On the black market, stallholders, street hustlers, waiters and hotel staff in Damascus, Aleppo and other tourist spots offer to change money at a rate of around S£50 to the US dollar; some black marketeers even take travellers' cheques and give you a cash advance on your credit card, although whether you feel it's safe to give your card details to such people is another matter. Changing money on the black market remains an illegal and risky practice for which caution and discretion are advised.

SENDING MONEY TO SYRIA

Having **money wired** from home is never convenient or cheap, and should be considered a last resort. Moneygram and Western Union do not operate in Syria, so the only way of sending money from overseas is **through banks**. In the UK, for example, high-street banks will transfer money to most branches of the Commercial Bank of Syria; their Damascus branch at no. 1 Mouaweia Street is probably the easiest place in the country to pick up money sent to you. The process costs about UK£20 (you may also have to pay a fee when the money is collected in Syria), and takes about three working days. Once funds are cleared in Syria, the money can be collected in US dollars or Syrian pounds.

COSTS

Accommodation varies from around UK£4/US$6 a night for a double room in a basic hotel to £150/$220 in Syria's most exclusive, business-oriented establishments. If you're on anything more than the most limited of budgets, you should bank on spending £15/$22 for a decent double room in a mid-range hotel, with prices rising perhaps to £20/$30 for a similar place in Damascus and Aleppo.

A basic sit-down **meal** of meat (kebabs or chicken), chips, a side salad and a soft drink rarely costs much more than £4/$6 in a local restaurant; however, falafel or *shwarma* can be had from street stalls or small eateries for as little as 50p/75c, and at the other end of the scale, a flash meal with wine or beer may cost double this in the Western-style restaurants in Damascus or Aleppo. Locally produced **beer and wine** tends to be cheap, with a half-litre bottle

of Al-Chark or Barada beer costing under £1/$1.50 in restaurants. European beers, however, sold mainly in hotels, are more expensive than back home. Local **soft drinks**, sold everywhere in small bottles, cost 15p/25c, twice that for drinks produced in Syria under licence from Western companies.

Transport within Syria is very inexpensive. Flying between Damascus and Aleppo, a distance of 370km, costs only £10/$15, and the same journey by Pullman bus costs just over £2/$3. The cost of a train ticket between these two cities is even less, at around £1.40/$2, with only a few pennies separating first- and second-class fares. The cost of local buses and microbuses, which you'll use a lot if you don't have a car, is absurdly low. If you rent a car you'll pay about £30/$45 per day for a Peugeot 205 or similar. Petrol is cheap, its price controlled by the state – around 30p/50c for a litre of "Super".

One of the biggest costs, which you can't do much to avoid, is the **entry charge** to museums and parts of some archeological sites, which can sometimes seem rather steep (local people sometimes pay only a tenth to a fifth of the tourist rate). Although many archeological sites outside the "big three" – Palmyra, Apamea and Bosra – are completely free, you should bank on spending around S£300 or S£400 to get into the principal sights and museums (such as the Aleppo citadel and archeological museum) and around S£200 to get into smaller regional museums.

If you're entitled to an **International Student Identification Card (ISIC)**, bring it along; in theory it should garner you a reduced entry charge of around a quarter of what non-cardholders pay, though in some places the officials won't understand what you're showing them and you'll have to cough up the normal price. You don't get anything off transport costs with an ISIC card.

BARGAINING AND BAKSHEESH

Bargaining is standard practice in souks (see p.52), but the only other people with whom bargaining is appropriate are **taxi drivers**, especially if you want to be taken a fair distance out of town, and **hotel owners**, particularly if you intend to stay more than three days.

Baksheesh – tipping for services – seems to make the Middle Eastern world go round, but things are much less pressured in Syria than in Turkey or Egypt. Unlike in Egypt and some other Asian countries, handing over money to speed along bureaucracy or to get yourself a seat on an otherwise crowded train or bus is not the done thing in Syria, and may cause offence or be misinterpreted. The most obvious examples of *baksheesh* you'll encounter in Syria are the tipping of hotel and restaurant staff, and payments to drivers who give you lifts in rural areas: waiters in any restaurant will expect you to round up the bill, perhaps to the nearest S£100, and if you're in a mid-range or expensive hotel, you'll be expected to tip the cleaners or porters. It makes sense to have some small-value notes (or US one-dollar bills) to hand for this purpose.

INFORMATION, WEB SITES AND MAPS

The Syrian government does not maintain tourist offices abroad, although their embassies may be able to provide you with the most basic maps and glossy handouts. Information is a commodity in short supply (and constant demand) in Syria, and it's best to be as fully prepared as possible before you leave home, particularly as far as maps are concerned.

MAPS

The best fold-out **map** of Syria is *Road Map: Syria* published by the Austrian cartographers, Freytag-Berndt; besides an excellent road map of the country at 1:800,000 scale, it contains detailed plans of Damascus, Aleppo and Palmyra. You can buy it from map stockists at home (see overleaf) or, in Syria, at English-language bookshops in Damascus (see p.108 and in bookshops in large luxury hotels throughout the country. The map of Syria published by Geoprojects (Beirut) is not nearly as accurate (or as widely available). The *Lonely Planet Travel Atlas* covering Jordan, Lebanon and Syria may be worth obtaining before you leave home; the maps it contains are accurate and detailed, but surprisingly there are no town or city plans.

Tourist offices in Syria give out a free map of the country, as well as a series of **regional maps**, which include local town plans and a certain amount of information in English, French or German (depending on which editions offices have in stock). It would be a good idea to stock up on these, but use them with caution – they are often poorly printed and compiled. Bear in mind that maps produced in Syria indicate that the Golan Heights (essentially part of Israel since 1967) and the Hatay (the finger of Turkey that juts down to the west of Aleppo, containing Antakya and Iskenderun) are both part of the country.

INFORMATION IN SYRIA

Major towns in Syria have **tourist offices** (generally daily except Fri 8am–2pm; some also open up again in the early evening). There is usually someone who speaks English in these offices, but most of the time they have little information to hand, and you may well find that people working on the reception desks in hotels are just as good a source of information. Indeed, probably the most useful thing these offices do is to distribute free maps. The English-language newspaper the *Syria Times* (see p.43) gives a random and far from comprehensive listing of exhibitions, talks, films and theatre shows in Aleppo and Damascus. Most archeological site offices sell maps or information booklets about the sites, some of which are horrendously dated.

MAP STOCKISTS

BRITAIN

Blackwell's Map and Travel Shop, 53 Broad St, Oxford OX1 3BQ (☎01865/792792, *bookshop.blackwell.co.uk*). Specialist map outlet of this national bookshop chain.

Daunt Books, 83 Marylebone High St, London W1M 3DE (☎020/7224 2295, fax 7224 6893); 193 Haverstock Hill, London NW3 4QL (☎020/7794 4006).

Heffers Map and Travel, 3rd Floor, in Heffers Stationery Department, 19 Sidney St, Cambridge CB2 3HL (☎01223/568467, *www.heffers.co.uk*). Mail order available from here; more maps and travel literature at their bookshop at 20 Trinity Street.

John Smith and Sons, 57–61 St Vincent St, Glasgow G2 5TB (☎0141/221 7472, fax 248 4412, *www.johnsmith.co.uk*). This long-estab-lished booksellers has a specialist map department.

The Map Shop, 30a Belvoir St, Leicester LE1 6QH (☎0116/247 1400). Domestic and foreign maps; mail order available.

Stanfords *sales@stanfords.co.uk* 12–14 Long Acre, London WC2E 9LP (☎020/7836 1321); 29 Corn St, Bristol BS1 1HT (☎0117/929 9966).

The Travel Bookshop, 13–15 Blenheim Crescent, London W11 2EE (☎020/7229 5260, *www.thetravelbookshop.co.uk*).

Waterstone's, 91 Deansgate, Manchester M3 2BW (☎0161/837 3000, fax 0161/835 1534, *www.waterstones-manchester-deansgate.co.uk*). Particularly good map department in this branch of the UK bookshop chain; mail order available.

IRELAND

Easons Bookshop, 40 O'Connell St, Dublin 1 (☎01/873 3811, *www.eason.ie*).

Fred Hanna's Bookshop, 27–29 Nassau St, Dublin 2 (☎01/677 1255).

Hodges Figgis Bookshop, 56–58 Dawson St, Dublin 2 (☎01/677 4754, *www.hodgesfiggis.com*).

Waterstone's, Queens Bldg, 8 Royal Ave, Belfast BT1 1DA (☎028/9024 7355); 7 Dawson St, Dublin 2 (☎01/679 1415); 69 Patrick St, Cork (☎021/276 522).

US AND CANADA

The Complete Traveller Bookstore, 199 Madison Ave, New York, NY 10016 (☎212/685-9007); 3207 Fillmore St, San Francisco, CA 92123 (☎415/923-1511).

Map Link, 30 S La Petera Lane, Unit #5, Santa Barbara, CA 93117 (☎805/692-6777, *www.maplink.com*).

Phileas Fogg's Books & Maps, #87 Stanford Shopping Center, Palo Alto, CA 94304 (☎1-800/533-FOGG, *www.foggs.com*).

Rand McNally ☎1-800/333-0136 ext 2111, *www.randmcnally.com* 444 N Michigan Ave, Chicago, IL 60611 (☎312/321-1751) and branches throughout the US.

Traveler's Choice Bookstore, 22 W 52nd St, New York, NY 10019 (☎212/941-1535, *tvlchoice@aol.com*).

Ulysses Travel Bookshop, 4176 St-Denis, Montreal (☎514/843-9447, *www.ulysses.ca*).

World of Maps, 1235 Wellington St, Ottawa, ON K1Y 3A3 (☎613/724-6776, *www.worldofmaps.com*).

World Wide Books and Maps, 552 Seymour St, Vancouver, BC V6B 3J5 (☎604/687-3320, *www.itmb.com*).

AUSTRALIA AND NEW ZEALAND

The Map Shop, 6 Peel St, Adelaide (☎08/8231 2033, *mapshop.net.au*).

Mapland, 372 Little Bourke St, Melbourne (☎03/9670 4383, *www.mapland.com.au*).

Mapworld, 173 Gloucester St, Christchurch (☎03/374 5399, fax 374 5633, *www.mapworld.co.nz*).

Perth Map Centre, 1/884 Hay St, Perth (☎08/9322 5733, *www.perthmap.com.au*).

Specialty Maps, 46 Albert St, Auckland (☎09/307 2217).

Travel Bookshop, Shop 3, 175 Liverpool St, Sydney (☎02/9261 8200).

Worldwide Maps and Guides, 187 George St, Brisbane (☎07/3221 4330).

SYRIA ON THE INTERNET

The Syrian government – not among the world's most liberal regimes – is rather suspicious of the **Internet**, and consequently the country has been slow to join the online revolution. However, the government has set up a few of its own Web sites, their contents ranging from (fairly basic) tourism-related pages to propaganda on the Golan Heights. For visitors, among the the most useful Web sites connected with Syria are those which have been established by upmarket private hotels, such as the *Beit Wakil* and the *Martini Dar Zamaria* in Aleppo (see p.221). Home-grown sites are identified by host names ending in *.sy*, rarer are those that end in *.lb*, which use Lebanese servers. For information about **getting online** in Syria, see pp.42, 111 and 238.

www.c-allen.dircon.co.uk/Countries/Syria.htm
Links to a huge variety of sites including those relating to history, current affairs, business, healthcare, economics, architecture and travel information.

www.emulateme.com/syria.htm
Facts and figures relating to history, government, politics and defence issues; even has current weather details.

www.syriatourism.org
Ministry of Tourism Web site, with text and photos relating to history, culture, and sights; it's most useful for its information on accommodation and other travel practicalities.

www.golan-syria.org
Extensive examination of history, culture and current political situation in the Golan Heights, posted by the National Information Centre in Damascus – so beware the predictable bias.

members.aol.com/syriatour
Articles on Syrian history and culture, and some excellent links, particularly relating to Syrian music, with details of upcoming concerts.

www.odci.gov/cia/publications/factbook/ geos/sy.html
www.middleeastnews.com/Syria.html
Fairly dry gazetteers of facts and figures relating to Syria, including defence information, transport, communications and the economy.

weecheng.simplenet.com/mideast/syria/ syria.htm
www.spectraweb.ch/~ajunge/Syria.html
homepages.ihug.co.nz/~artus/FactsSyr.htm
Three extensive accounts of personal visits to Syria, with photos and links to other similar sites; the second of these sites includes details of the author's attempts to learn Arabic in Damascus.

syria-online.com/tourism/
Travel-industry Web site, worth a browse for checking out latest situation as regards hotels and tour operators.

GETTING AROUND

As rail services in Syria are very sparse, you're most likely to rely on buses to get around; these come in all varieties, from luxury air-conditioned European-built vehicles to the ubiquitous cramped white microbuses that link most settlements on a regular basis. Syrianair has a limited network of ultra-cheap domestic flights, which can be useful for the longer distances even if you're on a relatively tight budget.

In **Ramadan** (see p.44), the holy month during which observant Muslims fast from dawn till dusk, some public transport services are reduced (or concentrated into the early morning period). Particularly affected are privately run microbuses and service taxis, whose drivers may prefer to set off after dark rather than in the afternoon. At this time of year, any bus or taxi journeys that aren't completed by sunset are bound to be interrupted by a long meal break, when the driver and passengers head off to break their fast.

TRAINS

Trains in Syria are very cheap and more comfortable than buses (though also slower), so it's a pity that using them is so difficult. No **timetables** are published in Syria, and trains often seem to run according to whim rather than to any sort of schedule. The only published source of information anywhere is the *Thomas Cook Overseas Timetable*, but even that is usually out of date. All this means that the only way of finding out the current situation is to ask at stations

themselves or at the **railway booking offices** in the centres of Qamishli and Deir Ez-Zur.

All passenger rail services within Syria are operated by **Chemins de Fer Syriennes** (CFS). The main **route** is Damascus–Homs–Hama–Aleppo–Deir ez-Zur–Qamishli, with a secondary route which runs from Homs along the coast through Tartous and Latakia and then through the mountains to Aleppo. Narrow-gauge routes run from Damascus up the Barada valley to Zabadani, and south to Dera and the Jordanian border, and on to Amman.

In practice, there is generally one train a day on the Damascus–Aleppo route, but Latakia, Tartous and Qamishli may only be linked with Damascus once a week. The most frequently served part of the network is Aleppo–Latakia, with three daily trains; it's also the most **scenic**, particularly close to Latakia, where the train navigates gorges and attractive, forested valleys by means of a series of viaducts and tunnels. There are usually two trains per week from Damascus to Zabadani, and two per week from Damascus to Dera, one of which continues to Amman.

All trains carry two classes of seats. First-class accommodation boasts air-conditioning, and sleepers on the Damascus–Qamishli route; second class is not air-conditioned and has slightly less leg room. Even those on a tight budget will easily be able to afford first-class travel: to give an idea of **fares**, a ticket for the six-hour journey from Damascus to Aleppo costs S£70 in second class and S£95 in first; a sleeper on the Damascus–Qamishli route S£800.

BUSES

Given that the road network is much better developed than the rail system, and that comparatively few Syrians own cars, it's not surprising that **bus transport** is by far the most convenient method of getting around. At the top end of the scale, inter-regional buses are inexpensive, frequent and comfortable, with competition between the various private **Pullman** firms – and the ailing state bus company, **Karnak** – ensuring a good deal for travellers. These buses cover all towns in Syria, and if you're in the country for any length of time you're likely to make considerable use of them. Some inter-regional routes are also covered by cheaper **micro-**

buses, but they're really too uncomfortable for any journey of a couple of hours or more; it's best to save them for shorter journeys, which they cover along with larger, older **local buses**.

For any form of bus travel between towns or cities, or even short trips out of town, you often need to show your **passport** before you board. It's as well to bear in mind that it is often considered inappropriate for men to sit next to lone women passengers – locals often arrange their seating so that the possibility of this does not arise.

KARNAK AND PULLMAN BUSES

Government-operated **Karnak buses**, coloured orange and white and air-conditioned, cover all the major centres in Syria, as well as linking Beirut and Amman with Damascus, and Beirut and Tripoli with Tartous and Latakia. Karnak buses tend to have their own designated stations in towns and cities, usually near the centre. The company has offices in the centres of most cities, selling tickets and giving information on their services; it's normally advisable to buy tickets in advance.

For many years the staple means of long-distance bus travel in Syria, Karnak vehicles, though comfortable enough, are beginning to look distinctly ancient in comparison with their snazzier **Pullman** competitors – Renault or other European-built luxury coaches operated by private bus companies, the biggest of which are Damas Tour, Al-Ahliah and Qadmous. Though there's little difference in terms of journey time, Pullman buses usually leave Karnak standing in terms of frequency, comfort and reliability. These vehicles, air-conditioned and very comfortable, usually feature pirated martial-arts videos or Egyptian TV comedies blaring away at the front, and a conductor who keeps passengers supplied with drinking water and boiled sweets at regular intervals. Pullmans run on major routes, most of which start or finish in Damascus or Aleppo; however, they tend not to serve international routes, and if you're travelling in the northeast, or between Damascus and the Hauran, you're likely to find Karnak more convenient.

The private bus companies tend to have offices in town centres, as well as at the bus stations themselves, where you can get information and buy tickets, though services are so frequent that you rarely have to wait long to get a seat to where you want to go. In Damascus, Aleppo and Homs, Pullman buses have a designated terminal some distance away from the town centre; in some small towns, Pullmans don't use a bus station at all, but pick up and drop off passengers outside the company office.

You'll pay slightly more on Pullman than on Karnak services. As a guide to **fares**, it costs S£170 for the five-hour journey between Damascus and Aleppo on a Pullman bus, S£110 with Karnak. Karnak and Pullman buses all run more or less to set schedules, with timetables sometimes displayed at bus stations or company offices; however, the bus operators don't produce timetable leaflets or booklets.

MICROBUSES AND LOCAL BUSES

Microbuses – white Mazda minivans known to locals as *meecro* – can be seen everywhere in Syria. They mostly serve smaller places, fanning out from towns into the surrounding countryside. Owned and operated by their drivers, microbuses do not run to timetables, simply leaving when they are full – which means that you'll sometimes wait a long time before enough passengers turn up, and that the vehicle is usually full to bursting when it finally sets off. Services tend to be frequent in the morning, but thin in the afternoon and all day on Friday. You should also bear in mind that some microbus drivers tend to ignore completely the rules of the road, treating their vehicles as racing cars and assuming their passengers are thrill-seeking visitors to an adventure theme park: some journeys beat anything that's on offer at Disneyworld.

Unlike Karnak and Pullman buses, microbuses can be flagged down anywhere along their route. In large towns they operate out of designated **stations**; in Damascus and Aleppo there are several of these, covering different destinations. Some of these stations have ticket offices where you have to purchase a ticket in advance; otherwise you'll end up paying once you're on the bus, when (at the request of the driver) everyone passes their money to the front and states their destination, with the required change somehow getting back to the right people in the same way. Sometimes the buses display their **destinations** in Arabic in their windscreens, but often you simply have to ask locals where the next vehicle headed for the town you want is parked.

Local buses which link towns with surrounding villages are ancient affairs, larger than microbuses but smaller than Pullmans; they're often adorned inside and out by an incredible array of ornaments, stickers, photographs and decorations. Middle Eastern pop music screeching out of tinny speakers is a feature that sets these buses apart from microbuses, which they resemble in terms of price and routeings. People are set down and picked up anywhere along the route, making journeys rather slow, but it's a good way to meet the locals, especially in remote areas. Local buses tend to operate from microbus stations, but are a dying breed, gradually being replaced by their zappy white cousins.

Fares on microbuses and local buses are very cheap: about S£25 for a forty-kilometre trip on the former, S£20 on the latter. Sometimes it's not clear whether you'll be catching a microbus or a large local bus when you buy a ticket; if you get the option, plump for the latter, as microbuses tend to be uncomfortable on long journeys – although journeys within some areas of the country (most notably the northeast and the Hauran) are only covered by microbuses.

SERVICE TAXIS

Shared **service taxis** (called *servees* by locals) are an institution all over the Middle East, though they're used much less in Syria than in Egypt or Jordan. Big, usually yellow, limousines (often American vehicles dating from the 1940s and 1950s), service taxis run set routes between towns and cities; passengers can get on and off where they want, provided it's along the taxi's route. They usually operate out of Karnak, Pullman or microbus stations, and are quite fast but relatively expensive compared to buses; you might find yourself paying up to S£500 per person for a trip from Damascus to Aleppo. Service taxis are most useful on international routes (eg Damascus to Amman or Beirut); internally, they only serve destinations on the Damascus–Homs–Hama–Aleppo road.

DOMESTIC FLIGHTS

Syrianair operates air services, usually using Tupolev 134/154 planes, between Damascus and Aleppo, Deir ez-Zur, Latakia and Qamishli. There are two or three flights a day between the capital and Aleppo, but flights to other centres are thrice weekly (or in the case of Latakia, once weekly). **Fares** are cheap: S£600 Damascus–Aleppo, for example, and S£900 Damascus–Qamishli or Deir ez-Zur. Given the time needed to travel from town centres to airports, however, air travel isn't actually much faster than the bus, unless you're heading for Deir ez-Zur or Qamishli.

Tickets can be bought from any Syrianair office – there's one in most towns. In some places the airline runs a bus out to the airport, but generally you have to use taxis to get to the airport.

DRIVING AND HITCHING

Driving in Syria is not an experience for the faint-hearted or road-wary, with traffic often moving at dangerous speeds and obeying few of the laws of the road that you are used to back home. Hazards include ambling animals and pedestrians, horse-drawn vehicles moving much slower than the general flow of traffic, occasional flooding after heavy rain, and potholed roads which can result in sudden swerves or blow-outs, depending on how much warning you get about them.

You drive on the right, but beyond that **rules of the road** are subject to interpretation. Lane discipline is practically non-existent, and on the highways and arterial roads of Damascus drivers weave in and out of lanes constantly, horns blaring at all times. A single long blast of the horn usually means "get out of the way, I'm coming through", and the largest vehicle on the road at the time is the one who normally gets right of way. On the open road, overtaking is usually done regardless of what's coming the other way, and the flow of traffic is fast whatever the state of the road. At night, headlights are rarely used beyond a warning flash at another car approaching, and the same daytime hazards – children, animals, carts and potholes – are of course still there, only practically invisible.

On roads in the desert (see also p.278) and the northeast you'll pass **police checkpoints**. You'll probably be asked to show your passport or driver's licence, but foreigners are usually treated with kid gloves. There's **signposting** in English on main roads, but it tends to be in Arabic only once you're into the backroads – especially in the mountains, where drivers with no knowledge of Arabic will experience some difficulty getting around.

The official **speed limits** are 60km per hour in built-up areas, 70km per hour on most open roads and 110km per hour on the main Damascus–Aleppo highway, which is a dual carriageway (this doesn't stop shepherds crossing it with their flocks on occasion).

CAR RENTAL

Renting a car pays obvious dividends if you want to see a lot of the country quickly, or, more particularly, to reach historic sites which are not

INTERNATIONAL CAR RENTAL AGENCIES

BRITAIN
Avis ☎0990/900500
Budget ☎0800/181181
Europcar ☎0845/722 2525

IRELAND
Budget Rent-A-Car In the Republic ☎0800/973 159; in Northern Ireland ☎0800/181181.
Europcar In the Republic ☎01/874 5844; in Northern Ireland ☎0845/722 2525.

US & CANADA
Avis ☎1-800/331-1084, www.avis.com

Budget ☎1-800/527-0700, www.budget.com
Dollar ☎1-800/800-6000, www.dollar.com
Hertz ☎1-800/654-3001, www.hertz.com

AUSTRALIA
Avis ☎1800/225533
Budget ☎13/2727

NEW ZEALAND
Avis ☎09/526 2847
Budget ☎09/375 2222

on public transport routes; the most obvious of these are the Dead Cities around Aleppo, and sites in the mountains accessible from Tartous or Latakia. If you don't want to drive yourself, then it's usually possible to hire a car with a driver.

In some places there are **small rental outfits** which charge very low rates, but they're only able to do this through offering no-insurance deals. You're strongly advised not to touch these firms with a bargepole, and instead to pay more at **established firms** such as Avis, Europcar or Budget, whose vehicles can be booked from abroad. This is, in any case, a good idea if you're planning to rent a vehicle, since most companies will tell you thay haven't got anything immediately available if you turn up without a reservation. Not surprisingly, the greatest choice of car rental outfits is in Damascus (see p.110). Elsewhere in the country the first place to look is one of the big luxury hotels; the *Cham Palace* chain has their own car rental arm, Chamcar, and Europcar and other companies operate through these and other hotels.

As a guide to **prices**, you'll probably pay as much as you would in Europe: Europcar in Damascus, for example, charges around US$40 a day, including insurance, for a small Peugeot 106, rising to US$75 for a Peugeot 406, and most other reliable firms charge about the same (these prices are for journeys limited to 100km per day over a minimum period of two days). Rental is always charged in dollars and, given the sizeable deposit that many firms demand if you pay by cash, this is one of the few occasions in Syria where you'll probably have no option but to use your plastic for payment – in which case no deposit is required.

Most firms insist that drivers be least 21 years of age.

PETROL AND BREAKDOWNS

Petrol stations are reasonably common in large towns and along major highways, but in desert areas it always pays to keep your tank well topped up. The Freytag-Berndt map of Syria recommended on p.27 indicates the positions of filling stations. Fuel is extremely cheap: many cars run on diesel *(mazout)*, with regular petrol *(benzin)* slightly more expensive.

In Damascus and Aleppo there are plenty of **repair shops** (details in the "Listings" for each city); elsewhere in the country you should be able to find a local garage with a competent mechanic. At either type of place, it's worth getting **oil filters** checked and cleaned to prevent dust from clogging the engine. Most Syrians drive Japanese and Korean cars, with European models comparatively rare and spare **parts** for them hard to find; whatever car you're driving, bring along as many replacement parts as you can (including a gearbox), and consult motoring organizations back home for advice before you set out.

HITCHING

In parts of Syria where there's minimal public transport – most particularly, in the mountains and around the Dead Cities – **hitching** is an accepted and routine method of getting around, with drivers **charging** unofficial rates for certain jouneys. Hitching in the desert, you're likely to be picked up by lorries or by one of the ubiquitous Bedouin pick-up trucks; in more densely settled areas (where there are more buses) you might find getting a lift actually more difficult than in remoter regions, and if you try hitching on main roads, you're much more likely to stop a passing microbus or local bus than a private vehicle.

For your own safety, **don't hitch alone**, or at night – only accept lifts when there are local people or fellow travellers doing the same. Local people themselves hitch a lot in out-of-the-way areas; foreigners who try to do so will quickly attract attention and are likely to be offered a lift somewhere without even asking for it first.

CITY TRANSPORT

All towns and cities have **taxis**, which are always coloured bright yellow; many are American cars from the 1940s and 1950s, which their drivers somehow manage to keep going despite the potholes and lack of spare parts. Fares are pretty low – no ride within Damascus, for example, should cost more than S£100. Most taxis have meters,

although not all drivers who have them use them, and more often than not you'll end up agreeing a price before you set off. Taxis are easy enough to hail in the street or to pick up at bus stations, but if your journey starts or finishes at one of the big hotels, you're almost asking for the fare to be inflated. In Aleppo there are also local **service taxis**, largely indistinguishable from normal taxis on the outside, which run set routes – essentially taxis operating as buses.

Syrian cities have **bus services** operated by two sorts of vehicle: ancient, lumbering, smoke-belching, jam-packed buses, and faster, smaller, newer microbuses. They're difficult to use as all destination signs and numbers are in Arabic (or simply not displayed at all), and there are no route maps or timetables published or displayed anywhere; even bus stops can be hard to spot. For this reason, few foreigners use city buses or microbuses, but the city centres are usually compact enough to walk around in any case.

ACCOMMODATION

Finding a bed for the night at the price you want is generally no problem in Syria. The only times when you might want to telephone in advance are if you are planning to arrive in Damascus or Aleppo late in the day, or travelling during busy holidays periods (particularly during the *eid*s – see p.44), or visiting Palmyra during its annual festival in May. There's only one youth hostel in Syria – located in the

citadel at Bosra – and a handful of fairly dreadful campsites, so most of the time you're left with no real option but hotels as far as accommodation goes; conveniently, a few of the hotels in Aleppo and Damascus even have decent dormitory accommodation.

Tourist offices know nothing about local hotels, so it's likely to be a matter of shopping around once you've arrived in a town. This is rarely a problem as hotels of a certain standard always tend to cluster around one area of downtown. Hotels come in all varieties from filthy, noisy, dirt-cheap hotels in city centres, where you will be certain to spend your night with a wide variety of insect life, up to huge five-star luxury places, including those of the Meridien and Sheraton chains.

The government ranks hotels from one to five stars, with the most expensive receiving a five-star de luxe category all of their own. By law, hotels must display their prices at the reception desk, but in all bar the most expensive you may be told that the rates shown are out of date. If you're planning to stay in four- and five-star places (price code ⑤ and above, according to our system), you should consid-

ACCOMMODATION PRICE CODES

In this book, all hotels have been categorized according to the **price codes** outlined below. They represent the minimum you can expect to pay for a **double room** in each hotel; note that prices do not tend to vary seasonally.

In categories ① and ② you pay in **Syrian pounds**, though hotel-keepers are unlikely to object if you offer them **US dollars**; in ③ and ④ establishments you are usually asked for payment in dollars (cash) but a bit of persuasion will allow you to pay in Syrian pounds, depending on the whim of the owner – always check before you agree to take the room, and to be on the safe side carry a fair-sized stock of US dollars with you if you're going to be using these places a lot. All establishments in category ⑤ and above will expect payment in dollars. Some places in band ④, and all in bands ⑤–⑧, allow guests to pay by **credit card** and **travellers' cheques**. **Bargaining** is possible in ① and ② hotels, and in ③–⑤ establishments if you're planning to stay longer than three days, or arrive late in the day when they're not busy and are keen to attract guests.

In category ④ places and above, **breakfast**, normally consisting of coffee or tea, boiled eggs, bread with various spreads and fillings, and olives or other fruit, is usually included in the price; you won't get a rebate if you choose not to have it. Some places in category ③ might provide an optional breakfast for around S£100; ① and ② hotels do not offer breakfast.

① under S£300/US$7	⑤ US$35–50/S£1500–2100
② S£300–600/US$7–14	⑥ US$50–90/S£2100–3900
③ S£600–1000/US$14–23	⑦ US$90–130/S£3900–5600
④ S£1000–1500/US$23–35	⑧ US$130 and over/S£5600 and over

er taking a package tour from your own country as you'll inevitably get much better rates. Whatever category of hotel you stay in, it's rare to find a double room with one large bed in it – twin beds are the norm; however, family rooms with three or four beds are easy to find. Lastly, bear in mind that the prices quoted above, and throughout the book, are for visiting Westerners; if you have a residence permit for Syria (known as an *iqaama*), you pay the rates Syrians pay – which can be up to eighty percent less in the most expensive places.

CHEAP HOTELS

The **cheap hotels** (one or two stars) charge about S£300 for a very basic single room, S£400 for a double. If you're a solo traveller and the hotel's fairly full you may end up sharing, but this is rare; more typically you'll be given a double room to yourself, and – if you're lucky – you'll only be asked to pay the single-room rate for this. Rooms are unlikely to have en-suite facilities, but will have a bed with a sheet or two provided, usually a fan, and perhaps a sink plumbed into the wall. Hot water is generally available in the evening and early morning; however, these hotels tend to be inadequately heated in winter, when it can get quite cold in Syria.

Some of these places are unhygienic and chronically dirty, with bedbugs and roach-infested

shared squat toilets; however, the Syrian government has ordered many of these hotels to clean up their acts in recent years and this is gradually becoming less of a problem. A number of cheap hotels even have TVs and fridges in the rooms nowadays. Hotels reviewed in the *Guide* were of a reasonable standard at the time of writing, but you should remember that in the cheap hotels rooms can vary enormously in terms of size, ambience and cleanliness, so it pays always to look at your room before you decide to take it.

In summer you'll want the window open, which will mean that street noise can be a real problem, so it makes sense to try to get a room at the back. In addition you should try to avoid hotels adjacent to mosques, unless you fancy being woken up by the dawn call to prayer from the *muezzin*.

In the accounts of Aleppo, Damascus and Hama, we've listed several backpacker-oriented hotels with decent **dormitory accommodation**. In Damascus and a few other large towns, there are also dorms used mainly by itinerant workers – avoid these unless you're really desperate.

MID-RANGE HOTELS

Mid-range hotels (three stars; ③–⑤ on our price code system) usually cost around $15/$25 for a single/double room, rising to $40/$50 in

Damascus and Aleppo. Facilities in these hotels will be en suite with hot water throughout the day, and you'll have efficient (but sometimes noisy) air-conditioning and a TV; breakfast will be available in the more expensive of these places, as well as perhaps a telephone and minibar. Generally the mid-range establishments we've listed in the guide are clean and friendly, with owners who speak a modicum of English and are often good sources of information about the local scene.

EXPENSIVE HOTELS

In Damascus, Aleppo and a few other touristed areas, **expensive hotels** are appearing which fill the wide gap between the mid-range and the luxury places. Typical rates are anywhere between $50 and $90 per night (⑥) for accommodation, classified as three or four stars, which isn't really much superior to the mid-range hotels. Normally there'll be a bar or a restaurant, the TV will be hooked up to receive satellite services, rooms will be carpeted and there will be central air-conditioning. Most of these hotels are modern but rather characterless, and are largely aimed at tour groups.

LUXURY HOTELS

International-standard **luxury hotels**, classified as four- or five-star and starting at $90 for a double, can be found in most large towns and tourist centres. Air-conditioned throughout, they tend to be oases of marble floors and shiny blandness. One of the advantages of the luxury hotels is that they can be **booked from abroad** in advance; you might also find that prices are much lower when you do so.

The less expensive of these places (price code ⑦ according to our system) have central air-conditioning, a bar and more than one restaurant, and usually a pool, snack bar and a shop; rooms have satellite TV, telephone, minibar and bath. Most of the Syrian-owned *Cham Palace* chain (in Paris ☎33-1.45.63.12.81 and in the US ☎1-202/785-0099, *www.chamhotels.com*), comprising several hotels in Damascus and others in Palmyra, Bosra, Hama, Safita, Aleppo, Deir ez-Zur, and on the coast just north of Latakia (the *Cote d'Azur de Cham* resort, the only apartment complex in the country) come under this category; they offer discounts if you book for several nights' stay. Band ⑧ hotels are confined mostly to Aleppo and Damascus, and usually provide all the above plus a nightclub, sporting and business facilities and a small-scale shopping arcade; they are the favourite haunts of visiting diplomats and moneyed business travellers from the Persian Gulf or Europe, and include the Damascus *Sheraton* (*www.sheraton.com*) and *Meridien* hotels in Damascus and by the beach in Latakia (☎020/7439 1244 in the UK, ☎1-800/543-4300 in North America, *www.lemeridien-hotels.com*).

EATING AND DRINKING

Syrian food typifies what you can find in the rest of the Levant but, because Syrians don't tend to eat out a lot, most of the best cooking is served up at home, and so the experience of the cuisine can be disappointing for foreigners. Especially if you're on a tight budget, you'll soon get tired of chicken, kebabs, falafel, hummus and salads; these make up the standard fare in most basic eateries, and are often all that's on offer in small towns and in the northeast of the country. However, in large towns or tourist centres the choice of food usually extends to pasta, pizza and burgers, while Damascus and Aleppo both offer

an excellent selection of restaurants of all standards serving Syrian and European fare.

WHERE TO EAT

Sit-down **restaurants** come in all varieties, from greasy chicken-and-kebab joints to pricey affairs which, outside Damascus and Aleppo, are almost exclusively attached to hotels. Especially worthwhile for those on a tight budget (or just in a rush), food purchased from **street vendors**, easy to come across in town centres (particularly around bus stations), is usually filling, tasty and extremely cheap. Every city and town also has its **pastry shops**, selling very sweet desserts, usually made from honey, syrup, pastry, cream and nuts in various combinations; many of these outlets double as sit-down places, in which case they may well do coffee and ice cream too. Best for the latter, though, are the **ice cream parlours** that have sprung up in Damascus and Aleppo; they're especially popular with families and couples out for an early evening stroll in summer.

Standards of **hygiene** in Syria are sometimes not quite up to scratch, so choose restaurants and food carefully: avoid meat dishes that look undercooked, and restaurants or stalls that look dirty. Salads can pose a risk (particularly if they have been washed in tap water); to be ultra-cautious, you might even want to avoid the chopped mint and parsley sprinkled onto most meat and kebab dishes. Fresh produce should be washed thoroughly (preferably in mineral water) before eating.

RESTAURANTS

Cheap restaurants can be found crammed together in the centres of all Syrian cities and towns, and in the smallest villages too. They don't have menus available, so it's just as well that they all sell basically the same limited range of dishes – a typical meal comprising chicken or kebab, side salad, chips and a soft drink costs around S£250 at one of these places. Only a few of the cheap places serve alcohol. In the larger or more touristy towns, you'll find **more expensive restaurants**, whose fare extends to pizza, pasta, and a variety of Arabic main dishes and desserts, and which serve alcohol (usually limited to bottled beers). A menu might be available in these places, but don't get your hopes up too quickly – usually most of what's written down isn't actually available.

Pizza and **burger joints**, modelled on Western chains, have appeared in the main cities

in recent years, as have slightly more expensive Western-oriented places serving unadventurous but filling pasta, meat and other dishes (and often Syrian food too). Some hotels catering to Western tastes offer an eat-all-you-want evening **buffet dinner**, consisting of meats, pasta and salads, with cakes or fruit as dessert. Chinese, French, Indian and Italian restaurants can be found in Aleppo and Damascus, but what they offer tends to be a pale imitation of the genuine article.

Whatever sort of restaurant you eat at, you'll get a glass of tap water, which should be safe to drink, and some unleavened bread put on your table. Western-style **cutlery** is always available, although some foods are usually eaten with hands, eg when dipping slivers of bread in hummus; note that it's customary to bring food up to your mouth using the **right hand** only.

Menus, where available, may not list **prices**, but waiters at the more expensive restaurants usually understand some English and so can give an idea of costs. At the end of your meal, your **bill** (*al-hesab*) will be itemized in Arabic, but the prices of dishes will be written down in both Arabic and "Western" numerals; a ten percent tip is usually expected.

FOOD

Lamb and chicken are the staple **meats** in Syria (Islam proscribes the consumption of pork, and beef is very hard to come by), occasionally supplemented by fish in coastal towns (especially Tartous). Locally produced **vegetables** and pulses include chickpeas, tomatoes, cucumbers, cabbages and lettuces; more appealing is the **fruit**, which includes peaches, grapes, olives, watermelons, pomegranates, pears, apples, figs and dates. All the fruit and vegetables, including the imported South American bananas (which are usually excellent and are available everywhere), are very cheap at produce **markets**, often located within souks or near central bus stations; the larger cities have **grocery stores** too, which are usually fairly well stocked with tinned and packaged food, though there are no Western-style supermarkets in Syria. A feature of many Syrian cities and towns are **nut stalls**, selling everything from peanuts to melon seeds and locally grown pistachios.

STREET FARE

Falafel, hummus and *fuul* are the staple **street snacks**. Eaten all over the Middle East, **falafel**

A FOOD AND DRINK GLOSSARY

GENERAL

bread	khobz	fruit	fawakih	salad	salata
butter	zibda	honey	'asal	salt	mileh
cheese	jibneh	ice cream	booza	soup	shorba
cheese (made from goat's milk)	shinklish	meat	lahm	sugar	sukkar
		mint	na'na'	vinegar	khal
		oil	zayt	yoghurt	laban
egg (boiled)	bayda (masloo)	pepper	filfil	vegetables	khadrawat/ khodar
fish	samak	rice	ruz		

MEAT

beef	lahm al-baqar	lamb	lahm al-kharoof	pork	lahm al-khanzeer
chicken	farooj	liver	kibda	steak	felay
kidney	kalaawi				

VEGETABLES

aubergine	bedinjan	green beans	fasolya	peas	bisella
cabbage	malfoof	lentils	'adas	peppers (hot)	fley fley hur
carrot	juzur	lettuce	khass	peppers (sweet)	fley fley heloo
cauliflower	arnabeet	mushroom	aesh al-ghorab		
courgette	koosa	olives	zaytoon	potato/chips	batatas
cucumber	khiyar	onion	basal	tomato	banadura
garlic	tum	parsley	badoonis		

FRUIT

apple	tufah	grapefruit	graybfroot	pineapple	ananas
apricot	mishmish	lemon	limoon	pomegranate	rumman
banana	moz	mango	manga	plum	khokh
dates	tamr	orange	burtuqqal	raspberry	toot
fig	teen	peach	durra	strawberry	frazeh
grapes	'anab	pear	njas	watermelon	batteekh

NUTS AND SEEDS

dry-roasted seeds	bizr	peanuts	fusto abeed	cashews	kashoo
		pistachios	fusto halabee	almonds	luz

DRINKS

arrack	'araq	milk	haleeb	water	miya
beer	beera	mineral water	miya at-taabiyya	wine	khamr
coffee	ahwa	fizzy soft drink	gazoza	yoghurt drink with water and salt	ayran
fruit juice	'aseer				
liquorice	soos	tea	shai		

DESSERTS AND SWEETS

coconut slice	isfinjiyya	rice pudding, very sweet and often topped with nuts	muhalabiyyeh
honey-soaked pastry, often filled with nuts	baqlawa	syrup-topped doughy pastry filled with ice cream or cream cheese	halawat al-jibna
ice cream	booza		

consists of deep-fried balls of chickpea paste with spices, served in a piece of unleavened bread (*khobz*) along with salad, pickled vegetables and sesame-seed paste (*tahini*). The meaty equivalent of a falafel is a **shwarma**, filled with either spit-roasted chicken or lamb (for the latter, layers of lamb or mutton are piled onto a vertical spit and heated before a gas-heated grill, and as the outer layers cook they're sliced off). To make **hummus**, often available alongside falafel, cooked and ground chickpeas are mixed with *tahini*, garlic and lemon; it's served as a side dish with main courses, or as a dip for bread or falafel. **Fuul** is a paste made from fava beans, garlic and lemon, and is often served doused in oil.

RESTAURANT MEALS

At cheap restaurants, **chicken** is usually roasted on spits in large ovens, rotisserie-style, while lamb is served up in **kebabs**, pieces of the minced meat pressed onto skewers and grilled over charcoal; both come with onion and chillies (and occasionally olives), with side dishes and dips of salad, beans, yoghurt, raw vegetables, olives, pickles and the ubiquitous hummus. **Chips** are also a popular side dish, available virtually everywhere. You might also come across **shishtaoo**, chicken kebab; **kibbeh**, meat pie made from ground lamb; and **borak**, a cheese-filled pastry.

In addition to serving up the same sort of fare as the cheaper eating places, mid-range restaurants usually offer **stews**, generally served on rice: *fasolya* is a green bean stew, *batatas* potato and *mulukhiyyeh* a stew made from a strongly flavoured leafy green vegetable similar to spinach. A pleasant change from chicken and kebabs, these stews nonetheless contain chunks of meat (usually mutton), often in a tomato purée base. Less frequently, you'll find **fatteh**, which is lamb, chicken or chickpeas cooked in a pot with rice, bread, pine-nuts and yoghurt; **maqloobeh**, rice mixed with chopped eggplant, lamb or chicken, occasionally sprinkled with walnuts or almonds; **basturma**, a veal dish; and **yalanje**, which consist of vine leaves stuffed with rice and meat or vegetables. Many of these restaurants also serve basic pasta dishes such as spaghetti, almost invariably accompanied by a minced meat and tomato sauce which is served on the side.

At **pricey** restaurants in Aleppo and Damascus, one of the particular gastronomic delights on offer is the Middle Eastern buffet, or **meze** (literally "table"). This is a shared experience, with six dishes perhaps sufficient for two people, although the number of dishes and diners is of course flexible. A meze tends to be a long, languid affair, particularly if eaten on terrace restaurants on summer evenings, when the meal becomes an ideal opportunity for both Syrians and visitors to talk the night away. Meze dishes are typically based on meat, cheese, or vegetables; some, such as hummus, or **mutabbal** (a creamy mixture of aubergine, onion, tomato, yoghurt, olive oil and *tahini*), are intended as dips for bread; and **tabbouleh**, a salad dish consisting of bulgar wheat, tomato, onion and parsley, is another common meze component. **Desserts**, if available in these restaurants, don't extend beyond fruit, sticky Arabic pastries or ice cream.

PASTRIES AND DESSERTS

Most Syrian **pastries** (generically known as *baqlawa*) are stuffed with honey, sugar, nuts and seeds, and are sold by weight or in bite-sized squares. Popular varieties include **kenaafeh**, a widely available Palestinian speciality consisting of layers of pastry and melted, creamy goat's-milk cheese, baked in syrup; and **mushabbak**, which is pastry cut into criss-crossing narrow strips and drenched in syrups. Larger pastry shops might also offer milk-based sweets such as **mahalabiyyeh**, a sweet rice pudding sprinkled with nuts; or **sahlab**, a hot, eggless custard made from milk, sugar and almond essence.

VEGETARIAN FARE

Vegetarians might well end up on quite a restricted diet in Syria, as so much of the savoury food on offer is meat-based, particularly at the cheaper restaurants; even where meat isn't among the visible ingredients, it's possible a meat stock has been used (in soups for example), or that the oil used in fried foods has previously been used to fry meat. That said, hummus, *fuul* and falafel are obvious, widely available snack foods that veggies can enjoy. For more choice it's best to head for the pricier restaurants (at cheaper places, hummus, chips and salad may be all that's suitable): mezes always come with some non-meat options, and Western dishes such as pizzas (it's usually possible to have them made without meat – ask for them "*bidoon lahm*") or pasta with cheese may be available. Checking into a hotel that serves **breakfast** (usually bread, jam, cheese, olives and boiled eggs) is a convenient way to fill up for the first part of the day.

DRINKS

Tap **water** in Syria is considered safe to drink, though many visitors prefer to buy bottled spring water, which is quite cheap and available everywhere, including the very cheapest restaurants and stalls. It's always as well to check the seal hasn't been broken, or you may be sold just plain old tap water. The most common brands are Boukein, bottled in the Barada Mountains west of Damascus, and Dreikish, which comes from the Anti-Lebanon Range near the Crac des Chevaliers.

TEA, COFFEE AND SOFT DRINKS

Tea (*shai*), drunk constantly by everyone, everywhere, is served black in small glasses, sometimes with mint or sage, and sweetened to taste. **Arabic coffee** is a bitter-tasting, green or grey, silty liquid which is drunk unsweetened. It's rarely served in coffee houses or restaurants, but you will see plenty of Syrians drinking it, perhaps sitting outside their houses in the late afternoon with a tin tray beside them on which is placed small glass tumblers and a long-spouted brass coffee pot. The coffee encountered by visitors is much more likely to be **Turkish coffee**, also drunk black, and served *ziyada* (sweet), *mazboota* (medium) or *saada* (plain); it's made by boiling beans flavoured with cardamom in a distinctive long-handled silver pot, letting it cool, then re-boiling it and serving it black in small cups, along with a glass of water to cool and freshen the palate. You rarely get more than a mouthful in one cup, and if you take a second swig you'll end up with what seems like a mouthful of silt – actually the settled grounds at the bottom of the cup. Turkish coffee is sold by vendors on many street corners, and many town centres have cavernous **coffee houses** which dispense endless cups of tea and coffee – though no food or other drinks – to their (usually exclusively male) clients until well into the early hours. It's good to hang out in these places if only to watch the locals discussing away an afternoon or playing cards or backgammon; a *nargileh* (hubble-bubble) is always on hand to help the pace amble along. If you're missing Western-style coffee, head for any four- or five-star hotel and order a "Nescafé". You should always avoid **milk** as it's unpasteurized, containing bugs which Syrian stomachs are used to but

which yours definitely won't be able to cope with; if you have milk with coffee, make sure it's been boiled first.

Soft drinks are very cheap and highly sugared. Locally produced brands of fizzy, garishly coloured lemon- and orange-flavour drinks come in tiny glass bottles which stallholders always want back, so you can't walk off with your drink. Cans of fizzy drinks produced by the Canada Dry company, including 7-Up and various orange and cola varieties, are available at inflated prices; at the time of writing, Syria was one of the few countries in the world where Coca-Cola and Pepsi were not on sale (except at duty-free places at airports and land border crossing points).

Fruit juice (*'aseer*) stalls can be identified by the string bags of fruit hanging out front; they produce thirst-quenching drinks by the glass, stallholders crushing the fruit in front of you. Popular varieties are grapefruit, lemon, orange, banana and watermelon, but note that some stalls put tap water or milk into drinks to dilute them.

In many large cities you'll see men dressed in ornate costumes carrying huge, elaborate jugs and wearing a belt which holds several small glasses. These characters are selling water or **liquorice**, the latter a brown-coloured and very bitter concoction – very much an acquired taste –made from the roots of liqourice plants.

WINE, BEER AND ARRACK

Some local **wines** are available, but most are best left alone if you place any value on the back of your throat; however, Nectar (red, white or rosé) and Napoleon (red) are recommended. Wine is very cheap (S£100–300 a bottle) at **liquor stalls**, which sit amid other shops in the centres of big cities, but is pricey in a restaurant, as only the most expensive places serve it. If you're after "local" wine and don't fancy the Syrian produce, bear in mind that Lebanon produces lots of excellent wine which is also widely available.

There are two local brews of **beer**, Barada from Damascus and Al-Chark from Aleppo. They taste about the same and can be quite thirstquenching when cold (but quite sickly when warm). In the more expensive hotels and in Damascus imported beer is available, but it's expensive. The local liquor **arrack** is similar to Greek *ouzo*, a clear, strong aniseed concoction which packs quite a punch; it's meant to be drunk with a meal, not on its own, and it's worshipped by some as a cure for upset stomachs.

MAIL AND COMMUNICATIONS

Post and telephone services are operated by the same government department and so often share the same building in any large town – sometimes labelled in the French style, PTT. Phone and post offices have been marked on the town maps in this book, and are usually clearly indicated on published maps.

POSTAL SERVICES

Syria's postal service is slow but generally reliable, with airmail **letters** taking a week to reach the UK and anything up to a month to reach the US or Australia. It speeds up the delivery process if you get someone to write the name of the country on the envelope in Arabic. Mailboxes in the street are red and marked *boite aux lettres*, but it's usually better to send mail from **post offices** (daily except Fri 9am–2pm, with seven-day opening and longer hours in Aleppo and Damascus). Private **courier firms** such as DHL have offices or agents in most large towns; the location of their offices in Damascus and Aleppo is marked on the maps of those cities in this book.

Sending a **parcel** abroad is a time-consuming business as the contents must be inspected before the parcel is wrapped in cotton, tagged, stamped and dispatched. It's best to go to one of the post offices in Aleppo or Damascus, where staff will do the necessary for you.

Receiving mail **poste restante** can be a bit hit-and-miss, since post office workers often file letters wrongly – something addressed to Mr John Smith, for instance, might end up being filed under M, J or S. Ask officials to check carefully, and get senders to underline your surname. Poste restante mail is always held at the central post office of any town, and should be addressed with the name of the recipient (with the surname underlined), followed by "Poste Restante", then the city or town, and finally "Syria". You need your passport to pick up any mail sent this way, and will be charged a small **holding fee** of S£10 or so.

TELEPHONE SERVICES

The Syrian **telephone** system is very gradually hauling itself into the modern world; improvements in international connections mean that phoning abroad is now probably easier and more reliable than placing domestic calls. Both domestic and international calls can be made from big **hotels** (who slap on a surcharge); from **telephone offices**, found in the centres of cities and large towns; or from the smart new silver-coloured **phone boxes** found in cities and larger towns. However, it isn't possible to make **reverse-charge (collect) calls** abroad from Syria.

Telephone offices (typically open daily 8am–8pm, except Fri until 1pm) can be found in the centres of large cities; we've given their locations throughout the guide. At a telephone office, you generally write down the number you want and give it to the clerk, who will dial it and direct you to a **booth** where you

USEFUL TELEPHONE NUMBERS

To **telephone Syria from overseas**, dial your country's international access code, then 963 for Syria, the area code minus the initial zero, and then the subscriber number.

For **telephoning overseas from Syria**, the international operator is on ☎143/144. International dialling codes from Syria include:

Australia ☎0061   Ireland ☎00353   New Zealand ☎0064   US and Canada ☎001   UK ☎0044

take the call. To make a call from a new phone box, you need a plastic **phonecard** (S£500), available at post and telephone offices, and at certain cafés and stalls; English-language instructions for using these cards are pinned up inside the phone boxes themselves. Inconveniently, when the credit on one phonecard is used up, it isn't possible to insert a new card and carry on talking; instead, you need to redial the number and have another phonecard handy to resume your conversation.

Syria's largest cities are even served by **mobile phone networks** now, and coverage is expanding to include smaller towns as well; if you have a mobile, check whether it's compatible with the Syrian network before bringing it out with you. There are older public **coinbox telephones** too, but these can only be used for urban calls (ie within that town), and take small-value coins – another problem, since these pieces rarely turn up in change. Lines from these coinbox phones are notoriously unreliable anyway; for all domestic calls, if there isn't a new phone box or telephone office in sight, call from a hotel – the surcharge on telephone calls within Syria made from hotels is much more reasonable than on calls to other countries.

INTERNATIONAL CALL CHARGES

International calls **cost** around S£150 a minute, so a phonecard pays for a conversation of just four minutes if you call abroad. A staff-assisted call overseas from a telephone office is charged at a slightly cheaper rate as a direct-dialled call (a 4min call overseas costs around S£400), though there is a minimum charge equal to the price of a three-minute call. Hotels don't offer good value on international calls made from their premises, usually slapping a hefty surcharge on the cost.

FAXES AND THE INTERNET

Fax machines were banned in Syria for security reasons until the mid-1990s, but most large hotels and telephone offices now operate them. You pay S£200 for the first page of a fax you send abroad from a phone office, and S£100 thereafter.

The Syrian government has been suspicious of email and the **Internet**, and the country has been among the slowest in getting wired up to cyberspace, though things may well improve with the accession of Bashar al-Assad to the presidency (he was once president of a different sort, heading the Syrian Computer Society). **Getting online** is still awkward, as there are just a few low-key places in Damascus (see p.111) and Aleppo (p.238) where you can access the Net and check and send emails. For Web sites containing useful information about Syria, see p.29.

THE MEDIA

Until recently, all Syria's newspapers were government-owned, with the exception of the Communist Party paper, launched at the start of 2001. The country's Arabic-language broadsheet and tabloid press are avidly bought – despite their being closely written and poorly printed, with few photographs. The news that people read is heavily controlled by the government news agency, SANA – the Syrian Arab News Agency – which also supplies TV and radio news reports.

ENGLISH-LANGUAGE NEWSPAPERS

The most reliable places to find **foreign newspapers** such as the *Guardian Europe* and the *International Herald Tribune* are the bookshops of the *Meridien*, *Sheraton* and *Cham Palace* hotels in Damascus, and in the English-language bookshops listed on p.108. Occasionally British newspapers such as *The Times* and *The Daily Telegraph* also turn up at these places too; a copy of the *Sunday Times* will cost you around five times the UK cover price. Usefully, the **library** of the British Council in Damascus has a selection of UK newspapers and magazines, and can be used by non-members free of charge. Outside Damascus it is virtually impossible to get hold of any of these papers; in Aleppo and other tourist centres, check in the big hotels – if they have anything at all it will be very out of date. Thankfully, the practice of selling foreign newspapers and magazines with articles about Syria torn out of them seems to be in decline.

Syria's **English-language newspaper**, the *Syria Times*, is supposed to be published daily except on Fridays, but actually appears erratically. Its main purpose seems to be to praise the Syrian leadership to the heavens whilst damning that of Israel to hell; much of the news it carries consists of outrageously boring reports of trade and diplomatic summits, and its coverage of foreign affairs is minimal. There is sometimes a good listings section, however, with details of exhibitions, concerts, lectures and museum opening times for Aleppo and Damascus. The *Syria Times* is available from some newsstands in Damascus and Aleppo, but again the big hotels are probably the best place to find it.

TV AND RADIO

There are two channels on terrestrial **Syrian television**. Channel 2 broadcasts news in English at 10pm every evening, a somewhat hysterical round-up of anti-Israel propaganda and fastidiously reported government business. Foreign news stories (particularly Northern Ireland) get a fair amount of coverage, but always in the later part of the bulletin. The weather forecast after the news is usually pretty accurate, and provides a nostalgic reminder of what weather reporting back home was like before forecasters developed charisma. Channel 2 also shows lots of English-language programmes – everything from recent BBC sitcoms and documentaries to 1970s American cop shows – subtitled in Arabic with their original soundtrack left intact.

The largest international hotels have CNN and other **satellite** channels (rarely BBC World) piped into hotel bars and rooms. Most TVs in the west, far north and far south of the country can receive, respectively, Lebanese, Turkish and Israeli television (in Aleppo you can usually pick up both the first two). These channels show a more commercially oriented, Western-influenced diet of game shows, pop music and sports programmes, movies and American soaps.

The Syrian Broadcasting Service also broadcasts **radio** news and features in English and other foreign languages; frequencies and broadcast times are given in the *Syria Times*. International short-wave broadcasters that can be picked up easily in Syria include the Voice of America, Swiss Radio International and the BBC, with many Syrians listening regularly to the BBC Arabic service; the BBC World Service in English (see *www.bbc.co.uk/worldservice* for frequencies) is also available on 1323 kHz medium wave.

OPENING HOURS AND PUBLIC HOLIDAYS

The working week in Syria runs from Saturday to Thursday, with Friday, the Islamic holy day, being roughly equivalent to Sundays in Western countries. Most government offices and banks are open from 8am to 2pm every day except Fridays and public holidays; shops and other offices usually open these same hours, and then again between 4pm and 7pm. The majority of restaurants are open on Fridays and holidays, when a few traders in cities operate limited opening hours. All these hours are reduced during the Muslim fasting month of Ramadan (see overleaf). In Christian quarters of Aleppo and other cities, things go on as normal on Fridays and shut down on Sundays.

However, the business hours, as well as public transport times (if they are even published), should be taken with a pinch of salt, and the museum and site opening times detailed in this book should be treated only as a rough indication of what actually happens; often things only open or start running when the official or driver concerned decides to turn up. Patience is something that travellers should bring to Syria in copious amounts.

HOLIDAYS AND FESTIVALS

Public **holidays** are closely observed in Syria, with Muslim and Christian festivals often meaning a day off for members of all the country's faiths. Much of the celebrating takes place at home though, so you probably won't see much in the way of festivities beyond streets decked out with coloured lights, with secular holidays additionally marked by military parades, organized political gatherings and fireworks (on Mt Qassioun in Damascus). Although the country works to the Gregorian (ie Western) calendar as far as business and government is concerned, it is the Hijra calendar that dictates Islamic holidays (see box below).

CHRISTIAN AND SECULAR HOLIDAYS

Government offices, banks, post offices and large companies are likely to be shut on New Year's Day (1 January), Revolution Day (8 March), Evacuation Day (17 April), Eastern and Western Easter (variable) and Christmas Day (25 December). Public transport (particularly microbuses) operate less frequently on these days, although the country by no means closes down, and most shops and stalls operate as normal.

ISLAMIC HOLIDAYS

Among the **Islamic holidays** celebrated in Syria (see box for dates in the coming years) are the first day of the Islamic New Year (*Ras as-Sana*), the birthday of the Prophet Mohammed (*Mulid an-Nabi*), the small feast at the end of Ramadan (*Eid al-Fitr* or *Eid as-Sagheer*), and the Big Feast (*Eid al-Adhah*), which celebrates the willingness of Abraham to sacrifice his son to God. These holidays, the *eid*s in particular, are marked by feasting, visiting relatives, and by taking children to rides and attractions which are often set up in parks. During the *eid*s many shops and offices

close for three days (sometimes all week if an *eid* falls midweek), and cities can be quiet as people head for the country. Needless to say, at such times public transport is seriously curtailed and **hotels** can get busy, making it wise to book in advance.

RAMADAN

The ninth month of the Islamic calendar, **Ramadan** commemorates the revelation of the Koran to Mohammed. During this month, devout Muslims must fast during daylight hours, letting neither food nor drink pass their lips; even smoking is not permitted while fasting (for more on Ramadan and other aspects of Islam, see pp.311–314). Business hours are much shorter during Ramadan, and many restaurants and shops do not open in daylight hours, though the former have extended opening hours after sunset, when the big evening meal (*iftar*) is a lively occasion, enjoyed by many who have fasted during the day. The meal starts as the prayer calls from the mosques indicate that night has fallen; after the *iftar* many head off to special prayers at mosques.

Not all Syrians are Muslims, and not all Muslims comply fully with Ramadan. Non-Muslims are not expected to follow suit, but daytime smoking or eating in public during Ramadan may cause offence, so be **sensitive** to local feeling. Most problematic to travellers is the curtailment of public **transport** during Ramadan, particularly microbuses and local buses (see p.31).

THE ISLAMIC CALENDAR AND MUSLIM FESTIVALS

Unlike the Gregorian calendar, the **Islamic calendar** uses lunar months (which last either 29 or 30 days), making the Islamic year eleven days shorter than the Gregorian year. Year on year, the lunar months (respectively named Muharram, Safar, Rabia Awwal, Rabia Thaani, Jumada Awwal, Jumada Thaani, Rajab, Shaaban, Ramadan, Shawwal, Dhul Qida and Dhul Hijja) therefore work their way slowly forwards through the solar year, as do Islamic festivals. The first day of the first year of the calendar is the date of the Prophet's migration (*hijra*) to Medina (16 July 622 AD); thus March 2002 AD sees the start of the Islamic year 1423 Anno Hijri (denoted AH). The Web site *www.solat.net* converts Western years to their Islamic equivalents. Below we list approximate dates for Muslim **festivals** and for the start of Ramadan (not itself a holiday); actual dates may vary by a day or so, depending upon on sightings of the new moon.

	Ramadan begins	Eid al-Fitr	Eid al-Adhah	Ras as-Sana	Mulid an-Nabi
2001	16 Nov	16 Dec	6 March	26 March	3 June
2002	5 Nov	5 Dec	23 Feb	15 March	23 May
2003	25 Oct	24 Nov	12 Feb	4 March	12 May
2004	15 Oct	13 Nov	1 Feb	22 Feb	1 May
2005	5 Oct	2 Nov	20 Jan	11 Feb	20 April

MONUMENTS, MUSEUMS AND RELIGIOUS SITES

An **admission charge** of between S£200 and S£300 is levied to look round most monuments and museums – from the Crac des Chevaliers and Palmyra's Temple of Bel to the murkiest local museum or dusty ruin; on top of that, many places charge extra for the right to take photos or use a video camera. In most places you can get a reduction in the price of admission if you present an ISIC card. Although you may begrudge shelling out S£200 to see what turns out to be a few glass cases and a custodian, remember that many sites, including most of Palmyra and Bosra, the Dead Cities and other desert sites, are open for you to wander round at any time and are completely free of charge.

MUSEUMS AND ANCIENT MONUMENTS

Syria's ancient sites and monuments are maintained by the **Syrian Antiquities Department**. Those few which have a custodian are usually open daily, although more minor sites may be closed on a Tuesday. None requires any special permits to allow you to visit, and if you want to scramble over a *tell* to see what's there in the way of excavations, then there's nothing to stop you doing just that. In some places you can see pieces of pottery and the like lying all over the place, but you should remember that removing any artefacts from any site is illegal.

Museums are mostly drab affairs, consisting of haphazard and poorly labelled (or just un-labelled) cases of artefacts. Most of the good stuff has been moved from provincial museums to the two main archeological collections in **Damascus** and **Aleppo**, but in **Sweida** in the south and **Deir ez-Zur** on the Euphrates you'll be pleasantly surprised by the quality of the collections displayed in their new museums. All museums tend to shut on Tuesdays (official opening times are detailed throughout the guide).

MOSQUES, CHURCHES AND MONASTERIES

Though all **mosques** are open to non-Muslim visitors, try to avoid visiting at prayer times, especially the main service of the week at noon on Fridays. No one is ever likely to object to your presence in any mosque, although only two – the Umayyad Mosque in Damascus and the Great Mosque in Aleppo – are classified as ancient monuments and so are used to seeing tourists.

Always take your **shoes** off at the entrance to a mosque; there should be no difficulty in leaving them there while you look round. Bare shoulders, shorts and short skirts may cause offence (at the Umayyad Mosque in Damascus, visitors in shorts are given a robe to wear), and women may be required to wear a headscarf. Most mosques are surprisingly relaxed places, with groups of people getting on with whatever they want – worshipping, sleeping, sightseeing or chatting. Attached

HIRING GUIDES

You have to look around quite carefully if you want an official, government-registered **guide**. Tourist offices, large hotels and travel agencies (in that order) are the best places to hire one; you shouldn't count on official guides being available on the spot (as they are at many Egyptian or Turkish ruins), except at Palmyra, Bosra and Apamea. Most other ruins are virtually deserted, and your most likely guides will be local children begging you to let them show you around, so that they can practise their English and earn a little *baksheesh*.

In towns and cities you may be approached by young men offering to show you around as **unofficial guides** – again, usually with a view to practising their English more than anything else. Many people you meet this way are unemployed teachers or lecturers, though they might turn out to be official guides touting for work independently if there aren't any tour groups around at that time. Whether you take them up on their offers is of course up to you, but agree on a price before you do so. Often these people don't actually want any money as they genuinely want to help and meet foreigners; even if you don't want to be shown around they will assist you in whatever way you ask, such as pointing out which bus to take or helping you bargain with a taxi driver. Such encounters rarely come with "strings attached" and can even lead to invitations to a guide's home later in the day, so (on either side) they make for a good way of meeting people.

to many mosques are **madrasas**, religious schools which sometimes boast fine architecture dating from Ottoman times. A few have been mentioned in the text, but unfortunately almost all of them are locked most of the time.

Syria abounds in Christian **churches and monasteries**. Churches are almost always locked, even those in the centre of Aleppo. Only St George's Monastery (p.188), near the Crac des Chevaliers, is used to seeing tourists by the busload; Deir Mar Mousa (p.120), an ancient monastery in the desert north of Damascus, provides meals and accommodation to travellers, although remoteness ensures that only a trickle of determined visitors come here. Other monasteries are secluded, working religious houses which don't welcome casual visits. As with mosques, it's best to dress conservatively to visit churches, though it isn't necessary to take your shoes off when entering a church, and women needn't wear headscarves.

TROUBLE AND THE POLICE

Syria is a remarkably safe country to travel in, with surprisingly little petty crime, cities which remain safe after dark and, despite a bus station bombing in 1996, next to nothing in the way of terrorism. Police are everywhere, in particular the feared secret police service, the Mukhabarat; however, beyond passport and other security checks few tourists will ever have cause to come into contact with them or their uniformed counterparts who make up a variety of civilian and military police forces. If you do have dealings with the police, expect civility and courtesy from them (few officers speak English though) — and a lot of paperwork.

PETTY CRIME

In Syria, **pickpocketing** and other types of theft are nowhere near the problem that they are in Turkey or Egypt. Nevertheless, it always makes sense to hang on to your things carefully in a crowded bus or a queue, and to keep valuables — including your passport, which you must carry around with you at all times — in a moneybelt around your waist or a pouch under your shirt. Casual **theft from hotels** is also unlikely, but given the poor security of both rooms and reception desks (which are often unstaffed and have no lockable storage areas), it makes sense to leave nothing to chance and to always carry your valuables with you. If you're **driving**, it's best to ensure that nothing valuable is visible in your car when you leave it.

Petty crime can take the form of **overcharging** by stallholders or taxi drivers (though sometimes this can amount to no more than a misunderstanding). To avoid being ripped off by the odd dishonest trader, you should be especially cautious over money and prices during your first few days in the country, until you've got a feel for typical prices for goods and services. However, remember that most Syrians are unfailingly honest and courteous, and you shouldn't let a cautious outlook spoil your trip, or be tempted to read anything sinister into the genuine offers of hospitality you receive.

EMERGENCY NUMBERS

Ambulance ☎110
Police ☎112
Fire ☎113
Traffic police ☎115

TERRORISM

In recent years tourists in Egypt, Turkey and Israel have been caught in the crossfire – or been the intended target – of extremist terrorists, but Syria has remained largely unblemished in this respect. The bombing of a Damascus bus station in 1996 was blamed on a Lebanese group, and remains an isolated incident; all the same, bus and train stations are security-conscious places, and you are likely to have your bags and passport checked when you enter them, with security at Damascus Airport likewise very tight.

The only potentially unsafe area in Syria is the northeast, which is occasionally at risk of absorbing some of the Kurdish separatist troubles from over the border in Turkey. For an update on the latest situation, you might want to ask the advice of your embassy in Damascus, or contact government advice services at home (in the UK ☎020/7270 1500, *www.fco.gov.uk/reference/travel_advice*; in the US ☎202/647-5225, *travel.state.gov/travel_warnings.html*). The area on the Turkish side of the border here is definitely a no-go area for Westerners at the moment.

THE POLICE

Syria has a strong tradition of maintaining tight internal security, backed up by compulsory conscription into the armed forces. Although there is a strong police or army presence in many places, the interest the police will take in you as a traveller is minimal, unless you're suspected of espionage, other anti-government activity or having anything to do with drugs.

One of the most obvious police units is the **traffic police**. Blessed with the almost impossible task of controlling traffic in larger cities, they stop cars for pedestrians to cross at intervals. The **municipal police** handle crimes like theft, and you'll need to contact them first in an emergency; there's a police station in even the smallest town. Flashily dressed **security police**, sharp-suited gentlemen in designer shades, are there to guard embassies and other important buildings in Damascus and Aleppo and shouldn't give you any trouble. There's no specific tourist police force.

The **Mukhabarat** is the internal Syrian secret police force, reporting to the Ministry of the Interior to pass on information relating to suspected anti-government activity. Although things are much more relaxed than they were in the 1980s, it is unwise to get into a conversation about internal politics with any Syrian, lest you put him or her in an awkward position (or say something you shouldn't and find out that it's a secret policeman you're talking to). Likewise, don't discuss Syrian politics or mention Assad (father or son) when talking with travelling companions in public spaces: this is a country where the walls have ears.

DIPLOMATIC MISSIONS IN SYRIA

If you find yourself in trouble, contact your **embassy** in Damascus (see p.110); the UK also maintains a **consulate** in Aleppo (see p.237). Diplomatic missions can advise on legal matters and replace lost or stolen passports, but will not be much help to you if you've been arrested, particularly if it's on narcotics charges (drug smuggling carries the death penalty in Syria). They won't lend you any money if you've run out or had it stolen, but as a last resort they'll get you back home – somehow.

CULTURAL ATTITUDES AND BEHAVIOUR

The reputation of Syrians for hospitality and friendliness isn't something dreamed up by government authorities to attract tourists: it's genuine and heartfelt, and you will encounter it wherever you go. In comparison to Egypt and Morocco, Syria is a hassle-free country to travel in, and you're unlikely to encounter people whose intentions are anything less than honest and friendly. However, it makes sense to know something of the dress and behaviour codes prevalent in the country, so that you can get the most out of your visit, avoid misunderstandings and return some of the respect which the Syrians naturally extend to you.

SYRIAN SOCIETY

The Syrians are an immensely proud people who regard their country as being at the **heart of Arab culture**: they are well aware of the extraordinary role the country has played in Islamic, Christian, Arab and pre-Arab history. There's an extraordinary diversity in the country: you'll see a surprising number of light-skinned, sometimes fair-haired people, who may have Druze blood in them, in addition to darker-skinned Kurds, who form an intriguing ethnic contrast to the bulk of the inhabitants.

In the cities there is a huge **social divide** between the urbane, wealthy elite, who could well have visited or lived in the West, and the vast majority, who are poorer and more traditional in outlook. Another contrast is between town and countryside: urban living in Syria has many similarities with the West (even the mobile phone has reached Syria's cities and larger towns), but in smaller places in the mountains, the desert and the northeast things are very different. Here, mules, donkeys and (much less often) camels are as important as four-wheel pick-up trucks for getting around, society is rigidly hierarchical and clannish, women tend to adhere much more to Islamic dress codes, and there is an often rigorous segregation along gender lines.

Families are extremely important within Syrian society; people can be seen in family groups everywhere – dressed to the nines enjoying an ice cream in the cities, or working together in the fields as a group in the countryside. Girls tend to stay firmly in the background, while their brothers might be engaged in anything from manning their father's stall in the souk to offering cups of tea to visitors at Palmyra or tending herds of animals in the countryside. Children usually stay at home until they get married, which typically happens when they are well into their twenties. The choice of a spouse is often heavily influenced by the family – particularly for women. There are no nursing homes for the elderly in Syria, and ageing parents are always looked after by relatives. A death in the family is sometimes marked by up to a year of mourning, a period during which women will wear nothing but black.

In their **personal relationships** Syrians are hugely more open with each other than Westerners: people greet each other with effusive cheek-kissing and genuine friendliness, and often walk around together arm in arm with same-sex relatives or friends. However, overt **displays of affection** between mixed-sex couples is very rare in public, beyond discreet holding of hands.

INTERACTING WITH SYRIANS

Despite being a country of barren deserts and forested mountains, Syria is not a country in which to seek solitude: concepts of personal space are different here than at home, and people will always take an interest in you at some point, particularly if you are a lone traveller. Sometimes this natural **curiosity** about foreigners can seem overwhelming and even intrusive, though it isn't meant to be. People will call out random, basic questions in English to you as you walk down the street; invite you to sit down with them and talk; or, in some places, simply stare at you and watch what you are doing. This won't happen in central Damascus or Aleppo but might be the case in out-of-the-way places where the arrival of a Westerner is unlikely to go unnoticed and unremarked on (particularly by young males, who occasionally try to get the attention of foreigners by whistling at them, which can be disconcerting at first).

Many Syrians seem flattered that you are visiting their country and will go out of their way to **offer assistance**. You will find that people break off what they are doing to jump in a taxi to help you get where you want to go, or to walk with you to show you exactly what you want to find, be it an obscure historic monument in a souk or the correct bus in a busy depot; payment is never expected for this sort of thing. In fact, people can sometimes be so keen to help you that they might point you in the wrong direction rather than admit they don't know. It's rare that these offers of assistance come with strings attached or a hidden agenda.

MAKING CONVERSATION

Everywhere you go, people will **ask** where you have been in Syria, who you are travelling with, which country you have come from, whether you are married or not, and how many children you have. If you do have kids, carrying photographs of them can be an excellent way of breaking the ice.

Beyond these standard questions, what people feel like talking to you about beyond the standard "where do you come from" usually falls into sexually stereotypical subjects: soccer and world news (and even how much you earn) if you're male, home and family life if you're female. As regards the former, if you're English, Syrian men will be keen to talk to you about the recent fortunes of Manchester United or Arsenal, and may even express surprise that teams other than these actually exist in the English football league. It's rare to find Syrians bringing up the subject of internal **politics**, recent political history, or the policies of Hafez or Bashar al-Assad, though more often than not they will talk about the situation in the Middle East; if you're from the UK, you might be told forcefully that the universally despised State of Israel was a British creation (which it was, in part), although you will never be held personally responsible for this. Female travellers may find that a discussion with Syrian women about families and children may progress on to the subject of the different status of women in Western and Arab societies, and the aspirations and changing roles of Syrian women.

or prolonged staring. Discomfiting though this sort of attention is, it rarely progresses beyond the verbal to the physical, and there are ways of dealing with it. Ignoring any comments might be the best way out, but don't be afraid of making a scene or asking for help from passers-by. Shouting '*ayb aleyk* – meaning "shame on you" – is usually enough to stop a situation developing. Remember that Syrian men would never have any physical contact with a woman they do not know – even shaking hands is sometimes regarded as taboo – so they can't claim unfamiliarity with Western culture as an excuse for their behaviour.

More generally, **eye contact** is often taken by men to denote some sort of come-on on your part, so try to avoid it if you think a situation might get threatening (and consider wearing dark glasses to reduce the possibility of misunderstandings); similarly, overt friendliness or gregariousness on your part towards Syrian males might be misinterpreted by them. Conforming to the local dress code also makes you less likely to be viewed as an easy target by Syrian men.

When dealing with behaviour of this sort it's as well to remember the **causes** of it. Deeply ingrained in Arab culture is the notion that women are inferior compared to men, arguably reinforced by traditionalist interpretations of the Koran and Bible. Syrian men have grown up in a climate of segregation, and sometimes do not leave home to get married until they are in their late twenties; women are often shielded from contact with men by their male relatives, who often have a strong say in whom they marry. Male behaviour stems from a sexual frustration born of ignorance, and from the images in Western media, which are seen as suggesting that Western women have a rather looser sexual morality than Syrian women. The possibility of marrying a foreign woman – with the expectation of obtaining an exit visa and residence abroad – is also attractive to many men.

WOMEN TRAVELLERS

As in many parts of the Middle East, Western women, particularly solo travellers, may unfortunately experience some sort of **harassment** from Syrian men. This can take the form of comments being made as Western women pass by, "kissy" noises, relentless and pointless chatting,

MEN TRAVELLERS

Male travellers do not face the same problems as women, but it's best to bear in mind some codes of behaviour when dealing with Syrian men and women. Firstly, Syria is not a country where men are likely to have any dealings with Syrian women beyond the most superficial social interaction, apart from possibly making friends with educated, urban women. In particular, women might be worried about retribution they could receive from male relatives if it is considered that they have taken an interest in a foreign man. For these reasons it's best to **exercise discretion** at all times when in female company.

Secondly, as a male tourist alone, you might come across sexual propositions from **other men**; these are rare, and however you deal with them, bear in mind that homosexuality is illegal in the country (see also p.56). You should also remember that same-sex touching is an accepted part of amicable interaction between Syrian men and rarely, if ever, has a sexual connotation.

MODES OF DRESS

Many Syrians take real care about their **appearance**, often to emphasize status or social class rather than out of being fashion-conscious; in this conservative society, Syrian women never wear miniskirts or have ultra-short hair, and Syrian men never wear earrings or grow their hair long.

Nowhere is the blend of culture and traditions which make up modern Syria more apparent than in how people dress. **Women** might be dressed from head to foot in black to fit in with Islamic traditions (this is particularly so in smaller towns and in ultra-conservative Hama), or they might wear Western-style clothes, even jeans and a blouse; many women wear what amounts to a blend of traditional and modern styles, wearing a headscarf which covers their hair, along with Western-style clothing. Women working in the fields often wear fantastically coloured skirts and headscarves, preserving their modesty as well as shielding them from the sun or wind.

The same contrast in styles can be seen on **men**. Traditional attire comprises the Arab gown, the *jalabiyyeh*, which can be of glistening white or of darker brown or grey, completed by a headscarf (*keffiyeh*), usually coloured red and white. You see males of all ages dressed in this manner, from small boys to aged patriarchs, and doctors and businessmen to beggars and shepherds. However, many middle-aged men wear suits, whereas boys and men in their twenties often prefer to don jeans, shades and a T-shirt with English slogans on it. Syrian men seldom wear shorts outside (except when playing sport) or go around without wearing a shirt which keeps the upper torso and upper arms covered.

The best advice for **visitors** is to fit in with what locals are wearing. Conforming to broadly conservative dress codes will endear you a lot to Syrians and give them the impression that you respect their culture. If you're in Syria in summer you'll most likely want to wear loose-fitting, pale-coloured cotton long trousers (*not* shorts) and a fairly baggy shirt (preferably tucked in), which will help you cope with the heat and achieve a fair degree of sartorial conformity. To discourage unwanted male attention, women may find it best to wear loose-fitting long skirts rather than jeans and long-sleeved shirts, and perhaps also a scarf to cover your hair and neck.

BODY LANGUAGE AND GESTURES

Arabs tend to use **gestures** a lot when communicating with each other: many discussions seem incomplete without furious motions of the hands and assertive body language. Even when speaking with foreigners, Syrians often communicate using gestures rather than words, assuming this will make them more easily understood. However, the meaning of many of these gestures is very different to their connotation in the West. **Yes** is indicated by a downwards movement of the head and eyes rather than by nodding, and **no** (or "not here – try somewhere else") by a backward tilt of the head and a raising of the eyebrows. Putting the hand over the chest (crossing one's heart, essentially) indicates that one is **sincere** or apologizing about something; it's also a polite way of declining an offer (of food or drink, for instance).

A gesture you see a lot (particularly when dealing with banks or officialdom) is the palm upturned with thumb and all fingers brought together to touch at the tips: this indicates that you should be patient and **wait**. An official drawing an imaginary line across the palm of his hand indicates that he wants to see your **passport** or some sort of transport or entrance ticket, depending on the situation.

Another piece of body language to learn is that when **eating** with your hands – handling bread or fruit, for example – you should pop the food into your mouth with your right hand only; the left is traditionally used for cleaning oneself in the toilet. Also, the **soles of the feet** are regarded as unclean in Islamic culture, and you should always ensure, when sitting or lying down, that you do not cause offence by pointing the soles of your feet at people.

HAMMAMS

One particular area of etiquette to get to grips with is what to do inside a **hammam,** or Turkish bath. Found all over the Arab world, hammams are the modern-day descendants of the multi-roomed Roman bathhouses, a place to meet as well as to get really clean. Most Syrian towns have a hammam, often located in the souk; in the guide, details have been given of hammams in the listings sections after the accounts of Damascus, Aleppo and Hama, although it's not difficult to seek out hammams in other places (maps from tourist offices indicate their locations).

The most important thing to realize in a hammam is that **nakedness** is taboo; you undress in private and move around the hammam wrapped in a linen towel known as a *fouta*. After stowing away your valuables in a locker, you put on some cumbersome wooden clogs (the floors are very slippery) and clomp off to the first room, which is usually the hottest. The heat is created by billowing steam, which draws the sweat from you, and with it toxins in your skin and body, which you then wash off when you move into the (thankfully cooler) adjacent room. Here either you wash yourself, from the basins of water filled by hot and cold taps, or a qualified **masseur** gets on with the business for you using a rough-textured glove: this can be a rather abrasive experience, but it's one which is guaranteed to remove even the most adamant of Syrian dust particles from your skin pores. After this you will probably want to head off back to the entrance lobby, where you can often rest up on a couch and sip away on a glass of tea, water or lemonade.

The hammams in Syria which are most used to seeing Westerners are the Hammam Nur al-Din, in the heart of the Damascus souk (p.111) and the Hammam al-Nasri, opposite the Aleppo citadel (see p.238). If you're new to the hammam experience you might, as a novice, feel more comfortable at these establishments, where a fair bit of English is spoken. The **price** at either is around S£400; other hammams, which you can use when you're more confident, won't set you back as much. Unfortunately, opportunities for **women** to use hammams are quite restricted; some hammams are only for men, while others have limited opening times for women (when men are excluded).

MINOR ANNOYANCES

Syrians will often push or jostle when standing in line, drive with aggressive disregard for pedestrians and other road users, and conduct arguments in public with raised voices and aggressive gesturing. Another thing which takes getting used to is the amount of **litter** everywhere: most Syrians drop empty packaging in the street with impunity, and sometimes it seems as if every scrap of waste ground in towns is stuffed with stinking garbage, and out in the countryside, fields can often seem awash with fluttering black plastic bags and scraps of packaging.

You will encounter some **begging** on the street in cities, and in rural areas you might find yourself pestered for money or pens (or just attention) by small children; the giving of **alms** to the needy is considered a tenet of Islam, but how much to give and on what occasions is a matter of personal choice. As a foreigner, it will always be assumed that you are rich, even if you think you aren't.

SHOPPING

The sprawling souks of Aleppo and Damascus offer one of the most enthralling shopping experiences of the Middle East. Amid the stalls, people, animals and noise of their dark, covered alleyways, it sometimes seems as if it's possible to buy almost anything, and indeed the souks do hold their share of offbeat items – from camel whips to caged songbirds.

However, the souks aren't really geared towards tourists (apart from certain curio shops in Aleppo and Damascus), and much of what they sell tends to be household goods, textiles and fresh meat. For souvenirs and craft products it's often best to head away from the souks, calling in at the **specialist antique shops** and **handi-craft souks** which have been set up (largely for tourists) in these two cities. Those shops that are particularly geared up to tourists sometimes quote prices in US dollars, and in the guide we've quoted prices the same way where appropriate. Aleppo and Damascus also have **modern shopping districts**, a wander round which can be as absorbing an experience as a visit to the souks, particularly after dusk in summer (when the souk stallholders have pulled down their shutters); the shops in these areas stay open well into the evening, making up for their period of closure in the afternoon, and do brisk business with the drifting hordes who window-shop whilst gorging on ice creams and reining in their children.

Outside the two largest cities, shopping opportunities are, however, rather more limited. Some towns, such as Hassakeh, Latakia and Tartous, don't really have a souk at all; in those that do, such as Homs and Hama, the souks offer a comparatively disappointing selection of goods. At least it's always easy to get hold of **day-to-day items** you might need, such as washing powder, cooking equipment, shampoos, soap, insect repellent and the like – all easily bought in souks and town-centre shops.

HOW TO BUY

Though the assertion that you're "only looking" is understood by merchants, they'll home in on you if they have an inkling that your casual interest can be translated into a sale, and it can be difficult to browse their wares in peace. Don't let yourself be pressured into buying something you don't want – if the sales pitch in one shop is too intrusive for comfort, go elsewhere.

If you let a **guide** take you shopping, he may well take you to shops where he gets a cut of the proceeds from custom he brings in – meaning you may end up paying more than you should. On the positive side, if his favoured shops don't have what you want, your guide may well know other shops that do, though you may need to be insistent to get him to take you there.

BARGAINING

A vital and memorable part of the souk experience is **haggling** over the price. It's a practised skill, to a certain extent, and can be great fun. How much below the original asking price the seller is prepared to go varies considerably from place to place; just turning away on your part after the initial price has been suggested might reduce it by as much as half. The one golden rule to follow is that you should never offer a price that you are not prepared to pay: once your bid matches the stallkeeper's expectation, the deal is done, and you'll cause a great deal of offence if you then walk away. You might also cause offence if you offer a price which seems insultingly low; but generally stallholders will discuss the price with foriegners in a genial manner, often with cups of sweet tea thrown in to smooth the negotiations along.

WHAT TO BUY

The most obvious **souvenirs** to buy are table-cloths, rugs, inlaid woodwork fashioned into items such as jewellery boxes and chess sets, and *nargileh*s (hubble-bubbles). Less obvious items to look out for include fabrics cut from the roll (especially the woven fabric, damask), gold and silver items (although finding genuine antique items can be hard), and clothing and leatherware. By far the best place to buy these items is the Old City and the handicraft souks in Damascus (see section on shopping in the capital, p.105), with Aleppo a close second; elsewhere the choice of what's on offer is comparatively much more limited, even in tourist-driven places such as Palmyra.

CARPETS, TABLECLOTHS AND TEXTILES

Damascus and Aleppo are both centres of **carpet** production, and there are several stalls in their handicraft souks, and in the main souks, where you can buy finely made woven rugs and knotted **kilims**. Most of these bear intricate geometric patterns (in line with the Islamic prohibition of the representation of people and animals in art) in restrained colours; many are made in factories in the city (or in a room above the stall itself), often by hand, though carpets from Iran, Azerbaijan and elsewhere are also on sale.

Aleppo is famous for its textile factories, and over half of its souk is given over to **fabrics** which you can buy off the roll (some of what's sold actually comes from East Asia). The souks in the largest cities sell **damask**, the heavy silk fabric with elaborate woven designs which is named after the capital; often it's made into attractive tablecloths, which are sold especially in the handicraft souk. Rather less appealing are the fabrics which depict well-known Syrian monuments, which tend to be aimed squarely at tourists.

SILVER, GOLD AND JEWELLERY

The Damascus and (particularly) the Aleppo souks have areas devoted to the sale of gold and jewellery. What's on offer is pretty similar at each stall, and although there's a good variety of items for sale, verifying the authenticity can sometimes be difficult.

Gold is sold by weight, even when in the form of jewellery, and is usually much cheaper than in the West. **Silver** jewellery, often quite chunky, is rather more genuine to the region, being a favourite of Bedouin tribespeople; silver necklaces and other items often come inlaid with amber and semiprecious stones. However, if you are told something on offer is an "antique", bear in mind that it isn't difficult to make silver look old. Even if you do find what looks to be the genuine article, it will often have been fashioned from a silver/copper alloy – although the degree of craftsmanship is often very fine.

INLAID WOODWORK

Wood items **inlaid** with mother-of-pearl –backgammon and chess sets, wooden jewellery boxes and the like – are on sale everywhere, from specialist shops in the Damascus and Aleppo handicraft souks to souvenir shops at airports and hotels. Look carefully at what you're buying if you don't want to end up with something which has more plastic in it than wood.

In the modern shopping districts of Aleppo and Damascus, it's even possible to buy elegant inlaid

furniture, usually fashioned from local oak or pistachio wood. The chairs, wardrobes and chests are all very nice to look at but it's difficult to see how you'd be able to get these items shipped home.

COPPER AND BRASSWARE

Platters, teapots, trays, candlesticks and other items made from **copper** and **brass** are easy to find, but the quality is often rather disappointing. Some shops, particularly in the handicraft souks in Damascus and Aleppo, also have swords and daggers on sale; these items are modelled on weapons which were traditionally carried by Bedouin, but are produced mainly for tourists these days.

CLOTHING AND LEATHER

In most cities and large towns there are numerous modern shops selling Western-style clothes, but the souks are the place to buy **traditional garments** such as a *jalabiyyeh*, the long gown worn by many Syrian males, or a *keffiyeh*, the traditional headcloth, usually red and white, which requires an *iqal* (headcord) to secure it in place. The same clothes shops also sell much brighter, gaudily coloured gowns, which Syrian women can sometimes be seen wearing. In the handicraft souk in Damascus there is a shop selling intricately embroidered gowns for women made by Palestinian refugees to traditional designs. **Brocade** is traditionally used by the Bedouin to make garments: you can buy items made from it in the handicraft souk in Damascus, and in the main souk too.

Leather items are a good buy in other parts of the Arab world (such as Tunisia and Morocco) but the quality of what's on offer in Syria is a shade disappointing. The country's few leather goods outlets are mainly in the handicraft souks of Aleppo and Damascus, where wallets, bags, shoes, sandals and jackets can be bought.

HUBBLE-BUBBLES

One of the best souvenirs to take home is a **nargileh** (hubble-bubble), the likes of which can be seen being gently puffed on in cafés and coffeehouses all over the country. Outlets selling these are ubiquitous: some *nargileh*s are newly made, others are antiques, and all are awkward to lug around with you and take on board an aircraft, so think carefully before you buy.

MUSICAL INSTRUMENTS AND RECORDED MUSIC

Arabic pop music can be something of an acquired taste, and if you travel on the cheaper buses you may even come to loathe it – it's not easy to ignore the repetitive (though often catchy) tunes blaring out from speakers at the front of these vehicles.

CDs of Arabic classical and pop music can be bought in smart music shops in Aleppo and Damascus. Many shops and stalls sell **cassettes** of the same sort of music, with modern shopping areas rather than souks probably the best places to look, though outlets are never difficult to find as they tend to play their tapes at full blast over their speakers, so you'll notice them whether you want to or not. Street vendors, too, often sell cassettes of Arabic music, spreading out their wares on mats in the evenings. Many of the artistes featured are Egyptian (Egypt being the home of the Arabic music and film industries), Iraqi or Lebanese; two Syrian names to look out for are Farid al-Atrache, who in his time (he died in 1974) successfully fused Western musical traditions with Arab ones, and George Wasouf, the country's most famous modern pop icon (for more details see p.319 in Contexts).

If you want to **make music** rather than play it, look out for *darbouka* drums, ouds (the Arabic predecessor of the lute), and flutes and other wind instruments, in specialist music shops in Aleppo and Damascus (see the accounts of the two cities for details). Musical instruments are also available in the souks, though what they sell is usually of inferior quality and meant for decoration rather than playing.

WORK AND STUDY

The sort of casual work that you can pick up in resort towns elsewhere in the Mediterranean isn't available in Syria, where finding work is difficult: your options are pretty much limited to teaching in Damascus or working on archeological digs elsewhere in the country. It's best to arrange employment back home before you leave for Syria; work and residence permits will be sorted out for you by your employers before you start. Opportunities for study are similarly limited, restricted essentially to learning Arabic.

TEACHING

The British Council in **Damascus** (PO Box 331105, Shaalan, Maisaloun St; ☎011/331 0632) and the American Language Center (PO Box 29, Rawda Circle; ☎011/332 7236) are just about the only two places in the country where you might find work teaching English as a foreign language. The former doesn't encourage casual work-seekers, and most teaching posts are filled by the British Council in London (☎020/7389 4931, *trs.britishcouncil.org*), who will interview you there before deciding whether to offer you a place. You can specify that you want to teach in Damascus – which might work to your advantage, since it isn't the most popular posting. Either way, you'll need a TEFL certificate and relevant experience. Once you've got a job, the British Council will arrange your flights and living accommodation.

Casual work is easier to come by at the American Language Center, which is always in need of teachers. If there's a post available and you're a native speaker of English, it's just possible that they'll employ you on the spot; a TEFL certificate, proven linguistic ability, teaching experience and a good university degree all improve your chances. Rates start at S£400 per hour but climb rapidly according to experience.

There's a remote possibility of teaching or private tutoring at the language faculty of the university in Damascus or elsewhere in Syria, but you'll need contacts to be able to do this; you might want to enquire through your embassy, through the bodies described above, or even through the Arabic departments of Western universities.

ARCHEOLOGICAL DIGS

Unless you're a trained archeologist, your chances of getting work on a dig in Syria are slim, to say the least; far more opportunities exist in Jordan, Israel and Turkey, where digs co-ordinated by Western universities are always in progress. Nevertheless, if you're determined, you could try contacting the Archeological Institute of America (656 Beacon St, 4th Floor, Boston MA 02215-2010; ☎617/353-9361): they produce an annual booklet listing current digs in the Middle East and other parts of the world which may require voluntary workers, entitled *Archeological*

Fieldwork Opportunities Bulletin (US$16; published by Kendal-Hunt, 4050 Westmark Drive, Dubuque, Iowa 52002; ☎319-589-1000).

STUDYING

Opportunities for study are limited to following a **course in Arabic**. Not surprisingly, given the city's historical role as one of the heartlands of Arab culture, Damascus has become very popular with students from all over the world as a place to learn Arabic. If you already have a grounding in the subject, head for the Arabic Teaching Institute for Foreigners, Jadet al-Shafei no. 3, PO Box 9340, Damascus (☎011/222 1538). A six-month course, with teaching in Arabic, costs about US$500, with classes held for three hours each morning. If you are a beginner, you might want to try asking expats at the American or British cultural centres, who should be able to put you in touch with one-to-one language tutors. The Institut Français runs Arabic courses for beginners, intermediate and advanced students, but teaching is in French, of course. Lessons take place in the evenings and courses run for about three months.

DIRECTORY

ADDRESSES Many Syrian streets simply do not have names, and the names of those that do are usually indicated in Arabic only, except in cities and larger towns where there are street signs in English. Sometimes, if a building is on an unnamed street, the nearest named street is used as the address on business cards and advertising literature – with attendant confusion over the exact location of the place.

BRING a hat, sunglasses and suncream in summer; warm clothes and wind- and waterproof jacket in winter; a universal plug – many sinks and baths don't have one; a water bottle; a torch – useful for exploring castles, and many out-of-the-way places are poorly lit at night; travel alarm clock for early trains and buses, and to get yourself up to enjoy the coolest part of the day in summer; earplugs to cut out the street noise in cheap hotels; a Walkman, to cut out the blaring pop

music in buses (or just to take refuge from your travelling companions for a while); a Swiss army penknife; a first-aid kit (see p.21); a small sewing kit for emergency repairs; a universal electric plug adaptor; an inflatable neck rest, for long journeys; and a sleeping bag, if you're travelling in winter and planning to stay in cheap hotels, where heating is often inadequate.

CHILDREN Kids are certainly welcomed in Syria, which is blessed with having one of the world's highest birth rates. Hotel rooms with three or four beds are easy to find, and you'll get discounts for children on most forms of public transport. Powdered milk and baby food are readily available, but disposable nappies are hard to come by. You might want to avoid visiting the country in the depths of winter or summer, when the weather can make travel with kids very wearing; you need to be especially careful over things like high temperatures and intense sunlight, which can affect children more severely than adults. Other things to be wary of are the busy traffic, which has a tendency to hoot rather than slow down if there's something in the way, and archeological sites, where unexpected holes, crumbling walls and unstable columns are rarely indicated or fenced off, making them less of the kids' adventure playground than they might initially seem. If you're travelling without children you'll often be asked whether you have any – carrying photographs of them is a great way of initiating conversations.

DEPARTURE TAX S£200 is payable on all international flights; this is usually not included in the price of air tickets, so set aside cash for the purpose if you're flying out.

ELECTRICITY The current used is 220 volts (North American appliances need a transformer to be used in Syria), 50 cycles, out of double round-pin sockets. In the event of a power cut (the supply can sometimes be erratic), the more expensive hotels fire up their generators; cheaper hotels keep a supply of candles.

EMERGENCIES Ambulance ☎110; police ☎112; fire ☎113; traffic police ☎115.

FILM AND PHOTOGRAPHY You can buy Western brands of print film (particularly Fuji products) in the centres of most large towns, and there are 24-hour film-developing outfits in Damascus and Aleppo. It's easy to find camera shops but difficult to get your camera repaired, or even to obtain new batteries for it. It's wiser to bring all photographic needs out with you, including any slide film, which is hard to buy in Syria. Be careful of getting dust in the shutter mechanism, a sure way to foul up your camera and ensure that you have no photographic record of your trip. Note that you should never take photographs of police or military installations, or of strategically sensitive things like bridges, railways stations, airports, dams or guarded public buildings. Men and children are usually

willing to be photographed, and may even get offended if you've got a camera with you but don't use them as a subject; women will normally deliberately steer clear of you if you're taking pictures.

GAY AND LESBIAN TRAVELLERS With homosexuality illegal and punishable by at least imprisonment, Syria is not an easy place for gay and lesbian travellers – although Robert Tewdwr Moss, in his book *Cleopatra's Wedding Present* (see p.323), provides a recent, readable account of a gay man's solo travels in the country; the *Spartacus Gay Guide* even lists some possible cruising areas in Damascus. The series of publications by Ferrari, PO Box 37887, Phoenix, AZ 85069, US (☎1-800/962-2912 or 602/863-2408) may also be worth a look: *Ferrari Gay Travel A to Z*, a worldwide gay and lesbian guide; *Inn Places*, a worldwide accommodation guide; *Men's Travel in Your Pocket* and *Women's Travel in Your Pocket*; and the quarterly *Ferrari Travel Report*.

LAUNDRY There are hardly any laundrettes in Syria, but many hotels will wash guests' clothes for them; the turn-around time can be anything from twelve hours to three days (in the cheapest places). Expect to pay about S£30 per item. Cities and larger towns have dry-cleaning facilities.

LEFT LUGGAGE There are no left-luggage facilities in Syria.

TIME Two hours ahead of GMT in winter; daylight-saving time is observed between the last weekend in March and the last in October, when Syria is three hours ahead of GMT.

TOILETS Public toilets are usually filthy and of the squat-hole variety; they tend to be found near main mosques and major bus stations in town centres. In cheap hotels you'll also find this style of toilet, with a floor-level tap supplied for washing yourself off. Toilet paper is rarely provided, and if you carry your own you shouldn't throw it down the hole – use the small bin provided. Western-style toilets can be found in mid-range hotels and the more expensive restaurants.

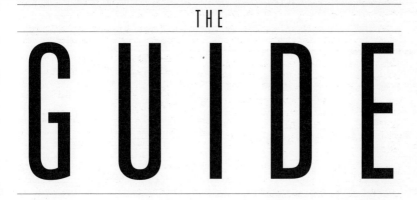

PART TWO

THE

GUIDE

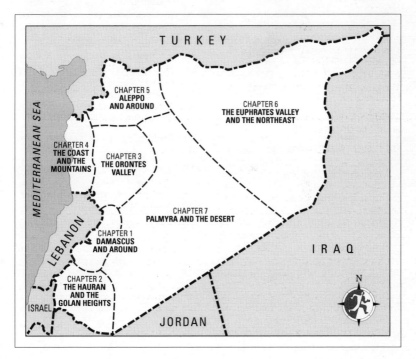

CHAPTER ONE

DAMASCUS AND AROUND

With a justifiable claim to being the oldest settlement on earth, and a huge number of beckoning historical sights, **DAMASCUS**, known to Syrians as *Dimashq* or sometimes *Ash-Sham*, is likely to be on every traveller's itinerary in Syria. Even if you wanted to, it would be hard to avoid the place: nearly all roads and railways in the country lead there, and its international airport is by far the most convenient point of entry into Syria from abroad. Damascus is a frantic, noisy, but fascinatingly diverse capital, where the contrasts which you can see all over the Middle East – between the developed and developing world, Christianity and Islam, Europe and Asia – are accentuated as in no other Syrian city. In the **Old City**, narrow, shady lanes, twisting and devoid of cars, seem to have remain unchanged for centuries; some of the architecture here is quite dazzling, and a deliberately unhurried wander beyond the more immediately touristy areas reveals a secretive, fascinating and often beguilingly silent world. The streets of **modern Damascus**, however, are anything but quiet, with screeching traffic competing for road space with horse-drawn wagons laden with goods destined for the souks. Assorted donkeys, tractor-engined three-wheelers, bicycles, modern Mercedes and vintage American yellow taxis are all thrown in for good measure, making crossing the road a triumph in itself and ensuring that the job of the hard-pressed traffic police is never dull. Men in chinos and shades smoke *nargileh*s in cafés, while women veiled in black from head to toe stroll around, accompanying children whose junior fashions would not look remarkable in London or Paris. The clamour of tongues in the markets includes Arabic, Turkish, Farsi (Persian) and European languages, haggling over anything from goats' heads (freshly severed) to clothes from Benetton. You'll need to spend a good few days in the city if you are to

---

ACCOMMODATION PRICE CODES

In this book, all hotels have been categorized according to the **price codes** outlined below, representing the minimum you can expect to pay for a **double room** in each hotel. Hotels in the ⑤–⑧ bands require payment in dollars. For further details, see p.35.

① under S£300/US$7	⑤ US$35–50/S£1500–2100
② S£300–600/US$7–14	⑥ US$50–90/S£2100–3900
③ S£600–1000/US$14–23	⑦ US$90–130/S£3900–5600
④ S£1000–1500/US$23–35	⑧ US$130/over S£5600

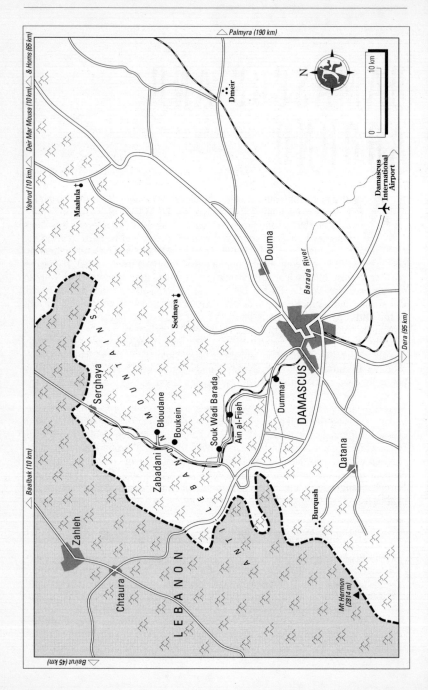

appreciate fully its diversity, history and chaotic charm. Although first impressions can often be disappointing – a lot of modern Damascus is very ugly, the public transport system is impossibly bewildering, and in summer the heat can be very wearying – once you take time to dig beneath the surface, Damascus, like a vast *tell*, reveals much more than a preliminary glance might suggest.

In fact, as an archeological site Damascus has yet to be investigated to its full depths. Most of Roman and pre-Roman Damascus still lies buried beneath the streets of the Old City, and the principal attractions for visitors are the reminders of the fine Islamic heritage which date from the era of the first Arab conquests. In the Old City, your priorities will be the stunning **Umayyad Mosque**, **Straight Street** and the **khans**, **madrasas** and hectic **souks** that stand between them. Of the Damascus museums, the archeological collections of the **National Museum**, in the New City, rank as a must-see survey of the history of Syria from stone-age times to the eighteenth century; other, smaller museums include those devoted to the Syrian armed forces, Arab epigraphy and the history of Damascus. When you're done with looking around the centre, don't ignore the attractions of the outer districts, most notably **Salihiye**, whose ageing mosques, mausoleums and madrasas line the narrow streets on the lower slopes of **Mount Qassioun**. The mountain's summit, providing magnificent views over the city and the desert beyond, allows you to appreciate the oasis-like nature of the capital's location. On the opposite side of the city from Qassioun, the **Saida Zeinab Mosque** is an important site of Shiah Islamic worship, an unusually striking modern building much frequented by visiting Iranian pilgrims.

Within day-trip range to the west and north of Damascus rises the fine, barren countryside of the **Anti-Lebanon Range**, the mountain borderlands where Syria, Israel and Lebanon meet. On warm summer days, Damascenes head by road or narrow-gauge rail line to the mountain resorts of **Bloudane** and **Zabadani**, near the source of the Barada River, for clean air, cool temperatures and fine views. Two pockets of Christianity to the north of the capital also make an easy and rewarding day-trip: the busy pilgrimage town of **Sednaya**, and the tiny, picturesque village of **Maalula**, one of the few places in the world where Aramaic, the language of Christ, is still spoken. Further afield, many of the places described in Chapter Two can be seen on day-trips from Damascus, with **Bosra** under ninety minutes away by direct bus. Even the **Crac des Chevaliers** (see p.184) can be visited on a long, but not impossibly long, jaunt from Damascus, although Palmyra is too far to be visited comfortably from the capital in a day.

Some history

Whether or not Damascus is, in fact, the oldest continuously inhabited settlement on earth is much disputed; Jericho and Aleppo are also claimants to the title. What is clear is that all three settlements, and many others in the Fertile Crescent (see p.150), were founded around 4000 BC when man first adopted settled farming practices rather than wandering around hunting and gathering. Damascus owes its existence to the **Barada River**, once a vital source of fresh water (though now little more than a putrid ditch running in a series of concrete culverts through the New City), its headwaters situated high in the Anti-Lebanon Range.

The city is first mentioned in written records dating from around 2500 BC found at Ebla and Mari. Most of the city's earliest history has been pieced together from ancient records found in locations as distant as Turkey and Egypt; it is clear from these that Damascus and its surroundings formed a city state during

Amorite, Aramean, Assyrian and Persian occupation of Syria, though never one of any great importance – even **Alexander the Great** largely ignored the city in 332 BC, leaving it in the hands of one of his generals before he himself pushed on. But it was under his appointed governor, **Parmenion**, that Damascus was systematically planned for the first time, with a grid pattern of streets which included Straight Street, mentioned in the Bible (Acts 9:11) and still the principal artery of the Old City.

Although the **Romans** ruled their province of Syria from Antioch (now Antakya in Turkey), Damascus assumed a certain degree of political importance during the seven centuries of Roman-Byzantine rule which began in 64 BC. They endowed the city with proper walls and gates, and built baths and temples, most notably refounding the former Aramean temple to Hadad to honour one of their own gods, Jupiter. At the time of the Christianization of the empire in the fourth century AD, the building was re-dedicated as a cathedral to St John the Baptist, whose head was entombed within. For around two hundred years Damascus was an important Christian centre and the city was the seat of a bishopric, but **Byzantine** rule from Constantinople was unpopular, and Damascus became rather a political backwater.

In 636 the city underwent a major change in its fortunes. Since the death of Mohammed in 632, Arab tribes from Arabia had been pushing northwards to capture Persian and Byzantine territory, bringing with them **Islam**; with the fall of Damascus to an army under Khalid ibn al-Walid, one of the greatest of Arab commanders, the city rapidly grew in importance as a trading and political centre. In 661 it was made the capital of the **Umayyad Empire** which, although it lasted less than ninety years, was to usher in an era of huge Arab expansion: by 732 Damascus was the centre of a vast empire which stretched from the Pyrenees to the Punjab. Although Mecca remained the spiritual capital of Islam, Damascus was the hub of political power, the site of a magnificent palace (of which no trace now remains) situated next to the equally grand **Umayyad Mosque**, which is the single most prominent reminder here of the city's short-lived golden age.

The growth of the Arab imperial possessions under the Umayyads was extraordinarily fast – in fact the pace of expansion was one of the major problems which beset the new empire. Lines of communication between Damascus and newly conquered territories – as far-flung as Spain and northern India – became rather stretched, and the Umayyads were beset with financial difficulties. Feuding Arab tribes fought for control of the empire; in 750 the Abbasi tribe, centred on Khorosan in Persia, pressed westwards and took Damascus, ushering in twelve centuries of rule of the city from distant seats of imperial power, the first of which was Baghdad. Under the **Abbasids**, Damascus lost ground as an Arab and Islamic centre, and from around 1000 control of the city was fought for by a variety of competing dynasties.

The capture of Jerusalem in 1099 during the First Crusade led to an influx into Damascus of Jewish and Christian refugees, and to the subsequent growth of the Salihiye district. The **Crusaders** fought for control of the city and attacked it in 1129, 1140 and 1148, but they never took it, and under the Muslim commander Nur al-Din and his successor **Saladin**, Damascus emerged as a bulwark against the Crusaders and its political and economic fortunes began to revive. In the first half of the thirteenth century it gained prominence as a centre of Sunni orthodoxy and teaching, but it wasn't until 1260 and the start of **Mameluke** rule from Cairo that the city once again assumed a political and cultural eminence. The

Mameluke Sultan Baibars spent most of his time here, and Damascus soon became an imperial centre second only to Cairo in importance.

Under the **Ottomans**, who ruled the city between 1516 and 1918, the fortunes of Damascus suffered under a succession of largely capricious and self-serving governors. Nevertheless a number of fine buildings were constructed during this time, albeit in a style transplanted from Constantinople and fused with local Syrian forms; the most notable examples are the Takiyyeh Mosque, near the National Museum, and the Azem Palace in the Old City. In the last few decades of Ottoman rule the rumbling conflict between Druze and Christians in Lebanon spilled over into rioting and a massacre of Christians in Damascus in 1860. It was during the Ottoman era, too, that the city became an important stop on the pilgrimage routes from Constantinople to Mecca. At the start of the twentieth century, with Syria increasingly coming under European influence, a tram network was constructed (the rails are still visible on Port Said Street), and rail links were established across the mountains to Beirut and into Arabia via Amman – the latter, known as the **Hedjaz Railway**, to ferry pilgrims on the hajj to Mecca and Medina.

The Allied victory in World War I resulted in the city coming under **French control** in 1920, after a brief Syrian administration lasting barely a year. This tantalizing glimpse of self-rule, combined with the deep unpopularity of the French administration, led to concerted resistance activities, and an uprising in 1925 was put down by a French bombardment of areas of the city that had fallen into rebel hands. The French finally left in 1946, after another major outbreak of civil unrest the year before, and upon the foundation of the modern Syrian state Damascus was the obvious choice for the capital – and the city at last assumed control of its own affairs, arguably for the first time since the seventh century.

After Ba'athist political victories in the early 1960s, and the stability brought by the **Assad regime**, Soviet-funded **industrial investment** took off, and suburbs expanded into the desert to the east and north of the city. Construction – both of industrial plants and of apartment buildings for their workers to live in – still continues apace, with precious little concern for the city's visual environment or air quality. Major problems familiar to many cities in the developing world, such as smog, high levels of ozone and carbon monoxide, and a lack of open space, are allowed to continue unchecked; future prospects for tackling them seem as bleak as the surroundings which the urban planners have chosen to create.

Orientation, arrival, information and city transport

The central area of Damascus encompasses a number of contrasting districts, which broadly fit into two areas, the Old City and the New City. At the heart of the **New City**, and of every visitor's mental map of the capital, is **Martyrs' Square**, marked *Al-Shouhada* on most maps but known to locals as *Plas Marjeh*. Traffic-clogged and unremarkable, this is a point of reference rather than a place to see, linked by Yousef al-Azmeh Street to **Yousef al-Azmeh Square**, a busy junction and another orientation point within the New City. It's between these two squares that most of the city's banks, airline offices, restaurants and mid-range hotels are located. Beyond Yousef al-Azmeh Square are the **Salihiye** shopping district and the **diplomatic quarter**, which occupies the lower, gentler slopes of **Mount**

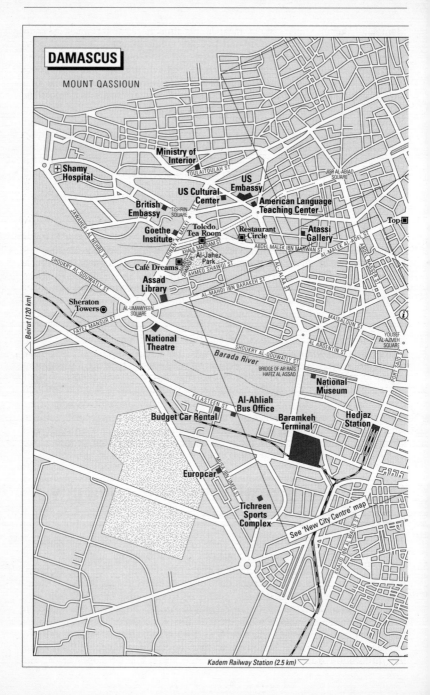

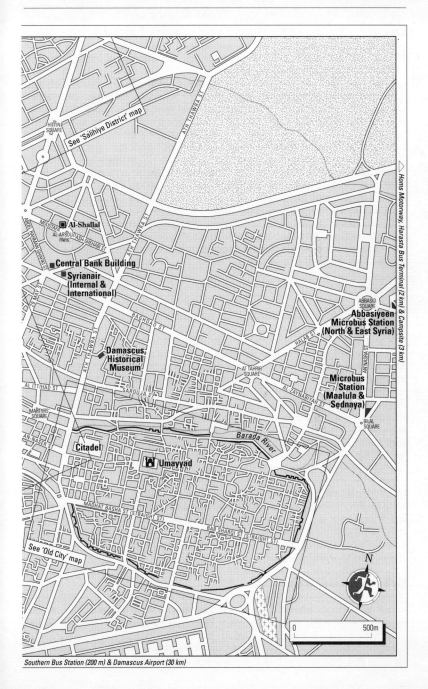

HITTIN SQUARE

See 'Salihiye District' map

ATH THAWRA ST

Homs Motorway, Harasta Bus Terminal (2 km) & Campsite (3 km)

ABDEL RAHMAN GHARQ ST

MOUSTAD

■ Al-Shallal

AL-ARSOUZI ASH SHEHABI ST PARK

■ Central Bank Building
■ Syrianair
(Internal &
International)

BAGHDAD ST

ABBASID SQUARE

Abbasiyeen
Microbus Station
(North & East Syria)

AN NASRIA ST

HALAB ST

Damascus
Historical
Museum

AT TAHRIR
SQUARE

AL-ZAYNABIYAH ST

Microbus
Station
(Maalula &
Sednaya)

AL ITTIHAD ST

SAROUJA ST

MARTYRS
SQUARE

BILAL
SQUARE

AN. NASER ST

Barada River

Citadel

🕌 Umayyad

MADHAT BASHA ST (STRAIGHT ST)

BAB SHARQI ST (STRAIGHT ST)

See 'Old City' map

N

0   500m

Southern Bus Station (200 m) & Damascus Airport (30 km)

Qassioun. Qassioun's rocky summit plateau, adorned with transmitter towers and military installations, is another useful point of orientation, as it can be seen from most parts of the city and provides the first glimpse of Damascus when approaching from the west or north.

West from Martyrs' Square are the **National Museum**, the **Baramkeh bus terminal** and **service taxi station**, as well as a **local bus and microbus depot**. Closer to the square, to its immediate south and west, is a jumble of streets lined with small eateries and stalls, the floors above given over to cheap hotels. In this relentlessly busy and lively area the main point of reference is the **Hedjaz Station**, linked by **An-Naser Street** to the **Citadel**, which stands at the entrance to the souks and the **Old City**. Walking along under the wrought-iron roof of the **Hamidiye Souk** will bring you to the **Umayyad Mosque**, which lies at the heart of ancient Damascus amid a dense network of covered markets. Heading south from here, you soon hit **Straight Street** which leads to the Christian monuments (and some good restaurants) at the eastern end of the Old City.

Beyond these central districts the ever-expanding residential sprawl is dissected by numerous fast urban highways, which can be used to reach far-flung bus and microbus depots and distant points of interest such as the **Saida Zeinab Mosque** on the southern outskirts.

Arrival

Damascus International Airport, the main gateway into Syria, is located 35km to the southeast of the capital. It's rather smarter than it used to be, but be warned that immigration formalities can be very slow. Once through the final passport checks you will find **exchange facilities** (open daily 24hr), a Europcar desk (you need to have reserved your vehicle in advance though; see p.32) and an **accommodation office** which deals exclusively with the various five-star hotels in the country.

The **private taxi** and **limousine offices** in the arrivals hall charge an extortionate $25 (payable in dollars) for a ride into the centre of town, so you're likely to want to use the airport bus or one of the more reasonably priced city taxis. The **bus** (daily 5.30am–midnight; S£10 payable on board) leaves every thirty minutes from next to the terminal building (turn right after coming through the main doors) for the 25-minute journey to its downtown terminus outside the *Kairawan Hotel*, a block northwest of Martyrs' Square. **Taxis** congregate at all hours immediately outside the main airport terminal entrance and can cost as little as S£100 with hard bargaining, but are more likely to set you back S£300; after midnight the drivers may well take advantage of their monopoly and try to push the price up beyond this. At all times you should agree a price before setting off – otherwise drivers might tell you at the end of the journey their meter is broken, and then make up a price they think you might pay.

By bus and service taxi

If you arrive in Damascus **by bus**, you'll be deposited at one of several depots which are spread around the city. **Luxury buses** from Lebanon, Jordan and southern Syria arrive at the **Baramkeh Terminal** (actually five terminals in one, each with its own entrances and exits), from where it's just a short walk east to Martyrs' Square. Karnak have their own terminal here, for their services from Amman and Beirut, as well as Cairo and Riyadh; next door is a terminal used by

MOVING ON FROM DAMASCUS

Damascus is the focal point of Syria's transport network and, though international bus, rail and air services from Aleppo are improving, remains the most likely international departure point from the country. As for moving on to other places within Syria, Damascus dominates the country's extensive road transport network and is the hub of its limited internal rail and air services.

By air

All **flights** from Damascus use the **International Airport**, with internal and international flights departing from the same terminal. The very reliable **airport bus** (S£10; 25min) departs every half-hour between 6am and 11pm from outside the *Kairawan Hotel*. If you're on one of the flights that depart Damascus at various odd hours of the night, you have no option but to take a taxi to the airport (the charge can be anything up to S£400); ask your hotel to arrange one for you as they can be hard to find in the very early hours, and the person at reception may be able to get a fair price for your journey.

Domestic flights are all run by Syrianair, with services to Aleppo, Deir ez-Zur, Latakia and Qamishli; tickets (under S£1000 one way) must be paid for in local currency. Flights to **Jordan and Lebanon** are infrequent and expensive, and often inconveniently timed; Syrianair operates services to Amman and Beirut, which are also served by Royal Jordanian and Middle East Airlines services respectively. Flying is a much more sensible option for **Turkey**, with reasonably priced services operated by Turkish Airlines and Syrianair to Istanbul and Ankara. For all international flights a **departure tax** of S£200 applies (only Syrian currency accepted), which must be paid at the booth just before passport control.

By Pullman and Karnak bus

At the **Harasta Terminal** (*Garaj Harasta* or *Garaj al-Pullman*), you will be besieged by touts offering seats on imminently departing services, but you can always shop around in the bus company offices which sit in a line between the departure bays. The most reliable firms are **Al-Ahliah** and **Zeitouni**, whose routes include Aleppo (S£150), Homs (S£70) and Hassakeh (S£300); the state-run Karnak, who maintain a desk in the Hatay company office (the first on the left just inside the terminal) charges about a third less. Other destinations served from this depot by these and other firms include Tartous, Latakia, Hama, Tadmor (Palmyra), and Deir ez-Zur. All these companies also have offices in central Damascus (see p.110). Harasta is also the place to come to pick up services to **Turkey** and **Europe**. Zeitouni offers some of the widest variety of routes, with a fare to Plovdiv and Sofia in Bulgaria of US$60. There is stiff competition on the Istanbul route, with most companies (see p.110) charging around S£1200.

From the **Baramkeh Terminal** (*Garaj Baramkeh*), Karnak services depart from their depot behind the service taxi area, heading to Beirut (S£175) or Amman (JD5 or US$6, with payment not possible in Syrian pounds; some of these are operated by Jordanian JETT buses), Cairo (S£2150) or Riyadh (S£1500). Luxury buses to **southern Syria** depart from a terminal beyond the yellow service taxi ranks and adjacent to the Karnak depot; their destinations include Dera, Bosra and Ezra, with fares around the S£60 mark.

By microbus and local bus

Microbuses and local buses **heading north** use the Abbasiyeen Terminal, by Abbasid Square in the northeast of the city. Fares here are around a half or a third

continues overleaf...

MOVING ON FROM DAMASCUS contd.

of what you pay at the Harasta Terminal, although journey times are liable to be longer and your journey will certainly be less comfortable. The most expensive fare from Abbasiyeen is around S£180 to Qamishli, while Aleppo costs S£80 and the more bearable hop to Homs S£40. Other destinations served include Deir ez-Zur, Dmeir, Hama, Latakia and Tartous. For Maalula and Sednaya, head to the depot on **An-Nasera Street**, 500m south of Abbasiyeen.

Microbuses to destinations **west and south of Damascus** leave from a noisy, chaotic depot within the Baramkeh Terminal, next to the Lebanon service-taxi terminal. Fares are typically low (S£20) for destinations including Qatana (for Burqush), Quneitra in the Golan Heights, and the hill resorts of Zabadani, Bloudane and Souk Wadi Barada along the Barada valley.

The southern bus station (*Garaj Dera* or *Garaj Bab Mousala*), reachable by city microbuses from halfway along Baroudi Street, 400m southeast of the Hedjaz Station, is used by microbuses and local buses for destinations in **southern Syria**. Fares to Sweida, Ezra or Dera from here are around S£30–40. There are no direct services to Bosra from here though, and given the cost and time to get out to this terminal, it's better to pay slightly more and travel in the better vehicles which leave from the Baramkeh Terminal.

By service taxi

From the northwestern corner of the **Baramkeh Terminal**, white service taxis, most of which have Jordanian and Lebanese plates, run regular trips to **Beirut** and **Amman** (S£400 to either destination); a smaller number of taxis run to **Irbid** in northern Jordan (S£300), with rather fewer serving the more minor centres of **Zarqa** and **Mafraq**. Service taxis heading to Amman, Zarqa and Mafraq use the border crossing at Nasib/Jaber on the Damascus–Amman highway; only taxis to Irbid use the older Dera/Ramtha crossing point. There are money-changing facilities and a tourist office at both border posts. Also operating from Baramkeh, rows of yellow Dodge and Chevrolet taxis serve destinations in **Saudi Arabia** (S£3000 to Riyadh), Beirut (S£400), and Syrian cities including Homs (S£100), Hama (S£150) and Aleppo (S£300).

By train

Train services from Damascus are slow, frustrating and often inconveniently timed, but they are extremely cheap. CFS operate trains out of **Kadem Station** to **Aleppo** via **Homs**, **Hama**, **Tartous** and **Latakia**, and to **Qamishli** via **Deir ez-Zur**. The Qamishli service is overnight and carries first-class sleepers (S£800) but may involve a change of trains in Aleppo. There's usually one train a day to Aleppo (S£80 first class, S£70 second class), and one a week to Qamishli, but it's worth enquiring at the information office in the Hedjaz Station for the current picture. CFS also operate a twice-weekly train from the Hedjaz Station south to **Ezra** and **Dera** and on to **Amman** (S£150). Occasionally trains are steam-hauled on the Syrian section of this line. Trains to **Zabadani** and **Serghaya** operate from the Hedjaz Station once a week.

luxury buses from southern Syria. White service taxis from Beirut and Amman arrive in the northwest corner of the Baramkeh terminal, near which is a noisy, chaotic depot used by microbuses from Syrian towns west of Damascus, including Zabadani, Bloudane, Souk Wadi Barada and Quneitra; yellow service taxis from Saudi Arabia and Beirut congregate behind the microbuses. Further afield, the **Harasta terminal**, 6km out in the city's northeastern suburbs, is where luxury buses from destinations to the north and northeast of Damascus, including Turkey and Eastern Europe, arrive. City microbuses (S£10) run from Harasta to Al-Ittihad Street, 200m east of its intersection with Yousef al-Azmeh Street, while a taxi ride into the city centre shouldn't cost more than S£60.

Microbuses arriving from northern Syria use the **Abbasiyeen bus station**, 3km east of the centre, from where local microbuses run to *Plas Marjeh*. Just to the south of Abbasiyeen, on **An-Nasera Street** by Bilal Square, is a small depot handling microbuses from Maalula and Sednaya. Microbuses from southern Syria use the **southern bus station** next to Yarmouk Square, 3km south of the centre. Local microbuses run to *Plas Marjeh* from all these outlying bus stations.

By train

The more central of Damascus's two train stations is the **Hedjaz Station**, terminus of the narrow-gauge trains from Amman via Dera and Ezra, and from Serghaya and Zabadani. The station is a short walk from the main areas of cheap and mid-range hotels. Mainline services from Qamishli, Aleppo, Homs, Hama and the coast use **Kadem Station**, located right out in the southwestern suburbs of Damascus; a free microbus or shuttle train service provided by the train company links Kadem and Hedjaz stations, timed to coincide with arrivals and departures. There are also plenty of city microbuses buzzing into the centre of town along the busy highway outside Kadem Station – just flag one of them down, and check that it's heading for *Plas Marjeh* or the central depot by the National Museum.

Information

The city's two **tourist offices** claim to be open 24 hours, seven days a week, but tend to be shut on Fridays (and at odd periods if they're short of staff). The main one is on 29 May Street, just up from Yousef al-Azmeh Square, with a smaller branch reached through a side entrance of the Ministry of Tourism building on Shoukry al-Qouwatly Street. The staff in both are friendly but, apart from their free maps of Damascus and other regions of Syria, have little information to impart. Hotel staff are often a better and more reliable source of information, particularly at the more expensive places. For entertainment listings, check out the English-language *Syria Times*, available from the bookshops listed on pp.108–109.

The best **map** of Damascus, far outstripping the tourist office freebie in terms of scale and quality of cartography, is on the reverse side of the locally published Avicenne map of Syria. Costing S£250 and available in all the English-language bookshops listed on pp.108–109, it shows the locations, addresses and phone numbers of embassies, banks, hotels, government buildings and hospitals, but is probably only worth investing in if you plan to stay more than a few days in the capital.

City transport

With distances in the centre of town easily walkable, you'll probably only need to resort to taxis or city buses and microbuses to reach the suburban bus depots, the few outlying sights or the airport. Trying to use the crowded white-and-blue **buses** and the smaller but ubiquitous white **microbuses** can be very frustrating. Both display their route numbers in Arabic only, there are no route maps published or displayed anywhere, and no information at bus stops (in any language) about which buses to take. Don't try asking at the tourist office, either – staff there will think it bizarre that you're even considering using a bus and will just tell you to hop in a taxi. In general, people wait at designated stops for the larger buses, and flag down microbuses anywhere in the street, but the best place to start fathoming out the situation is the **city bus and microbus depot**, situated underneath the flyover immediately west of the National Museum, about ten minutes' walk away from Martyrs' Square. There you can ask (and keep asking) and eventually you will get on the bus you want. Fares are very cheap – you'll never pay more than S£10 for a cross-town journey.

Fortunately, **taxis**, which are yellow and buzz around looking for trade at all hours of the day, are cheap too. You should insist that the driver uses the meter, but it's also sensible to discuss what the price is going to be before you start off, in case the driver tries to tell you that the meter is wrong, prices are out of date or some such, when you reach your destination. It shouldn't cost more than S£100 to travel between the centre and even the most far-flung suburban bus station; most journeys around town cost a lot less. You can simply flag a taxi down in the street – if you take one from or to an international hotel you're almost asking for the fare to be hiked up considerably, and possibly for it to be demanded in US dollars.

Accommodation

Virtually all **hotels** in Damascus are situated within ten minutes' walk of Martyrs' Square; they range from noisy, dirty, cockroach-infested dosshouses costing S£300 or less a night to five-star luxury in internationally owned chains such as the *Meridien*, where prices start at over $150 a night and head for the sky. Generally there should be no problem at all finding a place to stay, but booking ahead is advisable if you're arriving in Damascus late in the day in summer and you want somewhere decent. All hotels have a receptionist who speaks at least a modicum of English, and who will (usually grudgingly) show you a room before you decide to stay. Conveniently, hotels of a similar quality tend to cluster together in the same area, making room-hunting relatively easy, even if you're lugging a heavy pack around. The **cheapest** cram the area between Martyrs' Square and the Citadel; **mid-range hotels** (③–⑤) cluster around the Hedjaz Station (where the *Sultan* stands out) and the triangle formed by Yousef al-Azmeh, Port Said and Bahsa streets. Here you'll also find several hotels run by the Syrian-owned Alaa Towers group, but these tend to be rather overpriced and characterless mid-range options. Syrian-owned **top-class hotels** such as the *Cham Palace* can be found in the centre of town, with more recently built, internationally managed chains relegated to the outskirts.

The only alternative to hotels is Syria's one and only **campsite**, *Damascus Camping* (also known as *Harasta Camping*; ☎011/445 5870), situated just off the Homs motorway (from where it's clearly signposted) 4km northeast of the centre. Frequent city microbuses run there from Bahsa Street, 200m southeast from its intersection with Yousef al-Azmeh Street; you shouldn't have any trouble asking the drivers which one is heading for "Harasta". It's a small, scrubby site, really a courtyard rather than a field, but it has hot water, and showers, toilets and cooking facilities are available. You'll pay S£300 per person per day here, which is hardly worth it considering the inconvenience of getting in and out of the centre; it's much more popular with campervan owners than with those pitching tents.

If you're after an apartment to **rent long-term**, the first place to look is probably the noticeboard at the American Language Center (see p.54); after that, head for the accommodation rental agencies around the diplomatic quarter, such as Orient Flat Finder Agency on Al-Jalaa Street (☎011/333 3752).

South and southeast of Martyrs' Square

Packed into the area between Martyrs' Square and the Citadel, 250m to the southeast, are dozens of **cheap hotels**, all occupying the upper storeys of buildings which house shops, workshops, cheap restaurants and offices at ground level. It's a noisy, lively area, bounded by An-Naser Street, Ath-Thawra Street, Rami Street and Al-Furat Avenue, full of tiny lanes along which traders gather from well before dawn, selling caged birds, live poultry and all manner of meats and fresh carcasses. None of this is particularly conducive to a good night's sleep, but staying here ensures contact with a constantly changing community of travellers, and you're undeniably in the centre of things, with the souks, the National Museum, the Umayyad Mosque, the Hedjaz Station and all the major banks and offices under fifteen minutes away on foot.

There's actually very little to distinguish the hotels in this area, and your choice is most likely to depend on cleanliness rather than any other factors. Typically, you enter these hotels through a narrow ground-floor entrance which leads to a lift and a shuddery journey up to the first or second floor, where you'll find reception. The reception area will usually double as a communal room, with a constantly blaring TV and furniture in various states of collapse spread about. The bedrooms will be spread across two or three floors; some will come with a squat toilet, some will have just a wash basin, with communal facilities down the hall. Fierce competition has forced many of these hotels to install a TV and fridge in some of their rooms, though you may have to pay a bit extra for these. Most rooms have a fan and a window; remember that you'll probably want to keep the window open throughout the night, so if they've got a room which overlooks a quiet back alley, take it.

Most hotels here charge a similar sort of price (between S£300 and S£500). If you bargain, or even if you make your apologies and leave because you don't fancy what's on offer, you may find that you can reduce prices by S£100 or even more. Unless you're here during a public holiday, none of these hotels is really worth **reserving** in advance (except the *Omar Khyam*); in most, if you turn up late in the evening, they're more likely to lower the price rather than turn you away.

Basman, Rami St (☎011/221 8003, fax 224 6689). A little overpriced, but all rooms have aircon and fans. ⑤.

Najmet al-Shark, southwestern corner of Martyrs' Square (☎011/222 9139). A good option at this budget, in a noisy location but offering TV and fridge in its rooms. ②.

Al Raess, opposite the *Rudwan* on a street running off An-Naser St (☎011/221 4252). Clean, basic rooms with TV and fridge: a place that's good value in this price range. ②.

Rami Hotel, Rami St (☎011/221 9971 or 221 9972). Also called *Rami Palace,* this is a good-value mid-range hotel, offering single and double rooms, some with shower. Definitely a good place to head for – it's cleaner, quieter and much more bearable than the cheapies which line both sides of this street. ③.

Rudwan, off An-Naser St (☎011/222 1654). Clean rooms with shared showers in one of the better cheapies, located on one of the quieter streets in the district; the slightly higher price (it's at the upper end of this price category) reflects this. ②.

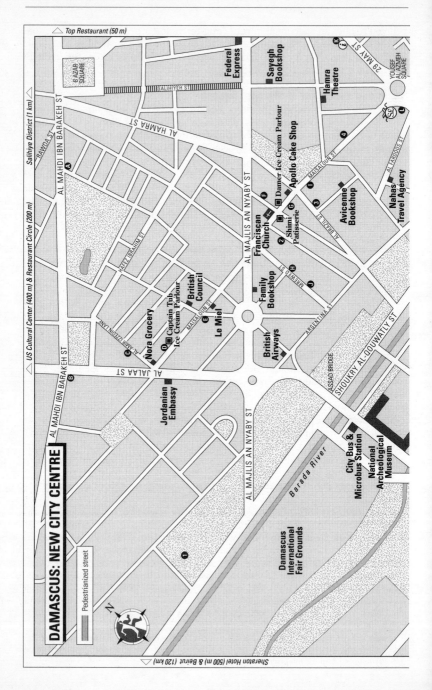

△ Top Restaurant (50 m)

DAMASCUS: NEW CITY CENTRE

Pedestrianized street

Federal Express

Sayegh Bookshop

Hamra Theatre

29 MAY ST

YOUSEF AL-AZMEH SQUARE

8 AZAR SQUARE

SALIHIYEH ST

AL HAMRA ST

RAWDA ST

AL MAHDI IBN BARAKEH ST

Salihiye District (1 km)

Damer Ice Cream Parlour

Apollo Cake Shop

MAISALOUN ST

AL CAHDOOS ST

Avicenne Bookshop

Nahas Travel Agency

AL BRAZIL ST

Shimi Patisserie

Franciscan Church

AL MAJLIS AN NYABY ST

HAFEZ IBRAHIM ST

Family Bookshop

MEHRET ST

US Cultural Center (400 m) & Restaurant Circle (200 m)

British Council

MAISALOUN S

Captain Tub Ice Cream Parlour

Nora Grocery

AL AMIN IZZEDIN LANE

Le Miel

British Airways

ARGENTINA ST

ASSAD BRIDGE

SHOUKRY AL-QUUWATLY ST

AL MAHDI IBN BARAKEH ST

Jordanian Embassy

AL JALAA ST

City Bus & Microbus Station

National Archeological Museum

AL MAJLIS AN NYABY ST

Damascus International Fair Grounds

Barada River

N

▽ Sheraton Hotel (500 m) & Beirut (120 km)

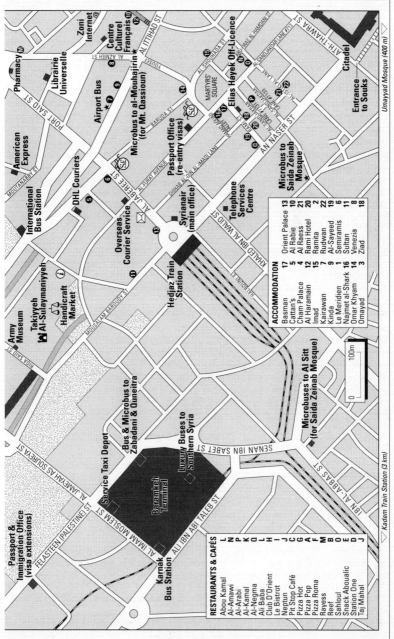

Al-Sayeed, Rami St (☎011/221 7893). Spartan but clean rooms although the location is rather noisy. ②.

Ziad, Rami St (☎011/222 9875). Approached along dingy covered alleyways lined with cavernous workshops, this is unquestionably the cheapest bed in Damascus. You get what you pay for, though: a cramped, stuffy dosshouse which sleeps three to four per room; it's cleaned itself up in recent years but is still only recommended if you're absolutely desperate. ①.

North of Martyrs' Square

Most of the hotels in this modern, soulless area of the New City occupy modern high-rise buildings in the triangle formed by Yousef al-Azmeh Street, Port Said Street and Al-Ittihad Street; for your money you'll get clean, carpeted rooms with en-suite facilities, air-conditioning, TV, fridge and minibar. As with the cheapies on the other side of Martyrs' Square, there's not much to choose between the hotels – the exceptions are the popular *Al-Haramain* and *Al-Rabie*.

Al-Haramain, off Al-Ittihad St, one block east of Yousef al-Azmeh St (☎011/231 9489, fax 231 4299). Situated along a narrow, shady lane lined with tailors' shops, this is an excellent cheap hotel, converted from a traditional Damascene house. The rooms are spartan but airy, with fans; the whole place has bags of character – even the wooden stairs are endearingly crooked. You can sleep on the roof for only S£100. Hugely popular: advance booking essential. ②.

Imad, Al-Shouhada St, just off Martyrs' Square (☎011/231 4225). Slightly dingy, high-ceilinged rooms with TV, air-con and fan. Rather cramped and a little overpriced, with street noise a problem unless you get a room at the back. ④.

Kairawan, off Al-Ittihad St (☎011/231 3338, fax 231 3343). Good rooms, all with TV and fridge, but lousy service and breakfast. ⑥.

Kinda, Al-Ittihad St (☎011/231 9760, fax 231 7438). Fairly ordinary, modern hotel popular with tour groups and (like the *Orient Palace*) with Iranian pilgrims. ⑤.

Omar Khyam, Martyrs' Square (☎011/231 2666). Old mandate-era hotel in a good position overlooking the square. The shabby, dark rooms have definitely seen better days, though here and there you can see traces of the former opulence showing through. ⑤.

Al-Rabie, off Al-Ittihad St (☎011/231 8374, fax 231 1875). Like the *Al-Haramain* two doors down, this is an old converted house, with a wonderful shady courtyard where travellers swap experiences until well into the night; the rooms are clean, though not en suite. One of the most characterful hotels in Syria and very popular, so it's worth booking ahead. ③.

Venezia, Yousef al-Azmeh St (☎011/231 6631, fax 231 4030). Well-appointed rooms with TV in a comfortable mid-range high-rise. ⑤.

Around Hedjaz Station

Hotels located around the Hedjaz Station are quiet and central, but generally pricier than those to the south and southeast of Martyrs' Square.

Cattan's, on a quiet side street off Shoukry al-Qouwatly St (☎011/223 9421). Decent, modern mid-range hotel which fills up quickly. Located just round the corner from the entrance to the green-tiled *Semiramis*. ④.

Orient Palace, opposite Hedjaz Station (☎011/223 1351, fax 221 1512). Dating back to colonial mandate times, and sharing with the train station an oddly melancholic charm. Plush foyer gives way to spacious if dim, shabby but very clean rooms, with TV, fridge and air-con throughout. Rooms at the back have balconies with good views of Mount Qassioun. A favourite with Iranian pilgrims, which gives the place an unusual ambience. Price includes breakfast. ⑤.

Semiramis, Al-Jaberee St (☎011/223 3555, fax 221 6797, *semirams@cyberia.net.lb*). Has a ghastly exterior fashioned from green and mauve tiles, which give it the appearance of an enormous bathroom. Inside, guests can enjoy a restaurant, nightclub with live music, gym, cinema and shops. The cheapest of all the luxury hotels. ⑧.

Sultan, Mousalam Baroudy St (☎011/222 5768 or 221 6910). The best mid-range option in Damascus, a small, friendly and justly popular hotel just up from the Hedjaz Station. The rooms are clean and have both fans and air-con, and there's a travellers' noticeboard and a library for guests to swap books. Get there early in the day or book in advance. ④.

North and west of Shoukry al-Qouwatly Street

A little way out from the centre lie several hotels. most of which fall into the luxury category and tend to be populated mainly by Western and Gulf Arab business travellers.

Cham Palace, Maisaloun St (☎011/223 2300, fax 221 2398, *chamdama@net.sy*). Modern hotel whose rather brutal brown-tiled exterior is something of a city-centre landmark, and whose atrium is a virtual forest of ornamental plants. Plush rooms and suites, with fitness centre, sauna, squash courts, shops, several bars and a roof top swimming pool. The most expensive city-centre hotel; among its many eating places are the only Chinese and revolving restaurants in Syria. ⑧.

Le Meridien, Noussair St (☎011/373 8730, fax 371 8661, *www.lemeridien-middleeast.com*). Fifteen minutes' walk from Martyrs' Square, this extremely smart hotel boasts several restaurants and snack bars, an outdoor pool and a business centre, plus the *Oasis Bar* on the ground floor, with an English-style pub (serving draught beer) in the basement. ⑧.

Omayad, Al-Brazil St (☎011/221 7700 or 223 5500, fax 221 3516). Luxury hotel where the quality of the rooms does not quite live up to the impressively grand foyer. Lower standards of service, but more character, a friendlier welcome and cheaper prices than the other luxury spots listed here. ⑦.

Ramita, Al-Manfaluti St, off Maisaloun St (☎011/331 6138). This very small, down-at-heel hotel, marooned far away from its sibling cheapies, is mercifully quiet, though basic, with OK rooms and shared bathrooms. Lower end of this price range. ②.

Sheraton Towers, Al-Umawiyeen Square (☎011/373 4630, fax 224 3607, *www.sheraton.com*). High-rise hotel set amid its own gardens on a roundabout 3km from the city centre, along the Beirut road. Shops, restaurants and business facilities, and a big outdoor pool. Rooms are priced according to what they call "luxury" (basically, size). ⑧.

The Old City

With so much of its fabric having been preserved and rehashed over the centuries, the **Old City** is just as much a place for wandering and absorbing as it is for seeking out specific sights. There is one obvious highlight, the **Umayyad Mosque**, one of the most famous monuments of Islam, but it is in the labyrinthine lanes of the **souks** that you will probably spend most of your time. These fascinating, vibrant bazaars offer the best opportunity in Syria for souvenir hunting, though their principal function is still to provide locals with their daily needs. Most of the Old City remains residential, and some of the grander historic homes are open to visitors; foremost among them is the **Azem Palace**, built in the eighteenth century by an Ottoman governor. **Straight Street** has been the main east–west thoroughfare of Damascus since Hellenistic times and was known to St Paul, whose stay in the city is commemorated by a couple of still-revered monuments. A full day would be enough to see the highlights of the route described below, two days would be more than enough to take in everything – though you could easily spend a couple more days further investigating the souks and narrow alleys of the Old City for yourself.

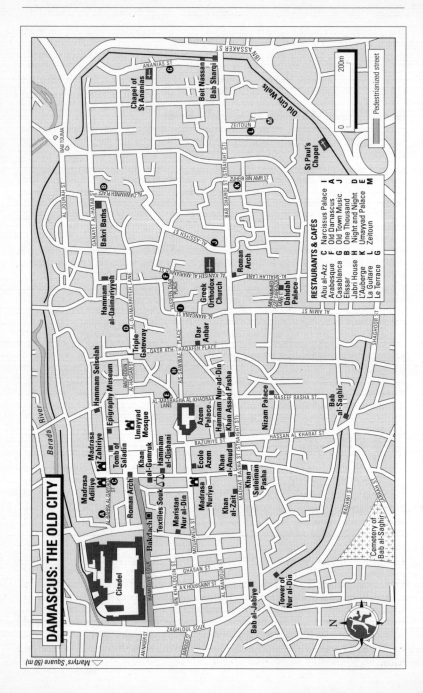

DAMASCUS: THE OLD CITY

RESTAURANTS & CAFÉS

Abu al-Azz	C
Arabesque	F
Casablanca	G
Elissar	B
Jabri House	H
L'Auberge	K
La Guitare	L
Le Terrace	G

Narcissus Palace	I
Old Damascus	A
Old Town Music	J
One Thousand	B
Night and Night	D
Umayyad Palace	E
Zeitoun	M

Pedestrianized street

0   200m

N

The Citadel

You can't help but notice this huge building, which stands right outside the main entrance to the souks and the Old City. Formidably intact and protected by twelve surviving towers, the **Citadel** was only retired as a prison in 1985, and since then substantial restoration has been taking place; it is not yet possible to visit the interior, though you may be able to gain access to the courtyard through one of the (usually guarded) entrances.

This has been a military site since at least Roman times, though little is known of the Roman or Byzantine fortifications underlying the site; what you see today largely dates from the thirteenth century when Damascus became a major centre of resistance to the Crusaders. Severely damaged during a fierce Mongol siege in 1400, the Citadel fell into neglect and, although the Turks used the building as a military base, their repairs were half-hearted; in 1912 Baedeker even reported that it was "shortly to be demolished". The Citadel survived, however, and the solidity of the exterior walls suggests that they will be here for some time to come.

Hamidiye Souk

Just to the south of the Citadel is the entrance to the cavernous **Hamidiye Souk**, which functions almost as a portal to Damascus's awesome history; indeed, in Roman times this street would have led to the western facade of the Temple of Jupiter, at the heart of the ancient settlement. It's slightly surprising therefore to find out that the Hamidiye Souk only came into its present form in the 1870s, the result of an urban renewal programme under the city's governor Rashid Nasha Pasha, who almost doubled the width of the street, built a couple of storeys of shops and offices on either side and put a corrugated iron roof on top. The vast roofing is pierced with holes creating an attractive star-like effect; these were put there deliberately in the 1870s to let sunlight in, though locals claim that the holes owe their presence to the French bombardment of the mid-1920s – the entire Hariqa quarter immediately to the south of the Hamidiye Souk was destroyed during this act of military vandalism.

Initially the shops in the souk are quite tourist-oriented, with a great variety of copperware, woodwork, carpets, swords, musical instruments, Arabic headscarfs and gold souvenirs. Invitations to change money or to look inside a shop are most persistent here, though after a firm but polite refusal you won't get hassled; of course if you do want to do some shopping there's no harm in taking up a no-obligation invitation for a cup of tea. Hawkers are numerous, mainly small boys or invalids, though they tend to sell quite mundane items such as pens or socks or the inevitable packs of Marlboro. Pretty soon the souk turns into a regular clothes market, with only occasional "Oriental Goods" stalls, announcing their cosmopolitanism with stickers that proclaim their ability to handle Mastercard, Visa and American Express. Smaller lanes branch off from the main concourse, stalls here selling anything from beach balls and sunglasses to spatulas and sweets. For a detailed account of what to buy in Damascus and where, see p.105.

Maristan Nur al-Din

About halfway along the souk is a short but fascinating southward diversion to the **Maristan Nur al-Din**, founded in 1154 with ransom money collected by the Muslim commander Nur al-Din from the Crusaders; what you see here today largely dates from restorations in 1283 and the eighteenth century. A functioning hospital until the early part of the twentieth century, the place now serves as a **museum of medical history** (daily except Fri 8am–2pm; S£150), well illustrating the sophistication of ancient Arab medicine which for centuries outpaced advances made in the West; public pharmacies have been around in this part of the world since the eighth century, and in medieval times Arab practitioners looked with horror upon the activities of their Occidental counterparts.

Probably the school's most famous pupil was Ibn al-Nafis Damishqui who, in the early twelfth century, revealed the secrets of the blood circulatory system three centuries before their "discovery" in Europe – only one of his many medical works was ever translated into Latin. Wince-inducing exhibits include some medieval circumcision scissors and an implement used to extract dead foetuses from the womb, though quite what the room of stuffed birds is doing here is anyone's guess. The building itself is also worthy of attention with its cool courtyard and richly decorated *iwan*s (open reception areas off the courtyard). The larger *iwan* opposite the entrance was used for consultations and teaching purposes (as illustrated by the mannequins), though the more intimate one on the south side has the more attractive decoration.

The Roman gateway

Emerging from the eastern end of the Hamidiye Souk, you are suddenly greeted with almost disorientating daylight and an extraordinary sight: a towering **Roman gateway**, or *propylaeum*, which formed the back entrance to the compound of the Temple of Jupiter. Running the short distance from the gateway towards the western facade of the Umayyad Mosque is a columned arcade, part of a Byzantine shopping complex dating to the early fourth century; today the stalls found along here sell mainly Korans and religious memorabilia. Before heading for the tourist entrance, in the north wall of the complex, it's worth briefly examining the curious patchwork of stone which makes up the mosque's awesome 100-metre-high walls; the lower part is made up of massive blocks which are Roman in origin, while the smaller blocks higher up date from the early Islamic period.

The Umayyad Mosque

Undoubtedly one of early Islam's most magnificent monuments, the **Umayyad Mosque** (daily 9am–5pm, open for prayers only Fri 12.30–2pm; S£50, including admission to the Tomb of Saladin) stands on a site which has been held sacred for at least three millennia, its chameleonic biography reflecting the monumental shifts in the history of the city. The compound of the Roman Temple of Jupiter would have stretched from the grand archway at the eastern end of the Hamidiye Souk right over to the monumental gate that lies half-buried beneath street level, some 120m beyond the eastern gate of the present-day mosque. Within this huge enclosure would have been an inner compound corresponding to the dimensions of the mosque today. In the late fourth century AD the temple was converted into a **church** dedicated to St John the Baptist, thought to cover roughly the same area as today's prayer hall. When the Arabs took Damascus in 636 the Christian population was initially allowed to continue worshipping here, though in the early eighth century Caliph al-Walid negotiated with the Christian community the ceding of the site in return for permanent rights to four other church sites in the city (including that of the present-day Greek Orthodox church).

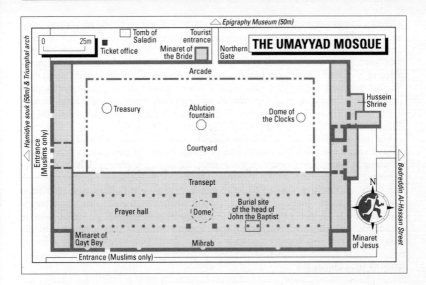

Between 708 and 715, hired Byzantine architects and craftsmen constructed essentially what you see today; it is said that the building work cost a total of four hundred chests of dinars and that eighteen camels were required just to transport the expense sheets. This was the first mosque in Syria to feature minarets, a *mihrab*, a *minbar* and ablution fountains, and it became the prototype for numerous other monumental Umayyad constructions, including those at Aleppo and Hama (and even the Great Mosque of Cordoba in Spain, constructed in 786). Over the centuries a number of disasters, both natural and man-made, have conspired to diminish the building's original splendour, the most serious of which was a major **fire** in 1893 (said to have been started accidently by a smoking workman involved in the repair of the dome) which destroyed much of the prayer hall. The mosque was rebuilt over a period of nine years by the Damascenes themselves, with seven brigades of volunteers being formed to work one day each week, and as such the building has come to embody something of the pride and spirit of the city – something Hafez al-Assad was no doubt aware of when he allotted S£300 million for the renovation of the courtyard and minarets, a process completed in 2000.

The courtyard and minarets

The ticket office for the mosque is near its northwestern corner; tourists enter through the mosque's northern gate, the **Bab al-Amara**, where the remains of the arcade that once connected the outer and inner walls of the Roman structure can be seen. From here you enter the marble-covered courtyard facing the magnificent facade of the prayer hall; on the right is a small octagonal building, elevated on eight recycled Classical columns, its beautiful mosaics thought to date from a thirteenth-century restoration. The early mosques all included a structure of this type, which functioned as a treasury for the Muslim community, but it's thought that the one here may have been symbolic. In the centre of the courtyard, the modern **ablution fountain** is said to mark the mid-point between Istanbul and Mecca, while on the eastern side is another domed pavilion, dating to the eighteenth century, popularly known as the **Dome of the Clocks** (until 1958 it housed the mosque's collection of clocks). Shiite pilgrims tend to gather in this part of the courtyard because a room off the eastern arcade contains the legendary burial place of the head of their revered leader Hussein, son of the Prophet's son-in-law Ali (for more on Shiah Islam, see p.313). After Hussein died at the hands of the Umayyads at the Battle of Kerbala in 680, his head was brought back to the Umayyad Mosque and put on public display as a warning to any future insurgents, though whether it was ever actually buried here is debatable.

The vast majority of the original **mosaics** on the prayer hall's exterior and arcaded walls have been lost in a succession of disasters over the centuries, but what is on show today is still an awe-inspiring sight, glistening ostentatiously in the sun. For the best appreciation of the surviving original work, look at the western arcade and in the darker sections of the transept. In accordance with Muslim prohibition, there are no representations of people or animals in the mosaics, which portray a lush, rolling landscape of orchards, fields and rivers populated by grand palaces and fantastical cities. It's not certain what exactly is being depicted here – some have suggested it is a representation of the city of Damascus, yet the eclectic nature of the design makes this unlikely; others say that it is the landscape of the Muslim paradise as referenced in the Koran, but this is anachronistic for the period. Perhaps a more likely explanation is that it is a subtle combination of the two: a portrayal of an Islamic paradise which is both physical, in that it represents Umayyad-held lands, and spiritual, in that it is clearly an idealized representation.

Above the northern arcade, a ninth-century structure to which an upper storey was added in the twelfth century, is the **Minaret of the Bride**. Its name derives from the story of a merchant who provided lead for the minaret's roof, and whose daughter subsequently married the Caliph. Rising from the southwest corner of the prayer hall is the late fifteenth-century **Minaret of Qayt Bey**, named after the Mameluke Sultan responsible for its construction, while at its southeastern corner is the **Minaret of Jesus**, built in 1247 on the site of an Umayyad structure. Though Muslims revere Jesus as one of the prophets, they reject the notion that he was the son of God, attributing this fallacy to the distorted beliefs of his followers; traditionally Muslims also believe that Jesus will come down from heaven via this minaret to lead the final conflict against the Anti-Christ just before the Last Judgement.

The prayer hall

You enter the **prayer hall** by one of the doors at either end, removing your shoes first. It's really its sheer scale which impresses – the interior is rather plain, the carpeting slightly threadbare. The building essentially follows the plan of the destroyed Roman triple-aisled basilica, except that the building is oriented not towards the east wall, where the altar would have been, but towards the south wall, in the middle of which is the *mihrab*, indicating the direction of Mecca. Recycled columns divide the area into three wide aisles running parallel to the south wall, reflecting the form of a Christian basilica, though in fact these aisles are of equal width. The entrance in the southern wall would originally have connected to the Umayyad Palace (now gone), and been reserved for the Caliph.

The present dome crowning the north–south transept dates from 1893, and in fact there is little here that predates the fire of that year, though the supports for the dome are eleventh-century, and some of the transept ceiling's exquisite original wood panelling can still be seen on the courtyard side, as can fragments of eleventh-century mosaic work on the transept's northern wall. A lavish marble monument commemorates the legendary burial site of the head of **John the Baptist**, who is revered by Muslims as one of the prophets; again this structure dates from after 1893, the former wooden mausoleum having been consumed in the flames. During the construction of the mosque in the early eighth century, it is said that workmen came upon a small Christian crypt containing a basket with the head inside. Today pilgrims shove money, prayer requests and candles into any crack they can find in the edifice.

North of the mosque

Exiting the mosque by its northern doorway, turn left at the end of the arcade and you'll soon pass the **Epigraphy Museum** (daily except Tues 8am–2pm; S£150), containing examples of Arab inscriptions and calligraphy written on everything from basalt to doeskin. The collection occupies a madrasa dating from 1420, which has only recently been restored after being bombed by the French in 1945. One famous former pupil of the school is Shoukry al-Qouwatly, independent Syria's first president. The two graves in the annexe to the main room are thought to belong to the founder Jaqmaq al-Argunsawi, governor of Damascus at the time, and his mother.

Just next to the ticket office for the Umayyad Mosque stands a red-domed building which houses the **Tomb of Saladin** (daily 10am–5pm; same ticket as for Umayyad Mosque), the military genius who united the Muslim world against the Crusaders (see p.205). It's a select location even if the building is not so impressive, and its understatedness is appropriate for the unassuming man that he was. Inside there are two sarcophagi: the rotting walnut one, said to contain the body of Saladin's faithful secretary, is original, whereas the marble one next to it, in which Saladin himself is thought to lie, appeared in the late nineteenth century. Kaiser Wilhelm II of Germany, passing this way in 1898, had the whole chamber restored, so keen was he to pay his respects to the great Arab military leader and to cement a Turkish alliance.

Madrasa Zahiriye and Madrasa Adiliye

West along the street from the Epigraphy Museum, the first right-hand turn leads to two buildings with impressive doorways standing opposite each other. On the east side of the street is the **Madrasa Zahiriye** whose entrance, boasting wonderful *muqarnas* (arrays of scallop-shaped recesses) work and inset with three marble bands bearing magnificently worked inscriptions, is a minor masterpiece. The building is today a library but also contains the **tomb of Baibars**, the Mameluke Sultan who virtually rid the Middle East of the Crusaders and who died in Damascus in 1277 (see p.82). You may have to ask someone to open the domed tomb chamber, which stands to your right as you enter the courtyard and also contains the tomb of one of Baibars' sons. Both tombs are plain marble affairs, but the interior mosaic decoration in the chamber is exquisite, echoing that of the Umayyad Mosque.

Opposite this building is the **Madrasa Adiliye**, dating from the early thirteenth century, the final resting place of Saladin's brother Al-Adil Saif al-Din, who became Sultan of Syria and Egypt in 1200 and was largely responsible for the reconstruction of Damascus's Citadel in the early thirteenth century. At the time of writing a complete renovation of the interior was under way; from the outside, you can at least admire the madrasa's impressive honeycombed *muqarnas* above the entrance, though it's rather overshadowed by the portal opposite.

BAIBARS

If Saladin did the donkey work in ridding the Middle East of the Crusaders (see p.205), it was **Baibars** who essentially completed the job. Over the centuries Baibars has acquired a certain notoriety, mainly because of his bloodthirsty fanaticism, and for the underhand nature of his dealings with his enemies – in stark contrast to the chivalrous and honourable Saladin. However, though Baibars certainly had no qualms about resorting to subterfuge or even assassination attempts, he was also a quite brilliant field commander and turned out to be one of Cairo's great builders, constructing bridges, mosques and roads throughout his domains.

Baibars was raised as one of the **Mameluke** Turkish slaves who were bought as young children by the ruling Egyptians and then brought up to form an elite brigade of soldiers. So loyal to their Sultan were the Mamelukes that when he died they were usually replaced. However, after brilliantly seeing off the Frankish threat in Egypt in 1250, the Mameluke battalions murdered the Sultan Turan Shah and successfully proclaimed one of their own, Aybeg, as successor. The most immediate threat they faced was not the Crusaders but the **Mongols**, who were defeated by the Mamelukes in 1260 at the Battle of Ain Jalut. Flushed with victory, the Mamelukes went on to take both Damascus and Aleppo; foremost of the generals in these campaigns was Baibars who, when refused the governorship of Aleppo, responded by murdering the Mameluke Sultan Qutuz and declaring himself his heir.

Baibars now turned his attention to the Crusaders; one target was ruthlessly attacked after the next, with the surrendering garrisons usually slaughtered upon capture. After the seizure of Antioch in 1268, Baibars sent Prince Bohemond of Antioch, who was holed up further south in Tripoli at the time, a charming little note describing what he would have seen had he been there: "knights prostrate beneath horses hooves, houses stormed by pillagers and ransacked by looters . . . crosses in the churches smashed, the pages of the false testaments scattered, the Patriarchs' tombs overturned and your Muslim enemy trampling on the place where you celebrate mass, cutting the throats of monks, priests and deacons upon the altars".

In 1271 both Safita and the Crak des Chevaliers fell to Baibars, but the following year, partly to consolidate his gains and partly to tackle again the threat of the resurgent Mongols, Baibars signed a ten-year truce with Prince Edward of England – though this didn't stop Baibars engineering an assassination attempt, while Edward was still in the Holy Land. Though Baibars died in 1277, the Mameluke war machine he had created rolled on: in 1291 Acre fell; soon after the Templars abandoned Tartous, then Arwad – and their great Middle Eastern adventure was at an end.

The south and east walls of the mosque

Back at the western facade of the Umayyad Mosque, you can either continue south through the souks to Straight Street (see opposite), or complete your appreciation of the mosque with a walk around its southern walls. About 30m along is the southern entrance, the **Bab al-Ziyadeh**; the mosque's windows are so high up along here because the Roman wall at this point was left substantially intact. A little further along, partially obscured by an electricity substation, is a Roman doorway, the original southern entrance to the Temple of Jupiter's inner compound, which was walled up when the prayer hall was built. With heavy irony, a Greek inscription over the blocked doorway, adapted from Psalm 145, reads "Your kingdom, Christ, is an everlasting kingdom, and your dominion endures throughout all generations."

Gold tends to dominate the souk at this point, more for the benefit of tourists from the Arab world than Westerners. As you walk further along the southern wall of the mosque a number of **woodwork** shops appear, many of them also serving as workshops where you can watch the vendor practise his trade. This is one of the best places to look for an inlaid chess or backgammon board and pieces, though anything from stools to cutting boards and spoons are on sale here.

At the corner, turn along the east wall up to the mosque's eastern gate, the **Bab an-Nofara**, a triple gateway that was once the principal entrance to the inner compound of the Roman temple, approached from the east along a colonnaded "sacred way". This ascended a broad flight of stairs to a columned porch which would have projected out from the gateway. Half-buried 100m along An-Nofara Lane (which turns into Badreddin al-Hassan Street), the avenue that follows the line of the sacred way, is the main entrance to the temple compound. Beyond lie the twisting streets of the old Christian quarter, though by this stage the traditional cafés by the mosque's eastern gate might prove a greater temptation than moving on; details of the **storyteller** who entertains at the café in the evenings can be found on p.104.

Through the souks to Straight Street

Running south of the remains of the triumphal arch at the end of the Hamidiye Souk, the narrow textiles souk, the Souk al-Haiyatin, runs all the way down to Straight Street. About 50m along here on the right is the **Khan al-Jumruk**, a seventeenth-century customs house in the form of an L-shaped hall topped with six domes. A few metres further on to the left is the former changing room of a public bath, the sixteenth-century Hammam al-Qishani (you can still see the characteristic tiled panels above the doorway), now simply part of the souk. Another 50m south is a crossroads of sorts; to the east is the way to the Azem Palace, but it's worth continuing straight ahead for another 10m to look at the Madrasa Nuriye on your right. This houses the **tomb of Nur al-Din**, one of the great military rulers of the Middle Ages and predecessor to Saladin (see p.205); the relatively plain tomb can be viewed from the souk through a grill just next to a water fountain.

Along the street leading east to the Azem Palace is a late eighteenth-century madrasa which now serves as a wonderfully diverse antiques shop, the **Azem Ecole**. Here you are free to browse without hassle collectibles such as inlaid wood, swords and goldware in evocative surroundings – a small courtyard arranged around a fountain. Continuing eastwards, you're soon in the heart of the perfume souk, which sells everything from well-known Western brands to odd-looking potions in unlabelled jars which you'll need a bit of help identifying: most stalls bear lists in English of the various aromas on offer.

Azem Palace

Through the perfume souk lies a small, relatively peaceful square and the entrance to the **Azem Palace** (Beit Azem), built between 1749 and 1752 by the Ottoman governor of Damascus, Assad Pasha al-Azem, who was previously the governor of Hama (where he had another impressive home; see p.161). Assad Pasha spared no expense in making his residence the most attractive in the city; a local barber, Shaikh Ahmad Al-Bidiri Al-Halaq, recorded in his diary how "every time he [Al-Azem] heard of an antiquity or a rare work of marble or porcelain he would send someone to get it – with or without the owner's consent". The house, which today houses the **Museum of Popular Arts and Tradition** (daily except Tues

8.30am–4pm, closed Fri 12.30–2.30pm; S£300), remained in the hands of the Azem family until 1920, when it was sold to the French Institute. Ownership reverted to the Azem family upon independence in 1945; in 1951 the house was purchased by the Syrian government, who installed the museum in it three years later.

The palace's most notable feature is its central **courtyard** which, with a cool pond and shady citrus trees, offers seductive respite from the bustle of the souk outside. As was typical, the building itself is arranged into three separate quarters: the *selamlek*, which was used for guests, visitors and official purposes; the *haramlek*, or family apartments; and the *khadamlek*, or servants' quarters. Red arrows and a few basic signs in French guide you on a tour of sorts of the rooms, which are adorned with a series of inscrutable wax dummies illustrating various aspects of traditional Arab culture – marriage, pilgrimage, school, the coffee-shop. Architecturally, the most interesting part of the palace complex is the private hammam; a claustrophobic succession of small rooms and narrow corridors lead you to the main steam room in the heart of the building. Next to the hammam is the main reception hall with a small fountain in the centre of its beautiful marble floor. Behind this is a second, smaller, courtyard set around which are a number of rooms illustrating various crafts – leather, glass, textiles and copper.

Souk al-Bazuriye

As you exit the Azem Palace, the broad street to the south, leading to Straight Street, is the spices and confectionery souk, the **Souk al-Bazuriye**. About 30m along on the left stands the twelfth-century **Hammam Nur al-Din**; it was used as a soap factory in the early years of the twentieth century before being pristinely restored and reverting to its original function as a bathhouse (see Listings, p.111 for details). Even if you don't want to use the facilities it's worth a peek in to see the gleaming white, Ottoman domed chamber; a series of photos in the hall gives some idea of the reconstruction process.

To your left, another 10m on and only a short distance before Straight Street, is undoubtedly the finest of the Damascene khans, the **Khan Assad Pasha**, built in 1752 by the same Ottoman governor who built the Azem Palace. Unfortunately the place is undergoing some major reconstruction (there are plans to turn it into a natural history museum), so all you'll be able to take in of the grand interior is a glimpse through the door – if it's unlocked and if there's no one stopping you. Opposite the entrance, in complete contrast, is the less impressive, rather dilapidated **Khan al-Amud**, which has been in continuous use as a warehouse since the seventeenth century and is still clogged with goods to be sold in the souks.

Straight Street

Since Hellenistic times **Straight Street** (the ancient Via Recta, now Madhat Basha Street and Bab Sharqi Street) has been the main east–west thoroughfare of Damascus. It was the Greeks who reoriented the city on a grid pattern based on rectangles 45m by 100m, and today's seemingly random streets and alleys still concur at many points with this ancient layout. Straight Street itself, however, was laid on top of an existing thoroughfare which skirted around existing buildings and low hills, so it has never completely lived up to its name. As part of their civic programme the Romans broadened Straight Street, lining it with columns; at that time it would have been some four times wider than at present, but over the centuries buildings have encroached onto the street and in places today there is barely enough room for pedestrians to walk along either side; indeed, if you haven't yet had your daily intake of exhaust fumes then this is a good place to come. The cell-like shops along Straight Street purvey anything from fruit and meat to cassettes and washing-up powder – there's little discernible order to it, though towards Bab Sharqi the pace is certainly much less hectic, and tourist-oriented antique shops proliferate.

Coming from the Souk al-Bazuriye, most of Straight Street stretches off to the east (left), but there are a couple of khans west along the street which might be worth a quick detour. After about 50m in this direction you'll see on your left the striped entrance to the early eighteenth-century **Khan Suleiman Pasha**. Its upper gallery is still intact, but the twin-domed roof which once covered the courtyard has long since collapsed. Another 50m westwards along Straight Street, on the opposite side of the road, stands the late sixteenth-century **Khan az-Zait**, once the depot for the olive-oil trade and today one of the more pleasant of the surviving khans, with an attractive tree-shaded open courtyard.

Nizam Palace and Dar Anbar

A couple of fine examples of old **Damascene residences** can be found a short way off Straight Street. Neither is an official museum though the doors to both are left unlocked in the mornings (except Fri) for visitors to look around. A short

---

TRADITIONAL DAMASCENE HOUSES

The uncompromising blank facades of most old **Damascene houses**, pressed hard against one another in the Old City and designed to preserve privacy, give little sense of the often spacious dwellings to be found within. The vast majority of the houses date to the eighteenth century when the city prospered under the governorship of the Azem family; indeed, most are smaller, less opulent versions of the Azem Palace. Traditionally the living quarters are arranged around one or more **courtyards**, typically with a fountain in the middle (supplied by spring water) and a clutch of sweet-scented citrus trees. Another typical feature is an **iwan**, an area open to the courtyard set into the side of the building and sheltered by its roof, which would be a place for relaxing and for receiving and entertaining guests. Most of the houses are built on two levels; in the past the family would have lived on the warmer upper storey during the winter while in the summer they retreated to the cooler ground floor and the courtyards. Popular tradition has it that serpents live inside the walls; it's said they can be heard breathing at night and some residents even leave food out for them, a kind of ritual offering to ensure they stay in their place.

Despite the uniformity of layout, each house had its own unique, busy decoration, adorning every wall, ceiling and cupboard. However, tables and chairs were relatively uncommon due to the scarcity of wood; even in the wealthiest houses, people would sit on cushions arranged around the walls. The vast majority of the houses did not have facilities for washing – the citizens used the city's hammams.

In recent decades the Damascene elite have moved out of the Old City to the more fashionable suburbs. While a few of the better-preserved houses are accessible to visitors, though without specific opening times, a number of others are being reborn as upmarket cafés and restaurants (see p.102); such metamorphoses are often the only means of ensuring the upkeep and preservation of what are now becoming increasingly dilapidated buildings.

way east of the Souk al-Bazuriye you can detour south off Straight Street to the **Nizam Palace** (Beit Nizam; signposted in English outside). This quiet, restful eighteenth-century Ottoman dwelling was the residence of the British consul for part of the nineteenth century, though it is now back in the hands of the Nizam family. Inside are three attractive courtyards with intricately decorated *iwan*s; none of the rooms is open to visitors, though some hustlers sitting around may demand *baksheesh* for a mini-tour. A little way further east along Straight Street and north up Qasr Ath-Thaqafeh Place is the **Dar Anbar**, built in 1867 as the residence of a wealthy Turkish merchant. It was turned into a school in 1887 and until 1936 housed the principal high school of Damascus. Today, it's a government-owned administrative building, though no one seems to mind you taking a quick look around its richly opulent courtyards.

From the Roman arch to Bab Sharqi

Back on Straight Street, the third-century **Roman arch** a little way to the east of the turning to Dar Anbar is a small but notable landmark. It once stood at the crossroads with the main north–south intersecting axis, but was lying completely buried and forgotten by the end of the nineteenth century, and was only excavated and re-erected after being accidentally discovered by workmen during the French Mandate.

The lane that leads south just west of the arch takes you via a signposted route to the **Dahdah Palace**, a grandly atmospheric example of eighteenth-century Syrian domestic architecture with a shady courtyard and intimate *iwan*. Visits are allowed in the mornings from 9am to 1pm; if the door is shut, press on the doorbell, though the warmth of the reception can vary dramatically.

The stretch of Straight Street to the east of the arch tends to be slightly less hectic, with the route dominated by antique shops and smart restaurants; there's also a small drinks store on the street which will serve a cheap beer, though the place seems to be a decidedly middle-aged male preserve. The northeastern segment of the Old City comprises the traditional **Christian quarter**, with a large, modern **Greek Orthodox church** just to the north of the arch. A Christian church is said to have stood on this spot since Byzantine times; during the 1860 massacre of the Christian population by the Druze (see p.304), three hundred people who were seeking refuge were consumed by flames when the church was burned down. The southeastern part of the Old City was the **Jewish quarter** until Hafez al-Assad allowed Syria's remaining Jews to leave the country in the early 1990s (see p.316).

Continuing on to the end of Straight Street, you finally arrive at the disappointingly plain eastern gate of the Old City, **Bab Sharqi**. Dating to the second century, though it underwent restoration during the French Mandate, it's the oldest existing monument in Damascus and the only Roman gate here to preserve its original form – a triple gateway, the central one designed for wheeled traffic and the ones either side for pedestrians.

On the trail of St Paul

St Paul the apostle once preached in the synagogues of Damascus, and the Old City contains a number of sights associated with his presence here. To reach the **Chapel of St Ananias**, formerly a house where Paul was reputedly given shelter by Ananias after his famously blinding conversion, take the narrow lane that leads north just before the Bab Sharqi for about 150m. On the way you'll pass another

---

ST PAUL

Paul, or Saul, was a Jew born sometime between 5 and 15 AD in Tarsus, Cilicia (southern Turkey); his double-naming was probably the result of him being born a Roman citizen, with Paul being his Roman name and Saul his Jewish name. At some point he became a member of the Pharisees, a Jewish religious sect which was based on strict adherence to the Law of Moses, and he received training from the respected Rabbi Gamaliel in Jerusalem, supporting himself, like the other Pharisees, with a manual trade – in his case tent making, which he probably learnt from his father. As a Pharisee, Paul was actively involved in the persecution of Christians in the period immediately after Jesus' death, and he was present at the stoning of St Stephen.

Around 35 AD, Paul was travelling to Damascus on a mission to rid the city of its Christians when, according to Acts, "suddenly a light from heaven flashed around him". The vision blinded Paul and he was led into the city by his companions where he waited for three days. Meanwhile, a Christian of the city named Ananias had a vision telling him to go to "the house of Judas on Straight Street" where he would find Paul. This he did, placing his hands upon him and curing his blindness; Paul was then baptized. At some point – whether immediately after or after having returned to the city at some later date is unclear – Paul preached in the synagogues of Damascus. This prompted a plot by the Jews of the city to kill him, but Paul **escaped** by night when his followers lowered him in a basket through an opening in the city walls.

Upon his escape, Paul immediately embarked upon a monumental mission of **conversion**, and founded a whole network of churches around the Eastern Mediterranean and throughout the Roman Empire. As such he has become known not simply as a follower of Jesus but as the **founder of Christianity**; it was he who led the way in preaching to Gentiles, a decision which changed the movement from a small sect within Judaism to a world religion. Paul is said to have been martyred during Nero's persecutions of the Christians, around 67 AD, though as a Roman citizen, he is thought to have been beheaded with a sword rather than crucified.

---

grand Damascene residence (signed in English above the door), **Beit Nassan**, featuring a finely decorated arcaded courtyard set around a fountain with an exceptionally decorated, if gently peeling, *iwan*. The chapel (daily: summer 9am–1pm & 4–7pm; winter 9am–1pm & 3–6pm) is located below ground level and entered via a stairway at the corner of a courtyard. The small, dank interior has a suitably reverential air, disturbed only by the steady stream of Western tourists. Although the attribution of the house to Ananias can be neither proved nor disproved, there is scientific evidence to suggest that the building is indeed contemporary with the events described in the Bible.

To continue on the trail of St Paul, retrace your steps and exit the Old City by Bab Sharqi, then turn right and walk for about 400m along the city walls until you come to **St Paul's Chapel**. This simple twentieth-century chapel built into the walls is said to mark the spot where Paul was lowered in a basket to flee the city (see box above). To gain entry to the chapel you have to walk through the break in the wall next to it; once inside you'll notice that the shrine incorporates the remains of a fairly unremarkable fourteenth-century Arab gateway, the Bab Kaysan. The donation boxes are for the benefit of the orphanage situated next door.

The New City

In many ways it's difficult to like the **New City**. Noisy and often frantically busy, and blighted in many places by ongoing construction work and ugly concrete freeways, it has none of the Old City's charm, history, forgotten corners, ancient mosques and quiet back streets. But the New City, which began life in colonial days, is where Damascus actually *happens*: at its heart is the commercial, governmental, and diplomatic hub of the capital. New suburbs are being added all the time as the city grows remorselessly, fed by Syria's high birth rate and migration from the countryside. Workers pour into the New City every day, creating nightmare traffic which, when not gridlocked, absolutely tears along, horns constantly blaring, making crossing the road something of a developed skill (it's interesting to watch the locals do it with consummate ease).

It's tempting to think of the New City as a homogeneous entity, but in reality there are many different aspects to this part of Damascus, with each district offering something new and different. The area around **Martyrs' Square** is the heart of colonial Damascus, where cheap hotels vie for space with bustling meat and livestock markets; close by is the distinctive early twentieth-century **Hedjaz Station**. A short way to the northwest of the station is the **National Museum**, housing the most important archeological collection in Syria, and to the north is **Yousef al-Azmeh Square**, a traffic circle which has superseded Martyrs' Square as the hub of modern Damascus. Hotels, airline offices, travel agencies, government departments and Western-style shops and fast-food restaurants cluster in this part of town, which is often surprisingly quiet during the afternoon but which comes alive again after dusk, when smartly dressed Syrians walk the streets, window-shopping and eating ice cream. At night the flashing neon outside the kitsch nightclubs, the glaring light from the shops and stalls, the wail of Arabic pop music and the clamour of people and traffic make this an exciting place just to wander.

Leading west from Yousef al-Azmeh Square, **Maisaloun Street** is one of the main arteries of the New City, running past some good mid-range restaurants and the dark-red exterior of the *Cham Palace* hotel to Al-Jalaa Street and the **Diplomatic Quarter**, which stretches west and north from here up the lower slopes of Mount Qassioun. This part of town is quieter than the heart of the New City, with shady villas occupying wide tree-lined avenues. Most are given over to foreign embassies, cultural centres, trade delegations and the like; also here are the European-oriented eateries of **Restaurant Circle** (see p.101). Very different again is the **Salihiyeh District**, an area of sloping, winding streets lined with outdoor vegetable markets and linking ancient mosques and madrasas. The whole of the New City is overlooked by **Mount Qassioun**, from where you can most easily appreciate the city's layout and size. In the south of the city, the **Saida Zeinab Mosque** is one of the most striking modern buildings in Damascus, a riot of gleaming colours and whitewashed arcades.

Martyrs' Square and the Hedjaz Station

It's no use pretending that **Martyrs' Square** (*Plas Marjeh*) is anything other than a traffic interchange with a grandiose name (the said martyrs were 21 Arab nationalists who were hanged on May 6, 1916 for their part in the Arab Revolt against Ottoman rule). Photographic prints of the square taken a hundred years ago (which you'll see hanging on the walls of many hotels and restaurants) show a rather elegant open space, with horse-drawn trams gathering outside the post office, and a small garden, ideal for the evening family stroll, in the centre of the square. The telegraph pole in the centre of the square proudly commemorates the establishment of the first telegraphic service in the Middle East, from here to Mecca, which allowed Damascenes to hear of the sighting of the moon confirming the start of Ramadan. Time has not been kind. The post office has moved away, the centre of the New City has shifted to the northwest, the whole square is overlooked by an enormous construction project which has been under way since the early 1990s and which dwarfs the poor telegraph pole, and the centre of the square is now a scrubby little area of shrubs sadly marooned inside the continuous circle of moving traffic. The ornamental bridges across the putrid Barada River just give the place an extra underlining of pathos; there are benches under the trees, the fountains sometimes work and there are often small boys wandering around selling tea, but this is decidedly not a place to linger. Taking any of the streets heading east from the square towards the Citadel will plunge you into the noisiest, liveliest part of the New City – an overspill from the souks, with tiny foodstalls with fresh carcasses hanging outside, metal workshops which stretch into dark recesses, and chickens and caged birds clucking and chirping away at each other in cages by the roadside, waiting to be sold. There's nothing specific to see, but a wander through this tightly packed network of streets and alleyways is an absorbing experience.

One building you shouldn't miss in this part of Damascus is the **Hedjaz Station**, a short walk away up Rami Street from the square and then right along busy An-Naser Street. It was built by the Turks in the early twentieth century for the pilgrimage rail route to Mecca and Medina, but now only the grandiose entrance hall hints at the station's once-vital role. The station becomes noisy and crowded when the infrequent trains roll up, but at other times a **bar** serving cheap beer in an elegantly restored Ottoman carriage on the main platform provides a haven from the noise and bustle in this part of the city and at least prevents the place from becoming a forgotten colonial relic; some of the abandoned wagons on the grassy sidings look as if they haven't been moved since Mandate days.

The Takiyyeh as-Sulaymaniyyeh complex

The main reason for following **Shoukry al-Qouwatly Street** to the west is to reach the National Museum (see p.91), but just before you get there you'll find a small clutch of interesting sights along Rida Said Street. The most obvious of these is the **Takiyyeh as-Sulaymaniyyeh Mosque**, part of an Ottoman complex which includes the Army Museum and the Handicraft Market. Unfortunately this modest mosque is rather lost next to the hulk of the National Museum, and its intimacy drowned by the traffic screaming along the adjacent main road, but once inside it's possible to appreciate the calmness of the gardens and courtyard, cooled by a fountain and shaded by trees.

The mosque was built in 1553 by **Sinan**, the greatest architect of the Ottoman era, whose most noted buildings in Istanbul (such as the Suleimaniye Mosque) are on a far more grandiose scale than this gracious, understated construction. Having been commissioned by the Sultan himself, Suleiman the Magnificent, Sinan set out to honour his master by designing a mosque which included both Turkish and Arab elements, thus reflecting Damascus's role as a vital stopping place on the pilgrimage from Istanbul to Mecca: the domed prayer hall, the slim minarets and the delicate sense of proportion are typically Turkish, whereas the alternating layers of black and white *ablaq* stonework forming the entrance arch were popular in Mameluke times.

Unfortunately this is as much of the mosque as many people will see, as the prayer hall is often locked (except during prayers) and you'll have to find the keeper to gain entry. It's worth persevering, as the walls inside are adorned with brightly painted tiles which are beautifully complemented by the coloured glasswork in the windows beneath the dome. Note also the sense of space that Sinan imparted to the interior by supporting the dome on arches which emerge from the wall, rather than on columns which would have interrupted the interior proportions.

The Army Museum
The name of the mosque derives from the building next door, which was originally a **tekke**, a monastery for whirling dervishes, before it was converted into a khan for travelling pilgrims. Now the fighter planes and big guns outside, all looking rather the worse for wear, identify the building as the **Army Museum** (daily except Tues 8am–2pm; S£5), which is often full of bored conscripts on their day off, being dragged round by their commanding officers to look dutifully at fairly mundane collections of weapons and armour. The whole place is a little surreal, with fighter planes shaded by the trees of the courtyard and collections of weapons crammed into cool archways. Recent episodes of Syrian military history, such as the wars fought against Israel in 1967 and 1973, are explained with unashamed bias, as is the fight for independence from France; photos on display depict the atrocities committed by the colonialists and the eventual ignominious departure of the French Army of the Levant. More honest and more interesting are displays relating to the former Syrian–Soviet space programme, which demonstrates the close ties which existed between Damascus and Moscow during the Cold War. Hafez al-Assad trained as a fighter pilot in the USSR in the 1950s, and in 1987 a Syrian was sent into space on one of the Soviet missions, coming back to earth in the capsule displayed here, which is adorned with multilingual instructions for the freeing of any cosmonauts inside it. The collaborative efforts came to an end as Syrian foreign policy shifted more towards the West during the 1990s and the Soviet space programme began to run out of money.

The Handicraft Souk
Entered through an archway adjacent to the Army Museum's coffee-shop, the **Handicraft Souk** (or "Artisanat", as local people refer to it) is a small area where traditional goods are made and sold on the premises. Everything from carpet-weaving and glassblowing to shoemaking and chessboard manufacture can be seen in action, and souvenir hunting is much more straightforward here than in the souks. Part of the market is set round the shady courtyard of the **Selimiye Madrasa**, built by Suleiman the Magnificent's successor, Sultan Selim II; weaving workshops and the like now occupy the cells where Islamic scholars once taught their students, though you can still see the high-domed prayer hall which opens off one side of the courtyard.

North across the busy Shoukry al-Qouwatly Street from the museum is a small shady **park**, with benches lining dusty walkways beneath trees, and sprinklers watering scruffy areas of shrubs and flowers. It's one of the few areas of greenery in the city centre; unfortunately the constant traffic nearby means that it's not exactly quiet.

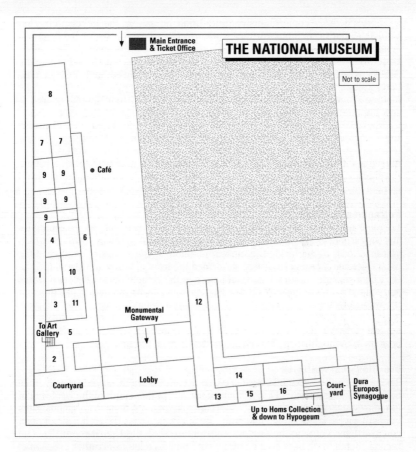

The National Museum

Housed in a purpose-built complex around a shady courtyard on Shoukry al-Qouwatly Street, the **National Museum** (daily except Tues 9am–6pm, 4pm in winter; S£300) shelters the bulk of artefacts unearthed from archeological sites in Syria over the past century and a half. If your itinerary allows, make it one of the last, rather than one of the first, things you see in Syria, to gain a better perspective on the ancient sites around the country that you have already visited. In size and scope the museum isn't a patch on similar museums in Ankara or Cairo, but it's definitely worth spending a good couple of hours or more wandering around its dimly lit galleries. If you only have time for the **highlights**, you should head to the synagogue, built in Dura Europos in the second century AD and transported to the museum piece by piece, looking in along the way on the stone-tablet archives from Ugarit which gave the world its first alphabet, the beautifully fashioned Byzantine-era manuscripts and jewellery, and the stonework and silk and cotton textiles from Palmyra – unearthed only in the twentieth century after being wonderfully preserved in the desert sands.

There's a dryly comprehensive **guidebook** on sale at the ticket office, but S£1000 is a lot to shell out for a book which lacks a contents list or index and so is rather difficult to use. Tagging along with a guided tour group might be a rather better idea as many of the exhibits are poorly labelled — mostly in French and Arabic, occasionally in English and sometimes not at all. In addition, bear in mind that exhibits are sometimes moved from one room to another, which can make looking around without a guide confusing. Most rooms are arranged by area or site, although there is also a broad organization of exhibits into three eras – pre-Classical, Classical and Early Byzantine, and Arab-Islamic. The **room numbering** shown on our plan and used in the text does not refer to any numbering system you'll find in the museum itself, but reflects the easiest way to get around the museum without too much backtracking. Once you're done with looking round, the shady **café** is a good place to cool off (the museum is not air-conditioned and can get hot and stuffy in summer).

Entrance and lobby

Looming up at you as you proceed from the ticket office, across the sculpture-strewn garden, is the museum's striking **monumental gateway**, through which you must pass to get inside the museum buildings. Once, these two huge stone pillars, semicircular in cross-section, formed the front entrance to Qasr al-Heir al-Gharbi, a seventh-century Umayyad palace in the remote desert between Homs and Palmyra. The honey-coloured pillars are carved with geometric designs, but the whole effect is rather crudely grandiose – you can only imagine that the gateway must have looked so much better in its original setting. Inside the **lobby** are several comprehensive, readable and well-illustrated accounts, in English, of the periods of Syrian history covered by the artefacts in the museum.

Pre-Classical galleries

The majority of the exhibits from pre-Classical times are displayed (mostly unlabelled) in a long gallery (**1**) which stretches part of the length of the west wall of the museum, but three individual rooms are given over to finds from specific sites in northern Syria. Heading right from the lobby, you pass through a small open courtyard and come to the first and most interesting, the **Ugarit** room (**2**). The reconstructed tomb here containing fifteen human skeletons is rather gruesome; assorted animal remains, weaponry, jewellery and ceramics are also included in the open sarcophagus, which dates from around 2000 BC. Close by is a tiny gold-plated statuette of the god El (Baal), his hand raised in benign greeting. Nearby are cases of stone tablets carved with probably the world's first alphabet, invented around 1400 BC by Ugarit merchants to record trading details (see p.202). To the right of the long gallery, which contains artefacts from a bewildering number of sites and eras, are rooms (**3** and **4**) devoted to the early Bronze Age sites of **Mari** and **Ebla**, which flourished around 2500 BC.

Arab-Islamic galleries

Return to the small open courtyard to gain entrance to the section on **Arab-Islamic art**, which roughly covers the seventh to the eighteenth centuries. You reach it through a vestibule (**5**) devoted to finds from **Raqqa**, a city on the Euphrates which flourished in early medieval times (see p.255); the principal exhibit here, given a case all to itself, is a twelfth-century mounted horseman, whose distinctly Asiatic facial features point to the belief that it was fashioned in

Chinese Turkestan. From the Raqqa room there are stairs to the upper floors of this wing of the museum, which house an **art gallery**. The paintings in its permanent collection range from the abstract to kitsch scenes of Syrian street life and legends, boldly executed in bright colours. Beyond the Raqqa room, the long gallery (**6**), displaying mostly coins and seals from Abbasid to Mameluke times, is fairly unexciting, although the weaponry from the early Middle Ages at the far end – notably some beautiful damascene swords – gives a good insight into the grisly violence of the times.

At the end of the long gallery, turn left to find a collection of carved wooden items from the thirteenth to the eighteenth centuries (**7**). The most striking piece here is an ornate sarcophagus (1250), whose faded original colours still cling determinedly to the wood ; close by is a prayer niche (1798), fashioned from beautifully carved cedarwood. Beyond this gallery you can see a reconstructed room (**8**) from an eighteenth-century Damascene house which was the home of one of Syria's prime ministers in the 1950s. It was moved here piece by piece between 1958 and 1962, and now serves as a meeting and function room (and so is closed to the public at times). Although some of the decorations are 1950s copies of eighteenth-century styles, the marble floor and timber panelling give a good sense of the former opulence of such residences during Ottoman times. Heading back in the general direction of the main lobby, through rooms which line the western wall of the museum, you can admire beautiful Korans and other early medieval Islamic manuscripts (**9**), before you come upon the medieval ceramics (**10**), with their intricate designs and colours intact. Beyond them, in a room (**11**) sandwiched between the long gallery and the Mari collections, is stonework from the same era, including a touchingly fashioned child's tomb dating from 1350. From here you can get back into the Raqqa room and head through the main lobby to the museum's east wing.

Classical and Early Byzantine galleries

The east wing is the most interesting and most carefully laid out of the museum's three sections. The first room (**12**) contains stonework, pottery and jewellery from various sites in the **Hauran**, although the most striking exhibit is an extraordinary mosaic from Latakia in northeastern Syria, in which the River Orontes is depicted as a god. In the centre of the room there's a magnificent Roman sarcophagus dating from the third century AD, boasting a representation of its incumbent lounging across the top as if his tomb were a stone-carved chaise longue.

Across from the Hauran room, against the back wall of the museum, is a room (**13**) devoted to exquisite textiles unearthed from the tower tombs in **Palmyra**. Used mostly to wrap the bodies of the dead, all the pieces were fashioned around eighteen hundred years ago and owe their high quality of preservation to the dry atmosphere and the absence of light in the tombs. The linens and wools were locally derived, but the dyes were Indian and the silks came from China – an indication of just how far-flung Palmyra's trading partners were.

Beyond the textiles you'll find a collection of Roman sarcophagi and other preserved stonework from Palmyra (**14**), and displays of early Christian icons and triptychs, one of which features St George and the dragon (**15** and **16**).

The Homs Collection and the Hypogeum of Yarhai

The steps leading up from just beyond room 15 lead to the **Homs Collection**, a valuable hoard of coins and jewels from Roman and pre-Roman times which were uncovered in the area around Homs in central Syria. Some of the coinage depicts such noted figures as Alexander the Great, who passed this way in 332 BC, and Philip the Arab, Roman emperor from 244 to 249 AD, who was born in Shahba, about 90km south of Damascus. Unfortunately, the stairs are usually roped off, though the curator in the main lobby may be willing to find someone to take you up there. Don't bother asking on a Friday, when there is only a skeleton staff present and the museum director (who has to give his permission for the room to be opened) doesn't come in.

Taking the stairs down from room 15 will bring you to the cool, dank **Hypogeum of Yarhai**, an underground tomb fashioned in 108 AD from the characteristic pale yellow stone of the Syrian desert; photographs on the wall show how it was moved in 1935 from the Valley of the Tombs in Palmyra to the museum. The whole tomb was given over to members of one family (the Yarhais), their mortal remains set into stone vaults with a bust of the deceased incumbent placed outside (the women are depicted partly veiled to represent death). The tomb has its own *triclinium* (dining hall) where funeral banquets would have been eaten.

The Dura Europos Synagogue

A doorway from just beyond room 16 brings you for an instant into a colonnaded courtyard and glaring sunshine, before you plunge into the sunken, rather musty atmosphere of the reconstructed **Dura Europos Synagogue**. The settlement from which the synagogue comes was established around 290 BC as a fortress town on the Euphrates in northeastern Syria. The building itself – in the form seen here – can be dated to 245 AD, and was hailed as a major archeological find when it was unearthed accidentally by the British army in 1920; other finds from Dura finished up in the Louvre and at Yale University, but this extraordinary synagogue stayed in Syria, and was moved piece by piece in the 1930s to this specially constructed wing of the museum.

The intimacy of the building is offset by the grandiose execution of its **wall paintings**, which the sand and dust had kept intact for so many centuries, their original colours still vibrant and the intentions of the artists still breathtakingly clear. Interestingly, the paintings depict the human form, something expressly forbidden in the Talmud; among other subjects, they portray the crossing of the Red Sea by the Israelites, the First Temple in Jerusalem and, immediately above the niche where the Torah scrolls were kept, Abraham sacrificing a ram (caught in the nearby thicket) instead of his son. The preservation of this building – it's by far the museum's most important feature – is all the more remarkable when you consider the recent fate of Syria's Jewish population and their places of worship (see p.316).

The Damascus Historical Museum

If your passion for old Damascene residences has been inflamed rather than sated by a visit to the Azem Palace, the short detour to the **Damascus Historical Museum** (daily except Fri 8am–2pm; S£150) is well worth the effort. The museum is slightly difficult to find; it's just off Ath-Thawra Street, immediately east of the northern ramp of the flyover, and to get there you'll have to walk through a military checkpoint, as there is a building belonging to the Ministry of the Interior here. Visitors to the museum are so rare that an attendant will be sent out with you to open the rooms specially for you.

The museum essentially consists of eight richly decorated rooms, most with their own mini-fountains, original to the property; these chambers, off a central courtyard, comprised the *haramlek*. The final room on the tour houses a fascinating large-scale model of the Old City as well as a selection of old photographs of Damascus, giving a fascinating insight into a time – only a hundred years ago – when it was possible to spend a pleasant afternoon walking along the banks of a tree-lined Barada river.

The Salihiye district

Not to be confused with the modern shopping precinct of the same name in the heart of the New City, the old **Salihiye district** is centred on Madaress Assad ad-Deen Lane, some 1500m northwest of the Old City walls, on the lower slopes of Mount Qassioun. Originally settled on in the twelfth century by refugees fleeing the marauding Crusaders, Salihiye used to be a completely separate town to Damascus and the two only became joined in the twentieth century. The name Salihiye means "holy" and the area is littered with numerous madrasas, mosques and mausoleums, though many of these have been adapted for modern-day purposes and are consequently not possible to visit; however, a wander through the district's evocative, winding lanes, crowded with bustling vegetable stalls, can still be heartily recommended.

It's best to begin at the busy traffic intersection called Jisr al-Abiad Square, on the north side of which stands the **Madrasa Maridaniye**, dating originally to 1213 (though the minaret was erected two hundred years later). The Turkish princess who endowed the building had the ill fortune to die on pilgrimage to Mecca and so is not actually buried here. From the madrasa, walk north up Afif Street and then turn down Madaress Assad ad-Deen Lane where, after about 30m, you pass on your right the permanently padlocked, early thirteenth-century **Mausoleum of Sheikh al-Faranti**; immediately after is a primary school, a former madrasa, whose square minaret is the only surviving example from the thirteenth century in Damascus. Another 20m on to your right is a thirteenth-century madrasa, whose pretty, copper-coloured, honeycombed doorway is worth particular attention. At this point the street starts to narrow considerably and busy stalls make progress slow – though the noise, smells and frenetic market activity are absorbing.

About another 200m down Madaress Assad ad-Deen Lane is the **Mosque of Sheikh Mohi ad-Din**, containing the burial chamber of the celebrated Sufi poet and philosopher who died in 1240 (the actual building dates to 1518). Though born in Spain, Mohi ad-Din lived in this street most of his life, having decided the district had the cleanest air after stringing up four pieces of fresh lamb around the city and monitoring their decay. His intimate, still-revered burial chamber can be reached via the stairway in the courtyard. The second tomb here used to house the body of the Algerian master-Sufi and patriot Abd al-Kader al-Jazairi (his corpse was returned to Algiers following independence), who led the tribes of Oran in resistance to the French for nearly fifteen years. In 1852, after five years' imprisonment, Abd al-Kader was banished to Damascus by Louis Napoleon with a pension equivalent to around £200,000 a year today, on condition that he never returned to his homeland. While in the city, Abd al-Kader devoted most of his time to study, living with five wives (adding and subtracting one from that number every year to stop him getting bored) and becoming a regular dining companion of the explorer, linguist and British consul Richard Burton, and his wife Isabel.

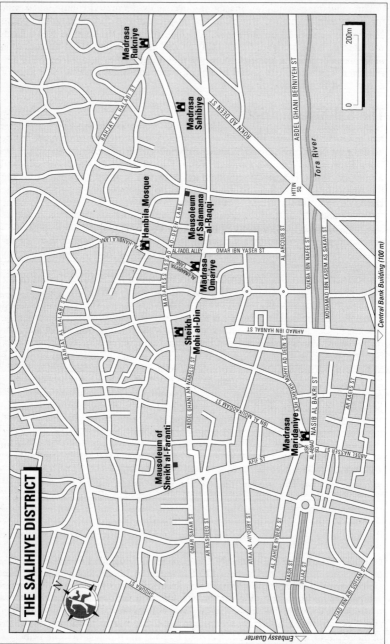

THE SALIHIYE DISTRICT

Madrasa Rukniye

Madrasa Sahibiye

Hanbila Mosque

Mausoleum of Salamana al-Raqqi

Madrasa Omariye

Sheikh Mohi al-Din

Mausoleum of Sheikh al-Faranti

Madrasa Maridaniye

Tora River

HITTIN SQ

Central Bank Building (100 m)

Embassy Quarter

200m

Walk on for another 70m, keeping left at the V-intersection, until you reach a small street ascending to your left, Al-Hanbila Lane. A short way up here is the **Hanbila Mosque**, built between 1202 and 1213 and thus the second oldest mosque in Damascus after the Umayyad Mosque, whose design it mirrors on a smaller scale; presently the building is undergoing extensive restoration. From the exterior it barely looks like a mosque but the minaret gives it away; the courtyard incorporates six recycled Classical columns, while in the prayer hall is a very fine *minbar* dating to 1207. Now return to and cross Madaress Assad ad-Deen Lane, continuing downhill for 50m; over the fence to your left lie the ruins of the **Madrasa Omariye**, the oldest building in the Salihiye quarter. From here you can return to complete your walk down Madaress Assad ad-Deen Lane, passing on the way the early thirteenth-century Mausoleum of Salamana al-Raqqi and the Madrasa Sahibiye – built between 1233 and 1245 and now a primary school – and ending up at the recently rebuilt Madrasa Rukniye.

Mount Qassioun

To the northwest of Damascus, overlooking the city, is **Mount Qassioun**, its summit strewn with a variety of transmission towers and military installations, making it an obvious point of orientation when you're in (or approaching) the city. At night Qassioun is even more distinctive — a curtain of orange and white specks of light, flecked here and there with the green lights of numerous mosques, dotting the hillside like a static fireworks display. It is not possible to get right to the top, but the perimeter road which runs around the summit leads past a collection of shabby cafés and drinking places, from whose terraces there are very good views over Damascus. Those who are supposed to have climbed this hill include Abraham, Jesus and Mary, and the Prophet Mohammed, who, according to legend, looked down from the summit and proclaimed that Damascus was a "paradise on earth"; indeed according to Arab folklore the mountain will be spared from the chaos and havoc of the Day of Judgement, which may be worth bearing in mind if you're staying in the city at the time.

Individual **landmarks** are quite difficult to distinguish from the top: the four towers of the Umayyad Mosque are easily discernible, rising above the crammed-in clutter of the Old City, but it's the broad avenues, busy traffic circles and high-rise hotels of the New City which are the most obvious focal points. More importantly, it is from Qassioun that it is most easy to appreciate Damascus's situation as an **oasis settlement**: green expanses of trees stretch away from the city to the east and south, with the desert beyond seen as just a sliver of yellow sandwiched between the woods and the sky. Damascus itself often appears to have precious little greenery and open space, but the view from Qassioun suggests otherwise: all over the New City are hidden parks and gardens, linked by avenues shaded by lines of trees.

There is no public **transport** up the mountain – either take a microbus from the bottom end of Yousef al-Azmeh to the Al-Mouhajirin district, from where a taxi should cost around S£50, or take a taxi from the centre of town, which should cost around S£150. Come up in the afternoon when the sun is behind you, leaving the slopes in shadow but casting brilliant light directly across the roofs and streets of the New City; even better, come at night, when the whole of Damascus glitters and sparkles and seethes below.

Saida Zeinab Mosque

Out in the southeastern suburbs, 8km from the city centre and close to the road which runs out to the airport, is the **Saida Zeinab Mosque**, where one of the granddaughters of the Prophet Mohammed is buried in a beautiful modern mausoleum. To get there by public transport, pick up a **city microbus** from halfway along the north side of Fakhri al-Baroudi Street, which runs parallel to An-Naser Street (on which is the Hedjaz Station); alternatively, catch a microbus from the northeastern end of Ibn al-Abbas Street, 400m south of Hedjaz Station, to the **Al-Sitt** suburban microbus station in southern Damascus, where you'll need to change onto another city microbus for the ride to the mosque. You'll probably find on either journey that people will guess where you're going and help you accordingly; the microbus fares should not come to more than S£20. A **taxi** can be expensive, since taxi drivers are unlikely to get a fare back into town; you'll need to agree on the fare before you set off (drivers will be reluctant to use the meter, telling you it's only for journeys within the city limits), so bargain hard – something like S£200 would be a fair price.

Zeinab's brother, Hussein, was slaughtered by the Umayyads at the Battle of Kerbala (southern Iraq) in 680 (she herself was taken into captivity in Damascus), during a complex series of events which split Islam into its two major factions: Shiah Muslims, who predominate in Iran, and Sunni Muslims, the majority in Syria and most Arab countries (see p.313). Many Shiah Muslims come from Iran to visit this shrine, which was constructed with money donated for the purpose by their revolutionary Shiite government – an act which further cemented political ties between Damascus and Tehran.

Pilgrims and worshippers at the mosque tend to be very conservatively dressed, as befits Shiah orthodoxy, and women visitors to the mosque have to don robes at the entrance, supplied by the custodian, to ensure that hair and necks are covered. Once inside, the most distinctive aspect of the building are the bold colours: blue, green and orange tiles, gaudy and brilliant in the sun, and curved into a myriad of geometric shapes, adorn the walls and arches of the main courtyard and the outside of the tall, slender minaret. The dome above the central prayer hall and tomb is covered with dazzling gold. Overlooking the courtyard is a minimalist clock, the final modernist touch. Non-Muslims are seldom allowed into the **central sanctuary**, where Zeinab's tomb lies behind silver railings which are kissed with touching reverence by the Shiite faithful. However, those who are with a group accompanied by a Syrian guide may find they are luckier than individual visitors; if you do manage to gain admittance, remember that there are separate entrances for men and women.

Eating

In comparison with the rest of Syria there is a relatively good choice of eating places in Damascus, so if you're only in the city for a short while, make the most of it. The city's **restaurants** range from street stalls which do filling, cheap meals of *shwarma* or roast chicken, right through to expensive Chinese, Mexican and Italian restaurants in the big hotels. Down Maisaloun Street in the New City are some of Damascus's best places for **ice cream** and **cakes**, both of which the locals consume with gusto.

Nora Grocery, on the corner of Maisaloun Street and Al-Jalaa Street, has a selection of foods not far off what you'd find in a supermarket, stocking dairy products, fruit juices, and alcoholic drinks among other items. For fresh produce, the best place to look is the **market** at the eastern end of Al-Ittihad Street.

Restaurants

Numerous undistinguished restaurants around the city serve inexpensive **Syrian** fare – kebab or chicken with salad, hummus or chips. The slightly pricier places tend towards a Western menu, meaning that there are only a few places where you can find good Arabic cuisine; most of these are concentrated in the Old City. For a quick snack, there are dozens of falafel places to fill up – particularly around Martyrs' Square – as well as a number of decent Western-style fast-food choices dotted around the New City.

Most **hotels** have attached restaurants which, generally speaking, are unremarkable places. However, the *Sheraton* can offer a very good Italian place called *Luigi's*, while the *Cham Palace* boasts the country's only Chinese restaurant and also its only revolving restaurant (on the fifteenth floor), as well as Japanese and Italian places. Not to be outdone, the *Meridien* has Tex-Mex specialities every Saturday at *L'Hacienda* and a 1930s-style restaurant with singers and dancers and international cuisine. The *Alaa Towers* chain also has decent restaurants in four of its hotels; the one on Ath-Thawra Street has views over the Old City.

The restaurants in the listings below have been categorized as cheap (under S£200 for a main meal), moderate (S£200–400) or expensive (over S£400).

The Old City

By far the most **atmospheric** place to eat, the Old City remains lively until well into the evening. Some of the restaurants here are fairly pricey, tourist-oriented affairs, where the Western-style muzak and sycophantic service may not be to everyone's taste; however, there are plenty of good alternatives. For an inexpensive bite, there are a number of decent falafel places lining Al-Qaimariyeh Lane, a short walk east of the Umayyad Mosque's eastern gate. The restaurants below are marked on the Old City map (p.76); the more tourist-oriented among these places are typically open daily, 1–5pm and 8pm–midnight.

Abu al-Azz, in the shoe souk, just north of the triumphal arch in the Hamidiye Souk. The best place in the Old City to sample some local delicacies without incurring great expense; just put yourself in the hands of the head waiter, who likes nothing more than to show off his meze to the passing trade. Traditional Arabic live music in the evening. Cheap.

Arabesque, Yasseen Diab Place, 100m north of the Roman arch. Aimed squarely at the tourist market, this place serves mainly Western dishes. The menus don't list prices. Make sure you've shined your shoes on the way here or they may not fancy serving you. Closed 5–8pm. Moderate.

Casablanca, Ananias St. Classy establishment, with a pianist in the evening. Serves a selection of delicious Western fish, steak and chicken dishes; very busy after 9pm. No prices on the menu. Moderate.

Elissar, Al-Dawamneh Place, south of Bab Touma. Housed in an atmospheric old house dating from the nineteenth century, the *Elissar* offers a variety of very tasty French and Syrian dishes, with an excellent choice of meze available. Particularly recommended is the *basturma*, a spicy veal dish. One of the best places in Damascus to try out Syrian cuisine. Closed 5–8pm. Moderate.

L'Auberge, Zuheir bin Amr St, just off Straight St, halfway between the Roman arch and Bab Sharqi. Excellent pizzas served in a pleasantly intimate interior. Cheap.

La Guitare, Zeitoun St. South off Straight St, 100m west of Bab Sharqi. Good Arab and Western cuisine – with a seafood and pasta bias – served up in a charming courtyard, with occasional live music in the evenings. Very popular with tour groups, so booking may be advisable in the evenings. Closed 5–8pm. Moderate.

Old Damascus, Al-Bahra Al-Daffaqa St. Just east of the Citadel. Standard Syrian fare (chicken or lamb kebab) in good, clean surroundings with friendly staff. Arabic traditional music is performed here in the evenings. Cheap.

Old Town Music, Al-Assiyeh St. Off Straight St near the Roman arch. Good Western food – with an emphasis on Italian dishes – and a pianist in the evenings. Moderate.

One Thousand Night And Night, Al-Qaimariyeh St, 150m east of the Umayyad Mosque. Doesn't quite conjure up the exotic atmosphere suggested by its name; offers a menu of Middle Eastern dishes, including a limited meze. Occasional live Arabic music laid on in the evenings. Cheap.

Umayyad Palace, Al-Masbagha Al-Khadraa Lane. Pricey joint, housed in a medieval grain warehouse, with Arabesque decor and a traditional Arab buffet. Despite the food being merely average and the lack of alcohol, it's popular with tour groups who come for the entertainment that gets laid on in the evenings – anything from circus troupes to whirling dervishes. Buffet S£700 per head in the evenings, half-price in the afternoons. Expensive.

Zeitoun, Zeitoun St, signposted beyond *La Guitare*. The menu here is limited to the usual chicken kebab and chicken fare, though the the ambience is a cut above, thanks to the pleasant courtyard – there's modestly priced beer, too. Cheap.

Around Martyrs' Square

This busy part of the New City, where most of the city's cheap hotels are situated, has a surprisingly poor choice of restaurants; most of the eateries here are simply inexpensive places to fill up in, with either lamb kebab or chicken being the only choice on the menu, and most don't serve beer. Numerous **juice** stores and falafel places line the south side of the square though, and there's also a very friendly and useful liquor shop called Elias Hayek, on Rami Street. The restaurants listed below are marked on the New City Centre map on pp.72–73.

Al-Amawi, Abu-Firas Al-Hamdani St. Predictable food in spruce surroundings with a friendly atmosphere; sheep's testicles – fried or grilled – are on the menu and the place also does a good breakfast spread. Cheap.

Al-Arabi, Al-Sandjakdar Lane #7131. This is actually two restaurants owned by the same people, of which the one further up the pedestrianized street is slightly more sassy. Unsurprising Middle Eastern menu, but it's popular with tourists and backpackers. Cheap.

Al-Negma, Rami St. Very popular with locals, and there's an English menu outside for perusal, though you'll find nothing out of the ordinary on it; decent breakfasts are also available. Cheap.

Sahloul, Al-Sandjakdar Lane #713. Agreeably clean establishment with very friendly service. The menu, an English version of which is available, is predictable enough, but there's an enticing selection of cakes on display. One of the nice things about this place is that they don't make you pay for any extras (bread, peanuts and the like) you don't touch. Cheap.

From Yousef al-Azmeh Square to Al-Mahdi ibn Barakeh Street

At the heart of this area is **Maisaloun Street**, which tends to be among the busiest parts of the New City at night; here there are a number of good restaurants to suit all tastes and pockets. The restaurants listed below are marked on the New City Centre map on pp.72–73.

Abou Kamal, first-floor restaurant on Yousef al-Azmeh Square. A cut above the ordinary with a healthy and popular selection of tasty Middle Eastern and Western-style dishes. A good place to indulge your passion for sheep's brains. Cheap.

Ali Baba, in the basement underneath the *Abou Kamal* on Yousef al-Azmeh Square. Intricately decorated wood panelling and hanging lanterns provide an atmospheric setting for some pleasing Middle Eastern and European eats (indeed, the same menu as the *Abou Kamal*). Cheap.

Club D'Orient, Mrewed St. Glitzy five-star establishment for the well-to-do, with a very good reputation. If you're looking for a Western-food blowout, this is the place to come. Expensive.

Al-Kamal, 29 May St. Bright spot serving a good, basic Western menu, with a Parisian café-style overspill onto the pavement. Meticulous service but slightly over-enthusiastic air-conditioning. Cheap.

Le Bistro, Maisaloun St, corner of Al-Brazil St. Part of the *Omayad* hotel, this bar-restaurant does a menu of Western dishes. It's expensive for what you get – though there's a good snack menu (pizza, burgers, spaghetti and the like) for those watching the cash. Moderate.

Neptun aka **Taj Mahal**, Mrewed St. If the Middle East still isn't quite east enough for you, check this Indian restaurant out. There's a buffet (S£700) in the evening. Expensive.

Pizza Hat, Maisaloun St, near the Franciscan church. Very popular pizzeria that also does a brisk trade in ice cream. Cheap.

Pizza Pop, Al-Mahdi ibn Barakeh St. The best pizza available in Damascus – they even fill the crusts. Impressive air-conditioning. Cheap.

Pizza Roma, just off Maisaloun St, opposite *Pizza Hat*. Very heavily modelled on *Pizza Hut* – so much so that the pizzas here taste exactly like theirs. Hard to beat for a quick no-fuss meal. Cheap.

Rayess, Yousef al-Azmeh St. Mountain lakes and golden beaches form the unlikely pictorial backdrop to your kebab and chips here. The food isn't special but there's a likeable provincial air to the place, which is patronized mainly by gently decaying middle-aged men. The management is more than happy if you just want to sit and drink beer. Cheap.

Reef, corner of Al-Jalaa St and Al-Mahdi ibn Barakeh St. Highly recommended, good-value menu of Eastern and Western grub with the odd Japanese speciality thrown in for good measure. Moderate.

Snack Aboualic, just off Maisaloun St beyond the Dar es Salam school. Very friendly, good sit-down Western fast-food joint, with takeaway service available. Cheap.

Station One, Maisaloun St, near the corner of Al-Jalaa St. Very enjoyable Western food, with the option of a special *plat du jour*, served in a classy ambience – though no beer. It also has a fast-food takeaway section. Moderate.

Restaurant Circle, the diplomatic quarter and Salihiye

At the heart of the most affluent part of Damascus, **Restaurant Circle**, off Abdel Malek ibn Marwan St, is a small green around which everything is either a restaurant, a café or an ice cream parlour. Here you'll find two cheap and cheery pizza joints – *Milano* and *Pizza New* (the latter even has a free delivery service, ☎011/333 8820), but no juice stalls or falafel shops. To the northeast, Salihiye's shopping precinct isn't the most fertile hunting ground for good food, though one or two places stand out. The restaurants listed below are marked on the map on pp.64–65.

Café Dreams, Ahmad Shawqi Place, by Al-Jahez Park. Classy coffee-shop with a limited menu of pizza, hamburger and steak. Cheap.

La Chaumiere, Restaurant Circle. Selection of Arab and French dishes with a good reputation for its seafood and meze. Moderate.

Le Chevalier, Restaurant Circle. Overpriced French menu (in French, and no prices either) catering mainly for diplomats; a good choice of fish though. Expensive.

Mr Steak, Restaurant Circle. Upstairs from the recently revamped *Café Vendome*. Does a pretty decent menu, with an emphasis on fish, and (unsurprisingly) steak. Moderate.

Al-Shallal, Moustafa ash-Shehabi St, opposite Al-Arsouzi Park. Good Middle Eastern cuisine but slightly out of the way. Cheap.

Toledo Tea Room, Khalil Mardam St. Coffee, beer and ice cream, in a select location with vehemently red decor. Good place to chill out. Cheap.

Top, at the roundabout where Abdel Rahman Ghafiki St and Al-Malek Al-Adel St meet. One of the brightest and best pizza/fast-food places, tucked away below ground level. Cheap.

Cafés, cake shops and ice cream parlours

Hubble-bubble cafés proliferate around Damascus; the best ones to head for are those by the eastern gate of the Umayyad Mosque, the *Ash-Sham* and the *An-Nofara*. The latter even has a storyteller in the evenings (see p.104), a tradition common before the arrival of radio and television. Rather smarter are a couple of early eighteenth-century Damascene houses which have recently been converted into cafés – try the *Narcissus Palace* on Al-Mangana Street or the *Jabri House* on As-Sawwaf Place. In the New City there are a couple of less atmospheric *nargileh* spots on Moutanabby Street; the one on the corner of Port Said Street is populated mainly by down-at-heel intellectuals and is good for an early morning coffee, while the other, much larger, establishment gets busy in the evenings and is popular with an elderly clientele.

For coffee with a more **Western-style ambience**, head for *Le Terrace* on the top floor of *Le Piano Bar* on Ananias Street in the Old City, or to one of the international hotels. Young people patronize Maisaloun Street's numerous patisseries and ice cream parlours in the evening, while the diplomatic quarter has its own selection of smart cafés patronized by sophisticated Damascenes. Down Maisaloun Street, try the *Damer* ice cream parlour or the *Apollo* cake shop – or further down the road, *Captain Tub* for ice cream and *Le Miel* for cake; also recommended here is the *Shimi Patisserie*, an inexpensive, family-oriented coffee and cake shop popular with the locals. For a relaxing coffee, the *Pit Stop Café* on Al-Amir Izzedin Lane is recommended for its sophisticated ambience, as is the *Café Vendome* on Restaurant Circle. In the Old City, easily the best place for an **ice cream** is the ever-popular *Bakdach* in the Hamidiye Souk which serves delicious bowls of the stuff, along with *muhalabiyyeh* and – in the mornings – *sahlab*, for a mere S£25.

Drinking and nightlife

Although many of the cheaper restaurants may be happy for you to sit and drink beer into the evening after your meal, or indeed in place of a meal (though the bill may well be upped by thirty percent if no food is eaten), proper **drinking holes** are scarce. The *Damascus Workers Club* off 29 May Street is a pleasant, cheap venue which operates as a restaurant, though many people just come here to drink out in the garden. Another reasonable option is the bar at the Hedjaz Station, installed inside the restored Ottoman train carriage permanently parked there (see p.89); a Barada here costs S£100. The rough-and-ready *Karnik*, off Martyrs' Square next to the *Siyaha* hotel, is populated mainly by holidaying Arabs come to loosen up, but may be useful in that most restaurants around Martyrs' Square are dry; it doesn't shut until around 1am. *Le Piano Bar* on Ananias Street in the Old City (closes 2am) is a popular and lively place with MTV and spirited karaoke in the evenings, though at S£140 for a Barada this is an expensive place for a tipple. In theory couples only are admitted, but individuals who turn up before the place has filled should be allowed in. Of course, all the more expensive hotels have bars selling imported European beer: the *Sheraton* has a "genuine" English pub, open until 2am, with red letter boxes and phone boxes, and draught bitter for S£220 plus fifteen percent government tax, while the *Fardoss Tower* has an intermittently open pub below decks where you can indulge your passion for European lager to your wallet's content. Alternatively, those after a more continental ambience (which continent is open to debate) may care to head for the *Bar L'Oasis* in the *Meridien*.

Nightlife

Damascus is not the place to go looking for a great night out – the clubs and discos tend to be rather tawdry, poorly attended and expensive, and by Egyptian, Israeli or Lebanese standards the nightlife is very quiet. Western-style **discos** are staged by the big hotels, but if they don't like the look of you they might say they're only for guests: Eastern European prostitutes tend to hang around the doors at closing time. One of the biggest discos is in the basement of the *Cham Palace*, where things don't usually get going until after 11pm; the *Meridien* and *Sheraton* also have discos.

Shows in **nightclubs** are very tacky and overpriced affairs, generally involving bored-looking East European women dancing on a stage under a flickering glitter ball to the accompaniment of Western dance music. The flashing neon, tatty décor and sycophantically attentive service may hold a certain kitsch fascination, if nothing else. You simply follow the neon into a subterranean world of sleaze at the *Semiramis*, on Salihiye Street, whereas the *Juhara*, reached up a flight of steps from Port Said Street, is a tad less sleazy; it costs around S£400 to get into either. Other places in the New City charge similar prices for a similar show: they're not difficult to spot along Port Said and Al-Jabaree streets and around the *Cham Palace*.

Entertainment

Damascus rather prides itself as being something of a centre for Arab and international culture, with **entertainment** ranging from concerts of Western or Arabic classical music to film screenings, plays and displays of oriental performing arts, such as whirling dervishes. However, the majority of these events occur ad hoc, and it's a shame that most are inadequately advertised in English; the *Syria Times* has a cultural events section, but the information they give tends to be vague and rudimentary, while the flyposters around the city are often months (even years) out of date and the staff at the tourist office can give the impression that they've never even explored the city. However, the various **cultural centres** around Damascus all run programmes of exhibitions and lectures outside the summer months (see p.110 for addresses), and the British Council and Centre Culturel Français both publish events calendars; a touch-screen computer situated in the foyer of the British Council building even has a "What's On" page.

Live music

It may go against the grain somewhat, but the best – or at least most regular – venues for hearing local musicians (anything from an exhibition of oud playing to raucous Middle Eastern pop) are the bars of the expensive hotels. Alternatively the *Umayyad Palace*, *Old Town Music*, *Old Damascus* and *Abu al-Azz* restaurants all lay on some form of **traditional Syrian music** (and folk dancing) as an accompaniment to your evening meal. Otherwise try the cultural centres or keep your eyes open for the flyposters around town; you can occasionally stumble upon some real treats – a free performance by the **Syrian Symphony Orchestra**, for instance. Easily the most attractive place used to stage concerts is the courtyard of the Azem Palace; ask at their ticket office to see if anything's on during your stay.

Cinemas

The best **cinema** in Damascus by far is in the *Cham Palace* (separate entrance on Maisaloun St), which shows many English-language films (up to £100; subtitled in French and Arabic) in pleasant surroundings. In the *Semiramis Hotel,* the Johno cinema presents different movies – usually recent American releases – at 7 and 9.30pm every night; the S£200 ticket includes a soft drink (or an alcoholic drink for an extra S£100). All the city's **cultural centres** (see p.110 for addresses) show films on a regular basis – though of course foreign-language films are normally shown with Arabic subtitles, if any at all. In early November Damascus hosts a week-long **film festival**; ask at the Tourist Information Office for details. Otherwise, there are dingy, threadbare cinemas all around Martyrs' Square: wander around for ten minutes and you'll encounter half a dozen, all showing the same Kung-Fu/Jackie Chan pap; tickets are around S£25.

Theatre

The **National Theatre**, situated in a new building on Al-Umawyeen Square, presents a varied programme of plays. Obviously there will be a serious language barrier if you don't speak Arabic, but European classics are also scheduled if you fancy trying your hand; the 2000 season contained adaptations of works by Gogol and Chekhov. Beyond this, there are a number of theatrical groups in the city – the University Theatre is quite active, as is the Institute for Dramatic Arts; the National Theatre's box office can provide information. **The Al-Hamra Theatre**, situated near the *Cham Palace*, is a popular ad hoc venue, but most of the time it functions as a cinema, and the staff have little information on forthcoming events to offer. Just west of the National Museum in the Damascus International Fair Grounds is a theatre which occasionally puts on drama productions as well as music concerts and dance displays, but the building is abandoned if there's nothing on, which is most of the year apart from during the main trade fair in late August.

Traditional entertainment

On many evenings, the *An-Nofara Cafe* by the eastern gate of the Umayyad Mosque plays host to a **performance storyteller**, enthroned on an ornate high-backed chair. He is one of the last of a long tradition of Syrian storytellers, once a feature of Ottoman-era coffee-houses but now a dying breed, a victim of the proliferation of TV and radio. The stories are likely to be from Middle Eastern epics such as the *One Thousand and One Nights* or the *Tale of Sultan Baibars*. The performance is watched by a largely male audience, who sit and smoke their hubble-bubbles when not banging their hands on the table-tops in noisy agreement with the storyteller's sentiments. If you're very lucky you might get someone to translate the stories for you, but even if you don't it's worth coming for the atmosphere

WHIRLING DERVISHES

The **whirling dervish** sect was founded in Konya, Turkey, shortly after the death of the Afghan-born mystic Mevlana Jelaleddin Rumi (1207–1273), whose poetry inspired their formation. The practice of whirling, however, long predates their inception; it had been practised by **Sufis**, a sect of Islam (see p.313). Mevlana's poetry gave voice to these ancient traditions, and the Mevlevi Order, to which all dervishes belong, has maintained and developed the traditions of whirling over seven centuries.

Dervishes undergo years of training before they are able to whirl – not unlike a ballerina pirouetting – between twenty and thirty times each minute without becoming dizzy, and their considerable skill often induces giddiness in an uninitiated audience. The dervishes' costumes and movements are laden with **symbolism**. They raise one hand to the heavens and lower the other towards the ground, signifying a unity of heaven and earth; their whirling white robes symbolize that the dancer has reached a state of floating between this world and an invisible one suffused with divine love. The dervishes' long white robes represent the death shroud of the ego, which is seen as an obstacle to spiritual contact between the dancer and God; their tall fezzes are the tombstones of the ego.

Though accompanied by musicians, usually playing flutes and percussion instruments, the dervish ceremony is intended to be a spiritual and religious experience rather than a theatrical show. Dervishes draw inspiration from the words in the Koran, that "wherever you turn is the face of God", and maintain that their whirling dance is intended as a sacred, serene ritual which is an aid to prayer and contemplation. Today, whirling dervishes use contemporary science to justify further their practice: everything revolves, they say, from protons and electrons whizzing round atoms, to blood pumping round the human body and the planets orbiting the sun. Although whirling dervishes remain popular in Turkey, only two troupes of dervishes now exist in Syria, in Aleppo and Damascus.

alone, which is laid-back or fraught with tension according to the mood of the tale being told.

Close by, the cool, spacious basement of the *Umayyad Palace Restaurant* (see p.100), wonderfully decorated with ornate woodwork and marble, is the only place in Damascus where you're likely to see **whirling dervishes** perform. The show, accompanied by musicians playing traditional instruments, usually begins at 9.30 every evening, and is open to diners only.

Shopping

The most obviously atmospheric place to do your craft and souvenir shopping is in the **souks of the Old City**, though you can often find similar products at cheaper prices in the stores that line the eastern section of Straight Street. These shops have the added attraction of being quieter than the souks, though many are Christian-owned and so are shut on Sunday. Many of the craft stores in the Hamidiye Souk and along Straight Street are aimed primarily at tourists and sell a variety of goods; however, those stores in the **Handicraft Souk**, located off Shoukry al-Qouwatly Street, between Martyrs' Square and the National Museum, tend to be specialist stores (though also aimed squarely at visitors). The shopping

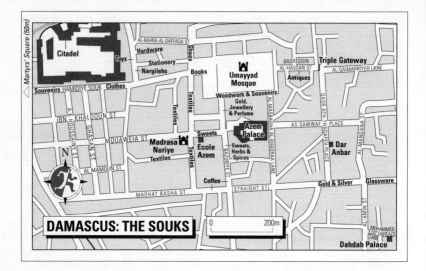

experience here is rather less authentically Middle Eastern than in the traditional souks, but looking around for what you want is easier and less hectic, and nearly all these stores take credit cards.

Antiques

The best selection of **antique** shops is in the **Old City**, where there's surprisingly little sales pressure if you just want to browse; indeed it often seems that the staff have little idea about what exactly they're selling. Beware that there is an industry in the making of modern "antiques"; most of the battered old gramophones you see are not actually old at all, just simply made to look that way. Aside from the places listed below, a succession of small odds-and-sods antique stalls line Badreddin al-Hassan Street, which leads off from the Umayyad Mosque's eastern door – or try the succession of shops that line the easternmost section of Straight Street between the Roman arch and Bab Sharqi.

Azem Ecole, just west of the Azem Palace, Old City. Sells everything from swords and pistols to genuine plastic wooden-inlay-style boxes; there's even a silk weaver in the foyer to prove that all the produce is locally made. Not cheap but a good place for a browse.

George Dabdoub, next to the Azem Palace, Old City. The busiest antique shop in Damascus, principally because the tour groups congregate outside on their way in and out of the Azem Palace. Besides selling all kinds of souvenirs, it has quite a large selection of antiques in the window and in one of the smaller rooms inside – anything from old irons to fragments of decorated tiles rescued from demolished hammams.

Dahdah Palace, Mohammad Ezat Dareaza Lane, Old City. Not a shop officially (see p.86), but the owner has a large selection of relics salvaged from the interiors of various old Damascene houses for sale.

Al-Khayat, opposite the Azem Palace, Old City. This souvenir store, popular because of its prime location, nonetheless has a window stuffed with all sorts of things from pots and pans to radios and sewing machines. Slightly more poky than Dabdoub.

Orientals Alaih, 3 Handicraft Souk. Silver, bronze and copperware on sale, plus *nargilehs*, teapots, ornaments, trays and bowls in abundance, as well as old radios and gramophones.

Carpets and kilims

The best place to look for a **carpet** or kilim in the **Old City** is at George Dabdoub (see p.106) or along the eastern stretch of Straight Street. Abou Elias, just off Straight Street on Al-Assiyeh Street near the Roman arch is also a particularly good choice; otherwise try the nearby Bazar Nazir on Straight Street itself. In the **Handicraft Souk**, store no. 45 sells a variety of rugs from Damascus itself and from Iran and Azerbaijan; here you can also buy a *sufra*, a Bedouin rug traditionally placed on the floor for people to sit on while they eat.

Clothes, textiles and leather

The Hamidiye Souk is predominantly a **clothes souk**, and although it's very much geared toward the locals, some of the more tourist-oriented shops sell such items as *keffiyeh*s and even belly-dancing costumes to passing Westerners. For the best selection of Damask **silk**, head along the **textiles souk** that leads south from the triumphal arch at the easternmost end of the Hamidiye Souk. Locally produced embroidered tablecloths are widely available around this area of the Old City, and can be found in most of the general craft shops located in the Hamidiye Souk and along Straight Street.

Several stores in the **Handicraft Souk** are also worth looking at. No. 36 sells tablecloths, which feature a good variety of different fabrics, colours and designs. Close by, at no. 39, there are beautiful hand-made embroidered clothes made by Palestinian refugees to their traditional designs: most striking are the women's long robes adorned with brightly coloured patterns. If you're after a silk tie, or want to buy silk off the roll, head for store no. 43, where the fabric is woven on site. There's a fair selection of **leather** bags, wallets and sandals at two places in the Handicraft Souk: store no. 59 specializes in footwear, while Ahmad Ali Adib has a good selection of bags and suchlike.

Copper and brassware

There's a huge amount of **copper** and **brassware** available in Damascus, although you have to look hard for good-quality items. One place to do this is Toby E. Stephan, located in the Hamidiye Souk in the **Old City**. Ahmad Sayha, on Straight Street in the Old City, sells mainly copper and brassware, though also a small selection of tablecloths and marquetry. More unusual offerings can be found in Kaka & Sons, also on Straight Street; they are swordsmiths with an impressively meaty selection in their window. The best-stocked of several stores in the **Handicraft Souk** is no.37, where trays, teapots and ornaments cram the groaning shelves.

Woodwork and furniture

Most craft shops in the **Old City** sell a selection of woodwork products, made in the small workshops in the northeastern quarter of the Old City; on Al-Assiyeh Street are a number of workshops where you can see craftsmen practising their trade – alternatively a number of the small shops along the street that runs by the southern wall of the Umayyad Mosque also function as workshops. For a specialist selling inlaid wood products, try Khalil Haddad on Straight Street, by the *L'Auberge* restaurant. Sanadiki, on the easternmost stretch of Straight Street just inside Bab Sharqi, has some truly remarkable examples of furniture decorated with mother-of-pearl. At Al-Wardeh al-Shamieh in the **Handicraft Souk**, you can browse round a good selection of wooden boxes, furniture, and backgammon and chess sets.

Nargilehs and glassware

A couple of **nargileh stores** can be found in the Hamidiye Souk opposite Toby E. Stephan's copperware store; prices range from $6 to $30. However, new and antique *nargileh*s are available from many other outlets, and you can even buy them (rather more expensively) in the airport's duty-free store, which is worth considering bearing in mind how awkward they are to carry around.

A cluster of good **glassware** shops can be found on Straight Street, just to the west of the Roman arch. In the Handicraft Souk, store no. 38 has a good selection of clear and coloured glassware products, including bowls and hanging ornaments. To see glass being blown at most times of day, follow Straight Street to Bab Sharqi, cross the busy road here, turn left and then (just before the water tower on your left) turn right along a side street to reach the Abou Ahmad Glass Factory (look out for the glass bottles hanging above the entrance to a short alleyway). They specialize in coloured glass products; you can get some great deals here and even have glass made to order.

Gold, silver and jewellery

Most of the shops in the **gold and silver souk**, situated along the street that heads south from the southwestern corner of the Umayyad Mosque, take credit cards, and their staff speak some English. A couple of good stores can also be found on the stretch of Straight Street between the Roman arch and the lane containing Dar Anbar; Abou Samra here specializes in elaborate trinkets with an Islamic tinge. Ahmad Alaf in the **Handicraft Souk** sells a good range of silver ornaments, picture frames, cutlery and jewellery, most of which is antique; there's nowhere to buy gold products in the Handicraft Souk, however. A succession of **jewellery** stores line the street that runs along the southern wall of the Umayyad Mosque.

Musical instruments

Al-Salka in Hamidiye Souk is the best place to buy **musical instruments** – ouds sell for anything up to $100 here. For instruments made primarily for decoration, check out numerous shops along the westernmost stretch of the Hamidiye Souk, where ouds (around $25) and drums are on sale. The Salihiye shopping district is a good place to buy **tapes** and **CDs** of Arabic music.

Paintings

In the **Handicraft Souk**, store no. 33 has an excellent selection of modern paintings by Syrian artists, which range in style from the abstract to the impressionistic. Favourite themes are Syrian scenes and people; both sketches and paintings on canvas can be purchased. If you're seriously interested in buying some Syrian art, check out the Atassi Gallery (see Listings, opposite), and the section in Contexts on contemporary Syrian artists.

Books

Damascus abounds in **bookstores**, but the only English books you'll find on sale in most of them are dictionaries and computer manuals. However, bookshops in the *Meridien*, *Sheraton* and *Cham Palace* hotels stock novels, guidebooks, newspapers, maps and postcards, and there are a few specialist bookshops, listed below.

Avicenne. Just off Maisaloun St, on a road running between the *Omayad* and *Fardoss Tower* hotels. Stocks English and French novels, guidebooks, children's books, periodicals and newspapers. Daily except Fri 9am–8.30pm.

The Family Bookshop, An-Majlis An-Nyaby St. Just west of the Franciscan church and Dar es Salam school. They have an excellent selection of English fiction, as well as periodicals and newspapers. Daily except Sun 9am–1.30pm & 5–8pm.

Librairie Universelle, Yousef al-Azmeh St. Here there's a limited choice of American, French and English paperbacks, both fiction and non-fiction.

Sayegh Bookshop, Salihiye St. Opposite the People's Assembly. Sells English-language textbooks in addition to a limited range of novels and non-fiction titles.

Listings

Airlines Most airlines maintain offices in the New City, between the Hedjaz Station and Yousef al-Azmeh Square. Air tickets are inevitably priced in US dollars, and all airlines take major credit cards; Syrianair takes only American Express, and if you want to pay for any of their international tickets in Syrian pounds you will have to change the required money at a bank at the special airline rate of exchange (the necessary paperwork to do this can be picked up from Syrianair offices). On Maisaloun St opposite the *Cham Palace* are Austrian Airlines (☎011/223 6001), Pakistan International (☎011/221 1581), Gulf Air (☎011/224 4203), and Iran Air (☎011/222 6431). LOT Polish Airlines (☎011/221 3441) is in an upper floor office next to the bank on the corner of Maisaloun Street and Yousef al-Azmeh Square. Around the corner, on the road linking Maisaloun St with Al-Moutanabby St, and situated either side of the *Fardoss Towers* hotel, are Turkish Airlines (☎011/222 1264), Alitalia (☎011/222 2262), Tarom Romanian Airlines (☎011/222 3332) and Saudi Arabian Airlines (☎011/231 2222). Around the next corner on Fardoos St, a block south of the eastern stretch of Maisaloun Street, are Malev Hungarian Airlines (☎011/222 7944), CSA Czech Airlines (☎011/222 5804), Iberia (☎011/222 6085) and KLM (☎011/221 3395). Nahas Travel and Tourism on Fardoos St (☎011/223 2000) represents a number of airlines which do not fly into Damascus, including TWA and Air Canada. On 29 May St, heading up from Yousef al-Azmeh Square, you'll find Aeroflot (☎011/231 7956) and Emirates (☎011/231 5211) on the right-hand side, Royal Jordanian (☎011/231 5577) on the left, and (on a side street) Cyprus Airways (☎011/232 4513). Air France (☎011/221 8580) is located in the second basement down in the *Meridien Hotel*; British Airways (☎011/331 0000), which represents British Mediterranean Airways and Qantas, is close by on Argentina St by the north end of the Assad Bridge. Free Hawk Travel and Tourism (☎011/332 6083), representing Qatar Airways and Singapore Airlines, is diagonally across from the *Meridien Hotel*, and Middle East Airlines (☎011/231 4998) is by the footbridge on Baruda St, across from the *Semiramis Hotel*. Egyptair (☎011/223 2158) maintains an office across from the Hedjaz Station. Syrianair's main office is also across from the Hedjaz Station, with other offices by the Central Bank (Baghdad St), on Fardoos St, and adjacent to the *Semiramis Hotel* (☎011/222 0700 or 223 2159 for all offices).

American Express Their agent is the Kaeou Shaar Group located in the Sudan Airlines office on the road linking Fardoos St and Al-Moutanabby St (☎011/221 7813). It isn't possible to obtain cash here using your card, nor can you buy travellers' cheques; they will hold post for you, though, and can organize tours (see "Travel agencies", below). In fact they'll probably be so pleased to see you that they'll give you a very useful free road map of Syria, just for putting your head round the door – whether or not you're an Amex customer.

Art galleries The art exhibition in the National Gallery has the best representative selection of modern Syrian artists, and is the obvious first stop. There are a number of small, private art galleries in the city, the most important of which is the Atassi Gallery at 39 Rawda St (☎011/332 1320), which exhibits the work of the best contemporary Syrian and Middle Eastern artists; they also publish a number of excellent art books dedicated to local painters, which are available in the bookshops listed on p.108. The various cultural institutes frequently put on art exhibitions; pop into the British Council or the French Institute and pick up their bi-monthly events calendars.

Banks and exchange Convenient branches of the Commercial Bank of Syria are on Yousef al-Azmeh Square and on Al-Jabaree St (both daily except Fri 8.30am–12.30pm), by the pedestrian footbridge; both change cash and travellers' cheques. If you get stuck, head for the branches at the *Sheraton* or *Meridien* hotels, which open on Fridays and in the afternoons, and don't mind changing cash or travellers' cheques for non-guests; their airport branch stays open 24hrs daily and changes cash and travellers' cheques. The booth outside the Yousef al-Azmeh Square branch is open daily except Fri 8.30am–7pm, but only changes cash. The exchange office on the west side of Martyrs' Square (daily 8am–7pm, Fri until 2pm) is a rather quicker place to change money or travellers' cheques than the banks.

Buses Zeitouni and Qadmoos have offices on Bahsa St, either side of the *Kairawan Hotel*, and Al-Ahlia has an office on Felasteen St, due west of the National Museum. Karnak have an office on Port Said St (daily 8am–2pm & 5–8pm; closed Fri pm; ☎011/231 6136). A set of offices located on the north side of Shoukry al-Qouwatly St, 200m west of the *Semiramis Hotel*, offer tickets to a variety of international destinations, mainly in Turkey, but also further afield in Romania, Bulgaria and Russia. Shopping around for what you want is easy; you'll pay around the same prices as are on offer at the Harasta Terminal (see p.69).

Camera shops Try Carmen Photo on the pedestrian mall opposite the People's Assembly on Salihiye St, or Pluto Photo Services on Maisaloun St, up past the *Cham Palace Hotel*. Both do developing and printing and sell new cameras, and can advise on camera repair.

Car rental Most firms and hotels require several days' notice before they can have a car ready for you. Europcar maintains offices at the airport (☎011/543 1536) and downtown on Musab ibn Umer St (☎011/211 7878, fax 211 1304), opposite the *Tichreen Hotel*. Their hotel offices are at the *Meridien* (☎011/332 2650), *Sheraton* (☎011/222 9300) and *Semiramis* (☎011/221 3813). Other major firms are Budget, Felasteen St (☎011/212 2220), and Avis, which is represented by Chamcar at the *Cham Palace Hotel* (☎011/223 2300). Most mid-range and upmarket hotels in the city can also organize a car for you, with or without driver.

Car repairs A number of car repair shops specializing in European models cluster around the Harasta station in northern Damascus close to (and signposted from) the main Damascus–Homs motorway.

Courier services DHL, Al-Jamhourieh St, 200m west of the *Semiramis Hotel* (☎011/223 8586); Federal Express, Al-Abed St, off 17 April Sq (☎011/442 0452); Overseas Courier Service, Omar bin Abi Rabia St, off Al-Jabaree St, round the corner from the main post office (☎011/223 6883).

Cultural centres The British Council is at Abdul Khareem al-Khalil St, off the western end of Maisaloun St (☎011/331 0631). The library (daily except Fri 9am–8pm) has many recently published UK books, magazines and journals, which can be read by non-members. Check the noticeboards or their monthly newsletter for details of films, theatre performances in English, exhibitions and other events. The American Cultural Center (☎011/333 8413) is off Al-Mansour St, behind fortress-thick walls in a leafy villa-lined street just up from the US embassy, but is much less welcoming to casual visitors; you are unlikely to be able to use the library here (daily except 1–5pm) unless you are a resident of the city or have a very good reason to do so. The Centre Culturel Français is opposite the *Alaa Towers Hotel* in a short street leading east off Yousef al-Azmeh St (daily except Sun 9am–9pm; ☎011/231 6181) and the Goethe Institut (☎011/333 6673) is at Adnan Malki 8, adjacent to the Indian Embassy. Both put on or advertise films, exhibitions and concerts, and you can browse the Goethe Institut's programme of events at their pleasant *Cafe Berlin*.

Dentists Emergency treatment is available at the Shamy Diplomatic Hospital (see "Hospitals"); for less urgent treatment, ask your embassy for a list of recommended dentists.

Embassies and consulates Australia, Faraby St, 6km west of city centre off the Beirut road (☎011/611 6730); Britain, Mohammad Kourd Ali St (☎011/373 9241); Canada, 4km west of city centre on the Beirut road (☎011/611 6692); Jordan, Al-Jalaa St (☎011/333 4642); US, Al-Mansour St (☎011/333 2315). New Zealand and the Irish Republic do not maintain embassies in Syria and their citizens should enquire at the British embassy for consular assistance. Most embassies are open from 8am to 2pm and are closed Fri & Sat, plus Syrian public holidays and national public holidays of the country concerned. Close to Martyrs' Sq is an office which deals with re-entry visas for those who want to visit Lebanon and return to Syria (see box, pp.114–115).

Emergencies Police ☎112, ambulance ☎110, fire ☎113, traffic police ☎115.

Hammams Located down Bazuriye St in the heart of the souk, Hammam Nur al-Din (daily 8am–11pm; men only) is one of the oldest in Syria and the staff, who are accustomed to seeing tourists, can speak some English. The basic deal here including massage comes to S£125; add-ons including "abrasive cleaning" might push the cost up to S£250. Prices are the much the same at Hammam Selselah, a short way east of the Epigraphy Museum. Cheaper and friendlier than the others are the Bakri Baths, tucked away in the northeast corner of the Old City amid charming narrow alleyways. The above are open from 8am to midnight and are for men only; women can try the Hammam al-Qaimariyyeh on Zuqqaq Hammam St in the Old City, which has daily women-only sessions in the afternoon.

Hospitals The main hospital for foreigners is the Shamy Diplomatic Hospital on Jawaher al-Nahro St, northwest of the city centre (☎011/373 4960). Here you will be assured of prompt and excellent service from English-speaking medics; a consultation with a doctor costs S£500.

Internet access You can access the Web three floors up in the Assad Library on Umawiyeen Sq, 2km west of Martyrs' Sq (daily except Fri 9am to 1pm; S£2 per minute; take your passport). Connections aren't reliable, though (some email sites may even be blocked) and every site you access (or even try to access) will be written down on a form and filed away. The site which the officials are most keen for you to access is the Syrian Government's site about why Israel should give back the Golan Heights. Flyers on the noticeboards of the *Al-Haramain* and *Al-Rabie* hotels (see p.74) may indicate addresses of places where you can access the Web, including email and chat services, although the legality of these access points is doubtful and they certainly do not advertise widely. One of these is Internet Zoni, (☎011/232 4670, *zoni@net.sy*), located in the Abbedin Building east off Yousef al-Azmeh St. All the cultural centres have Internet access but their computers can only be used by those signed up on courses; there's no harm asking them whether casual visitors can go online, though.

Laundry Most hotels can do your laundry for you. A good city-centre laundry is the Technical Laundry, across the road from the Cham Cinema on Maisaloun St; they charge per item (but don't do underwear).

Opticians Two good opticians are situated close to each other across the small street running off Salihiye St by the People's Assembly.

Pharmacy The best in Damascus is the Kanawati Principale on Yousef al-Azmeh Sq. There's also a pharmacy in the Shamy Diplomatic Hospital.

Phones The installation of shiny new public telephone boxes, which take both coins and phone cards and can be found all over the city centre, has made it unnecessary to use the big Telephone Services Centre (daily 8am–10pm) by the Hedjaz Station on An-Naser St, unless you're having difficulty getting connected or want to send a fax (S£75 per minute to Europe and North America; bring your passport). Phone cards are available at the Telephone Services Centre and from certain shops in the downtown area (look for their window stickers).

Post office The central post office is on Al-Jaberee St (daily except Fri 8am–7pm). The poste restante counter in the post office is the only one in Damascus; there is a small payment to be made if letters are collected, and you should take your passport with you. If you're an Amex customer, you can have mail sent to their office (see p.109).

Swimming pools The *Cham Palace*, *Meridien* and *Sheraton* hotels will let non-guests use their outdoor pools for around S£500. The Tichreen Sports Complex on Musab ibn Umer St, 800m southwest of Hedjaz Station, has a huge public indoor pool (S£50).

Thomas Cook Represented by Nahas Travel and Tourism on Fardoos St (daily 8am–7pm). Though you can report stolen travellers' cheques here, they can neither replace them nor sell you new ones.

Travel agencies Most companies offering flight bookings and car rental are on Port Said St, Yousef al-Azmeh St and the small alleyways linking them; the best is probably Nahas Travel and Tourism on Fardoos St (☎011/223 2000). If you are after organized tours of Damascus or Syrian sights, ask at the travel agencies associated with the big hotels, or try Adonis on Moutanabi St (☎011/223 6272) or American Express (see p.109); prices and duration of tours, and whether or not you have a guide, are negotiable.

Visa extensions The main office for visa extensions is on Felasteen (Palestine) St, 300m west of the Baramkeh Terminal's service taxi depot and close to the big Syrian Arab News Agency (SANA) building (daily except Fri 8am–2pm). Look for the photographers and typists in the street; the office for visa extensions for foreigners is upstairs (and signposted in English). A month-long visa extension is normally ready for collection the next working day after you apply; three passport-style photos are required.

West of Damascus

Although the **Barada River** is little more than a rubbish-strewn ditch as it flows through Damascus, it is an ancient and fabled river, celebrated in II Kings 5 in the Old Testament as having curative properties superior even to the rivers of Israel. If the marsh near Damascus Airport into which the river drains makes for something of an ignominious lower end, its source region, in the **Anti-Lebanon mountains** northwest of the capital, is altogether more inspiring. The landscape around the Barada headwaters is wild and barren, consisting in the main of rocky mountain ridges broken by narrow valleys forged by the Barada's tributaries. **Burqush** sits atop one of these ridges, a remote Byzantine and Roman site where the remains of a sixth-century basilica are set in stunning scenery. Across the border in Lebanon, the extensive Roman ruins at **Baalbak** make for a fairly easy day-excursion from the city; easier to get to are two bland resort towns (both linked to the capital by a narrow-gauge rail line), **Zabadani** and **Bloudane**, where there's nothing much to do except savour the clean air and relaxed atmosphere.

Zabadani and Bloudane

Zabadani, 45km northwest of Damascus, and its neighbour Bloudane are shamelessly summer-oriented resorts where Syrians and foreign visitors come simply to cool off. In truth, half the fun of visiting the area is travelling on the rickety **train** which makes the weekly journey up from the capital; there's nothing specific to see, and in the cooler months there's not a lot of point coming here. The train usually continues beyond Zabadani to **Serghaya**, a dull, ugly settlement located just before the Lebanese border, which cannot be crossed here by road or rail. Beyond Serghaya the rail lines disappear into the undergrowth, but one day they may be uncovered and restored so that trains can once again continue to Beirut. However, the track on the Lebanese section suffered from bombing during the war in Lebanon, and is still in a far from usable state.

Of the two resorts, **ZABADANI** is larger and busier, but is actually a fairly dull place, its shops full of tourist kitsch and its restaurants blaring Western pop music at full volume. If you've made it all the way up here, it's better to pick up a microbus (S£20) to **BLOUDANE**, a tranquil resort accessible by a steep, winding seven-kilometre road from Zabadani. The microbuses leave from Zabadani's main square – once out of the train station, turn left, then left again across the railway lines to reach it. A spring in Bloudane provides the mineral water bottled as Boukein, the most widespread brand available in Syria. The air is fantastically clean up here, and the views (far superior to those in Zabadani) encompass the whole of the upper Barada valley, as far as the Bekaa Valley across the border in

Lebanon. If you have some spare cash, you can quite happily spend it on a drink or meal at the *Grand Hotel* (see overleaf), whose outdoor terrace **restaurant** is probably the best-situated of any in Syria.

Souk Wadi Barada

The route the train takes up to Zabadani goes through **SOUK WADI BARADA**, a picturesquely situated though otherwise fairly ordinary town where some minor ruin-spotting is possible. Immediately north of the settlement, the rail line and road pass through a tunnel and a steep gorge, on whose upper slopes you can see remains of Roman rock-cut burial caves – accessible by a bit of tricky scrambling – and a cutting, dug into a terrace on the mountainside, which once carried the Roman road from Baalbak to Damascus (the remains are scant though, the road having been washed away on many occasions by the floods which it was supposedly constructed to avoid). The Romans knew Souk Wadi Barada as **Abilia**, after Abel, supposedly murdered here by Cain and buried on a summit to the west at a spot now marked by a Druze holy place; the buildings in the modern town utilize pieces of Roman masonry left over from ancient Abilia, of which nothing now remains.

Practicalities

The narrow-gauge **rail line** is served by a train sardonically nicknamed the **Zabadani Flyer**, which operates occasionally (currently Fri & public holidays; S£30 one way) from Damascus's Hedjaz Station. Hauled by 100-year-old steam engines, the train, jammed with families laden with food for their day out, takes three hours to struggle up to Zabadani. The first part of the journey is along tracks laid tramline-style through the streets of Damascus, with the train hair-raisingly competing for space with the usual jumble of trucks, horse-drawn carts and perpetually hooting taxis and private cars. Beyond the city limits the line hugs the valley side, coping with steep rock outcrops and narrow gullies by means of a bewildering succession of bridges, tunnels and cuttings; so infrequent are the trains that locals use the tracks as a parking lot for their cars and trucks, and passengers are roped in at regular intervals to move offending vehicles if their owners fail to respond to the train's fierce whistling. With only one service there and back (currently leaving Damascus around 8am and returning from Zabadani at 2pm) on the days the train runs, there's no possibility of breaking your journey at Souk Wadi Barada (microbuses up to Zabadani and Bloudane don't pass through), and not a great deal of time to look round Bloudane or Zabadani on a day-trip from Damascus unless you head back to the capital by microbus.

Duller but faster are the **microbuses** (S£20; 45min) which depart a couple of times an hour (and infrequently for Souk Wadi Barada) for the resorts from the Baramkeh Terminal in Damascus (see p.66); microbuses serving Bloudane do not pass through Zabadani, which is actually no bad thing. The quickest route **by road** is to take the motorway towards Beirut (signposted from the centre of Damascus), turning off to Zabadani shortly before the Lebanese border; to stop off at Souk Wadi Barada, use the route via Dummar to reach Zabadani, which will take you through Souk Wadi Barada and the gorge.

ACCOMMODATION AND EATING

Most people head up this way for no more than a day-trip, but if you're considering the possibility of staying over, you can certainly pass over the claims of drab

Zabadani in favour of its loftier neighbour. The first two **hotels** you come to in **Bloudane** face each other across an open square. The *Akel* is a very pleasant modern place, though lacking in character, with decent rooms (☎011/712 8604; ⑤); the *Grand* is a much classier hotel, with tennis courts, an open-air swimming pool and a **restaurant** with fabulous views across the valley (☎011/227551; ⑦). A three-minute walk up the main road from these hotels is the much cheaper *Dahabiyeh*, a small place with a genial owner and some balcony rooms with a view (☎011/712 7462; ②). If you're driving up to the resorts – by whatever route – then you might want to investigate one of the many small restaurants which have sprung up along the roadside on the Zabadani turn-off from the Damascus–Beirut highway; attractively situated on the valley slopes, they're good for a drink or cheap meal.

Burqush

The border between Syria and Lebanon, to the west of Damascus, is a sensitive area, so travel in the region is hampered by military activity, road blocks and the presence of numerous no-go areas. The most obvious place to head for is **BURQUSH**, where fairly scant Roman and Byzantine ruins are set amid awe-inspiringly bleak scenery within 5km of the border. The main focus of the site is

---

BAALBAK

No visitor to Syria should miss out on the opportunity to visit the awesome ruins of **BAALBAK**, arguably the archeological highlight of a trip to the Middle East and an easy day-trip into Lebanon from Damascus. The site essentially consists of two huge **temples**: the Temple of Jupiter is much the larger, though only the massive podium on which it stood and some awesome columns remain today; the Temple of Bacchus, though very much in the shadow of its neighbour, is incredibly well preserved, and both dwarf any Classical remains in Syria.

There is evidence for settlement here dating back to the third millennium BC, though hardly any written history refers to the place until the Greeks arrived in the fourth century BC, and nothing in Baalbak today predates the Roman takeover in 64 BC. Entrance to the site (daily: summer 8.30am–7pm; winter 8.30am–4.30pm; S£400 or LL10,000) is via a grand monumental stairway, rebuilt from scratch in 1901, which leads up to the temple complex. Passing through the huge portico, you enter a small hexagonal courtyard which leads to a larger square courtyard. From here, steps lead up to the **Temple of Jupiter**; once the largest such edifice in the Roman empire, though ruined by a succession of earthquakes and almost completely dismantled during the construction of a Byzantine basilica. All that remains of the temple today are six of the original 54 monumental columns which would once have surrounded the cella, each an awe-inspiring 2.5m in diameter and 20m high. Equally impressive is the sheer size of the stone blocks used to form the podium on which the temple stood, the largest of which measures 19m by 4m by 3m and weighs over 1000 tonnes.

The town of Baalbak was once one of the centres of Hezbollah resistance to the Israelis, and was where many Western hostages, including Terry Waite and John McCarthy, were held during the Lebanese war. Now though, the war has long ended and Baalbak generally quite safe to visit, though obviously it pays to be alert to the ever-changing security situation in the region.

a ruined sixth-century **Byzantine basilica**, built above a narrow ridge of moun-tainside flattened off to form a plateau – it's difficult to fathom how anyone got the enormous stone blocks used to build the three-aisled structure up here. The basilica was built on the podium of a former Roman temple, thought to date from the first century AD, itself constructed on a site used for religious purposes for at least four hundred years prior to that. On all sides there are more blocks, some jumbled around like bizarre geological outcrops, others recognizably forming the outlines of buildings. More than the remains, though, it's the superb **views** which are the most arresting aspect of the location – sweeping down onto the Damascus plain on one side, and encompassing steep, dusty hills on the other, their surfaces grazed almost bare by the wandering herds of camels and goats you might see on the journey up here.

Practicalities

To get to Burqush, you have to make for **Qatana**, 26km west of the capital, and served by plenty of microbuses and buses from the Baramkeh Terminal (S£10, 30min); it's also perfectly possible to drive there from Damascus (use the Quneitra turning off the main Beirut road). Once you get to Qatana things become less straightforward; you need to arrange a taxi, or ask a local driving one of the ubiquitous pick-up trucks in the main square, to get you the rest of the way,

---

Practicalities

Syria thinks of Lebanon as being part of "Greater Syria", and so there is no Lebanese embassy in Damascus (and no Syrian embassy in Beirut), but EU, Australian, Canadian and US citizens can obtain a **Lebanese visa** for US$16 at the border on the Damascus–Beirut highway. If you have a single-entry Syrian visa and want to make a short visit to Lebanon before returning to Syria, you should first visit the passport office on al-Furat Avenue in Damascus (see map, p.72) just west of Martyrs' Square. They will telex your details to the border post at Jdayde where your passport will be stamped accordingly when you cross into Lebanon. On your return to Syria (which must be by the same route) you'll have to pay for another Syrian visa.

It's possible to visit Baalbak on an **organized tour** from Damascus (see pp.111–112 for a list of travel agents); this costs around US$150 for a day-trip, including lunch, transport in a private car and hire of an English-speaking guide. To get there independently, take a Baalbak **service taxi** from the Felasteen Street station in Damascus (S£400; 2hr 30min including border formalities). In view of the length of the trip, it's best to make an early start, especially as demand tends to dry up by late morning and you may end up having to hire the whole taxi (which costs at least S£800) if you get there late. To catch a service taxi back from Baalbak, walk down the road that heads away from the entrance to the ruins; the office is on the left, just beyond the crossroads. Alternatively, take a regular microbus down the Bekaa Valley to **Chtaura** and pick up one of the Beirut–Damascus micros from there.

Baalbak is not an especially large site, so you don't need to spend more than two or three hours there; should you wish to **stay** overnight though, the place to head for is the *Palmyra Hotel* (☎00961/08/370230; ⑤, credit cards not accepted), a ten-minute walk from the entrance to the ruins on the main road heading south. Built in 1874, the hotel possesses a wealth of history not dissimilar to that of the *Baron* in Aleppo (see p.219) and is much bet-ter maintained than its Syrian cousin.

Syrian **currency** is accepted in Baalbak – both in the town and at the entrance to the ruins. Just along from the *Palmyra Hotel* is a bank, open on weekday mornings, which will change cash – otherwise try the hotel itself or ask the souvenir sellers or in the souk. There are no cash machines in Baalbak.

as local drivers will be best placed to negotiate military road blocks and cope with the complete lack of signposting. A fair price for the thirty-minute ride from Qatana to Burqush is S£300–400, with bargaining. Be prepared at any point in your journey to find yourself joined by a soldier as an escort, and have your passport handy in case you need to show it at one of the army roadblocks. Burqush is situated well away from metalled roads and can only be reached by a ten-minute walk up a steep hill from a farm track; you'll need some water and protection from the sun if you come on a hot day.

Northeast of Damascus

It's the area to the **northeast** which provides the most varied opportunities for excursions around the capital, the diverse places of interest in this region providing welcome relief from the bustling souks and choked streets of the big city. West of the main Damascus–Homs highway, the Anti-Lebanon mountains reach heights of more than 2000m, the slopes peppered with a myriad of small towns and villages. The most attractive of these are **Sednaya** and **Maalula**, both Christian enclaves, the former a popular pilgrimage centre dominated by a large convent, the latter a much more characterful town, huddled dramatically beneath an escarpment and famed for its use of Aramaic, the language spoken by Jesus. To the east, out in the desert on the road to Palmyra, is **Dmeir**, a former Roman settlement which grew up on the intersection of two major caravan routes, its main (indeed only) attraction being a brilliantly preserved temple. Each of these three towns is an easy day-trip from Damascus. The farthest-flung destination out this way is the fabulously situated desert monastery of **Deir Mar Mousa**, reached by a time-consuming journey through parched, forbidding scenery.

Sednaya

High in the barren hills 27km north of Damascus lies the small Christian settlement of **SEDNAYA**, crowned by the castle-like **Convent of Our Lady**. A steady flow of chattering pilgrims is drawn to the convent by its miracle-inducing image of the Virgin, said to have been painted from life by St Luke. Legend further has it that the convent is situated on the spot where Noah planted the first vine after the Flood, and indeed the town produces its own sickly-sweet wine. The convent was established in 547 when, during his wars with the Persians, Justinian and his army were encamped here, and it's no surprise to learn that a miracle has become attached to its foundation, too. The story goes that while he was out hunting deer, the emperor was suddenly overwhelmed by a bright light; the deer he was pursuing then changed into a woman dressed in white, who commanded him to build a church and convent on the site. This he did, installing his sister as the first mother superior.

It's not known when the icon of the Virgin was brought here, but during the Middle Ages a succession of miracles associated with St Luke's handiwork turned the place into the most popular pilgrimage centre in the Middle East after Jerusalem. According to *The Travels of Sir John Mandeville* (which purported to be an account of journeys in the parts, and were very widely read at the time), the icon dripped a mysterious oil which was given to pilgrims "for it heals of many sicknesses; and the men say that if it be kept well seven year, afterwards it turns into flesh and blood" – furthermore, a nearby river was said to flow only on Saturdays. With such an astonishing press, it's hardly surprising that not all visitors were impressed by what they found. Henry Maundrell, writing in 1697, remarked with horror that the convent was "possessed by twenty Greek monks and forty nuns who seem to live promiscuously together, without order or separation", although he did comment favourably on the "most excellent" local wine. His verdict is certainly open to question, but one thing you should try to get hold of is a jar of the delicious locally produced **honey**; beekeeping is one of Sednaya's oldest industries.

Today the Greek Orthodox Church runs the church, having wrestled control from the Greek Catholics some two hundred years ago. The convent **complex** is very modern and rather maze-like, with stairways winding all over the vine-covered courtyards, leading eventually up to the roof, from where there are some splendid views over the town and down onto the arid plain below. The centrepiece **Chapel of the Virgin**, chock-full of icons dating from as far back as the fifth century, is usually very busy (with a huge surge of visitors on the main pilgrimage day, Sept 8); the reputation of the icons has had the curious effect of attracting a large number of Muslims to the shrine, particularly on Fridays, many of them women seeking help to conceive – often they are allowed to stay overnight in the church, sleeping next to the icon for luck and nibbling the candles to pass the time.

Most of Sednaya's twenty **other churches** are also modern buildings, though between the convent and the microbus station is a small, square Roman structure which has been converted into a church dedicated to St Peter. Particularly striking is its refurbished door, constructed by placing a slab of stone in the old doorway and cutting a smaller hole out of it to ensure that worshippers would have to bow upon entering. In the escarpment opposite the town are a number of caves used by the early Christians, variously as meeting places, dwellings and burial chambers; to get inside them, you need to arrange for a guide from the convent. The large white cross on the horizon marks the location of the **Convent of St Thomas** (a fairly stiff 2km hike along a rough road), another converted Roman monument with a great view, as well as a large grotto thought to have served as either a burial chamber or possibly a meeting place for priests.

Practicalities

Sednaya can be reached in forty minutes by a frequent microbus service (S£12) from the Bilal Square station in Damascus. For a place to stay, there's a **hotel**, the *Touristic* (☎012/595 0358; ④), fifteen minutes' walk from the convent along the main road in Sednaya. A number of **restaurants** line the road just before you reach town; in Sednaya itself there is the *Al-Massaya*, situated on the main road and offering a traditional Syrian menu, or the restaurant in the *Touristic*.

Maalula

Nestled in a harsh landscape 58km away from the Damascene city bustle, **MAALULA** is simply the most enchanting town in Syria, its attractive pastel-coloured houses gripping the slopes of a dramatic escarpment rising out the desert on an epic scale. The combination of the monumental landscape and pretty

---

ARAMAIC

Brought into the Middle East around 1000 BC, **Aramaic** is a Semitic language, closely related to Hebrew, and was originally the language of the Arameans (see p.300). It was spoken by the Jews of Palestine when Jesus was alive and thus by Jesus himself, as well as by the early Apostles; many books of the Old Testament were originally written in Aramaic, as were many of the Dead Sea Scrolls found at Qumran, Palestine, in 1947.

Aramaic remained widely spoken in Syria up until the Muslim conquest of the seventh century, but as the Arabic language became widespread, the old tongue hid away in the mountains – though even in the fifteenth century it was so widespread that Franciscan missionaries had to learn it in order to carry out their work.

Maalula apart, the nearby villages of Jabadeen and Bakha also claim to be Aramaic-speaking, and a form of it is spoken in a number of communities in the northeast of Syria by people who arrived there in the twentieth century from Iraq. However, **Arabic** is now taught in schools and used as the everyday means of communication throughout Syria. Even in Maalula, the arrival of the mass media and the emigration of many of the younger generation from the village have left the language largely the preserve of literary scholars. Though the locals are belatedly trying to pass the rudiments of their language on, so far these attempts have mainly taken the form of cassettes and CDs of folk songs sung in Aramaic, available in the souvenir shops next to the convent.

---

houses, as well as the refreshingly cool air, make it one of the most relaxing and aesthetically pleasing destinations in Syria. Besides its striking location, Maalula is also famed as an extraordinary pocket of Christianity, for not only is this small settlement packed with tiny churches, as well as containing a large monastery, but it is also one of the very few places in the world where **Aramaic** – the language that Jesus used – is still spoken.

It's especially worth heading up to Maalula during one of the three main festival dates: September 14, for the exaltation of the Holy Cross; September 24, for the Feast of St Tekla; or October 7, for the Feast of St Sergius. Large crowds flock to the village during these festivals and the place comes alive with pageantry, folklore displays, music and dancing. On the night of the Feast of the Holy Cross huge fires are lit on top of the hills of Maalula, an old tradition commemorating the events of 325 when St Helen is said to have found the Cross in Jerusalem; to spread the news back to Constantinople a chain of huge bonfires was lit between the two cities, with Maalula being one of the chosen sites. Another magical time to head up here is in winter, when the fallen snow transforms the place into an unforgettable picture-postcard scene.

The Convent of St Tekla

The Damascus microbus usually drops you off at the small roundabout in the centre of town, from where the right-hand fork winds uphill to the **Convent of St Tekla**. Legend has it that Tekla was an early convert of St Paul from the town of Iconium (in what's now modern Turkey), whose radical views led to her being sentenced to death by burning by the governor of the town – who also happened to be her father. The story goes that just as Tekla was about to step towards the flames, the skies above suddenly darkened and a huge downpour quenched them. Disappointed but undeterred, Tekla's father ordered her to be thrown to the lions instead but, sensing her innate goodness, the lions merely nestled at her feet. By now rapidly losing patience, he ordered his daughter's head to be hacked off; Tekla, however, managed to flee the town, aided by a spot of cross-dressing. Pursued across many lands by her father, she eventually came to Maalula where she is said to have found refuge in a cave and eventually settled down. It wasn't until the 1960s that the Pope finally conceded that Tekla's story was all just bunkum, and her name was struck off the official list of saints.

The convent building itself, uncompromisingly modern, is snugly located under a cliff. Stairways inside the complex lead up to Tekla's reputed **grotto**, where sacred water – reputedly a cure for flatulence – trickles from the ceiling. Beyond the convent is a narrow gorge, said to have been formed miraculously: while fleeing from the pagans, Tekla prayed for help, and the mountain which barred her passage split, letting her through. The gorge manages to retain its charm despite the extensive graffiti on its walls; up the sides are many burial niches, carved into the rock.

The Church of St Sergius
Where the gorge ends, turn left up and beyond the incongruous four-star *Safir Hotel* to the small Greek Catholic **monastery**; its distinctive low doorway requires you to bow in order to enter. Inside, accessed via the monastery's courtyard, is the **church of St Sergius** (*Kaneesat Mar Sarkis* in Arabic, named after a Roman soldier reputedly martyred at Resafe; see p.258), containing icons dating to the thirteenth century. An intimate early fourth-century structure, the church is built on the site of a pagan temple. Indeed, the church's unusual early Christian central and northern altars both have rims around them, reflecting the traditional form of a pagan altar; the rim would have been used to prevent the loss of blood during sacrifice, though in fact it's likely no sacrifices were ever undertaken on these altars as they lack the holes necessary to allow the blood to run away (the southern altar is a modern replica of the two older ones).

A souvenir shop has recently opened up in the monastery courtyard, stocked up with cassettes and CDs of folk songs and religious music, mainly sung in Aramaic. It's a good place to try some Maalulan **wine** which, at S£200 a bottle, is not exactly cheap, but it's far more palatable than the ditchwater they sell in the souvenir shops next to the Convent of St Tekla for half the price.

Cut into the hillside beyond the monastery are a number of litter-strewn **caves** thought to have been inhabited in the Stone Age, and known to have been in use, for living, worship or burial, in the first few centuries after Christ. Following the road on down brings you back to the village and the roundabout, from where you can pick up a microbus back to Damascus; on the way you pass some more caves cut into the opposing rock face, some of which may be accessed by dodgy-looking ladders.

Practicalities
Microbuses (every 30min; S£12) run to Maalula from the Bilal Square station in east Damascus, taking just under an hour to complete the journey. No buses cover the 25km between Sednaya and Maalula, so to combine the two in one visit, head first for Sednaya, from where you can hire a microbus or taxi to Maalula for around S£300 (there are fewer vehicles available for hire in Maalula).

Maalula's four-star *Safir* **hotel** (☎011/777 0250; ⑤) is especially geared up for tour groups; all rooms are en-suite and boast TVs and fridges, and there's a restaurant and swimming pool too. The square by the convent in Maalula has a cheap sit-down place to **eat**, or if you fancy something a bit more classy, try the *Mar Sarkis* located near the *Safir*, or the restaurant in the *Safir* itself, which does Arabic and Western dishes.

Dmeir

DMEIR is a dusty, inconsequential sort of place today, but during the Roman period it was an important fortified post standing at the crossroads of the Homs–Palmyra and Damascus–Resafe caravan routes. One remarkable remnant survives from this period, the **Temple of Zeus Hypsistos**, still intact up to roof level. The temple stands in an excavated depression some 5m deep in the centre of town, just beyond the main crossroads to your right as you approach from Damascus; it's usually kept locked but ask around the surrounding houses, one of whose inhabitants has the key. Numerous inscriptions survive on the monument, one of which dates it to 245 AD; carved portraits in relief in the interior may be of Philip the Arab (see p.139), the emperor at the time, and his wife. The discovery of an altar (now in Paris) dedicated to the Semitic sky god Baal-Shamin suggests that this site was used earlier by the Nabateans (see p.300) in the first century AD. The temple later served as a Christian church and then as an Arab fortress; indeed the locals sometimes refer to it as the *qalaa*.

A couple of kilometres east of Dmeir, by the side of the main road and right next to an air-force base (photos not advised), are the scant remains of a late second-century **Roman military camp**. There's precious little of substance to see apart from a few crumbling walls and a lot of fallen masonry, but it's a small detour with your own transport.

Practicalities

There are **microbuses** to Dmeir from the Abbasiyeen Terminal in northeast Damascus; the journey takes just under an hour (every 30min or so; S£15). As Dmeir isn't the most compelling attraction in its own right, you might consider taking it in while travelling between Damascus and Palmyra, as it's on the main road between the two (microbuses stop here en route, though Pullmans don't). There are no hotels in Dmeir; for a quick bite, there are some **falafel** places along the main road.

Deir Mar Mousa

Located at the head of a precipitous gully amid some of the harshest and most uncompromising desert scenery anywhere in Syria, **DEIR MAR MOUSA** (the Monastery of St Moses the Ethiopian – the son of an Ethiopian monarch who didn't want to inherit the throne) is a lengthy but very rewarding day-trip from either Damascus or Homs. Getting to the monastery requires time, patience, a little expense and a short burst of fairly strenuous leg-work. The first part of the journey is by microbus to **Nabek**, a small, dusty town situated just to the east of the main Damascus–Homs highway and around 80km from either city.

From Nabek, the road climbs east over a high ridge; once over the crest there are fine views across fabulously bleak and featureless plains, which stretch endlessly into the haze, cut through only by the jet-black of the bitumen road. After fifteen minutes' drive from Nabek there's a signpost pointing out a left turning to the monastery along an unmade track, which is easy to follow. Another fifteen minutes later the track terminates at the mouth of a gully cut into a steep limb of dusty hills by seasonal rains; the monastery buildings are clearly visible from here and take around twenty minutes to reach on foot, up a well-made path.

St Moses himself is reputed to have founded a monastery in this inhospitable location over 1400 years ago. It fell into neglect in the seventeenth century and was abandoned; the present restoration work is the result of the combined efforts of an Italian Jesuit, Father Paolo, and the Syrian Catholic communities of Nabek and Damascus. There is now a permanent community of around four or five monks and nuns here, including the multilingual and very friendly Father Paolo himself, who will probably give you an English-language copy of the monastery's newsletter. As you come in through the main gate, you'll find the **church** is the square, windowless building to your left, reached through a door you must crouch to pass through. This intensely gloomy, three-aisled building almost seems to breathe venerability, its frescoes dating from the seventh and eleventh centuries. Beyond the church is a terrace with great views across the gully and down towards the desert plains. Other buildings on the site include dwellings for the monks and nuns; among these is a hermitage set apart from the main group of buildings and clinging to the steep, rocky slope.

Practicalities

Microbus connections between Nabek and Damascus (from the Abbasiyeen Terminal, see p.69) or Homs (microbus station) are very frequent (around 1hr from either; S£20). Buses travelling between Damascus and Homs will drop passengers for Nabek on the highway, from where it's a two-kilometre walk to the centre of town, although getting a lift in a taxi or passing local traffic shouldn't be too difficult. Microbuses which begin or terminate their journey in Nabek will stop on the main square - really an elongated street – on the east side of which is a **taxi office**. Here you can usually negotiate a price of around S£400 for a ride out to the monastery including a two-hour waiting period for you to look round, which should be plenty. If the office is closed, you might end up paying up to S£700 to one of the drivers for the journey. Getting drivers to understand where you want to go shouldn't prove a problem: there's no reason for visitors to come to Nabek other than to travel out to the monastery.

Given the time it takes to reach Deir Mar Mousa, and the fact that the monastery's main attraction is its wonderful setting, the opportunity for an **overnight stay** here is an attractive one. You won't be expected to pay for your bed; a contribution to monastic funds is in order, though, or you might consider bringing food, which may well be pooled with the monastery's own supplies. Facilities are understandably basic – there's a phone, and electricity, and water from a well – but the spectacle of watching the desert sunrise from the terrace outside the church more than makes up for the lack of creature comforts. When you're ready to depart, you can use the phone to ring the taxi office in Nabek to get a vehicle to meet you at the bottom of the path to the monastery.

travel details

Trains
Hedjaz Station to:

Amman (Jordan; 2 weekly; 9hr); Dera (2 weekly; 4hr); Ezra (2 weekly; 2hr).

Serghaya (1 weekly; 3hr 30min); Zabadani (1 weekly; 3hr).

Kadem Station to:

Aleppo (1 daily; 6hr); Hama (1 daily; 5hr); Homs (1 daily; 3hr); Latakia (1 weekly; 7hr); Tartous (1 weekly; 5hr).

Deir ez-Zur (1 weekly; 11hr); Qamishli (1 weekly; 15hr).

Pullman and Karnak buses
Frequent departures from Baramkeh Terminal to:

Dera, Bosra, and Ezra (60–90min to each destination).

Frequent departures from Harasta Terminal to:

Aleppo (5hr); Deir ez-Zur (6hr); Hama (3hr); Hassakeh (8hr); Homs (2hr); Latakia (5hr); Tadmor (Palmyra, 3hr); Tartous (3hr).

Microbuses and local buses
Abbasiyeen Terminal to:

Aleppo (6hr); Deir ez-Zur (7–8hr); Dmeir (1hr); Hama (3hr); Homs (2hr 30min); Latakia (6hr); Nabek (1hr 15min); Qamishli (10hr); Tartous (4hr).

An-Nasera Street (Bilal Square) depot to:

Maalula (55min); Sednaya (40min).

Baramkeh Terminal to:

Qatana (for Burqush), Quneitra, Zabadani, Bloudane and Souk Wadi Barada.

Southern bus station to:

Sweida, Ezra and Dera (60–90min to each destination).

Service taxis
Baramkeh Terminal to:

Amman (Jordan; 3hr); Beirut (Lebanon; 3hr); Irbid (Jordan; 2hr 30min); Mafraq (Jordan; 2hr 30min); Zarqa (Jordan; 3hr).

Domestic flights
Damascus to: Aleppo (2 or 3 daily; 1hr); Deir ez-Zur (2 weekly; 1hr); Latakia (1 weekly; 1hr); Qamishli (3 weekly; 1hr 15min).

International buses
Baramkeh Terminal to:

Beirut (3hr; departures at half-past each hour); Amman (Jordan; 2 daily; 3hr); Beirut (Lebanon; departures at half-past each hour; 3hr).

Harasta Terminal to:

Istanbul (Turkey; 30hr).

CHAPTER TWO

THE HAURAN AND THE GOLAN HEIGHTS

The roads running south from Damascus pass at first through fertile agricultural country, across plains of wheat where nothing interrupts the flat horizon apart from huge grain silos. A speciality of the region is watermelon, sold along the roadside off wooden tables groaning with the weight of the huge fruits. Gradually, however, the countryside becomes desolate and barren, as fruit farms and fertile cropfields give way to some of the starkest and emptiest desert in Syria.

This is the **Hauran**, an area of rough steppe and grassland interspersed with strange volcanic basalt formations which stretches across the border into Jordan. It was from these black rocks that the Romans built their desert garrison and trading settlement at **Bosra** which, with its well-preserved streets and magnificent theatre, is by far the most important attraction of the region. With fast, easy bus connections linking Bosra to Damascus, it's quite possible to see nowhere else in the Hauran and still come away satisfied. However, the other, less accessible sights in the region are attractive for their very remoteness, and justify a longer stay. On the way to **Dera** – one of two places where it's possible to cross the Jordanian border – is a Byzantine church at **Ezra**, the supposed burial place of St George. **Sweida**, northeast of Bosra and rather cut off from the rest of the Hauran, has an outstanding **archeological museum** and some interesting Roman ruins to visit nearby at **Qanawat** and **Shahba**.

Through peaceful occupation by the Greeks, Nabateans, Romans, Byzantines and Arabs, the Hauran has had a largely quiet existence, shepherds, traders and cultivators forming the backbone of traditional life here. The major interruption to this peace came with the **Battle of Yarmouk River**, fought in 636 AD near Dera, which marked the end of Byzantine rule in Syria and the introduction of

---

ACCOMMODATION PRICE CODES

In this book, all hotels have been categorized according to the **price codes** outlined below, representing the minimum you can expect to pay for a **double room** in each hotel. Hotels in the ⑤–⑧ bands require payment in dollars. For further details, see p.35.

① under S£300/US$7	⑤ US$35–50/S£1500–2100
② S£300–600/US$7–14	⑥ US$50–90/S£2100–3900
③ S£600–1000/US$14–23	⑦ US$90–130/S£3900–5600
④ S£1000–1500/US$23–35	⑧ US$130/over S£5600

Islam to the country by the new Arab rulers who invaded from the south. Since then, nothing of any great historical note has occurred in the Hauran, unlike on the **Golan Heights**, the mountainous area southwest of Damascus which has been the focus of fierce dispute for over thirty years. In the demilitarized zone here, it's possible to make an unusual and unforgettable visit to the ghost town of **Quneitra**, razed by Israeli soldiers in 1973.

Syria's **Druze** community (see Contexts, p.315) is estimated to number something over a hundred thousand today, concentrated mainly in the Hauran and the Golan. Easily recognizable by their black clothes and white headscarves (the moustaches the older men often sport are emphatic, even by Syrian standards), the religious elite of the Druze add a distinctive visual presence to the landscape of these parts.

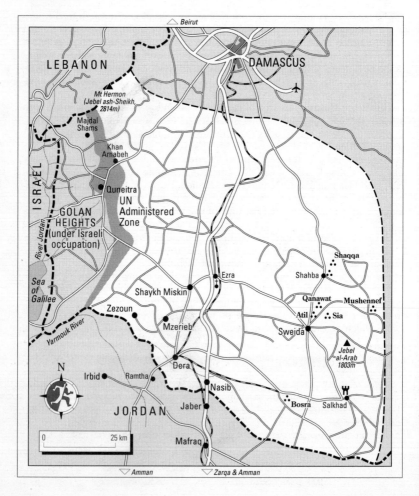

There are two road **border crossings** between Syria and Jordan: at **Nasib/Jaber** on the Damascus–Amman highway (used by buses travelling between the two capitals), and at **Dera/Ramtha** (service taxis run frequently between the bus stations in the two towns; S£170).Unfortunately you can't pick up any Damascus–Amman buses in Dera, but once you get to Ramtha you can get a bus to Irbid or Mafraq, from where travelling on to Amman is straightforward. One **train** a week (on Sun) stops in Dera on its way from Damascus to Amman, a service recommended only for people with plenty of time on their hands.

A single-entry **visa** for Jordan is available on the spot at the border to citizens of the EU, US, Canada or Australia; it costs anything between JD15 and 40, depending on your nationality. Citizens of other countries, those who want multiple-entry visas or those who just want to be on the safe side can apply for a visa in advance at the Jordanian embassy in Damascus (see p.110). Visas purchased in advance are usually slightly more expensive than those bought at the border, but you may feel that the extra is worth it for the added peace of mind (and reduced hassle).

Bosra

Although its magnificent Roman theatre is statistically the country's number-one tourist attraction, **BOSRA** tends to be written off as Palmyra's poor relation by many visitors to Syria. This is a pity, for though it lacks the grandeur and epic desert setting of Palmyra, Bosra can boast not only impressive Nabatean and Roman remains but also some of the oldest and most important Christian and Muslim monuments in Syria. The local black **basalt** out of which the town is built gives it a strangely sooty complexion, and the density of the stone has allowed it to last astonishingly well: the old Roman bath complex still boasts its roof, shops on the main thoroughfare are still capable of being used today, and the first jolting sight of the huge theatre, brilliantly preserved within an Ayyubid fortification, is simply one of the most memorable in Syria.

Like many of the ruined towns of the Hauran, Bosra is also remarkable in that it is still inhabited today, many of its shapeless modern dwellings made from the ruins of Roman ones. As you take a stroll down the decumanus maximus you may encounter gaggles of children on their way home from school or eager young antique-sellers ready to invite you for a cup of tea in their premises off the ancient street. The only part of Bosra which you have to pay to enter is the citadel and theatre complex, though to gain entry to the old mosques, which are usually kept locked, you will have to pay some *baksheesh* to the custodian; there are always some children around to help you find him in exchange for some more *baksheesh*.

Some history

Bosra's grid pattern of streets is thought to have been laid out in Hellenistic times, though the irregular layout of the eastern half of the city suggests it may have assimilated an earlier settlement. What is clear, however, is that the town remained unimportant until the first century BC, when King Aretas III incorporated it into the **Nabatean** kingdom. Thereafter the town prospered, and in 70 AD the Nabateans transferred their capital from Petra to Bosra because of the latter's

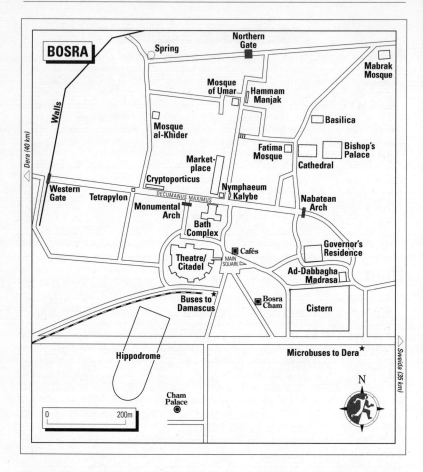

greater commercial potential. After the Nabatean kingdom was conquered by the **Romans** in 106, Bosra was made capital of the province of Arabia, and the area around Bosra became a major centre for the production of corn. The town benefited greatly from the trade of the **Via Trajana**, the Roman road that linked Damascus to Aqaba, and was ambitiously expanded during the late second century; its wealth was such that it even began minting its own coinage during the reign of the emperor Philip the Arab (see p.139).

During the Christian era Bosra became the seat of an archbishopric, entailing the construction of a major cathedral in the sixth century. According to Islamic tradition, Mohammed stopped off in Bosra as he travelled with a caravan to Syria at the age of around ten, and it was on this occasion that he was first revealed to be a prophet (by a Christian priest, Bahira). In 632 AD Bosra became the first Byzantine city to fall during the opening phase of the Arab expansion – a number of early mosques were built here, and Bahira's house became a revered Muslim site. The town remained important both for caravan traffic and as a stopping point on the pilgrimage to Mecca, but its fortunes slowly declined as the region became increasingly politically unstable. During the long Crusader struggles Bosra was attacked at least twice by the Franks, and in 1260 it was devastated by a Mongol invading force before once again suffering great damage during the disputes between Cairo and Damascus in the fourteenth century. The caravan routes were subsequently moved west, through Dera, where things were safer; by the mid-nineteenth century Bosra had only a token population, allowing the resettlement here of a large number of **Druze** in the aftermath of their bloody disputes with the Maronites in Lebanon (see p.304).

The citadel and theatre

Bosra's **citadel and theatre complex** (daily: summer 9am–6pm; winter 9am–4pm; S£400), the centrepiece and highlight of the ancient site, combines one of the most remarkably preserved theatres in the Roman world with one of the finest examples of Arab military architecture in Syria. The complex has an imposingly formidable look, having been constructed with defence rather than grace in mind, but is no less impressive because of this. For most of the year the complex and main square (linked to the citadel by a bridge over the ditch which surrounds the whole structure) are crowded with busloads of tourists and visiting parties of schoolchildren, but during the heat of July and August you pretty much have the place to yourself.

Dated on stylistic grounds to the late second century AD, the theatre was first fortified by the Umayyads in the latter part of the eighth century, though by far the greater part of the work was done by the Ayyubids in response to the Crusader threat of the early thirteenth century. The semicircular fortification which encases the entire theatre boasts two large towers at its northwestern and northeastern corners, and five smaller towers along the curve. A number of Arab buildings, among them a palace and mosque, were built within the citadel (indeed the Swiss adventurer Burckhardt, passing this way in 1810, didn't even realize there was a theatre inside), though these were removed during the **reconstruction** programme which took place between 1947 and 1970.

Access to the theatre is gained through a maze of dimly lit **passages** and stairways; the sudden contrast between the claustrophobic corridors and the huge space that the theatre occupies can initially be quite disorienting. The stage, backed by a long gallery, is 100m wide, and there are some 37 tiers of seats in all, making this one of the largest theatres in the Roman world, with capacity for an estimated fifteen thousand spectactors. The earth and sand that had filled most of the lower part of the theatre had done a remarkable job in preservation, so most of the reconstruction effort was directed at the stage area (the pristine columns being very obvious recent additions) and the upper rows of seats. Fittingly, the acoustics are excellent: anything you say as you wander about the stage can be heard right up to the topmost tier.

The upper ramparts of the Ayyubid fortifications house an unexciting **folklore museum** and a café, while on the terrace are a collection of Roman carved remains whose lack of finesse only makes clear the difficulty of carving in the dense local basalt. From the ramparts the outline of a **hippodrome**, thought to have had a seating capacity in the region of thirty thousand, is visible in the fields by the *Cham Palace Hotel*; this spot is where chariot races would once have taken place.

Along the decumanus maximus to the western gate

The substantial remains of the Roman **bath complex** lie on the north side of the citadel. This would have been one of the city's main social institutions, with citizens normally coming here to wash at least once a day – the facilities were free to all. Presently the building is undergoing extensive restoration by the French Archeological Institute in an effort to preserve its crumbling mortar roof; look beneath your feet and you'll see patches of the original mosaic floor which lies unexcavated beneath a thin layer of soil. The baths' northern entrance faces the main east–west axis of the town, the **decumanus maximus**, once resplendent with colonnades and recently excavated down to its Roman level; most of the columns have been recycled into other buildings over the centuries but some of the bases still remain. It's likely that most of Bosra's roads would have featured such colonnades, used to shade the pavement and their shoppers – it's still possible to do some shopping here as several enterprising young businessmen have taken over premises along the eastern stretch of the track in order to sell souvenirs.

Across the decumanus maximus from the baths is the Roman **marketplace**, the four tall columns at its southeast corner signifying the remains of a **nymphaeum** or public water fountain, built some time in the second century. On the opposite side of the north–south street from this are the fragmentary remains of a **kalybe**, a pagan open-air shrine in which statuary would have been displayed; one striking column remains but most of the stonework has been rearranged over the centuries. Walking westwards down the decumanus maximus brings you to the substantial **monumental arch** built in the early third century in honour of the Third Cyrenaica Legion, the Arabian province's principal military force, which had been garrisoned in Bosra since 123 AD. Though partially reconstructed in Arab times, its design is typically Roman, comprising a high central arch with a smaller one on each side.

On the north side of the road some 50m west of the arch is a large, cool underground warehouse, called a **cryptoporticus**, used to store products before their export and only rediscovered in 1968; the horizontal slits in the south wall were designed to admit light and air. The entrance is at its western end but unfortunately the locals tend to use the place as a huge rubbish bin, so it's not always pleasant to look inside. At the major cross street by the entrance once stood a tetrapylon, though today only traces of the outer ring of columns and the bases of a couple of pillar stumps can be made out. About 200m on is the well-preserved **western gate**, a fine monument that would once have been adorned with statuary; the Roman road underneath still provides excellent service today. The **walls** stretching either side are not in such a good state of preservation though, much of the stonework having been used in the fortification of the theatre, with only the blocks that were too immense to be carted off remaining.

North of the decumanus maximus

Back at the cryptoporticus, the road leading north runs past the tiny twelfth-century **Mosque al-Khider**, built near the spring that supplied the town with fresh water and partially constructed from recycled Classical remains. From here you can head east to the **Mosque of Umar**, built on the site of a pagan temple and dated by inscription to 720/1, making it the third oldest surviving mosque in the world. Despite some reconstruction in the twelfth and thirteenth centuries, the mosque has survived without extensive remodelling and so is of exceptional

Herbs and spices in the Damascus souks

Prayer mats in the courtyard of the Umayyad Mosque, Damascus

Colonnade in the Roman city of Shahba

Umayyad Mosque, Damascus

Café storyteller, Damascus

The cardo maximus at Apamea

The Roman theatre at Bosra

Norias (medieval waterwheels) on the Orontes at Hama

The Crac des Chevaliers

Blue Beach near Latakia

Fishing boats on the island of Arwad

Smoking a water pipe on a wall at Arwad

The narrow-gauge train along the Barada Valley

historical value; indeed it is one of only three surviving mosques which retain the form of Islam's earliest mosques. (Based on the plan of Mohammed's house in Medina, these were basically square-shaped enclosures which had covered arcades running around each side, thus creating a courtyard, in the middle of which was a fountain; one of the arcades would be twice as deep as the other three and this functioned as the prayer hall.) Most of the materials used in the building of the Mosque of Umar were recycled from antiquity – possibly from the pagan temple – and a number of Greek and Latin inscriptions have been found on the columns which hold up the basalt-tiled roof. Though heavily rebuilt during the thirteenth century, the mosque's square minaret is contemporary with the rest of the structure; this form of minaret originated in Syria and was probably inspired by the local square towers which functioned as hermits' cells.

Beyond the Mosque of Umar is a recently restored Mameluke bath complex, the **Hammam Manjak**, late fourteenth-century in origin and thus one of the last major buildings to go up before the town's fortunes dramatically waned. The building is usually shut unless there's a tour group being shown around, but you can walk round to the back of the complex for a view over the bath chambers, set behind a reception area that would have sported an expansive dome. About 100m east of the bath complex is a third-century Roman **basilica**, a well-preserved rectangular building converted for Christian worship in the fourth century, and said to be the place where Bahira met the prophet Mohammed (an alternative tale says the site is where the young Mohammed rested before he first entered Bosra). Some 250m along the surfaced road heading northeast from here is the recently restored twelfth-century **Mabrak Mosque**, supposedly marking the spot where the camel carrying the first copy of the Koran to Syria knelt to rest; a stone which apparently bears the imprint of its kneecaps can be seen in the mosque's westernmost section. In the easternmost section of the building is a madrasa, established in the twelfth century, which is notable for its unusual cruciform plan.

South of the basilica are the remains of an early sixth-century **cathedral**. This is an important building in the history of Christian architecture, as it was one of the first churches to be constructed with a circular dome over a square base; the idea had been used in secular buildings before, but its translation to Christian usage was a southern Syrian idea. The emperor Justinian used it as a model for cathedrals in Constantinople and Ravenna which are still standing, and it's also a direct ancestor of the Dome of the Rock in Jerusalem, built some two hundred years later. Behind the cathedral can be seen, meshed into some modern dwellings, the remains of a **bishop's palace**, while almost opposite is the simple **Fatima Mosque**, parts of which have been dated back to the eleventh century, though the minaret is fourteenth-century.

The eastern end of the decumanus maximus

South of the cathedral, at the eastern end of the decumanus maximus, is an early second-century **Nabatean arch**, thought to have formed the entrance to a palace. Just to the south are the remains of a large two-storeyed dwelling constructed around a courtyard, which may have been the Roman **governor's residence**. A little to the south again lies a huge **cistern** measuring some 120m by 150m by 4m deep, which is today a popular swimming hole with the local boys, despite its slimy-green complexion. The lack of major rivers or sufficient natural springs in the Hauran necessitated the use of open tanks like this as reservoirs, even up until the early part of the twentieth century: the British aristocratic traveller Gertrude Bell, passing this way in 1905, remarked that "the traveller may consider himself fortunate if he be not asked to drink a liquid in which he has seen the mules and camels wallowing". The cistern is on a hillock to allow the water to be easily channelled throughout the settlement, particularly to supply the baths and fountains. The original construction probably dates back to Nabatean times, with substantial further development undertaken by the Romans; the cistern is only half as deep as it once was, thanks to all the debris accumulated inside over the centuries. Its popular name today, the Al-Hajj cistern, attests to its importance for the pilgrim caravans. The **Ad-Dabbagha Madrasa**, a thirteenth-century construction restored in the 1980s, stands by the northeastern corner.

Practicalities

Given the lack of decent cheap accommodation in Bosra or nearby Dera, most budget travellers visit on a day-trip **from Damascus**. A direct luxury **bus** to Bosra, run by Challal Tours, departs from the microbus station in the Baramkeh Terminal (every 2hr; 1hr 30min; S£50); it stops on the main square by the citadel and theatre complex, with the last bus back at 8pm. Beware that this service seems prone to last-minute cancellation if demand is low, so ask about the times of the buses back while on the outward journey or at their Bosra office, which is situated a short distance down the street which runs westwards from the western gate. As an alternative, travelling between Bosra and Damascus **via Dera** (see p.132) is uncomplicated (total journey time 2hr 15min); until the late afternoon there are frequent microbuses from Bosra to Dera, which arrive at and depart from the south side of the huge cistern. There are no buses between Bosra and Sweida (see p.140); the thirty-minute taxi journey between the two is usually quoted at S£400, though skilled negotiators may be able to knock S£100 off that.

Bosra's **train station**, opposite the citadel, is only served by trains during Bosra's **festival**, every odd-numbered year, when a programme of concerts and drama is staged in the amphitheatre during the last two weeks of September; contact the tourist office in Damascus (Bosra doesn't have a tourist office) for programme information. The trains that run at this time connect Bosra with Dera and Damascus – for details, ask at Damascus's Hedjaz Station.

A couple of hundred metres south of the citadel is Bosra's one **hotel**, the *Cham Palace* (☎015/790 881, *www.chamhotels.com*; ⑦); among its luxuries are full air-conditioning, several bars and restaurants, and a swimming pool. The only alternative if you want to stay overnight is the **youth hostel** installed within one of the towers of the citadel; it offers clean if somewhat basic dormitory accommodation for S£200 per person. **Eating** possibilities include the overpriced **restaurant** within the citadel and a number of cheap fill-up places around the main square – or for those looking to splash the cash, a short walk away is the *Bosra Cham Palace* restaurant (oddly enough not installed inside the hotel).

The southwestern Hauran

A fast highway and breathtakingly slow train line head south of Damascus to Dera, 104km away, but only a detour to the Byzantine church at **Ezra**, reached after some 75km of monotonous travelling, might tempt you off the train or road. Indeed, there's really not much reason to stop in Dera, aside from using it as a base from which to tackle the border crossing to Jordan at Ramtha or to visit Bosra; your fellow travellers will mostly be frustrated truckies, whose vehicles line the sides of the road running up to the busy frontier post.

Ezra

A dusty, ugly place, overlooked by a huge grain silo that's visible for miles around, the small town of **EZRA** has one unusual sight, its extraordinary Byzantine **Church of St George**, the purported resting place of St George (*Mar Jorgis*), who is much venerated by all Middle Eastern Christians. Located 3km out in Ezra's northern suburbs (a taxi there and back from the crossroads in the town centre costs S£200, including a wait), the church is usually kept locked, but it won't be long before someone in this residential district alerts the keeper of the key, who lives nearby, to the fact that there are visitors.

THE LEGEND OF ST GEORGE

What little is known about **St George**, the man who became the patron saint of England – a place of which he had probably never heard – is submerged in myth and legend. George was probably a soldier; he was martyred at Diospolis (now Lod in central Israel) in around 303 AD, during the persecutions of the early Christians in Palestine instigated by the Roman emperor Diocletian. In the centuries following his death a cult surrounding him grew up and became widespread in Palestine and Syria, and later in Europe. Stories of his deeds were around in England since at least the early eighth century, when he was mentioned in the writings of the Venerable Bede, the first English historian. In 1098 he was said to have been seen aiding the Crusaders at the Battle of Antioch, with the result that many of the soldiers returning to Europe further popularized his cult. Richard I placed himself and his crusading army under the protection of the saint in 1191, and two centuries later – at least according to the histories on which Shakespeare drew – Henry V, speaking to his soldiers at the Battle of Agincourt, again invoked George as the patron of the English army.

In the fifteenth century the most famous myth surrounding St George was translated and published for the first time by the English printer William Caxton, in the *Golden Legend*. The story centred around a fire-breathing **dragon**, whom the terrified citizens of a country tried to appease by offering the king's daughter as a sacrifice. George intervened and fought the dragon, reducing the beast to tame captivity, and told the relieved citizens that if they accepted Christianity he would rid them of the monster. The king and people agreed, whereupon George baptized fifteen thousand men and then killed the dragon. He accepted no reward but asked the king to maintain churches in his country, and to show compassion to the poor.

George did not become **patron saint of England** until Edward III (1327–77) made him the patron of the newly founded Order of the Garter; in 1348 Pope Benedict XIV ratified him as Protector of the Kingdom of England. Yet George was a much-venerated figure all over medieval Europe, and today there are still churches dedicated to him in Venice, Rome, Verona and Istanbul; many other churches and cathedrals include a portrayal of his story in stained glass or on murals. After the Reformation his popularity declined in continental Europe but remained solid in England. Indeed, a much later legend records that he once visited England, coming from the west through that part of the Irish Sea now known as St George's Channel – a set of events which is about as likely as him taming the dragon.

The building is one of the oldest churches in Syria, its survival accountable to the fact that it was solidly fortified to protect the town's minority Christians in times of religious persecution. Its intimate scale, the ancient and claustrophobically dark interior, and its slightly incongrous setting on the edge of town where modern dwellings give way to wheat fields, all add to its appeal. Over the middle portal of the western entrance, the inscription which dates the church to 515 AD remarks that in the place "where once idols were sacrificed . . . there are now choirs of angels". Though the dome is modern, the rest of the church has remained largely unaltered since Byzantine times. The interior arches, the unusual shape – an octagonal arrangement of internal columns and arches which sit within solidly square outer walls – and the dark stone give the place an intimate, sombre feel. In a side chapel, the supposed **tomb** of St George, decorated with venerable pictures of his supposed visage, is well looked after by the Greek Orthodox community which worships here. Despite its remote location, the church is visited by a fair number of the pious and the curious, most of whom diligently record their names in an absorbingly polyglot visitors' book.

Close by are two more churches which are worth a brief look. Just next door is the ruined **Church of St John** (whom locals know as Mar Yuhanna), of which the most discernible part is a set of arcaded columns fashioned, characteristically, from the black basalt of the region (see p.137). From here, and with St George's behind you, turn left (along the road running parallel with the arcaded columns), then take the first right and then first left to reach the **Church of St Elias** (*Mar Elias*), which is an enticing mix of ancient and modern styles. Above one of its portals, ancient Christian inscriptions point to the church's foundation in the sixth century, but if one of the Greek Catholic priests opens up the building you can see the twentieth-century dome, its coloured glass windows throwing bold pools of light onto the walls and floor of the airy nave. The church follows an unusual architectural style for this part of Syria, that of an east-west-oriented cruciform plan rather than the dome-over-square structure which can be seen in St George's Church and in the cathedral at Bosra.

Practicalities

If you're **driving**, simply leave the main Damascus–Amman highway at the junction for Ezra, and you'll find yourself in the town almost immediately. Frequent **microbuses** make the hour-long journey to Ezra from the southern bus station in Damascus. Microbuses also connect Ezra with Sweida (30min) and Dera (change at Shaykh Miskin, total journey time 45min). **Trains** from Damascus to Dera pass through Ezra, but with only two services a week they're not much of an alternative.

Buses and microbuses stop at the crossroads in the centre of town. Some fairly ordinary places to **eat** can be found around the centre, though there's nowhere to stay in the town.

Dera

DERA is an important border town, and the most obvious place to stop off if you're travelling between Damascus and Amman, but although it's a lively place, with a history of settlement which stretches back over two thousand years, there's little of specific interest here. The town's attractions – such as they are – include a fairly unremarkable thirteenth-century Ayyubid **mosque**, parts of which were built with stones plundered from the Roman **theatre** which lies

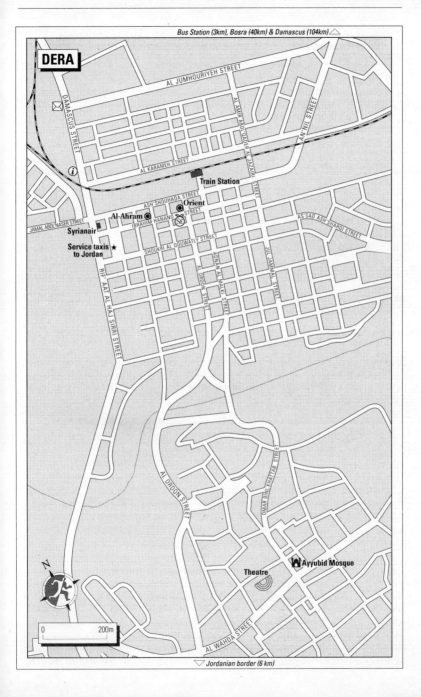

DERA

Bus Station (3km), Bosra (40km) & Damascus (104km) △

AL JUMHOURIYEH STREET

DAMASCUS STREET

AL AMIR ABD QADER AL JAZAIRI STREET

AN' NIL STREET

AL KARAMEH STREET

Train Station

ASH SHOUHADA STREET

Orient

JAMAL ABDUL NASER STREET

Al-Ahram

BRAHIM HANANO STREET

AS'SAD ASH SHARQI STREET

Syrianair

Service taxis
to Jordan

SHOUKRI AL QOUWATLY STREET

ADNAN AL MALKI STREET

JUL JAMMAL STREET

RIF' AAT AL HAJ SIRRI STREET

AL ORDON STREET

AL ORDON STREET

OMAR BIN KHATTAB STREET

Ayyubid Mosque

Theatre

N

0 200m

AL WAHDA STREET

▽ Jordanian border (6 km)

LAWRENCE OF ARABIA AND THE "DERA INCIDENT"

T.E. Lawrence served out World War I as an adviser to Emir Feisal, the ruler of Mecca, guiding the Arab forces in their disruptive guerrilla tactics against the Turks. The rail terminus of **Dera** was a prime target for such activities, standing as it did between Damascus (and therefore Constantinople), and Amman (and thus Jerusalem and Medina). Accordingly, in November 1917 Lawrence went on a dangerous reconnaissance mission to Dera to determine with what ease the town itself might be taken. According to his *Seven Pillars of Wisdom*, Lawrence was wandering through the streets when he was apprehended by a Turkish officer and taken to see the governor of the town. After successfully repelling the governor's sexual advances, Lawrence was severely beaten and then flogged; when subsequently left alone in a room, he managed to escape through a window.

However, Richard Meinertzhagen, a friend and fellow intelligence officer, insisted that Lawrence confided in him that he had been stripped and bound and sodomized by the governor and his servants, but had chosen not to reveal this in his book because it was too "degrading". Recently reissued, Lawrence's 1922 private publication of *Seven Pillars*, nearly a third as long again as the finished version of 1926, refers to what took place "that night in Dera" as "defilement"; this version of events is corroborated by a letter written by Lawrence in 1924 to George Bernard Shaw's wife, Charlotte: "About that night. I shouldn't tell you, because decent men don't talk about such things . . . I gave away the only possession we are born into the world with – our bodily integrity."

On a political note, the 1922 manuscript emphasizes the duality of Lawrence's position – helping the Arabs overthrow Turkish domination but knowing as a British agent that it was destined to be replaced with rule by the Allied powers. It was a position that confirmed Lawrence as an outsider on both sides. When the British army's advance into Syria began in September 1918, Lawrence was given the task of helping destroy the lines into the Dera terminus to prevent the arrival of Turkish reinforcements. This he successfully completed and the Turks fled from the town, making its capture a formality. The British army then proceeded on to Damascus alongside the Arabs and an Australian force, and Lawrence's role was at an end. At the subsequent peace conferences the English promises to the Arabs concerning the creation of an independent Arab state were duly revealed to be empty, and the mandates (see p.304) were imposed.

across the road. Although it's possible to pick out parts of the stage and seating of the theatre, a lot of the site is indistinguishable rubble, and Bosra it most definitely isn't. To get to these places, which lie 2km south of the centre, head south on the Jordan highway, then take the road veering off it to the left before the river, following this up the hill and beyond until the mosque appears on your left. Probably a better bet for wasting some time, however, is a wander around the town's central **railway station** for a look at the vintage steam trains and Ottoman carriages which stand marooned on discarded lines. If you've got an afternoon to kill, and you've already visited Bosra and Ezra, you could head off for the scenic **Yarmouk Gorge** (see opposite) which lies to the west of the town, and makes an ideal brief excursion.

Practicalities

Dera is something of a transport hub for this part of Syria, with frequent **microbus** connections from Bosra (45min) and Damascus (1hr 30min). **Karnak** operates one service a day between Damascus and Dera (1hr 30min), and numerous **Pullman** buses also ply the route; unfortunately no buses connect Dera with Sweida (see p.140), which is more conveniently approached from Damascus. The **bus station** is 3km from the town centre; taxis tend to accumulate outside the station or else you can simply hop onto one of the local microbuses on their way into town. There's a twice-weekly **train** service on the narrow-gauge line from the Hedjaz Station in Damascus (4hr); the **station** in Dera is centrally located one block north of the main street.

By far the best **hotel** in town is the dollar-priced *Orient* (☎015/240 971; ④) – also known as the *Al-Chark* – on Ibrahim Hanano Street in the centre of town. It offers spotless rooms with TVs that pick up an entertaining blend of Syrian, Jordanian and Israeli transmissions; the hotel's **restaurant** is the best bet for a sit-down meal here, though a number of falafel joints can be found on Ibrahim Hanano Street. Also on this street is the *Al-Ahram* (☎015/230 809; ③), which offers a number of rooms of varying quality; check what you're getting before you book in, as the crusty linen in some of the rooms looks decidedly unenticing.

West of Dera: the Yarmouk Gorge

The area west of Dera consists of unremarkable irrigated wheatfields and undulating scrub. Cutting a swath through the otherwise flat countryside is the Yarmouk River, whose spectacular **gorge**, located around 20km northwest of Dera, is worth a visit if you have a vehicle and a free afternoon (microbus connections here are unfortunately very poor). Along the road from Dera towards the village of **Zezoun**, the first indication of nearby attractive scenery is a sign pointing to the **Tal Shahib Falls**, which are unfortunately only active following

---

THE BATTLE OF YARMOUK RIVER

The **Battle of Yarmouk River** signalled the end of over six hundred years of Roman/Byzantine rule in the Middle East, and as such is one of the most important events in Syrian, and indeed Arab, history. The beginnings of the Arab triumph go back to 629 when a band of three thousand raided the town of Mutah at the southern end of the Dead Sea. In 630 Mohammed personally led a successful expedition of thirty thousand men to the nearby oasis of Tabuk, with subsequent negotiations seeing the capitulation of a number of towns stretching into southern Syria. After Mohammed's death, the Arabs under the first Caliph, Abu Bakr, undertook a full-scale invasion of Syria which culminated in 636 at Yarmouk River. The Byzantine forces were manoeuvred into a tight position between the Yarmouk and its tributary the Ruqqad and, with the Ruqqad bridge controlled by the Arabs, the Byzantine eastern line of communication was cut and victory sealed. Most of the defeated army was slaughtered, the emperor Heraclius declaring, "Farewell, O Syria, and what an excellent country this is for the enemy."

It's not clear exactly why Mohammed decided to extend his influence into Syria (there was certainly no overwhelming missionary zeal behind the expansion), though it's probable that he would have viewed the people of Syria and Palestine as natural brothers to the inhabitants of the Arabian peninsula – they were, after all, from the same Semitic stock, and certainly held little loyalty to the emperor in Constantinople. The campaign would prove to be the spark for a remarkable story of conquest which led the Arabs all the way along North Africa, up into Spain and by 732 to the banks of the Loire.

periods of rain. Although the gorge is fairly deep at this point it's better to press on to the village itself, at whose northwestern end, straight across from the roundabout, is a restaurant overlooking the most dramatic and accessible part of the gorge. The views are undeniably splendid; the steep walls of the gorge, dusty and barely vegetated, are blinding to look at in the glare of the sun, and the often fierce desert wind adds to the sense of desolation. The railway tracks that can be seen here form a stretch of the old branch of the Hedjaz line between Dera and Haifa (in what's now northern Israel). At the bottom of the gorge, the Yarmouk has been reduced to little more than a trickle by the extraction of water along its length for irrigation and domestic use.

Reached by a turning off the Dera–Zezoun road, the small **boating lake** at **Mzerieb** is an unusual feature in an area otherwise starved of water. Many of the pedaloes and rowing boats here have awnings as protection from the sun, but the strong Hauran winds which often ripple the surface of the lake mean that if you take one out, you might have to battle hard to avoid going in one direction only. The shores of the lake are lined with **cafés** blaring out pop music, popular with families on a day out.

The southeastern Hauran

In the southeast of the Hauran are a clutch of interesting ancient sites, grouped around the largest town, **Sweida**. The Roman remains at **Shahba** (which could be visited en route to Sweida from Damascus) and **Qanawat** are the most obvious draws, but all of the sites here are much less frequented than Bosra or even Ezra, and Sweida itself, despite its fine museum, doesn't give the impression of being used to seeing many tourists. However, for those with time on their hands who want to get off the beaten track, this is a good area to spend a couple of days exploring. Sweida is the only viable base in the region, though given the poor state of its accommodation, and the lack of public transport from Bosra, it may well be worth considering tackling this part of the Hauran from Damascus; a trip to Shahba, then Qanawat via Sweida – taking in the Sweida museum on the way back – is perfectly feasible in one long day.

Shahba and around

Thought to be the only town in Syria the Romans built from scratch, **SHAHBA**, 20km north of Sweida, is one of the most important architectural legacies of their rule in the East. Designed in a rough square on a rigid grid plan, it was founded by the emperor **Philip the Arab** in 244 (see p.139), who subsequently raised its status to that of a colony and named it Philippopolis. At his death in 249, however, the vast building plans had not been completed, and the town had only a token population. Only during the nineteenth century was the town substantially repopulated with Druze from Lebanon; today Shahba retains a remarkable proportion of the original Roman walls, roads and public buildings.

Most of what remains of the ancient settlement is to be found a little way west of the present-day roundabout and transport hub at the centre of the town, which was the intersection of the two main Roman arteries. The street leading west from the roundabout still retains its Roman basalt paving stones; about 50m along is a flight of steps leading up to four tall **columns** which once formed the portico of a

VOLCANIC HAURAN

Much of western Syria bears the scars of tectonic activity; plate movements deep within the earth have caused volcanoes and earthquakes to occur periodically over comparatively recent geological times. The **Hauran**, and the desert to the north as far as Palmyra, is pitted with **volcanic cones**, distinctive landforms whose defensive potential has been recognized throughout the ages; the Arab castle at Palmyra, and Qalaat Shmaimis in the desert east of Hama, are both built on top of former volcanoes which have risen above the flat plains surrounding them. But volcanic activity further south has been much more dramatic: rising to a height of 1800m, the volcanic massif of the **Jebel al-Arab** (or Jebel Druze), located east of Sweida, is a giant compared to other volcanoes in the country, and moreover was responsible for spilling runny lava for hundreds of kilometres in all directions, over the course of successive eruptions. Although Jebel al-Arab (like all volcanoes in Syria) has been inactive for millions of years, it has left the landscape of the Hauran with an indelible characteristic: the lava which it spilled has solidified to black, sometimes glassy **basalt** rock, which forms the single most distinguishable aspect of the scenery over hundreds of square kilometres of desert and scrub. These flat, stark and inhospitable plains stretch into Jordan where yet more archeological sites exist, all built from the dark stone.

Around Dera and Ezra the basalt tends to be obscured by scrubby vegetation or wheatfields, although here and there stubborn extrusions of rock rise above the landscape in sometimes weird geological formations. Further east, particularly around Shahba, the landscape becomes more distinctively volcanic. The thirteenth-century castle at **Salkhad** is built on one of the numerous volcanic cones of the Jebel al-Arab, and around Shahba itself the rock has been quarried for more than two thousand years. The Romans used the basalt rock in their construction of Shahba and, most strikingly of all, Bosra, but you can see it in many other less well-known structures too, such as the Roman theatre at Dera or the ruined fifth-century basilica at Ezra. The rock can also be seen in many other parts of Syria, where it forms the dark bands of the alternating white and black patterns of tiles or bricks known as **ablaq**, which became widely used in the thirteenth century and is a distinctive aspect of Mameluke architecture.

temple, but which now form the rather impressive entrance to somebody's house. Continuing west from here, you'll find yourself in the **forum**, its dusty, littered basalt paving reminiscent of a school playground; at its far end is a **kalybe**, a shrine that would probably have displayed statues of Philip the Arab's ancestors, some of whom he proclaimed gods.

Behind and to the north of the kalybe stand the confused remains of a **palace**, though the modern dwellings that have been incorporated into it make exploration difficult. On the forum's south side is a minimally decorated, well-preserved **temple**, thought to have been erected in honour of Philip's father, an Arab chief; in the early years of the twentieth century this building housed the local school. A nine-rowed (partially restored) **theatre** stands just beyond this; again decoration is minimal, probably because of the difficulty of carving into the dense local basalt.

Back at the roundabout, the substantial, slightly daunting remains of the **Roman baths** lie off the east–west road a couple of minutes' walk south. Built on an imperial scale, and far larger than a town of Shahba's size could ever justify, the baths were never completed. Across the road from the baths is a **museum** (daily except Tues: summer 9am–6pm; winter 9am–4pm; S£250) containing some early fourth-century **mosaics**, helpfully labelled in English, which were found in a private house on this spot (the museum was built over them). One in particular stands out, a poignant portrayal of Orpheus entrancing a group of animals with his lyre.

Practicalities

Situated on the main road that links the two, Shahba is easily accessible from Sweida (20min) and Damascus (southern bus station; 1hr); microbuses to and from either are frequent until late afternoon. Buses running between Damascus and Sweida sometimes use Shahba's ring road and so bypass the town (you can ask to be let off to walk the last 1km). Being a small town, Shahba takes no more than a couple of hours to explore; afterwards it's quite possible to head down to Sweida (and even visit the ruins of Qanawat, with an early start) on a day-trip from Damascus, which is certainly worth considering as there are no hotels in Shahba and the accommodation situation in Sweida is dire. Shahba has no sit-down restaurants but a number of falafel stalls line the main street.

Shaqqa and Mushennef

Frequent microbuses ply the route between Shahba and **SHAQQA**, an eight-kilometre journey that takes only ten minutes and costs a mere S£5. Though you

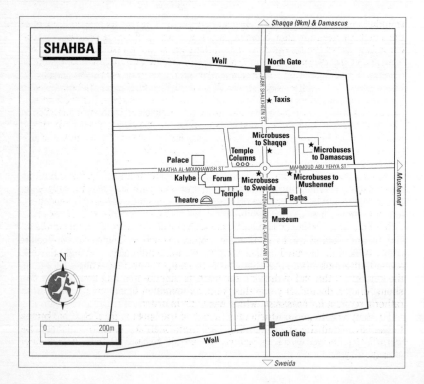

PHILIP THE ARAB

Marcus Julius Philippus, better known as Philip the Arab, was born the son of a local chieftain in the Roman province of Arabia around 204AD. He first came to prominence as praetorian prefect in the army of the emperor Gordian III who was killed in 244 – some say by Philip's connivance – while fighting the Persians. Philip was declared the new emperor by the local Roman legions and proceeded to conclude a quick peace with the Persians in order to cement his position back in Rome. He spent most of the next two years attempting to re-establish Roman control over the Danube regions, before returning to Rome in 248 to preside over the spectacular celebrations that marked the one-thousandth anniversary of the founding of the city. In an attempt to establish a dynasty Philip then deified his father and declared his young son joint ruler in Rome. However, that same year a rebellion broke out amongst the Danube legions; Philip sent his trusted ally Trajan Decius to quell the revolt – which he did so impressively that the following year the legions declared him to be their new emperor. Philip immediately set off to meet Trajan in battle near Verona and was killed, along with his son, in the fighting. During the fourth century Philip was declared by some Christian writers, including St Jerome, to have been Rome's first Christian emperor, but though he ended the persecution of Christians in Rome, there is no evidence to suggest he ever adopted the religion.

wouldn't guess it today, Shaqqa was at one time the most important settlement of the northern Hauran after Shahba, and was even declared a bishopric in the Christian era. At the far eastern edge of the village, just up from the bus shelter, is a very well-preserved **palace**, featuring a grand doorway topped by a semicircular arch and flanked on either side by two smaller entrances; this was probably the residence of the Roman governor. Unusually for the Hauran, nobody lives in it so it's worth pushing the door open for a look inside the main hall; note in particular the ingeniously designed ceiling, formed completely from short stubby blocks of basalt – the Hauran is notoriously short of wood and so the whole of the building had to be made from basalt stone. Visible from the entrance to the palace is a stocky, square tower, around 300m away, which forms part of a sixth-century monastery (this one does have someone living in it).

Twenty-five kilometres to the southeast of Shahba, in the middle of the reclusive village of **MUSHENNEF**, lies a second-century Roman **temple**, located on the edge of a small artificial lake where the winter rains would have been collected, and now incorporated into an amalgam of modern dwellings. Indeed the front of the temple has been completely (and haphazardly) rebuilt, though the northern, western and southern walls are as original; some of the carving on them is remarkably well executed considering the unsuitability of the raw material. Ask around for a look inside the temple; a pugnacious old woman living nearby has the key, and at the end of the visit she tends to point to her chest, moan a lot and shout "doctor, doctor" at you – this is not an invitation to call an ambulance but rather a request for *baksheesh*, which would be in order.

The only way to get to Mushennef by public transport is from Shahba: **buses** there leave from the street running east from Shahba's main roundabout. Be warned that services back to Shahba are infrequent, and virtually non-existent after midday.

Sweida

The chief highlight of **SWEIDA**, 100km south of Damascus, is undoubtedly its **museum**, as most of the evidence of the town's long history was lost during the first decade of the twentieth century, when its ancient remains were used by Ottoman troops to build a barracks; the ruins of the temple, basilica and mosque described by Baedeker in 1876 have now all gone. Recently though, the Roman town gate on Hafez al-Assad Street has been reconstructed and the small Roman theatre (more properly an odeon, or concert hall) just beyond has also seen some belated attention. Indeed, this part of town has an odd feel to it, the main street (Hafez al-Assad St) having been extended, widened and lined with offices and shops. This triumph of modern-day Syrian town planning contrasts bizarrely with the haphazard ancient stonework and often starkly rural scenes that directly abut it.

The museum

Sweida's **museum** (daily except Tues: summer 9am–6pm; winter 9am–4pm; S£300) is an incongruously huge modern building on Qanawat Street, a kilome-

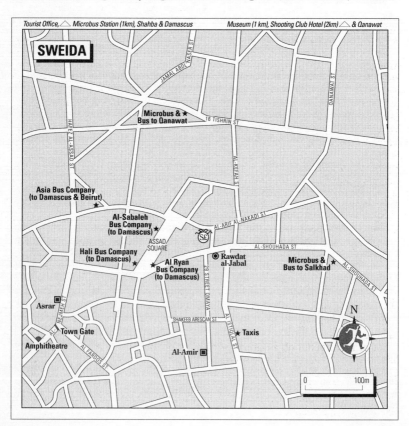

tre or so northeast of the centre. Opened in November 1991, under the auspices of the French Archeological Institute and partly funded by the French oil multi-national Total, it houses an impressive and well-laid-out collection, covering the history of the Hauran from the Stone Age to the early Arab occupation. The unusually excellent labelling is in French and Arabic, though the numerous examples of early weaponry, finely decorated ceramics and black basalt Roman statuary are entertaining even if you can't read either language.

Most interesting of all the museum's artefacts is the set of well-preserved **mosaics** from Shahba. The most famous – and one of the largest – is entitled *Artemis Is Surprised Whilst Bathing* and dates from the middle of the third century AD. Surrounded by magnificent garlands of fruit and foliage, the naked goddess Artemis, bejewelled and attended by four nymphs, is shown being surprised by the huntsman Actaeon, whose head emerges from the shrubbery in the top left-hand corner. The poignancy of the story lies in the fact that Artemis was obliged to turn Actaeon into a stag – which was then devoured by his own hounds – because the gods could not allow themselves to be seen without permission. On the first floor of the building is a decidedly less compelling folklore exhibition.

Practicalities

Staff at the **tourist office**, by the main bus station on Hafez al-Assad Street, are polite enough, but a map of almost stunning inaccuracy is all they have to offer. **Microbuses** from Damascus (south station) take just over ninety minutes to reach Sweida, pulling in at the bus station on Hafez al-Assad Street at the northern edge of town, as do microbuses from Shahba. Luxury bus companies, whose offices in Sweida are grouped around the main square (Hafez al-Assad Square), offer frequent and slightly quicker services from Damascus's Baramkeh Terminal into the evening. There are also microbus connections **from Ezra**, 44km to the northwest along a good road, useful for breaking your journey from Damascus to visit the Church of St George (see p.131). Reflecting the substantial Druze population of the town, there's a luxury-bus service **to Beirut** run by the Asia Company (who also do the Damascus run); their terminal is located on the street that leads off the northwestern corner of Hafez al-Assad Square. It's possible to use Sweida as a base from which to visit Bosra, 35km south; though there are no buses between the two, taxi drivers in the town are prepared to make the trip for around S£400.

Unfortunately, the choice of **accommodation** in Sweida is pretty rum. The town has just one hotel, the *Rawdat al-Jabal* (☎016/221 347; ①) on Al-Shouhada Street, an uncompromisingly spartan budget establishment which is permeated by some very odd smells. The only alternative is the *Shooting Club* (☎016/231 929; ④), 3km away along the road to Qanawat; staff here will be not so much pleased as astonished to see you, and for the price they charge it's easy to see why – the service is lousy, the rooms are dingy and the en-suite bathrooms indelibly stained.

You're much better off as far as **restaurants** go, the pick of the crop being the bright and clean *Al-Amir* which serves very tasty Arabic food at affordable prices. The service is exceptional for Syria – the waiters even refrain from smoking when serving – and the all-year Christmas decorations can only serve to heighten the cheer. A good alternative, serving regular chicken or kebab fare, is the *Asrar* on Hafez al-Assad Street.

Around Sweida

For dedicated **ruins** buffs the region around Sweida holds many fascinating treasures barely acknowledged, it seems, by the people who live among (and occasionally in) them, let alone by professional archeologists. Only the area of the Dead Cities around Aleppo (see p.239) can match this area in terms of the preservation of the ancient remains to be found here, but whereas the former are noted principally for their isolation, the villages and towns around Sweida are very much inhabited. The casual scenes of everyday existence in and among the ruins furnishe them with a unique charm; this is one place where Syria's archeological heritage really comes to life.

Atil

Two small, remarkably intact **Roman temples** can be found just 6km to the north of Sweida, by the main road in the small dusty village of **ATIL**. Any microbus between Sweida and Shahba will let you off at the north end of the settlement; from there head eastwards up the hill and ask around for the exact location of the temples – the local children will be more than happy to adopt you for an hour or so in return for some *baksheesh* (and will probably try to sell you some lumps of Classical masonry). The temples, about 200m apart, were both built to the same design in the mid-second century; the better-preserved of the two is free-standing while the other now forms part of someone's house – the owner doesn't mind a polite request to view the interior and may even offer you coffee and grapes.

Qanawat and Sia

Like many towns in the region, the modern settlement of **QANAWAT** has grown up within an ancient Roman one, providing a disorienting mesh of past and present. It's a fascinating place simply to wander around: ancient columns have been haphazardly incorporated into humble modern dwellings, noisy children play among jumbled ruins and goats shelter peacefully by stonework that has stood undisturbed for centuries. During the fourth century Qanawat became the seat of a bishopric, with an impressive **church complex** that is the main focus of interest for visitors today. After the town was taken by the Arabs in the seventh century, decline set in; by 1810 the Swiss explorer Burkhardt reported only two families living in this "ruined city", but in recent decades the town has been substantially repopulated by Druze.

The Qanawat **bus** leaves from 16 Tishrin Street in the centre of Sweida (every 30min; 15min; last bus back to Sweida at about 4pm), and will drop you off right outside the main church complex. The site's custodian is usually there from about 9am to late afternoon; ask at the café next door if nobody's around. Entry (S£150) to the site is via the western building, a second-century Roman **basilica** which, in the fourth or fifth century, was enterprisingly reoriented east–west from the original north–south in order to serve as a church; an altar was placed at the eastern end (of which nothing remains) and a wall constructed across the three semicircular niches that you see at the southern end. A few of the columns which would once have formed part of the portico of the original northern entrance to the building are still standing. Originally built as one, the atrium and southern building were bisected by a three-doorwayed wall in the fourth century, with the area to the south being converted into a second church. East–west orientation here was achieved by placing a raised semicircular platform against the eastern

wall, upon which would have stood a bishop's throne; today you will find a large stone bowl here, used for baptisms, while just over the wall at this point are several magnificently carved tombs made for the Byzantine clergy.

Taking the road that heads north from the complex brings you to a path which leads sharply down to the Wadi al-Ghar – fortunately the rubbish is piled so high that you can cross the stream without getting your feet wet (alternatively head down to the bridge). A short walk away are a dinky **theatre**, still in quite good condition, built into the hillside, and a curious, highly photogenic building (probably a temple) usually filled with water from the wadi. Just to the south of the complex lies a huge underground **cistern** whose roof slabs still remain, just beyond which are the ruins of a second-century **temple** dedicated to Zeus.

Qanawat has no hotels and no sit-down restaurants. Indeed the only place for a **snack** seems to be the fly-infested falafel joint next to the café by the entrance to the ruins; starvation may be a more attractive option.

SIA
According to the 1876 edition of *Baedeker's Guide to Syria and Palestine*, the **Nabatean temple complex** at **SIA** (a three-kilometre walk or hitch southeast from Qanawat – there are no buses here) was "one of the most interesting in

the Hauran, resembling in style the Herodian Temple at Jerusalem". Unfortunately this magnificently preserved edifice was almost completely dismantled (along with a similarly dated temple in Sweida) by Turkish soldiers during the first decade of the twentieth century, its masonry used to construct a barracks.

To reach Sia from Qanawat, follow the road (Roman in parts) that leads beyond the tower; the ruins are situated on a small, narrow hill, identifiable by the three buildings visible on the horizon from Qanawat. Two terraced courtyards once stood at Sia, each preceded by a gateway; today there's just a mess of rubble, with the original paving stones only exposed in the far left-hand corner of what would have been the innermost courtyard. Next to this are the foundations of a minor temple dedicated to Dushara (the Nabateans' sun god) and some steps which once would have led up to the Temple of Baal-Shamin, dating back to 37–32 BC, now surviving as bits of the "modern" farm building standing here.

Salkhad

The early thirteenth-century **castle** that tops the volcanic cone above the otherwise unremarkable town of **SALKHAD**, about 25km southeast of Sweida, was constructed by the Ayyubids to aid in the defence of Damascus while the Crusaders were occupying Jerusalem. From the centre of the town it's an obvious fifteen-minute walk up to the castle, but as it's situated in a military zone, be prepared to answer the calls of any uniformed personnel and to show your passport. No photographs are allowed here, but you are free to wander at will through the labyrinth of subterranean vaults, containing two huge cisterns that still hold vast quantities of water; a torch would be useful to appreciate their full dimensions.

Microbuses from Sweida leave every thirty minutes or so from Ash-Shouhada Street, dropping you off in Salkhad's main square after 45 minutes. There are no microbuses between Bosra and Salkhad, but taxis will cover the ground for around S£250. All there is by way of places to get **food** are some falafel stalls and shops in the main square.

The Golan Heights

For over thirty years, the **Golan Heights** *(Al-Jawlan)*, captured from Syria by Israel in 1967 during the Six-Day War, have rarely been far from Middle Eastern headlines. The Syrian position under Hafez al-Assad always remained firm – no peace until the whole of the Golan returns to Syria – and unsurprisingly this is the line that has been taken by Bashar in the early days of his presidency. Most of the Golan Heights remains under Israeli control, and the only part of the area which can be visited from Syria is the town of **Quneitra**, in the demilitarized buffer zone supervised by the United Nations.

Around fifteen thousand Syrians remain on Israeli-occupied land (about the same number of Israeli settlers live here), the vast majority **Druze** whose communities were divided by the Six-Day War. Divided Druze families here are forced to communicate with one another across the divide using megaphones; as marriage outside the sect is expressly forbidden, occasionally courtships are carried out this way. In March 1999 the Syrian–Israeli border was even briefly opened to allow seven Syrian brides to enter Israel to marry; relatives who hadn't spoken to each other face to face for over thirty years were reunited for an hour in the neu-

THE POLITICS OF THE GOLAN HEIGHTS

Before the **Six-Day War**, the borders of Syria stretched as far west as the eastern shore of the Sea of Galilee (Lake Tiberias), encompassing the **Golan Heights** to the east and north of the lake. The fact that the lake, Israel's largest reservoir, is fed by meltwater from the heights, and the sheer altitude of the terrain, illustrate well how the Golan is not a simple strip of land to be bartered in return for peace – Damascus itself is visible from its peaks, and between 1948 and 1967 these mountains were regularly used by Syrian artillery to launch bombs into northern Israel.

In May 1967 Israel began massing troops on its border with Syria in response to sporadic Syrian guerrilla attacks on settlements in the Galilee. Support for Syria was immediately forthcoming from President Nasser of Egypt, who ordered the Straits of Tiran, at the entrance to the Red Sea, to be closed to Israeli shipping, effectively shutting the Israeli port of Eilat. Jordan and Egypt then signed a mutual defence pact, all of which prompted Israel into taking pre-emptive military action against its adversaries: in a predawn raid on June 5, the Israelis wiped out the Egyptian Air Force on the ground, and within six days were in control of Gaza and the Sinai Peninsula, the West Bank (including East Jerusalem) and the Golan Heights. The United Nations negotiated a ceasefire on June 11, and on September 22 passed Security Council **Resolution 242** which called for Israeli withdrawal from the territories it had occupied, and for all countries of the Middle East to live in peace with their neighbours within recognized boundaries. Syria refused to accept the resolution as it implied Syrian recognition of the right of the state of Israel to exist, but this hasn't stopped Syria justifying its stance over the Golan by quoting UN calls for Israeli withdrawal from the heights; Israel has refused to withdraw on the grounds that its pre-1967 boundaries were not secure.

In October 1973, Syria and Egypt launched a surprise attack on Israel to try to regain their lost territory. The resulting **Yom Kippur War** lingered on for months; there was fighting in the Golan until the following May, but very little ground was made by either side. A shaky truce between Syria and Israel, arranged by the then US Secretary of State Henry Kissinger, resulted in Syria regaining a few small areas and in the establishment of a complex UN-administered **buffer zone** to separate the two countries' armies. Israel gave up some of the territory it captured in 1967 to create the zone, but not before its troops had razed the town of **Quneitra** to the ground in a gratuitous act of defiance. In 1981 Israel formally annexed the part of the heights it controlled and began establishing **Jewish settlements** there.

In the peace negotiations of the mid-1990s, the Syrians claimed that Israel had made a tacit promise to withdraw fully from the heights in return for a full peace, but a formal agreement was never reached. The spectacular breakdown in Israeli–Palestinian relations during the autumn of 2000 pushes the issue of the Golan Heights well down the list of Israeli priorities for the foreseeable future.

Recently the conflict over the Golan Heights has been transferred to **cyberspace** as each side proclaims its inalienable historical right to control the territory. The Israelis have been heavily excavating the area since the 1970s in an effort to find evidence to justify their position there, claiming that the Golan was a part of "Israel" back in the Iron Age, with the first Arab settlers only appearing in the Hellenistic period, a couple of thousand years later. The Syrians allege the Israelis have been selective with their findings and insist that the region was inhabited by people of "Arab Semitic origin", the Amorites, back in the third millennium BC. Check out *www.golan-syria.org* and *www.golan.org.il* for the conflicting propoganda.

tral zone before the women tearfully bade their loved ones goodbye, handed in their Syrian passports and passed over to the Israeli side.

The anniversary of Israel's annexation of part of the heights in 1981 is usually marked by pro-Syrian demonstrations in and around the Druze village of **Majdal Shams**, within the Israeli-controlled area. Most of the people here call themselves "Syrian Arabs" and the couple of hundred of Druze who have accepted Israeli identity cards since the annexation have been made social and religious outcasts by the wider community. However, some 75 percent of children in a Golan Druze high-school poll in 1999 voted that they would prefer to remain in Israel (conversely, more than half the Golan's Jewish settlers voted for Ehud Barak in the 1999 Israeli elections, thus giving tacit approval to his peace manifesto which, if any deal was made with Syria, would almost certainly involve giving back the Golan).

Quneitra

Of all the places to visit in Syria, the ghost town of **QUNEITRA** will probably have the biggest emotional impact. When Quneitra was handed back to Syria in 1974 President Hafez al-Assad stood among the ruins and made a grand speech pledging to rebuild the town, though in the event the place was left completely untouched, probably for its propaganda value – for Syrians, Quneitra has become a potent symbol of Israeli belligerence.

The circumstances by which Quneitra was lost in 1967 reflect the sadly chaotic nature of the Syrian military campaign. At 8.45am on June 10, while Syrian troops were being directed north of the town under heavy bombardment to aid in the defence of Damascus, government radio officially announced that Quneitra had fallen. It was over two hours before a correction was broadcast, but by then a tactical redeployment by the Syrian army had turned into a desperate rush to get back to the "safe" side of the town; the Israelis took full advantage of the confusion and by the end of the morning had seized Quneitra for real. The road to Damascus was open at this point, but any assault on the capital would have been a vastly ambitious move by the Israelis and by late afternoon both they, and the Syrians, were happy to agree to a ceasefire. Over the next few months Quneitra's seventeen thousand citizens, and up to seventy thousand more people from the occupied region, were forcibly driven from their homes to join around thirty thousand others who had departed during the fighting. Since then only four hundred of the estimated fifteen thousand people left in the Israeli-occupied Golan have been allowed to return to Syrian-controlled land.

The first sight of the flattened houses on Quneitra's outskirts is the most dramatic; many of the unscathed roofs simply lie on top of a mass of rubble, leaving the impression of a building that has imploded. You will then probably be taken to the hospital by your military escort, its smashed interior strewn with broken tiles and riddled with bullet holes – a sign above the entrance reads "Destructed by the Zionists and changed it to firing target". Similar scenes of destruction are repeated at the town's desecrated church and mosque, at the broken husk of the local cinema and in the empty cells along the main shopping street.

Oddly enough there is a working **restaurant** in the town, situated right next to the barbed wire that signals the end of Syrian-controlled land; the owner can offer a pair of binoculars for a view of the Israeli early-warning station on the hill opposite. In the distance you can see the magnificent snow-capped mountains that feed

Lake Tiberias; certainly the Israeli side of the fence looks much more fertile and lush than the scrubland which characterizes the Syrian side. At Quneitra's final Syrian checkpoint you can just about make out the "Welcome to Israel" signs about 100m away across no-man's-land. Heading back, you can pause at the town **museum**, which has nothing to do with recent history but contains a collection of bits and bobs largely dating from the Byzantine period, incongruously providing relief from the devastation in the rest of the town.

Practicalities

Permits are required to visit Quneitra; to obtain one, take your passport to the Ministry of the Interior (daily except Fri 8am–2pm), next to the Kuwaiti embassy on Toulaitoulah Street in Damascus. You apply at the booth outside the building, and the whole process takes about ten minutes; the pass, which is free, is valid for one day (either the same day or the following one).

Microbuses for Quneitra depart from the station in the Baramkeh Terminal. Make sure the driver knows where you want to go and has seen your permit; he may take you to a UN-Syrian checkpoint just beyond the town of **Khan Arnabeh**, or simply drop you off in the town itself, from where you have to pick up another bus to the checkpoint. At the checkpoint, the Syrian Army takes your permit and organizes a **military escort** (who will probably not speak English). You might be given a walking tour, or be asked if you want to hire the bus to take you around (S£200 would be an appropriate sum to pay the driver, though he'll probably start the bidding at S£300). **Photographs** are permitted, but not of UN personnel or installations. The town's **restaurant** does the usual chicken and kebab fare, though you may not have time to savour it as your guide may want to usher you back to the checkpoint, where you catch a bus back to Khan Arnabeh.

travel details

Trains
Dera to: Amman (Jordan; 1 weekly; 5hr); Damascus (2 weekly; 4hr).

Ezra to: Damascus (2 weekly; 2hr 30min).

Pullman buses
Bosra, frequent services to: Damascus (1hr 30min).

Dera, frequent services to: Damascus (1hr 30min).

Sweida, frequent services to: Damascus (1hr 30min).

Karnak buses
Dera to: Damascus (1 daily; 1hr 30min).

Sweida to: Damascus (1 daily; 1hr 30min).

Microbuses and local buses
There are frequent services as follows:

Dera to: Bosra (45min); Damascus (1hr 30min); Shaykh Miskin (30min).

Ezra to: Damascus (1hr); Shaykh Miskin (15min); Sweida (30min).

Quneitra to: Damascus (1hr).

Shahba to: Damascus (1hr); Mushennef (30min); Shaqqa (10min); Sweida (20min).

Sweida to: Atil (10min); Damascus (1hr 30min); Ezra (30min); Qanawat (15min); Salkhad (45min); Shahba (20min).

Service taxis
Dera to: Ramtha (Jordan; frequent; 30min).

CHAPTER THREE

THE ORONTES VALLEY

Bounded by the mountains and forests of the coastal strip to the west and the parched expanse of desert to the east, the **Orontes Valley** is a popular destination for travellers wanting to see something of provincial Syria on their way between Damascus and Aleppo or the coast. Within this small area history and the terrain have conspired to throw up plenty of contrasts: Roman ruins lost in the desert, crumbling medieval castles, bustling towns with busy souks, and dramatic but peaceful countryside along the banks of the **Orontes River**. Getting around is fairly straightforward, though you'll need to have your own transport to reach the more out-of-the-way sites.

Dominating the region, the Orontes rises in the Lebanese mountains near Baalbak, entering Lake Qattinah (first dammed in the second millennium BC and now providing the region with drinking water) before flowing through the outskirts of the industrial city of **Homs**, Syria's third largest city and a natural focus for travellers, if only because the main traffic arteries in the region lead there. Further north along the river's course, **Hama** is altogether more agreeable, with its reasonably intact old quarter and shady riverside parks and restaurants from where you can watch the *noria*s, ancient, groaning waterwheels which have been turned by the water of the Orontes for centuries.

Beyond Hama the river enters the plain of the **Ghab**, a marshy, verdant area bordered by arid plains and hills which shimmer in the heat of summer; intensively cultivated, the Ghab is one of the most productive farming regions in Syria. Here the course of the river is rather indistinct, its sluggish flow causing it to divide into many channels and stagnant reed beds; beyond the Ghab the Orontes follows a more definite course as it flows north, entering Turkey near Jish ash-Shughur; it then makes an abrupt turn westwards, passing through Antakya before emptying into the Mediterranean.

The region immediately around Homs offers little of interest (though the city is linked by microbus to the magnificent Crac des Chevaliers; see p.184), but there are plenty of places worth seeing in the Ghab and in its mountain and desert

---

ACCOMMODATION PRICE CODES

In this book, all hotels have been categorized according to the **price codes** outlined below, representing the minimum you can expect to pay for a **double room** in each hotel. Hotels in the ⑤–⑧ bands require payment in dollars. For further details, see p.35.

① under S£300/US$7	⑤ US$35–50/S£1500–2100
② S£300–600/US$7–14	⑥ US$50–90/S£2100–3900
③ S£600–1000/US$14–23	⑦ US$90–130/S£3900–5600
④ S£1000–1500/US$23–35	⑧ US$130/over S£5600

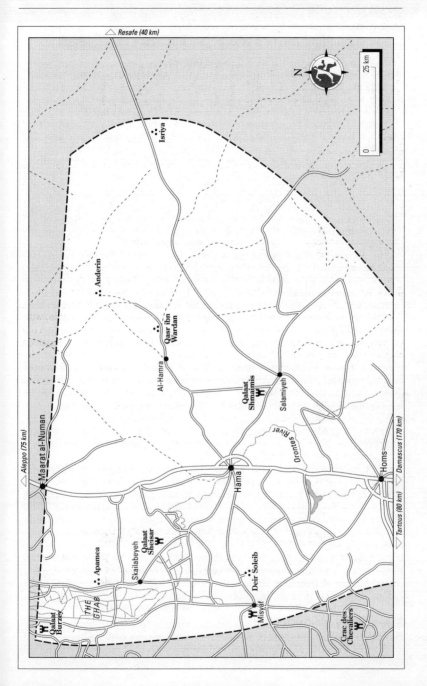

THE ORONTES RIVER AND FERTILE CRESCENT

Almost all the historical sites in this region were first settled because of their proximity to the **Orontes** River, or *Nahr al-Assi*, the "rebel river", in Arabic, because unlike the Jordan, the Yarmouk and other rivers in Syria, it runs from south to north. The river's importance to agriculture has ensured that the region has been both densely settled and frequently fought over. The Crusaders built the Crac des Chevaliers to guard the main route running between the coast and the Orontes, while at Kadesh (now Tell Nebi Mend, southwest of Homs near the border with Lebanon), a Bronze Age fortress city by the river, the Egyptian Pharaoh Ramses II fought a major battle against the Hittites around 1285 BC over control of the valley and Syria (see p.154).

In biblical times the Orontes, along with the Jordan, formed the western part of the so-called **Fertile Crescent** – the watered and settled arc stretching from Jerusalem to the head of the main route running between the Tigris and Euphrates forming its eastern section. It was here that some of the world's earliest settled societies originated, with some village sites dated to around 8000 BC, and here that the ancient states of Babylonia, Assyria and Phoenicia flourished.

In more recent times, Syrian extraction of water from the Orontes has drawn complaints from the Turkish government, mindful of the necessity of keeping the fertile farmland of the **Hatay** (around Antakya) well watered. However, the fact that the Hatay is regarded by the Damascus government as part of Syria means these grumblings have been largely ignored; besides, the Syrians accuse the Turks of taking more than their fair share from the Euphrates before it enters Syrian territory.

fringes. Obvious destinations **around Hama** include the spectacular Roman ruins of **Apamea**, the Assassin fortress at **Misyaf** and the extravagant Byzantine desert palace at **Qasr Ibn Wardan**, beyond which lies the well-preserved Roman temple of **Isriya**, emerging from the parched plains in fantastic isolation.

Homs

Syria's third city, **HOMS** is ugly without being unpleasant, and busy without the big-city stress of Damascus or the confusing sprawl of parts of Aleppo. Its university, one of only four in the country, is a specialist engineering foundation, whose large student population gives Homs a more lively air than other towns in the region. The modern housing developments and building sites which surround the city provide an ungainly but appropriate introduction: there's virtually nothing left of its ancient past, and the centre adds up to little more than a succession of busy traffic intersections, low-rise office buildings and a workaday souk. Homs does, however, make a convenient base to travel out to Crac des Chevaliers (see p.184), the monastery at Deir Mar Mousa (see p.120) and possibly Palmyra (see p.282) before pushing north to the more obvious attractions of Hama (see p.156).

Some history

Homs has been an important trading centre since ancient times, when its wealth challenged even that of Palmyra, the next great caravan halt on the long trek from the Mediterranean to India and China. Known as **Emesa** during the Roman period, the city was ruled by a dynasty of priest-kings, guardians of a black stone – representing the sun god – that resided within the **Great Temple of Bel**. In 187 AD **Julia Domna**, daughter of the priest-king, married the local Roman commander Septimius Severus, who became emperor six years later. Under his patronage the city was ambitiously expanded; the Great Temple was completely rebuilt and came to rival the magnificent edifices at Baalbak and Palmyra.

Under Julia Domna's grandson **Elagabalus**, who was proclaimed Emperor Marcus Antoninus in Emesa at the age of 14 in 218, the town was raised to the status of a metropolis. The black stone was removed from the Great Temple and taken to Rome, where the sun-worshipping cult took hold. Elagabalus's reign, however, which was characterized by all manner of excess and depravity, was murderously cut short by the praetorian guard in 222. The black stone was sent back home, although Emperor Aurelian gave the cult official status in Rome later that century; he had prayed to the black stone at Emesa on his way to confront the Palmyrene princess Zenobia (see p.284), and credited it with aiding his subsequent victory.

The cult of Bel survived in Emesa until the fifth century, by which time **Christianity** had begun to take a strong hold. The most noteworthy remnants of the city's ancient past are two churches, though Christian catacombs dating from between the third and seventh centuries have been found under houses in the old quarter of Homs (unfortunately they are in a perilous state and so can't be visited). In the wake of the Muslim conquest, Homs became an important settlement once more and the famous Arab commander Khalid ibn al-Walid is today buried in the city's main mosque. Homs managed to resist the attentions of the Crusaders despite their relative proximity at the Crac des Chevaliers, coming instead under the control of the Zengids of Aleppo during the early twelfth century. There is little trace of the Great Temple of Bel left today, and the walls and city gates of the ancient city were largely demolished during the Ottoman period; the citadel is now no more than a mound. Otherwise, Homs is an unapologetically modern city: industrially, it's the most important in Syria, boasting the country's largest oil refinery and standing at the heart of its vital phosphate industry.

Arrival, information and accommodation

The centre of Homs is compact, with most of the hotels, shops and public services clustering around **Qouwatly Street**. The **Karnak and microbus stations** are next to each other over a kilometre to the north, with the **Pullman bus station** 500m beyond them. If you're arriving on a microbus from the south (along the Damascus road), you'll probably be dropped off in the centre; otherwise, catch a taxi (S£50 maximum), or city microbus heading into town. The best way to cover the 1500m northeast from the **train station** to the centre is to get a city taxi (S£25). **Service taxis** from Aleppo and Damascus terminate on Qouwatly Street, opposite the museum.

Homs has a small **tourist office** (daily except Fri: summer 8am–2pm & 5–9pm; winter 8am–2pm & 4–8pm), in the park off Qouwatly Street. The staff are very friendly and can provide a few glossy brochures and a free map, but little practical information.

Accommodation

It's never difficult to find a **place to stay** in Homs, though the choice can hardly be described as inspiring. The city's budget hotels all tend to be located in the centre; in summer the lack of decent air-conditioning can make them quite airless

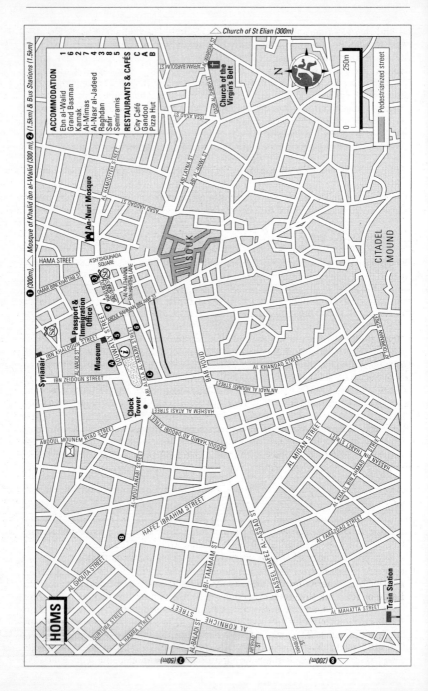

HOMS

△ Church of St Elian (300m)

ACCOMMODATION
Ebn al-Walid 1
Grand Basman 6
Karnak 2
Al-Mimas 7
Al-Nasr al-Jadeed 4
Raghdan 3
Safir 8
Semiramis 5

RESTAURANTS & CAFÉS
City Café C
Gandool A
Pizza Hut B

Church of the
Virgin's Belt

SOUK

CITADEL
MOUND

N

0   250m

Pedestrianized street

An-Nuri Mosque

HAMA STREET

A'SH'SHOUHADA
SQUARE

Passport &
Immigration
Office

Museum

Syrianair

Clock
Tower

Train Station

① (300m), △ Mosque of Khalid ibn al-Walid (300 m), ② (1.5km) & Bus Stations (1.5km)

OMAR BINI KHATTAB ST

IBN KHALDOUN STREET

IBN ZEIDOUN STREET

AL-WALID STREET

AL-HAMIDIYEH STREET

ABDOUL RAHMAN BIN AWF ST

OUWATLI STREET

ABI ALA AL-MAARI STREET

ABI ALA AL-ATASI STREET

ABDOUL MOUNEM RYAD STREET

ABDOUL HAMID AD-DROUBI STREET

AL-MOUTANABI STREET

HAFEZ IBRAHIM STREET

AL GHOUTA STREET

QURTUBA STREET

AL-BALADI ST

AL-HAMRA STREET

AL KORNICHE STREET

ABI-TAMMAM STREET

AR RIYAD ST

TARABLUS ST

AL MAHATTA STREET

BASSEL HAFEZ AL-ASSAD ST

HAFEZ AL-ASSAD ST

AL FARAZDAQ STREET

AL MIDAN STREET

HASSAN IBN THABET STREET

KHALID BIN AHMAD STREET

OMAR STREET

AT-TURKMAN STREET

AL KHANDAQ STREET

BAB HOUD

AN NADI AL HOMSI STREET

HASHEM AL HOMSI STREET

AL-MUTHANNA IBN HARTHA LANE

ASAD HADDAQ ST

ABI LAYNA ST

ABI AL-HAWL ST

ISSA ASAD ST

QUSI AS-SUHFI ST

FARRAH BARSOUM ST

△ ① (50m)

△ ⑧ (200m)

– and the traffic noise can be a problem. Best in the mid-price bracket are the *Karnak* and *Al-Mimas*, both far enough away from the main thoroughfares to be much quieter.

Ebn Al-Walid, Kinana St, off Hama St (☎031/223 953). The pick of the bunch of cheap hotels near the mosque of Khalid ibn al-Walid, with friendly staff and functional if bare rooms, some with en-suite bath. ①.

Grand Basman, off Abi Alala al-Maarr St (☎031/235 700). Located in a small shopping arcade, this has acceptably clean if soulless rooms with tatty en-suite bath; it's overpriced and not especially friendly, though. ③.

Karnak (☎031/233 099). Above the Karnak bus station. One of the endearingly peculiar chain of government-run hotels: this one is octagonal, very spruce and usually completely empty. Ironically it's arguably the best-value hotel in the city, its rooms boasting TV, en-suite bathrooms and air-con. ③.

Al-Mimas, Al-Baladi St (☎031/220 224). Somewhat lost over in the west of town and slightly overpriced, though the rooms are agreeably clean and its location negates the problem of traffic noise; all rooms have a TV and fridge. ④.

Al-Nasr al-Jadeed, Al-Muthanna bin Haritha Lane (☎031/227 423). The best of the cheapies in the city centre, with a friendly proprietor who speaks good English. The rooms, spartan and functional, are clean and have shared facilities. ②.

Raghdan, Qouwatly St (☎031/225 211). A similar deal to the *Grand Basman*, but slightly cheaper and cleaner, and much friendlier. ③.

Safir, Ragheb al-Jamali St (☎031/412 400, fax 433 420). Luxury hotel situated near the train station. All rooms here have air-con, TV, radio and minibar, and guests have the exclusive use of the hotel's tennis courts and enticing swimming pool. ⑧.

The City

After you've seen the very modern **Mosque of Khalid ibn al-Walid** and two semi-interesting **churches**, one of which, **St Elian**, is claimed to contain the oldest surviving frescoes in Syria, there's not much to do in Homs beyond drifting among the crowds in the souk and the main shopping areas. Homs does boast a city **museum** (daily except Tues 9am–6pm; S£300), at the clock-tower end of Qouwatly Street, opposite the tourist office, but it's a dingy place that seems in a permanent state of upheaval. If you do decide to venture inside, prepare yourself for a series of boring, ill-defined exhibits, some of which are unlabelled even in Arabic. At the end of your tour the curator may try to sell you some "antiques".

The mosques

From ash-Shouhada Square, outside the souk, head 300m north up Hama Street to reach Homs's only edifice of any real note, the **Mosque of Khalid ibn al-Walid**, which sits in a well-manicured park. Its bright tin roof glinting in the sun, the mosque dates from the last days of Turkish rule in Syria (1908–13), but its courtyard makes use of Mameluke *ablaq*-style stonework. Inside the spacious interior is the **mausoleum** of Khalid ibn al-Walid who led the Arab forces at the Battle of Yarmouk River in 636, a confrontation which overturned nearly six hundred years of Roman rule in Syria (see p.135). The surrounding park, one of the few peaceful spots in the city, is a good place to find a shady tree, eat ice cream and people-watch. The only other important mosque in Homs is the **Great Mosque of an-Nuri**, thought to have been built by Nur al-Din (see p.303). Situated in the drab souk, the building itself is unremarkable, but it stands on the

THE BATTLE OF KADESH

The **Battle of Kadesh** was the culmination of a trial of strength between the **Hittites**, based in central Turkey, and the **Egyptians**, under Ramses II, determined to restore Syria to their empire. The two armies met in combat around 1285 BC outside the city of Kadesh (now called **Tell Nebi Mend**, 25km southwest of Homs), the earliest major battle in history whose sequence of events is known, thanks to the chronicles of the Egyptian poet Pentaur. The Hittite army based at Kadesh withdrew from the city, concealing itself from the view of the Egyptian scouts, then, as the Egyptians started to camp outside the city, a detachment of Hittite chariots detoured around the settlement to launch a surprise attack. With magnificent fortitude Ramses gathered his forces together and drove back, stalling the advance; the late arrival of a detached Egyptian regiment eventually allowed the pharaoh's escape. This action was commemorated by Ramses on many monuments throughout Egypt as a victory, but the evidence of a surviving Hittite treaty with the city of Aleppo and a number of Hittite seals found at Ugarit suggests that Syria remained in the Hittite sphere of influence in the decades following the battle. Direct microbuses run to Tell Nebi Mend from Homs, but there's precious little to see save a large mound with a few modern dwellings on top, and a lot of scrawny goats.

To archeologists, however, the Battle of Kadesh has a far wider significance in that it played a major role in the detective story (unravelled in O.R. Gurney's definitive study *The Hittites*) which revealed the importance, indeed the very existence, of the Hittite empire. Ramses II had celebrated his "victory" at Kadesh over a people he called the Hatti, but nothing connected these people to the enigmatic Hittites, known only through a couple of unforthcoming biblical references. In 1812 the famous Swiss explorer Johann Ludwig Burckhardt became the first Westerner to notice the presence of a number of inscribed basalt stones incorporated into houses in the Hama souk; these were only finally properly made available to historians in 1872 when a missionary, William Wright, visited the city with the Syrian Turkish Governor, who ordered the stones to be removed and sent to the museum in Constantinople. In the following decade connections were made between the stones and similar inscriptions, also undeciphered, found at various sites in Turkey, leading to the conjecture that a vast empire at one time must have filled much of Turkey and Syria. The final piece of the jigsaw fell into place with the discovery of the Hittite **royal archives** at Boğazköy in central Turkey in 1906. These included a number of tablets written in decipherable Babylonian cuneiform, which not only identified Boğazköy as the ancient capital of the Hittite empire, but also revealed a Hittite copy of a peace treaty made with the Egyptians which matched exactly Ramses' treaty with the Hatti after the Battle of Kadesh.

site of the Great Temple of Bel, of which all that remains are a few blocks of Roman masonry in the courtyard.

The churches

Four hundred metres east of the Great Mosque of an-Nuri is the most important Christian monument in Homs, the **Church of the Belt** (Kaneesat al-Zunnar), named after a piece of cloth said to have belonged to the Virgin Mary that was found underneath the altar during a 1953 renovation; the belt is kept in a showcase in a special room and is a surprisingly unedifying piece of cloth. The church interior cosily resembles that of a modern English parish church, complete with cheap iconography, insubstantial wooden pews and gently peeling paintwork; indeed the present structure only dates from the mid-nineteenth century, although it's claimed that this has been a site of Christian worship since 59 AD.

The same back road that leads to the Church of the Virgin's Belt brings you, 300m further east – turn right where it ends down Tarafa bin al-Abd Street – to the **Church of St Elian** (Kaneesat Mar Elian); usually the only way to get inside is to rattle for attention on the gate enclosing the building. The church is dedicated to the son of a Roman officer who was martyred at the hands of his own father in 284 for refusing to renounce Christianity, and indeed is said to have been founded in 432 on the very site of the martyrdom, with Elian's remains placed in a sarcophagus in the crypt. A major renovation of the church in 1970 led to the discovery of some colourful **murals** of Christ, Mary, the prophets and the Apostles which had been brilliantly preserved under a layer of plaster. These date back to the twelfth century at least and, if the claims of some experts are to be believed, possibly right back to the sixth century, making them the oldest surviving church paintings in Syria. The rest of the church is covered with modern, and quite garish, paintings depicting the life of St Elian.

Eating and drinking

The numerous cheap eateries around Qouwatly Street will satisfy anyone seeking a snack, but actual **restaurants** are pretty thin on the ground. The *City Café* on Abi Alala al-Maarr Street is about as jazzy as it gets in Homs; its unspectacular pizza and hamburger menu is compensated for somewhat by the first-floor vantage point over the city centre. At the end of Al-Moutanabbi Street is the good-value *Pizza Hut* – an imitation of the Western chain – which serves very filling pizzas for between S£75 and S£200, and has menus in English. The railway station has an ambitiously large restaurant, complete with cloakrooms, which offers cheap chicken and kebab fare and beer, but it's usually unnervingly devoid of patrons. A much better bet for a sit-down meal – though the staff are unused to serving in the daytime, and once again chicken and kebabs predominate – is the slightly tatty first-floor restaurant at the Karnak bus terminal. The *Safir* hotel also has a couple of restaurants, which sell overpriced Syrian and international dishes. The biggest of the city's **cafés** is the outdoor *Gandool* on the north side of Qouwatly Street; no food or beer is served here, but it's a good place to chill out and watch endless games of backgammon.

Listings

Airline Syrianair has an office on Ibn Khaldoun St, north of the immigration office (☎031/238 809).

Banks and exchange Change cash and travellers' cheques at the branch of the Commercial Bank of Syria just off Ibn Khaldoun St (daily except Fri 8am–12.30pm). Cash only may be changed at a booth a block south of the eastern end of Qouwatly St (daily except Fri 8am–8pm).

Bookshop The *Safir* hotel has the only useful shop with English-language books.

Buses Departures are frequent to Aleppo, Hama and Damascus, and it's not usually necessary to book ahead, though you may want to check in advance about departures to Palmyra.

Microbus departures to Crac des Chevaliers from the microbus station are very frequent in the mornings, but tend to thin out in the afternoons.

Car rental Universal on Ibn Khaldoun St (☎031/468 666) is a Europcar agent; they speak English but don't always have cars available. The *Safir* hotel has a Mercedes available for rental but only with a driver; examples of return fares (including waiting time) are $36 to the Crac des Chevaliers and $68 to Palmyra.

Pharmacies Try Modern Pharmacy on Al-Moutanabbi St or City Pharmacy on Abi Alala al-Maarr St.

Phones There's a telephone office (daily 8am–8pm) at the western end of Qouwatly St by the clock tower; card phones are down the side of the building, while phone cards are available in the building itself. It's also possible to make phone calls from the post office.

Post office North of the clock tower, on Abdul Mounem Ryad St (daily except Fri 8am–4.30pm).

Service taxis Departures from outside the *Al-Khayyam Hotel* on Qouwatly St; destinations include Aleppo, Damascus and Hama and (in Lebanon) Beirut and Tripoli.

Travel agents Universal and Al-Borg, both on Ibn Khaldoun St, deal with most of the major airlines. The *Al-Mimas* hotel on Al-Baladi St has a travel agency attached which books flights and organizes local tours.

Visa extensions The Immigration Office is located on the third floor of an office building on Ibn Khaldoun St (daily except Fri 8am–2pm).

Hama

With its pleasant riverside parks and groaning water wheels turned by the Orontes, **HAMA** boasts one of the most relaxed and picturesque city centres in Syria. To some the place may seem too much of a well-oiled museum piece – it's usually busy with coach parties photographing themselves beside the carefully restored water wheels – but there's no denying that the city has charm, and with so many other sights in the vicinity (see p.163), it's possible to spend three or four worthwhile days based here. However, beyond the obvious attractions of its carefully manicured gardens, there are less appealing aspects of Hama which soon become apparent. Like Homs, Hama has grown exponentially during the last few decades, and its suburbs, which sprawl in every direction from the centre, are as shabby and uninviting as any in Syria. Despite the massive building programme, evidence still remains – in the form of shell-pocked buildings and bullet-scarred walls – of the 1982 **Hama Massacre**, a brutal government suppression of a local uprising which represents the worst atrocity perpetrated by Hafez al-Assad's regime in Syria.

Hama's provincial air reflects a **history** spent away from the political spotlight and the major foreign trade routes. Evidence of human settlement here dates back to around 1100 BC when the small kingdom of **Hamath** was ruled from the citadel hill. During the Seleucid era the town, renamed **Epiphania**, became an administrative centre of minor importance, a role which continued through the Roman and Byzantine eras. Because of its location Hama suffered badly in the disputes between Damascus and Aleppo during the eleventh and twelfth centuries, but emerged to gentle prosperity in the Ayyubid period, through Ottoman times and up to the present. For many centuries the city has been a centre of **Sunni Muslim orthodoxy**, and there is a much greater feeling of conservatism here than anywhere else in Syria, with many women wearing traditional black veils which cover their heads completely.

THE HAMA MASSACRE

Peaceful and visibly prosperous though it may be today, in 1982 Hama witnessed the savage quelling of a civilian revolt by the Syrian army, which resulted in the deaths of anything between 5000 and 25,000 people. What became known as the **Hama Massacre** has never been any great secret inside or outside Syria, and although few in the country are willing to talk about it, everybody knows it happened; it was, after all, intended as a warning that any dissent against the established order would be met swiftly with cruel violence.

In the late 1970s opposition to the Assad regime was mounting on many fronts, with widespread calls for democratic reform of the corrupt, Alawite-dominated government. Basic human rights were being violated by the secret police, and Syria's military intervention in Lebanon was proving unpopular with the army and the intellectuals, as well as with the general populace, the arrival of Lebanese refugees deepening the existing housing crisis. The most active opposition came from the fundamentalist **Muslim Brotherhood** who wanted to replace the regime with a system based on Sunni orthodoxy. During the late 1970s and early 1980s the Brotherhood launched a series of terrorist attacks in the main cities and even made an unsuccessful attempt on Assad's life; the regime reacted with mass arrests and a series of summary executions. On the outskirts of Hama, one of the strongholds of the Brotherhood, guerrillas ambushed a security checkpoint on April 21, 1981. The government responded three days later by shooting dead an estimated 350 men, completely at random, leaving their bodies in the streets.

On February 2, 1982, sensing an embryonic revolt, the government sent special army units into Hama to arrest members of the Brotherhood and confiscate guns. However, when the soldiers entered the Barudi quarter of the old city they found armed members of the Brotherhood ready to meet them. The Brotherhood won the first round of fighting, and the call went up from microphones on the city's minarets for a *jihad*, or holy struggle, to be waged against Assad. In the ensuing uprising, about a hundred policemen and party officials were killed, guns and ammunition were seized from the local police headquarters and the old city was barricaded. The Syrian army responded quickly and with massive force: up to thirty thousand men were brought into Hama from all over Syria, commanded by Rifaat al-Assad, the president's brother, and artillery units bombarded the city. The Brotherhood fought back strongly, but on February 22 Rifaat was able to claim victory for the government and promptly flattened the city centre, bulldozing what was left of the houses and leaving countless bodies (of people already dead from the bombardment) buried underneath the rubble. An estimated third of Hama's centre was destroyed, leaving some seventy thousand people homeless. (This is why much of the city looks so modern today; in the area where the *Apamee Cham Palace* now stands, for example, there used to be an ancient *noria* and a cluster of domed houses with projecting verandas overlooking the river.)

The Hama Massacre resulted in the immediate annihilation of an extremist terrorist organization which in any case had little widespread support. But this swift, brutal show of force – and the widespread human rights violations which characterized the ensuing national state of emergency – enabled Hafez al-Assad to silence the wider opposition, ultimately securing the future of his regime as one of the most stable in the Middle East.

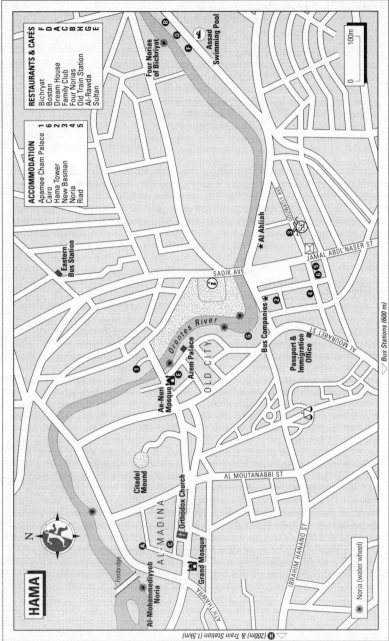

HAMA

N

Al-Mohammediyyeh
Noria

Footbridge

AL-MADINA

Citadel
Mound

Orthodox Church

Grand Mosque

AL THAWRA

An-Nuri
Mosque

Azem Palace

OLD CITY

Orontes River

Bus Companies

Passport &
Immigration
Office

AL MOUTANABBI ST

IBRAHIM HANANO ST

Noria (water wheel)

SADIK AVE

Eastern
Bus Station

Al Ahliah

JOUWATY AVE

JAMAL ABDL'NASER ST

AL MOURABET ST

Four Norias
of Bichriyat

Assad
Swimming Pool

▷ Bus Stations (600 m)

▷ (200m) & Train Station (1.5km) H

ACCOMMODATION

Apamee Cham Palace 1
Cairo 6
Hama Tower 2
New Basman 3
Noria 4
Riad 5

RESTAURANTS & CAFÉS

Bichryat F
Bostan D
Dream House A
Family Club C
Four Norias B
Old Train Station H
Al-Rawda G
Sultan E

0   100m

0

Arrival and information

From the **train station**, over 2km west of the centre, it's possible to pick up a local bus to the corner of Sadik Avenue and Qouwatly Avenue in the centre of town, though it's worth asking the driver before you get on, as not all buses from the station end up there. The **bus stations** for **microbuses** and **local buses** are opposite each another on Al-Mourabet Street, from where the centre is a ten-minute walk – or short bus ride – to the northeast; however, buses to and from Qasr Ibn Wardan use the eastern bus station, about 400m north of the centre. **Pullman buses** will drop you in the very centre of town at their company offices, most of which are near Sadik Avenue. All the main things to see in Hama are within walking distance of one another and the main hotels, so you're unlikely to need city transport unless you're going out to the train station.

There's a small **tourist office** (daily except Fri 8am–2pm) in the gardens in the centre of town. As usual, they try their best but the staff haven't really got that much to say and on occasions can be downright misleading; the **map** of Hama they dole out is highly inaccurate. Hotels are probably a better source of information, particularly the *Noria*.

Accommodation

One of the reasons travellers have a tendency to linger in Hama is the city's very good selection of **hotels**. Two of the best **budget** options in Syria are next to each other on Qouwatly Avenue: the *Cairo* (☎033/237 206, fax 511 715; ②) and the

---

MOVING ON FROM HAMA

By Pullman and Karnak bus

Pullman and Karnak buses depart Hama from outside their respective bus company offices. The **Karnak** office is in the *Cafeteria Afamia*, overlooking the main *noria*s in the centre of town; they operate services to Homs, Damascus and Aleppo. Next door is the Qadmous company serving Homs, Damascus, Aleppo, Latakia and Tartous; next to this in turn is An-Nawras which, in addition to the five towns served by Qadmous, runs buses to Qamishli and Raqqa. Al-Ahliah, the best of the four companies, is located 100m east down the same road and has frequent services to Aleppo, Damascus, Homs, Latakia, Raqqa, Idleb and Tartous.

By microbus and local bus

From the microbus station, **microbuses** head for Homs (S£20), Skailabeyeh (for Apamea; S£20), Salamiyeh (for Qalaat Shmaimis; S£20) Misyaf (S£20). **Local buses** also serve these destinations (similar journey times and fares), plus Aleppo and Damascus (both 3hr; S£50).

By service taxi

There are departures to Aleppo, Damascus and Homs from outside the microbus station.

By train

There is one train a day to Damascus (S£70/50 in first/second class) and to Aleppo (S£60/40), as well as a weekly, overnight train to Qamishli via Deir ez-Zur.

Riad (☎033/239 512, fax 517 776; ②) are both quite disarmingly clean and offer a variety of rooms with constant hot water and optional en-suite bathrooms and satellite TV. A bed in a shared room costs around S£250 at either hotel; in summer you can sleep on the roof at either place (S£200), with proper beds provided. In addition both hotels are very useful sources of information, giving out free maps and organizing tours to Apamea and the Dead Cities (see p.239). Hama has a few decent **mid-range** places and one **upmarket** hotel, listed below.

Apamee Cham Palace (☎033/525 335, fax 511 626, *www.chamhotels.com*). East of the river, near the road bridge 400m north of the centre. Five-star luxuries are on offer here, including tennis courts and a swimming pool, plus a variety of bars and restaurants. ⑦.

Hama Tower (☎033/226 864). Located a block north of the *Noria*, with clean though rather spartan rooms and polite, if slightly muddled, staff. ④.

New Basman, Qouwatly Ave (☎033/224 838). Recently spruced up, this boasts very clean, spacious rooms with air-con, though you should ask for a room at the back as it's next to a busy traffic junction. ④.

Noria (☎ & fax 033/511 715), Qouwatly Ave. Run by the same management as the *Cairo* opposite, this is likewise spotless. Aimed at tour groups, it boasts well-appointed rooms with satellite TV and air-con. ④.

The City

The **gardens** stretching north of the city centre along the east side of the Orontes are the easiest place to see Hama's water wheels, or **norias**, in action, and as such are the most obvious attraction here. Immediately to the west of here, across the river, are the quieter streets of the **old city**, at the centre of which is the **Azem Palace**, the governor's residence in Ottoman times, now an excellent **museum** of Hama and the surrounding region, the exhibits often taking second place to the resplendent rooms and crumbling courtyards. Although it saw some of the fiercest fighting during the 1982 uprising, the prosperous Al-Madina quarter

---

NORIAS

Syria's wooden **norias**, huge water wheels up to 20m in diameter, were built to supply water to places near the Orontes. They were first developed in the Byzantine period, though those *noria*s that remain in Hama – seventeen in all – date from Mameluke and early Ottoman times; similar wheels were developed in Egypt, Portugal and Spain, with one fine example still standing in the Andalucian city of Córdoba. The *noria*s would have scooped up water from the river and deposited it onto a narrow **aqueduct** (only a few of these survive in Hama), whose top end would be adjacent to the wheel. Built on a downward gradient and supported by elegant stone arches, the aqueduct took the water off to nearby mosques and public buildings; out in the countryside the same principle was used for the irrigation of fields, using much more complex aqueducts.

The thing which will probably surprise you most about the *noria*s is the **noise** they make: a whining, almost mournful groan as the wheel turns in its central support. Out in the countryside, along the Orontes or in the Ghab, you can often hear a *noria* before you see it, and in the central gardens of Hama that run up towards the *Apamee Cham Palace Hotel* the sound is constant and relentless – except when the water level in the Orontes is too low to make the wheels turn, as can happen particularly in late summer.

around the **Great Mosque** is worth exploring, too. Away from the river, just five minutes' walk west of the centre, is Hama's **souk**, refreshingly little visited by tourists.

West and east of the city centre, along the Orontes, are more *noria*s, and you could do a lot worse than allow yourself to finish up (and cool off) ten minutes' walk east of the centre at the **Four Norias of Bichriyat**, where some of the tallest wheels grind away. Local kids swim in the river here, riding up on the wheels and then spectacularly jumping off the stone supports at the top. On the south bank are three decent restaurants (see overleaf) from whose shady terraces, pleasantly cooled by the spray from the *noria*s, you can observe all this mad activity while sipping a cool beer or two; well-to-do families are drawn here for their evening stroll, something akin to the Italian *passegiata*.

The old city

Immediately to the west of the river, as it makes an abrupt turn northwards in the centre of town, is the **old city**. Its narrow streets, shady and deserted on hot afternoons, are a good place for aimless ambling and offer occasional glimpses of life going on behind barred windows or inside gated courtyards – everything from raucous family arguments to private gatherings of men smoking *nargileh*s. The main sight here is the **Azem Palace** (*Beit al-Azem*; daily except Tues 9am–6pm; S£150), the expansive and beautiful former residence of Assad Pasha al-Azem, Ottoman governor of Hama until 1742 when he assumed a similar office in Damascus (see p.83). The building itself is a draw, although many parts are rather ramshackle and still recovering from the events of 1982. Those rooms which survived the crossfire, or which have been restored, give a good impression of the extravagant lifestyle led by Ottoman overlords of Syria in the eighteenth century, with the most striking aspects of the decor being the wooden panelling and inlay work, and the eighteenth-century furniture.

Most of the palace is given over to a rather haphazard **museum**, with some rooms displaying historical artefacts from Roman and other times, others left bare or with enough finery intact to indicate further the lavish lifestyle of the Pasha. The most interesting of the rooms is the **Royal Hall**, a bare-walled though still rather grand room accessed from the upstairs courtyard, in which the Pasha slept under a beautifully carved wooden ceiling. In other rooms leading off this courtyard you'll find an unedifying display of costumes and rituals from local life, displayed by bemused-looking mannequins.

A couple of minutes' walk northwest of the palace, the **An-Nuri Mosque** was built in the late twelfth century by Saladin's uncle, Nur al-Din, under whose command Muslim forces gained important victories against Crusader outposts in the mountains west of Hama. It's an intimate building, shady and secretive like many small mosques, with a striking minaret comprising bands of alternating yellow limestone and black basalt. Very close by are more *noria*s, one of which can be observed from the *Sultan Restaurant* (see p.163), reached by a tunnel very close to the mosque.

The Al-Madina quarter

Few visitors seem to venture away from the carefully tended flowerbeds of the main parks and the peeling decay of the old city into **Al-Madina**, but there are a couple of things worth seeing amid the modern roads and well-heeled apartment buildings. West of the An-Nuri Mosque is the site of the **citadel**, which is today no more than a mound. Excavated in parts by Danish archeologists, the site yielded evidence of occupation dating back to Neolithic times, but now there is nothing more than a carefully landscaped picnic area here, popular with families on Fridays. From the roadway leading up to the summit of the hill you get a good view of the area flattened during the 1982 rebellion. The *Apamee Cham Palace* sits marooned at the centre of a site where once there were streets lined with houses, but where now there is only waste ground; the still-standing houses surrounding the area bear the scars of bullet holes and hasty demolition of neighbouring buildings.

Three hundred metres to the west are the two buildings that have traditionally formed the religious centre of the town. Founded in the eighth century by the Umayyads on a site previously occupied by a Byzantine basilica and various pagan temples, the **Great Mosque** (*Jami' al-Umawi*) has been completely restored after its almost total destruction in 1982. Its layout reflects the old basilica plan: the prayer hall has three aisles, and the domes on top were built in the form of a cross. Besides the prayer hall, the most distinctive features of the mosque are the vaulted porticoes which surround the courtyard, the design of the two minarets, one a square tower dating from Zengid times, the other Mameluke and octagonal; and the black and white patterns in the brickwork.

To the northeast of the mosque stands the **Orthodox Cathedral**, grand, modern and usually closed outside Sunday services. A five-minute walk away on the river banks are two more *noria*s, one of which, the **Al-Mohammediyyeh**, is the largest in Hama, and can be viewed from a spacious open-air café on the opposite side of the river.

The souk

Back in the city centre, a five-minute stroll west brings you to Hama's **souk** which – unlike the covered bazaars of Damascus and Aleppo – mostly comprises open-air alleyways lined with stalls crammed with racks of cheap clothing, shelves of washing powder and kitchen utensils. There's hardly anything specifically aimed at tourists here, which means the stall-owners are all the happier to assist the few foreigners who drop by. To reach the heart of the souk, take the fourth lane on the left as you walk up Ibrahim Hanano Street; after 200m this lane passes the Hammam Al-Assadiyya (see Listings, opposite).

Eating and drinking

It's very easy to eat well and cheaply in Hama, though there is little variety on offer; your choice of restaurant will be determined more by the surroundings and ambience than by what's on the menu. Modest eating places serving kebab and chicken can be found on or near Qouwatly Avenue; next door to the Al-Ahliah bus-company office, for example, is a café which does inexpensive pizza and hamburgers. If you're feeling flush though, you could venture into one of the restaurants at the *Apamee Cham Palace Hotel*; its terrace is very popular with affluent locals on a Friday night, when there is sometimes an Arabic pop singer.

At some point during your stay, make sure you try the town's **speciality**, the sweet cheese-filled pastry dessert called *halawat al-jibna*; it's available in most of its restaurants and in any number of cake shops along Qouwatly Avenue, often served with ice cream as a topping.

Bichryat, Bostan and the **Four Norias**. Situated next door to one another by the Four Norias of Bichriyat. All three restaurants are generally quiet and provide regular Syrian fare and a beer for around S£200, to the eerie accompaniment of the groaning water wheels. Of the three, the *Bichryat* has the most varied menu (which includes pizza), but the *Four Norias* has the widest and most attractive riverbank terrace. In winter it's too cold to sit outside, and as the interiors of these restaurants are not very attractive you may prefer to eat somewhere else.

Family Club. Al-Madina Quarter, next to the Great Mosque. Serves a good variety of moderately priced Western and Syrian dishes. One block to the north is *Dream House*, which does similar fare; both places serve alcohol, though it's their soft drinks which make them popular with locals chilling out in the evenings.

Old Train Station, cnr of Abdul Mounem Riyad St and Ibrahim Hanono St, about 1500m west of the centre. The very inexpensive restaurant here offers occasional live music and gets very busy on Fridays when there is much consumption of arrack and impromptu dancing between 3pm and 8pm. However, the building itself is not as evocative as it might sound, its innards having simply been ripped out and replaced with tables.

Al-Rawda. Right in the centre of town, on the west bank of the river. Offers pleasant views of the river and gardens and reasonably priced food. About S£200 for a meal and drink; no beer.

Sultan. Next to the An-Nuri Mosque. Offers diners the opportunity to sit right next to a *noria*, watching its unceasing rotation through glass panes; here you'll pay slightly more than at the *Al-Rawda* for the rather better atmosphere.

Listings

Airline Syrianair is on Alamen St (☎033/239 977).

Banks The Commercial Bank of Syria on Qouwatly Ave changes cash and travellers' cheques (daily except Fri 8am–2pm & 5–8pm); cash advances on credit cards can be obtained at the *Noria* hotel, albeit with a fairly hefty commission.

Car rental There is a branch of Chamcar at the *Apamee Cham Palace Hotel*.

Hammam The Hammam Al-Assadiyya in the souk charges S£115 for bath and massage (early morning–midnight; men only).

Post office A large, modern building on Qouwatly Ave (corner of Sadik Ave), which also offers telephone services (daily except Fri 8am–4.30pm).

Swimming pool The open-air Assad Pool is ten minutes' walk east from the town centre, opposite the *Bichryat* restaurant.

Tours The *Noria, Cairo* and *Riad* hotels all have drivers available to run to any itinerary you want, certainly worth considering for the desert sites of Qasr Ibn Wardan and Isriya (see pp.172–173) or a tour of some of the nearby Dead Cities (see p.248) where public transport is unreliable. Prices are reasonable: around US$50 for around five passengers in a vehicle for a whole day, depending on how long you want to stay there and how many of you there are.

Visa extensions The Immigration Office is hidden away on the third floor of a building on Al-Mourabet St in the centre of town (daily except Fri 8am–1pm); look for a sign at street level in English, "Passports".

Around Hama

The most popular excursion from Hama is to the Roman ruins at **Apamea**, where extensively unearthed remains of the streets, buildings and fortifications of this former desert trading centre make for a full day's visit – though bear in mind that the bus service back to Hama is thin from mid-afternoon. **West of Hama**, other ideas for excursions include a number of ruined castles, the most interesting and accessible of which is at **Misyaf**, while nearby **Deir Soleib** offers a couple of remarkable ruined Byzantine churches. It's also straightforward to visit the magnificent Crac des Chevaliers (see p.184) from Hama, travelling via Homs. **East of Hama** there is less of note to visit – and far fewer people looking around what sights there are. Two roads head out across the desert plains: one southeast to Salamiyeh via another impressive castle, **Qalaat Shmaimis**, the other northeast to the flamboyant Byzantine palace at **Qasr Ibn Wardan** and the ruinous Byzantine settlement of **Anderin**. Further east again is the Roman temple at **Isriya**, possibly the remotest tourist sight in Syria. Another option for a day-trip is the Dead Cities around Maarat al-Numan (covered on p.248), located halfway between Hama and Aleppo and conveniently approached from either centre.

Hama is a fairly good transport hub, and the sites described in this section are all reachable on day-trips – which is fortunate, since there are no hotels available at any of them. However, to reach the sites east of Qalaat Shmaimis, you need to arrange your own transport in Hama.

Apamea and around

Most visitors to Hama – in fact, most visitors to Syria – make it to **APAMEA**, and although the tour buses which start pitching up here from mid-morning onwards detract somewhat from the excitement of its desolate location, it's still well worth the effort of seeing the place, even if you have only a passing interest in things Roman. Like Palmyra, Apamea was a **desert trading post** on the long trek from the Mediterranean to Central Asia, and the remains, well preserved by the dryness of the climate, form one of the most important archeological sites in the Middle East. Several eras of history threaten to sweep you off your tired feet here: the site is essentially **Roman**, with important additions from the Byzantine era, but there is a **citadel** dating from early medieval times, and along the dusty main road in **Qalaat Mudiq**, the modern part of the settlement which takes its name from the citadel, there's even an Ottoman caravanserai (now the site museum).

To get to Apamea **from Hama**, take a **microbus** 45km northwest to Skailabeyeh, where you change onto another microbus for further 9km to the north; remember to ask for **Afamia**, the local name, rather than Apamea, the Roman name which has stuck among English-speakers. Total journey time should be no longer than an hour, but note that buses tend to dry up around 4pm, and anyone travelling here on a Friday should prepare for longer waiting times. About 25km out of Hama is a ruined Arab castle, **Qalaat Sheizar** (see p.168), hardly essential viewing but an easy break in the journey between Hama and Skailabeyeh.

In summer Apamea gets so scorchingly hot that looking round the site is unpleasant at any time other than early to mid-morning or late afternoon. This, however, leaves only a short time to see what is, in fact, a huge and absorbing set of archeological remains (there are no hotels here to make it easier). A slightly overpriced **café** right in the centre of the site is the only place hereabouts for refreshments.

Some history

Apamea was founded around 300 BC by **Seleucus**, ruler of northern Syria and Mesopotamia following the death of Alexander the Great, and was named after Seleucus's Persian wife. During the Seleucid period the town became an important trading post, linking Latakia with Palmyra and eventually Persia and the Asian interior. After conquest by the **Romans** in 64 BC Apamea became an important garrison town and was dramatically rebuilt, its population expanding to about 500,000, of whom an estimated 380,000 were slaves. A huge rebuilding programme had to be undertaken following an earthquake in 115 AD, so the famous colonnaded main street as seen today dates only to around 180 AD.

Apamea's fortunes declined with the end of Byzantine rule, but it re-emerged into brief prominence in the early twelfth century when it was occupied by the **Crusaders**. However, after further earthquakes in 1157 and 1170 almost completely destroyed the town, the population moved to and refortified the old Roman acropolis on the hill overlooking the Ghab. During Ottoman times, this village within the walls, Qalaat Mudiq, became an important stopover point on the pilgrimage route from Istanbul to Mecca.

The site

The microbus from Skailabeyeh drops you outside the museum, from where a track runs past the museum entrance to the main site, a ten-minute walk. Arriving **by car or taxi**, it's best to leave the main road at the well-marked turning just to the north of the museum, which heads up around the northern edge of the citadel and brings you up to the cardo maximus, the long, columned street which formed the heart of the Roman city. **Tickets** for the site must be purchased in the small booth opposite (S£300 for combined entry to the site and museum).

The best place from which to get your bearings is the café by the cardo maximus; the modern road leading up here follows the line of a decumanus, one of several roads which intersected the cardo maximus at right angles – part of the Hellenistic grid pattern of streets bequeathed to the Romans. Along the cardo maximus is a long line of **columns**, the site's most immediate draw, with the remains of several interesting buildings along its length. The churches and Byzantine cathedral south and east of the café are very ruinous, but the Roman houses along the road to the east are better preserved and easier to appreciate, despite – or because of – their smaller scale. Finally, there's the decrepit Roman theatre and the medieval citadel, both of them on a lavish scale but with little to recommend them save the fine views over the site, and over the plain of the Ghab, from the entrance to the latter.

NORTH ALONG THE CARDO MAXIMUS

The most obvious feature of the site today is the **cardo maximus**, which was the main street and showpiece of Roman Apamea, built to show off the prosperity of the city. Aligned precisely north–south, it runs longer than the main thoroughfares in either Damascus or Palmyra, its high, fluted columns, mostly reconstructed during the twentieth century, striding energetically across the desert. Following the earthquake of 115 the cardo maximus was rebuilt starting from the north end, where the Classical sobriety of the columns contrasts vividly with a freer, more ornate style towards the southern end, reconstructed several decades later. The empty consoles projecting from many of the columns would once have supported busts of eminent citizens; most of these have long since been lost, destroyed or carted off to museums in Aleppo and Damascus, though some can be seen in the museum beneath the citadel. The ruts made by chariot wheels can still be seen in many of the paving stones on the street, while beyond the columns, where there once stood elegant doorways, there are now just vacant openings taking you into weed-strewn areas of rubble.

Strolling north along the cardo maximus from the café, the first remains you come to, on the left, are of the **agora**, the long, narrow marketplace, not all of

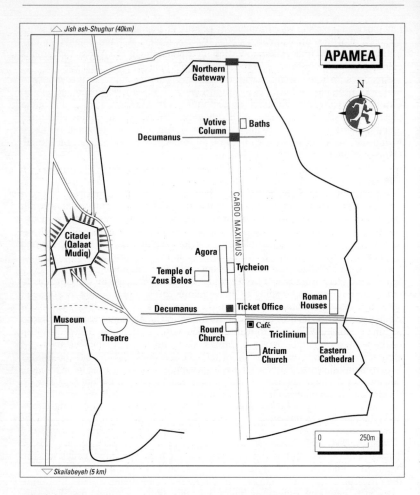

which has been excavated, which runs for 150m beside the main street. Over the hill beyond this are the scant remains of the **Temple of Zeus Belos**, which was dismantled in 384 as Christianity took hold in the Roman Empire. Back on the main drag you can see on the east side of the street a series of columns with spiral fluting, the direction of the spiral on one column alternating with that on the next, a technique unique to Apamea. Their elegance formed a suitable counterpoint to the formerly grandiose (though now ruined) façade of the **tycheion** opposite, where Tyche, the protecting goddess of the city, was worshipped.

About 600m north of the *tycheion* stands the single most striking feature of the cardo maximus, a **votive column** which once marked the intersection with a decumanus. Heavily restored and reconstructed, the column is little more than an ostentatious showpiece, architecturally useless but intended as a grandiose and permanent monument to the city's power and wealth. On your right, 150m beyond the column, are the **baths**, built in 117 AD by Emperor Trajan but now rather the worse for wear. No restoration has gone on here, so it's possible to appreciate the scale of the original building but not its layout, which would have comprised two large halls for the warm and cold baths. At the end of the cardo maximus is a second-century **northern gateway** under which would have passed the road to Antioch, now in Turkey but in Roman times the seat of the provincial government of Syria. Of the 6km of city **walls**, which were refortified by the emperor Justinian during the sixth century, this is the best-preserved section – though that isn't saying a great deal.

THE SOUTHERN END OF THE CARDO MAXIMUS

Immediately south and east of the café building are large areas of ruins, mostly fallen stones from churches and civic buildings which are now hard to distinguish. Closest to the café are the scant remains of the foundations of a **round church**, dating to the sixth century. The jumbled collection of masonry opposite marks the **atrium church**, of similar dating, dedicated to SS Cosmas and Damian, twin brothers who worked as healers without charging fees; one of their services was a process called incubation, whereby a sick person could spend the night in their church in the hope that they would be cured by their dreams.

East over the brow of a low hill, yet more fallen stonework on the right marks the vast site of **the eastern cathedral**, which also dates mostly from around the sixth century; the remains of the walls reach up to 4m high in places. It's just possible to appreciate something of the cathedral's layout: the building was entered by steps from the decumanus, and the floor of the narthex, the entrance hall which spanned the width of the church, can still be seen. On the west side of the cathedral is a *triclinium* consisting of eighty rooms arranged around a courtyard, which points to its possible use as a governor's residence; on the southeast side, a series of rooms was used for baptisms and other ceremonies. Some of the most intricately decorated stonework and mosaics that were found in these two sets of buildings can be seen in the site museum.

Less monumental than the cathedral are the excavated remains, to the north, of **Roman houses**. You can still make out the main courtyards, lined with columns, which would once have also had central fountains, benches in the cool arcades and marble paving. The intimate scale of the buildings here makes them one of the most interesting parts of the whole site, although they seem to be overlooked by most visitors.

THE THEATRE AND CITADEL

Located behind modern houses between the cardo maximus and the main road, the **theatre** probably dates from the late second century AD and would have been one of the largest in the Roman world. It was certainly the largest in Syria, with a stage almost a third as big again as that in Bosra, but its ruinous state makes estimating seating capacity difficult, as many of the blocks have been taken away for building works elsewhere in the town. The theatre is perhaps best appreciated from a distance rather than close up, though the scant remains are hardly impressive from whatever angle you view them.

The formidable **citadel** of Apamea, **Qalaat Mudiq**, occupies a spectacular position, overlooking the Orontes Valley on one side and the desert on the other. A fort was first established on this hill in Seleucid times; later on it became an Arab bulwark against the Crusaders, who captured many of the castles on the western side of the valley and were in fact in control of this castle between 1106 and 1149.

Inside the walls is a small village with its own stores, stalls and a small mosque, outside of which hustlers sell "antique" coins and other artefacts supposedly found around the ruins. A wander through the warren of streets indicates that villagers' homes occupy and utilize parts of the ruins of the fortifications which stood here; but the most striking aspect of the citadel is the fantastic **view** over the Ghab from the former entrance gateway, the distant rocky mountains often lost in haze. Some parts of the plain are mere marsh, others are intensively farmed, the fields dissected by numerous natural channels and irrigation ditches.

The museum

Hard by the modern main road, the **museum** (daily except Tues 9am–6pm; S£200) occupies an eighteenth-century Turkish caravanserai, which was used by trading convoys as a warehouse and rest place and is now a cool retreat from the blistering heat of the desert in summer. Housed in the dark, cavernous rooms which line the courtyard are artefacts from Apamea and nearby Roman settlements, mostly dating from between 230 and 370 AD and labelled only in Arabic.

The mosaic set into the ground as you enter the building depicts Socrates and the Sages, with the philosopher surrounded by his followers in a composition that's strongly reminiscent of typical portrayals of Christ and his disciples. Look out also for the two bulky, functional sarcophagi nearby, which were found in the same tomb and date from around 230; the first one you come to is that of a former legionary and has an inscription dedicated by his wife. Immediately around the next corner is another fairly well-preserved mosaic, measuring over 7m in length, entitled *The Judgement of the Nereides*. Found in the eastern cathedral, it depicts a beauty contest, judged by Poseidon (fourth figure from right), who has declared Cassiopeia (nude figure, third from left) to be the loveliest maiden. Unfortunately many of the other mosaics here are fragmentary, and there's not actually that much else which grabs the attention.

Qalaat Sheizar

Microbuses running between Hama and Skailabeyeh pass through **Maharde**, a small roadside town 25km due northwest of Hama. Rising above the town, with the road on one side and a steep gully on the other, are the ruins of **Qalaat Sheizar**, a castle founded by the Arabs to defend the west bank of the Orontes. In early medieval times, when Apamea was in the hands of the Crusaders, the castle was used as a base from which to mount attacks against the European armies – and so came under attack itself. Now little remains of the castle, although the ruins on the summit make for an interesting wander; it's an unproblematic couple of minutes' walk from the road, and once you've looked round you can easily flag down a passing microbus for the journey on to Hama or Skailabeyeh. The castle is within sight – and earshot – of a *noria* which supplies water to nearby fields.

Misyaf and around

Numerous microbuses ply the forty-kilometre route west from Hama to **MISYAF**, a fairly dull junction town which nevertheless contains the best-preserved of the **Assassin castles**. The initial view of the castle as you descend the road from Hama is the finest, especially in the early morning when it emerges from the mist like something out of a fairy tale.

THE ASSASSINS

The strange and fearsome Shiite Muslim sect known as the **Assassins** (*Hashashin* in Arabic) earned their popular nickname, probably in the eleventh century, from their reputed use of hashish to prepare themselves for attack or conflict. This reputation, however, is recorded only in travellers' tales (most famously those of Marco Polo), and probably only serves to illustrate outsiders' long-term bewilderment at the Assassins' motives and beliefs.

The first recorded references to the sect date to the period of political and religious fragmentation in the late eleventh century, when they were essentially a terrorist group in Persia, based around a small territorial holding that emerged upon the death of the Fatimid Caliph Mustansir in 1094. In the late eleventh century the Assassins began to expand their influence into Syria, leading to a backlash against them from orthodox Sunni regimes in Damascus and Aleppo; as a result, the Assassins retreated into the mountains, basing themselves at the castle of **Misyaf** which they acquired in 1140. The sect then undertook a policy of killing anyone who might threaten their independence, whence the term "assassin", brought back to Europe by the Crusaders, derives its present meaning. Murder, as practised by the Assassins, was more than just a means of political expediency, it was an act of devotion, even piety; daggers were almost always used and the killer made no attempt to escape – indeed to escape alive from such a mission was regarded as shameful.

The Assassins were particularly active between 1163 and 1193 under the leadership of **Rashid al-Din Sinan**, dubbed the "Old Man of the Mountains" by the Crusaders. He sponsored the assassination in 1172 of Conrad of Austria, the King of Jerusalem, and in 1176 even dared to make an attempt on the life of the orthodox Sunni leader Saladin, who was laying siege to Misyaf. The story goes that Saladin was awoken by nightmares to find on his bed a poisoned dagger and a piece of paper with the words "you are in our power" written on it, which he was convinced had been left by Sinan himself. Duly frightened, Saladin made a hasty retreat, asking for Sinan's pardon and calling off his campaign against the Assassins.

The sect's strength diminished during the late twelfth century as the Sunnis extended control from Damascus and Aleppo, and much of their coherence was lost in 1260 with the sacking of their Persian headquarters in Alamut by the Mongols. In the early 1270s Sultan Baibars (see p.82) defeated an Assassin rebellion and placed their castles under Mameluke governors, effectively destroying their political identity and reducing them to a harmless minority. The sect's members sought refuge in the mountains; during the nineteenth century many settled around the Syrian desert town of Salamiyeh, southeast of Hama, though the largest remaining group is in India and Pakistan.

From the microbus station, you can easily get a taxi to the castle, which is situated on top of a rocky crag rising pimple-like from the centre of Misyaf (otherwise it's a twenty-minute hike up). The plan of the castle (daily: summer 9am–6pm; winter 9am–3pm; S£150) is fairly conventional: there is a central keep enveloped by an outer wall with square bastions and a large gatehouse, all of which are further protected by the steep rocky slopes below. The mess of stonework used in the castle's construction reflects both the poor quality of Assassin renovation and the fact that this site has been fortified since Hellenistic times; the Classical masonry used in the walls suggests the existence of a nearby

Roman settlement from which building materials were pilfered. Today, the outer walls and towers remain in pretty good shape, though the keep has been unsubtly restored using concrete. A visit needn't last long as it's quite a small place, but tourists here are rare and the guardian may decide to make a fuss over you, plying you with tea and dusty tourist-office posters.

Deir Soleib

The small, unassuming village of **DEIR SOLEIB** plays dispassionate host to a couple of fascinating **Byzantine churches**, fairly well preserved and not dissimilar to those found in the Dead Cities around Aleppo. No buses run all the way to the village, which lies 9km east of Misyaf and south off the main road to Hama, so ask a microbus driver travelling back to Hama to drop you at the turning and then walk or hitch the last 6km; bear in mind when returning that buses along the main road dry up around 2pm. Alternatively, simply negotiate a price with a taxi driver in Misyaf (S£150 one way from the town's microbus station would be fair). Two kilometres west of the village, in the middle of a fig grove (to the left as you approach the village from Misyaf), is the first church, dated stylistically to the sixth century. The pale stone walls and the semi-domed apse which protrude from the rear of the church are well preserved, though the decoration here is minimal save for a few Byzantine crosses; an unusual cruciform font carved out of a single piece of rock can be seen in the baptistry off the southern end of the narthex. The church, though a three-aisled basilica in form, is almost square inside; a gallery reserved for women would once have run along the upper levels of the side aisles. Immediately to the south of the church stands a mausoleum with three sarcophagi lining the interior walls; substantially intact, it was probably built for important clergy. The second Byzantine church, reachable only on foot, can be found 2km southeast of Deir Soleib. Dated by an inscription above the central portal to 604–605 AD, it's much more ruinous than the first, but its setting, a jumble of masonry surrounded by stillness, is absorbing.

Qalaat Burzey

West of Apamea the marshy, fertile **Ghab depression**, a huge geological gash in the earth's surface which also caused the low-lying areas of the Dead Sea further south, opens up around the Orontes River. Scorchingly hot in summer, the valley is crossed by a dense network of minor roads, with principal roads running north–south on either side.

Dramatically situated on a steep bluff 34km northwest of Apamea, **Qalaat Burzey** (also Mazra or Barzuya) is the principal site of archeological interest here, offering magnificent views over the Orontes valley to the east. Back in Seleucid times a castle already stood here protecting the route between Latakia and Apamea, though what can be seen today dates from the eleventh century when the Crusaders occupied the site. The walls were apparently impregnable, the castle's defensive strength concentrated at its main entrance, which would have been through the western wall; however, in 1188 Saladin took the castle after a series of fierce raids. The ruins, scattered across a barren hillside, are fairly insubstantial, but it's possible to pick out the watchtower, two levels of fortification, a large chapel and the rectangular keep, which is an Arab construction.

Getting here requires you to rent your own transport in Hama or Homs, as public transport options are severely limited. To reach the castle, take the main road which runs along the western edge of the valley from Misyaf towards Jish ash-

Shughur; about 2.5km north of the village of **Jooreen** the road skirts a small artificial lake, and from here you must walk along a track and then scramble up a
steep boulder-strewn slope to the ruins, just visible from the road.

East of Hama

As soon as you head east beyond the built-up limits of Hama, the **desert** begins.
You get the same jam-packed minibuses and lunatic truckies careering along the
desert highways as you do everywhere else in the country, but the difference in
this part of Syria is the scenery: the desert here, unlike the pancake flatness of
the eastern and central desert, is rocky and hilly, and venturing out into it is an
absorbing experience in itself, never mind the archeological sites hereabouts, the
highlight being the remarkable desert complex of **Qasr Ibn Wardan**.

Qalaat Shmaimis
Rising out of the desert with breathtaking aplomb atop the summit of a steep volcanic cone, 20km southeast of Hama, are the remains of **Qalaat Shmaimis** (free
access at all times), a thirteenth-century Ayyubid fortification. It's set at least a
kilometre back from the road, and the scramble up to it is a strenuous one, so consider coming here either by taxi or as part of a tour organized by one of Hama's
hotels, rather than by simply hopping off one of the many buses that plod along
the road to **Salamiyeh**, 5km southeast of the castle. As the drawbridge has disappeared, you'll need footwear with a good grip to get up the slippery slope and
inside the castle; there is a cave here which looks like it might be an entrance, but
the real entrance is just to the right. Once there, as is so often the case in Syria,
the remains offer nothing but a disappointing jumble of masonry. However, the
views from the ramparts, across the windswept plains and over towards distant
grey hills, are predictably superb, and it's the breezy and utterly silent remoteness of the place which grabs the imagination most.

"BEEHIVE" HOUSES

Travelling past the villages that hug the desert roads to the east of Hama, you're
bound to notice the proliferation of traditional "**beehive**" houses, their name deriving from their distinctive shape. About 5m in diameter, they are built of mud and
straw, their design originating in the round houses of the Neolithic period, the
foundations of which have been unearthed in the Levant, particularly in Jordan.
Under their conical ceilings, beehive houses have just one chamber inside; some
– seemingly incongruously – boast electric lighting and appliances. The dwellings
are kept at a level temperature – relatively cool in summer, warm in winter – by the
trapping of air within (each house has only one entrance and no windows) and by
the insulation provided by their thick walls.

Nowadays very few people live in these buildings, which are used more for storage; the locals reside instead in the faceless concrete houses that stand side by
side with the "beehive" houses. Both the *Cairo* and *Noria* hotels in Hama organize
tours which will allow you to see inside one; alternatively, with your own transport,
simply stop off nearby and look around, and you'll probably be invited inside. As
head of the household, the father of the resident family will dominate conversation
with visitors, while the children scamper in and out and the mother maintains an
equilibrium between the two.

Qasr Ibn Wardan

One of the most flamboyant Byzantine constructions in Syria, **Qasr Ibn Wardan**, lies 62km northeast of Hama. It was completed in 565 AD, the last year of the reign of Emperor Justinian, who had attempted to restore to the empire much of the land lost in the East since Rome's heyday. In order to secure the conquests of his military commander Belisarius against the Persians, Justinian constructed a series of fortifications along the Euphrates, including formidable Halebiye (see p.261) and Resafe (see p.258); however, Qasr Ibn Wardan was probably designed to keep tabs on the Bedouin and to serve as the residence of some important military commander – possibly even Belisarius himself, who died one year after its completion.

To enter the complex (no set times; S£150), the key must be obtained from the genial guardian who lives in the house closest to it. The fey extravagance of Qasr Ibn Wardan has much more in common with the architecture of Constantinople, including the distinctive red-brick and black-basalt banding of the imperial capital; the centrepiece of the site is the **palace**, access to which is by a broad vaulted hall. Beyond are a series of rooms to the left and right, mainly residential quarters and ceremonial rooms, and a stairway leading to the second-floor dormitory area, where you can look down onto the courtyard and the restored stables at the far end. A calendar and sundial can be made out among the stone slabs which litter the courtyard; the basalt floor of the courtyard is original as are the patches of mosaic floor in some of the interiors. Note also the traditional Byzantine carved crosses above the doorways. The rooms on the western side of the courtyard formed a baths complex, and feature a sixty-metre-deep well (helpfully kept covered).

The **church** next to the palace is much smaller than a regular congregational church would have been and so was probably a private church connected with the palace, or a chapel. Pillars divide the church into three aisles and some of the original blue and white floor tiles remain. The staircase on its northwest side leads to an upper storey, probably reserved for women according to Byzantine tradition. The somewhat clumsy nature of the carvings together with the unusually tall nature of the building in relation to its dimensions has led to speculation that the architect was not from Constantinople but rather a local imperfectly mimicking the forms of the capital. The last building in the complex is a **military barracks**, 100m to the south of the palace, which at one time would have been the largest building of the three, though nothing much remains of it today.

It's best to arrange your own **transport** in Hama to get to Qasr Ibn Wardan, though microbuses (S£15) from the small eastern station in Hama run as far as the dusty town of **Al-Hamra**, 16km short of the site. To cover the remainder of the journey, you'll have to negotiate with one of the local taxi drivers (S£300 there and back is a fair price) – it's a small place so it won't take long for you to get noticed.

Anderin

Though an extensive site, dating back to at least the second century AD, **ANDERIN**, 25km beyond Qasr Ibn Wardan, offers nothing but a mass of ancient rubble emerging from the landscape. Little is discernible here apart from a Byzantine church and barracks, though at one time this would have been a settlement of some importance, with a further nine churches. However, the town was built largely of mud-brick, something increasingly prevalent further east of here, and has almost entirely disintegrated, the more substantial stonework having been pilfered even as recently as the last couple of decades. No buses, or indeed proper roads, reach out to Anderin (the last 3km of the trip is slow going along a bumpy desert track), so if you don't have a car you'll have to pay someone to take you there, either from Hama or Al-Hamra.

Isriya

The Roman town at **ISRIYA** was built at the crossroads of two trading routes which ran respectively from Resafe to Salamiyeh and from Qinnesrin, 30km south of Aleppo, to Palmyra. Once the settlement would have boasted a citadel attesting to its defensive importance, but today only the white limestone **temple**, dating from the third century, stands on the citadel mound. The eastern doorway of the stocky building contains impressively elaborate decoration, similar to and contemporary with examples at Baalbak (see p.114) in Lebanon. Inside, a staircase to the right of the doorway takes you up to what would have been the terrace. The improvised Bedouin graveyard situated in front of the temple lends the place a curious air of sanctity, but the most remarkable aspect of Isriya is its sheer remoteness – this must be one of the loneliest outposts of Syrian archeology.

Isriya is about ninety minutes' drive (there are no buses here) from Salamiyeh along a new paved road that continues on across the desert to Resafe (see p.258). Alternatively, there is a desert track stretching the 40km or so between Isriya and Anderin, but a four-wheel drive and a guide (best arranged in Hama) are needed for this journey.

travel details

Trains
Hama to: Aleppo (1 daily; 2hr 30min); Damascus (1 daily; 5hr); Homs (1 daily; 1hr 15min).

Homs to: Aleppo (1 daily; 4hr); Damascus (1 daily; 3hr); Hama (1 daily; 1hr 15min); Latakia (1 weekly; 4hr); Tartous (1 weekly; 2hr).

Pullman buses
Frequent Pullman buses **from Hama** cover the same routes as Karnak, plus Latakia (4hr); Qamishli (8hr); Raqqa (4hr); and Tartous (2hr). **From Homs**, Pullman buses run to the same destinations as Karnak.

Karnak buses
Hama to: Aleppo (4 daily; 1hr); Damascus (4 daily; 3hr); Homs (4 daily; 1hr).

Homs to: Aleppo (3 daily; 2hr 30min); Damascus (3 daily; 2hr); Hama (2 daily; 50min); Latakia (2 daily; 3hr); Palmyra (2 daily; 2hr 30min); Tartous (2 daily; 1hr).

Microbuses and local buses
Hama: frequent services to Aleppo (2hr 30min); Damascus (4hr); Al-Hamra (40min); Homs (1hr); Maarat al-Numan (1hr); Misyaf (35min); Salamiyeh (30min); Skailabeyeh (40min).

Homs: frequent services to Aleppo (3hr 30min); Crac des Chevaliers (1hr 15min); Damascus (3hr); Hama (1hr); Tartous (2hr).

Service taxis
Hama to: Aleppo (1hr); Damascus (3hr); Homs (1hr).

Homs to: Aleppo (2hr 30min); Beirut (Lebanon; 3hr); Damascus (2hr); Hama (50min); Tripoli (Lebanon; 2hr).

CHAPTER FOUR

THE COAST AND THE MOUNTAINS

Along Syria's Mediterranean coastline it's the **towns**, rather than the shore itself, which are the main attractions: **Tartous** boasts a reasonably intact old quarter and an attractive seafront, and **Latakia** has a cosmopolitan, European air about it that's unique in the country. If you're on the lookout for **history**, you'll find it dotted all along the coast, encompassing remains from the Bronze Age to the Middle Ages – and usually cheek-by-jowl with modern beach resorts, oil refineries or military zones. Undoubtedly the principal draw is just north of Latakia at **Ugarit**, where you can see the remains of a city which rose to prominence around 3000 BC and whose scribes and civil servants had a hand in inventing what was probably the world's first written alphabet. The Crusaders, whose castles are a major attraction in the mountains, have left their mark in the old city and cathedral at Tartous, on nearby **Arwad**, Syria's only island, and further north along the coast at **Qalaat Marqab**. Scant Roman remains can be seen at **Jableh**, south of Latakia, and Phoenician ones at **Amrit**, near Tartous, although neither spot is a patch on similar sites up in the mountains or elsewhere in the country. Unfortunately, if it's swimming and sunbathing you're after, it's only north of Latakia that there's anywhere clean enough to allow you to be wet or horizontal – a lot of the coast consists of uninspiring industrial complexes and dirty beaches.

Rising up behind the coastal plain, the rugged **Jebel al-Ansariya** – the extension of the Anti-Lebanon Range – has the strongest identity of any region in Syria: its climate, scenery and wildlife are different from everywhere else in the country, more akin to upland areas of Greece or Cyprus. Winters are cold and wet, with snow likely in January and February, and chilly, rainy days the norm until the end of April. In the summer it's generally cool and cloudy; while the rest of the country gradually wilts under months of drought, the mountains often expe-

---

ACCOMMODATION PRICE CODES

In this book, all hotels have been categorized according to the **price codes** outlined below, representing the minimum you can expect to pay for a **double room** in each hotel. Hotels in the ⑤–⑧ bands require payment in dollars. For further details, see p.35.

① under S£300/US$7	⑤ US$35–50/S£1500–2100
② S£300–600/US$7–14	⑥ US$50–90/S£2100–3900
③ S£600–1000/US$14–23	⑦ US$90–130/S£3900–5600
④ S£1000–1500/US$23–35	⑧ US$130/over S£5600

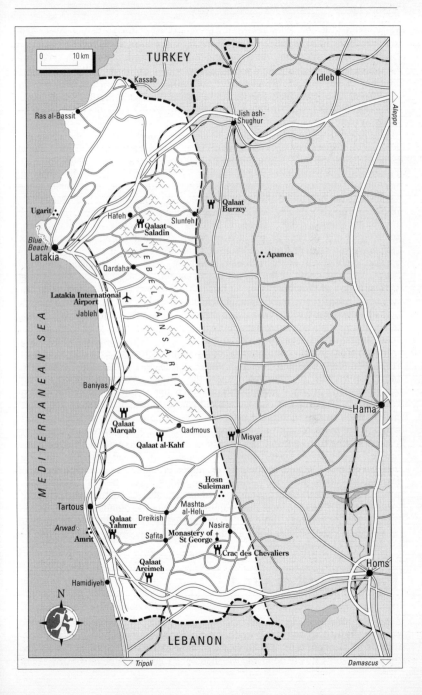

rience short, heavy thunderstorms, particularly in the early evenings. The scenery tends to be grassy limestone moorland in the south, with villages hidden by steep bluffs and overlooked by ruined castles, but further north there are forests of spruce and pine, and valleys dotted with churches and stone-built farmhouses. The people of the mountains are initially more reserved than city- or desert-dwellers, and many follow the Christian or Alawite faiths, which partly accounts for the mistrust with which they have traditionally been regarded by other Syrians.

It's in these mountains that most of the points of interest in this region are found, the major draw undoubtedly the **Crac des Chevaliers**, the magnificent Crusader fortress built during the twelfth century to protect the vital upland route linking Tartous with Homs. Now a regular stop for tour buses, which rumble up here from Damascus or, increasingly, from cruise ships docked at Tartous, the Crac shouldn't be missed. Also worth a visit is the Greek Orthodox **Monastery of St George** very nearby, and in the same area lies **Safita**, a modern town which boasts the imposing keep of the Crusaders' **White Castle**. Higher up in the mountains, and difficult to reach with or without your own transport, are the remains of an ancient Roman temple at **Hosn Suleiman**, a site of worship (of various deities) for centuries, impressively situated amid desolate moorland scenery. In the north of the region the Crusaders established another base at **Qalaat Salah al-Din**, taken in 1188 by the Muslim general whose name it bears, and now an impressive ruin, dramatically surrounded by woods and steep valleys.

With **accommodation** possibilities in the mountains rather limited, you'll most likely find yourself staying in Tartous or Latakia and making day-trips inland from there; both towns are easily reachable by road from Damascus and Aleppo. Away from the coast **public transport** becomes limited and sporadic, and you may be relying on slow, irregular buses or whatever transport locals can provide. The more you venture off the beaten track, the more interest and curiosity – and therefore offers of help – you will attract. With patience and perseverance you can reach all the places in this chapter without your own wheels, although you might find yourself having to fork out hefty wads of cash to locals if you want to reach some of the more obscure places; good humour and a sure sense of how much you are willing to spend on transport are necessary prerequisites for negotiating lifts in this way. If this doesn't appeal but you still want to see more than the Crac des Chevaliers, consider **renting a car**, either in Latakia or, planning ahead, in Damascus, Homs or Aleppo – this is the region in Syria where it's most worthwhile, although the lack of good maps and inadequate signposting pose problems for drivers. Perhaps the most disappointing aspect of the mountains is the lack of opportunity for **hiking** – there are no designated paths or trails, and no maps to let you guide yourself, so any walking you'll end up doing is most likely to be along roads between villages.

Tartous and around

The charming small fishing town and former Crusader stronghold of **Tartous** is a pleasant base for excursions to the Phoenician remains at **Amrit** and over to the island of **Arwad**, as well as up to the Crac des Chevaliers and other, lesser monuments in the mountains. The former Crusader **cathedral** (now a museum) and the nearby **Old City** are definitely worth looking round, and the **harbour** is lively,

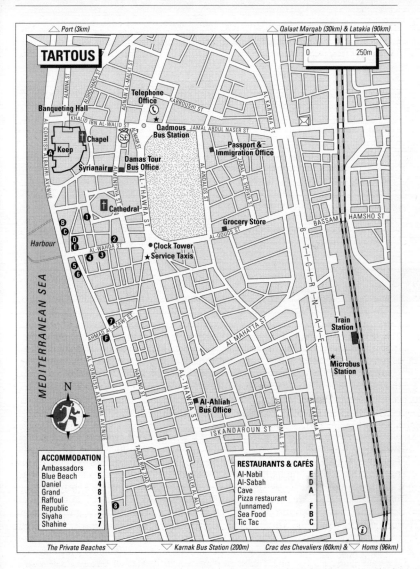

but the litter-strewn beach and string of scrawny fish restaurants along the water-front form a rather less attractive aspect to the city.

Tartous

Founded by the Phoenician colony on Arwad, **TARTOUS** remained an important settlement through Hellenistic and Roman times. It subsequently became a major

TEMPLARS AND HOSPITALLERS

Most Crusaders tended to come and go from the Holy Land according to whim or circumstance; the only permanent standing armies in the East were comprised of the **Templars** and **Hospitallers**, into whose hands most Crusader fortifications eventually passed. The basic concept behind the formation of those two military orders was to combine a monk's way of life with the knightly ideal. Hugh of Payens, a knight from France, was reputedly the first person to come up with the idea; in 1119 he, along with eight of his companions, swore to the patriarch of Jerusalem to be obedient, poor and chaste, and to protect the pilgrims travelling on the dangerous road from Jaffa to Jerusalem. The king of Jerusalem gave them special rooms – erroneously thought to have been part of the Temple of Solomon – in the royal palace, and the men subsequently became known as the Templars. Undoubtedly influenced by them were the Hospitallers (or Knights of St John), originating from a community of laymen who had founded a Christian hostel in Jerusalem in 1070. Initially their role was purely charitable, but in 1136 they became militarized when they took over the running of a castle near Ascalon in Palestine. Other castles soon came under their protection, initially garrisoned by knights whom the Hospitallers paid for the purpose, but by the 1150s the Hospitallers were carrying out all military duties themselves.

The only sworn allegiance of the Templars and Hospitallers was not to a local leader, but to the **pope**. This fact, combined with the autonomy afforded by their immense wealth (derived from the many gifts of land in Europe they received), and the increasing impoverishment of the nobility in the Holy Land, ultimately contributed to the undermining of the local rulers and the fragmentation of Crusader-held lands. Indeed, the Templars and Hospitallers ended up bitter **rivals**, almost to the point of open warfare in 1243 when the former entered into an alliance with the Ayyubids in Damascus. The Templars were eventually suppressed in 1312 following the expulsion of the Crusader armies from the Holy Land; their wealth and possessions were given over to the Hospitallers, who retreated first to Rhodes and then finally, in 1530, to Malta.

Christian stronghold, and by the fourth century a chapel, claimed to be the first dedicated to the Virgin, had been built here. An earthquake in 487 largely destroyed the chapel but left its altar miraculously unscathed; this was later incorporated into a cathedral built by the Crusaders in 1123, which became a popular pilgrimage site. In 1152 control of Tartous passed to the **Knights Templars** (see box, above), who extensively fortified the town, transforming it into their most significant base after their headquarters in Acre. The Templar garrison was forced to blockade itself in the castle keep in 1188 when Saladin's forces raided and destroyed much of the town (including the cathedral), but their final defence held strong and Tartous remained in Crusader hands until their very last days on the mainland in 1291. The Templars clung on to Arwad for eleven more years before a final withdrawal to Cyprus.

Tartous is now Syria's second most important port after Latakia – although you'll probably see nothing of the docks, which are located a fair distance to the north of the city. It's an unhurried place, centred around an attractive harbour from which the boats to Arwad leave. The **town centre** is marked by the clock tower along Ath-Thawra Street. **Al-Wahda Street** runs inland from the harbour towards the clock tower, and is lined with the town's cheaper hotels and restaurants; to the north of this street is the **Old City**, whose two focal points are the **cathedral** (now a museum) and the **keep** and the **city walls**. Running south from the harbour is an attractive sea front *corniche*, the setting for the town's beaches and the better hotels.

The cathedral

Tartous's **cathedral**, in a small square to the north of Al-Wahda Street, has a flat, expressionless facade – the result of a solidly defensive reconstruction following its mauling at the hands of Saladin's troops – and the best that can be said of the early Gothic three-aisled interior is that it's grim but impressive. Following the Crusaders' departure from Syria, the building served a variety of purposes: in 1697 the pilgrim Henry Maundrell reported that it had become a cattle shed, filled knee-deep with excrement, while in the nineteenth century it was put to use as a mosque, before being commandeered by the Turkish army during World War I. In the Mandate era the cathedral was substantially restored, and it now houses a sporadically interesting, if poorly laid-out, museum (daily except Tues: April–Sept 9am–6pm; Oct–March 9am–4pm; S£300). Most noteworthy among the exhibits are some marble sarcophagi from Amrit and an 800 BC black stone carving of the god Baal; coins, costumes and fragments from all periods and in no discernible order make up the rest of the display, with only a handful of faded French labels to assist those who don't read Arabic.

The keep and city walls

In Crusader times the walled city of Tartous formed a large rectangle, its western facade lapped by the sea and its other three sides protected by a deep ditch filled with sea water. Little remains of these outer fortifications apart from a small, square **tower** marking their southwestern corner, by the harbour at the end of Al-Wahda Street. In the northwest corner of the city was a fortified inner compound protecting a banqueting hall, a chapel and a keep. Today a small square occupies its courtyard, its western side occupied by the **keep**, where the Crusaders holed themselves up while Saladin was busy razing the town; its forbiddingly dark interior is usually kept locked. The western face of the keep would have met the sea directly in Crusader times; from the modern-day road that runs past it you can see a small postern gate in its sloping wall, probably the exit used by the Templars on their final retreat from the mainland to Arwad. Little remains of the great hall to the north of the square, where the knights would have met and deliberated, though the chapel in the northeastern corner is far easier to recognize. The surrounding streets make for good exploring: they're set in a tightly weaving maze, reflecting the original medieval plan, although here and there they are spoilt by the confusing incursion of modern buildings.

The beaches

Tartous's **seafront**, which is promenaded for a couple of kilometres heading south from the harbour, is ideal for a relaxing stroll while you watch families at play on the beach or follow the progress of the small boats which bob out to the tiny island of Arwad. The succession of colourful stalls selling all the regular seaside accessories, and numerous cafés, restaurants and ice cream parlours provide the place with a distinct holiday atmosphere. However, despite the antics of the locals, the polluted sea is not fit for swimming, and the stretch of beach from the harbour south to and beyond the ruins of Amrit is strewn with litter; walking on the sand (which should on no account be done barefoot) is often much less pleasant than a stroll along the road. Sometimes there are groups of local schoolchildren out on the beaches, engaged in a community-service clean-up, but they're fighting something of a losing battle – although the situation has definitely improved in recent years.

The best beaches are located a couple of kilometres south from the Old City, where there are privately owned stretches of sand which are allied to the nearby holiday-home complexes. You can gain access to these beaches for a small amount or by renting one of the grubby chalets (around S£500 a night); enquire at one of the beach huts if you want to do either.

Practicalities

Microbuses from all destinations in the mountains, as well as from Homs, Latakia and Damascus, arrive at the **microbus station** on 6 Tichrin Avenue. Just to the east is the **train station**, served by just one passenger train a week travelling in either direction along the coast. The centre is easily reached on foot from either station – head north along 6 Tichrin Avenue, then west along Al-Quds Street. Qadmous are the **Pullman** kings in these parts; they've got their own handy terminal on Jamal Abdul Naser Street, 400m north of the clock tower, with frequent timetabled services to and from Aleppo, Baniyas, Damascus, Homs and Latakia. Midway between the Qadmous terminal and the clock tower, a short way west from Ath-Thawra Street, is the office of Damas Tour, outside which their buses from Damascus and Latakia stop. **Karnak**, on Tareq bin Ziad Street (it's best to get a taxi north into the centre from their terminal), offer less frequent services on the same routes as Qadmous, and have a daily departure to Beirut via Tripoli. **Service taxis** hang around the clock tower on Ath-Thawra Street, and also do the run into Lebanon (as well as Damascus, Homs and Latakia), but they're far more expensive.

The **port** is situated well to the north of the city centre; here cruise ships can often be seen docked incongruously amid the aged freighters. There are no scheduled ferry services from Tartous, though the shipping agency offices on Khalid ibn al-Walid Street can tell you if any last-minute cruise tickets are available to casual travellers; it's unlikely, but it makes for a stylish way of leaving the country.

The **tourist office** (daily except Fri 8am–2pm) is situated on 6 Tichrin Avenue, 600m south of the microbus station; as usual they're very nice people, but are unable to provide you with anything beyond free hand-out maps. Efficient **exchange** services are offered at the Commercial Bank of Syria on Khalid ibn al-Walid Street (daily except Fri 8am–1pm). The immigration office, for **visa extensions**, is off Jamal Abdul Naser Street, east of the park (daily except Fri 8am–2pm). Just east of the junction of Jamal Abdul Naser Street and 6 Tichrin Avenue is the **post office** (daily except Fri 8am–10pm); the **telephone office** is on Ath-Thawra Street, just north of the Qadmous bus terminal. There's a **pharmacy**, Al-Iman, opposite the *Daniel Hotel* on Al-Wahda Street.

ACCOMMODATION

Most of the cheap **hotels** are situated near the harbour on Al-Wahda Street, with a number of decent mid-range establishments lining the seafront.

Ambassadors (☎043/220 183). Very similar to the neighboring *Blue Beach*, though not quite as good value. ③.

Blue Beach (☎043/222 746), off Al-Wahda St. Very friendly, offering basic, clean sea-facing rooms with balcony and private bath. ③.

Daniel (☎043/220 582), Al-Wahda St. The best of the cheap hotels, and consequently often full; the rooms, most of which are en-suite, vary dramatically from the clean to the downright grotty. On no account take a room without a fan in summer. Breakfast is available. ②.

Grand (☎043/315 681), Al-Cornish Al-Bahri Ave. The foyer is as grand as you get in Tartous; other parts of the hotel give an impression of having seen better days, but the rooms are excellently appointed, with satellite TV, fridges, efficient air-con, and balconies with a view of the sea in most cases. ⑤.

Raffoul (☎043/ 220 616), across the road from the cathedral, 150 north of Al-Wahda St. This is one of the cheapest options in town, offering a small number of clean, quiet rooms; if it's locked, ask for the proprietor at the small shop on the corner immediately south from the front door. ①.

Republic (☎043/222 580), Al-Wahda St. Reasonably clean doubles are available here, though the showers are unappealing. ①.

Shahine (☎043/221 703, fax 315 002), Ahmad al-Azawi St. Selection of spruce if slightly over-priced rooms in a characterless high-rise hotel which is often full. The restaurant on the top floor has a good view over the town and sea, as do many of the rooms, although there are no balconies. ④.

Siyaha (☎043/221 763), Al-Wahda St. Very basic hotel; rooms have fans and are just about acceptable, but street noise can be a problem. Lone travellers might get a bed in a room with others with bargaining, but the dingy entrance from the busy street sets the scene for an uninviting hotel generally, and this place is recommended only if other places are full. ②.

EATING AND DRINKING

Eating in Tartous focuses firmly on **seafood**, in terms of both the location of restaurants and what they serve. By far the best place to sample locally-caught fish is the *Cave*, whose cavernous interior is built into the walls of the Old City; on offer here are shrimps, octopus, sea bass and salads, with meat dishes in the winter. The other restaurants specializing in the local catch are the unappealing *Al-Nabil* and *Al-Sabah,* and the much better and more expensive *Sea Food*, where there's a greater variety of dishes and some outside seating. At *Tic Tac* you'll find pizza, spaghetti or other snacks on offer, and there's a good pizza place across the road from the *Shahine Hotel*. The *Grand Hotel* has a good restaurant serving *meze* and Western fare at reasonable prices. There are a few restaurants along the southern beaches which serve the usual Syrian cuisine for slightly inflated prices, although they're quite nice places to chill out by the sea.

Arwad

Of the many Syrians who come to Tartous for a beach holiday, the majority make the journey over to **ARWAD**, the small island that rises invitingly on the horizon 3km off the coast. There are no beach facilities here at all though, and no hotels or good restaurants either, just a bunch of tacky eating places and juice stalls along the harbourfront. It's easy to romanticize Arwad, to talk of its traffic-free narrow lanes that wind up to the remains of its Crusader fort, of the sight of small boats being repaired along the shoreline and fishermen repairing their nets along the harbour. However, it's very difficult to ignore the island's unsavoury side: the stinking rubbish lying piled up everywhere; too many people crowded into too small a space; the recent proliferation of ugly, faceless concrete buildings; the shamelessly polluted sea and slime-covered beaches. All this is a great shame, as you get the feeling that – if they tried – the Syrian authorities could make Arwad a really pleasant place.

Tacky though it may be today, the island has an illustrious and ancient **history**, encompassing Phoenician and Crusader settlement. Arwad is mentioned in the Bible: Genesis 10:18 records that the original settlers were descendants of Canaan, one of Noah's grandsons. During Phoenician times Arwad was a prosperous maritime state (the name derives from the Phoenician word for "refuge"), but the Romans, who took control in 64 BC, didn't really take much notice of the place, although St Paul is said to have visited the island on his journey to Rome. Arwad was the last Frankish settlement in the Middle East to fall to the Muslims; the mainland Crusader strongholds of Acre and Tartous had fallen in 1291, but the soldiers in Arwad grimly held on until 1302 when they finally retreated to Cyprus – and the history of the Crusades in the Middle East came to a decisive end. The **Crusader fort** (daily except Tues 9am–4pm; S£150), at the highest point of the island, remains Arwad's main point of interest. That's not saying much, however, as all you get for the entry charge is a look around a poor museum and the chance to clamber over some crumbling fortifications – though the view over the rooftops across to Tartous is a fine one.

Practicalities

As long as it's not too rough, compact **boats** crammed with families and picnic baskets ply the route from the small harbour in Tartous throughout the day, a journey of about twenty minutes; beware that, even if the seas look fairly calm, the journey in these small vessels can be quite stomach-churning. Boats back to the mainland run until sunset – be sure not to get stranded. You pay for your trip (S£20 return) only when you come back from Arwad, at the ticket booth by the harbour entrance there. There are open-air **fish restaurants** clustered around the harbour, with not much to choose between them; drinks at these places are rather expensive, but there are cheaper, much smaller (and more enticing) cafés on some of the narrow streets around the fort.

Amrit

AMRIT, 8km south of Tartous, was founded by the Amorites sometime in the third millennium BC and developed by the Phoenicians as a religious centre to complement their settlement on Arwad. Its virtual abandonment during the early second century has meant the rare survival of Phoenician ruins without extensive remodelling by later generations. Set in a largely deserted agricultural area, with the sea glistening in the background, the peaceful remains may well induce you to stay longer than you expected. A rusted sign has, for many years, announced the impending arrival of a luxury beach resort along here, but there's scant evidence that it's going to happen in the foreseeable future.

The most important monument at Amrit is a **temple** dating to the late fourth century BC, an early and considerably less elaborate antecedent of the Temple of Bel in Palmyra. It consists of a large court cut out of the rock, in the centre of which is a well-preserved cella where the image of the resident god Melqart would have been placed. The court was flooded by a local spring (a feature unique to this site) whose supposed healing properties are the most likely explanation for the existence of the temple. This sacred pool was surrounded on three of its sides by a colonnaded arcade which has been recently reconstructed. Remnants of a

stadium can be seen across the choked river from the top of the unexplored *tell* next to the temple, though the only way to get a closer look is back via the road.

Situated on a small ridge 700m south of the temple are a pair of tall funerary monuments, known as the **spindles**; they soon come into view if you follow the path that leads behind the temple to the gap in the barbed wire fence and then continue walking southwards. The two make a decidedly odd couple: one is relatively plain, though it has a pyramid-shaped hunk of stone for a "head"; the other has castellated markings near its domed top and four battered lion sculptures around its base. The latter are a Persian influence which, along with the Greek and Egyptian styles found at the site, illustrates the Phoenicians' susceptibility to outside influences through their extensive trading links. Each spindle stands atop a small burial chamber – a torch is useful for a look round inside.

There are many other monuments, mausoleums and burial chambers in the vicinity, the best of which is a huge two-storeyed cube-shaped **mausoleum**, once topped by a pyramid, and known as the Burj al-Bezzaq (Snail Tower). Containing two burial chambers, it undoubtedly belonged to one of Amrit's most important families; its most impressive feature is the colossal blocks of stone used in its construction. To get to the mausoleum, walk inland from the spindles to the main highway, then 1km south along the road to where the turning (right) is signposted in English; follow the road off the main highway until it curves left, when you should take the dirt track which goes straight ahead – the monument can be seen down at the end of a small track heading through the trees to your right after about 50m.

Practicalities

To get to Amrit, take the Hamidiyeh **microbus** from Tartous, making sure the driver knows where you want to get off. You will probably be dropped off where the main road forks; follow the minor one which runs nearer the coast and the Amrit temple comes into view on your left after about 2km (just after the army base). As the area is partially a military zone, it would be wise not to be too tactless in your wanderings and photography. Going back, simply flag down any bus heading back into town along the coastal road, or you could walk it along the beach in a couple of hours.

Inland from Tartous

Inland from the industrial sprawl of modern Tartous the mountains begin, often shrouded in mist or low cloud whilst the town languishes in the sun on the coastal plain. The uplands here are cool and green, with villages built of stone on hillside terraces and clustering around dirt tracks which are barely motorable. Some of the settlements eke out a pretty meagre existence, their streets occupied by ragged children – tending equally ragged goats and chickens – who stop and stare whenever a stranger appears.

The **Crusaders** were immediately attracted to a landscape such as this: sparsely settled, simple to farm and easy to defend and control. They built some of their most enduring architectural monuments here, supreme among them the impregnable fortress of **Crac des Chevaliers**. Nowhere else in the mountains is as commercialized or popular as the Crac, though **Safita**, where you can see the remains of the Templars' White Castle, is busy turning itself into something of a mountain retreat for the well-heeled. The Roman temple at **Hosn Suleiman**, the area's other highlight, is interesting to clamber round and wonderfully situated amid some desolate scenery.

Tartous is by far the best base for exploring this part of the country: there are **accommodation** possibilities at Safita and around the Crac des Chevaliers, but they're recommended principally for those with their own transport. Only a limited number of **buses** grind along the twisting upland roads, making forward planning essential. Hitching or paying for lifts may be a necessity, but it's highly unlikely that you'll get stuck anywhere. Safita is the main public transport hub in the mountains, and it would be easy to combine a trip there with a visit to Hosn Suleiman, possibly taking in the compact **Qalaat Yahmur** on the way back. It's just about possible to visit the Crac des Chevaliers and Safita in one day (ignoring Hosn Suleiman), but as there are no direct microbuses between the two, it probably makes more sense to do separate day-trips to each from Tartous.

The Crac des Chevaliers and around

Set on a high, wind-swept ledge above a rocky valley, with superlative views across the mountains in every direction, the **CRAC DES CHEVALIERS** (daily: summer 9am–6pm; winter 9am–4pm; S£300) is quite simply an essential stop for anybody travelling in Syria. You won't find a better-preserved Crusader castle anywhere – it's still as formidable now as it must have been the day the Knights Hospitallers surrendered it. A visit here is easily combined with one to the nearby Monastery of St George. **Microbuses** run to the Crac from Homs only, though it's quite feasible to approach from either Hama, via Homs, or from Tartous, which entails changing micros on the way; see p.188 for details of routes to the castle.

A little history

Archeological evidence suggests that the site may have been occupied by the **Egyptians** during their struggle with the Hittites for dominance in Syria, which culminated in the Battle of Kadesh (see p.154) around 1285 BC. In 1031 the **Emir of Homs** built a new fortification here, and it was still a prime defensive location when the **Crusaders** arrived on the scene in the early twelfth century. The **Knights Hospitallers** gained control of the castle in 1144, completely rebuilding the place and fortifying it so well that it survived two major Arab assaults in the late twelfth century. However, during the thirteenth century the Crusader presence in the Holy Land thinned out considerably, leaving the Crac increasingly isolated and occupied by a garrison of only two hundred men (it could house four thousand). In 1271 **Sultan Baibars** (see p.82) began a siege of the castle, managing to breach the outer wall but finding the inner defences solidly impregnable. To resolve the stalemate he sent a forged letter into the castle, supposedly from the Grand Commander of the Order in Tripoli, urging surrender, and the depleted and dejected Hospitaller garrison hastily accepted the Sultan's offer of safe conduct to the sea. Within twenty years the Crusaders would have disappeared from the mainland.

The castle remained in use during the Mameluke period but as the foreign threat disappeared its strategic importance lessened. A village grew up inside the castle; in 1909 T.E. Lawrence reported that the regional governor was living in the keep, and that the castle had recently "withstood a siege on the part of a neigh-

THE BUILDING OF CRUSADER CASTLES

Many knights headed off home after Jerusalem was taken on the First Crusade, leaving at most only five thousand men to defend their conquests. With such small numbers left behind, and reinforcements tending merely to trickle in, their gains could only be held with a network of imposing **fortifications**. The Crusaders chose the most inaccessible **locations** they could find, usually on the tops of steep mountains, making communication with neighbouring castles much easier and siege much more difficult – indeed there was often no suitable terrain for besiegers to use mangonels or ballistas to lob missiles into the castle.

Though military architecture in the early twelfth century was much more sophisticated in the East than in Europe, the Byzantine castles the Crusaders came across were essentially fortified camps, with the stonework often hurriedly improvised. **Crusader castles** had to be long-term residences for permanent garrisons, much stronger and easier to defend than their Byzantine counterparts, and so the Crusader castle builders were forced to become pioneers in their field, adapting and developing both European and Byzantine models; walls were made taller and thicker, and the freestanding Norman keep was largely jettisoned (though a good example survives at Safita) in favour of a more solid construction located in the weakest point of the curtain wall. The Byzantine use of **machicolations** – projecting galleries situated near the tops of the walls used to rain down missiles on invaders – was adopted; so too was the practice of placing towers along curtain walls for added protection, with round towers supplanting the traditional square ones to allow a wider firing range and withstand bombardment more robustly.

As the castles increased in size, their entrance **gateways** became much more sophisticated and complicated; the supreme example of this is at the Crac des Chevaliers, which has a long winding passageway into the inner courtyard, and the deepening of the ditch at Qalaat Salah al-Din also illustrates the Crusaders' concern to make their entrances as impregnable as possible. At the bigger castles a second defensive wall was often built, a concept which had been used to defend cities in the East, such as Constantinople in the fifth century and Baghdad in the eighth, but never castles.

The most serious threat the castles faced was the **mining** of one of the towers – assailants would dig a tunnel underneath, then burn the supports so that the tower would collapse; the outer rings of both Marqab and the Crac were penetrated in this manner. Yet the reason these castles eventually fell was that they were woefully **undermanned**; when they were put under sustained attack with no prospect of a relieving force arriving, morale among the community inside collapsed, as exploited to the full by Saladin (see p.205) and Baibars (see p.82).

bouring district with complete success". The villagers were turfed out by the French Antiquities Department in 1934 who declared, with just a hint of Gallic superiority, that the Crac was "a monument of France".

The castle

The plan of the castle is that of an inner and outer line of defences, each strengthened by towers, the inner wall raised upon a large **glacis** – a smooth artificial slope – making it much higher than the outer wall, and thus a formidable obstacle to anyone who had managed to breach the outer ring. Before entering the castle it's worth completing a circuit of the **outer walls** to gain a full appreciation of its defences, and also to wind your way onto the hill behind that provides the

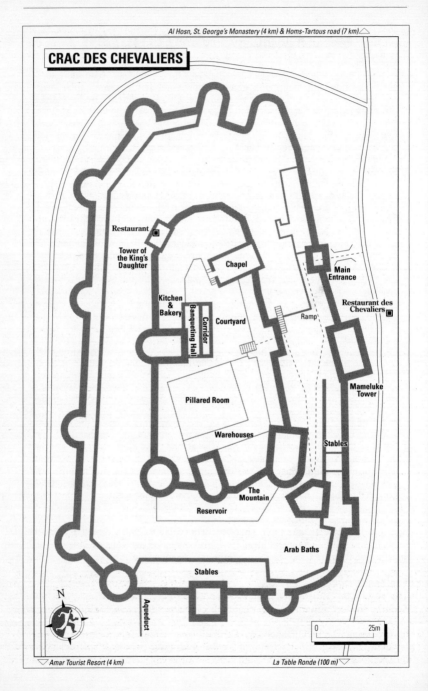

Al Hosn, St. George's Monastery (4 km) & Homs-Tartous road (7 km)

CRAC DES CHEVALIERS

Restaurant

Tower of
the King's
Daughter

Chapel

Main
Entrance

Kitchen
&
Bakery

Corridor

Banqueting Hall

Courtyard

Ramp

Restaurant des
Chevaliers

Mameluke
Tower

Pillared Room

Warehouses

Stables

The
Mountain

Reservoir

Arab Baths

Stables

N

Aqueduct

0   25m

Amar Tourist Resort (4 km)

La Table Ronde (100 m)

classic Crac photo opportunity. The south side, being the most easily approached, was the most vulnerable point of the castle; a ditch was dug to try to isolate the fortifications from the ridge and it is here that the walls are thickest and towers most tightly grouped. Despite these efforts, however, this is where Baibars managed to break through, successfully mining one of the towers; the southern wall you see now is an Arab reconstruction. The **aqueduct** (which looks like a bridge) would have fed water into the reservoir which is between the inner and outer defences.

FROM THE ENTRANCE TO THE SOUTHERN OUTER WALL
The **entrance** is on the castle's eastern side, through a dark, sloping passageway which would in Crusader days have boasted four gateways; the wide sloping steps were designed to allow horses to enter. The first tower along to the left is Mameluke in origin; next along is a long hall thought to have functioned as a stables, beyond which is a room giving access to the ramparts above the stables (which have seen some very obvious recent restoration). On the left, through a gateway at the point where the passageway doubles back on itself, are the remains of an **Arab baths** complex, while the castle's **reservoir**, filled with sickly green stagnant water, lies to the right. The reservoir stands at the bottom of what Baibars' besieging forces called "the mountain" – a huge glacis some 25m thick at its base. Why exactly the mountain was built has been the subject of some fierce debate: possibly it was an added protection against earthquakes (which had severely damaged the site in 1157, 1170 and 1201), or it might have been constructed to prevent mining (though as it stands on solid rock mining was hardly an option). Another theory suggests that it could have been used to produce a smooth surface to prevent it being scaled – T.E. Lawrence attempted to climb it in 1909 and only got halfway up. Perhaps the simplest and best explanation, however, is that it was built so that no besieger who had breached the outer defences could shelter beneath the inner walls of the castle.

Running along the southern line of defences is a long, unsupported vaulted chamber that probably functioned as the castle's main **stables**. Stairs lead up from here to its roof, from where you can gain access to the three **towers** that line the southern **outer wall**. The central square tower was rebuilt by Qalaun in 1285; inside the main room is a huge central pillar which almost fills it, and a staircase which heads up to the top – the best place to gain a full appreciation of "the mountain". From here you can complete the **circuit** of the outer walls, either by walking along the top of them or returning to ground level and continuing along the gap between the inner and outer walls. This allows you to admire the three sets of arches that decorate the exterior of the **tower of the king's daughter**, in the northwestern part of the inner wall. The lowest set originally concealed machicolations used to allow missiles or liquids to be rained down on any attacking force; when the Crusaders rebuilt the tower these machicolations were filled in and new ones built above the uppermost arches. At the end of the circuit, a staircase in the eastern section of this space gives access to the inner castle.

THE INNER WALLS AND COURTYARD
The alternative route to the inner part of the castle from the stables is to return to the entrance passageway at the point where it doubles back on itself, and continue along it to reach a set of steps leading into the castle's **courtyard**. Directly opposite across the courtyard from here is a graceful thirteenth-century **corridor**, its roof attractively divided into seven vaulted bays, whose delicately carved

Gothic doorways and windows fit incongruously with the Crac's starkly function-al military architecture. A Latin inscription on the far right-hand window reads, "Grace, wisdom and beauty you may enjoy, but beware pride which may alone tar-nish all the rest." From here two doorways admit you to an austere **banqueting hall**, a century older than the corridor but also Gothic in style. Behind this is a 120-metre-long **chamber** which would once have been filled with the castle's stocks and provisions, as well as housing the kitchen and bakery; the remains of the oven, more than 5m in diameter, can be made out on the floor just to the left as you enter, while to the right (running along the wall) are twelve medieval toi-lets. The **pillared room** to the south of the courtyard was probably used as a gen-eral area for storage, accommodation and cooking; the remains of oil jars can be seen embedded in the ground of the warehouses beyond. Across the courtyard is a twelfth-century **chapel**, a simple construction with little Christian decoration save some traces of painted rosettes on the north wall. After the Crusaders left, this was converted into a mosque, of which the *minbar* still remains.

The staircase by the chapel leads up to the northern ramparts; immediately in front of you here is the **tower of the king's daughter**, which hosts a **restaurant** that also sells souvenirs. A narrow staircase leads up to the roof, from where on a clear day you may be able to spot the tall keep of the White Castle in Safita (see opposite), which gave the Crusader garrison here a quick means of communicat-ing with the coast by relaying signals via Safita; it's also quite easy to make out the Monastery of St George (see below) across the valley to the north.

Finally, you can cross over the court to the **southern ramparts** that sit above the "mountain". The three towers here served as the final line of defence in the castle and provided the accommodation quarters for the most important of the knights; the interior of the southwestern tower is particularly attractive, featuring some delicate ribbed vaulting and skilfully carved rosettes. Being the tallest parts of the castle the roofs of these towers provide the most breathtaking views over the surrounding countryside, though hold on tightly to your hats as the wind up here can get surprisingly strong.

The Monastery of St George

Four kilometres away as the crow flies, the Greek Orthodox **Monastery of St George** (daily 9am–8pm; free), founded in the sixth century, is a relatively easy addition to sightseeing at the Crac, though the building itself will take up little of your time. It's a working monastery, built mostly during the last hundred years, with only a few medieval parts still intact. The peaceful chapel in the first court-yard to the right as you enter dates to 1857; descend into the lower courtyard for a look at a more interesting thirteenth-century one, recently restored after flood-ing, whose solemn interior features a remarkable 300-year-old ebony **iconostasis** made in Aleppo. This chapel might be locked, but wait around for someone to open it for you.

Practicalities

The only direct **microbus to the Crac** is the frequent service from Homs (1hr 30min; S£20), but it's easy enough to reach the castle from Hama by catching a connecting bus to Homs (1hr). Getting there from Tartous isn't hard either: take one of the frequent Homs-bound microbuses (S£15) and ask to be let off at the Crac turn-off on the motorway, where you can pick up the Homs–Crac microbus (S£5); the whole journey takes a couple of hours. Remember to ask for *Qalaat al-*

Hosn, the Arabic name for the Crac, **al-Hosn** being the name of the village immediately below the castle. About 25km along the highway from Tartous to Homs is
another (signposted) Crusader fortification, **Qalaat Areimeh**; however, though
the views from the ramparts are good, the remains are disappointing and the trip
only recommended for those with their own transport or prepared for a stiff walk.

The microbus service back to Homs from the Crac dries up mid-afternoon, but
taxi and microbus drivers hang around the castle entrance all day, and the
Restaurant des Chevaliers situated right in front of the entrance can get hold of a
taxi for you. No microbuses run between the Crac and the **monastery**, so you'll
have to negotiate a ride there with a taxi or microbus driver at the castle entrance
(about S£100). To get back to Tartous or Homs from the monastery, either hitch
or walk twenty minutes back along the way you came to the main road which
heads off to Nasira, where you can pick up a microbus towards Homs; for
Tartous, get off this microbus at the Homs–Tartous highway and catch another
microbus to Tartous from there.

ACCOMMODATION AND EATING
Around the Crac, the *La Table Ronde* (☎031/734 280; ③) is the only place to **stay**
in al-Hosn itself, with a limited number of basic rooms available and a spot to pitch
a tent (S£150). The management here are, however, in the process of financing
the construction of a new hotel on the hill overlooking the castle which is due to
open in 2001. Signposted 4km beyond the castle is the *Amar Tourist Resort*
(☎031/730 512; ⑤; June–Sept) offering apartments and double rooms along with
a restaurant and pool. There are three places here for **food**: the overpriced restaurant in the tower of the king's daughter, the *Des Chevaliers* near the castle
entrance, and *La Table Ronde* 200m up the hill beyond the main entrance: all rus-
tle up the standard Syrian fare of kebab or chicken and chips.

Along the road to the **monastery** are a number of good **hotels**. The clean and
friendly *Al-Khoudr* (☎031/730 245; ④) is virtually next door to the monastery, and
1km east of this is the very plush *Al-Wadi* (☎031/730 456, fax 730 399; ⑥), one of
Syria's best luxury hotels, where all rooms have TV, telephone and fridge, and
bars, restaurants, tennis courts and a swimming pool are thrown in for good measure. Just 200m along, the *Al-Naaim* (☎031/730 422; ③; June–Sept) is a decent
(and more decently priced) choice boasting clean en-suite rooms and a terrace
restaurant with great views of the Crac. Next along, the *Al-Riad* (☎031/730 402;
③) is also open in summer only; it's clean but basic and ultimately overpriced,
though you can camp here for US$6.

Safita and around

Standing seemingly aloof amid peaceful mountain scenery, the burgeoning
town of **SAFITA** is signposted across the mountains by its distinctive **keep**, all
that remains today of the **White Castle** of the Templars. A Crusader fortification was originally built here in the early twelfth century, but it was razed by
Nur al-Din in 1171; what can be seen today, a pale-coloured, windowless, square
stone keep rising above the roofs of the highest point of the town, dates from
the early thirteenth century. Upon the approach of Baibars in 1271, the Templar
garrison was commanded by the Master of the Order in Tartous to leave the
castle, an action which left the Crac des Chevaliers out on a limb; it fell only two
months afterwards.

Safita has a maddeningly impatient and claustrophobic air, its narrow streets choked with busy shoppers and relentlessly noisy traffic, making progress slow and wearing. Any one of the steep, winding alleys from the main road will lead you up to the keep, which maintains irregular opening hours but is generally shut in the early afternoon; try asking around for the key at the adjacent restaurant if necessary. Upon entry to the keep it's slightly surprising to find inside a fully functional **church**, dedicated to St Michael and serving the town's Greek Orthodox community; the windows of the church were originally firing slits. The entrance fee to the keep is a donation in one of the boxes provided. A narrow stairway leads up to a spacious room where the garrison would have been housed, with a further set of stairs taking you up to the crenellated terrace and some fine sweeping views; from here communication was made with other castles via signal fires. Just to the east of the keep is one of the castle's original gateways and part of the thirteenth-century wall.

Practicalities

Safita acts as a traffic hub for the mountains, with frequent microbuses making the half-hour journey (S£20) up here from Tartous, as well as services from Mashta al-Helu, Hosn Suleiman and Homs. To get here from the Crac des Chevaliers, catch a Homs microbus back to the Homs–Tartous motorway, where you can hail a Homs–Safita microbus (total journey time about 1hr 15min). The tiny **microbus station** is located 100m down the hill from the small central roundabout.

For a **place to stay**, the *Safita Cham Palace* hotel (☎043/531 131, fax 525 984, *www.chamhotels.com*; ⑥ except Jan–March ⑤), off the western end of the main street (on the right, set back a little from the road, as you enter from Tartous) has a pool and a restaurant with fine views from the terrace, though it's the luxury chain's smallest and least opulent establishment. A ten-minute walk east of the mini-roundabout near the bus station on Ali Yehia Street is a signposted but unnamed hotel (☎043/521 221; ③) which has reasonable rooms. There are a couple of **restaurants** next to the keep which serve standard Middle Eastern fare at moderate prices and boast great hillside views.

Qalaat Yahmur

Any journey between Tartous and Safita could be easily broken with a visit to the minor but well-wearing **Qalaat Yahmur**, 10km southeast of Tartous, an interesting complement to the larger fortifications in the mountains. The small, stocky castle is a twelfth-century Crusader reconstruction of a Byzantine fortification and consists of a stubby square tower surrounded by a very well-preserved outer wall. Just 2km from the main road, the castle, in the village of **Beit Shalluf**, is now given over to the housing of animals, but it's OK to nudge past them for a view into the interior. The upper storey of the tower can be reached via an external stairway; two watchtowers stand at the southeast and northwest corners of the outer wall, both Arab additions. It's easy to hail a micro back at the main road to continue on to Tartous or Safita.

Mashta al-Helu and Dreikish

Nestling in the southern mountains is the resort of **MASHTA AL-HELU**, 18km northeast of Safita (from where there are frequent micros; 30min) though signposted from just about everywhere. It's got a number of decent **restaurants**, overlooking some sweeping mountain scenery, and numerous ice cream stores in the centre of town, but lacks any real character and hardly justifies a special trip. There are two hotels: the four-star *Mashta al-Helu Resort* (☎043/584 000, fax 584 060; ⑥), a luxury residence with tennis courts, a swimming pool located on a terrace with magnificent views (S£200 for non-residents to use), restaurants and coffee-shops; and the much cheaper *Al-Widian* (☎043/581 298; ③), which boasts a shady **restaurant** next to a natural pool.

Dreikish, 7km north of Safita, is a name that will probably be familiar to you as it's plastered across the labels of most bottles of mineral water in Syria, but though the place is styled by local literature as another mountain retreat, it holds even less allure than Mashta al-Helu and isn't worth the time of day.

Hosn Suleiman

A ruined temple situated within a sheltered natural amphitheatre in the mountains, **HOSN SULEIMAN** can be approached via a direct **bus** service northeast from Safita (every 60 or 90min; 30min; S£20); buses back dry up around midday so bear this in mind when planning your day's schedule. This wild and rocky location, surprisingly verdant and cool (and usually very quiet unless a tour bus rolls up), consists of gigantic half-collapsed ruins which were a site for cult worship for thousands of years. From around 2000 BC the Canaanites were worshipping their god Baotocecian Baal here (the patron of the Phoenicians at Arwad); the site subsequently became a cult centre for the followers of Zeus Baotocecian, a hybrid of Baal and his Greek equivalent, Zeus. The Roman temple, the remains of which can be seen today, was probably built between the middle of the first century AD and the end of the second. Worship of various pagan cults took place here well into the fourth century, by which time Christianity had been firmly adopted as the religion of the Roman Empire.

The temple consists of a large rectangular building, built from huge blocks up to 10m in length, enclosing a central raised area (the **cella**, with its one remaining column) which housed the altar, now little more than a tumbled mass of masonry and boulders. There are four impressive entrances, the most elaborate of which is the northern gateway, set into the most substantial part of the remaining walls. Above the eastern gate an inscription in Greek, dated to 171 AD, records the dedication of the temple by local people, who had collected the funds needed to build it. If you cross the road you can see the scant remains of a monastery, believed to have been a separate temple adapted later on for use as a Christian convent and basilica, but now pleasingly overgrown by an apple orchard.

The coast between Tartous and Latakia

Frequent buses and microbuses bowl along the motorway between Tartous and Latakia, 80km north, past a series of dull towns, sprawling industrial complexes and intensive farms that are well watered by winter and summer rains. The view from a passing vehicle is not enticing, but there is scope to break your journey and get away from the road if you want to. **Baniyas**, with its huge oil refinery, gives access to **Qalaat Marqab**, a mountain-top Crusader stronghold, and further on at **Jableh** you can see the remains of a Roman theatre and wander round an attractive fishing harbour before pushing on. Both places would also be easy to visit on day-trips from either Tartous or Latakia, but the less compelling Ismaili fortress of **Qalaat al-Kahf** is really only worth visiting if you have your own transport.

Qalaat Marqab

From afar **QALAAT MARQAB** (daily: summer 9am–6pm; winter 9am–5pm; S£300) rivals even the Crac with its foreboding presence. Though the majority of the site is being taken over by a tenacious marrying of rubble and undergrowth, the castle still stands as one of the most formidable examples of Crusader castle-building in Syria. First fortified by the Muslims in 1062, the site passed into Crusader hands in the early twelfth century, though it wasn't until 1186 that the **Knights Hospitallers** came here; they spent the next twenty years or so converting it into one of their major strongholds. Though powerful enough to withstand sieges in 1204 and 1280 (Saladin didn't even attempt to breach it during his 1188 campaign), dwindling manpower and the loss of the Crac in 1271 led in 1285 to the castle's fall – mining by Baibars' successor Sultan Qalaun resulted in the collapse of the south tower, after which the beleaguered knights inside surrendered in return for a peaceful escape to Tartous and then Tripoli. The tower was rebuilt under Arab occupation, and the bands of white marble in the stonework observable from outside are a distinctive Mameluke autograph. During the Ottoman period the castle was converted into a prison.

The castle's defences were heavily weighted towards its weakest point in the south, which is by far the best-preserved section. The long stairway outside the castle leads up to the main entrance tower where the ticket office is situated; to reach the main **courtyard** from here, exit to the right to get between the line of inner and outer defences, then head down to the inner gateway. At the southern end of the courtyard is a spacious twelfth-century **chapel** (declared a cathedral in 1188, and converted into a mosque after Qalaun took the castle), a very early example of the Gothic style; indeed most of the arches can't seem to make up their mind whether they are pointed or rounded. In the small sacristry to the left of the apse you can see a fragment of a fresco depicting the Last Supper, which was uncovered in 1987.

South of the chapel are a barracks and the remains of the great hall, built over a massive cistern, and beyond that is the solemnly dark granite keep, boasting walls 5m thick; stairways lead up to the roof of the keep and some awesome **views** over the Mediterranean and the industrial town of Baniyas. Back in the courtyard, the rooms that line the eastern side are thought to have functioned as storage chambers or possibly kitchens; on the other side of these is a cavernous hall, probably once used as a warehouse. The large area of the castle to the north of the courtyard is badly overgrown and largely ruined, the area having been heavily built over after the Crusaders left. An Arab cemetery and Ottoman khan may be rooted out amongst the mess of rubble – indeed this part of the castle was inhabited until the 1950s.

Practicalities

It's easy to **reach Baniyas** by microbus from Tartous to the south or from Jableh or Latakia to the north. Microbuses to **Zaoube** (every hour or so) wind their way up the six-kilometre road to Marqab from Baniyas microbus station, though you could always take a taxi to save time waiting; buses back dry up in

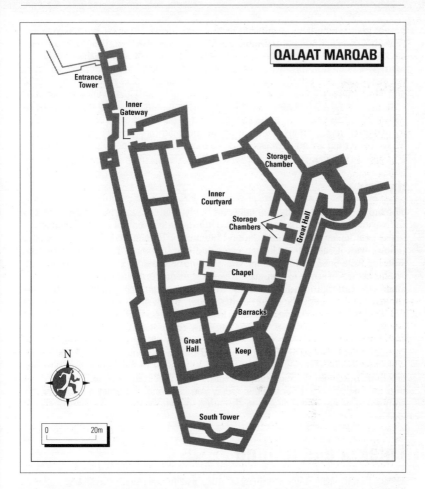

the early afternoon. Approaching by car, you need to enter Baniyas, take the old coast road south and head up the mountain from there. In the hills above the highway just before the town, look out for a basalt **watchtower** built at the same time as the castle and designed to protect the coastal road and the important Crusader settlement at Baniyas. There is a **restaurant**, the *Al-Nejmeh*, situated just beneath the castle – or you could fill up at the café in Baniyas microbus station.

Qalaat al-Kahf

To the southeast of Qalaat Marqab, about 30km away by an almost bewildering succession of winding mountain roads, is the Ismaili fortress of **Qalaat al-Kahf**, sitting on a peaceful ridge between two wild gorges. The road up to the castle is barely good enough for vehicular traffic, and the castle itself is mostly ruins, though it does feature a remarkable entrance passageway inscribed in Arabic and carved from solid rock, which gives the place its name "Castle of the Cave". The fortress was built in the early twelfth century by a local lord whose son sold it to the Assassins (see p.169), one of eight acquisitions the sect made between 1132 and 1140. Baibars finally captured the castle in 1273, and it remained in use until Ottoman times, finally being razed in the early nineteenth century. To **get there** without your own transport, the easiest thing to do would be to catch a microbus to the town of Qadmous, 24km east on the main road between Baniyas and Misyaf, and then arrange transport with a local from there, possibly by motorbike (cheaper than a car, so bargain accordingly).

Jableh

The only settlement of any size between Baniyas and Latakia is **JABLEH**, just to the west of the main coastal highway. Little trace remains of the town's ancient history as an important port under Phoenician, Roman and Byzantine rulers, though with its attractive cliff-top cafés and two harbours, Jableh is worth considering for a brief stopover along this part of the coast.

The centre of town is dominated by a large modern stadium, next to which stands the **bus station**. Just to the southwest of this are the remains of a **Roman theatre** (daily except Tues 9am–2pm; S£100), much of it overgrown and falling down. The first eleven rows of seating are well preserved, their yellow stone glinting in the sun, and it's now undergoing slow restoration work by archeologists. Nearby is a mosque, built on the site of a church dating from Byzantine times, containing the **shrine of Ibrahim ben Adham**, a local mystic and Muslim saint who died in 778. Over on the waterfront, 500m west of the bus station, are two small **harbours** for fishing boats, the older of which is thought to have been cut into the rock by the Phoenicians. Here, you can smoke a quiet *nargileh* or get something to **eat** while taking in the attractive views from a couple of cliff-top cafés.

Latakia and around

Syria's fourth largest town and the country's principal port, **LATAKIA** comes as a pleasant surprise after the drabness of much of the the coast, and is a very pleasant (though not typical) introduction to provincial Syria for those arriving from Turkey. It's a thoroughly modern place, prosperous and cosmopolitan, with a lively student presence and a diverse cultural and sporting life. The wide boulevards lined with palm trees, the bustling street cafés and restaurants, and the shops brimming with designer labels (even if they are fakes imported from Turkey) give the place a distinctly cosmopolitan feeling, though there are no seafront hotels, tempting fish restaurants, beaches (grubby or otherwise) or attractive Tartous-style *corniche* road here. Latakia is easily visited without realizing its port function, the maritime facilities hidden away behind high railings. It's a ten-minute walk from the city centre to a view of the water, and otherwise only the stiff sea breeze cutting through the town confirms its coastal location.

Although there's very little to see in Latakia itself, its good selection of hotels and excellent transport connections make it a worthwhile base for seeing the surrounding area. Nearby lie the remains of the former Phoenician city of **Ugarit**, and if you've grown weary of looking at beaches along the coast tainted by scattered garbage, then take heart – the **Blue Beach**, just north of the city, is the cleanest in Syria, although you have to pay for the pleasure of using it. Slightly further afield are the black beaches at **Ras al-Bassit** (see p.209) and, inland, the Crusader castle, **Qalaat Salah al-Din** (see p.204), both easily accessible from Latakia.

Some history

Though there is evidence to suggest continuous settlement here stretching back to at least 1000 BC, Latakia only came to prominence in the wake of Alexander the Great's conquests, when it was transformed into a major city of the **Seleucid** empire. Renamed in honour of Laodicea, the mother of Alexander's general Seleucus I Nicator, it developed into an important port, usurping Arwad's previous dominance and becoming the main supplier of wine to the Hellenistic world. The town was briefly declared capital of Syria in the late second century AD by Septimius Severus, though that role soon reverted to Antioch (now Antakya in Turkey). Devastating earthquakes in 494 and 555 badly damaged Latakia, but it was rebuilt by Justinian before being seized by the invading Arab army in 638. After capture by the Crusaders in the autumn of 1097, the town oscillated between Muslim and Christian control for nearly two centuries until it was decisively retaken by Qalaun in 1287.

Latakia benefited from a small but influential Venetian trading colony from 1229 until 1436, but after their expulsion the town settled on a long path of decline. By the end of the nineteenth century it was no more than a minor fishing village with a population in the region of six thousand; in 1876 Baedeker mentioned its "squalid, poverty-stricken appearance". The town's fortunes were revived during the **Mandate** era when the French made it the capital of their new Alawite state; with the formal creation of Lebanon and the handing back of the Hatay region to Turkey, Latakia suddenly found itself in the role of modern-day Syria's major **port**, the new government having little choice but to expand and develop the city.

Arrival and information

The **city centre** is marked by Latakia's main mosque, which stands at the western end of 14 Ramadan Avenue; the majority of the hotels and restaurants are within walking distance from here. Running south from the mosque to the port is Ibrahim Hanano Street, the main shopping area.

Near the eastern end of 14 Ramadan Avenue, 500m from the mosque, is the **service taxi station**; within walking distance to the northeast, on Al-Jalaa Street, is the station for **local buses and microbuses**. Pullman and Karnak **buses** use the new terminal just beyond the **train station** on Abdel Qader al-Housayni Avenue, where all the major companies have their offices. From here, a taxi is the best option into the centre. There are no buses from the **airport**, 25km south of the city near **Jableh**, but a taxi into town from there costs around S£300.

The unsigned **tourist office** (daily except Fri 8am–7pm) is at the eastern end of 14 Ramadan Avenue, opposite the *Riviera Hotel*; the staff here are very friendly and knowledgeable, though all they have to hand out is a free map.

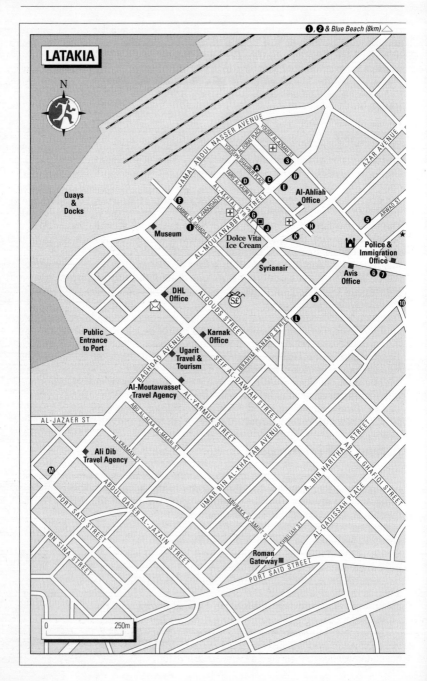

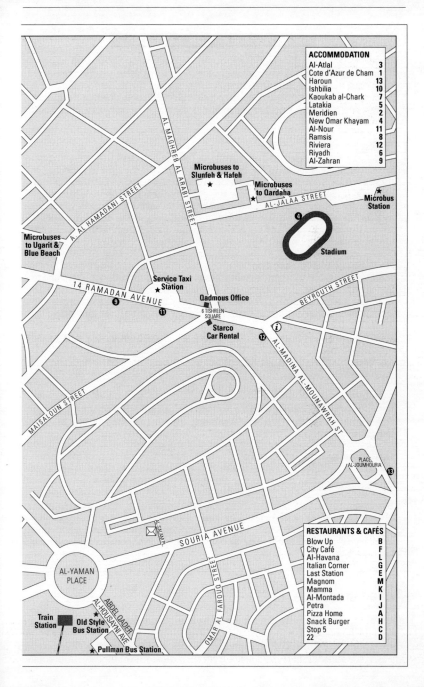

ACCOMMODATION

Al-Atlal	3
Cote d'Azur de Cham	1
Haroun	13
Ishbilia	10
Kaoukab al-Chark	7
Latakia	5
Meridien	2
New Omar Khayam	4
Al-Nour	11
Ramsis	8
Riviera	12
Riyadh	6
Al-Zahran	9

Microbuses to Slunfeh & Hafeh

Microbuses to Qardaha

Microbus Station

AL-JALAA STREET

AL MAGHREB AL ARAB STREET

A. AL HAMADANI STREET

Microbuses to Ugarit & Blue Beach

Stadium

BEYROUTH STREET

Service Taxi Station

14 RAMADAN AVENUE

Qadmous Office

6 TISHREEN SQUARE

Starco Car Rental

AL-MADINA AL-MOUNAWRAH ST.

MAISALOUN STREET

PLACE AL-JOUMHOURIA

AL-SALAM P.

SOURIA AVENUE

AL FAROUQ STREET

RESTAURANTS & CAFÉS

Blow Up	B
City Café	F
Al-Havana	L
Italian Corner	G
Last Station	E
Magnom	M
Mamma	K
Al-Montada	I
Petra	J
Pizza Home	A
Snack Burger	H
Stop 5	C
22	D

AL-YAMAN PLACE

Train Station

Old Style Bus Station

ABDEL QADER AL-HOUSAINI AVE.

OMAR AL FAROUQ STREET

Pullman Bus Station

MOVING ON FROM LATAKIA

By air
There are two **flights** a week from Latakia airport (both Fri), one to Damascus (S£500) and one to Cairo (US$160). It's best to buy tickets in advance at the Syrianair office, as the price is upped considerably if you buy them at the airport to travel on the same day. There is no bus to the airport; a taxi there should cost around S£300.

By ferry
In the past ferries have run from Latakia to Volos in mainland Greece via Cyprus and Crete, and also down to Alexandria via Beirut, but at the time of writing all of these were in abeyance. For the latest information ask at the Ali Dib travel agency on Abdul Qader al-Jazain St; one day the shipping agency office on Al-Jazaer Ave may reopen. If you find that it's still impossible to leave Syria by sea, you could pick up one of the regular service taxis for Beirut, from where there are plenty of ferries to Egypt, Cyprus and Greece; transit visas for Lebanon (US$16) are available at the border.

By Pullman and Karnak bus
Most long-distance services, including buses to Antakya in Turkey (S£175) and to Beirut (S£200), use the Karnak and Pullman bus station off Abdel Qader al-Housayni Ave. The major companies have offices here; Al-Ahliah, Qadmous and Karnak (which serves Aleppo; Damascus, via Tartous and Homs; and Beirut via Tripoli) also have offices in the centre of town (see p.201). Unless you're really counting the pounds, you can safely ignore the clapped-out station next to the Pullman station on Abdel Qader Al-Housayni Ave, which has old-style buses serving Aleppo and Damascus (via Tartous and Homs), not renowned for their comfort or air-conditioning (fares are about half the price of the Pullman services).

By microbus and local bus
For most local destinations head for the local bus and microbus station on Al-Jalaa St; however, micros for Ugarit, via Blue Beach, leave from behind the school on 14 Ramadan Ave.

By service taxi
Service taxis to Aleppo, Damascus, and Tripoli and Beirut in Lebanon depart from the station on 14 Ramadan Ave. The Beirut trip costs S£500 per person.

By train
Three trains a day run to Aleppo (3hr 30min; S£55 first class) – and for once this is a good alternative to the bus, the trains being cheaper and quicker and offering much more leg room. The service down the coast to Tartous and on to Homs runs just once a week.

Accommodation

Most of the city's excellent selection of **hotels** congregate around the western end of 14 Ramadan Avenue; cheapies to avoid on the avenue itself include the *Afamia* and the *Ferdos*. The very cheapest places are in the noisy area just to the north of the mosque here, and apart from the *Latakia* have little to differentiate them. Latakia's **luxury** hotels are located not in the city centre but on Blue Beach, 8km to the north (a taxi ride there from the centre costs about S£250).

Al-Atlal, at the port end of Yousef al-Azmah St (☎041/236 121). Its quiet location away from the city centre, friendly owner and reasonably clean rooms make this one of the better budget options. ②.

Haroun, Place Al-Joumhouria (☎041/427 140; fax 418 285). A bit dull but probably the best value for its price; the rooms are very clean and all have a bath, TV and fridge. Pity about the inconvenient location. ④.

Ishbilia, Omar bin al-Khattab Ave (☎041/473 921). A reasonable selection of rooms located high enough up to neutralize some of the traffic noise, though the showers are dingy. Prices seem open to negotiation, but bargain hard. ②.

Kaoukab al-Chark, 14 Ramadan Ave (☎041/238 452). Reasonable if basic rooms; you pay extra for an en-suite bathroom. ②.

Latakia, on the second floor of a building on Arwad St, off Yousef al-Azmah St, north of the mosque (☎041/479 527). The best of numerous similar cheapies next to the mosque (beware the wake-up call). A variety of rooms are available, some with shower and toilet, and the English-speaking owner is prepared to bargain. ①.

New Omar Khayam, Al-Jalaa St (☎041/228 219). Right next to the stadium, near the microbus station. Quite a bright little place, with modern amenities and nicely appointed rooms. ④.

Al-Nour, 14 Ramadan Ave (☎041/423 980). A rather soulless place with a selection of uninspiring, if acceptably clean, rooms. ③.

Ramsis, Ibrahim Hanano St (☎041/238 058). A pretty good deal, with fairly clean rooms and an owner who speaks basic French. ①.

Riviera, 14 Ramadan Ave (☎041/421 803, fax 418 287). One step into the beautifully air-conditioned reception area tells you that this is the best place to be in downtown Latakia, if you have the money. The staff are all professional and friendly, and speak very good English; all rooms are equipped with TV and fridge. ⑥.

Riyadh, 14 Ramadan Ave (☎041/239 778). A clean and comfortable option, with the possibility of a room with a balcony at the front, or a quieter room at the back. All rooms are air-conditioned and en-suite, though they don't have TVs and tend to be a little cramped. It's a little overpriced, though wavering at the reception area can generally knock a few dollars off. ④.

Al-Zahran, 14 Ramadan Ave (☎041/425 128). A noisy location, though don't be put off by the grubby entrance as there are a number of acceptably clean rooms with balcony and bath inside. ①.

Blue Beach

Cote d'Azur de Cham (☎041/228 691, *www.chamhotels.com*). A resort in itself with its own private beach, swimming pool, mini-golf, tennis courts and all the usual bars and restaurants. Reached by an underground tunnel from here is the *Cote D'Azur Residence*, an apartment block set back from the sea; the rooms are essentially self-contained apartments with kitchenettes. Both ⑦.

Meridien (☎041/428 736/7, fax 428 732, *www.lemeridien-hotels.com*). On its own stretch of beach, which non-guests can pay to use, this hotel boasts a swimming pool, restaurants, bars, tennis courts and even, in summer, all-night karaoke on the beach at its *Piano Bar II*. ⑦.

The City

The city's **museum** (daily except Tues 8am–6pm; S£300), on Jamal Abdul Nasser Avenue, is housed in an old Ottoman khan which served as the Alawite governor's residence during the French mandate. It's not especially good value, but there are some interesting examples of pottery, glassware and inscribed clay tablets from nearby Ugarit, and the exhibits have been thoughtfully labelled in English. The final room features an incongruous selection of contemporary paintings which won't detain you.

A rare surviving testimony to Latakia's ancient past (which is featured on the sides of the city's taxis) is the four-sided **Roman gateway**, or *tetraporticus*, on Port Said Street in the southern part of the city. Dating to the late second century, this would have marked the eastern end of the ancient Roman city; occasional Classical columns litter the surrounding streets. Its sturdy, and highly unusual, near-cubic shape ensured its survival through the several major earthquakes which devastated much of the old settlement.

The beaches
The road north out of the city centre towards Ugarit passes after about 8km the *Cote d'Azur de Cham* complex, situated on **Blue Beach**, at the landward end of the Ras ibn Hani promontory. Here the sands are spotless and the sea clean; non-guests can pay S£250 to use the hotel's private beach, go swimming, waterskiing and windsurfing in crystal-clear blue water, or just lounge under the palms. Less crowded is the beach at the *Meridien Hotel*, further up the road running west along the promontory; slightly less of an eyesore, the hotel charges the same as the *Cham* for similar facilities. People using these two private beaches tend to be mostly Europeans (who come here because it's warmer than back home) and Arabs from the Persian Gulf area (who come because it's cooler), and you're unlikely to meet any Syrians.

The couple of kilometres of Blue Beach running up to the *Cote d'Azur de Cham* are occupied by holiday complexes, where getting onto the sand is a lot cheaper: you pay around S£50 at one of numerous turnstiles. This stretch tends to be a lot livelier and untidier than the hotel beaches, and on Fridays it can be claustrophobically busy.

Most **microbuses** heading out from Latakia to Ugarit pass the stretch of beach in front of the holiday complexes and stop outside the *Cote d'Azur de Cham* complex; you will probably have to walk from here if you want to get to the *Meridien* (5–10min along the road).

Eating and drinking

Latakia offers a good selection of inexpensive **restaurants**, although it can at times feel as if the city is hell-bent on offering the ultimate pizza challenge. For some good stand-up Western fast food head for *Snack Burger*, located just off Azar Avenue, to the north of the *Mamma* restaurant. There's not much to choose between the cheap falafel and chicken haunts at the western end of 14 Ramadan Avenue – just roll up and choose the one which looks cleanest.

Most of the choices listed below are on or near Al-Moutanabby Street, a popular spot with the country's youth: watch them, decked out in smart Western clothes, as they self-consciously preen themselves over an early evening ice cream (the *Dolce Vita* parlour on Al-Akhtal Street is recommended). You can eat a main course at any of the places listed below for under S£300, and usually much less; many of the restaurants listed also double up as **bars**. Latakia also has a few smart **coffee-houses**; try *City Cafe* or *Al-Montada* on Gabrel Al-Sahada Street, or head down Baghdad Avenue where there are a number of places to sit and watch the world go by.

Blow Up, Al-Moutanabby St. Standard Syrian fare in relaxed ambience with a decent bar. First-floor window seats are available for people-watchers.

Al-Havana, Ibrahim Hanano St. A bright spot with friendly staff and an absorbing view over a busy inner-city square. You can come here just to chill out over a beer if you want; its musical selection only confirms the ubiquity of the Spice Girls.

Italian Corner, Al-Moutanabby St. Reasonably priced and popular place, but the pizzas are a bit too fluffy and short on toppings. A small selection of chicken and steak dishes also available, plus full bar.

Last Station, Al-Moutanabby St. Very pleasant Western dishes and ambience; slightly older crowd than usual though the prices are very affordable.

Magnom, at the southern end of Baghdad Ave. Decent, cheap place serving a limited menu of Western fast food (pizzas, burgers, lasagne), cheekily announced by a familiar-looking yellow "M" sign.

Mamma, Azar Ave. Good pizza/hamburger joint for a quick sit-down meal, though slightly cramped.

Petra, Al-Akhtal St. The luminous decor with a Greek mythological theme here provides the pleasing background to some very tasty eats. There's a good selection of Western and Arabic food, including the usual Italian dishes so popular in the city, and a full bar is available.

Pizza Home, Sultan Basha Alatresh St. Cheap and cheerful pizza joint.

Stop 5, Al-Moutanabby St. Serves the best pizza in town, as well as a limited number of other Western dishes. Intimate place with efficient service and an English menu; European beer available.

22, Faris Alkhun St. Another good pizza-oriented sit-down place, where your ale comes in a genuine beer-mug. The décor is nautically themed, though the serviettes bear the logo of Syrianair. Burgers, lasagne and spaghetti are also available.

Listings

Airline Syrianair is on Baghdad Ave (daily 9am–6pm; Fri until 1pm).

Bookshops The only decent selections are in the luxury hotels on Blue Beach.

Buses Besides the bus company offices at the bus station, Al-Ahliah maintains an office on Yousef Shahrur Place, near the central mosque; Qadmous is at the eastern end of 14 Ramadan Ave; Karnak has its office just off Baghdad Ave in the centre of town.

Camera shops Numerous shops on Baghdad Ave sell Kodak or Fuji film and offer developing services.

Car rental Starco (☎041/416 502) is a local car rental company situated at the eastern end of 14 Ramadan Ave opposite the Qadmous bus company office; little English is spoken but cars are in theory available for upwards of $40 a day. Avis have an office on 14 Ramadan Ave (☎041/478 310) and also in the *Meridien*; prices range from S£4000 to S£17,500 a day depending on the car.

Couriers A DHL office is located directly opposite the telephone office.

Exchange The Commercial Bank of Syria (daily except Fri 8.30am–1.30pm & 5–8pm) is on Baghdad Ave; the exchange booth has a separate entrance all to itself and is very efficient. Their branch in the *Meridien* on Blue Beach is open daily 8am–2pm & 5–8pm.

Hospital Latakia's main hospital is the Assad University Hospital, the large building located opposite Syrianair on Baghdad Ave.

Pharmacies There are two situated opposite each other at the western end of 14 Ramadan Ave and a couple more nearby at the northern end of Ibrahim Hanano St.

Post office The main post office is slightly out of the way near the train station, on Al-Salam Place (daily except Fri 8am–6pm).

Telephones The telephone office is located on Seif Al-Dawiah St; hawkers linger outside selling phonecards for a small markup as the office doesn't always have them in stock.

Travel agents Numerous travel agents on Baghdad Ave and around the main shopping district can book flights. Examples include Al-Moutawasset on Al-Yarmuk St which represents Air France, Alitalia, Royal Jordanian and Turkish Airlines, and Ali Dib, on Abdul Qader al-Jazain St, which acts for KLM, Lufthansa and Qantas.

Visa extensions The immigration office (daily except Fri 8am–2pm) is situated on the second floor of the police station on 14 Ramadan Ave opposite the mosque. Service here can be extremely slow and frustrating. There's a photographer's just behind the police station for passport-style photos.

Ugarit

The area stretching along the coast to the immediate north of Latakia is very fertile, with richly productive orchards hidden behind high cypress trees. About 16km along stands the site of **UGARIT** (Ras Shamra; daily: summer 9am–6pm; winter 9am–4pm; S£200), discovered in 1928 after a local farmer's plough hit a large piece of masonry buried in the soil; he contacted the French colonial authorities, whose archeologists began excavating the area the following year.

What the farmer had found were the remains of one of the most powerful and wealthy cities in the Middle East. First settled in the **Neolithic** period (very

---

THE TABLETS OF UGARIT

Now housed in museums as far apart as Aleppo and New York, the clay **tablets** found at Ugarit have provided invaluable evidence concerning the history of language and writing. It's debatable whether the **alphabet** imprinted upon them actually is, as claimed, the world's first – similar claims are made for alphabets developed by ancient civilizations in Crete, Cyprus and Egypt – but it's certainly one of the very earliest, devised between 1400 and 1300 BC when Ugarit was at the height of its power as a trading and mercantile centre. The alphabet has thirty letters (no vowels and no accents) in all, in sequence and pronunciation similar to modern Arabic; the letters are formed using triangles and stalks arranged at different angles and in different combinations.

Besides mundane inventories of goods received at the port, and royal and political correspondence (indicating a high level of administrative efficiency), the tablets contain mythical and religious texts. One tells the story of Kart, a king who had no son and who departed for faraway places looking for a woman who would bear children for him. Another story tells of Akhaat, the son of King Daniel; one day the boy was eaten by eagles and, as a result, all the plants in the world suddenly died. The tablets also include the first known **musical text**, which has rhythm and short notes. It was deciphered and played by a musicologist at University of California at Berkeley in the 1970s, who declared it to "sound very familiar to us, and to be part of the international musical heritage".

Some of the material on the tablets is quite ethereal; a will written using the alphabet declares: "Starting from today, I, Yaremano, give up all my properties to my wife Baydawe, and two sons, Yataleeno and Yanhamo. If one of my sons treats his mother meanly, he must pay five hundred pieces of silver to the king. Beyond that, he should take off his shirt, leave it on the door handle, and go out into the street. But the son who treats his mother with respect and consideration, will be given all her property." Aphorisms found on tablets include advice such as "Do not tell your wife where you hide your money" and "A life with no light does not deserve less than death".

roughly, around 7000 BC), Ugarit rose to prominence around 3000 BC when it traded extensively with Cyprus and Mesopotamia; one of the finds the French archeologists made was a shipment of a thousand perfume flasks from Cyprus, unearthed from a city warehouse and believed to date from this time. The city's most important feature for today's archeologists and historians was the palace library, where in 1948 clay tablets were unearthed covered in one of the earliest known **alphabets**. Ugarit had lain abandoned and uninhabited since a disastrous fire, caused by Philistine raiders, destroyed the place in 1180 BC. Subsequently the site had been gradually covered by soil and silt, becoming indistinguishable from the fertile land along the rest of the coastal plain. Being far older than the Roman sites in Syria, the settlement has far less still standing today, and to the uninitiated the waist-high pieces of stone wall enclosing extensive areas of rooms, with narrow streets separating the buildings, won't mean very much; Ugarit's fascination lies more in its age and history than in what's left to see.

The site

There are only a couple of areas of the site where you can make out the remnants of specific structures. **The Royal Palace** (late fourteenth to thirteenth century BC) forms the largest collection of buildings, consisting of over ninety rambling rooms and six courtyards, which you enter through the original (and still very well-preserved) gateway to the city, located to the immediate right of the path up from the ticket office. At one time the palace was the largest and most opulent in western Asia, including courtyard fountains, burial chambers and even a piped water and sewerage system, its grandeur reflecting the wealth of the city itself.

At the highest point of the site, to the northeast of the palace, and a fair distance from the ticket office, you can see the foundations of the **temples** dedicated to Baal and to Dagon, the god of the underworld, although it's hard to discern anything much of interest. Baal, the prime figure mentioned in the mythical texts found at Ugarit, was considered to be the son of the god El, creator of the universe, source of all wisdom, and the god of storms, rains and hills; Ugarit's Temple of Baal was famous over the whole of the Near East, and records show that priests received offerings from as far away as Egypt. Between the two temples in the former house of the high priest, many chants and other religious texts written on stone tablets were found by archeologists.

As you look around you'll see numerous **wells** and **water courses**, particularly around the courtyard of the main palace; water played an important part in funeral rites here, and it was believed that the dead had to have water near them. Ugarit was a port town and the sea once came right up to its walls; after it was abandoned the harbour silted up and the Mediterranean retreated, leaving a dry area of scrub between the site and the sea. The blue water can be glimpsed through the trees from the ruins, but you can't get down to the sea at this point as the area is occupied by the military.

Practicalities

The site of Ugarit is usually pretty busy by Syrian standards, being close to Latakia and the nearby resort hotels, but it's easy to reach and worth looking round for an hour or so. From Latakia, there are frequent **microbuses** from behind the school on 14 Ramadan Avenue to the site (stopping outside the entrance), or you could take a taxi (S£250). If you want a really detailed look round, it's well worth buying a detailed **plan** of the site at the ticket office and trying to listen in on any guided tours which might be taking place. Otherwise, there are helpful little blue signs all over the site pointing out the remains.

Inland from Latakia

The most obvious attraction in the mountains east of Latakia is **Qalaat Salah al-Din**, an impressively situated, well-preserved Crusader castle, much admired by T.E. Lawrence, among others. Such is the castle's allure, it's easy to overlook the other possible destinations in the area, which have a contemporary rather than historical appeal. **Slunfeh** is a mountain resort popular with day-trippers from Latakia who want to escape the muggy air of the coast, while at **Qardaha**, former president Hafez al-Assad lies entombed in a purpose-built mausoleum which has become something of a point of secular pilgrimage – or at least curiosity – for Syrians.

Qalaat Salah al-Din

In 1909 T.E. Lawrence visited the Middle East as an undergraduate researching a thesis on medieval architecture, and declared **QALAAT SALAH AL-DIN** (Saladin's Castle; daily: summer 9am–6pm; winter 9am-4pm; S£300) to be "probably the finest example of military architecture in Syria". The castle certainly provides a good example of an early Crusader fortification which was not reworked by the Templars or Hospitallers, though under Arab control it underwent a number of facelifts: the lower terrace became home to a small town while remains of a mosque, palace and bathhouse can be found in the castle proper. Though it has not survived as well as Crac des Chevaliers and lacks the foreboding presence of Qalaat Marqab, a visit here leaves few feeling shortchanged.

The castle only ever occupied – rather than commanded – the ridge on which it was built, and in July 1188 Saladin easily breached the vulnerable walls of the lower court; the overstretched garrison within surrendered without much of a fight. It was only in 1957 that Qalaat Salah al-Din was renamed after its Arab conqueror; previously it had been known as Saone, or Sahyun.

The castle

The Phoenicians first fortified the site in the first millennium BC, but what can be seen today largely dates to the twelfth century, courtesy of the Crusaders. The castle's eastern defence, described by Lawrence as "the most sensational thing in castle building", is a massive **ditch** cut from the rock; indeed it's hard initially to take in the fact that this is man-made. Most of the ditch-digging was probably done in Byzantine times and finished off by the Crusaders, leaving only an improbably tall stone needle to support a drawbridge. The castle **entrance** is located up the steps at the end of this uniquely improvised ravine.

Immediately to your right on leaving the ticket office are two well-preserved **towers**; in the lower section of the first one are some of the stone balls thrown over the castle walls by Saladin's troops in 1188. Beyond the second is a courtyard, with the formidable, two-storeyed **keep** (its walls are over 5m thick) in the middle of its eastern side. Although the ground floor sees little natural light, the stairways inside have been helpfully illuminated and the first floor has windows; the stairway continues up to the roof from where there are fine views all round. South of the keep are the castle's pillared stables and a huge cistern – now home to a skittish colony of birds – while the former **drawbridge entrance** to the castle is just to the north of the keep, though a look down the sheer sides is not recommended for vertigo sufferers. The more ruinous northeastern section of the castle is Byzantine in origin, as is the wall that runs parallel to the eastern defence.

SALADIN

One of world's most brilliant military leaders, **Saladin**, the great unifier of the Levant against the Crusaders, was nonetheless revered by the Franks for both his military skill and his sense of honour. At the end of the eleventh century the Crusaders entered a politically fractured land, a chaotic mess of independent city states; within a few decades the whole of the eastern Mediterranean coast was under Frankish control. The first ruler to offer any form of unified Muslim resistance to the invading armies was **Nur al-Din**, the Zengid regent who united Aleppo and Damascus. Having been raised at Nur al-Din's court, Saladin made his military reputation by thwarting Crusader interest in Egypt during the 1160s; the Zengids became the new ruling force in Egypt, and Saladin the effective ruler.

Nur al-Din died in 1174, leaving only an 11-year-old son as heir, and Saladin deftly moved into the obvious vacuum, largely through the power of his purse. His only major opposition to unifying the Muslim world came from the **Zengids** in Aleppo, and over the next ten years Saladin waged small-scale wars against them and the Crusaders. It was not until 1186, when the Zengids finally capitulated, that Saladin was ready to engage the Franks in a full-scale campaign. On a boiling-hot July day in 1187, thirty thousand knights were caught by surprise at **Hattin** (west of Lake Tiberias) on their way to Palestine to relieve the Muslim siege of Tiberias, and were defeated by Saladin's army. After the battle, Crusader garrisons toppled one by one until in October of that year, Jerusalem was finally recaptured. The peaceful evacuation of its Christian population was in marked contrast to the mass slaughter of Muslims that had accompanied the Crusaders' entry into the city 88 years previously.

However, Saladin's decision at this point to abandon the siege of **Tyre** (in what's now southern Lebanon) was to prove costly, as it became the rallying point for the Third Crusade, support for which arrived in large numbers in 1189. Two years later, further armies arrived under the command of King Philip of France and King Richard the "the Lion-Heart" of England. The Crusaders immediately seized much of the coastline but were far too weak to attempt to penetrate inland. In September 1192 Richard, anxious to return home and realizing Jerusalem could not be taken easily, agreed to a treaty, honoured by Saladin, which gave the Franks the right to visit Christian shrines in the holy city.

Constant campaigning had by this time taken its toll on Saladin, who entered a rapid physical decline and **died** in Damascus on March 4, 1193, at the age of 54. An austere man, Saladin was without great personal wealth at his death, but his achievements were monumental, both in military and political terms. Much of his success came about not simply by force of arms but by the strength of his personality; many chronicles, both Muslim and Christian, testified to his sense of honour and justice. Ibn Shaddad, his friend and biographer, wrote: "I have heard people say that they would like to ransom those dear to them with their own lives, but this has usually been a figure of speech, except on the day of his death. For I know that had our sacrifice been accepted, I and others would have given our lives for him." Yet Saladin's unification of Muslim territory was never institutionalized, and, in the absence of any able successor, much of his work was lost in squabbles and divisions within decades of his death.

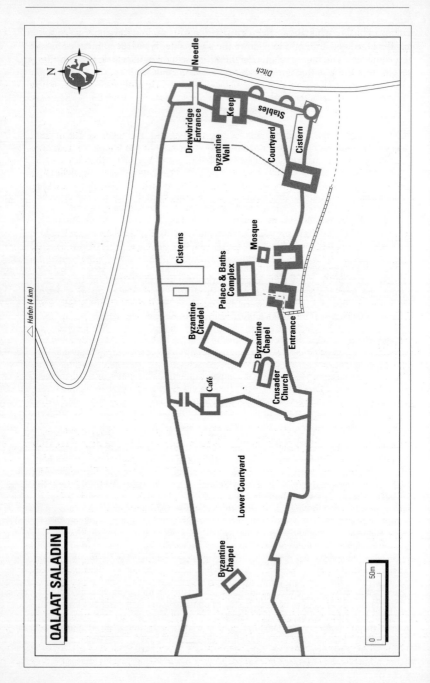

QALAAT SALADIN

N

Hafeh (4 km)

Needle

Ditch

Drawbridge Entrance

Keep

Stables

Byzantine Wall

Courtyard

Cistern

Cisterns

Mosque

Palace & Baths Complex

Byzantine Citadel

Byzantine Chapel

Entrance

Café

Crusader Church

Lower Courtyard

Byzantine Chapel

0   50m

Back towards the centre of the castle, opposite the entrance gateway, is the main evidence of Arab inhabitation of the site: a late thirteenth-century **mosque** (presently undergoing a fairly substantial reconstruction) and a twelfth-century palace complex featuring some discernible **baths** and a particularly attractive stalactited *muqarnas* carving above the palace entrance. Heading from here towards the northern walls, you can't miss the awesome Crusader **cistern** along the north wall, some 32m long and 10m deep, next to which is another smaller version. A short walk west of here is a **café**, situated where the upper terrace looks down upon the lower one; the latter is permanently choked in undergrowth, making progress slow, but you can venture across it to a small, suffocated **Byzantine chapel**. Returning to the café and continuing eastwards you'll pass, on your left, the bare remains of the main Crusader church, while, on the top of the hillock, is the badly ruined inner segment of the **Byzantine citadel** – difficult to climb up to and not particularly rewarding once you get there.

Practicalities
Local **buses** or **microbuses** between Latakia and Slunfeh will take you as far as the village of **Hafeh** (40min from either starting point), from where you must either catch another microbus 4km south to the castle or walk or hitch the rest of the way; at the end of the village is a sign in English directing you there. There's nowhere to stay in Hafeh; for **food**, there are a number of falafel options along the main road, and on the way to the castle you pass a **restaurant** perched on a ridge opposite, from where there are great views of Qalaat Salah al-Din.

Slunfeh

The most welcoming of Syria's mountain resorts and, in summer, one of the coolest places in Syria, **SLUNFEH** has developed into quite an exclusive retreat for the well-to-do, as well as a popular day-trip for the citizens of Latakia. There's little to do here except stroll through the town, appreciate the fresh mountain air and enjoy the dramatic views.

Frequent **microbuses** from Latakia (1hr) via Hafeh, and occasional microbuses from Aleppo, drop off at the small **station** located a two-minute walk from the main street (Alsayed al-Raeis St). For a **place to stay**, there's the *Slunfeh Grand* (☎041/750 606; ⑤; June–Sept), right in the centre of town on the main street; it's comfortable enough, with clean, en-suite rooms and an attached restaurant, though slightly overpriced – and curiously only the wedding suite has a TV. The busy main street is awash with **restaurants** and cheap eateries.

Qardaha

The town of **QARDAHA**, 20km east of Latakia, has little of intrinsic interest save for the fact that it is the birthplace (and final resting place) of **Hafez al-Assad**, the late president of Syria and the man largely credited with restoring Syrian pride after the debacle of the 1967 war. Indeed, a visit to the domed, purpose-built mausoleum here provides a fascinating insight into the lofty ambitions of the man who for three decades defined Syria's place in the world, as well as underlining the esteem in which he is held by the local – primarily Alawite – community.

The first thing of note when approaching the town from the coast is that the road up here is not some rough, winding track but a very grand (and usually very sparsely travelled) four-lane motorway. When Assad died in 2000 his body was flown to Latakia and then taken up this road to Qardaha for burial; all the walls, doors and even trees in the town were painted black to greet the procession, and they remain so today, providing the place with an eerily sombre ambience.

The only thing to see in town is the **mausoleum** itself, incredibly popular on Fridays, when busloads of people head here from Latakia and the surrounding towns. The atmosphere is by no means formal or stuffy – attire is casual and children tend to run around the place shouting. Though huge, the mausoleum is relatively plain inside; Hafez al-Assad lies in the centre of the hall in a plain coffin, while in a side annex is his eldest son **Bassel**, who died in a car accident in 1994. A talented equestrian and the obvious successor to Hafez al-Assad before his untimely death, Bassel is still, it seems, a genuinely popular figure, and children often bend forward to kiss his coffin. Security is not particularly tight in Qardaha and the presence of Westerners should not cause too much of a stir, though there are a number of besuited gentlemen standing around the mausoleum to direct mourners and keep an eye on things.

Practicalities

Frequent **microbuses** head up to Qardaha from the microbus station in Latakia (1hr). The mausoleum is situated a ten-minute walk east from the crossroads where the microbus stops off. A short taxi ride from the centre of town is the only place to **stay**, the government-run *Karnak* hotel (☎041/843 231; ④), a huge, dimly lit place which is (understandably) usually completely empty; waiters here make no effort to hide the stains on their T-shirts.

North of Latakia: Kassab and Ras al-Bassit

The stretch of mountainous coastline between Latakia and the Turkish border forms one of the most surprising, and attractive, landscapes in Syria. Here you'll find gorse-covered slopes dotted with stone farmhouses and tiny churches, and deep ravines and valleys carpeted with forests of pine and spruce. Most of the inhabitants are poor farmers, surviving on the limited agricultural potential of the land, or urban rich, whose gated and guarded villas line many of the roads leading towards the sea.

KASSAB is the principal town in the region, an attractive place situated in a bowl in the mountains about ninety minutes by road north of Latakia, and very close to the border. It's more like a hill town in Greece or Sicily than a typical Middle Eastern settlement; indeed, you'll see far more churches than mosques here, while many of the inhabitants speak Turkish as their first language. There's nothing specific to see, but it's pleasant to wander round, taking in the views across the hills and enjoying the cool, clean air. During late August the town's population swells from three thousand to around thirty thousand, as Syrians flock here to escape the summer heat and many locals rent out their rooms and houses. For foreigners wishing to **stay**, the best bets are a short walk up the hill, past the church, from the main square and crossroads: the *Al-Rawda* (☎041/711 008; ③) and the nearby *Amira* (also known as the *Princess;* ☎041/711 007; ②; May–Nov) both provide decent, clean rooms. Moving on from the square, heading around to the right, you come to the *Al-Moukhtar* (☎041/710 049; ②), which is rather basic but has some rooms with attractive balconies. Still more hotels are situated on the road up into the town from Latakia.

The formidable entrance to the Aleppo citadel

Coppersmith near the Aleppo souk

Qalaat Saladin

Bedouin woman with hay-laden horse at Serjilla, near Aleppo

Ruins at Serjilla

St Simeon's Basilica, with the stumpy remnants of his pillar

The Euphrates River glimpsed through a Roman arch at Halebiye

Along the banks of the Euphrates

Roman monumental gateway, Palmyra

Harvesting wheat in northeastern Syria

Footbridge over the Euphrates, Deir ez-Zur

The desert near Palmyra

From the dusty crossroads in the centre of Kassab, where buses from Latakia stop, a road heads west over the hills to **RAS AL-BASSIT**, where you'll find black sand beaches running north along the rugged coastline towards the Turkish border. The road twists and turns, then crosses over a low pass before dropping down to a long valley and finally leading to the sea. If you have your own transport, it'll be hard to resist eating at one of the cheap hotel restaurants along the mountain road, and if you do you'll probably find yourself joined by groups of well-to-do families who live in the whitewashed villas nearby. The **beaches** themselves are relatively litter-free and impressively situated against the mighty backdrop of Mount Casius just over the Turkish border, whose summit was held sacred by both the Phoenicians and the Greeks. The southern stretch of beach is the most developed, lined with numerous chalets, restaurants, cafés, table-football tents and even some basic video-game arcades. There is one **hotel** here, the slightly overpriced *Bassat Tourist* (☎041/429 668; ⑤), which has decent rooms and its own restaurant and swimming pool. Bare chalets along the beach and main road cost in the region of S£1000 a night.

Microbuses between Latakia and Kassab are fairly frequent; in summer the last one back to Latakia leaves at around 8pm. There is, however, only one scheduled departure from Kassab down to the beaches (at 10am; 30min), so you may well have to hire a taxi to take you down there (S£300 would be a fair price though the driver will probably attempt to charge you more). Direct microbuses between Latakia and Ras al-Bassit (not routed via Kassab) are very frequent in summer (50min), less so out of season. Just before entering Kassab the road from Latakia swings past a **border post**, where you can ask the bus to stop if you want to cross over into Turkey – be warned, however, that there's not much traffic on the Turkish side. Nor are there any buses from Kassab into Turkey, so all in all it's probably easier simply to catch a direct service from the Pullman station in Latakia.

travel details

Trains
Latakia to: Aleppo (3 daily; 4hr); Damascus (1 weekly; 7hr); Homs (1 weekly; 4 hr); Tartous (1 weekly; 2hr).

Pullman buses
Pullman buses from Latakia run frequently to all the same destinations as Karnak, and also to Antakya in Turkey. From Tartous Pullman buses depart frequently to the same destinations as Karnak, except Beirut and Tripoli.

Karnak buses
Latakia to: Aleppo (2 daily; 4hr); Beirut (Lebanon; 1 daily; 9hr); Damascus (2 daily; 5hr); Homs (2 daily; 2hr 30min); Tartous (2 daily; 1hr); Tripoli (Lebanon; 1 daily; 5hr).

Tartous to: Aleppo (2 daily; 5hr); Beirut (Lebanon; 1 daily; 8hr); Damascus (2 daily; 4hr); Homs (2 daily; 1hr 30min); Latakia (2 daily; 1hr); Tripoli (Lebanon; 1 daily; 4hr).

Microbuses and local buses
Latakia, frequent services to: Baniyas (1hr); Hafeh (40min); Jableh (30min); Kassab (1hr 15min); Ras al-Bassit (50min); Slunfeh (1hr); Tartous (1hr 30min); Ugarit (20min).

Safita, frequent services to: Dreikish (20min); Homs (1hr 30min); Hosn Suleiman (40min); Mashta al-Helu (30min); Tartous (45min).

Tartous, frequent services to: Amrit (15min); Baniyas (30min); Damascus (5hr); Homs (2hr); Jableh (1hr); Latakia (1hr 30min); Safita (45min).

Service taxis
Latakia to: Beirut (Lebanon; 9hr); Damascus (5hr); Latakia (1hr); Tripoli (Lebanon; 5hr).

Tartous to: Beirut (Lebanon; 8hr); Damascus (4hr); Homs (1hr 30min); Latakia (1hr); Tripoli (Lebanon; 4hr).

Domestic flights
Latakia to: Damascus (1 weekly; 1hr).

CHAPTER FIVE

ALEPPO AND AROUND

Aleppo, Syria's second city, is a bustling, cosmopolitan centre which offers visitors an intoxicating blend of neon-lit modernity, vibrant souks and ancient, often spectacular architecture. Relaxed, comparatively green and uncluttered, it's instantly more appealing than Damascus, with none of the brutal concrete architecture or abandoned building sites which beset the capital. Aleppo can boast road, rail and air connections with the rest of Syria, north into Turkey, and an increasing number of direct air links to Europe and other parts of the Middle East; hotels and restaurants that are at least equal to those of Damascus in quality and variety (and, unfortunately, price); and a long and eventful history that has bequeathed it an impressive array of ancient monuments, crowned by its largely medieval **citadel** and fabulous **Great Mosque**. It's worth kicking back here for a few days, at the very least.

Cropping up at astonishingly regular intervals across northwestern Syria, in the parched, empty scrubland beyond the fertile depression to which Aleppo owes its existence, are the so-called **Dead Cities**; these ruins of Roman and Byzantine settlements are easily visited on day-trips from Aleppo. Pre-eminent among them is the complex surrounding the **Church of St Simeon**, commemorating the mystic who spent nearly forty years sitting on top of a stone pillar. Such was Simeon's notoriety that pilgrims once travelled here from as far afield as England just to get a look at him from the base of his pillar; now it's bus-loads of tourists who form the curious, picking over the sad remains of the pillar – reduced to a stump by all the pilgrims chipping away at it – and wondering what all the fuss was about. It's also worth making time for the more homely Dead Cities **around Maarat al-Numan**: the taverns, baths, churches and ordinary houses of these small provincial towns are remarkably well preserved and usually completely deserted save for passing shepherds. Equally remote and often appealingly devoid of tourist hordes are the ruins of the third-century BC town of **Cyrrhus**, up near the Turkish border, and **Ebla**, a 5000-year-old city state whose remains can be seen partly excavated in a windy *tell* just off the main Aleppo–Damascus highway.

ACCOMMODATION PRICE CODES

In this book, all hotels have been categorized according to the **price codes** outlined below, representing the minimum you can expect to pay for a **double room** in each hotel. Hotels in the ⑤–⑧ bands require payment in dollars. For further details, see p.35.

① under S£300/US$7
② S£300–600/US$7–14
③ S£600–1000/US$14–23
④ S£1000–1500/US$23–35

⑤ US$35–50/S£1500–2100
⑥ US$50–90/S£2100–3900
⑦ US$90–130/S£3900–5600
⑧ US$130/over S£5600

ALEPPO

ALEPPO (Halab in Arabic) has a history rivalling that of Damascus in terms of scope and complexity, and like the capital – though with less justification – it claims to be the oldest inhabited settlement on earth. The city's 2000-year-old mercantile tradition, far more deeply rooted than that of Damascus, has given Aleppo a **cosmopolitan air** which the capital significantly lacks. Many of the cheap hotels are occupied by itinerant buyers and sellers from Turkey, Armenia and Russia, who noisily display their wares at bus stations, in the souks and on the street, and there's a high proportion of Armenian, Kurdish and Turkish immigrants, who own many of the restaurants, hotels and market stalls in the city centre. There's also a significant **Christian minority**, many of whom still live in the medieval **Jdeide Quarter** and worship in its ancient churches. Another distinctive Aleppo landmark, the **Baron Hotel**, has been owned and run for over fifty years by a woman from the English Lake District and is a unique reminder of the city's colonial past and European outlook.

There were already European trade and diplomatic delegations in Aleppo in the Middle Ages; more recent colonial ties with Europe are manifested in the wide avenues and extensive, fountain-strewn parklands of the **New City**, which in summer provide a cool haven from the clamour of the souks of the **Old City**. It's in the souks that trade comes together with the other major activity on which the city's economy is based, the manufacture of textiles; in the huge area of warren-like covered markets and open khans, dozens of stalls sell Aleppo-made silks and other fabrics, cut to order from the roll and made in modern factories in the suburbs.

Divisions within Syrian society are more apparent in Aleppo than in any other Syrian city. The western districts, around the university, comprise smart apartment blocks, expensive hotels, western-style sports and leisure centres, and tree-lined streets dotted with the occasional French-style *patisserie*. The area to the south of the citadel, on the eastern side of the city, couldn't be more of a contrast; here there are dusty, pock-marked streets, hordes of straggly (and usually very friendly) children, low-rise concrete-box houses and an abundance of load-bearing and wagon-pulling mules. Nowhere in the city is this social polarization more apparent than in the elegant surroundings of the city park, where wealthier families dressed in European clothes eat ice cream and talk busily on mobile phones as the Kurdish shoe-shine boys and water-sellers look on, eager for custom or *baksheesh*. Even more than the wealth of historical monuments, it is these contrasts which form the most abiding impression of Aleppo for visitors, and make a thorough exploration of the city so worthwhile.

Some history

The earliest mentions of Aleppo are recorded on stone tablets found at Mari, on the Syrian Euphrates, which date from around 2000 BC. From this time onwards Aleppo was the capital of a succession of prosperous city states, governed by the Amorites, the Hittites (after the Battle of Kadesh in 1285 BC; see p.154), the Assyrians, the Persians and, after 333 BC, by the Seleucid dynasty, founded by one of Alexander the Great's generals, who named the city **Beroia**. Virtually nothing remains of these settlements, nor of later Roman and Byzantine occupation, although history records a visit in the fourth century by **St Helena**, mother of Constantine the Great, in honour of whom a Christian cathedral (later turned into the Madrasa Halawiye) was founded.

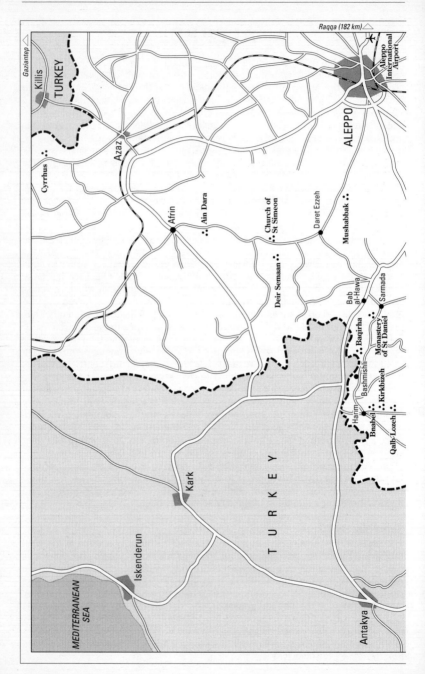

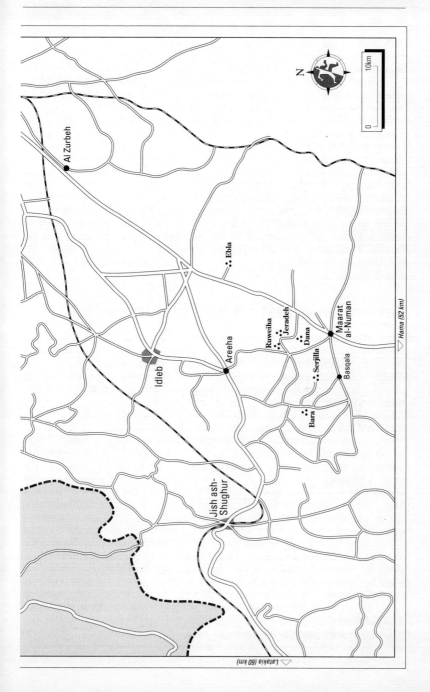

The importance of the city grew after the Arab invasion of Syria during the seventh century; the Umayyad dynasty built the Great Mosque adjacent to the site of the Madrasa Halawiye, and the city was fortified anew, allowing it to repel two attempts at capture by the Crusaders in 1098 and 1124. By the 1180s the victorious Saladin considered Aleppo important enough to make his son **Al-Zaher Ghazi** city governor, and it was he who extensively rebuilt the citadel, which became the cornerstone of Aleppo's defences.

The later Middle Ages saw renewed prosperity for traders, as the city became a natural stopping place on the main overland routes from the Mediterranean to China. By 1800 Aleppo was the largest city in Syria, with sizeable Kurdish, Armenian, Jewish and Christian communities, but the development of new sea routes to the Far East led to a gradual decline in fortunes. In 1939 Iskenderun, for centuries the natural seaport for Aleppo, was ceded by France to Turkey, and the redrawing of the Turkish–Syrian border less than 40km from the city meant that much of its hinterland was cut off. However, Aleppo's international outlook continued unabated by the decline in trade: there was a train service from here through Turkey to the Asiatic side of the Bosphorus, where it linked up with the Istanbul–Paris Orient Express in the 1930s, and the French colonial administration laid out tree-lined streets and a spacious, leafy city park in the manner of European capitals.

Arrival, information and city transport

The centre of town falls conveniently into very distinct areas, and once you've got the basic layout clear, finding your way around is very easy. At the heart of the New City, a useful point of reference is **Baron Street**, around which most of Aleppo's hotels are located. To the southeast are the **souks** of the Old City, east of which lies the **citadel**; northeast of Baron Street and northwest of the citadel is the old **Jdeide Quarter**.

Chances are you'll arrive in Aleppo by bus. Confusingly, there are at least eight **bus stations** in Aleppo (including the city-bus station, south of Baron Street behind the *Amir Palace Hotel*), but the good news is that seven of them are right in the centre of town (see map, p.217), within easy walking distance of all the hotels. The exception is the **eastern bus station** (marked on the map on p.215), at the northeastern end of Qadi Askar Street and 3km east of the centre, used by ordinary buses or microbuses from the northeast of the country (principally Raqqa and Deir ez-Zur); from this station, you can catch a bus to the city-bus station or a taxi into the centre (the latter ride costs around S£25). Local buses and **microbuses** from destinations north, west and south of Aleppo use the depot on the street which forms the southerly extension of Baron Street; about 500m to the west, on Ibrahim Hanono Street, is the station used by **luxury Pullman** buses. Humbler versions of these use a station immediately south of the city-bus station; some bus services from Beirut and Tripoli (Lebanon) also end up here. Privately run **international bus** services terminate a minute's walk west of the southern end of Baron Street, with **Karnak** buses arriving round the corner from here, on Al-Walid Street.

From the **train station**, it's a fifteen-minute walk south across the city park to Baron Street; note, however, that the daily train from Damascus usually gets into Aleppo at around 11pm – not the most convenient of times to start hunting for

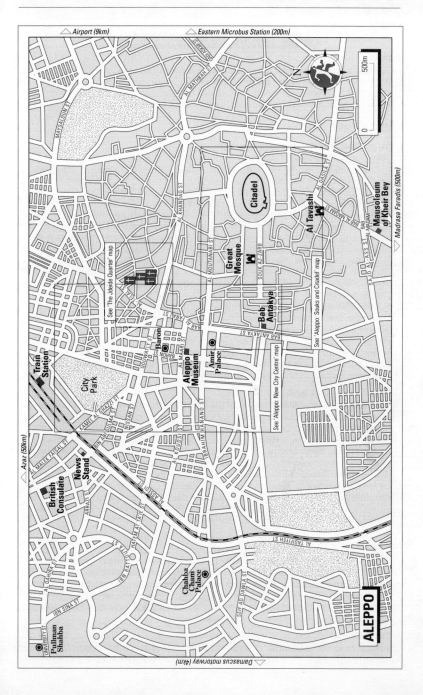

Airport (9km)

Eastern Microbus Station (200m)

500m

0

Citadel

Al Tavashi

Mausoleum of Kheir Bey

Madrasa Faradis (500m)

Great Mosque

SOUK AZ-ZARB

Bab Antakya

See 'The Jdeide Quarter' map

Baron

See 'Aleppo Souks and Citadel' map

Train Station

City Park

Aleppo Museum

Amir Palace

See 'Aleppo New City Centre' map

Azaz (50km)

British Consulate

News Stand

Chahba Cham Palace

University St

Pullman Shahba

ALEPPO

Damascus motorway (4km)

MOVING ON FROM ALEPPO

By air
The airport bus leaves from outside the international/Karnak bus station (every 30min; 40min; S£10). From Aleppo, Syrianair flies daily to Damascus (S£600), twice weekly to Beirut, Rome, Frankfurt, Paris, Stockholm and Athens; and once a week to Amsterdam, Munich, Berlin, Istanbul and Madrid. Foreign airlines operating out of Aleppo include British Mediterranean Airways (twice weekly to London Heathrow) and Austrian Airlines (twice weekly to Vienna).

By Pullman and Karnak bus
From the luxury **Pullman** station on Ibrahim Hanono St, there are frequent departures to Damascus (S£150), via Hama and Homs, with less frequent services to Deir ez-Zur, Latakia, Qamishli, Raqqa and Tartous. Shopping around the various windows for what you want is easy; booking in advance is possible but not really necessary.

Aleppo is one of the few places in Syria where you might want to use **cheaper Pullman** services; their depot, south of the city-bus station (behind the line of low-rise apartment buildings), is clean and well organized, with a good sit-down café on the left as you enter. Shop around at the windows for destinations and times you want; as a guide, most companies charge S£90 to Damascus and S£250 to Beirut.

Karnak buses leave from the area round the corner from their hassle-free office on Baron St (daily 7am–8pm). As a guide, services to Damascus cost around S£130, to Amman S£430 and to Beirut S£250; Karnak also serves Deir ez-Zur, Hama, Homs, Latakia and Tartous.

Offices around a square immediately west of the southern end of Baron Street run coaches to destinations in Turkey and Europe. The place is less hectic than other bus stations in Aleppo, and it's easy to shop around for what you want. Buses are usually modern and comfortable, but it might be a good idea to ask to look at the vehicle before you part with your money. A through fare to **Istanbul**, for example, is around S£1200, with a change of bus likely in Antakya (the fare up to here from Aleppo is S£250); a through service to **Sofia** in Bulgaria (S£3000) is operated by Zeitouni Tours, with an office off Baron St.

By microbus and local bus
The depot on the southern extension of Baron St is the departure point for all the places around Aleppo covered in the second part of this chapter, including Afrin, Azaz (from where there are taxis to the Turkish border post; once you've crossed the border on foot you can get another taxi to Killis, then a bus to the nearest large town, Gaziantep), Daret Ezzeh, Harim, Idleb, Maarat al-Numan; there are also services to Damascus, Hama, Homs and Latakia from here. You buy tickets at the windows in the cavernous entrance hall, or on the bus itself; keep asking for the destination you want and eventually you'll be shown the right bus. It costs a mere S£60 to travel to Damascus, taking six hours – an uncomfortable amount of time to spend in one of these vehicles. Among the destinations served from the **eastern bus station** are Deir ez-Zur (7hr) and Raqqa (4hr); change at Raqqa for services to Qamishli and Hassakeh.

By taxi
From opposite Bab Antakya, **service taxis** head out to Damascus (S£500) and to Beirut (S£600); other destinations covered include Homs and Hama. It's worth considering travelling to and into **Turkey by taxi** if you want to head for **Gaziantep**, the nearest town where you can pick up the Turkish train network. Hiring a taxi (ask at your hotel) from Aleppo to the border (which you cross on foot, a walk of 15min or so), and another taxi from the border to Gazientep, costs around US$50 all in all (drivers most likely want to be paid in US currency) and takes three to four hours.

By train
Aleppo is served by **trains** to Istanbul (S£500/350 first/second class), Damascus (S£90/60), Qamishle (S£400 in sleeper; otherwise S£140/90) and Latakia (S£60/40).

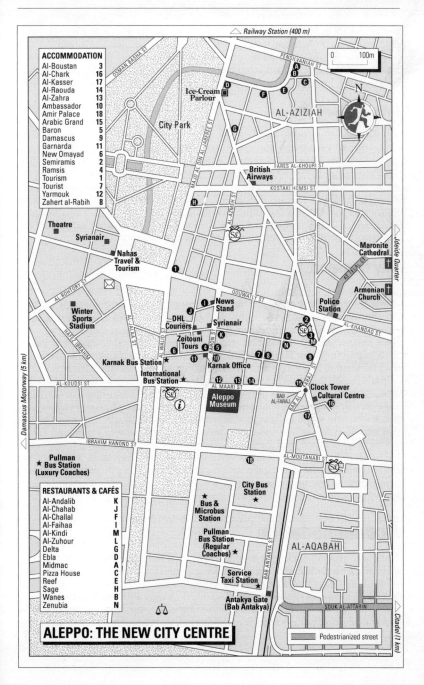

△ *Railway Station (400 m)*

0   100m

ACCOMMODATION
Al-Boustan	3
Al-Chark	16
Al-Kasser	17
Al-Raouda	14
Al-Zahra	13
Ambassador	10
Amir Palace	18
Arabic Grand	15
Baron	5
Damascus	9
Garnarda	11
New Omayad	6
Semiramis	2
Ramsis	4
Tourism	1
Tourist	7
Yarmouk	12
Zahert al-Rabih	8

PENSILVANIAH ST

AL-AZIZIAH

OSMAN BASHA ST

Ice-Cream Parlour

City Park

MAJD AL DIN AL JABERE ST

British Airways

FARES AL-KHOURI ST

KOSTAKI HOMSI ST

Maronite Cathedral †

Theatre

Syrianair

AL AZIMZH ST

ATFA ST

△ *Jdeide Quarter*

Nahas Travel & Tourism

Armenian Church †

AL BOHTORY ST

OOUWATLY ST

Police Station

Winter Sports Stadium

HAFEZ IBRAHIM

AL WALID ST

News Stand

DHL Couriers

Syrianair

AL-KHANDAQ ST

Zeitouni Tours

BARON ST

AL JALAA ST

Karnak Bus Station ★

International Bus Station ★

Karnak Office

AL-KOUDSI ST

AL MAARI ST

BAB AL-FARAJ

BAB AL FARAJ ST

Clock Tower
Cultural Centre

Aleppo Museum

i

IBRAHIM HANONO ST

AL-MOUTANABI ST

Pullman ★ Bus Station (Luxury Coaches)

RESTAURANTS & CAFÉS
Al-Andalib	K
Al-Chahab	J
Al-Challal	F
Al-Faihaa	I
Al-Kindi	M
Al-Zuhour	L
Delta	G
Ebla	D
Midmac	A
Pizza House	C
Reef	E
Sage	H
Wanes	B
Zenubia	N

City Bus Station ★

★ Bus & Microbus Station

Pullman Bus Station (Regular Coaches) ★

AL-AQABAH

BAB ANTAKYA ST

△ *Damascus Motorway (5 km)*

Service Taxi Station

Antakya Gate (Bab Antakya)

SOUK AL-ATTARIN

△ *Citadel (1 km)*

ALEPPO: THE NEW CITY CENTRE

Pedestrianized street

accommodation. **Service taxis** from Damascus, Homs, Hama and Beirut terminate opposite Bab Antakya, the western gate into the Old City. The **airport**, which has currency exchange facilities (daily 24hr), is 9km east of the centre along the road to Raqqa; there's a dedicated bus (every 30min, S£10) which will get you to the New City, dropping you off outside the Karnak and international bus stations.

Information

The **tourist office** (daily except Fri 8.30am–3pm; ☎021/222 1200), with unusually helpful and knowledgeable staff, is located in a pavilion opposite the museum in the New City. Here you can hire English-speaking **guides** for S£1500 per day. Staff have a useful, free city **map** to hand out; however, a much better one appears on the fold-out Freytag-Berndt *Road Map: Syria*, available in the **bookshop** at the *Amir Palace Hotel* close by. Either the bookshop or the tourist office can provide information on festivals and other **events** in the city. The *Syria Times* is also a good source of information on Aleppo events, but can be difficult to find; try the newsstands on Baron Street or the *Amir Palace* bookshop.

City transport

It's unlikely you'll feel much of a need to use the crowded **microbuses** or the smoke-belching, jam-packed blue or orange **buses** which form the bulk of Aleppo's city transport. These leave from the **city-bus station**, a chaotic, bewildering place strewn with wind-blown rubbish of all descriptions; it's located directly behind the *Amir Palace Hotel*. As usual, there are no published or posted timetables or indications of routes, so you'll just have to ask for help from locals (who'll think you're mad for wanting to go anywhere by bus); tickets are purchased on the bus.

You're much more likely to resort to your own two feet, or to **taxis**, for getting around; these yellow, often clapped-out American-built limousines can be hailed anywhere in Aleppo. Ask the driver to use the meter, though often you'll be told that it's broken or out of date, in which case you'll need to agree on a fare before you set out. A ride across town shouldn't cost more than S£40 – although you're asking to be charged over the odds if your journey starts or finishes at one of the big hotels. Some of the taxis are actually shared city **service taxis**, which run set routes, picking up and dropping off people as they go; they're difficult to distinguish from the normal taxis, apart from the fact that they're often carrying a carload of passengers instead of people in ones or twos.

Accommodation

There's no shortage of **hotels** in Aleppo, covering the full price and quality range, and they're rarely full; what's more, looking around for somewhere to stay is easy, as most are concentrated in the area around Baron Street and Bab al-Faraj (the former location of a city gate, now marked by an ugly 100-year-old clock tower). Prices are, however, higher than in other parts of Syria (with the exception of Damascus), and Aleppo's role as a trading centre might mean that you find noisy sessions between sellers (often Russians and Armenians) and buyers actually taking place in your hotel, at all hours of the day and night. Street noise can be a problem too, especially in cheaper places.

THE BARON HOTEL

Since its opening in 1909 the **Baron** has been the most famous and talked-about hotel in Syria, although nowadays its fame rests solely on its illustrious list of former guests, and has little to do with the rather sorry condition which currently besets the place. The hotel is managed by **Coco Masloumian**, a direct descendant of one of the two founders, brothers who, like many of their kinsfolk in the 1890s, fled the Turkish pogrom in Armenia and sought refuge in Aleppo. The brothers decided to open a hotel in what was then the chic European part of town, not far from the train station (where part of the Orient Express terminated) and with a terrace overlooking a marsh, where game could easily be shot for the hotel's dinner table. Incorporating the best of oriental hospitality and European standards of luxury, the hotel developed a reputation which quickly spread, and its guest list grew to include Kemal Atatürk, Theodore Roosevelt, Lady Louis Mountbatten, the aviators Charles Lindbergh and Amy Johnson, the writer Agatha Christie and her archeologist husband Sir Max Mallowan (many of whose finds are now on display in the archeological museum), and, most famously of all, T.E. Lawrence (of Arabia), a copy of whose bill can be seen in the TV lounge. Coco Masloumian's English wife Sally, who co-manages the hotel, married him just after World War II when she was a nurse working in Aleppo; she, like the hotel itself, is one of the few remaining links that Syria has with its colonial past.

Although modern office blocks now rather dwarf the humble *Baron*, it remains the most distinctive building on the street. Ninety years after its opening, the hotel still retains some of its original charm – although none of its famed luxury; the rooms are airy but bare and shabby, with plumbing that has a mind of its own and beds and furniture which have seen better days. You can no longer shoot game from the terrace, as the former marsh has long since been drained and built over, but sipping a cool beer on the terrace while gazing down upon the busiest street in Aleppo will no doubt compensate.

The hotel's **bar** is by far its most noted feature nowadays, a meeting point for travellers and expats who sink with ease into the faded armchairs and read back copies of *Time* magazine or gather on the terrace in the cool of summer evenings – when the ancient French thermometers pinned to the wall indicate that the temperature has at last dropped to something bearable. Lots of people drink here just to savour the atmosphere, secretly glad that they're not actually staying – although the place is usually booked solid, with many guests asking to be put up in Lawrence of Arabia's old room (he actually occupied several during his many stays). If you do decide to stay, then be prepared for plenty of noise from the street outside, in addition to night-time rumblings from the pipes and perhaps even the sounds of Agatha Christie's typewriter, as her ghost rewrites *Murder on the Orient Express* in the room she used as her study.

Rock-bottom dosshouses can be found along Al-Maari Street and the roads leading off it, and around the Bab al-Faraj Street clock tower, many of them located in the upper floors of apartment blocks. Some of these places are intolerably unhygienic and unsafe, with bedbugs and superior types of armour-plated insect life coming as standard, although many have gone to some lengths to clean up their acts over recent years. Prices start from as little as S£125 a night in a dormitory bed in the city's only backpackers' **hostel**, while single rooms in the **cheapest hotels** start at around S£200; we've earmarked the best of a pretty bad bunch below. In all these hotels (and even some of the slightly more expensive ones), a little haggling might reduce the price, particularly if you're staying for a few nights.

Apart from the *Al-Boustan*, by Bab al-Faraj, all the **mid-range** hotels we've listed are located on Baron Street or roads immediately leading from it, often above airline offices or travel agencies. The **top-of-the-range** big boys include the *Amir Palace*, close to Baron Street, and two five-star establishments a taxi ride from the centre, out in the western suburbs close to the university; much smaller, though nearly as expensive, are the two characterful hotels in old converted residences in the Jdeide Quarter.

Budget

Arabic Grand, Bab al-Faraj (☎021/221 1375). In a prime but noisy location by the clock-tower intersection, this hotel has clean, reasonably spacious single, double and triple rooms, some offering a good vantage point on the street below. ②.

Al-Chark, 50m southeast of Bab al-Faraj (☎021/223 9122). Cleaner and quieter than others at this price around the clock tower, this place has double rooms without bath, but no singles. ②.

Damascus, Bab al-Faraj (☎021/221 0786). In a noisy location overlooking the clock-tower intersection. Basic but bearable for a night or two. ①.

Al-Kasser, Al-Masaben St (☎021/223 9365). The rooms here have fans, en-suite squat toilets and, unusually, a spacious balcony overlooking the street below; however, there's no hot water. ②.

Al-Raouda, Al-Maari St (☎021/223 3896). Basic hotel with double rooms only and separate bathrooms on both its floors. ①.

Tourist, off Al-Maari St (☎021/221 6583). The forests of pot plants in the foyer and on the landings set the tone for this justifiably popular hotel, boasting scrupulously clean, spacious rooms, some en-suite. When there's enough demand, the management organizes minibus trips to sights around Aleppo. ②.

Yarmouk, Al-Maari St (☎021/221 7510 or 222 7990). A popular hotel praised by many budget travellers and filling up quickly as a result. It's very good for its price, with a choice of doubles or singles with or without bath. ②.

Zahert al-Rabih, off Al-Maari St (☎021/221 2790). Like the *Tourist* opposite, this is a backpackers' favourite; the rooms are perfectly acceptable, if a bit cramped. Besides boasting email facilities and a travel library at reception, it organizes transport out to Qalaat Semaan and other places around Aleppo. ①, dorm beds S£125.

Al-Zahra, just off Al-Maari St (☎021/222 0188). Acceptably clean option; occupies the floor below and uses the same lift as the *Assia Hotel* (a place which cannot be recommended). ②.

Mid-range

Ambassador, Baron St (☎021/221 0231). A small, rather soulless hotel, with air-con singles, doubles and triples available, though not breakfasts. ③.

Baron, Baron St (☎021/221 0880, fax 221 8164). Though this legendary hotel is a tourist sight in itself (see box, p.219), tales abound of shabby rooms and antiquated plumbing; a lot of guests seem to spend their time sitting around the (very convivial) downstairs bar, slagging the place off. It's overpriced and many rooms are without shower or bath; all the same, booking in advance is advised if you want to stay. Usefully, the hotel organizes transport, with a guide, out to the sights in the vicinity of Aleppo; you don't need to be staying here to take advantage of this. ④.

Al-Boustan, Bab al-Faraj (☎021/221 7104 or 221 7456). Located just north of the clock tower, this is a small, well-appointed hotel. Well worth a look. ④.

Garnarda, just off Baron St (☎021/222 4298). Clean, spacious rooms with rather elderly fittings. ④.

New Omayad, on a side street between Baron and Al-Walid streets (☎021/221 4202). Good rooms with air-con in a quiet location, away from the noise of the traffic. ⑤.

Ramsis, Baron St (☎021/221 6700). Opposite the *Baron*. Rather overpriced for what it is (the plush foyer is there to make you forget how shabby the rooms are), though the rate does include breakfast. ⑤.

Semiramis, Bab al-Faraj (☎021/221 9991). Rooms here are basic and minimally furnished, but do have air-con. No breakfast. ③.

Tourism, Al-Walid St (☎021/225 1602, fax 221 9956). Superior to the other mid-range options in terms of facilities on offer, and size and comfort of the rooms. It's a bit soulless, but if you want a centrally located, well-appointed hotel and can't quite afford the *Amir Palace*, this is the place to head for. ⑤.

Expensive

Amir Palace, Ibrahim Hanono St/Al-Raies Square (☎021/221 4800, fax 221 5710). Luxury high-rise, with TV, central air-con and all mod cons. Cheaper and more central than the other hotels in this class. ⑦.

Beit Wakil, Sissi St (☎021/221 7169, fax 224 7082, *www.beitwakil.com*). Housed in a refurbished sixteenth-century Aleppo residence, this Jdeide Quarter hotel has sixteen air-con rooms, satellite TV and modern bathrooms partly modelled on traditional hammams. The decor is sumptuous throughout, with arabesque ceilings and attractive courtyards incorporating marble fountains shaded by jasmine and lemon trees. It also boasts restaurants serving Arabic and Western cuisine, and a bar down in the ancient cellars. ⑦.

Martini Dar Zamaria, 100m east of Jdeide Sq (☎021/363 6100, fax 363 2333, *www.syria -guide.com/hotel/zamaria/INDEX.htm*). Like the *Beit Wakil*, this hotel is an old converted Aleppo residence. A similar sort of deal: the décor features coloured-glass windows, ornate wooden ceilings and marble floors, and there's central air-con and satellite TV in every room. Also has a restaurant, café and bar. ⑦.

Chahba Cham Palace, Al-Koudsi St (☎021/222 1600, fax 227 0150). Not only does this huge place boast comfortable rooms with satellite TV and central air-con, it also has an outdoor pool, tennis courts, a fitness centre and sauna, not to mention a business centre, several restaurants and bars and a disco. However, the inconvenient location (a 20min walk from Baron St), bland sheen and impersonal service can be rather wearing. ⑧.

Pullman Shahba, University St (☎021/266 7200, fax 266 7213). Smaller, less impersonal and better value than the *Chahba Cham Palace*. All rooms here have TV and central air-con, and there's a café/snack bar and two restaurants. ⑧.

The City

The area of town between the *Amir Palace Hotel* and the citadel is taken up by the **souks**, which for many travellers are the principal attraction of Aleppo. Dark, noisy and crowded with animals, traders and shoppers, the souks form one of the largest areas of covered market anywhere in the world, a labyrinthine network of passages broken only by the open courtyards of mosques and by the quadrangles of medieval **khans**, the combined inns and warehouses used by merchants in Ottoman days. The **Great Mosque**, which lies in the northern part of the souk area, is an unmissable haven of glacial calm after the bustle of the markets.

Just beyond the eastern end of the souks is the **citadel**, the defensive and administrative heart of medieval Aleppo, its distinctive ramparts and formidable towered gateway depicted in tourist posters around Syria. Although the rooms of the tower have been splendidly restored to give some flavour of the city's wealth during the Middle Ages, the citadel's most alluring aspect is the view over the whole of Aleppo from the upper walls. The area south of the citadel consists of streets lined with artisans' workshops, mosques and madrasas, and is a good place to head for if the tourist crowds in the souks and citadel become wearing.

To the northwest of the citadel is the **Jdeide Quarter**, traditionally home to Aleppo's Christian community, where, in addition to churches belonging to the major sects, the fascinating **Museum of Popular Tradition** can be visited. If the churches are locked and the museum doesn't grab your attention, it's still well worth exploring this district, as it's another good place to escape the crowds: most of the streets are quiet, traffic-free lanes, narrow and twisting, with tall, shuttered houses whose upper floors often overhang the street to give welcome shade.

Although the city's main hotels, restaurants, shops, transport and business facilities are found in the **New City**, the **National Museum of Aleppo** is the only specific tourist sight here. Also in this part of the city is the pleasant **city park**, a shady area of paths, greenery and fountains, laid out in the late 1940s like a Paris park, with refreshment stalls and a children's pleasure park thrown in for good measure. Especially worth spending time in on warm afternoons or during the early evening in mid-summer, the place is unique in Syria, where urban greenery is something of a rarity, and beats hands-down any of the scruffy public parks in Damascus. Late in the day the park is the arena for Aleppo's Mediterranean-style *passegiata*, when families dressed up to the nines wander the paths and sit by the numerous gushing fountains, consuming copious amounts of ice cream.

The souks and Great Mosque

An incredible array of goods is sold in the **souks**, ranging from whole, fresh animal carcasses (with entrails available in a separate bag), to jewellery, fabrics, clothing, ornaments, shoes, nuts, spices and household goods. Whether you want a packet of washing powder or a genuine antique *nargileh*, this is the place to come. The souks are divided into sectors, with traders in each zone selling one particular thing, which makes shopping and shopping around easy. Little pressure to buy is exerted by the traders, most of whom talk genially on mobile phones while drinking endless tiny cups of strong, sweet tea, which you may be offered yourself in the course of your discussions over what's on offer. Don't forget to bargain fiercely for what you want – often the price can be got down to a half of what was originally suggested, and with so many traders selling much the same sort of thing, arriving at a fair price is always easy. The souks **open** from about 10am to 5pm, except on Fridays when virtually all traders close up (you can still walk through the passageways at any time). If it's souvenirs and handicrafts you're after – inlaid backgammon boards, ornate copperware and the like – you're better off looking in the designated **handicrafts souk** (see p.228) to the south of the citadel (see also p.238 for more shopping recommendations).

The best way to get your bearings in the souk proper is to spend a little time walking up and down the **main street** (its western half named Souk al-Attarin, the rest named Souk az-Zarb), an ancient highway aligned west–east through the middle of the souks. After a first pass down this road, it's well worth diving off into the narrower, mercifully donkey-free lanes to the sides. In addition to what's described below, you'll encounter more khans (none of them particularly special) and tiny mosques (most of which are hidden from view and/or locked), but more importantly you'll find yet more things on offer, sold by traders as willing to

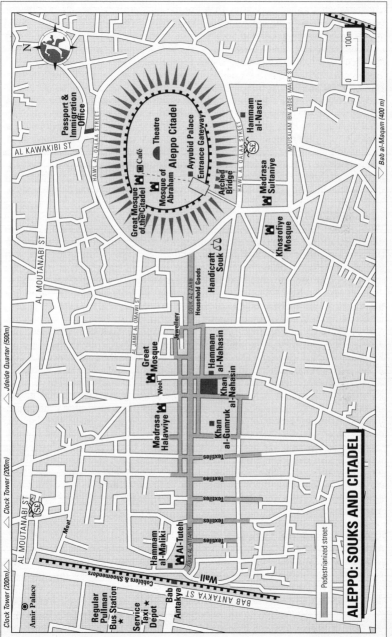

ALEPPO: SOUKS AND CITADEL

practise their English on you as they are to sell you their wares. Don't be surprised if you end up buying something you never actually wanted, from a trader who says he's been to London and asks you how Arsenal are doing: after you've been immersed in these tunnels for a few hours, you'll realize that the off-beat comes as standard in the Aleppo souks.

From the meat souk to Bab Antakya

Just east of the *Amir Palace* hotel, one area of the souks you might want to look at first (or go out of your way to avoid) is the **meat souk**, located to the north of the main trading area. Here every stall is almost hidden by the array of fresh animal carcasses hanging from hooks along the souk's single passageway, and the blood drains freely into gutters from the entrails and separate cuts sitting on the trays along its length. Between the meat souk and the main entrance to the souks through Bab Antakya are dozens of **shoemenders** armed with ancient sewing machines, who might come in handy if your own footwear is approaching a state of collapse.

Souk al-Attarin

Wider than the other passageways, **Souk al-Attarin** starts at **Bab Antakya**, located southeast of the *Amir Palace*, across the road from the service-taxi depot; this was the medieval Antioch Gate into the Old City and is thought to stand on the site of a Roman triumphal arch. Just beyond the gate a flight of stone steps leads up to the left and onto the Old City **ramparts**, from where there are good views across the New City. Halfway up the steps is the **Hammam al-Maliki** (see p.238), set amid small dwellings which act as a reminder that the Old City is a residential as well as a mercantile quarter.

Back down the steps, Souk al-Attarin undertakes a couple of twists which take it round the **Al-Tuteh Mosque**, supposedly constructed from pieces of the old Roman triumphal arch (and usually closed); east of here the street becomes completely straight and plunges into murky gloom under an arched roof pierced by regular holes through which sunlight streams and rain cascades. This covered alleyway lined with stalls selling pots and pans and other kitchenware gives a flavour of the souk as a whole: the district consists of narrow, often claustrophobic and thoroughly disorienting weaving passageways crammed with bustling people, laden donkeys, wooden carts piled high with anything from freshly-slain carcasses to blocks of ice, and even the odd pick-up truck, groaning slowly along the cobbles as people press their backs to the walls to let it past. As you head east, the kitchenware is followed by clothing and material stalls, the nuts, spices and coffee souks, and then more fabric-sellers, with everything on offer from bulk-import material from the Far East to locally woven, intricately patterned textiles which you can buy off the roll.

Khan al-Jumruk and Khan al-Nahasin

Around 400m east of Bab Antakya, and below a high dome in the ceiling punctured by four windows, a huge set of oak doors on the south side of the street marks the entrance to the **Khan al-Jumruk**. It's easy to walk past the khan without noticing – look for the high railing which bars the passageway to vehicles, and the plaque on the wall indicating the dates of the khan's foundation in both the Gregorian and Islamic calendars. After passing through a short, dark tunnel you emerge in the spacious courtyard of this former Ottoman customs house, laid out in the usual khan style: stables and warehouses on the ground floor, accommodation above (reached by the upstairs gallery). In the sixteenth century this was the headquarters for the English and Dutch consulates and trade missions, a self-contained and inward-looking diplomatic sanctum whose design itself reduced contact between European traders and their Muslim counterparts. The Europeans were not allowed out of the building at night, for reasons of their own safety, and although some hunted or played sport in the surrounding countryside (or even made a pilgrimage to Jerusalem), by all accounts the merchants led a fairly restricted and isolated life, often drinking away their boredom in the khan's own ale house. The English trade mission, founded by Elizabeth I in 1581, closed in 1791, and since then the building has been used by souk traders, today selling textiles and fabrics in far less cramped surroundings than their colleagues along the covered lanes. On Fridays the place is eerily empty and silent, save for stray cats sunning themselves on the stones and chasing wind-blown pieces of loose fabric left by careless traders.

East of the entrance to the khan is an intersection; the worshippers' entrance to the Great Mosque is clearly signposted to the north here, while a southward turn brings you to the **Hammam al-Nahasin**, a bathhouse dating from the thirteenth century, where you can still sweat away in the hot room or come under the skilled care of a masseur. Right opposite the bathhouse is the entrance to the **Khan al-Nahasin**, where footwear is sold among the archways and raised galleries of the former residence of the Venetian consul. It's a welcome arena of sunshine, but the architecture (spoiled by accretions through the ages) is nothing special.

The Great Mosque

The **Great** (or **Umayyad**) **Mosque** is an airy retreat from the rest of Aleppo, almost hermetically sealed by solid medieval stonework from the noise and clamour of the city. It was founded in 715 AD by Caliph al-Walid I, and probably completed by his brother and successor Caliph Suleiman two years later, thus following hard on the heels of, and attempting to emulate, the other great Umayyad foundation, the Great Mosque in Damascus. Earthquakes, fires and bouts of rebuilding, however, mean that what you see today dates mostly from medieval times.

There are entrances on all four sides, from the souks on the south and east, from a public square on the north, and from a small lane on the west side (leading up from the intersection 20m beyond the Khan al-Jumruk), which is the **entrance for non-Muslims**. Unless you're Muslim, it's best to avoid visiting during prayer times, as you might feel awkward walking round the place as people are worshipping – although you're unlikely to be asked to leave if you do show up then.

Inside, the mosque's architecture is curiously artless, grandiose without being in any way beautiful or graceful. In summer the courtyard is hot and devoid of shade, people generally lingering among the cool colonnades which run along three sides, worshipping, sleeping, talking or sitting in family groups. A distinguishing feature of the long, narrow **prayer hall** is a reliquary, draped with beautifully embroidered cloth, which is said to contain the head of Zacharias, the father of John the Baptist.

More appealing architecturally than any of this is the 47-metre-high square **minaret**, one of the finest in Syria, which was built as a free-standing construction by the Seljuk Turks in 1092. Each side is adorned with attractive wooden carvings, stylized Kufic script and inlaid stonework, with none of the panels identical to any other. The earthquakes which have regularly beset Aleppo through the ages have caused the tower to lean visibly from the vertical.

Madrasa Halawiye

Opposite the tourist entrance to the mosque is a shabby building which, more than any other in Aleppo, reflects the city's varied history. Formerly the theological school attached to the Great Mosque, the **Madrasa Halawiye** stands on the site of the **Cathedral of St Helena**, founded in the sixth century in honour of the mother of Emperor Constantine; it was only in 1124, after four centuries of co-existence with the Great Mosque built in its garden, that the cathedral was commandeered by the Muslim ruler of Aleppo and turned into a madrasa, in response to the thoughtless wrecking of Islamic monuments by the besieging Crusader army.

The place is often locked, but if a tour group shows up or there's a custodian present, you'll probably get a look in (and should expect to pay an entry charge of S£25). The building is entered from the street by a flight of stone steps leading down to a shady courtyard, which is lined with the former cubicles of students. Once you're at the foot of the steps, the **prayer hall** is through a wooden door straight ahead of you. Inside, all that's left of the ancient basilica are the six columns with ornate capitals, supporting the dome of the left *iwan* in a semicircular arrangement; the hall itself is a strikingly serene space, its thick prayer mats and high ceiling giving it an air of intimacy which the Great Mosque lacks.

Souk az-Zarb

Back on the main west–east lane, which soon becomes the **Souk az-Zarb** to the east of the Great Mosque, are more stalls selling fabric and household goods; here you can buy cockroach repellent and cheap jewellery, and there's at least one stall selling bars of soap which have been sculpted into designs such as houses and jugs. Passages to the north lead to the **gold souk**, where a succession of cramped stalls sell an array of glittering jewellery pieces. Many of the outlets here sell much the same sort of stuff, but there are also stalls selling carpets, bridal dresses and antiques. East along the street, close to the citadel, what's on offer is more tourist-oriented; here you encounter traders who'll flog you a *keffiyeh* or a fez, and there are also *nargileh*s, brightly coloured head scarves and damask tablecloths on sale. After a short uphill section, the street finally emerges into the open on Hawl al-Qalaa, the road at the foot of the citadel mound.

The citadel

As well as being the most distinctive feature of Aleppo's skyline, the **citadel** (daily except Tues 9am–4pm; S£300, additional charge for cameras and camcorders) is the city's major historic monument, with a regular stream of tour buses disgorging their loads outside the main entrance from early morning onwards. Not surprisingly, the small, steep-sided mound on which the citadel sits has been in use for defensive purposes since Bronze Age times (around 1600 BC); less obviously, the hill has also been accorded religious significance over the centuries, and it's thought that both the Greeks and the Romans worshipped various gods here in addition to using the site as an army base. Most of what can be seen of the defences now is the result of rebuilding and strengthening by a series of rulers between 1150 and 1400, their efforts hampered by the repeated adverse attention of Crusader and Mongol armies. During the later Middle Ages the city began to grow around the citadel mound, somewhat nullifying its defensive role, and the Mamelukes developed the place as a showpiece royal palace, turning the tower bastions into magnificent state rooms but doing next to nothing with the area inside the old walls.

What remains today falls into two separate parts: in the formidable entrance gateway are a succession of restored rooms, linked by passages and stairways, which formed the Mameluke palace; beyond that, on the open summit of the mound, are two mosques, plus a ramshackle collection of remains of the various fortifications which once stood here. It's a disappointing place in some ways, spoilt both by thoughtless restoration work and by shameful neglect, though the Mameluke state rooms and dramatic views over Aleppo from the ramparts are truly memorable.

The entrance gateway

The only way into the citadel is across a fine stone **entrance bridge**, its supporting arches and rising rampway straddling the (now dry) moat; opposite the entrance are several cafés serving coffee, tea and soft drinks to weary tourists. At the top of the bridge lies the **entrance gateway**, a spectacularly formidable feat of early medieval engineering, incorporating several storeys. After coping with missiles being thrown from the upper storeys, potential invaders would have had to negotiate the twists and sudden darkness of the passageway which curls around inside the gateway. Small wonder, then, that the citadel in its present form was never successfully captured.

After 1400, when the threat of Mongol invasion was severely reduced, the gateway took on much more of a ceremonial function, and the interior was altered accordingly. To see the rooms used as a palace by the Mameluke rulers, turn right after crossing the bridge, pass through the first set of huge steel doors, and then follow the passageway as it swings abruptly left; ahead is a door set at the top of a short flight of steps. Beyond the door you pass through several dull halls (once domestic quarters, kitchens and an armoury, and now left bare) before reaching the grandiose **throne room**, the centrepiece of the royal palace. Extravagantly restored, the main feature of the room is the ornate wooden ceiling, carved with profuse geometric shapes and patterns to wonderfully luxuriant effect.

Inside the walls

Beyond the main gateway, the flat, windy summit of the citadel **mound** is crossed by a central, paved and stepped path which runs to the café by the north wall. Much of the summit is a weed-infested jumble of half-excavated ruins, worth little more than a casual glance. On the right as you emerge from the passage through the gateway are the scant remains, little more than waist-high, of the **Ayyubid palace**, built in 1230 but destroyed by later Mongol invasions (which prompted the building of the much more solid defences you've just walked through). The fourteenth-century palace baths have undergone recent restoration, but apart from that all you can make sense of here is a maze of former courtyards and rooms.

Further along the path, on the left, there's rather more that's worth looking at in the **Mosque of Abraham**, dated to 1167 and probably founded by the Muslim commander Nur al-Din. Abraham, who is especially revered by Muslims, as well as by Christians and Jews, because of his adoption of monotheism, is believed by Muslims to have stayed and worshipped at this spot on one of his frequent journeys across the desert; the site is also thought to have been a resting place of the head of John the Baptist (said to have eventually finished up in the Umayyad

Mosque in Damascus). The building is rather plain and austere, as is the **Great Mosque of the Citadel** a little further on – although the latter, built in 1214 by the Ayyubids has a certain serene beauty; it's a small, sombre but well-proportioned affair, with a plain, square-towered minaret standing not far away, overlooking the citadel's northern walls, and a cloistered courtyard and trees that provide some relief from the starkness of the rest of the citadel.

Next to the Great Mosque of the Citadel, in what remains of a nineteenth-century Ottoman barracks, is a small **café** serving coffee and a limited selection of soft drinks and snacks. The fare may be ordinary, but the spot is the greatest attraction of the summit, commanding a stunning view over the domes, minarets, walled courtyards and rooftop gardens of central Aleppo. From the café you can follow the **citadel walls** around the mound, though in some places they've crumbled almost to nothing. In the eastern part of the summit, the modern open-air **amphitheatre** has no historical right to be here, but it's impressively used for occasional shows – in recent years, for example, it has been the setting for a performance of Purcell's opera *Dido and Aeneas*, and for a number of performances by whirling dervishes (see p.105).

South from the citadel

Apart from the **Madrasa Faradis**, considered by many to be the most beautiful of all Aleppo's Islamic buildings, there's little specific to see in the area to the south of the citadel, and many of the Islamic monuments covered in this section are locked for most of the time. Nevertheless, an hour's walk from the citadel entrance gets you right away from the tour groups, into an area of Aleppo which still retains many ancient touches, though you'll have to look for them carefully, along backstreets and behind houses and shops.

Hammam al-Nasri and the handicrafts souk

To the east of the citadel entrance, the **Hammam al-Nasri** is the best-appointed baths in Syria, spruced up in 1985 by the government with the specific aim of luring in tourists, and their presumed fistfuls of dollars. It's not the most authentic hammam experience, and carries a comparatively hefty price tag (see "Listings", p.238, for details of this and other Aleppo bathhouses), but for the uninitiated this may be the best place for an introduction to the complex business of having a Turkish bath.

Behind the cafés opposite the citadel entrance, the **handicrafts souk** is another tourism initiative by the Syrian government, a bright and airy L-shaped hall where copperware, fancy footwear and textiles, woven and brocaded rugs, inlaid wooden backgammon and chess boards, musical instruments (mainly of the drumming and strumming kind) and brightly coloured earthenware are on sale. For souvenirs, this is the place to come: the choice is better, though prices are higher, than in the main area of the souks, where you'll spend much more time looking for exactly what you want.

South to Bab al-Maqam

Immediately south of the handicrafts souk is the **Khosrofiye Mosque**, a high-walled building with a spacious courtyard. The oldest Ottoman mosque in Aleppo, it was built in 1537 by Sinan, who went on to become the most famous architect of imperial Istanbul; unsurprisingly, the five domes above the portico and the tall, slender minaret are in the Turkish style. Opposite the mosque stands the

Madrasa Sultaniye, a religious school built in the early thirteenth century, with a particularly fine *mihrab* in the (usually locked) prayer hall; also in this building is the tomb of Sultan Al-Zaher Ghazi, a son of Saladin and governor of Aleppo, who founded the mosque and initiated much of the fortification work on the citadel.

One of the original gates into the city, **Bab al-Maqam**, lies a few minutes' walk to the south. To reach it, head south from the start of the citadel bridge, down an avenue lined with shops and workshops (the road between the mosque and the madrasa intersects this). About 200m south from the citadel is a junction surrounded by all manner of small metal forges and meat shops, with the usual hanging carcasses outside; turn right (southwest) here along Bab al-Maqam Street, which gradually becomes more residential, narrow dusty lanes leading off it into a district dense with low-rise dwellings and stalls. On the right after about 100m is the sixteenth-century **Al-Tavashi Mosque**, its facade lined with slender columns (and its door usually firmly shut); five minutes further on is Bab al-Maqam itself, a solid stone structure whose fifteenth-century arches now provide shade for traders and animals.

From Bab al-Maqam to the Madrasa Faradis

Immediately beyond Bab al-Maqam is a small, busy intersection, clogged with traffic and donkey carts laden with produce for the markets which line the surrounding streets. Cross over the main east–west drag here (Sajd al-Ass Street) and take the road which runs diagonally right from the intersection, heading southwest (and running parallel with, and to the right of, a street with two distinctive minarets along it). On the left after 40m is the sixteenth-century **Mausoleum of Kheir Bey**, a plain, domed building whose patron was in fact buried in Cairo, posted there on diplomatic business after this, his intended tomb, had been completed.

After 300m the road forks; take the right-hand fork, which runs straight through the middle of a large cemetery. At this point the urban landscape changes and you enter a visibly poorer, but vibrant, part of the city, populated by grimy children and mangy animals. This is well off the beaten Aleppo tourist track and your appearance in this part of the city will not go unnoticed. Around 200m or so from the fork in the road, turn left following the south side of the cemetery wall. This lane is unmarked, running between the gravestones on the left and walled buildings on the right. It looks as though it leads nowhere, but after 100m you reach the **Madrasa Faradis**, founded by the widow of governor Al-Zaher Ghazi in 1234. Entered through a small door on the right, its cool central courtyard, whose shallow pool reflects the domes and sky, is lined with arcades supported by ancient columns; inside everything displays a restrained simplicity and charm, especially the main prayer niche which is richly inlaid with marble.

The Jdeide Quarter

Lying northwest of the citadel and east of Baron Street, the **Jdeide Quarter** is a fascinating warren of serpentine, traffic-free lanes, lined with medieval houses whose upper floors overhang the streets. Large, ornate and distinctly private, these dwellings have shut themselves away, architecturally and socially, from the rest of the city, and while some still remain private houses, others have been converted into schools and ecclesiastical residences, their intricate wooden decorations and inlay work firmly barred from public view; some have recently been renovated and turned into rather swish hotels (see p.221) and restaurants (see p.235).

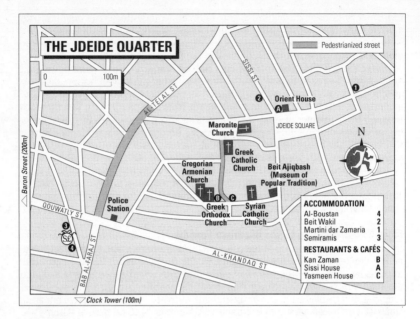

The quarter is the traditional home of Aleppo's large **Christian community**, and although there are only a few specific sights to aim for, it's a wonderful area to wander round, particularly during the afternoons when all is shady, shuttered and silent. Things are different on Sunday mornings, however, when, to the accompaniment of pealing church bells, clergymen scurry along the lanes with cassocks billowing, hurrying past well-to-do families making their sedate way to church.

There are several ways of approaching the Jdeide Quarter, but the easiest **route** from the New City is by **Al-Telal Street**, a pedestrianized thoroughfare which leads northeast from the city's main police station (itself just north of the clock tower; you'll recognize the police station from the railings and armed guards outside). Its start marked by an archway built over the paved road, Al-Telal Street is lively and modern, lined with pharmacies, clothes shops, photo-processing labs and stores selling electrical gear and cassette tapes. Few of the other streets in the quarter have names or are marked on maps, and it's easy – perhaps even preferable – to get pleasantly lost; before immersing yourself completely in the maze of narrow passageways, however, you should at least make an effort to find the **Greek Orthodox** and **Armenian** churches, plus the **Museum of Popular Tradition**, which constitute the main sights of the area. It's worth noting that the churches are locked most of the time, except on Sunday mornings, when seeing them may mean just poking your head round the front door during a service.

The churches

At the northern end of the pedestrianized zone on Al-Telal Street, take the street on the right to a pleasant square, where you'll see the **Maronite church** facing you, with the smaller **Greek Catholic church** to the right. Both are late nineteenth-century constructions, neither particularly interesting, with uninspiring stonework – and firmly closed doors. From this attractive square, turn south along a narrow lane which twists and turns a number of times, passing two restaurants, the *Kan Zaman* and the *Yasmeen House* (see p.236). Shortly after the restaurants there is a T-junction; a short distance west along from here, on the northern side, is the **Greek Orthodox church** which – unlike most of the district's other churches – usually keeps its doors open and is worth looking round. Built in the 1860s, it has an ornate if rather fussy iconostasis, and a shady, leafy courtyard, containing the grave of a former Russian diplomat. A little further on along the same street is the late medieval **Gregorian Armenian church**, its decorations including fifteenth-century paintings, carvings and icons.

The Museum of Popular Tradition

Back at the T-junction, heading east brings you almost immediately to the Syrian Catholic church on the left (usually closed), beyond which (again on the left) is the **Museum of Popular Tradition** (daily except Tues 8am–2pm; S£200). It's the architecture which captures the attention as much as the museum, though: the building, known as **Beit Ajiqbash**, is one of the few examples of the homes built by Aleppo's wealthy Christian business families that is open to public view. Built in 1757, the house has a delightful central courtyard, planted with trees and cooled by a splashing fountain, around which, in the main living rooms, some wonderfully preserved wooden wall panels and ceilings, meticulously carved and painted, and richly inlaid eighteenth-century chairs and tables can be seen. The other parts of the museum are disappointing, consisting of hackneyed displays of clothing, weapons and the like that seem quite out of place here – though it's worth persevering for the views across Aleppo from the upstairs terrace.

The National Museum of Aleppo

Just 150m south of the *Baron* hotel, the **National Museum** (daily except Tues 9am–6pm; S£300) chronicles the history of Aleppo and northern Syria from earliest times to the Ottoman era, its main displays being archeological finds from various sites in the Jezira in northeastern Syria. Housed in a purpose-built pavilion around an open courtyard, the collection is nicely set out in airy rooms and reasonably well labelled, with a detailed guidebook available at the entrance (S£150); however, the exhibits are moved around a fair bit, so what you see may not bear much relation to what's in the guide. A visit is especially rewarding if you've already been to the sites from which the majority of the finds come (such as Mari, Ugarit and Ebla).

Ground floor

You enter the museum building past some bemused-looking statues fashioned from black basalt which were unearthed from Tell Halaf in northeastern Syria; 3000 years old they may be, but their eye-popping expressions render them an unintentionally amusing introduction to the museum. To the right of the ticket desk is a room designed for a mosaic collection, which, when it is finally installed, promises to be one of the museum's highlights.

•**Prehistoric section**. Housed in the first room to the right of the entrance are figurines that probably represent the Mother Goddess, as well as stone tools and pieces of pottery found in a 1990 dig at Tell Kashashuk in the northeast. However, the most interesting exhibit here is the reconstructed skeleton of a Neanderthal child, aged two, who lived in middle Palaeolithic times and was probably killed by a flint weapon that was found with the bones; the body was buried at a site around 60km northwest of Aleppo. Also in this room are the finds from Tell Halula which have been unearthed by a Spanish archeological mission. Principal among them are some extraordinary paintings, now faded to almost nothing, which are the oldest example of human representation in artwork found in the Middle East, dating to around 6000 BC.

• **Tell Brak**. Most of the pieces in this room were unearthed in the 1930s by the British archeologist Sir Max Mallowan, husband of Agatha Christie, at Tell Brak

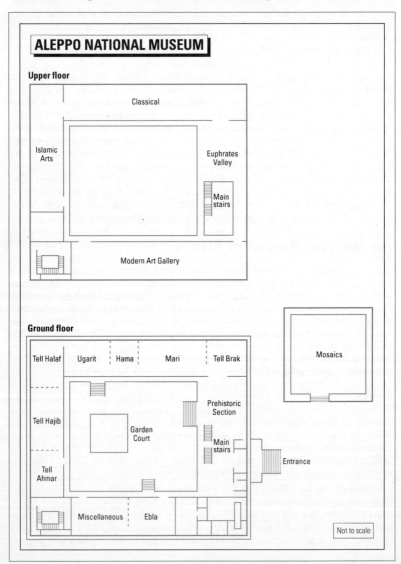

and other sites in northeastern Syria (see also p.272). Mallowan gave a lot of the best finds to the British Museum in London, and what grabs the attention most here are the necklaces fashioned from beads of different shapes and materials and the stone tablets written in cuneiform script, all of which date from around 3000 BC.

• **Mari**. The most interesting exhibit from this Bronze Age (c.1700 BC) site is the Golden Lion, made from (now oxidized) bronze, with its sad, benign eyes. Also striking is the statue of the Spring Goddess, whose vase once flowed with water which came through pipes built inside the statue.

• **Hama**. Dating back to around 1000 BC, the finds from the region surrounding Hama include ceramic pieces and the like; against one wall are two lions which guarded the citadel in Hama around 800 BC.

• **Ugarit**. The most significant discovery made at Ugarit, a major Bronze Age trading centre on the coast near Latakia, was the temple archives, dating from around 1200 BC and written in what is believed to be the world's first alphabet; the language used by the scribes and merchants in Ugarit was Akkadian, at that time the principal language of diplomacy and trade in the eastern Mediterranean. Some of the tablets from the archives can be seen inside one case; other cases contain a variety of secretarial paraphernalia – cylinder seals, weights and the like – and a beautiful statuette in gilded bronze, depicting a bearded deity with ox horns, sitting on his throne and holding a child on his knee.

• **Tell Halaf**, **Tell Hajib** and **Tell Ahmar**. Upon entering the room, you're greeted by two enormous statues of seated women from Tell Halaf, 70km northwest of Hassakeh. Dating from around 1000 BC, the statues are thought to represent members of the Halaf ruling dynasty; between them is part of the facade of what must have been a glorious temple palace, featuring a winged sun-disc being transported by mythical figures, one of which is half-man, half-bull. Unfortunately, many of the other finds from Tell Halaf, excavated by German archeologists in the 1930s, were taken to Berlin and were destroyed in Allied bombing raids in World War II. Further on, the most important Iron Age finds from Tell Hajib, in the northern Jezira, are intricate, clearly Egyptian-inspired ivory carvings, inlaid with precious stones and decorated with coloured glaze; one design depicts the birth of the Egyptian god Horus, who sits on top of a lotus flower. Close by are paintings which once adorned the royal palace at Tell Ahmar (also in the northern Jezira), completed around 850 BC and clearly the reflection of an egomaniacal regime: the king is shown scorning vanquished leaders, holding receptions and communing with humble-looking deities. The enormous obelisks at the far end of the room are of King Esarhaddon, who reigned from 680 to 661 BC. Immortalizing himself on these and other similarly sculptured stones, the king is shown in larger-than-life form, towering over his vanquished foes. In the rooms that follow the Tell Ahmar display, there's little of immediate interest, except perhaps some stone tablets from Ebla, and pottery pieces from Al-Ansari, a Bronze Age settlement very close to Aleppo.

Upper floor

The collections on the upper floor do not fit in with the chronological ordering of the ground floor and, on the whole, are not as absorbing.

• **Euphrates Valley**. There's little labelling in English in the first of the upstairs rooms, which contains mainly finds from early sites along the Euphrates. Most of these settlements flourished during the fourth and third millennia BC, their livelihood based on river trade with Babylonia and other, more important Euphrates settlements further downstream. The designs – of clay figurines, bronze and stone vessels, and animal sculptures – are fairly unsophisticated and pale in comparison with some of the beautiful finds from later settlements downstairs.

• **Classical section**. The most interesting of the upstairs galleries is that devoted to finds from Roman-era sites in Syria, particularly Palmyra. Coins, statuary, glass and bronze objects and mosaics are on display, but most prominent here is a tombstone found at Manbij, 90km east of Aleppo: the sculpture is of an elegant, seated woman, with a Greek inscription carved into the stone which reads simply and poignantly, "Rest in peace, Marta".

• **Islamic arts**. Only a tiny hint is given here of the richness of Islamic art fashioned in Syria from the eighth century onwards. The gold and silver coins produced by successive Arab dynasties are very fine; also prominent, in the corner, is the astrolabe – a fussy, mathematically complex device consisting of a myriad of globes and rings, used by early medieval scholars for determining the altitude of stars and planets. In the centre of the room is probably the single most interesting exhibit of the upstairs galleries, a model of the old city of Aleppo, with walls and gates, markets and mosques appearing as they do today.

• **Modern art gallery**. This ever-changing selection of paintings gives you something of a feel for Syrian modern art; most works are boldly realistic portraits of Syrian scenes and people, although there are a few more abstract works too. For a run-down of modern Syrian art and artists, see p.317 in Contexts.

Eating

There's an excellent variety of **restaurants** in Aleppo, from greasy chicken-and-kebab stalls to classy joints set up in restored eighteenth-century houses. If you're heading off into the sticks next, particularly eastward, the food options quickly become much more limited, so enjoy the culinary diversity while you're here.

For a quick bite, the spotless *Al-Faihaa*, just off Baron Street, near the junction with Qouwatly Street, is good for **falafels**. Those homesick for **Western-style snack food** can head for the café on the ground floor of the *Amir Palace Hotel* on Ibrahim Hanono Street, where tasty, if somewhat overpriced, sandwiches, pizzas, cakes and the like are served. A range of **ice cream** flavours, as well as a variety of sticky cakes and pastries, can be had at the ice cream parlour on Majd al-Din Al-Jaberee Street, opposite the eastern edge of the city park.

Self-catering travellers should head to the **grocery stores** along Baron and Al-Maari streets; the fruit and vegetable **market** which is situated immediately southeast of the entrance to the *Amir Palace Hotel* is also worth a visit. The quality of what's on offer is variable, although prices are incredibly cheap and there is a good variety of local and imported produce on offer, from bucketloads of pistachio nuts to South American bananas.

Restaurants

Aleppo's **restaurants** can be neatly grouped according to area: as a rule, the cheapest places are around Baron Street, with the mid-range and Western-oriented options in Al-Aziziah, just east of the city park; the most luxurious eating places the city has to offer are in the smartest hotels in the university district to the west, and in the Jdeide Quarter. In the listings below the restaurants have been categorized as cheap (under S£200 for a main meal), moderate (S£200–400) or expensive (over S£400). Restaurants in the upmarket hotels and those recommended in Al-Aziziah serve alcohol unless otherwise stated.

Baron Street and around

All the restaurants listed in this area are in the cheap category.

Al-Andalib, Baron St, next to the *Baron Hotel*. Very pleasant rooftop restaurant overlooking Baron St, serving chicken, kebabs, chips and salad, but not much else.

Al-Chahab, off Baron St. Limited range of kebab, chicken, chips and salad, with pigeon thrown in as an option for good measure. The main reason for eating here is the spacious open-air section, shaded by greenery and very pleasant on summer evenings.

Al-Kindi, 100m north of Bab al-Faraj. Long, narrow restaurant with efficient service and very filling portions of chicken or kebabs; there's also a counter at the far end where you can choose sweet pastries and the like for dessert. Slightly more upmarket than others in this area.

Zenubia, 100m northwest of Bab al-Faraj. Good, intimate kebab house.

Al-Zuhour, opposite the *Zenubia*, northwest of Bab al-Faraj. Large, basic, breezy but welcoming restaurant, where the tasty shish kebab comes with barbecued onions and tomato, and there's plenty of bread and salad.

Al-Aziziah

Al-Challal, on road linking Majd al-Din Al-Jaberee St with Pensilvaniah St. Elegant, good-value restaurant with terrace. Extensive menu of *mezze* and main dishes, served by very friendly Kurdish waiters. Moderate.

Delta, on northwards extension of Yousef al-Azmeh St. Bland, defiantly could-be-anywhere place, decked out in shiny chrome with soft muzak to accompany their international (pizzas and pasta) and Syrian fare; filling if unadventurous. Mid-range.

Ebla, on road linking Majd al-Din Al-Jaberee St with Pensilvaniah St. The lowest-priced establishment in this quarter, with an excellent range of food that includes starters, desserts, European dishes and lots of affordable Syrian dishes to try out, including fried brain and brain salad. Cheap.

Midmac, just off road linking Majd al-Din Al-Jaberee St with Pensilvaniah St. The name and familiar "golden arches" logo are a rip-off of McDonald's, but the shady terrace and nice interior décor make this a more elegant establishment than its Western near-namesake. Kebab, chicken, steak, veal, pizza, spaghetti and of course burgers and fries are all on offer, with lots of varieties of ice cream for afters. No alcohol. Moderate.

Pizza House, just south of Pensilvaniah St. Imitator of the similarly named Western chain, set back a little from the other restaurants in this district on a side road. Pizza, burgers, pasta, soft drinks, cakes and ice cream. No alcohol. Cheap.

Reef, on road linking Majd al-Din Al-Jaberee St with Pensilvaniah St. Extensive menu with European food and beer; tables spill out onto a canopy-covered pavement terrace. A good, comparatively inexpensive place to try out a Syrian meze. Moderate.

Sage, Majd al-Din Al-Jaberee St. Swish-looking place that's much less expensive than you might judge from the outside; the Syrian and international food is good, though the choice is limited. Cheap.

Wanes, on road linking Majd al-Din Al-Jaberee St with Pensilvaniah St. The favourite eating place of Aleppo's expat community. European-oriented, with pleasant food at slightly inflated prices. Moderate.

The Jdeide and university quarters

The three **Jdeide Quarter** restaurants listed (marked on the map on p.230) are sumptuously housed in former Aleppo residences, each one restored to good effect, as are the restaurants in the *Beit Wakil* and *Martini Dar Zamaria* hotels, which are also in this district and have expensive restaurants serving very good Syrian fare. The attractive roof top, terrace or courtyard eating areas at *Beit Wakil*, *Sissi House* and *Yasmeen House* are open only in summer; *Kan Zaman* and the *Martini Dar Zamaria* have indoor seating only.

Kan Zaman. New restaurant in Jdeide Quarter, serving traditional Syrian dishes such as *yalange* (aubergine stuffed with rice) amid beautiful surroundings. Moderate.

L'Italiano, *Pullman Shahba Hotel*, University St. This top-class hotel over in the university quarter boasts a very good Italian restaurant – the only one in Aleppo. The outside terrace is not particularly enticing, overlooking the main road, but the food on offer is good, including soups, salads, pasta, pizzas (with a choose-your-own-topping option), chicken escalope and seafood dishes. Moderate.

Sissi House. In what was once the elegant home of a wealthy Christian family (restored accordingly to good effect), this beautifully furnished Jdeide Quarter restaurant serves good traditional Syrian dishes, with not much change out of S£700 for a meal for two without wine – though the food is not quite as good as the ambience might suggest. To get there, follow the long, straight passage east along the northern wall of the Maronite Church. Expensive.

Yasmeen House. Also in the Jdeide Quarter, this restaurant includes an outdoor section, along the terraces and in the courtyard of an eighteenth-century residence. The cuisine is exclusively Syrian, with enticing meze and main courses that you choose from a folder of photographs, proffered by well-informed, English-speaking waiters. The entrance is opposite the *Kan Zaman*. Expensive.

Drinking, entertainment and nightlife

All over the centre of Aleppo, particularly along Al-Maari Street and Baron Street, and around the clock tower, there are big **coffee-houses** where you can sit and drink nothing but Turkish coffee until the early hours of the morning. The clientele is almost exclusively male, engaged in chewing the fat, playing cards or backgammon, or just puffing on a *nargileh* and watching the world go by; women are likely to find these places uncomfortable, particularly if they go there alone. For Western-style coffee, the *Amir Palace* hotel is by far the best place in Aleppo. **Fruit juice stores** and **liquor stalls** can be found on the small alleyways leading west from Bab al-Faraj Street, and around the clock tower and the *Damascus Hotel*.

There are no stand-alone **bars** in Aleppo, so if you want something alcoholic but don't fancy paying to get into one of the sleazy nightclubs, you'll have to go to a hotel. The most popular hangout in Aleppo, both with tourists and resident Westerners, is the ground floor and terrace bar in the *Baron Hotel* (see p.219); the armchairs have seen better days but are comfy, and the décor hasn't changed much since the 1950s, but the inflated prices keep all but the most well-heeled Syrians away. The tables out on the terrace provide a great opportunity for watching people Baron Street, but there's little shade and on summer afternoons it's definitely preferable to be inside. The downstairs bar at the *Amir Palace* is a bland sort of place, but this is where you'll find the best range of drinks on offer in central Aleppo.

Entertainment and nightlife

Aleppo goes to bed quite early, and by midnight most of the activity is centred on the sleazy **nightclubs** along Baron and Qouwatly streets. It's hard to recommend any of these places, but you'll find them soon enough if you want to – just follow the flashing neon, and be prepared to part with about S£400 for an evening of belly-dancing and the like. The alcohol flows quite freely, and most of these joints are a magnet for prostitutes and their pimps, who manage the brothels next door.

For something a little more edifying, there are two **theatres** in the city: an open-air amphitheatre on top of the citadel mound (see p.228), where **whirling dervishes** (see p.105) occasionally perform, and a more conventional indoor performance venue on 17 April Street, just west of the main post office. To find out what's on, try to pick up a copy of the *Syria Times*, ask at the tourist office or, more reliably, visit the venues themselves.

There are at least a dozen **cinemas** in Aleppo, all of them along Al-Azmeh Street (the northern extension of Baron Street), Qouwatly Street or around the clock tower. Most show an endless diet of Jackie Chan films and other martial-arts pap, but occasionally more interesting stuff turns up – anything from 1970s Michael Caine movies to recent European and American arthouse and main-stream works. Almost everything is subtitled in Arabic and French, so there's usually something around with an English soundtrack that's worth seeing. Prices are extremely low (about S£30), but the cinemas are fleapits, with lousy projection and sound quality, and an audience which normally insists on talking throughout the film. The posters pinned up outside and in the lobbies indicate what's showing that day; films sometimes change on a daily basis.

Listings

Airlines The following all have offices at the southern end of Baron St: Air France (☎021/223 2238); KLM (☎021/221 1074); Turkish Airlines (☎021/224 5955); Alitalia (☎021/222 2721). Syrianair has an office on the west side of Baron St, a short way north of the *Ramsis* hotel, though their main office (☎021/222 0501/2/3 or 224 1232; daily 8.30am–5.30pm, Fri until 2.30pm) is up by the southwestern corner of the park, immediately north of the post office. British Airways is on Kostaki Homsi St (☎021/227 4586); Nahas Travel and Tourism (☎021/222 2512), just up from the main post office, represents Austrian Airlines, Singapore Airlines, Thai International, United Airlines, Air New Zealand, Lufthansa and British Midland. All these airlines take most major credit cards.

Banks and exchange The "no.1" branch of the Commercial Bank of Syria (daily except Fri 8.30am–noon) is on Al-Moutanabi St, on the right as you walk east from the *Amir Palace Hotel*; they change cash and travellers' cheques, as does the branch on the east side of Al-Azmeh St (the northern extension of Baron St), which is open until 1pm (but likewise closed Fri). Both banks insist that you show the initial purchase receipt when you change travellers' cheques. The three exchange booths located respectively on the corner of Bab al-Faraj and Qouwatly St, adjacent to the tourist office and opposite the citadel are open daily 8am–8pm, but change cash only. All these places will exchange Turkish lira and most other Western and Middle Eastern currencies.

Bookshops The bookshop in the *Amir Palace Hotel* sells a limited range of English-language novels, guidebooks and coffee-table tomes about Syrian art, architecture and cooking.

Car rental Some travel agencies along Baron St offer car-with-driver rental for S£3500 per day upwards. To rent a self-drive car, contact the Europcar desk (☎021/266 7200) at the *Pullman Shahba Hotel* on University St.

Car repair Most Western makes of car are catered for at Mitsubishi Service, a block south-east of the *Baron Hotel*, on a road running parallel with Baron St (☎021/221 673). There's also a string of car repair shops along the eastern end of Al-Koudsi St.

Consulates The UK maintains a consulate (☎021/266 1206 or 267 2200; daily except Fri 8am–3pm) on the corner of Abu Firas al-Hamadani St and Muhammad Said al-Zaim St, due west of the train station; look out for the large signs of the Palmyra Languages Centre next door.

Couriers DHL is down a side street west along from Syrianair's Baron St office (☎021/221 4808).

Emergency services Police ☎112; ambulance ☎110; fire ☎113; traffic police ☎115. The main police station is on the major intersection 200m north of the clock tower.

Hammams Designed for tourists, the Al-Nasri (men Mon, Thurs & Sat 5pm–midnight, plus all day Tues, Wed, Fri & Sun; women Mon, Thurs & Sat 9am–5pm) opposite the entrance to the citadel is the best-appointed bathhouse in Syria; prices start at S£365 for use of all the rooms. Locals use the Hammam al-Nahasin (daily 8am–midnight; men only) opposite the Khan al-Nahasin in the souk, and the Hammam al-Maliki (same times; women only noon–6pm) by Bab Antakya – turn left up the steps after coming through the gate from Bab Antakya St. Both these hammams are much cheaper than the Al-Nasri.

Hospital The University Hospital is 5km west of the city centre at the north end of Haoul Albaldeh St.

Internet access The *Zahert al-Rabih* hotel offers its guests online facilities; if you are not staying there, they might allow you to go online anyway (for a small fee) or direct you to any recently opened public-access Internet cafés.

Newspapers The small bookshop in the *Chahba Cham Palace Hotel* and the newsstand on Bin Abi Sultan St (see map on p.215) sometimes sell rather elderly copies of the *International Herald Tribune* and other Western newspapers. Newsstands on Baron St sometimes have the *Syria Times*.

Pharmacies At the corner of Qouwatly St and the pedestrianized Al-Telal St are two excellent pharmacies.

Phones and faxes The falafel joint opposite the post office sells phone cards for use in the public phone booths around the city centre. Faxes can be sent from the post office.

Post office The main post office (daily 8am–8pm, Fri until noon) is at the north end of Al-Jalaa St, opposite the southern rim of the city park – you can't miss the huge transmission mast on the roof.

Shopping Try Babylon Antiques at the corner of Baron St and Al-Maari St, for antiques; next door there's a good selection of carpets and rugs in Jabaseh and Co. Rugs the size of a large table-top can be bought here for S£1000, and there's a good variety of designs and colours available. On the northwestern corner of Jdeide Sq, in the Jdeide Quarter, Orient House is a fascinating shop crammed with all manner of paraphernalia, including teapots, ornaments, books (mostly in French), bottles, ancient telephones and gramophones, copperware, and black-and-white prints from yesteryear. On the ground floor of the same building is a silverware shop. Otherwise try the shops in the handicrafts souk (see p.228). For cassettes of Arabic and Turkish music, head to the dozens of tiny stalls lining the western end of Qouwatly St.

Swimming There's a huge, modern indoor swimming pool in a building called Grand House, just up from the *Pullman Shahba Hotel* on University St, west of the city centre (men Sun, Tues & Thurs 6–10am & 3pm–midnight; Mon, Wed, Fri & Sat 6am–midnight; women Sun, Tues & Thurs 10am–3pm; S£150). The *Pullman Shahba Hotel* lets non-resident mixed-sex couples use their outdoor pool for S£700 per day.

Visa extensions Apply for these at the office just north of the citadel (see map, p.223). There's a photographic shop opposite which does passport photos (four needed).

AROUND ALEPPO

From the constant offers of taxi drivers and travel agency touts in downtown Aleppo, you'd think that the **Church of St Simeon** was the only place worth visiting in the city's vicinity. It's true that this ruined church and the pilgrimage complex that surrounds it is a compelling excursion, but you'd be missing out on a lot if you made it the only place in the area that you saw. The St Simeon complex is just one of a huge number of so-called **Dead Cities** around Aleppo, ruined

THE DEAD CITIES

The so-called **Dead Cities**, easily the best-preserved relics of the Byzantine world, consist of an estimated 780 towns, villages and monastic settlements in what was once the hinterland of **Antioch** (present-day Antakya in Turkey), the most important city of the Roman and Byzantine Middle East. Many of these sites originated in the first centuries after Christ as the country estates or summer resorts of the wealthier citizens of Antioch. The settlements slowly grew up to house the tenacious farmers who cultivated the dessicated land, and a monastic boom from the middle of the fourth century to the end of the sixth century led to the construction of sixty monasteries in the region. The area was a wealthy one, its prosperity founded upon the production of **oil** from olive orchards and **wine**, and their export, through Antioch, to the rest of the Byzantine world.

However, the devastating economic effects of successive wars led to the slow abandonment of the settlements: the struggle between the Byzantines and the Sasanian Persians in the sixth and early seventh centuries saw the destruction of many of the settlements and their orchards, and during the Persian occupation of Antioch, all international trade through the town ceased; then, once the Arabs had taken over the city later in the seventh century, the Byzantines imposed a trading boycott on their old possessions. The resulting political insecurity and economic hardship forced the peasants who occupied the Dead Cities back to self-sufficiency on the more cultivable plain of Amuq, to the northeast of Antioch. The area was largely abandoned by the tenth century, and has only in the last century been in any way repopulated; it is a remarkable testament to the Roman and Byzantine farmers that its barren limestone hills could ever support a population. The very lack of woodland in the area meant the Byzantine settlements had to be constructed almost entirely from limestone, as a result of which they have survived, largely undisturbed, in great numbers and often in an astonishing state of preservation.

Roman-Byzantine settlements dating from a century or so either side of 500 AD; we've described in detail only a handful of the most interesting and accessible in this section, but there are dozens of other more remote and decaying sites to keep serious ruins buffs happy, especially around Maarat al-Numan.

The most popular and accessible clutch of ruins lies to the **northwest** of Aleppo: in addition to the St Simeon complex, this area contains the remains of a Hittite temple at **Ain Dara**, and **Cyrrhus**, a former Roman city right on the Turkish border. To the **southwest** of Aleppo are the major Bronze Age dig at **Ebla** and the remote, surprisingly intact Dead Cities around **Maarat al-Numan**, of which Serjilla, in particular, and Ruweiha are the most interesting. The few sites to the **west** of Aleppo, more difficult to reach and generally in a much poorer state of preservation, are really only of specialist interest.

It would take a week or more to visit all the historical sites around Aleppo, but for most people two or three days will be rewarding enough. **Renting a car** in Aleppo is recommended, as public transport is unreliable, even if the distances are short. To hire a car with a driver, go to the tourist office or ask at the *Baron Hotel* (whether or not you're staying there); reasonable prices would be S£1500 for a trip to the St Simeon Complex and Ain Dara, S£2500 if you were to add Cyrrhus to this list, S£1500 to travel west to Harim and Qalb Lozeh, and S£3000 to visit the sites around Maarat al-Numan. Alternatively, the *Tourist* and *Zahert al-Rabih* hotels can organize minibus transport out to sights around Aleppo. It's worth visiting the Aleppo tourist office beforehand to pick up their useful **map** of the area; the Arabic version is handy in case your driver doesn't understand much English. With or without a vehicle, the most sensible way to see the region is on a series of day-trips from the city.

Northwest of Aleppo

Most visitors to Aleppo will find themselves making a trek out to the remains of the monumental **Church of St Simeon**, erected in the fifth century to revere the famous pillar-sitting ascetic. Less interesting destinations are the messy Roman ruins at **Cyrrhus**, up by the Turkish border, and the recently restored tenth-century BC temple complex at **Ain Dara**, remarkable more for its age than aesthetic impact. Attempting to visit all three is only feasible with your own transport; otherwise, it's better to tackle Cyrrhus as a morning trip from Aleppo, and spend a long day combining visits to Ain Dara and St Simeon.

Qalaat Semaan

The most popular and rewarding day-trip from Aleppo is the church complex of **Qalaat Semaan** (daily: summer 10am–6pm; winter 9am–4pm; S£300), its scale, which never fails to take visitors aback, and the finesse of the carvings combining to produce one of the most awesome sets of remains in the country. The object of all this architectural attention, Simeon, joined the community of monks in the settlement of **Telanissos** – the present-day village of **Deir Semaan** – in the early fifth century; following his death in 459, his remarkable life was commemorated by this huge church complex, the largest in the world at the time. On the hill above Telanissos, the complex was built by the monastic authorities between 476 and 491, using funds donated by pilgrims; its four separate basilicas, in the form of a cross, are centred around the **pillar** on which Simeon spent most of his time on earth. Telanissos became almost entirely given over to the housing of pilgrims visiting the church, and in the early sixth century a *via sacra* was built leading up from the village. The hastily built **wall** that surrounds the church is a tenth-century Byzantine fortification, hence the site's local name.

Despite the fame of the place, getting to St Simeon by **public transport** could be a lot easier. Microbuses from the Baron Street station in Aleppo to the nearest village, **Daret Ezzeh**, are frequent and take an hour, but onward minibuses are very infrequent; you'll probably have to negotiate with a microbus or taxi driver to take you the final 8km north to the complex (S£300 is a fair price), or even hop in the back of someone's truck (see p.33 for advice). If you're using your own transport from Aleppo, you might consider making a stop at the overgrown basilica church at **Mushabbak**, visible 1km south of the highway, 5km before you reach Daret Ezzeh. Dating to the late fifth century, it was probably built to serve pilgrims on their way out to St Simeon; it's not as stunning visually as many of the Dead City sites, but its state of preservation – up to roof level – is remarkable.

The complex

Entry to Qalaat Semaan is via the **ticket office** on the eastern side of the hill; here there's also a handy **café**. Climbing the ridge from here gives a view of the **church** on the right, announced by its glorious **narthex**, and the more modest

SAINT SIMEON

Born the son of a shepherd in the region of Antioch around 390, **Simeon** joined the monastic community at Telanissos sometime around 410–412, following a revelatory dream; he was to spend the rest of his life there. His asceticism soon manifested itself in some unusual behaviour: wearing spiked girdles which drew blood, and in summer burying himself in the ground up to his chin. From this he progressed to chaining himself to a rock in the middle of a roofless enclosure on the hill next to the village. His conduct naturally provoked much attention, and soon people were coming from miles around to witness his piety, seek advice and ask for miracles. To avoid people attempting to touch him, Simeon took to standing on top of a **pillar**, at first 3m high, but later extended to 6, 11 and finally 18m; a railing around the top prevented him from falling off in his sleep. As the pillar grew in height, so did Simeon's reputation (he was dubbed Simeon Stylites, from the Greek for pillar, *stylos*), and he began to attract pilgrims from as far away as Britain and France.

From his perch Simeon preached twice daily to warn against earthly vices and speak of the heavenly joys to come. He diligently took time to answer every question asked of him, even giving the Byzantine emperor some advice on doctrinal disputes. However, he resolutely refused to let women into his sight, even cold-shouldering his mother; one woman who dared breach this rule was said to have dropped dead on the spot. Simeon used to pray while bending his body, arms outstretched, touching his head to his toes like a human hinge. He did this repeatedly, and to pass the time the pilgrims below would keep count; on one occasion Simeon had completed over 1200 of these manoeuvres before the counter gave up.

Simeon **died** in 459, at the end of a remarkable 38-year stint on top of his pillar. Six hundred imperial troops immediately swooped in and took his body away for burial in Antioch (it was later moved to Constantinople). His life and example spawned many imitators, the best-known being St Daniel (409–93) in Constantinople, and St Simeon Stylites the Younger (517–92), who lived on a mountain on the outskirts of Antioch.

baptistry on the left. The church's triple-arched entrance is one of the most dauntingly impressive sights in the country, not only in terms of scale but also for its decoration, with each arch topped by a triangle and beautifully ornamented; note particularly the acanthus leaves carved as if swaying in the breeze, a floral decoration that originated here and spread throughout the Byzantine empire. On entering, it becomes plain that each of the church's four basilicas is sizeable enough to be a major church in its own right. The bare limestone façades lend the place an austere dignity, though when it was built the interiors would have been plastered and painted, and the floors decorated with multicoloured paving, traces of which can still be made out through the dust and dirt.

The south, west and north basilicas were never used for religious services, only for the assembly and organization of pilgrims, the major ceremonies taking place in the **east basilica**, which is larger than the other three and bent slightly off axis to orientate it towards true east. Its interior columns were lost during the sixteenth and seventeenth centuries when the building was occupied by local aristocracy, but the attractive floral decoration on the apse has survived. The hill had to be extended artificially to accommodate the **western basilica**, the most ruinous of the four, though it compensates with a mighty view down onto the

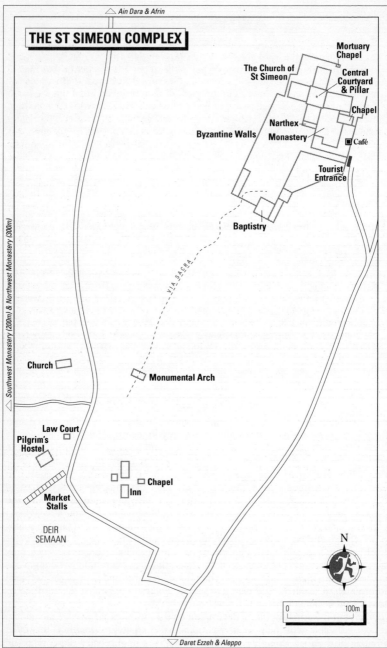

THE ST SIMEON COMPLEX

Ain Dara & Afrin

Mortuary Chapel

The Church of St Simeon

Central Courtyard & Pillar

Chapel

Narthex

Byzantine Walls

Monastery

Café

Tourist Entrance

Baptistry

Southwest Monastery (200m) & Northwest Monastery (300m)

VIA SACRA

Church

Monumental Arch

Law Court

Pilgrim's Hostel

Chapel

Inn

Market Stalls

DEIR SEMAAN

N

0   100m

Daret Ezzeh & Aleppo

confusing remains of Deir Semaan, and across the Afrin valley that stretches lazily beyond.

The four basilicas meet at a **courtyard**, at the centre of which is all that remains of Simeon's **pillar**. It's a slightly bizarre sight, a stumpy block of stone – the rest having been whittled down over the centuries by souvenir-hunters – sitting in pride of place among the magnificent ruined arches. Streams of tourists merrily ascend the block, wave at each other, get their picture taken and then jump off, their elevated moment of asceticism having passed. The square courtyard was converted into an octagon by the creation of four corner exedras, and the effect of the huge arches and intricate decoration is one of opulence and grandeur – this is where you feel the full force of imperial patronage that backed the project. The original domed wooden roof over the courtyard collapsed during an earthquake in 528 and was not replaced.

Just beyond the north basilica, within the Byzantine walls, are the remains of a small **mortuary chapel**, its lower level carved out of rock. The U-shaped building forming a courtyard with the church's southeastern walls is a **monastery** that was used to house resident and visiting clergy (non-clerics would have been accommodated down in Deir Semaan). Note the small chapel which would probably have been used for the daily services in the complex – the east basilica being employed only on Sundays and feast days.

Back on the path – in fact the final stage of the **via sacra** which led up from Deir Semaan – which culminates in the great south narthex, head on to the **baptistry**, 200m away, a square building cunningly concealing an octagonal interior which would originally have been topped by a wooden roof. Mass baptisms for converts would have taken place here at the semicircular font (still surviving against the left-hand wall of the building) before entry to the church. From here you can easily spot the most obvious remnant of the *via sacra* which once linked the village to the church – an **arch**, halfway up the hill, which has undergone some recent reconstruction. Unfortunately the path is blocked by the complex's Byzantine wall; to reach Deir Semaan from the church today, you need to head back out to the modern road, turning right onto the Afrin road at the bottom of the hill, a good ten-minute walk from the baptistry.

Deir Semaan

An agricultural settlement was founded at **DEIR SEMAAN** (then Telanissos) sometime in the first centuries after Christ, followed at the beginning of the fifth century by a monastic community. Simeon's antics on the hill above soon transformed the village into a pilgrimage centre, a role which was cemented with the construction of the church complex after his death in the late fifth century; the village continued to serve the pilgrimage trade until it died out in the twelfth century.

Deir Semaan covers an extensive area, and the incursion of a modern-day **village**, built from and among the ruins, makes discerning the ancient constructions difficult – indeed much of a visit comprises trampling around people's back gardens and over their improvised fences. Plans have been in place for around thirty years to relocate the villagers before the ancient ruins become completely obliterated, but the will to implement them seems lacking. The site, entered using the modern road, is always open, so ignore the cheeky young shepherds who attempt to charge entrance fees to the old buildings where they tend their sheep.

On the west side of the modern road, near the bottom of the *via sacra*, stands a **church** whose western facade is largely intact, though it's a modest building worth only brief exploration. About 100m south of this, again by the road, is the ruin of a **law court**, behind which are the remains of a **pilgrim's hostel** (or *pandocheion*) and eleven **market stalls** strung along the town's old east–west axis. Around 200m southwest of these, the **southwest monastery** is fairly intact; consisting of three colonnaded buildings and a large chapel grouped around a courtyard, it would have housed pilgrims as well as resident monks. About 150m north of this is another remarkably preserved complex, the **northwest monastery**, also comprising a number of accommodation blocks and a church. Both are just over the brow of a slight hill and can't be seen from the road, but it's worth walking a short distance up the dusty track to see these monuments. The most remarkable ruin at Deir Semaan, though, is the huge two-storeyed pilgrims' **inn** east of the modern road at the base of the hill; this impressive building, much of which still survives, was the major *pandocheion* in the village. A bridge behind leads to a terrace cut from the rock, beyond which is a **chapel**, half-hewn from the rock, containing a number of burial niches.

Ain Dara

The sizeable mound of **Ain Dara**, rising out of the fertile plain 17km north of Deir Semaan, conceals a history stretching from the fourth millennium BC through to the sixteenth century. The most obvious reminder of this is a tenth-century BC Hittite temple which is being restored by a team from Japan; atop a hillock about 400m west of the road across cultivated fields, it is now a somewhat incongruous mixture of ancient masonry, concrete and scaffolding. Elsewhere on the site, you may feel slightly short-changed as so little of any consequence remains standing.

Only a small area of the *tell* has been extensively excavated, with most of the attention focusing on the **temple complex** (tickets from the building at the bottom of the path; S£150). On the pathway to the entrance are a couple of huge stone lions – it is thought that the temple may have been devoted to Ishtar, a goddess of fertility, often symbolized by lions. The paved courtyard in front of the temple features a well and basin used for ritual handwashing before entering the precinct. Imprinted on two large limestone blocks in what was once the temple doorway are giant footsteps; theories abound as to their import, the most likely being that worshippers believed the marks signified the presence of a god here. Before going through, check out also the winged sphinxes and lion figures that decorate the walls and guard the entrance, some of which are in surprisingly good condition; inside, however, the small antechamber and main cella are badly worn and evoke little.

To get to Ain Dara from Aleppo by public transport, you need to make for **Afrin**, from whose small bus station you catch a microbus the final 10km south. The microbus **from Aleppo** to Afrin loops along the main road that runs past the turn-off for Azaz, making it just about possible to combine visits to Cyrrhus (see below) and Ain Dara in one day. Microbuses **from Deir Semaan** to Afrin, via Ain Dara, are very infrequent, so if you're coming this way, you would be advised to pick up any traffic passing, paying the driver appropriately for his trouble (see p.33).

Cyrrhus

The dramatic location of the ruins at **Cyrrhus**, set against the backdrop of the Turkish mountains, goes some way towards compensating for their relatively paltry condition. Founded around 300 BC to cement Seleucid control of the region, the settlement was taken over by the Romans and then refortified by Justinian in the sixth century. Cyrrhus was occupied briefly by the Crusaders five hundred years later, but disappeared from the pages of history soon afterwards.

The only way to get to Cyrrhus without your own car is to take a **microbus** from the Baron Street local bus station in Aleppo to the village of **Azaz**, 51km north, and then bargain with a taxi driver to cover the last 28km there and back (S£300–500 is a reasonable fare). On the way your driver will have to negotiate a couple of interesting Roman humpback **bridges** which still serve their original purpose, though crossing them can be hair-raising – they have steep ascents and descents, narrow approachways and no sides.

Approaching the site, just outside the south gate you pass a hexagonal Roman **tower tomb** dating to the third century, the lower floor of which houses the tomb of the Muslim saint Houri, giving the site its local name, *Nabi Houri*. The complex is surrounded by bare Byzantine walls, which follow the line of the Hellenistic defences; about 200m inside the south gate is the **theatre**, originally larger than Bosra's and partially restored by the French during the 1950s. The seating embedded into the hillside is quite well preserved, but there's no trace of the free-standing upper tier, and the rest is largely a jumble of masonry, the stage wall having collapsed during an earthquake. Crowning the hill above the theatre are the scant remains of the citadel; it's worth stumbling up through the undergrowth for the terrific views on a clear day across to the Turkish mountains.

West to Harim and Qalb Lozeh

What few ancient sites there are due west of Aleppo, along the road to and beyond fortress-crowned Harim, lie scattered and neglected for the most part, with nothing that lives up to the St Simeon complex in aesthetic or historical significance. This area is recommended only for ruins buffs and those with their own transport: microbuses run as far as Harim, but if you want to continue to the impressive church of Qalb Lozeh, you'll have to bargain with taxi drivers to take you there. You need at least a day to see everything here, and should bring plenty of water and food (there are few shops of any kind around) and your passport, as Harim is right on the Turkish border.

Driving west from Aleppo along the road towards Bab al-Hawa, you pass on the left after about 40km – just before the turning for Daret Ezzeh – a remarkably preserved stretch of second-century **Roman road** marching 1200m into the distance. Most of the Roman roads that criss-crossed the whole of Syria have long since disappeared, but this stretch was built more solidly than most in order to accommodate a steep slope, and was restored during the French mandate.

Five kilometres west of the Daret Ezzeh turn-off, before you've reached Bab al-Hawa, turn south off the main road to the village of Sarmada. Two kilometres west of the village you pass, embedded in the hillside on your right about 400m from the road, the impressive remains of the **Monastery of St Daniel**, which dates to the late sixth century and thus the last phase of the monastic blossoming of the Dead Cities. Just 4km beyond this is the turn-off, signposted in English, to **Baqirha**, the site of a well-preserved Roman temple dedicated to Zeus, consisting of a cella preceded by one surviving column of what was a four-columned portico; the monumental gateway also survives, dated by inscription to 161. Down the hill are the jumbled remains of a Byzantine town, where two early sixth-century churches can be identified in the chaos, the western one once forming part of a monastery. Like many of the Dead Cities, it is the setting which is the most attractive aspect of the site – bleak, uncompromising and desolate.

Beyond the Baqirha turning the road follows an impressively high ridge, from which several Turkish towns across the border can be seen, before descending onto plains to arrive at the largest settlement in these parts, **HARIM**. A pleasant provincial town dating back to Byzantine times, Harim is crowned by an Ayyubid **castle** (free admission), built in response to the Crusader threat in the late twelfth century. The conical sides of the castle mound were pared down and paved with smooth stone to prevent scaling, and the whole structure was then surrounded by a moat. The inside of the castle is utterly dilapidated, but the ramparts offer fine views over the town, which is a little more colourful than most, the locals having painted their houses in pastel shades in preference to the dull concrete tones which characterize most Syrian towns.

A five-kilometre drive due south from Harim, via some unremarkable ruins at Bnabel and the more substantial Byzantine settlement of Kirkbizeh, leads to the small village of **QALB LOZEH**, whose **church** (S£200 if custodian is present), fashioned from cream-coloured stone, is one of the best-preserved and most attractive ecclesiastical monuments in Syria. Built around 460, probably as a stopping point for pilgrims on the way to view St Simeon's pillar, it's the earliest Syrian example of a Roman basilica on a monumental scale, now incongruously surrounded by the low houses of the village. In its style, the church's lavish semicircular entrance arch with its three-storeyed flanking towers is a direct precursor to the grand Romanesque cathedrals of medieval Europe. The original wooden roof of the nave has long since collapsed, though over the two side aisles some of the stone slates of the roofs survive – these roofs would have been flat to allow light into the church from the windows above the nave. The projection of the apse beyond the basic rectangular form of the building was a new idea, and remarkably its semi-domed roof and intricate decoration have survived intact. Wandering around here is an eerily silent experience, save for the occasional noises of the clucking hens, barking dogs and the cries of the village children for *baksheesh* if other foreign visitors show up.

Southwest from Aleppo

To the southwest of Aleppo, accessible from the major highway to Hama and Damascus, are the least-visited desert sites in this area of Syria. The easiest to get to by public transport is **Ebla**, a Bronze Age settlement interesting more for its antiquity than for the little you can see there today. Finds from the site are displayed in a good museum in the largest town hereabouts, **Idleb**, which also boasts two decent hotels; making it a potential base for exploring the ancient sites in this area, though you'll need your own transport from here. Further south, the Roman-Byzantine sites to the west and north of **Maarat al-Numan** are remote and practically deserted; little effort has been made to restore them, yet the state of repair of the buildings in **Serjilla**, in particular, is remarkable. It's best to visit these Dead Cities with your own transport, but even then the poor state of the roads, the lack of signposting and the fact that there are so many similar-looking sites out here make getting around difficult and time-consuming.

Idleb

There's not a great deal to be said for **IDLEB**, although the town does boast a surprisingly good **museum** (daily except Tues 9am–4pm; S£200) on Al-Thawra Square, which is the first traffic circle you reach coming into Idleb from Aleppo. It starts unpromisingly with a folklore collection, an array of dead birds around a fountain and some mediocre paintings, before perking up with a fine selection of Roman-Byzantine gold and silver coins. Upstairs the Ebla collection is a very worthwhile accompaniment to the site (see below): all the exhibits are well illustrated and explained in English, and there's even a reconstruction of a royal archive room. A final section of the museum exhibits displays from various local *tell*s.

Idleb is only fifty minutes by road from Aleppo. The bus station, used by services from Aleppo and Latakia, is 500m southeast of the centre. There's no tourist office in Idleb itself; if you're coming here from Aleppo, pick up a regional map from the tourist office there, as it has a street plan of Idleb on the back. Idleb has two hotels: the central *Grand Hotel* (☎023/221 137; ④) on Al-Malky Street offers decent **rooms** and an attached **restaurant**, while the brand-new *Carlton* (☎023/241 623; ⑥) is awkwardly located away from the centre but offers four-star facilities at a price more reasonable than similar places in Aleppo. A bank and post office are situated on either side of the *Grand Hotel*.

Ebla

Unless you know a lot about archeology, or have an unusually vivid imagination, you won't find much to appreciate at the important Bronze Age site of **Ebla**, though its location amid scorching, flat and often very windy desert plains, 45km southwest of Aleppo, is certainly compelling. Once a powerful and agriculturally rich city state, Ebla rose to prominence in the centuries leading up to 2400 BC. By 1600 BC, however, the city had been destroyed by Hittite forces, although a settlement of some sort persisted here; in 1450 BC the Egyptian Pharaoh Thutmose III stated on a monument at Karnak that the Egyptian army marched through Ebla on its way to the Euphrates, and nearly three thousand years later the first Crusader army passed by and recorded that the place had changed its name to Mardic. Since 1964 Ebla has been excavated by an Italian team, and at any time of the year there might be someone at the archeologists' office who can guide you around the remains. The most important find has been fifteen thousand **clay tablets**, recording aspects of the economy and administration of the city, which have been shipped off to museums in Aleppo and Damascus and are slowly being deciphered and translated.

Any local **bus** or microbus travelling between Aleppo and Hama can drop you on the highway at the turning for Ebla; from there it's a walk of twenty minutes or so east along a road that runs through a dusty desert village, in which there are a few beehive houses built of dried mud bricks (see p.171). Turn right at the fork in the road in the village; at the next fork, about 3km from the highway, a modern brick building serves as **site ticket office** (the site is open at all times, and the entrance fee of S£100 is collected during the ticket office's irregular opening hours), café and small **museum** – best visited after looking round the remains so as to put what you've seen into some sort of context. This is as far as drivers can get – the site itself is a little further southeast along the road, just over the brow of a small hill.

Approaching the site from the ticket office, the first thing you come to is the ring-shaped **outer mound**, which gives a good impression of the huge scale of the city; thirty thousand people once lived within these walls, which were pierced by four monumental gateways, of which the best-preserved is on the southwestern side. Most of the excavation and (rather crude) reconstruction work has taken place around the site of the **Royal Palace** on the furthest part of the central area of the citadel, revealing residential areas and underground burial chambers; most clearly discernible is a stairway leading down into what was once a huge audience chamber.

The Dead Cities around Maarat al-Numan

The Dead Cities to the southwest of Aleppo are centred around a modern market town, **Maarat al-Numan**, 20km south of Ebla on the main highway and exactly halfway between Aleppo and Hama, making either city a good base from which to visit this area (Maarat al-Numan itself doesn't have accommodation). There are dozens of ruined Roman-Byzantine sites all over the surrounding countryside, of which the three described in this section – **Bara**, **Serjilla** and **Ruweiha** – are the most interesting and the easiest to get to. Other ruins set against the skyline can be seen in whatever direction you look, many of them wholly deserted and inaccessible by motorized transport.

Maarat al-Numan itself is easy to get to by public **transport**, as most buses travelling between Aleppo and Hama stop there. However, to get beyond Maarat, the only option for those without a car is to negotiate with taxi drivers at the bus terminal or main square in the town, or with any willing vehicle owners (see p.33). Distances are too great to make walking a viable option, and the lack of traffic in the desert here makes hitching difficult – and even potentially dangerous, if you end up getting stranded. If you're driving yourself, beware the lack of signposting and the poor roads, and be prepared to take a few wrong turnings in places.

Maarat al-Numan

MAARAT AL-NUMAN is a dusty, sprawling, unattractive place, centred on an east–west main street. At the eastern end of the street, a ten-minute walk up the road from the **bus station** on the main highway, stands a sturdily built Ottoman **khan**, supposedly the largest in Syria, which now houses an extensive collection of Byzantine **mosaics** (daily except Tues 9am–4pm; S£300). Unearthed from village sites around Maarat, the mosaics once adorned the houses of the local rich; it's a superb collection, featuring fantastically preserved, bold images depicting (mainly) birds, animals and geometric designs. As usual the dry desert climate has done a good preservation job. The museum was opened in 1987 and, not surprisingly, sports a garish mosaic of Hafez al-Assad above the entrance. There's not much by way of places to **eat** in town, save for the usual falafel and kebab places on the main street.

Bara (Kafr)

The modern village of **Kafr** and the ruins of **Bara** seem almost to grow into each other, with the villagers using parts of the ancient site for olive and citrus orchards. To reach Bara, head 10km west from Maarat to **Basqala**, then turn off onto a signposted road which leads 5km north to Kafr.

An important religious centre in the late fifth century, Bara contains the remains of at least five churches. The major focus of the ruins is two **pyramid**

tombs, which are obvious from the village; a tarmac road runs past the first, the larger of the two. Built for folk who could afford to be buried in style, the tombs are excellently preserved, and carry restrained Classical carvings with the Christian "chi-rho" symbol visible in many parts of the design. From here it's interesting to scramble around the substantial but haphazard remains of churches and ordinary houses that surround the tombs. The large building which stands alone on a slight rise to the southwest of the pyramid tombs, reached along a confusing network of metalled roads, is a former monastery, **Deir Sobat**, whose walls are very well preserved (parts of it have been recently reconstructed).

Serjilla

From Bara a road runs east, climbing slightly into more barren terrain. The insubstantial ruins of **Bauda**, scattered along the southern side of the road after 4km, include another pyramid tomb. After another 3km the road terminates in a shallow bowl at lonely **Serjilla**, a beautifully preserved Roman provincial town and one of the most absorbing ancient sites in Syria. Smaller and more manageable than Palmyra or Apamea, Serjilla has no grand colonnaded avenues or ostentatious theatres; there are simply modest town houses, a tavern, public baths and a small parish church, all now used for shelter by herds of goats.

Near where the road ends, on the left, the **necropolis** area contains a large stone sarcophagus, while down the hill are the remains of the **public baths**, small in scale but beautifully intact. Beyond the baths, the **tavern** would have been an unremarkable building in its day, but now, with its perfectly preserved two storeys and its frontage marked by a double portico of three columns on each level, it is one of the most perfectly preserved Roman buildings of any type, anywhere. Just above it is a small triple-naved **church** dating from around 370 AD or earlier, which has been enlarged several times. One of the side buildings contained three sarcophagi, thought to be those of local church or civic dignitaries, which have since been removed. Many other buildings run on beyond this central cluster, the former residential areas of the town gradually giving way to desert; on the horizon, other Dead Cities can be seen, which can be approached simply by walking towards them across the plains.

Ruweiha

The route to Ruweiha, 12km north of Maarat al-Numan along the back roads, takes you past several less interesting Dead Cities. Heading out of Maarat along the highway to Aleppo, turn left (west) 4km north of town and after another 3km you come to the ruins of **Dana**. Here there's a recently reconstructed pyramidal-roofed tomb, dated by inscription to 324 AD, the year that Emperor Constantine made Christianity the official religion of the Roman Empire. About 500m to the north of these remains, reachable only on foot, stands **Qasr al-Banat**, a well-preserved three-storey building thought to be a former monastery, with its associated (and much more ruinous) church close by. The road leading north from Dana then brings you, after about 3km, to the scattered remains of **Jeradeh**, of which the most obvious survivor is a sixth-century, six-storey tower.

Turn left at the road junction at Jeradeh and you reach **Ruweiha** after 2km. Set in a desolate landscape, the ruined buildings of this extensive site are used by settled Bedouin as dwellings, with the spaces between the houses given over to the rudimentary cultivation of figs and watermelons. Look out for the fifth-century **columned basilica**, close to the road and fairly easy to distinguish amid the piles of overturned boulders; nearby an odd structure supported on eight columns might once have been a tower lived in by a recluse. Thereafter the most obvious place to aim for, though a long way back from the road, is the **Church of Bissos**, one of the largest ruined churches in northern Syria. Although much of the building has collapsed, many of the arches spanning the nave remain, giving an impression of the building's original extent. The domed tomb nearby is that of Bissos, the church's benefactor, who may have been a local priest or bishop.

travel details

Trains

Aleppo to: Damascus (1 daily; 6hr); Deir ez-Zur (1 daily; 4hr); Hama (1 daily; 2hr 15min); Homs (1 daily; 4hr); Istanbul (Turkey; 1 weekly; 36hr); Latakia (3 daily; 3hr 30min); Qamishli (1 daily; 6–7hr); Raqqa (1 daily; 2hr 15min).

Pullman buses

From the Ibrahim Hanono Street station and the regular Pullman station to:

Damascus (5–6hr), via Hama (1hr) and Homs (2hr), with less frequent services to Deir ez-Zur (4hr), Latakia (4hr), Qamishli (5–6hr), Raqqa (3hr) and Tartous (5hr).

Karnak buses

From the Karnak bus station to:

Amman (Jordan; 1 daily; 9hr); Beirut (Lebanon; 3 daily; 7hr); Damascus (4 daily; 5hr); Deir ez-Zur (1 daily; 4hr); Hama (4 daily; 1hr); Homs (2 daily; 2hr); Latakia (2 daily; 4hr); Tartous (2 daily; 5hr).

Microbuses and local buses

From the depot on the southerly extension of Baron Street to:

Afrin (1hr 15min); Azaz (1hr); Damascus (6hr); Daret Ezzeh (1hr); Hama (2hr); Harim (1hr 15min); Homs (3hr); Idleb (50min); Latakia (4hr); Maarat al-Numan (1hr).

From Aleppo's eastern bus station to:

Deir ez-Zur (7hr) and Raqqa (4hr); change at Raqqa for services to Qamishli and Hassakeh.

Service taxis

For long-distance journeys from Aleppo, these congregate across the road from the Bab Antakya. You will be besieged by touts as soon as you walk up, with fares to Damascus offered at S£500 per person and to Beirut for S£600 per person; other destinations covered include Homs and Hama.

Flights

Aleppo to: Damascus (up to 5 daily; 1hr); Beirut (Lebanon; 2 weekly; 1hr 30min).

International buses

Apart from the Karnak and Pullman services above, there are private buses from Aleppo's international bus station to:

Istanbul (at least 1 daily; 24hr) via Antakya.

CHAPTER SIX

THE EUPHRATES VALLEY AND THE NORTHEAST

The history of Syria east of Aleppo is dominated by the **Euphrates**, its valley cutting a luxurious green swathe through the desert, supporting the principal towns of **Raqqa** and **Deir ez-Zur** in the same way that it once allowed a succession of ancient city states to thrive. The narrow strip of farmland along the river is the most obvious feature of the region for travellers, a humid streak of settlement that cuts through the otherwise parched landscape, buzzing with the activity of cultivators and tractors, the chugging of diesel-engine irrigation pumps rarely out of earshot. Though the two modern settlements are of limited appeal in themselves (apart from the riverside restaurant and excellent museum in Deir ez-Zur), they both offer a reasonable selection of hotels and so make decent bases for excursions out to the astonishing variety of **archeological sites** along the river valley. Travelling to and between the main towns is fairly easy: there are good bus links between Deir ez-Zur and Damascus (via Palmyra) and between Raqqa and Aleppo, and frequent microbuses and Pullmans buzz along the main road beside the river.

The wealth of visible evidence of human occupation in this region ranges from the era of the first settlers on this part of the Fertile Crescent to the time of Saladin's campaigns during the Middle Ages. From Raqqa you can travel west to **Qalaat Jaber**, a medieval castle perched above **Lake Assad**, the huge reservoir created by damming the Euphrates at **Ath-Thawra**; and to **Resafe**, an ancient

---

ACCOMMODATION PRICE CODES

In this book, all hotels have been categorized according to the **price codes** outlined below, representing the minimum you can expect to pay for a **double room** in each hotel. Hotels in the ⑤–⑧ bands require payment in dollars. For further details, see p.35.

① under S£300/US$7	⑤ US$35–50/S£1500–2100
② S£300–600/US$7–14	⑥ US$50–90/S£2100–3900
③ S£600–1000/US$14–23	⑦ US$90–130/S£3900–5600
④ S£1000–1500/US$23–35	⑧ US$130/over S£5600

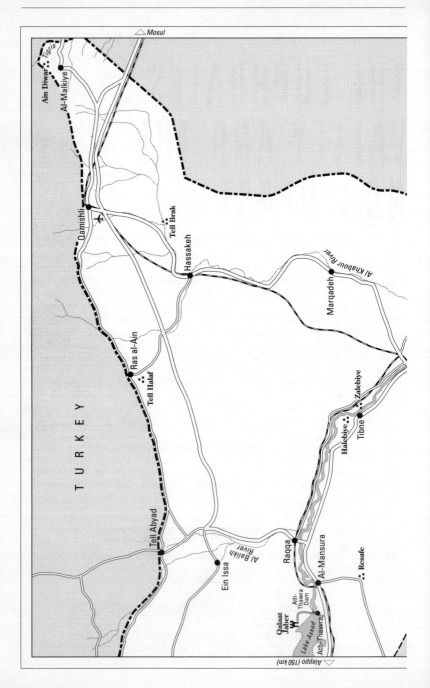

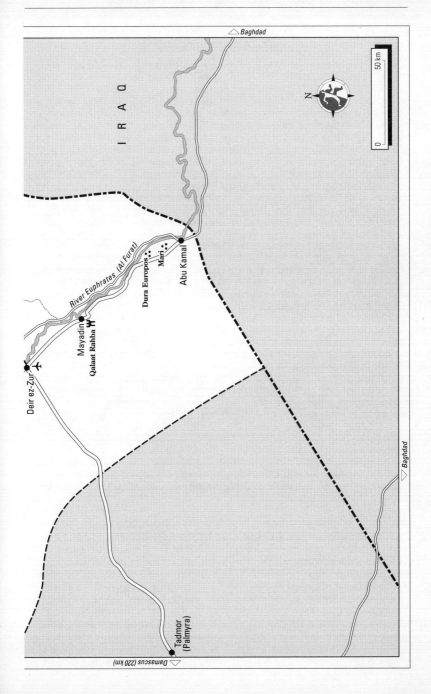

The longest river in western Asia and the region's life-blood, the **Euphrates** – along with the Tigris – forms the eastern part of the Fertile Crescent, the great arc of cultivation stretching all the way to the Jordan and Orontes rivers in the west (see the box on p.150). The legendary wealth and power of the state of Mesopotamia (the "land between the rivers" and, according to tradition, the location of the Garden of Eden), in present-day Iraq, derived from the trade and agricultural advantages brought by the Tigris and Euphrates, and at various times the Babylonians, Sumerians, Assyrians and early Muslims strove for control of the rivers. Other great settlements supported by the two rivers included the Sumerian cities of Ur, Uruk (biblical Erech), Lagash and Nippur, all founded between 5000 BC and 3000 BC; later on, Babylon (on the Euphrates) and Nineveh (on the Tigris) became great and glorious capitals. Not as important or powerful were the ancient cities that grew up along what is now the Syrian part of the Euphrates, the largest of which were Mari and Dura Europos, both located close to the point where the river enters Iraq.

Control of the waters of the Euphrates is still a matter of bitter contention: for many years Turkey, Syria and Iraq, through all of which the river flows, have argued about how this vital commodity should be distributed, disagreements which have occasionally threatened to spill over into armed conflict. In the 1960s, the **damming** of the river at Ath-Thawra in Syria allowed the Euphrates to be regulated and its water used for extensive agriculture along the banks; two decades later, however, the Syrians were blaming the frequent failures of electricity supplies across the country on Turkish activities further upstream on the Euphrates, which interrupted (unintentionally or otherwise) the flow of water to the hydroelectric turbines on the dam. It remains to be seen what the political and environmental fallout will be if and when plans for large-scale dams and reservoirs on the Turkish Euphrates reach fruition.

The name of the Euphrates (*Nahr al-Furat* in Arabic) is always linked in history with that of the **Tigris** (*Nahr Dijlah*), which flows parallel to it through Iraq. The two merge in a huge swamp in southeastern Iraq, the Shatt al-Arab – by that stage most of the Euphrates' water has already been used for farming or has simply evaporated away – and eventually drain into the Persian Gulf. The Tigris, which grazes the Syrian border but does not flow through it, is shorter but commercially more important, by virtue of having a deeper channel than the Euphrates; the important Iraqi ports and cities of Mosul, Basra and Baghdad line its banks. Until such time as Iraq is open to tourists, the ruins of the cities along the Syrian part of the Euphrates are the only easily visited reminders of the rivers' ancient civilizations.

walled city situated amid barren desert. In the opposite direction lie the Roman remains at **Halebiye** and **Zalebiye**, two former fortress towns which face each other across the river between Raqqa and Deir ez-Zur. Undoubtedly easier to get to and more interesting are the sites between Deir ez-Zur and the Iraqi border: the remains of **Mari**, first settled over five thousand years ago; the ruined medieval castle of **Qalaat Rahba** and the ancient Roman city of **Dura Europos**.

Known in Arabic as the the **Jezira**, **northeastern Syria**, beyond the Euphrates, is part of the homelands of the **Kurds**, one of the world's largest ethnic groups to whom history has denied a political homeland. Syria's Kurdish minority is small and somewhat less persecuted than those of neighbouring Turkey and Iraq (see the box on p.274); nonetheless, the area has long been seen by the Damascus regime as being naturally hostile to it. Rather devoid of attractions for visitors, the northeast consists mostly of flat desert, its numerous *tell*s – mounds which mark the sites of long-buried former cities – uninteresting except to the initiated archeologist. The two main towns, **Hassakeh** and **Qamishli**, are dull and visually unappealing; the only specific sight is the impressive bridge at **Ain Diwar**, right in the northeastern corner of the country on the Turkish border – it takes some getting to, but those who do make it are never left unimpressed by the magnificent scenery of the Tigris valley.

Raqqa and around

Although **RAQQA** – the first place of any real size you come to if you head east from Aleppo – was once the summer capital of Abbasid-ruled Syria, next to nothing of its former glory remains; nowadays the place is little more than a busy market town and transport interchange. The river can occasionally be glimpsed from the Aleppo road, but the first time you get to see theEuphrates properly is as you cross the road bridge just south of the town. Here the river is a series of sluggish, braiding channels, with families picnicking and children playing and bathing from the muddy beaches which line the banks and islands.

Orientation in Raqqa is easy, as Al-Jalai Square, in the centre of town, is marked by a clock tower (which chimes like an electronic version of Big Ben), and by the huge masts on top of the post office, visible from beyond the town's limits. The choice of hotels and restaurants is fairly poor for a place of this size, but with your own transport you could easily spend two or three days using Raqqa as a base to visit the medieval fortress of **Qalaat Jaber**, perched on a promontory above Lake Assad, and the ancient cities of **Halebiye** and **Resafe**, to the east and west of town respectively. Local buses from Raqqa cover only parts of the routes to these sites, so visitors without their own transport have to shell out for taxis or lifts, or be prepared to trudge long distances along the desert roads.

The Town

Founded in Hellenistic times, possibly by Alexander the Great himself, Raqqa was developed in the Byzantine era into an important fortress on the front line with the Persian empire. In 772 the Abbasid Caliph Al-Mansur completely rebuilt the town, endowing it with the horseshoe-shaped **walls** (once lined with a hundred towers) that survive in part today; the design mirrored the circular plan of the capital Baghdad, with Raqqa in the role of second capital, controlling northeast Syria. In 1258 the town was razed by Mongol invaders and depopulated, only being revived after centuries of slumber by the construction of the Ath-Thawra Dam and its promotion to provincial capital in the 1960s.

The best place to see what remains of the Abbasid walls is at the partially reconstructed southeastern corner of the old city, by the sturdy brick **Bab Baghdad**, the only surviving town gate, dating to the twelfth century. Follow the walls north from here for about 200m (try to ignore the stench from the improvised rubbish tip), and on the left will appear the **Palace of the Maidens** (*Qasr al-Banat*), a ninth-century residence centred around a small courtyard with four *iwan*s and a fountain, all of which have survived relatively well, though the site is inhabited by annoyingly excitable dogs and pesky kids. To the northwest of here up Saif al-Daula Street is the largely ruinous, if expansive, **Great**

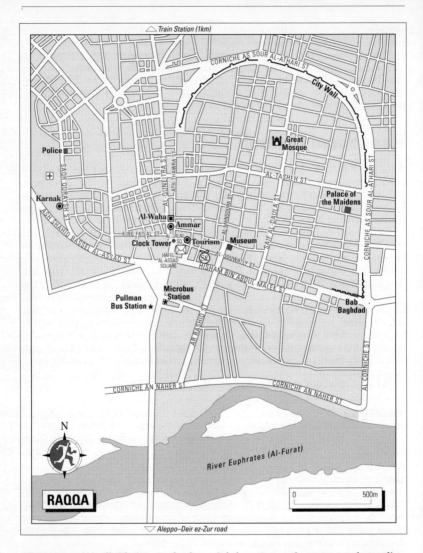

△ Train Station (1km)

CORNICHE AS SOUR AL-ATHARI ST

City Wall

Great Mosque

AL-TASHEH ST

Police ■

Palace of the Maidens

Karnak ◉

SAQR QURAYSH ST

ATH-THAWRA ST

AL-QUNEITRA ST

AL-TASHEH ST

ASH-SHAHID BASSEL AL-ASSAD ST

Al-Waha ■ Ammar

KING FAISAL ST

AL-JALAI

Clock Tower ● SQ.

Tourism

Museum

HAFEL AL-ASSAD SQUARE

AL-JANSOUFIA ST

SAIF AD-DAULA ST

AL-ROUWATLY ST

HISHAM BIN ABDUL MALEK ST

Pullman Bus Station ★

Microbus Station

AR RASHID ST

Bab Baghdad

CORNICHE AS SOUR AL-ATHARI ST

AL CORNICHE ST

CORNICHE AN NAHER ST

CORNICHE AN NAHER ST

N

River Euphrates (Al-Furat)

RAQQA

0   500m

▽ Aleppo–Deir ez-Zur road

Mosque, originally dating to the late eighth century; the tower and standing colonnade, deriving from Nur al-Din's reconstruction of the mosque in 1165–66, are all that remain of a building that was once 100m square with eleven towers. On the way back from here to the main square is a small **museum** (daily except Tues: summer 9am–6pm; winter 9am–4pm; S£200) displaying a range of unexciting and (largely) unlabelled remains, mainly from the excavations of local *tell*s; a recent effort has been made to spruce the place up and there are now some useful information sheets in English dotted around, but all in all it's not really worth the entry charge.

Practicalities

Karnak and Pullman buses stop off at the **Pullman bus station**, 400m south of the clock tower; the **microbus station** is situated directly opposite. The Pullman companies have their offices at the Pullman terminal, as does Karnak, who operate just one service a day, to Damascus via Aleppo, Hama and Homs. At the opposite end of town, 2km north of the centre, is the **train station**, with services from Damascus and Qamishli; a taxi into the centre from here costs no more than S£50, or you can reach Al-Jalai Square on foot by turning left out of the station and carrying on south down the road.

For a place of its size, the town offers surprisingly few services: there is no tourist information office in Raqqa, nor is there a Syrianair branch or travel agent. Equally, you can forget any ideas you might have had of renting a car; the nearest places to apply for visa extensions are Aleppo or Deir ez-Zur.

The **post and telephone offices** are next door to each other around the clock tower on Al-Jalai Square (daily except Fri 8am–6pm). To **change money**, head to Qouwatly Street, where the exchange branch of the Commercial Bank of Syria is located on the first floor of an office building; it's not easy to find, though, as it's not signed in English. The main hospital is located about 100m north of the *Karnak Hotel* on Saqr Quraysh Street.

Accommodation

The best **place to stay** in town is the *Karnak Hotel* (☎022/232 265; ④), located on Saqr Quraysh Street in a residential district ten minutes' walk west of the centre. Run by the government bus company, it carries nostalgic echoes of state-run hotels in the old Eastern Europe, with a cavernous, tatty lobby and bored staff; guests must feel like they have the run of the whole place, as it's as though hardly anyone ever stays here. That said, each room is comfy and carpeted, and comes with TV, a fridge and efficient air-conditioning.

Right in the centre are two basic **hotels**, neither with en-suite rooms: the *Ammar*, immediately north of the clock tower (☎022/222 612; ②), is bare but marginally cleaner than the dimly lit *Tourism* on Qouwatly Street (☎022/220 725; ③), where each room comes complete with malfunctioning television and a fridge that might as well be an oven.

Eating and drinking

The choice of **restaurants** in Raqqa is decidedly uninspiring. The terrace of the *Karnak Hotel* is a good place for a relaxing beer, but their kebab is consistently undercooked and the chicken leaves a very odd aftertaste. Qouwatly Street has some fairly ordinary chicken-and-kebab places dotted along it; otherwise the best place is the *Al-Waha*, just to the north of the clock tower, which serves a reasonably tasty *shishtaoo* for S£200.

Qalaat Jaber

Just off the main Raqqa–Aleppo road, **Ath-Thawra** is an ugly, confusing town, built to accommodate workers on the dam and then given over to those whose houses were drowned as Lake Assad filled. The only reason for coming here is to continue on to **Qalaat Jaber** (daily except Tues 9am–4pm; S£300), 30km northwest of town along a road that passes right over the dam itself. A lot of Syrians

---

LAKE ASSAD

One of the largest lakes in the Middle East, **Lake Assad** is an artificial creation, resulting from the building of the **Ath-Thawra dam** on the River Euphrates in the 1960s. The dam's turbines now provide the bulk of Syria's electricity, and control over the river's flow has been a boon to agriculture across the entire region. Less pleased by this than the farmers and the government were the inhabitants of the villages upstream of the dam, which were flooded as the lake filled; hundreds of people were forcibly rehoused in the ugly town of **Ath-Thawra**, at the lake's southern end.

Along with villages, the lake's creation flooded numerous ancient monuments: many were documented by UNESCO archeologists before the waters rose, and some were moved, Abu-Simbel-style, up to higher ground. In the centre of Ath-Thawra, for example, is a 27-metre-high minaret, originally attached to a mosque in the now-submerged village of Maskana. Also moved, to the north end of the lake, was the tomb of one of the first Ottoman sultans, Suleiman Shah, who drowned in the Euphrates near Qalaat Jaber. Although the Turks were kicked out of Syria at the end of World War I, they had a clause inserted in the Treaty of Versailles stipulating that a small garrison of Turkish troops should guard the tomb, an arrangement which continues to this day.

---

come here, mostly on Fridays (the place is virtually deserted for the rest of the week), to swim or fish in the lake, the castle forming an impressive backdrop to the narrow beaches along the lakeshore.

Today Qalaat Jaber is situated on a rocky promontory lapped by the shores of the lake, though once it overlooked the Euphrates valley from on high, guarding an important crossing point on the river. The first records of a castle here date from 1087; it was taken by the Crusaders in 1104 but remained in Frankish hands for less than fifty years. In the late twelfth century, and then again in the fourteenth, it was refortified as an Arab stronghold, surrounded by massive outer defensive walls. The only break in these defences was an arched **entrance gateway**, the most impressive part of the structure today. It's pleasant to stroll around the walls, enjoying the magnificent views across the lake, but a lot of the place is rubble and ruin. The interior of the castle is mostly bare apart from an isolated brick minaret, and recent crude restoration work seems to have involved not much more than pouring concrete into gaps in the medieval brickwork.

Practicalities

The castle is difficult to get to without your own transport: you have to take one of the frequent microbuses from Raqqa to Ath-Thawra (50min), and then a taxi (S£350 return) to complete the journey. You may wish to combine a visit here with one to nearby Resafe, also hard to reach by public transport; S£1200 would be a reasonable price to hire a Raqqa taxi for both places. A small **refreshment** place next to the castle entrance serves soft drinks and a limited range of snacks; staff here will unlock the castle for you if it's shut when you arrive.

Resafe

Half buried in sand, **Resafe** is one of Syria's most characterful desert ruins, a city whose glistening gypsum walls and astonishingly grand **basilica** appear to rise out of the ground in the middle of nowhere. No buses run to the site; **from**

Raqqa, you have to either hire a taxi (around S£700 return) or catch a microbus to the village of **Al-Mansura** (30min), which stands at the turning off the main Aleppo road, and arrange a lift from there (S£200). It's a long hard drive here **from Hama**, via a sealed road which has recently been extended across the desert via Salamiyeh (see p.171) and Isriya (see p.173).

Some history

Resafe's **origins** go far back – it's even mentioned in the Old Testament, as Receph in II Kings and Isaiah – though it remained a minor caravan settlement between Palmyra and the Euphrates until after the fall of Dura Europos in 256, when it was fortified by the emperor Diocletian in response to the Sasanian threat. In the early fifth century a *martyrium* was built here to commemorate the death of **Sergius**, a Christian Roman soldier reputedly martyred for refusing to offer sacrifices at the Temple of Zeus in Antioch sometime in the early fourth century. A cult grew up around the Sergius story, and in the mid-fifth century Resafe became a major site of pilgrimage, eventually being renamed **Sergiopolis**.

According to the Greek passion of Sergius and Bacchus, Sergius suffered a particularly painful martyrdom: being forced to run to Resafe from the fort of Tetrapyrgium, nails having been driven upright into the soles of his shoes, before his final execution. Yet the passion contains some major anachronisms, and this, combined with the fact that the cult of Sergius did not arise until over a century after his supposed death, has led many historians to question whether he even existed; it's plausible that Sergius's story was simply a reworking of several different pre-existing texts, and that the passion was concocted after the discovery of an anonymous burial site near Resafe.

During the sixth century a large basilica was constructed to cope with the number of pilgrims, and the city walls were rebuilt. Nevertheless, the town fell to the Persians early in the following century, thus weakening Byzantine control over the region and paving the way for the subsequent successful Arab invasion. A sacking by Abbasid troops in 750, combined with a devastating earthquake in the late eighth century, contributed to the decline of the city, though it continued to house a small Christian population right up until the thirteenth century.

The site

Tickets to the site (S£150) are sold at the café by the eastern gate to the city. Directly in front of you as you approach from the café is the **Basilica Church of St Sergius**, officially renamed the Basilica of the Holy Cross in 1977 following the discovery of a dedicatory inscription; this grand edifice was built in the 550s to accommodate the increasing numbers of pilgrims to Resafe. The leaping arches which divide the side aisles from the nave are very grand, though you can see from their construction that the builders didn't quite get it right first time, for each of the three arches subsequently had to be supported by two smaller ones underneath – and the southeastern arch had to be filled in completely. Though most of the fine stone carvings and colourful mosaics for which the church was once famed have been lost, the inner walls have recently seen some partial reconstruction, and if you explore the area behind the nave you can still find some traces of original wall paintings.

West of here are the ruins of a second **basilica**, dating from the late fifth century; part of its apse still stands, and you can just about work out where the original entrance was. Unimpressive today, this would at one time have been nearly as big as the main basilica, and is thought to have housed the bones of Sergius before they were carted off to Constantinople. West of here again is the first of the city's huge **cisterns**, which look more like massive underground cathedrals; signs in Arabic point out the dangers of standing too near the edge of these massive constructions, which would have contained enough water to supply the population for up to two years.

About 100m north of the cisterns, along the partially excavated main north–south thoroughfare, are the jumbled remains of a Byzantine khan. A further 100m north is another ruined **church**, dating to the 520s; part of the apse survives while a number of huge pink columns litter the nave. A number of sarcophagi belonging to bishops have been found here, implying that this may have been the episcopal church of Resafe, as distinct from the other churches, which were used by the pilgrims. Its design is an ambitious example – only slightly later than the similar Bosra cathedral (see p.129) – of an attempt to construct a square-planned building with a domed roof.

The city's partially restored **northern gate** is not only a fine piece of workmanship but also impressive as a defensive construction. Outside are the remains of an outer gateway and a hallway; note the intricate decoration of the pillars here. From inside the gate you can climb up and walk along the upper gallery, built to allow defenders quick and easy access around the walls. The northern walls are by far the best-preserved and afford an overview of the site, now largely bare apart from the ruins already mentioned; most of the city's buildings were constructed of mud and have disintegrated over the centuries. The holes in the sand all over the site are said to be the result of informal diggings by the local Bedouin, busy looking for hidden treasure.

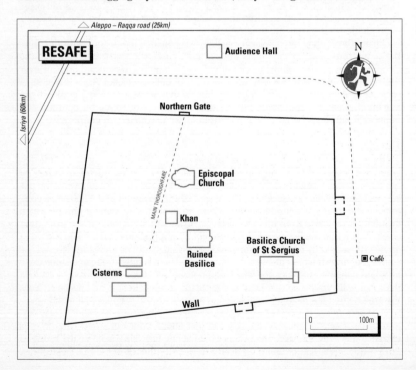

Just outside the northern walls and the entrance to the city is a late sixth-century **audience hall** that once belonged to Al-Mundhir, the chieftain of a Christian Arab tribe, the Ghassanids, who were allies of the Byzantines and largely controlled the desert between Palmyra and the Euphrates. The building is presently under restoration, drifting sand having done a good preservation job over the centuries.

Halebiye and Zalebiye

The twin Roman fortresses of **Halebiye** and **Zalebiye** lie on opposite banks of the Euphrates at a rather desolate spot midway between Raqqa and Deir ez-Zur. There's nothing much to see at Zalebiye, on the northeast bank, but Halebiye comprises a series of well-preserved walls, fortifications and former barracks which rise above the river on a steep hillside.

There are two ways of approaching by **public transport**, neither of them easy. On the southwest bank of the river, frequent microbuses and buses along the Raqqa–Deir ez-Zur road will drop you off at **Tibne** (40min from Deir ez-Zur), but from there you have to resort to lifts from locals, or a stiff two-hour walk north along the desert road, to get to Halebiye. Fewer buses and microbuses run along the road on the northeast bank of the river from Raqqa to Deir ez-Zur, but these vehicles drop you at a turning only thirty minutes' walk from Zalebiye. Don't be excited by the presence of a **train station** just 2km from Zalebiye – the once-weekly services on the Raqqa–Deir ez-Zur line arrive there in the middle of the night. Hiring a **taxi** from Deir ez-Zur to take you to Halebiye, Zalebiye and back to Deir ez-Zur costs around S£1500; it's best to ask your hotel to negotiate a price and arrange for a taxi to pick you up. Getting from one fortress to the other involves crossing a rickety modern bridge across the river and takes about 45 minutes on foot, or a quarter of an hour in a vehicle.

Halebiye

Halabiye was founded in around 265 AD by Zenobia, the rebel leader of the Palmyrenes (see p.284), but most of what can be seen today is the result of refortification three hundred years later by the emperor Justinian, who made the settlement one of the key forts along Byzantium's eastern flank. Justinian was particularly keen to secure Byzantine rule in Syria, which by that time was a Christian stronghold, but Halebiye was unable to resist capture by the Persians in 610 AD. Occasional military use was made of the fortifications during the first years of Arab rule in Syria, but earthquake damage took its toll and eventually it was abandoned to the desert foxes and itinerant shepherds.

Usually deserted, the site (S£150 if a custodian is present) is bleak and very impressive, particularly as the setting sun throws shadows over the stark hills and casts a warm glow over the stones and the river. You can make some sense of the place by studying the plan by the main entrance gate: the banks of the Euphrates here are lined with walls and other defences, which also spread up the hillside, where they are punctuated by massive square bastions; on the opposite side is a well-preserved **praetorium**, a three-storeyed, thick-walled building which housed the troops. Overlooking it all, and a fair clamber uphill across fallen pieces of masonry, is the **citadel**, the only part of the site historically used by the Arabs (as a lookout post); not surprisingly, the view from there is particularly stunning.

Zalebiye

Zalebiye has a history mirroring that of Halebiye, but is far smaller, its ruins much more scattered and indistinct, impressively situated though they are on a steep rocky bluff above the river. If you arrive by bus, simply head up to Zalebiye along the road which runs alongside the river. To reach Zalebiye from Halebiye, walk or drive a short distance (15min on foot) north up the road from Tibne to the river bridge; cross this and turn right (south) along a very rocky track – best walked if you value the underside of your vehicle – across irrigated farmland (30min on foot). Along the southwest bank of the river, before you cross the bridge, the scant remains of Roman rock-cut **tombs** and **funerary towers** can be seen dotting the hillside; the latter, containing several burials per storey, were for the upper echelons of Roman society.

Deir ez-Zur

Much more attractive than Raqqa, with a good range of facilities, hotels and restaurants, **DEIR EZ-ZUR** (often just "Deir" in local parlance) is the most appealing base for travellers on the Syrian Euphrates. There's a distinctly oriental feel about the place, with its chaotic confusion of traffic, bicycles and animals, and its colourful, pungent markets. Gliding incongruously through all this are the sleek stretch limos of oil executives from the Persian Gulf, come to do business with Al-Furat, the Syrian state oil company: in 1984 extensive **oil fields** were found around Deir ez-Zur, which currently produce 600,000 barrels a day, earning Syria over US$2 billion a year in exports – a minuscule amount compared to the earnings of Gulf states, but a major boon for a poor country like Syria. In the near future gas fields too will be developed here, following the signing of a major deal with the French oil multinational Elf.

Laid-back and unhurried (this is one of the hottest places in Syria during the summer), Deir ez-Zur is a good place to stay for two or three nights, travelling out by day to the fortresses of Halebiye and Zalebiye to the northwest, and the ancient remains of Mari and Dura Europos to the southeast (see p.266). Visiting the unusually good archeological **museum** apart, there's nothing much to do in Deir itself except sit on the terrace at the riverside restaurant overlooking the bridge, or watch the local lads diving off the nearby **pedestrian suspension bridge**, the town's most distinctive feature.

Arrival, information and accommodation

The town is centred on the 8 Azar Square intersection, around which are most of the places to stay. If you arrive at the **train station**, 2km out on the northern outskirts of town, there should be a CFS bus waiting to take you to the train booking office, one block northwest of the main square. The **microbus** and **Pullman terminals** are both south of the centre, a short taxi ride from the downtown hotels; **Karnak buses** will deposit you outside the Karnak office, right next door to the train booking office. Deir's **airport** is on the Abu Kemal road, 7km out from the centre; shuttle buses timed to coincide with flights operate between it and the Syrianair office, 500m north of the main square. The **tourist office** is located 200m from the main square, on a street that runs southwest off Khalid bin Walid Street; as usual a map and a friendly chat are the only reasons to venture here (daily except Fri 9am–2pm).

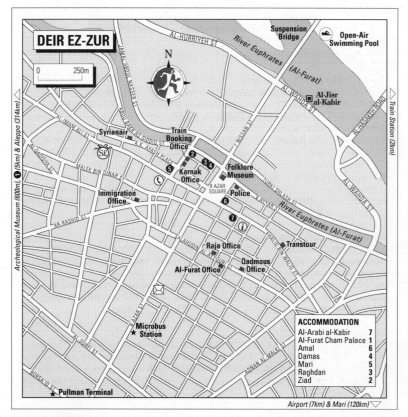

Airport (7km) & Mari (120km)▽

Accommodation

Accommodation is fairly easy to come by in Deir, with **hotels** catering for everyone from impoverished backpackers to Kuwaiti oil executives.

Amal, Khalid ibn al-Walid St. Dingy, basic but just about acceptable place prominently situated right on the main square. ①.

Al-Arabi Al-Kabir, Khalid ibn al-Walid St (☎051/222 070). Brighter than the other cheapies in town, with clean rooms and bathrooms. ②.

Damas, Abou Bakr Assiddiq St (☎051/221 481). Basic but acceptable hotel overlooking an arm of the Euphrates, and one of the better cheapies. Beds in shared rooms available for S£100. ②.

Al-Furat Cham Palace (☎051/225 418, fax 225 950, *www.chamhotels.com*). Five kilometres west of the town centre along the main road to Raqqa. Built for oil executives and tour groups, this is one of the most characterless, overpriced hotels of the *Cham Palace* chain, though facilities include two restaurants, two bars, a large outdoor pool, a gym and tennis and squash courts. ⑧.

Mari (☎051/224 340). A block north of Al-Ma'moun St. Larger and newer than the *Raghdan*, but not as good value; the rooms and showers are clean, but it's all rather soulless, and the tatty foyer with its permanently closed arcade of small shops indicates that the place has definitely seen better days. ④.

MOVING ON FROM DEIR EZ-ZUR

By air
There are weekly Syrianair flights to Damascus (S£600 one way) and to Kuwait.

By Pullman and Karnak bus
Karnak runs to Aleppo and Palmyra from outside its office, situated at the far end of a closed-in shopping arcade; the office can be tricky to find as it's not signed in in English. There are frequent **Pullman** departures for Damascus (via Palmyra) and Aleppo, with occasional services to Raqqa, Qamishli, Hassakeh, Homs, Latakia and Abu Kamal. All the regular Pullman companies have offices at the Pullman terminal, while Qadmous, Al-Furat and Raja also maintain offices along Salahudin al-Ayyoubi Street, a few minutes' walk south of the main square; only the Qadmous office is signed in English. Most Pullman and Karnak services to Aleppo don't stop in Raqqa, dropping passengers off instead on the highway at the turn-off (about 4km away), so a microbus may be more convenient for this journey.

By microbus and local bus
From the microbus station, local buses and microbuses head out to **Raqqa** and to **Hassekeh**, from where there are microbuses on to **Qamishli**; services to these towns are much more frequent than Pullman buses. The same is true of microbuses to Abu Kamal, which are thus a better way of getting to either **Mari** or **Dura Europos** than Pullmans; however, doing the long treks to Aleppo or Palmyra by microbus is only recommended for those really short of money.

By train
Currently one nightly service, with sleepers available, operates down to Damascus (via Aleppo). In the opposite direction, the Damascus–Qamishli train stops in Deir ez-Zur pretty much when in feels like it, sometime in the early hours of the morning. CFS buses for the station leave from the train booking office an hour before train departures.

Raghdan, Khalid ibn al-Walid St (☎051/222 053). Definitely the best mid-range option, a quiet if rather elderly hotel with air-con and spacious rooms. ③.
Ziad, Abou Bakr Assidiq St (☎051/214 596, fax 211 923). With clean, spacious, modern rooms, this new kid on the block is giving the long-established *Mari* and *Raghdan* a run for their money; excellent value. ④.

The Town

Opened in 1996 under the auspices of the Free University of Berlin, Deir ez-Zur's **archeological museum** (daily except Tues 9am–6pm; S£200), a one-kilometre walk west of the central square, is one of Syria's very best, well laid out and thoughtfully presented, with some excellent reconstructions, including prehistoric housing and even a Mari temple. The exhibits mostly cover the period before the Islamic era in Syria, with particularly good sections on nearby Mari and Dura Europos, and the various local *tell*s; however, the final sections bring the story up to date, looking at the history of Deir ez-Zur in the last century, and at the progress that has been made in farming the difficult agricultural land of the surrounding steppes. Everything here is labelled, intelligently and in great detail, in English. Deir ez-Zur's other museum, on the main square itself, is far less compelling, housing an odds-and-sods **folklore collection** (daily except Tues 9am–1pm; S£150), which encompasses a motley collection of weapons, teapots and other paraphernalia.

Half a kilometre northeast from the main square is the town's **suspension bridge**, pictured on tourist posters in hotels across Syria. Built in the 1920s, it's an elegant structure over 500m in length, crossing the languid Euphrates as the river glides past a clutch of verdantly green islands. Adjacent to the far end of the bridge is the very popular open-air **swimming pool**.

Eating and drinking

There's precious little variety among the cheap **restaurants** in the centre of town, mainly chicken-and-kebab places around the central square. Most visitors seem to end up at the *Al-Jisr al-Kabir* restaurant overlooking the Euphrates at least once; again, you're probably in trouble if you don't like kebab, chicken, salad or chips (about S£150 per person), but the relaxing setting is unbeatable, especially in the afternoon. After dusk, however, the mosquitoes begin to emerge, and then it might be best to head away from the river to the rooftop restaurant of the *Mari* hotel, which offers slightly more choice at a slightly higher price.

The *Al-Furat Cham Palace Hotel* offers the most variety in terms of eating and drinking. There's a **bar**, and at lunchtimes and in the afternoons their American-themed *La Louisiane* restaurant offers a variety of pasta dishes, sandwiches and the like; in the evenings you can join the tour groups and expat oil men at the hotel's overpriced *Four Seasons* restaurant, which has a buffet or a menu of Syrian specialities, including fish, grilled meats and meze, not to mention a good selection of wines.

Listings

Airlines Syrianair have an office on A.K. Ayash Place (daily except Fri 8.30am–12.30pm).

Banks and exchange The bank (daily except Fri 8.30am–12.30pm), on Al-Imam Ali St, takes an age to change cash or travellers' cheques; the *Al-Furat Hotel* can change money otherwise.

Car rental At the *Al-Furat Cham Palace Hotel*, you can rent a Peugeot 205 for US$40 per day (minimum rental period three days); the local Europcar agent, Transtour, is on Khalid ibn al-Walid Street, but there is a minimum one month wait for a car here.

Pharmacy Several of these can be found down Al-Imam Ali St.

Phones The telephone office (daily 8am–10pm) is on Al-Imam Ali St; usefully, it contains a counter which sells stamps (daily except Fri 8am–1pm).

Post office The large and modern main post office (daily 8am–8pm, Fri until 1pm) is on 8 Azar Street.

Swimming pools More inviting than the pool by the suspension bridge is the open-air pool at the *Al-Furat Cham Palace Hotel*, which non-residents can use for S£200; it's a long walk or a short taxi ride to get to from the centre, but the pool's setting, on a ledge high above a magnificent curve of the Euphrates, is unbeatable.

Visa extensions The immigration office (daily except Fri 8.30am–12.30pm) is at Ar-Rashid St, five minutes' walk west of the main square.

Southeast from Deir ez-Zur

Of the attractions between Deir and the Iraqi border, the closest to the city is a ruined medieval castle, **Qalaat Rahba**, most noteworthy for its views across the surrounding countryside. **Mari**, a full two hours' drive from Deir and close to the border, was first settled nearly five thousand years ago, but its remains are rather insubstantial compared to the largely Roman garrison town of **Dura Europos**, stunningly located on the banks of the Euphrates about an hour and a half from Deir.

The road out to these sites crosses parched, dusty scrubland which is broken in places by welcome bursts of verdant irrigated fields, watered by the Euphrates as it cuts through the desert in a series of broad curves. **Microbuses** from the depot in Deir are reasonably frequent along this road; with a reasonably early start (particularly in summer, when the torrid heat makes visiting these sites in the afternoon rather unpleasant), it is possible to see all these places in a day-trip from Deir using public transport.

Qalaat Rahba

Worth a stop, if time permits, on the way to Dura Europos and Mari are the ruins of **Qalaat Rahba**, 2km south of the village of **Mayadin**, itself 44km southeast of Deir on the road towards the Iraqi border. Buses from Deir stop in the centre of the village, from where it's a manageable walk along an obvious desert track to the castle.

Qalaat Rahba had only a short military career: it was built by Nur al-Din in the mid-twelfth century as part of his Syrian unification strategy, but fell out of use following the Mongol invasions of the late thirteenth and fourteenth centuries. The remains are impressively poised from afar and, with quite a good portion of the castle's inner fabric surviving, including a well-preserved central keep, the effect is not entirely diminished when you take a look up close. There are also some glorious sweeping views across the desert from the ramparts.

Dura Europos

The initial sighting of the walls of **DURA EUROPOS** across the parched desert plain from the main road raises expectations like no other site in Syria and, although little remains within the walls above foundation level, the expansive ruins (open at all times; S£150) lend themselves to a relaxed appreciation. The historical importance of Dura only came to light in 1920 when British soldiers digging trenches here came across some wonderfully preserved **wall paintings**; previously the place had been dismissed as an unremarkable Arab fortification. The site was initially excavated in 1922–23 by a French team, but the more significant work was done by a Franco-American effort of 1928–37, written up by one of the American project directors, Clark Hopkins, in *The Discovery of Dura Europos* (see p.324).

Microbuses to Dura Europos from the main microbus station in Deir ez-Zur are very frequent, passing the site after about eighty minutes. The same buses head on to Mari and can be flagged down on the main road.

Some history

Dura Europos was established around 290 BC to defend the route between Apamea and Seleucia-on-the-Tigris, two major **Seleucid** military bases. From 113

BC the town came under the influence of the Parthians, while the Romans established themselves just to the northeast at Circesium; their mutual economic interests along the Euphrates were recognized by a treaty signed in 20 BC. However, in 164 AD the Romans took over the town, establishing a major **garrison** and embarking upon a substantial building programme. Dura's demise was sudden: in 256 the Sasanian Persians captured the town and, rather than occupy the site, decided to destroy it and banish the inhabitants, leaving the chaotic region without a substantial stronghold for centuries to follow.

The site

The main western gateway, the imposing **Palmyra Gate**, consists of two bastions, linked by a passageway over the arch; now barred by a grille, it's believed to date to around 17 BC and thus the days of Parthian rule. You gain access to the site through a gap in the wall about 50m to the right – look out for the armed ticket-seller (the weapon is to take care of wild dogs) parading around on his motorbike.

Unfortunately for visitors, Dura Europos is most famed for monuments which have been taken away from the site. The **chapel**, dating to 231 (and thus one of the world's earliest identified places of Christian worship), was located by the present site entrance before being transported wholesale to Yale University in the

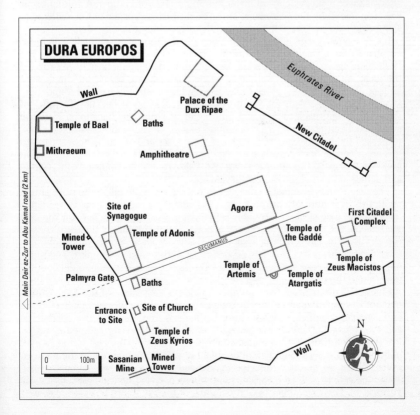

1930s. As with all early churches, it was originally a private house which was converted into a place of worship. The walls of the chapel – like Dura's synagogue – were adorned with paintings (here depicting Christ's miracles); a stone basin was found inside, believed to have been used as a font.

The Dura **synagogue**, now one of the most celebrated exhibits in the National Museum in Damascus (indeed the museum was built to house the synagogue; see p.94), was situated between the first and second towers to the north of the gate, where you can just about make out its pillared courtyard. Ironically, the synagogue owes its remarkable state of preservation to the **siege** by the Sasanians in 256, which led to the final downfall of the town: anticipating the siege, the defenders of Dura piled huge amounts of sand and gravel against the town walls in an effort to prevent them from being mined; all the buildings closest to the walls were also filled with sand, thus preserving their interiors. However, the Sasanians, undeterred by the strengthening of the walls, succeeded in mining the second tower north of the Palmyra Gate, under the protection of a ramp; archeologists have found skeletons in the mine bearing coinage from 256 and thus roughly dating the city's fall. Timbers supporting the roof of the mine would have been burned, causing it, and the tower above, to collapse; the attackers would then have rushed over the wall via the ramp and short ladders, and Dura must have fallen quickly thereafter, as there is no evidence of major fighting in the town proper. A second tower was also mined by the Sasanians, at the southwestern corner of the settlement, and outside the wall there the hollow of the original mine can be seen.

It's best now to walk into the town along the **decumanus**, originally colonnaded, that leads from the Palmyra Gate. To the left after 300m is the site of the Hellenistic **agora**, the main marketplace around which would have been grouped the most important civic institutions; in the Parthian era, bazaar buildings were built on the open space, which today is a slightly confusing mess of foundation-level walls. To the right of the decumanus at this point lies the **Temple of Artemis**, dating back to Seleucid times, with Parthian modifications. Note the small attached theatre, where ceremonies of some form would have taken place, witnessed by the city elite whose names were inscribed on the benches. Next to this are a couple more **temples**, one dating to 31–32 AD dedicated to the Syrian goddess Atargatis, the other serving two Palmyrene gods known as the Gaddé and dating to the mid-second century AD.

The decumanus eventually collapses into a wadi. On the hill to the right at this point, **the first citadel complex** was constructed by the Greeks as a residence for the chief magistrate. It probably remained in use as a residence, for the civil governor of the town, after the construction of a **new citadel** in the early second century BC, the ruins of which stand across the wadi alongside the Euphrates. Over the centuries the river has eroded most of this second complex, and today only the western face survives; the view across the river from the top is the best thing about the place.

Further along the river bank are the remains of the **palace of the Dux Ripae**, built for the commander of the Roman garrison during the heavy militarization of Dura against potential Sasanian attack in the early third century; two courtyards and the remains of an arcaded corridor overlooking the river can just about be made out along with a private baths complex. Unusually, the rest of the Roman military camp was situated within the main town, between here and the western walls, taking up nearly a quarter of the settlement. This was almost a self-contained colony with its own baths and temples, including the first-century AD **Temple of Baal** identified by the columns at the angle of the north and west walls, where British troops discovered the frescoes (now in Damascus) that alerted the world to the importance of the site. Just to the south of this, the early third-century **Mithraeum** was dedicated to the Persian god Mithras, who was especially popular with the Roman legions; unfortunately this has been so thoroughly excavated that only the bare foundations remain.

Mari

Sweltering on the bleak, featureless plains near the Iraqi border, **MARI** (S£200 if custodian present), first settled around 2900 BC, is the most significant Mesopotamian site that can be easily seen, given the difficulty of visiting Iraq. Its most famous ruler was **Zimrilim** (1775–1760 BC), who endowed the city with its major monuments – only for them to be destroyed during the sacking of the city by the Babylonians in 1759 BC. Mari has attracted the attention of archeologists, mostly French, since 1933, and investigations at the site are still going on. Chunks of pottery poke out of the dust here and there, discarded by archeologists as they worked, but there isn't all that much here to grab the eye today, though the intimacy and manageability of the remains are appealing. Most of the important finds are in Damascus, Aleppo or the Louvre in Paris, including the **state archives**, which consist of fifteen thousand stone tablets detailing the household accounts of the Royal Palace and the administrative records of the kingdom.

TWO COUNTRIES, ONE PEOPLE

Although Syrians often refer to Syria and **Iraq** as "two countries, one people", relations between Syria and its larger, oil-rich neighbour to the east have always been somewhat strained. Saddam Hussein and Hafez al-Assad came from rival wings of the socialist Ba'ath Party, which have been at loggerheads since the 1970s. By the time war broke out between Iraq and Iran in 1980 (over disputed oil fields at the head of the Persian Gulf), it was inevitable that Assad would voice support for Iran. This resulted in Iraq and Syria breaking off diplomatic and trading ties, and the only land crossing between the two countries, at **Abu Kamal**, was sealed to all traffic. Things might have got better in 1988 with the ending of the Iran–Iraq War, but instead, two years later, they worsened with Saddam's invasion of Kuwait: Syria gave full support to the UN coalition against Iraq, and even sent troops to assist in Operation Desert Storm in early 1991.

Since then, however, the situation has been gradually thawing. UN sanctions against Iraq allow Saddam's regime to sell oil in exchange for food and medical supplies; Syria, needful of oil and possessing an efficient food industry, saw a role for itself in fulfilling this "oil-for-food" deal. In the first six months of 1997 Syrian companies won contracts worth US$20 million to supply Iraq with permitted food and medicines, and in May of that year the border at Abu Kamal was opened for the first time in fifteen years. A populist advance was made in the summer of 1997 when Iraqi singers Kazem al-Saher and Elias Khodr gave live concerts in Damascus, attended by hundreds of their Syrian fans who, up to then, had only been able to hear them on tape. The border is still closed to all but carefully controlled trade and diplomatic traffic, but there are signs that the two countries are on the way to re-establishing full ties, with the resumption of the **train** service between Aleppo and Mosul in July 2000 and Syria's defiance of the UN air embargo in October of that year, when it sent food and medical supplies to Baghdad.

The most important part of the city is the **Royal Palace**, now protected from rain by a modern roof: Zimrilim used the wealth accrued through trade to build this vast residence, which had over three hundred rooms and covered an area measuring 200m by 120m. To get some idea of the scale of the place, wander round the excavated rooms which are grouped around two central courtyards and defended by five-metre-thick walls. Elsewhere on the site are five temples and the foundations of a **ziggurat**, a pyramidal tower built in many Mesopotamian towns, which would once have been surmounted by a temple.

The site lies just off the main road, 10km north of the dull border town of **Abu Kamal**, increasingly busy as a stopping point for long-distance trucks as they prepare to cross into Iraq; **buses and microbuses** from Deir ez-Zur (2hr) and Abu Kamal (30min) stop by the short track over to the ruins, which are well signposted. By the entrance to the site is a small tent-like **café**, which shelters the occasional tour-bus groups from the heat of the sun; if you come here independently you're likely to have the whole site to yourself.

The northeast

Little visited by tourists, the area of Syria to the northeast of the Euphrates, known as the **Jezira**, is a plateau dissected by wadis and broken by areas of wheat cultivation; from time to time low-rise villages consisting of concrete-box houses, ragged children and mangy animals emerge from the bleakly monotonous plains. In winter it can be bitterly cold here, especially if there's a north wind blowing off the mountains of eastern Turkey; in summer the heat is torrid and can be dangerously intense, and the towns have a siesta which lasts late into the afternoon, with many shops not opening their shutters until 6pm and trading well into the evening. Prosperous city states grew up here in ancient times, evidenced by the numerous small *tell*s emerging from the plains, which have been picked over extensively by archeologists but are of no real interest to the uninitiated.

The economy of these parts revolves around agriculture and oil: there's little specific to interest the traveller, although **Hassakeh** and **Qamishli** are pleasant towns in which to rest up for a night or two before pressing on to eastern **Turkey**, which is the reason most travellers come here. The only true sight is at **Ain Diwar**, where the arch of a former Roman bridge is surrounded by the fabulous scenery of the **Tigris valley**. To get there, or indeed anywhere in the region, requires perseverance and time, as distances are long and public transport rather

---

TRAVELLING INTO SOUTHEASTERN TURKEY

You can cross into Turkey at three border posts in this region – most conveniently at **Qamishli**, but also at **Ras al-Ain** and **Tell Abyad**, further west. Until recently, travelling in southeastern Turkey was a risky venture: the uprising by the Kurdish separatist group the PKK involved shoot-outs, curfews, a heavy military presence and kidnapping of foreign tourists. Things calmed down in the very late 1990s and at the time of writing the region is pretty trouble-free; nevertheless, **check** with embassies or government advisory services at home (see p.47) for details about the latest situation before confirming your itinerary here. For further information, see the most recent edition of the *Rough Guide to Turkey*.

poor. It takes at least four hours by road, for example, to travel from Deir ez-Zur to the border town of **Qamishli**, the largest settlement in the region and a pleasant jumping-off point for both Ain Diwar and Turkey.

Hassakeh

HASSAKEH, the northeast's second town, is a charmless modern settlement, 180km north of Deir ez-Zur, with absolutely nothing of interest. The **bus station**, used by services from Aleppo, Qamishli and Deir ez-Zur, is in the north of town, the **train station** in the northwest; from either station it's about twenty minutes' walk (or a short taxi ride; under S£100) into the centre, marked by Istiqlal Square, with its coloured fountains. The **tourist office** is here, reached by taking a dingy covered passageway from the square (signposted). Also centrally located are the **bank** and **post office**, both in the centre of town on Jamal Abdul Nasser Street; the **passport and immigration office** is located a little way south of the centre (look out for the railings outside the building and the blue sign above the door – it can be hard to spot).

If you need somewhere to stay here, head for the centre of town and ask for the *Ugarit* (☎052/227 000; ②), near the clock tower by the souks, which is among the

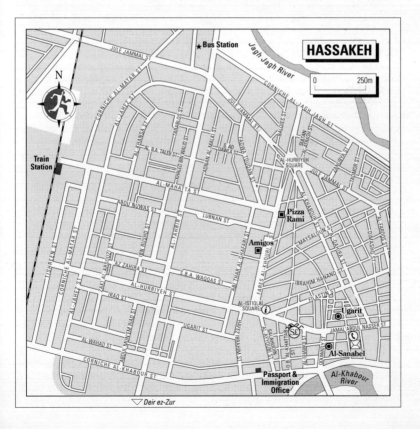

TELL BRAK AND AGATHA CHRISTIE

The area of Syria northeast of the Euphrates has more than its fair share of **tells** – "the rubbish heaps of history", as Robert Tewdwr Moss memorably dubbed them in *Cleopatra's Wedding Present*. Sometimes four or five of these bald, sun-scorched mounds can be seen rising above the horizon at any one time, breaking the monotony of the otherwise flat horizon. They are of no interest to the casual visitor: unless a dig is actively in progress only bare rock is in evidence. For archeologists, however, no *tell* hereabouts has revealed more than **Tell Brak**, which you can see clearly from the Hassakeh–Qamishli road, at the village of the same name.

Tell Brak was excavated extensively in the late 1930s by the archeologist **Sir Max Mallowan**, and further digs have taken place periodically since then. Mallowan's most famous discovery was the remains of the Eye Temple, dating from around 3000 BC and named after the hundreds of offerings he unearthed, all of them idols depicted with one enormous eye. Teams of British archeologists have also discovered remains of a **Mitannian palace** (c.1500 BC) and an **Akkadian fortress**, built on the site a mere two thousand years ago. More recent still is a nearby **Byzantine fort**, whose outline, invisible at ground level, was picked up by French aerial surveys in the 1920s.

Mallowan was married to the British writer of detective fiction **Agatha Christie**, who accompanied him on many of his digs in what is now Jordan, Turkey and Syria during the 1930s. She tells of her travels in Syria in an unusual little book entitled *Come, Tell Me How You Live*, first published in 1946 and reprinted in a number of editions since. Renting the bat-infested house of a local sheikh, she let her husband get on with the spadework at Tell Brak while she tended the sick and catalogued the finds. Villagers were offered *baksheesh* on top of their regular pay for any objects they unearthed; at one point, in their haste to acquire still more *baksheesh*, the men dug so furiously that part of the pit collapsed on top of them, killing a number and sending the rest off in flight across the desert. But the next day, she records somewhat insensitively, those same men were back, digging enthusiastically and seemingly with "no care for their lives at all. . . They were laughing about the deaths and making dumb show of the whole thing this morning during the work! Max says death isn't really important out here."

Christie's curiosity about all aspects of Syrian life is infectious: in her epilogue to the "inconsequent chronicle" she admits that she loves "that gentle fertile country and its simple people, who know how to laugh and enjoy life . . . who have dignity, good manners, and a great sense of humour, and to whom death is no terrible. *Inshallah*," she announces as a hopeful conclusion, "I shall go there again, and [I hope] the things that I loved shall not have perished from this earth."

best budget **hotels** in Syria. Each of its rooms is immaculately clean and features a TV and fridge, and prices can be bargained down if things are quiet. The town's most expensive hotel is the *Al-Sanabel* (☎052/311 477; ④) on Qouwatly Street, to the south of the clock tower, though it's not much better than the *Ugarit*.

Plenty of reasonable **restaurants** (mainly chicken-and-kebab joints) congregate on Fares al-Khouri Street; strolling up from the fountains on Istiqlal Square you'll pass a cavernous café, of the usual coffee-and-backgammon variety, before reaching *Amigos* (daily from 8pm), where the town's trendy young things hang out, gorging themselves on pizza and enormous cheeseburgers. A little further up the street on the right, *Pizza Rami* is rather more cramped and sells only pizza, but is slightly cheaper (daily from 5pm).

Qamishli

It's the presence of the frontier with Turkey, less than 1km from the centre, which is
the most obvious feature of **QAMISHLI**, with Kurds, Turks and Syrians seeming to
mingle here in almost equal numbers. There's nothing to see in the town itself, but
you'll probably end up spending a night here as you press on elsewhere; transport connections by road, air and rail are the best in the region, and with time to spare it's well
worth making the effort to travel out to the **bridge** at Ain Diwar, 80km to the east.

Practicalities

Qamishli's main street runs east–west, past the obligatory statue of Hafez al-
Assad and the town's central Commercial Bank of Syria branch. Most visitors
arrive at one of two **bus stations**: Hassakeh and Deir ez-Zur microbuses use a
terminal a kilometre or so southwest of the centre, from where it's not hard to
reach the main street on foot, but you'll probably want to get a taxi into town if you
arrive at the main terminal, 4km east of the centre, where coach services from
Aleppo and Damascus, and microbuses from Raqqa, terminate. From the **train
station**, 6km out on the northeastern outskirts of Qamishli, it usually quite easy
to flag down a passing microbus on the main road. There's a **railway office**
around the corner from the *Chahba* hotel, although no English is spoken here.

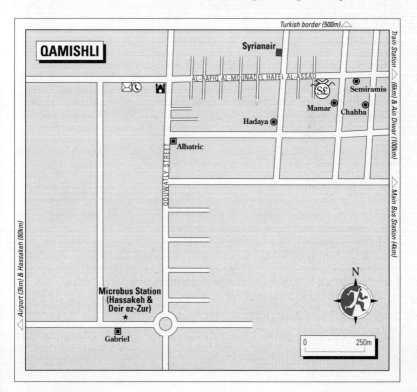

THE KURDS

Of the one million **Kurds** living in Syria, the vast majority are divided between Aleppo and the towns and villages of northeastern Syria. Little is known about the origins of this ethnic group: it is thought they were originally a nomadic people in central Asia, who came to settle in the mountain territories of what is now eastern Turkey and northern Iran. Although there are about twenty million Kurds in the Middle East today, spread through contiguous region covering Syria, Turkey, Iraq, Iran and parts of the former USSR, they have never been grouped in a state of their own; among obstacles faced by those campaigning for a **united Kurdistan** are that Kurds speak four languages (all of which have their roots in Farsi, the language of modern Iran), are divided in religious loyalty between Sunni and Shiah Islam, and are traditionally organized into powerful rival clans.

In **Turkey** and **Iraq**, which have much larger Kurdish populations than Syria, the Kurds are seen as a serious threat to internal stability. Saddam Hussein used poison gas to wipe out many Kurdish villages in the mountains of northern Iraq, which he assumed to be significant areas of dissent against his Ba'ath Arab regime, and in Turkey the militant **PKK** has been fighting for an independent, Marxist Kurdish state in the southeast of the country since 1978. At the height of the troubles, the Ankara government accused Syrian Kurds (and the Syrian government) of harbouring many PKK members, who use the northern part of Syria as a base for incursions into southeastern Turkey, an accusation fiercely denied by Syria. The capture by Turkish authorities of the group's leader, Abdullah Ocalan, in 1999 has meant that the situation in eastern Turkey has calmed down considerably of late.

In **Syria** the Kurds are seen as less of a threat than in Turkey and Iraq, mainly because there are fewer of them and because many have abandoned traditional Kurdish territories in the northeast to live in Aleppo or even Damascus. Nevertheless, any show of Kurdish solidarity is treated as a form of dissent against the government: in their August 1997 report on Syria, for example, Amnesty International alleged that thirteen Syrian Kurds were arrested in February and March of that year after they illegally celebrated *Nawruz*, the Kurdish New Year festival, in the province of Aleppo.

Plenty of microbuses for the centre pass by the **airport**, 3km out on the road to Hassakeh; a taxi into town costs around S£200. It takes around ten minutes to walk to the **border post** from the *Chahba Hotel*; the Turkish town of **Nusaybin** is located just beyond the frontier post, from where onward transport is available.

The **post office** is located on the main street very close to the Assad statue; and there's a **Syrianair office** just north of the main street. Unfortunately the town's **passport and immigration office** has closed.

Hotels in Qamishli are all at the eastern end of the main drag, which becomes the road out to Al-Malkiye (for Ain Diwar) and the train station. The *Chahba* (☎053/420 874; ②) is a dreadful place, dingy and cramped, and accessed through a covered area of workshops. Only slightly more expensive but much better value is the *Mamar* (no phone; ②), on a side street running south from the main road, with clean rooms, air-conditioning and TV. Located on the main road between these two, the *Semiramis* (☎053/421 185; ③) is easily the best hotel in Qamishli, where visiting oil executives stay in cavernous doubles with fan, air-conditioning and TV. The other hotel which quotes its prices in dollars is the *Hadaya* (☎053/420 141; ②), but the rooms, clean if very basic, are somewhat overpriced.

Along the main street are various kebab-and-chicken **restaurants**. For something different, head for the *Gabriel Restaurant*, opposite the Hassakeh microbus terminal, which is open for pizzas and other meals from about 8.30pm onwards, and has a very pleasant outdoor terrace. A short distance south of the main street is the much cheaper *Albatric*, where you can gorge on hamburgers or pizzas with fries at any time of the day or into the evening.

Ain Diwar

Though it never enters Syria, the River **Tigris** forms part of the frontier with Turkey for a short stretch; at one point, **AIN DIWAR**, one arch remains of a **bridge** built originally by the Romans. The site is remote and heavily militarized, being so close to Turkey and Iraq, and not surprisingly, it takes time and expense (not to mention luck) to get there; but the effort is worth it, for the stunning location as much as the arch itself.

Taxis from Qamishli, which congregate outside the *Chahba Hotel* at the western end of the main street, will get you to the bridge and back comfortably in a morning (S£1500 or less). If you don't want to spend this much, take a **bus** to **Al-Malkiye**, the nearest town of any size to Ain Diwar, and pick up a taxi (around S£350) the rest of the way. The road on from Al-Malkiye ends just beyond the village of Ain Diwar at a **police station** overlooking the Tigris valley, which forms a stately curve cut through the hills; the policemen here are friendly and helpful, having nothing to do all day but stare through their binoculars at Turkey, and treat visitors with interest and respect. You can't see the bridge from the police station, but on a clear day it's possible to gaze beyond Turkey to the mountains in northwestern Iran – one of the most exciting views anywhere in Syria.

To get to the bridge itself, right down in the valley, you have to travel in a police four-wheel-drive vehicle or, at least, carry on in your own vehicle with a police escort. Beware, however, that the track down to the bridge crosses many irrigation streams and ditches, and so will be impassable if it's rained recently. Surrounded by marsh and rushes, the solitary arch is a sturdy affair, constructed from basalt and inlaid on one side with sandstone panels depicting the signs of the zodiac. The Roman camp of Bezabda once stood on this side of the river, and the bridge was built to give access to Roman-occupied Anatolia. There's no way of crossing the Tigris here now, though you can hear the steady bumping and rolling of Turkish trucks as they bounce over the potholes on the other side of the river – the only thing, apart from the cicadas, which disturbs the peace of the location.

travel details

Trains
Qamishli to: Damascus (1 daily; 14hr) via Hassakeh (1hr), Deir ez-Zur (3hr), Raqqa (4hr), and Aleppo (7hr); first-class sleepers are available on this overnight service.

Buses and microbuses
Deir ez-Zur to: Abu Kamal (frequent; 2hr 30min) via Mayadin (1hr), Dura Europos (1hr 20min) and Mari (2hr); Aleppo (frequent; 5hr); Damascus (frequent; 6hr); Hassakeh (3 or 4 daily; 4hr); Palmyra (frequent; 2hr); Qamishli (3 or 4 daily; 5hr).

Hassakeh to: Deir ez-Zur (2 or 3 daily; 4hr); Qamishli (frequent; 1hr).

Qamishli to: Al-Malkiye (2 daily; 2hr); Aleppo (2 or 3 daily; 5hr); Damascus (2 or 3 daily; 10hr).

Raqqa to: Aleppo (frequent; 2hr 15min); Damascus (frequent; 7hr); Deir ez-Zur (frequent; 2hr 15min); Hama (frequent; 3hr 30min); Homs (frequent; 4hr 15min); Qamishli (2 or 3 daily; 4hr).

Domestic flights
Deir ez-Zur to: Damascus (3 weekly).

Qamishli to: Damascus (3 weekly; 1hr).

CHAPTER SEVEN

PALMYRA AND THE DESERT

The main Damascus–Aleppo highway roughly marks the division between the green, mountainous western part of Syria and the vast **desert** of the southeast, which stretches into Iraq and Jordan. It is surprising that any human habitation could survive in such desolate surroundings, and it is tempting to romanticize – as much of Arab mythology does – both the landscape and the people who make this astonishing environment their home. However, this is not the desert of popular imagination, with endless rolling sand dunes as are found in Arabia or the Sahara; nor does this part of Syria boast the spectacular scenery of the Jordanian desert. Instead the Syrian desert consists for the most part of flat, rocky and seemingly infinite plains, where the glare of the sun, the intensity of the heat and the sheer emptiness are extraordinary to witness.

Dotting the desert scene are the black goat-hair tents of the **Bedouin** (see box, pp.292–293), nomadic herders who drive their camels, sheep and goats from place to place in search of grazing land as they have done for millennia, their lifestyle little affected by the twenty-first century save perhaps for a few modern cooking utensils and beat-up Nissan trucks. On the main roads and tracks, a few tiny villages – ramshackle collections of crude concrete-box houses and traditional mud-brick beehive dwellings (see p.171) – break up the monotony of the plains, but for large stretches of the seven-hour road journey between Damascus and Deir ez-Zur there is no evidence of any human activity; the only other permanent signs of life hereabouts are occasional cement works, oil installations and army camps.

No settlement can be established in such an area without a regular supply of water; at a site just over 200km northeast of Damascus, a last geological fold in the Anti-Lebanon Range creates the right conditions for a spring, reliable enough

---

ACCOMMODATION PRICE CODES

In this book, all hotels have been categorized according to the **price codes** outlined below, representing the minimum you can expect to pay for a **double room** in each hotel. Hotels in the ⑤–⑧ bands require payment in dollars. For further details, see p.35.

① under S£300/US$7
② S£300–600/US$7–14
③ S£600–1000/US$14–23
④ S£1000–1500/US$23–35

⑤ US$35–50/S£1500–2100
⑥ US$50–90/S£2100–3900
⑦ US$90–130/S£3900–5600
⑧ US$130/over S£5600

to have supported ancient **Palmyra**. This ruined city, emerging from the desert beside a vast oasis of palm trees, is the highlight of many a visit to Syria, and remains one of the most exotic and absorbing destinations in the Middle East despite the rising swell of tourism to the site. Travelling to, staying in and looking round Palmyra (and its modern adjunct **Tadmor**) is very straightforward, the only drawbacks being the considerable distances to cover on foot around the site, and, in summer, the dust, flies and intense heat.

Although volcanic ridges break the surface here and there (most notably around Palmyra), the Syrian desert is otherwise just a scorched void; you can forget any visions you may have had of hiking or driving through the desert to visit long-forgotten sites in the middle of nowhere. Palmyra aside, the only points of interest in the Syrian desert are the fortress of **Qasr al-Heir al-Sharqi**, well

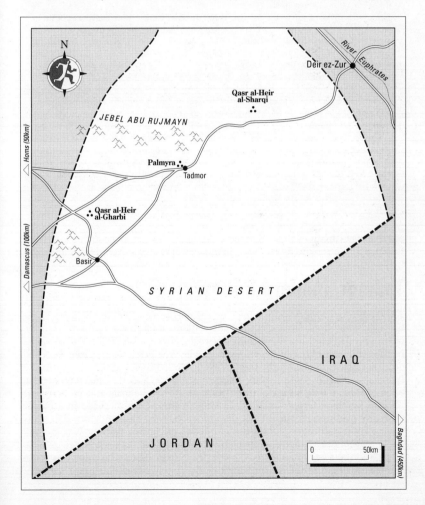

TRAVELLING IN DESERT REGIONS – SOME ADVICE

The main **desert highways** linking Damascus and Homs with Palmyra and Deir ez-Zur are busy roads, travelled by plenty of trucks, buses, army vehicles and private cars, and fuel and food stops are fairly regularly spaced. Disappearing off at frequent intervals are desert tracks, little more than wheel-ruts cut into the dust which mostly lead off to remote Bedouin settlements. Driving these twisting, multi-branching tracks is highly inadvisable without a knowledgeable guide: there are no adequate maps, and no signs or points of reference to orientate you, and in no time at all you'll be simply (and seriously) lost. The only occasion on which you need to use them is if you decide to travel out from Palmyra to **Qasr al-Heir al-Sharqi**, but this is too dangerous to attempt on your own, and we recommend you hire a car with a driver in Palmyra.

If you're **driving yourself on the main highways**, there are several points to bear in mind. Always take spare supplies of water and fuel, and be prepared for frequent police **checkpoints**. Traffic moves fast on these highways, overtaking aggressively, and often making no use of headlights at night. Gaping potholes can be a problem: regular drivers on these routes seem to know where the main ones are, but to the uninitiated they appear out of the blue without much warning, so check the spare tyre before you set out, and keep a steady hold on the wheel. In addition, look out for animals, either in groups or singly, usually being herded by children. There is plenty of passing army and police traffic should you need help or have an accident.

The **Bedouin** (see pp.292–293) are incredibly hospitable and will come to the assistance of anyone in trouble. Their black tents are very distinctive and, if you chance upon a Bedouin camp, it is highly probable that you will be invited in to take tea with them or have a meal (except in Palmyra where they see lots of visitors). Be warned, though, that most Bedouin keep semi-wild dogs, which have no respect for their masters' traditions of hospitality.

worth a visit (though you need to hire a car and an experienced driver to get you there), and the remote Roman sites to the east of Hama (covered in Chapter 3).

Tadmor (modern Palmyra)

TADMOR, the modern service town on the northeast side of the Palmyra ruins, takes its name from the ancient Semitic settlement on this site. Apart from the buzz of hotels and kitsch shops along the west end of Qouwatly Street, which must be the single most concentrated tourist area in Syria, it's a sleepy place, knocked dead on summer afternoons by the stultifying heat (and consequent siesta). All the facilities you need while visiting Palmyra are here, and thankfully nothing in Tadmor is more than twenty minutes' walk away from the main area of the ruins.

Lined by characterless buildings, Tadmor's streets are arranged in a rigidly obsessive grid pattern; the only visible evidence of the oasis to which the settlement owes its existence is the mass of trees in the hollow between Tadmor and the Temple of Bel. (Water used to gush out of the ground at the Efqa spring, located next to the *Cham Palace Hotel*, but it dried up in 1994.) The **museum** is the one specific sight in the modern town, conveniently situated right on the main square.

Arrival, information and accommodation

Most **buses and microbuses** drop passengers off in the main square, outside the archeological museum and within comfortable walking distance of all hotels but the *Cham Palace*. The exception is if you arrive on a Qadmous bus from Deir ez-Zur, in which case you'll be dropped at their depot on the northeastern edge of Tadmor, from where you have to use **local transport** to reach the centre of town; this tends to be worked by pick-up trucks which offer an unusual alternative to taxis. The **tourist office** is centrally situated on the traffic circle just off the square (Mon–Thurs, Sat & Sun 8am–2pm & 5–8pm, Fri 8am–2pm), but staff here aren't especially knowledgeable.

Accommodation

With tourist numbers in Palmyra mushrooming, there's a wide choice of **hotels**, and new ones in every category are appearing every year; fierce competition keeps prices down and availability up. If you choose a hotel right on Qouwatly Street, try to get a room at the back – noise from the road can be a nuisance at night. Air-conditioning is not as vital here as elsewhere as it gets quite chilly at night, although you may be glad of a cool retreat in the middle of the day. In winter it can get cold, so make sure you choose a hotel that's adequately heated.

BUDGET

New Afqa (☎031/910 386). One block north of the post office. Good hotel away from traffic noise, with clean, simply furnished rooms and friendly staff who can organize trips out to Bedouin settlements in the desert. ② without air-con, ③ with.

Citadel (☎031/910 537, fax 912 970). In the main square. Managed by friendly, English-speaking staff, this is a decent hotel with very clean rooms boasting fans and heating, though they vary considerably in size and standards of décor. ③.

New Tourist Hotel, Qouwatly St (☎031/910 333). Old hotel with cramped and dingy rooms that catch a lot of street noise. Until recently it was the only budget lodging in Tadmor, and is consequently still something of a backpackers' meeting place; you can exchange views

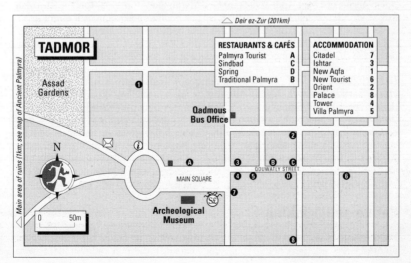

with other travellers via their polyglot noticeboard, but nowadays it's possible to do a lot better than this for somewhere cheap to stay. ②.

Orient (☎031/910 131, fax 910 700). On a quiet street one block north of Qouwatly St. A modern hotel; rooms are clean and functional, with fans and heating, and there's a restaurant as well. ③.

MID-RANGE

Ishtar, Qouwatly St (☎031/913 073, fax 913 260). One of the best-value hotels in Tadmor, with clean rooms and genial owners, though street noise can be a problem. All rooms have TV, fridges and air-con. ④.

Palace (☎031/911 707). One block south of Qouwatly St. Good, quiet hotel with nicely appointed, though rather small, air-con rooms. ④.

Tower, Qouwatly St (☎031/910 116). Good-value hotel with and a first-floor lounge. The rooms are clean and en-suite, each with air-con, a TV and fridge. Unsurprisingly popular with tour groups. ④.

UPMARKET

Cham Palace (☎031 912 231, fax 912 245). Located 3km from Tadmor, beyond the ruins, on the Damascus road. Rising from the greenery of the surrounding oasis is this low-rise, 250-room bunker, where guests can enjoy the use of the *Oasis Disco*, tennis courts and swimming pool – or simply cool off in their marble-floored bathrooms. Bedouin visits, sightseeing tours and transport to the Arab castle at sundown are all laid on. ⑧.

Villa Palmyra, Qouwatly St (☎031/910 156, fax 912 554). The only upmarket hotel in the centre of Tadmor, with modern rooms, each with TV, minibar and air-con. There's a lobby bar and a restaurant on the top floor. ⑥.

Zenobia (☎031/910 107, fax 912 407). Located just north of the main area of ruins. A smaller, much more attractive hotel than the *Villa Palmyra*, with a cool outdoor bar and terrace restaurant. ⑥.

The Palmyra Archeological Museum

On the main square in Tadmor, the **Palmyra Archeological Museum** (daily except Tues: April–Sept 8am–1pm & 4–6pm; Oct–March 8am–1pm & 2–4pm; in Ramadan 8am–3pm; S£200), established in 1961, isn't as good or absorbing as it ought to be, largely because a lot of the Palmyra finds have been moved to Damascus (and other museums throughout the world). If you do decide to visit, come after seeing the site proper, so that you can appreciate the collections in their archeological context.

In the rooms to the right of the main entrance hall, which the arrows suggest you visit first, there are collections of **ceramics and mosaics** removed from private houses in Palmyra. Also in this section are an excellent model showing how the Temple of Bel originally looked, and an interesting guide (in French only) to the Palmyrene alphabet. Heading on round, it's the collections of **funerary and religious art** (more simply reached by turning left from the main entrance hall) which are particularly absorbing, featuring huge late second- and third-century AD statues which once adorned the tombs of wealthy Palmyrenes and which provide ample demonstration of their opulent lifestyle. The intricate designs of the women's headbands and jewellery have been astonishingly well preserved.

Eating and drinking

For a slap-up meal, head to one of the **restaurants** in the upmarket hotels, where **alcohol** is served; there are no stand-alone bars elsewhere in Tadmor. In the town centre are three cheaper eating places, the *Spring*, *Traditional Palmyra* and *Sindbad*, catering to the budget traveller/backpacker market; all three offer mainly chicken and kebabs, plus Western-style pasta or sandwiches, and tempt potential customers with offers of free, sweet tea; prices are generally slightly higher (and the food slightly better) than at similar establishments elsewhere in the country.

Al-Nakhil, *Cham Palace Hotel*. International cuisine, including pasta, smoked salmon, meat dishes and fruit desserts. A meal here for two with wine leaves you little change from S£1000 – not particularly good value; the unappetizing view from the window is of a dusty car park.

Palmyra Tourist Restaurant, on the main square. Every visitor to Palmyra seems to end up here at some time or other. Despite being an obvious tourist trap, it does offer reasonable value; the limited range of food on offer is well prepared, and the spacious, shady terrace is especially cool and attractive in summer.

Sindbad, Qouwatly St. Cheap and cheerful budget joint, with Western snacks and the usual Syrian fare – hummus, chips and kebabs.

Spring Restaurant, Qouwatly St. Kebabs, chicken and chips, along with sandwiches and desserts such as yoghurt, are served in this friendly place situated close to all the cheap hotels.

Tourist Oasis Restaurant, on the road between Tadmor and the ruins. Nothing special at all – it serves the usual kebab, chicken, chips and beer – and the flies are a nuisance.

Traditional Palmyra Restaurant, Qouwatly St. A good breakfast venue and a cheap option for any meal, serving Syrian, Lebanese and Turkish dishes. Despite the kitsch décor – camel whips, cheap local musical instruments and the like – it's probably the best of the three backpacker-geared budget restaurants in this part of the street.

Villa Palmyra Hotel. Most evenings, the top-floor restaurant of this plush hotel on the main street serves an excellent, if pricey three-course buffet (S£400 excluding drinks), with attentive service. At other times you can choose from a fairly extensive menu of Western and Syrian dishes.

Zenobia Hotel. The attractiveness of the hotel's outdoor terrace restaurant belies the undistinguished Arabic and Western fare they serve up. Nonetheless, with column capitals as tables and with great views of Palmyra, it's an atmospheric place for a leisurely meal, particular at dusk when you can watch the sun sink slowly over the ruins and the air cools surprisingly quickly. A meal for two with beer here costs around S£600.

Listings

Banks and exchange The Commercial Bank of Syria's exchange booth (daily 9am–1pm and 6–8.30pm) on the main square takes cash and travellers' cheques, as does the exchange desk at the *Cham Palace Hotel*.

Buses Karnak buses operate from their office on the main square, Qadmous services from their office just north of the main square. Microbuses and other local buses can be picked up on the main square; to reach the small square where they have their main terminal, head east from the main square along Qouwatly St for five minutes.

Phones There are card-operated phones (accessible 24hrs) outside the post office.

Post office Next door to the tourist office, on the central roundabout (daily except Fri 8am–2pm).

Shopping The shops along Qouwatly St sell a variety of goods, mainly tourist-oriented souvenirs including rugs, musical instruments, inlaid wooden items and clothing; most shops sell a mish-mash of everything and are open into the evening. However, compared to the souks in Damascus and Aleppo, the choice here is limited and the prices somewhat higher.

Swimming pools The *Cham Palace* lets non-guests use their pool for S£300, but much better is the pool filled straight from a spring, located amid cool oasis greenery opposite the *Zenobia Hotel*.

TADMOR PRISON

Though one can wax lyrical about Palmyra's romantic ruins and idyllic location, the town that abuts it has a more unsavoury side, playing host to Syria's largest and most notorious jail. The well-concealed **Tadmor Prison** has been used predominantly as a holding place for political prisoners, mainly Islamic extremists, though army officers who fell out with the regime and members of the secular opposition have also been incarcerated here. In the late 1970s the prison became infamous when tales of torture, mutilation, isolation and imprisonment without trial or even reason became widely documented; by far the most ignominious episode in the prison's history occurred on June 27, 1980 when, in retaliation for an attempt by the Muslim Brotherhood on President Hafez al-Assad's life, a special unit shot dead around five hundred prisoners in their cells.

The Syrian authorities do not allow international observers into the prison, but reports from ex-internees tell of cells typically 5m by 20m in size, each holding up to seventy prisoners – the figure rising to two hundred in the aftermath of the 1982 Muslim Brotherhood uprising. In the most crowded cells inmates have to sleep either in shifts or by crouching on the floor. The extremities of heat and cold in Palmyra make life in Tadmor prison especially harsh, with each inmate issued with only four thin blankets doubling as a mattress. Though President Bashar al-Assad granted an amnesty to six hundred political prisoners in 2000, conditions in the prison remain abysmal, and the Syrian authorities still refuse to answer queries from human rights groups concerning the fate of individual detainees.

Ancient Palmyra

Though no more than a twenty-minute walk from the hotels in the centre of Tadmor, the ruins of ancient **PALMYRA** cover a huge area; approaching Tadmor from Damascus or Homs gives a fair impression of the ruins, since the road sweeps past the Temple of Bel and the monumental gateway before entering the modern settlement. As most of the site has to be visited on foot (ideally over the course of several separate visits in view of its scale), it's a good idea to get a perspective on the history and **layout** of the site before visiting, so you can make the most of the place. The site is most easily thought of as falling into four distinct parts: the **Temple of Bel**, the religious centre of the Roman city, still provides a good glimpse of its former magnificence despite being altered through subsequent use as part of the Arab fortifications; the **great colonnade** links the Temple of Bel with Diocletian's Camp, and along its length are the remains of the theatre, the agora, temples and other Roman buildings; the hills to the southwest of the city are dotted with dozens of underground and tower **tombs**; and lastly there's **Qalaat ibn Maan**, the Arab castle which gives a great overview of the site.

Seeing Palmyra requires a day at the very least, several if you want to do the place justice. You're free to wander around the bulk of the ruins at any time, but the Temple of Bel has specific opening hours, and the interior of the funerary towers can only be visited on official tours. In summer, early morning and late afternoon are the best times for sightseeing; your impression of the place will be somewhat compromised if you end up trudging round the ruins in the hottest part of the day, so spending the afternoon under a tree or in a café is a good plan of action. Wear a hat around the ruins – there's precious little shade – and take something to drink with you, rather than paying over the odds for cans and bottles sold by the hawkers who tend to congregate around the monumental arch and the tetrapylon. In winter, be prepared for rain, even snow. At any time of year, the light on the pale stones can be blinding, so take a pair of sunglasses – which will also protect your eyes from the dust and sand that are frequently blown around by the desert winds.

Some history
Since earliest times, nomads have recognized the attractions of the **springs** at Palmyra, and there is evidence that Neolithic man settled and farmed the land around the Efqa spring. Records dating from around 1800 BC, found at Mari on the Euphrates, contain the first written evidence of the city's existence, referring to a desert fort at **Tadmor** (the name meant "guard post"). For at least two millennia the city was little more than the seat of a minor desert chief, forever in the shadow of Petra, the wealthy Nabatean capital in what is now the Jordanian desert, which was better positioned to be the western focus of trade routes across the desert to the interior of Asia.

When the Roman emperor Trajan annexed the kingdom of Petra in 106 AD, however, the fortunes of Palmyra suddenly began to look up: Antioch (modern Antakya in southern Turkey) emerged as the centre of Roman power along the eastern Mediterranean coast, and the treasures found in the increasingly prosperous and powerful kingdom of Parthia to the east of the Euphrates caught the attention of the Romans. Trade routes between Antioch and Parthia were

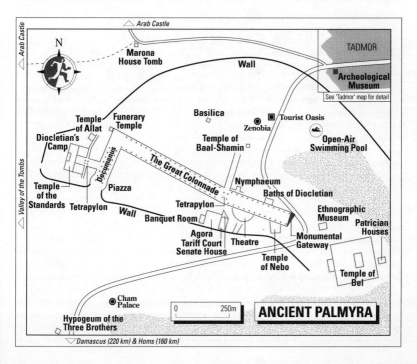

ANCIENT PALMYRA

QUEEN ZENOBIA

Zenobia is one of the most fascinating and controversial figures in the ancient history of Syria, a reputedly beautiful Arab queen who dared to defy the Romans, and whose strength and courage provide inspiration to sentiments of Arab and Syrian nationalism to this day. She rose to prominence as the wife of **Odenathus**, the ruler of Palmyra from 252 until his murder in 267. Recognizing the increased threat the Romans felt from the Persian Sasanian dynasty, Odenathus took great pains to curry favour with his imperial overlords, and led campaigns against the Sasanians on behalf of Rome. After his death, his charismatic and powerful wife ruled Palmyra as regent on behalf of their young son, Wahballat, and immediately reversed policy towards Rome. Under Zenobia, Palmyrene armies captured Bosra and campaigned as far away as Turkey and Egypt, apparently as part of her designs on ruling the eastern part of the Roman Empire from Palmyra, leaving the western half under Roman control.

Not surprisingly, the Roman emperor **Aurelian** had other ideas, and launched a campaign against the Palmyrenes, defeating them at Emesa (Homs) in 272 and pressing on to attack and occupy Palmyra itself. Zenobia fled the city eastwards on a camel, probably planning to reach Persia to seek the support of the Sasanians for a campaign against Aurelian, but was captured by Roman forces as she tried to cross the Euphrates. Palmyra was formally surrendered to Aurelian; however, after a revolt there in 273, the Romans sacked the place, burning, destroying and murdering at random. Zenobia was taken to Rome in chains and shown off as a vanquished ruler who had dared to challenge Roman authority; contemporary reports say that she suffered the humiliation of being paraded through the streets in a full victory cortege that included elephants and gladiators. After being imprisoned in the city for a time, Zenobia seems to have met an untimely death at the hands of the Roman authorities.

In 1997 Zenobia was the subject of a 22-part **Syrian TV** series, *Al-Abadid* ("Anarchy"), partly shot in Palmyra, with Raghda, one of the most beautiful and famous of Arab film stars, in the central role. Watched by millions of people throughout the Arab world, the series portrayed Zenobia's struggle against the Romans as a metaphor for Syria's contemporary defiance of Israel. In the face of frequent assertions by some historians that she was herself Jewish (a rather galling notion to those anxious to promote her as an icon for anti-Zionist sentiment), the series also took great pains to point out her Arab identity; her most likely ancestors were Cleopatra and the Greek rulers of Egypt. In a similar political vein, disunity among her followers was the reason for Zenobia's defeat, according to this dramatization of her life – the subtext being a plea for a united Arab stance against Israel, which, despite the popularity of the series from Abu Dhabi to Beirut, seems highly unlikely to materialize.

established, and Palmyra, which lay between the two, quickly emerged as the most important **caravan city** of the western desert.

Virtually all that can be seen in Palmyra today dates from a comparatively short period of its history – the second and third centuries AD. Within thirty years of the fall of Petra, everything from silk and ebony to slaves and dried foods were being traded through Palmyra, and its **merchants** began to flaunt their individual and collective wealth, endowing the town with grandiose monuments, temples and palaces; many had statues of themselves erected on the columns lining the main streets. One particularly wealthy merchant, named **Male Agrippa**, obviously thought that there wasn't much point in all this flamboyance unless someone important came to look at it, and in 129 he personally paid for a state visit of the Roman emperor Hadrian to the city – after which it was briefly renamed Palmyra Hadriana. Not content with imperial patronage, Male Agrippa later funded the virtual rebuilding of the city's most famous monument, the vast **Temple of Bel**. Yet despite the sudden rise of a wealthy merchant class, Palmyrene society remained largely tribal and agricultural rather than urban, its power and wealth enjoyed only by a privileged few.

Palmyra had been nominally incorporated into the Roman province of Syria during the reign of Nero (54–68 AD), and throughout the second century the Romans maintained a small garrison in the city, but their political influence was limited; the Palmyrenes were wealthy enough to be able to guard their independence from Rome jealously. In 224, however, the Parthian dynasty in Persia was replaced by the **Sasanians**, who were hungrier for territorial gains than their predecessors and began to threaten Roman rule in Syria. This upset the delicate balance of power in the area, and in 273 the Romans under Emperor Aurelian sacked Palmyra (after it had been held for a while by the legendary **Queen Zenobia** – see box opposite) and brought it under direct control. By 300 Emperor Diocletian, alert to the continued military threat from the east, had established a huge fortified camp in Palmyra and strengthened the walls, transforming the city from an ostentatious showpiece into a military stronghold. Under the Sasanians, Persia was a military threat rather than a source of trading riches, and decline set in at Palmyra; by the time the emperor Justinian refortified the walls in the sixth century, the city was a virtual ruin.

In the twelfth century there was a brief revival of interest in the city, when the Mamelukes refortified the walls of the Temple of Bel and constructed a **castle** on a prominent site overlooking the city, much of which by then had crumbled to nothing. In Ottoman times the site was finally abandoned to the desert winds, visited only by sheltering nomads – and also by some of the very first **European travellers**, among them Englishmen Wood and Dawkins, who published *The Ruins of Palmyra* in 1753. Their engravings of designs found in the ruins influenced the Neoclassical architectural movement in Britain, where several eighteenth-century stately homes (such as Blair Castle and Drayton House) boast Palmyra-style ceilings and cornices.

The Temple of Bel and around

The vast **Temple of Bel** (daily: summer 8am–1pm & 4–6pm; winter 8am–4pm; S£300) is by far the best-preserved (or reconstructed) of the city's monuments and the site's main focal point; this seems only fitting, as Bel (a Babylonian pronunciation of Baal, meaning "master") was the supreme deity of the Palmyrenes, equated with the Greek god Zeus. Its cella was built in 32 AD to replace a Hellenistic temple, which itself was constructed on a sacred *tell* dating back to the Bronze Age (2200–1500 BC); the last phase of building took place in the late second century, when the monumental entrance gateway was added.

Before going inside, take a look at the curious patchwork **walls**, their haphazard assortment of stonework being the result both of numerous reconstructions following earthquakes, and of twelfth-century reinforcement when the main entrance gateway was turned into a keep, and the cella into a mosque; indeed the gateway today gives no hint whatsoever of the great pillared portico and huge 35-metre-wide stairway that once preceded it. The **ticket office** is to the left of the gateway and has a good selection of guidebooks; personal guides, who hang

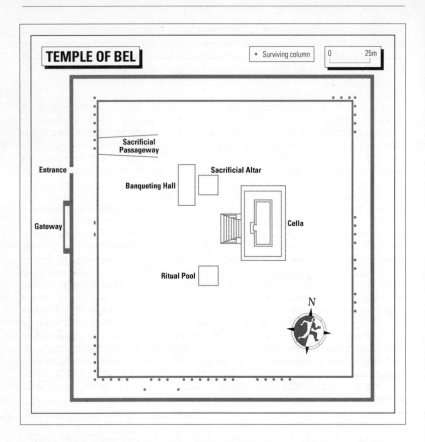

around outside or at the ticket office, ask for S£200, though they can easily be bargained down to S£150 if you've dressed down for the occasion.

The courtyard

The temple **courtyard** once housed a small town; in 1876 Baedeker reported that the settlement consisted of "about fifty huts, partly built with fragments of columns and ancient materials, and arranged in long lanes . . . the traveller may enter the houses and mount upon the roofs without scruple, the wives and families of the peasantry being much less shy than the ladies in towns". The town was removed by the French in 1929, the inhabitants resettled in Tadmor; today local guides will point with pride to the former location of their family's house. Though it feels like a vast exposed space today, the compound would have had a wooden roof, supported by occasional pillars (mostly re-erected in the 1960s) which surround it.

The centrepiece of the courtyard is the huge **cella**, reached via a broad flight of stairs. To the left as you approach is the **sacrificial altar** (note the passageway for the unlucky camels, cattle and sheep that leads up to it from next to the ticket office); to the right are the remains of a **ritual pool** for the washing of hands and the knives used at the altar. Right beside the altar are the foundations of a long **banqueting hall**; clay tokens found here were used as invites to ritual banquets.

The cella

The **cella** was the holiest part of the temple, accessible only to the priests, where, besides Bel, Yarhibol (a solar god) and Aglibol (a lunar god) were worshipped. Its soaring entrance **portal**, reconstructed by the French in the 1930s, leans visibly from the vertical. To the right of the portal are some interesting carved **cross beams**, used to link the peristyle with the wall, and these still have traces of their original colouring; depictions on the first beam include a temple with a fruit-laden altar, the moon god Aglibol (identified by the crescent at his shoulder) and a combat between some divinities and the forces of evil, while on the second is a procession featuring a camel and some veiled women.

The **entrance** to the cella is slightly off-centre; the original entry point was to the south, but the building was reorientated to accommodate two shrines. This arrangement concurred with Semitic tradition (and was used in the Temple of Jerusalem); the northern shrine would have been the holier of the two, with the southern one probably holding a portable statue of Bel used in religious processions. Both shrines would have been concealed – behind either a screen or curtain – except at important moments of a service, a tradition which survives today in the use of the iconostasis in Orthodox churches. The roof of the **northern shrine** consists of a single stone, carved with images of the seven planetary divinities – with Jupiter in the middle – encircled by the signs of the zodiac. On the lintel is a very worn but identifiable eagle with wings outspread, which represents the god Bel presiding over the stars (and thus also the fate of men). The **southern shrine** is simpler but still marvellously decorated, if defiantly sooty – this is the work that so interested Dawkins and Wood and made such an impact on English architecture in the latter part of the eighteenth century (see p.285). Sacrifices would probably have taken place on the roof, reached via the staircase beside the southern shrine, which is now too unsafe to climb.

The ceiling of the cella, like that of the courtyard, was originally of Lebanese cedar. In the walls, note the holes in the joints between the blocks of stone: most of the bronze which was used to fasten the blocks together has been greedily removed over the centuries; only at base level has some been left to strengthen the walls against earthquakes. Traces of faint **frescoes** on the interior walls recall the Byzantine era, when the temple was converted into a church; in the twelfth century it was turned into a mosque (and a **mihrab** was added in the wall of the southern shrine), a function which persisted right up until the clearing of the temple interior in 1929. The back of the cella is its most photogenic side, the columns here reconstructed by the French antiquites department in 1938. Just behind the cella are some recently excavated remains of the previous **Hellenistic temple**, while in the northeastern corner of the courtyard you can ascend some steps for a view over the oasis of olive and palm trees (unfortunately all on private land).

The patrician houses and the ethnographic museum

Behind the temple are the remains of a couple of **patrician houses**, dating to the third century; you can make out the plan of a series of rooms grouped around central pillared courtyards, but the most interesting elements of these houses, their mosaics, have been moved to the Palmyra and Damascus museums.

Northwest of the temple is an **ethnographic museum** (daily except Tues 8.30am–2.30pm; S£150), housing a reasonable collection of Bedouin and local traditional costume, all labelled in English. It's situated within a late nineteenth-century Ottoman governor's residence, which was used as a military prison during the French mandate.

Along the great colonnade

The **great colonnade** which forms the main axis of Palmyra is not a straight line but changes direction twice along its 1200-metre journey, once at the triple-arched **monumental gateway** – a wedge that bends the street round towards the Temple of Bel entrance – and then again at the tetrapylon further west. Built in the early third century, the gateway reflects the traditional Roman form of one high central arch flanked by two smaller side arches; the central arch was built high enough to accommodate camels and as a further concession to these very useful beasts, the great colonnade was left unpaved. Note in particular the brilliantly intricate and varied carvings that adorn the gateway: from acorns, palm trees and intertwining floral designs to bewilderingly complex geometric patterns.

Just beyond the gateway are the low remains of the late first-century **Temple of Nebo**, dedicated to the Mesopotamian god of wisdom; its construction was largely funded by the Elahbel family, who also built the best-preserved of Palmyra's tower tombs (see p.292). Had it not been for the need to avoid the cella of the Nebo temple, the main colonnaded street would probably have run in one straight line from the Temple of Bel to the funerary temple situated at the far western end of the site; as it was, the northern end of the Temple of Nebo (and one side of what was a rectangular colonnade within its courtyard) was sliced off to accommodate the rebuilding of the main street in the late second century AD. The plan of the temple essentially reflects that of the Temple of Bel; today only the cella podium (faced by an outdoor altar) and some surrounding column bases from the original courtyard survive.

The eastern end is the best-preserved section of the colonnaded main axis, though most of the **columns** along the street were re-erected in the twentieth century. The horizontal projections from the columns are brackets upon which the busts of civic notables – largely officials, military men and businessmen – were placed; many of the inscriptions beneath, giving details of the people depicted, are still legible, though the busts have all now gone. (Back in 1876, Baedeker reported that numerous examples of these were available for the traveller to buy, and suggested that "not more than 30–40 [piastres] should be paid" as they were "generally of rude execution".)

A little way up, across the colonnaded street, four tall Egyptian red-granite columns mark the entrance to the **Baths of Diocletian**. These date from the reconstruction of Palmyra in the early fourth century, though a bath complex had probably been situated here for about a century prior to this. The identifiable octagonal room was the dressing room (note the paving stones, which are original, and the drain in the centre), beyond which is the colonnaded main pool; however the rest of the complex barely survives above foundation level.

Around the theatre and the tetrapylon

A short walk west of the Diocletian baths is the **theatre**, which was buried in sand until the 1950s. Though the lower seats have since been restored and the stage

THE PALMYRENE TARIFF

The Syrians have often been refered to as "the middlemen of antiquity", with goods passing through here on their way between Western Europe and places as far away as India and China, and it was trade that formed the basis of Palmyra's wealth. The **taxes** and financial laws to which to the citizens of the town and passing merchants were subject are listed on the **Palmyrene tariff**, a huge stone slab (nearly 2m by 5m) dated to 137 AD and found in the tariff court, providing a fascinating insight into the economic life and customs of Palmyra at the time.

Perfumes formed an important part of the commercial flow, and according to the tariff stone, these were very heavily taxed; also specifically mentioned are dried fish – once considered a great delicacy in Palmyra, whose supplies of the stuff came from Lake Tiberias – as well as olive oil and cattle. Oddly enough the slab reveals that a monthly tax was levied on prostitutes – equal to the amount the prostitute charged for her services; this practice was probably based on the similar tax established in Rome by the emperor Caligula. Water being the most valuable of Palmyra's natural assets, it's not altogether surprising to find that water rates were also levied: one payment of 800 denarii entitled a merchant to use the springs whenever he liked – not bad value considering a caravan could consist of up to one thousand camels.

façade largely reconstructed, there would have originally been another two storeys on the façade and tiers of seating higher up, probably constructed out of wood. The building has been dated to early in the second century, thus predating this part of the great colonnade, and its presence – along with that of the Temple of Nebo – may well have dictated the street's change in direction, the theatre probably losing the dressing rooms behind the stage when the street was laid out.

At the back of the theatre are the remains of the **senate house**, the debating arena for the city's governing body. A compact, strangely shaped building, it underwent some degree of amputation during the construction of the street that curves around the theatre. To the south of the senate house is a large courtyard area known as the **tariff court**, after the discovery here of a five-metre-long inscribed stone slab (transported to St Petersburg in 1901) listing the Palmyrene tax arrangements for goods entering or leaving the city (see box, above). The court's main entrance was through the huge southern doorway which – like the monumental gateway's central arch – was built high enough for camels to enter. West of here, the early second-century **agora** is surrounded on all sides by a portico, which would at one time have been bordered by up to two hundred columns, upon whose brackets would have stood busts of senators, soldiers and caravan leaders; the presence of empty slots for more brackets on the surrounding walls suggests that space on the columns ran out at some stage. At the agora's southwestern corner is a small **banqueting room** with some attractive maze-like carvings and some bare remains of benches around the walls.

Back on the great colonnade, head for the **tetrapylon**, a grouping of four sets of four columns marking a slight bend in the road and the intersection of a cross street; impressive centrepiece to the ruins though the tetrapylon is, only one of its columns is original, the rest having been reconstructed in concrete in the 1960s. Standing just to the east of this on the main street are the pitiful remains of a **nymphaeum**, a public water fountain.

West of the tetrapylon

The oldest part of the great colonnade, dating from the early second century, lies west of the tetrapylon. This stretch of the street has been only partially excavated and is narrowed considerably in places by the shops which would have encroached onto it. At the far end of the great colonnade stands a late second-century **funerary temple** – basically an elaborate mausoleum – which has recently been restored with a large quantity of concrete (and not much subtlety); there's a crypt underneath, but it's not possible to get inside this.

Diocletian's Camp

A left turn from the western end of the great colonnade brings you onto the broad decumanus, the area west of which is **Diocletian's Camp**, essentially a fortified city within a city; it was established by the emperor Diocletian about thirty years after Aurelian's destruction of Palmyra in 273 (prior to this the Roman garrison had its camp near the site of the Palmyra Archeological Museum). Small boys from local Bedouin families who live around here make an enterprising business of selling cups of tea to thirsty visitors.

About 200m down the decumanus, a right turn into a narrow avenue takes you past the pitiful remains of a smaller, second tetrapylon before you arrive at the sloping monumental stairway heralding the **Temple of the Standards**; little of the structure survives today, but for a good view back over the site, ascend the winding staircase of the inner shrine. Directly behind the temple is a burial cave which still has four badly worn sarcophagi, while just to the northeast are the scant remains – a doorway, a podium and a few columns – of the second-century **Temple of Allat**; a fierce-looking early first-century AD lion found here has been reconstructed and now stands in front of the Palmyra Archeological Museum. The decumanus largely peters out here, but would have ended at an oval **piazza** – an unusual feature in Roman town planning (the only other example is at Jerash in Jordan); only a few pillars now remain around it. The piazza would have opened out behind the southern gate to the city, which was the main entrance leading in from Damascus – probably the reason the decumanus is wider than the main colonnaded axis.

Around the Temple of Baal-Shamin

Returning to Tadmor from Diocletian's Camp and the great colonnade, you can easily take in the interesting ruins which lie near the *Zenobia Hotel*. The best-preserved of these is the **Temple of Baal-Shamin**, dedicated to the deity who as "lord of the heavens" – and thus of fertilizing rain also – was naturally an important god in Roman Syria (he was often equated with Zeus). Though the temple dates to 17 AD, its main focal point, the cella, was added in 130, and owes its remarkable state of preservation to its conversion into a church during the Byzantine period, when the entrance doorway was moved to the western wall. In the 1950s a Swiss team carefully restored the cella to its original form, and today it is not only one of the most intact monuments on the site but also one of the few to have been fully excavated; on the ground to the north and south of the cella you can see two colonnaded courtyards which formed part of the huge temple complex.

About 150m west of the temple, six columns (but not much else) identify the remains of a sixth-century Christian **basilica**. Apart from this, little of the area north of the great colonnade has been excavated from beneath the dust and sand that has accumulated over the centuries, though two peristyles do stick out like sore thumbs; these would have once formed part of the central courtyards of houses belonging to wealthy Palmyrenes. The well-preserved northern **wall** of the settlement dates from Diocletian's fortification of Palmyra, and was reinforced by Emperor Justinian in the sixth century; by the northern gate, which would have been where the modern road cuts through the wall on the way into Tadmor, are the remains of a military barracks.

The tombs

Two basic types of tomb are found in Palmyra, **tower tombs** and **hypogea** (underground chambers). Used for burials up until the third century, the tower tombs are the older of the two, dating back perhaps as far as Hellenistic times, though one was built as late as 128 AD; some tower tombs also have underground chambers, representing a transitional phase leading up to the era of the hypogea, dated examples of which are known from between 81 and 251 AD. The tombs are mainly found in two areas, the Valley of the Tombs on the south side of Diocletian's Camp, and the southwest necropolis by the Damascus road.

Although it's possible to wander round the more decrepit tower tombs by yourself, the only way to get inside the two fascinating reconstructed tombs – the Tower Tomb of Elahbel and the Hypogeum of the Three Brothers – is on one of the official **tours**, as they are kept locked at other times; tickets (S£150; 1hr) must be bought at the window just outside the museum entrance. The only drawback to these otherwise enjoyable trips is that the quality of guide can vary dramatically; you could get a local with basic English earning some extra money, or a university lecturer topping up his government salary in his vacation. **Buses** (additional fee payable) timed to coincide with the tours leave for the Tower Tomb from outside the Palmyra Archeological Museum at 8.30am, 10am, 11.30am (not Fri) and 4pm (the afternoon departure is at 2pm Oct–March, 1.30pm in Ramadan), subsequently heading on to the hypogeum. Use of these buses is optional – you can simply make your own way out at the appropriate time to join a tour if you've bought a ticket; note, however, that you'll need your own transport (taxis accumulate outside the museum at tour times) to see both reconstructed tombs, as it isn't possible to get from the tower tomb to the hypogeum on foot before the latter is closed.

The Valley of the Tombs

Stretching back for about 1km behind Diocletian's Camp is the **Valley of the Tombs**, a bleak place where the tombs range from ruinous stacks to extremely well-preserved edifices. Many of the hypogea here are still waiting to be discovered, having been buried in a tenth-century earthquake; others have collapsed and been raided in the intervening centuries. The most obviously photogenic batch of tower tombs – unfortunately not included on the official tour – lie in a row on the hill opposite Diocletian's Camp. You can head up there for a peek through the grille at the front of the prominent and impressive **Tower Tomb of Iamliku** (on the right of this grouping), which has undergone some restoration; dating to 83 AD, it would have had room for up to two hundred burials.

It's possible to continue west along the valley path for about 500m beyond this, passing an enticing selection of tombs, some merely rubble, others plain but well-preserved examples which you can climb inside and explore. By far the largest and most intact is the **Tower Tomb of Elahbel**, which stands three storeys high and would have had room for no fewer than three hundred incumbents (a hypogeum lies underneath, but it isn't possible to get inside this). Funds for its construction, and for the Temple of Nebo, were provided by the family of Elahbel, one of the most important in the city, and their status is reflected in the splendour of the tomb, built, according to the inscription above the entrance, in 103 AD. The iron grille door replaces what would originally have been two massive stone ones hewn from the quarries to the north of the city. Inside, traces of the original colouring indicate how rich the decoration would have been: grand pilasters stretch up to the ceiling, and remarkably dignified busts representing deceased family members look down upon you from all angles. It is refreshing to see these *in situ* for once, rather than ripped out of context in the corner of some anodyne museum. A narrow staircase leads up to the roof, from where there is a fine view back over the valley.

The southwest necropolis

The tower tombs of the **southwest necropolis**, just beyond the *Cham Palace Hotel* by the main road to Damascus, are unremarkable, but the site does contain an astonishing underground chamber, the **Hypogeum of the Three Brothers**, dating to the second century and restored in 1947. An inscription in Aramaic above the entrance records the names of the brothers who built it, and the fact

---

THE BEDOUIN

The **Bedouin** – whose name derives from the Arabic for "desert wanderers" – live in the deserts of Syria, Iraq, Jordan and Israel, and in all the countries of the Arabian peninsula and North Africa. They were once a race fiercely adherent to ancient nomadic traditions and tribal loyalties, though many Bedouin have now resettled (either under compulsion or voluntarily) in permanent desert communities and large cities. Some, however, are still traditional desert-dwellers, living in makeshift goat-skin tents and tending their herds of goats or sheep – even if many have abandoned camels for pick-up trucks. Back in the days of the Silk Road, the Bedouin held positions of importance as suppliers of pack animals to the caravan merchants, and patrolled trade routes giving guidance and military protection to the convoys as they crossed the dangerous terrain from oasis to oasis. Now, the Bedouin have lost much of their former political strength, though many city-dwelling Arabs – despite having a reputation for looking down on them – still celebrate the Bedouin's status as legendary Arab heroes.

Tribal loyalty is the bedrock of true Bedouin nomadic communities. A complex web of relationships attaches every Bedouin to an extended family: the *fakhida* is a network of cousins, down to the fifth generation; a *fakhd* is made up of several of these groupings, and forms part of a tribe, each member of which, in theory, shares one common ancestor. Tribal connections are expressed in Bedouin **dress**: the male headdress, known as the *ghutra*, is a large square of cotton, coloured according to the traditions of each individual tribe and folded around the head to give protection from heat, dust and flies. Most Bedouin men and boys also wear a loose-fitting, ankle-length gown called a *thawb*, made of cotton and usually coloured white, grey or black, which buttons up at the neck like a nightshirt. Women wear long-sleeved dresses or gowns, sometimes multicoloured, occasionally black; sometimes kohl, a black cosmetic, is rubbed around the eyes to keep out the glare of the sun; intricate designs

that some of the chamber's capacity of 360 bodies was later sold off to other families. The stone doors and the frescoes inside are all original, with the three brothers represented inside circular frames at the end of the main corridor. Other paintings deal with the theme of the soul overcoming death, including a depiction on the ceiling of Ganymede being carried by the eagle of Zeus, and another of Achilles achieving immortality in battle. The right wing of the hypogeum contains the sarcophagi of the three brothers; in the left wing is a funerary monument to Male, the most important of them, who died in 142 AD.

Qalaat ibn Maan

Fourteen hundred years separate the building of Palymra's Arab castle, **Qalaat ibn Maan**, which sits atop a precipitous volcanic cone to the west of the ruins, and the construction of the town over which it presides. The date of the first fortification on the volcanic cone is unclear, though it seems likely that a castle was built here in the twelfth century. What is certain is that in the early seventeenth century a Lebanese emir, Fakhr al-Din, built the present edifice to secure his control over this part of the Syrian desert. However, his plan to provide a territorial bulwark against encroaching Ottoman power failed dismally: he himself was captured by the Ottomans in 1635 and later executed in Istanbul. The castle was abandoned thereafter, and is now in a poor state of repair – when you get up here

may be painted onto other exposed parts of their skin. As in cities, veils are only sometimes worn over the face. In the desert, women are much less visible than men and may retreat into their own private tents when strangers approach – while the men of the community welcome the visitor hospitably.

Nowadays, most Bedouin herd goats or sheep, driving them – using dogs, donkeys, camels, assorted family members and Nissan pick-ups – from place to place in search of pasture. Camel herds are rare in Syria, though groups of these rather ragged beasts can still be seen from the desert roads and tracks; they are much more common further south in the Arabian deserts and the Sahara. Occasionally, the Bedouin hunt desert animals and, if the soil is good enough, cultivate a few crops. Traditional Bedouin **meals** comprise a meat dish and a communal bowl of rice, eaten first by the men (though cooked by the women), followed by endless small cups of coffee, flavoured with cardamom. To suit their surroundings the ablutions before prayers may be performed with sand rather than water.

Bedouin **hospitality** – to fellow tribespeople, Arabs and foreigners alike – is famous, a tradition, stemming from the harshness of the environment, of looking after any stranger who emerges from the desert. For centuries it's been the subject of comment by Middle Eastern travellers, and nowadays many tour groups are given the opportunity to "take tea with the Bedouin"; in Palmyra children approach independent visitors with similar offers, which are more likely to be an authentic experience, although *baksheesh* is expected. In **remote** desert regions, visitors who happen across a Bedouin settlement will find the hospitality they are given almost overwhelming. If you are invited into a tent, remember to remove your shoes upon entering. All visitors are made welcome, though in general Bedouin men do not shake hands with foreign women. You will probably be offered a shot of bitter black coffee followed by sweet, sickly tea and possibly some food. The keys to the few desert sights (such as Qasr al-Heir al-Sharqi) are often held by Bedouin, and tea is offered as a matter of course when visitors turn up.

you'll probably be disappointed both by the crude restoration work that's been done in places, and by the fact that there really isn't much to see inside the walls. In truth, though, the main attraction is not the castle itself but the **view** from its ramparts, encompassing the ancient ruins, the oasis and the modern town on one side, and the rocky spine of the Jebel al-Tadmoria on the other, all fringed by the pale desert, flecked with the characteristic black tents of the Bedouin.

Technically the castle is **open** from noon until 8pm, with an entry **charge** of S£150, but these arrangements depend largely on the custodian at the main gate: you may well come up here to find there's no one around and you get in for free. The best time to visit, however, is when the sun is setting over the arid hills to the west, a magical photographic occasion, not easily forgotten despite the inevitable crowd. To get to the castle **by car**, follow the road from the roundabout in Tadmor, which winds up the hill from behind. Heading there **on foot** (40min from the roundabout), you pass a number of funerary monuments en route, most of them pretty ruinous, though it is worth pausing at the **Marona house tomb**, one of the two solid square buildings constructed as a mausoleum for the family of a wealthy Palmyrene merchant in the early third century. The track to the castle, which branches off from the road at a point by the Marona house tomb, is steep but well marked, and affords a number of irresistible backward glances over the site. Thankfully, cold **drinks** are usually on sale at the castle entrance.

Qasr al-Heir al-Sharqi

It takes time, patience and expense to reach **Qasr al-Heir al-Sharqi** (the last bit of its name, meaning "eastern", indicates it's one of two such castles either side of Palmyra), but once there it's hard not to be impressed by the arid splendour of the setting, and the improbable sight of the bright orange walls rising out of the desert plain. The original purpose of the complex, which was constructed around 700, remains unclear, though it was probably built by the Umayyads to consolidate their control of the region in the face of local tribal wars, and to develop the site as a caravan stop between Syria and Mesopotamia. It wasn't until the thirteenth century that the complex was abandoned, probably as a result of the Mongol invasions. The drama of the castle's setting today goes a long way towards making up for some fairly disappointing remains – they certainly don't compare favourably with the ruins of Resafe (see p.258), which has a similar ambience and is at least accessible by a proper road. A sibling castle, **Qasr al-Heir al-Gharbi**, 110km west of Palmyra, has a similar history, but what remains of it now is very disappointing and not worth the effort of a visit; its most interesting feature was the grand gateway that now forms the entrance to the National Museum in Damascus (see p.92).

About 5km before reaching the site, remains of the **outer walls** of the settlement can be seen; their circumference would have stretched some 18km, encircling a huge area of gardens, as well as a civilian town and the castle buildings that survive today. Once at the **main site** you'll find two enclosures facing each other, the smaller and better-preserved of which, to the east, is thought to have served as a **khan** (the key to this is available from a local Bedouin), though it probably also had a military function as it has two-metre thick walls and only one entrance. The interior is a disappointing mess of rubble, though it's possible to climb up the walls at various points. Between the buildings stands a **minaret** which, if contemporary with the other buildings, would be the third oldest in Islam; however, its construction remains something of a mystery – it may have started life as a watchtower, as there is no mosque attached.

The **western enclosure**, some six times larger than the eastern one, contains an identifiable grid pattern of streets, in the centre of which is a small square and a cistern. Though its interior is largely ruinous, parts of a mosque survive in the southeastern corner, and the residential and administrative buildings that filled the rest of the site are easy to make out. Curiously, three of the four gates of this building were walled up very shortly after construction, reflecting the fact that this was built according to a traditional city plan rather than specifically for this location. Outside and about 50m to the north of the minaret are the remains of a large **bath house**, of which just the foundations survive.

Practicalities

The thirty-kilometre desert track from the main highway to the castle is extremely confusing (there are dozens of similar tracks made by the Bedouin, and no signposts), and in wet weather you need a four-wheel drive to avoid getting stuck in the mud. Until the proposed tarmac road to Qasr al-Heir al-Sharqi is built, the only sensible way of **getting there** is to hire a car with driver in Palmyra (S£2000 is the typical going rate): ask around outside the entrance to the museum, where drivers congregate to take people out to Palmyra's tombs, or at your hotel. In summer, drivers often want to make an early start to avoid the heat of the day, so expect a 6am or 7am pick-up, arriving back at midday. In any case, remember to take plenty of water with you as you won't find any on the way.

travel details

Pullman and Karnak buses
From the Qadmous office to:
Damascus (3hr); Deir ez-Zur (2hr).

From the Karnak office to:
Damascus (4 daily; 3hr); Deir ez-Zur (7 daily; 2hr); Hassakeh (1 daily; 5hr); Homs (2 daily; 2hr); Qamishli (1 daily; 6hr).

Microbuses and local buses
Infrequent services from the microbus terminal and main square in Tadmor to:
Damascus (3hr), Deir ez-Zur (2hr) and Homs (2hr).

PART THREE

THE
CONTEXTS

THE HISTORICAL FRAMEWORK

Juxtaposing Mediterranean, Anatolian and Arabian cultures, modern Syria is the political descendant of a bewildering succession of independent city states and of long periods of control by external imperial powers; what follows is an outline of events, from prehistoric times to the present-day rule of President Bashar al-Assad.

PREHISTORIC TIMES

Man's first permanent settlements were established along the **Euphrates River** around twelve thousand years ago. This is where crops were first planted, and where wild animals were first domesticated and managed; villages grew up where the soil was fertile and the supply of water most abundant. The mastery of food production led eventually to surpluses, which in turn allowed the possibility of specialization, and then trade between individuals and settlements.

It is thought that Aleppo, Damascus and Hama all have their origins in the **Neolithic period**. Each claims to be the oldest continually inhabited settlement on earth, though the archeological investigation necessary to substantiate their claims is obviously impractical. Among Syria's numerous *tell*s – artificial mounds formed by the accumulated debris of centuries of occupation – the most interesting Neolithic site for the non-specialist is at **Ugarit**;

tools imported from Suphan Dagh in eastern Turkey dating back to the eighth millennium BC have been found here, suggesting that trade was sophisticated even at this early stage. Furthermore, a style of pottery known as "Halaf pottery", dating to the sixth millennium BC and originating from **Tell Halaf** in northeast Syria, has been found all over northern Syria and Iraq, testifying to the spread of some kind of homogenous culture over a wide area. The Bedouin still lead lives not too dissimilar to that of the prehistoric herdsmen, while the distinctive **beehive houses** found in northern Syria, particularly in the area east of Hama, have their counterparts in the Neolithic round houses from roughly the same areas, which were developed as man moved away from caves and rock shelters out into the open.

THE BRONZE AGE (3000–1200 BC)

The development of trade saw the rise of wealthy mercantile centres at **Ugarit**, **Mari** and **Ebla**, which developed into powerful city states with commercial contacts as far away as Egypt, Cyprus and Mesopotamia. Arguably the first major empire to emerge in the region was that of the **Akkadians**, founded in Mesopotamia around 2340 BC. At its apogee the Akkadian empire stretched from the Mediterranean coast to the Persian Gulf, though it only lasted two hundred years. Around 2000 BC the established pattern of trade was disturbed by the influx of the **Amorites**, a Semitic people from the Syrian desert. After an initial period of upheaval which witnessed the decline of Ebla, a number of major Amorite city states emerged: Mari in particular enjoyed renewed prosperity, and the kingdom of Yamkhad (Aleppo) became the main power in the north, taking over Ebla's old trade. Around 1759 BC Mari was razed by another Semitic people, the **Babylonians**, under Hammurabi, but Yamkhad and the other Amorite kingdoms in the north of Syria managed to resist the Babylonian threat and developed substantial trading links with Persia and India.

During the fifteenth and fourteenth centuries BC Syria became a battleground between three major powers, the Egyptians, the Hittites and the Mitanni. Indo-Europeans in origin, the **Hittites**, whose empire was based in central Turkey, had removed the Babylonians from the region around 1595 BC; by the late fourteenth century BC they had absorbed the **Mitanni** – a non-Semitic people of obscure origin based in the northeast – through a series of marriage alliances. The **Egyptians** meanwhile had been developing trading links with the Syrian coastal cities since the twentieth century BC, and by the end of the fourteenth century BC they felt ready to square up to the Hittites, who had by this time extended their influence as far south as Damascus. The decisive battle was fought in 1285 BC at **Kadesh** (present-day Tell Nebi Mend, near Homs), during which Ramses II was ambushed by the Hittite cavalry and was lucky to escape with his life (for more, see box on p.154).

The coastal region remained largely untroubled during the conflict between the Egyptians, the Hittites and the Mitanni, allowing **Ugarit**, **Jableh** and **Arwad** to prosper as trading centres. The Semitic **Canaanites**, who had settled on the Mediterranean coast around 2000 BC, were probably the first people to develop a form of writing that used letters rather than words or syllables; their alphabet consisted of thirty letters, similar to modern Arabic in sequence and pronunciation, and indeed the language contained some words which are still in use today.

THE IRON AGE (1200–333 BC)

Hittite dominance of the region was brought to an end around 1200 BC by the aggressive migration of the **Sea Peoples**, a coalition of tribes from around the Aegean who are thought to have variously ended up in Palestine, Anatolia and Sardinia. All the coastal cities were razed, including Ugarit, though they subsequently revived under the **Phoenicians**, descendants of the Canaanites. The Phoenicians' massive expansion of sea trade led to the creation of over fifty colonies around the Mediterranean and the spread of the Phoenician script (developed from its Canaanite predecessor).

In the aftermath of the chaos created by the passing of the Sea Peoples, the **Arameans**, a Bedouin people of Semitic origin, migrated into central and northern Syria. Their language, Aramaic, took hold across the Middle East, and a thousand years later was being spoken by Jesus; it still survives in certain isolated villages today, most notably Maalula near Damascus. Around 1000 BC, the north of Syria was absorbed by the **Assyrians**, based in northern Mesopotamia, who adopted the Aramaic language and its neo-Phoenician

script. In 612 BC the Assyrian capital Nineveh was captured by the **Babylonians**, who took over its prosperous western possessions; this was the time of the legendary palaces and hanging gardens of Babylon. Babylon fell in 539 BC to the **Achaemenid Persians**, who rapidly took over the whole of the Middle East and Asia Minor.

THE HELLENISTIC PERIOD (333–64 BC)

Persian incursions into Greece eventually provoked a pan-Greek expeditionary force led by **Alexander the Great**. The struggle was decided over a series of battles in 333 BC, the greatest at Issus in southern Turkey. Eventually Alexander managed to march his army all the way down the Syrian coast, ending up in Egypt and founding the port of Alexandria. When he died aged 33 in 323 BC in Babylon, he had created an empire bigger even than the Persians', which changed the whole orientation of the region; Syria, save the coast, had until then had been essentially eastward-looking, but now it looked to Greece and then Rome for its government and ideas – while Rome became susceptible to ideas, especially religious ones, from the East.

On his death, Alexander's new empire was divided between his two most able generals: Ptolemy took over Egypt, southern Lebanon and southern Syria (including Damascus), while Seleucus took northern Syria, Mesopotamia and Asia Minor – Antioch (modern-day Antakya in Turkey) became the capital of the **Seleucid empire**, and **Apamea** was founded as its military headquarters. In 198 BC the Seleucids took over southern Syria, but Greek manpower never exceeded fifty thousand and within a hundred years, as their lack of numbers began to tell, the empire began to crumble: the Arab Nabateans took Bosra and Damascus, while the Parthians made inroads in the east and the Armenians sniffed around in the north.

THE ROMAN PERIOD (64BC–395 AD)

In 64 BC the Roman legate Pompey invaded the Seleucid empire and formally created the **Roman province** of Syria; Damascus was brought under direct Roman rule in the early part of the first century AD, and in 92–93

Palestine was integrated. The Roman period saw Syria flourish economically; Syrian merchants became wealthy middlemen in the East–West trade in luxuries like silk and precious stones, and the country became a major area of cultivation, grain and wine being its specialities. Numerous roads were built and many new settlements sprang up, particularly in the hinterland of Antioch (where what became the Dead Cities were founded) and in the Hauran. In 106 the annexation of the Hauran was completed with the creation of the province of Arabia, with **Bosra** as its capital; Bosra and Qanawat were then extensively replanned.

In turn, Syria also had its influence on Rome: in 187 Septimius Severus, a Libyan general in the Roman army, married Julia Domna, a high priest's daughter from Emesa (Homs). Soon afterwards he became emperor, and upon his death Julia became effective ruler in Rome behind her son Caracalla; the line produced two further emperors, Elagabalus and Alexander Severus. In the mid-third century **Philip the Arab**, from Shahba, also briefly ruled the Roman Empire (see p.139).

The main threat to the Romans came from the **Parthians** to the east, who by the late second century had become a major source of concern – as a consequence **Dura Europos** was reinforced and **Palmyra** taken under direct rule. In 224 the Sasanians took over Persia from the Parthians and in 256 they took Dura Europos. Four years later they captured the emperor Valerian himself at Edessa in southeastern Turkey. Valerian was subsequently tortured and killed, leaving the Romans happy to enlist any local help they could; they turned to Odenathus, the Palmyrene prince, who campaigned deep into Sasanian-held lands. Odenathus was killed in 266 but his wife **Zenobia** had even greater glory in mind, declaring herself Roman empress, sending forces to Egypt and attacking Antioch. Emperor Aurelian had no choice but to confront Zenobia head-on, defeating her army just outside Homs in 272. Forced to flee Palmyra when Aurelian placed it under siege, Zenobia was captured on her way to the Euphrates and sent to Rome as a prisoner; after a further revolt in 273 Palmyra itself was razed.

It was **Emperor Constantine** who first gave official recognition to **Christianity** in 313, though Syria (and especially Antioch) had been strongly Christian since the first-century mis-

sions of St Paul. Before 313 Christian churches had merely been adapted houses (as at Dura Europos for example), but during the fourth century they began to adopt the grandeur of major public buildings. In 392 Christianity was declared by the emperor Theodosius I to be the official religion of the Roman Empire, and subsequently flourished under imperial patronage; pagan temples were either destroyed or adapted for Christian use, and by the fifth century Syria was littered with churches.

THE BYZANTINE PERIOD (395–636)

In 395 the Roman Empire was officially divided into east and west; the western half fell to German invaders in 476 but the **Byzantine** eastern half called itself Roman right up until the fall of Constantinople to the Ottomans in 1453. Despite troubled frontiers and internal church divisions Syria continued to prosper economically: Antioch thrived on its olive oil exports, the Hauran became intensely cultivated and building projects multiplied – indeed, no other area of the Byzantine Empire contains such a wealth of architectural evidence from this period as Syria, with its numerous villages, churches and monastic remains, pride of place going to the basilica devoted to St Simeon, northwest of Aleppo.

During the reign of Justinian (527–65) the empire won back much of the land lost since its heyday, though the continuing **Sasanian** threat led to a number of defensive projects along the Euphrates, including the fortifications at Resafe and Halebiye. The two sides locked horns in an epic struggle covering the late sixth and early seventh centuries, resulting in a mutual exhaustion that paved the way for a completely new force to emerge in the region.

THE ARAB CONQUEST, THE UMAYYADS AND THE ABBASIDS (636–1097)

After the death in Mecca in 632 of **Mohammed**, who had founded Islam and united the Arabian tribes, his successors went about extending their influence in the area north of the Arabian peninsula. Caliph Omar succeeded in conquering all of present-day Syria, Lebanon, Israel, Jordan and Egypt – with the decisive battle for Syria taking place in 636 at **Yarmouk River** (see box on p.135) – while under his successor Caliph

Othman all of Persia was captured. Yet the events following Othman's assassination in 656 led to the first and greatest Islamic division, that between Sunnis and Shiites. Othman's natural successor appeared to be Ali, husband of the prophet's daughter Fatima, but he was opposed by the governor of Syria, **Moawiya**, who eventually triumphed in 661, founding the **Umayyad dynasty** and moving the capital from southern Iraq to Damascus where his power base lay. Shiites, who still follow Ali's line to this day, represent about ten percent of all Muslims and are found mostly in Iran and the Indian subcontinent.

The Caliphs' rule sat quite easily on the basically Christian population because it rested more on tax incentives than coercion, but the growth of the Islamic faith was slow. Major building projects were embarked on, especially under Khalid ibn al-Walid (705–15) who was responsible for the Umayyad Mosque in Damascus (the Great Mosque of Aleppo also dates from this period). Military conquests led to Umayyad rule extending almost to the borders of China and including Afghanistan, Pakistan and the west coast of India – in the west, all of north Africa, most of Spain and even southern France came under Arab control.

In 750 the Umayyad line was replaced by the **Abbasids** from Persia, who transferred their capital from Damascus to Iraq (Kufa first and then Baghdad after 762). As a consequence Syria became a blind spot; the only significant remains in the country from this period are to be found at Raqqa on the Euphrates. With the western possessions neglected, Egypt and then the other North African possessions broke away from Abbasid rule, while revolts in Syria in the mid-ninth century encouraged the spread of Shiism. In the mid-tenth century the Abbasid empire fragmented and Syria became a confusing free-for-all as the Egyptian Fatimids, Seljuk Turks and Byzantines all dipped their fingers in the pot – though none was strong enough to take a firm hold. Sunni and Shiite tensions grew, and it is in this period of turmoil and uncertainty that the region's confusing religious make-up largely originated, with Shiism engendering numerous offshoots. The **Druze** (see p.315) arose out of the teachings of Caliph Al-Hakim of the Fatimid dynasty, one of many sects thought to have been founded upon a belief in the Caliph's divinity, though only the Druze have survived to the present day. It was also at this

time that the Christian **Maronites** (see p.316) holed themselves up in the mountains of Lebanon; tensions between the Druze and Maronites would rumble on for centuries.

Syria's political history at this point can only be related at local level. In the north, first the Hamdanid dynasty (944–1003), then the Bedouin Mirdasid (1023–79) controlled Aleppo, each retaining a large degree of independence from both the Byzantines and the Seljuk Turks (who were in theory controlled by the Sunni Abbasid caliphs in Baghdad); meantime, the Shiite **Fatimids** held the upper hand in the south. In the late eleventh century the **Seljuks** gained supremacy in the region as a whole, defeating the Byzantines at the battle of Manzikert in 1071, before taking Damascus in 1075 and Jerusalem in 1078. However, by 1095 the Seljuk-held lands had divided between two rival dynasties: one with its power base in Damascus, the other based in Aleppo.

THE CRUSADES (1097–1260)

Although it is true that the rule of Caliph Al-Hakim in the early eleventh century saw the widespread destruction of churches in the Holy Land (including that of the Church of the Holy Sepulchre in Jerusalem), by the end of the century the situation in the East for pilgrims and Christians was not particularly grave within the contexts of a war-torn region. It was more the pleas for military assistance from the Byzantine emperor Alexius I (along with vague promises of unification of the Western and Eastern churches under the primacy of Rome) that prompted Pope Urban II to call, at the Council of Clermont-Ferrand in 1095, for a **crusade** to reclaim Jerusalem. What Alexius was probably hoping for was a small battalion of mercenaries, but what he got instead was a 100,000-strong largely French army which arrived in Constantinople in 1097; Antioch was taken in June 1098 after a nine-month siege, and the fractured Seljuk states provided little further resistance to this massive force. In 1099 Jerusalem was captured amid scenes of great carnage when the entire Muslim population was massacred; Tartous and Latakia soon fell too, though Tripoli was not taken until 1109 and an assault on Aleppo in 1125 failed. After the Second Crusade in 1148 the defence of most of the inland conquests was left to two autonomous orders of knights, the **Templars** and **Hospitallers** (see box on p.178), who, because of their small numbers, relied principally on the forbidding nature of their castles such as Marqab, Saone (Saladin) and the Crac des Chevaliers.

The first inroads against the Crusader presence were made by **Zengi**, local ruler of Aleppo (1128–46), and his son **Nur al-Din**, who took Damascus in 1154 and for the first time united Syrian resistance to the Crusaders. His achievements were built upon by his nephew **Saladin** (see box on p.205), a Kurd from Iraq who founded the **Ayyubid** dynasty (1176–1260), named after his father Ayyub. By 1186 Saladin had completed the unification of Arab lands from Baghdad to Cairo, and in 1187 he was able to recapture Jerusalem after the decisive battle of Hattin, before sacking Tartous and Latakia and taking Saone after a three-day siege. This in turn provoked the pan-European Third Crusade, which in the 1190s recaptured most of the coastline and in 1192 secured access for pilgrims to the Holy Sepulchre; in 1227 Jerusalem was handed back by treaty to the Crusaders, though it returned to Muslim hands in 1244.

THE MAMELUKES (1260–1516)

Following a palace coup in Cairo, in 1260 the Ayyubids were replaced in Syria by the Egyptian **Mamelukes**, who had been an elite of slave troops of central Asian or Turkish origin, specifically raised from a young age to serve their Ayyubid rulers. When they replaced the Ayyubids, they continued to draw their court, administration and army leaders from the same class of slave troops, with each sultan being specially chosen and groomed for the purpose.

Under the military brilliance of **Baibars** (see box on p.82), the Mamelukes managed to inflict a defeat on a foe far more dangerous than the Europeans; the **Mongols** under Genghis Khan had swept into Persia in 1220 and with their taking of Baghdad in 1258, seemed on the point of overwhelming the whole of Syria and Egypt. However, at the Battle of Ain Jalout in Palestine in 1260, the Mamelukes decisively halted this progress and the region breathed a sigh of relief (though the Mongols sporadically wreaked havoc for another couple of centuries, most famously with Tamerlane's destruction of Damascus in 1400). Baibars now turned his attention to the Crusaders; in 1268 Antioch was captured from them, in 1271 Safita and the Crac

des Chevaliers. Baibars' successor Qalaun took Marqab in 1285 and Latakia two years later. The Crusaders lost Tartous in 1291, but a Crusader garrison clung on to Arwad until 1302 – their departure signalling the end of the Crusader presence in the Middle East.

With their enemies out of the way, the Mamelukes enjoyed a long and stable period of rule. Even though their capital was in Cairo, they endowed Aleppo and Damascus with many monuments; some of these survive today, most notably the wealth of **mausoleums** in the Salihiye district of Damascus (see p.95).

THE OTTOMAN PERIOD (1516–1918)

In 1516 the Mamelukes were defeated north of Aleppo by a new Turkish power, the **Ottomans**, bringing Syria once again under rule from Constantinople (by now named Istanbul), though this time as a backwater. The Ottoman Empire was huge, stretching from the Caucasus to Bosnia, and under Suleiman the Magnificent (1520–66), Serbia, Hungary, Rhodes, Mesopotamia and the whole of North Africa save Morocco was added. As a result, Aleppo was opened up to the West and flourished as the main trading city in the Levant. The role of Damascus in administering and accommodating pilgrims from Turkey on the annual hajj did much to further its economy, as witnessed by the khans and souks built at this time.

Under the Ottomans, Syria was divided into three administrative districts (Aleppo, Damascus and Raqqa), each governed by a **pasha**, who was responsible ultimately to Constantinople but nevertheless able to act with a geat deal of independence. Yet the Ottomans' grip over Syria was surprisingly loose, with local families often exercising power in practice. Though the Syrians had to put up with a great deal of inefficiency and corruption from its overwhelmingly indifferent Turkish governors, some important modernizations did occur in the late nineteenth century, such as improvements in civic amenities and sanitation. In 1863, the region's first paved road since Roman times was built to connect Damascus and Beirut; the Beirut–Damascus–Hauran rail link was established in 1894; and in 1908 the Hedjaz rail line linking Damascus to Medina was inaugurated.

EUROPEAN INTEREST AWAKENS

At the end of the eighteenth century foreign powers, particularly Britain, France and Russia, began to cultivate spheres of influence where they could concentrate their trade. Syria became part of the French orbit, and when in 1831, Syria was occupied by an Egyptian force, the Ottomans and the Western powers reacted by stirring up a Druze rebellion and blockading Beirut with an Anglo-Austrian naval force, forcing an Egyptian evacuation in 1840. As set out in the Anglo-Ottoman Commercial Convention of 1838, Syria was opened to unrestricted European trade – which largely ruined Syria's embryonic manufacturing industry.

In 1860 the **Druze-Christian troubles** in Lebanon spilled over to Damascus; Muslims invaded the Christian quarter and went on a three-day killing spree, destroying all the principal churches and engulfing an estimated 2500 Christians in the flames. The Turkish chief of police even joined in the killing, luring Christians out of hiding with promises of safety and then shooting them. At the end of the massacre the remaining Christian women were driven naked through the streets and sold to the Bedouin. Europe was horrified and demanded action; the Turkish Sultan responded by ordering the immediate execution of 150 people, including the city's governor and chief of police, who were strung up in the streets. Lebanon was subsequently declared to be a separately administered state within the Turkish empire – the origins of the modern Lebanese state.

THE END OF OTTOMAN RULE

In the late nineteenth century the **French** made increasing inroads into Syria after extending considerable loans to the Ottoman authorities; as a result, ports were built to open up the Syrian market, much to the detriment of local producers. This led to a certain amount of anti-European and anti-Ottoman feeling among the Arab elite, and at the start of the twentieth century a number of societies had sprung up in Aleppo, Beirut and Damascus advocating **Syrian independence**.

Widespread Arab nationalism emerged after 1914, when Damascus was made the general headquarters of German and Turkish forces in the Middle East. Turkish indifference and incompetence aggravated food shortages during World War I, leading to starvation, the outbreak of a number of serious epidemics, and an intensification of anti-Turkish feeling. In 1916 an **Arab revolt** broke out, encouraged by the British, which was immediately answered by the hanging of 21 Arab nationalists in Damascus and Beirut on May 6; the places of execution are now commemorated as Martyrs' Square in each city, and the anniversary as Martyrs' Day. The Arab revolt is best known today in the West for the role in it played by T.E. Lawrence, "of Arabia" (see box on p.134).

THE FRENCH MANDATE (1918–45)

British troops entered Damascus on October 1, 1918 alongside the Arab forces of **Emir Feisal** of Mecca. The British had led the Arabs to believe that the defeat of Turkey would lead to the Arabs being granted a state; however, under the secret 1916 **Sykes-Picot treaty** the British had already agreed a partition of the Middle East with France. Furthermore, the 1917 **Balfour declaration** intimated British support for the creation of a Jewish homeland in the region.

On Feisal's return from the Paris Peace Conference of May 1919, his supporters immediately organized elections wherever possible; a parliamentary government was even set up, with Feisal being declared **king of Syria**. However, at a conference in San Remo, Italy, the French and British partition of the Middle East was confirmed, with Britain handed **mandates** over Palestine and Jordan, and France over Lebanon and Syria. In theory the mandates were designed to bring these former Ottoman territories to full independence under the supervision of the great powers as soon as possible; in reality, however, the difference between mandates and colonies was hard to distinguish.

The French immediately attempted to divide and rule, carving Syria up into three districts, with Lebanon being treated as a fourth. Heavy censorship was imposed, printing presses were confiscated, theatres were closed and the *Service des Renseignements* was set up, precursor of the modern Syrian intelligence service, the Mukhabarat. When confronted with local **resistance** in October 1925 the French shelled Hama, killing over three hundred people. A Druze revolt in the Hauran, which spread to Damascus, led to the French doing the same to the capital in October 1925 and February and May 1926; several neighbourhoods, including those around the Hamidiye Souk, were destroyed as a result, and around three thousand people died.

The continued rebellion, now taking the form of a series of strikes, eventually produced a more conciliatory line from the French. In 1936, following the British granting of some autonomy to Egypt and full independence to Iraq, the newly elected left-wing Popular Front government in France drafted a treaty providing for Syrian independence (though with French consultation on foreign policy). This was ratified by the Syrian parliament, but not by the French government before its fall from power, when it was replaced by a right-wing cabinet anxious to maintain control over its Middle Eastern possessions, especially with the new prospect of oil in the northeast of Syria.

German aggression in Europe led France to cede the **Hatay** region (including Antakya, the old Roman capital of Syria) to Turkey in 1939 in an attempt to ensure Turkish neutrality in the event of a future war. The Hatay had been declared an autonomous state in 1937, and parliamentary elections had been fixed to ensure a Turkish majority – despite the fact that they were outnumbered by Arabs and Armenians in the region. (Syrians are still aggrieved by this chain of events to this day, and maps published in the country depict the Hatay as part of Syria.) In 1940 France fell to Germany, and the following year Syria was invaded by Allied forces, with the mandate being placed under Free French control.

Syria's economy stagnated under the French mandate, but a modern administrative system was introduced, many roads and public buildings were built and a state education system was founded, along with a university in Damascus. Mains water and electricity were introduced to all major Syrian towns, and irrigation and reforestation projects set up; indeed the land area under cultivation increased by some fifty percent, while the population rose from two to three-and-a-half million. More significant for today's visitor was the creation of a department of antiquities to preserve and administer the country's architectural heritage; most notable is its work at Apamea, the Crac des Chevaliers and Palmyra.

INDEPENDENCE AND THE RISE OF THE BA'ATH PARTY

At the end of World War II, Syria's **independence** was finally proclaimed and the country

was admitted into the United Nations, though French forces did not finally leave until April 1946; indeed in 1945 there was some renewed French bombing of Damascus in response to a Syrian reluctance to sign a new Franco-Syrian treaty as a precondition to withdrawal.

The 1948 **Arab-Israeli conflict** was a reaction by the Arabs to the United Nations General Assembly's voting to partition Palestine into an Arab and a Jewish state, and an expression of their refusal to recognize the existence of the state of Israel. The subsequent **defeat** of the Arab powers led to great internal political instability in Syria, and 1949 witnessed three separate military coups in the country; free elections were not held again until 1954, and the army remained the single most important force in Syrian politics.

During the early 1950s, in response to American backing of Israel, Syria developed close ties with the **Soviet Union**; the United States attempted to destabilize the Syrian government by dumping wheat stocks into Italy and Greece, Syria's major export markets, but the disclosure in 1957 of an American plot to install a pro-Western military dictatorship in Syria only served to push the country into the arms of a newly emerging voice of Arab nationalism, Egypt's Gamal Abdel-Nasser.

THE BA'ATH PARTY

Nasser's rise coincided in Syria with that of the **Ba'ath Party**, which was dedicated to the creation of a unified Arab state. The party was founded in 1941 by two young Syrians, **Michel Aflaq** and **Salah al-Din Bitar**, the former a Christian, the latter a Muslim; both had discovered socialism while they were students in Paris in the early 1930s. Upon returning to Syria, Aflaq and Bitar began careers as teachers, also taking an active interest in domestic politics; in 1935 they helped found and edit a left-wing journal noted for its challenging articles on the major social, political and literary questions of the day. In 1942 both gave up teaching to engage in full-time politics; 1946 saw the first publication of the party newspaper (*Al-Ba'ath*), and the first party congress was held the following year.

Aflaq put forward three essential tenets of the Ba'ath movement – **Arab unity**, **freedom** and **socialism**. To him, the struggle for Arab unity was not simply a question of throwing off political oppression but also one of inspiring a comprehensive rebirth of Arab culture, character and society: to "explain to ourselves and to the nation something more profound than politics – namely the Arab mind and soul". Personal as well as national freedom was seen as essential for the deepening of the nation's moral and intellectual life, and socialism was regarded as the ideal social order which would allow the Arab people ultimately to fulfil themselves. Thus the three tenets were fused into one somewhat mystical alliance. Notable by its absence is any mention of Islam – Aflaq tended to view Islam more as "an expression of Arab genius" than as a method of ordering society.

Although Aflaq's speeches were criticized by some as being mere woolly rhetoric – inspirational but vague in terms of detailed social and economic policy, by 1954 the Ba'ath Party had six thousand registered members. It was the elections of that year that marked the entry of the party into mainstream Syrian politics; two years later the Ba'ath Party tasted power for the first time, as part of a government of national unity.

UNION WITH EGYPT

In February 1958 a referendum in Syria approved formal union with Egypt and the formation of the **United Arab Republic** (UAR). The new country was to have one president and cabinet, but two separate councils ruling Syria and Egypt. However, the Ba'ath had overlooked the authoritarian nature of Nasser's regime; upon union, all important decisions affecting Syria were taken within Nasser's immediate private circle and soon Syria lost all control over its own affairs. The union's economic policy merely extended inappropriate Egyptian policies to Syria, with disastrous consequences, and nationalization and redistribution of private enterprises proved unpopular with Syrian merchants and businessmen. Soon locals began to complain of the stifling of Syrian trade and manufacturing, and of unfair competition from their Egyptian counterparts; rumours were rife that Syria was full of Egyptian spies and secret police, and that the country was being flooded with Egyptian peasants.

DISORDER AFTER UNION COLLAPSES

Nasser's nationalization decrees of July 1961 proved to be the final straw for the UAR. On

September 28 of that year, Syria was taken out of the union by a military **putsch** led by Abd al-Karim Hahlawi. The reforms of the UAR era were rescinded in Syria, and there was a period of **political infighting** and stagnation, which in 1963 allowed a coup by the military committee of the Ba'ath Party. Nationalization of banks and insurance companies was immediately reintroduced, and a land law was implemented limiting the size of private holdings.

The following year a number of the larger industrial firms in Aleppo and Homs were taken under government ownership, a new labour law protecting workers' rights was passed and a General Peasants' Union formed. These moves provoked demonstrations and rioting in the major cities, which led to a power struggle within the Ba'ath Party between moderates and extremists. The latter emerged on top in February 1966, when General Salah Jadid became president with the backing of the commander of the air force, **Hafez al-Assad**, a member of the Alawite minority; many of the moderates in the party, including Aflaq, were arrested. A **command economy** was introduced and communists were included in the cabinet, provoking further demonstrations in 1967, when the regime reacted by using its workers' militia to restore order.

THE SIX-DAY WAR

In June 1967, Israel launched the **Six-Day War**, in retaliation for incursions made by Syrian guerrillas in the Golan Heights, Egypt's closure of the Red Sea to Israeli shipping and the signing of a mutual defence pact between Egypt and Jordan. Israeli troops, in a lightning pre-emptive military action, captured the West Bank from Jordan, Gaza and the Sinai peninsula from Egypt, and the **Golan Heights** from Syria.

Apart from leaving Syria with a bloody nose, the war severely harmed the country economically, as Israeli air strikes had targeted large factories and the Homs oil refinery. The loss of the Golan Heights was also a massive dent to the Syrian regime's prestige, prompting yet more protests during 1968 and 1969, largely organized by Islamists reacting to the perceived atheism of the regime. Extremists and pragmatists – the latter led by Assad, then Defence Minister – fought for power in the next couple of years. Assad, reinforced by the widespread popularity of measures relaxing import restrictions and subsidizing private factories, was able to bring off a coup in November 1970, becoming president the following year.

SYRIA UNDER HAFEZ AL-ASSAD

The presidency of **Hafez al-Assad**, which lasted until his death from a heart attack in June 2000, aged 69, was to a large extent defined by the scars of the Six-Day War; it was upon his dealings with Israel that his reputation for being a shrewd, determined operator was largely founded. Although Assad was careful not to engage the Israelis in a full-scale conflict after the Yom Kippur war of 1973, his intervention during the Lebanese civil war and support for the Palestinians made him a constant thorn in the Israelis' side. His repeatedly stated refusal to make any peace without the full return of the Golan Heights and the conclusion of separate deals with the Lebanese and Palestinians not only enhanced his reputation as a pan-Arab leader but also restored to Syria much of the dignity lost during the 1967 debacle.

Assad's calculated participation in **Operation Desert Storm** against the occupying Iraqis in Kuwait is another case in point. Despite some popular support for Iraq at home, Assad reasoned that by joining the alliance he could not only help teach his old adversary Saddam a lesson but also gain US goodwill. This was especially valuable to Syria – which had hitherto been within the Soviet orbit – in the wake of the realignment in Soviet foreign policy under Gorbachev, rendering continued Soviet support for Syria much less likely. In the event, Syrian troops didn't participate in any fighting, but the rewards were indeed forthcoming: three billion dollars' worth of aid from Saudi Arabia, a new relationship with Washington and an American blind eye to Syria's dominance in Lebanon.

Against Assad's steadfastness in foreign policy must be set a lack of development at home, where – despite some attempts at economic liberalization in the late 1980s and early 1990s – the **economy** largely stagnated under government mismanagement; corruption and cronyism were two charges frequently levied at a ruling elite which had grown wealthy on the back of Syria's small-scale oil exports and the exploitation of drugs grown in the Bekaa Valley in Lebanon under the auspices of Syrian troops.

There was also a darker side to his presidency, for Assad allowed little room for people to

express their grievances against the regime. Ironically, the president who began his rule with a tour around his country to meet the population at first hand was hardly ever seen in public following an attempt on his life in 1980; in the wake of this, Syria became a virtual **police state**.

INTERNAL DISSENT AND REPRESSION

Regarded as a liberal at the time of his rise to power, Assad initially set out to broaden the basis of his support with further political and economic reforms: food prices were cut, restrictions on travel and trade revoked, the security forces purged and political prisoners freed. In 1970 he took the ostensibly democratic step of creating the **National People's Assembly**, whose members were first elected by popular vote in 1972; they were supposed to represent the people's voice, but turned out to be a rubber-stamping body with little authority to debate major political and economic issues. A system of locally elected councils was also created, but with memories of the 1955–58 chaos still fresh in his mind, Assad ensured real power lay with the president and his small circle of trusted advisors.

The first rumblings of discontent with Assad's rule came in 1973 when the publication of a draft of Syria's new constitution provoked rioting by Islamists. Not only did the proposed constitution not put forward a state religion, but it did not even stipulate that the head of state should be a Muslim; there was of course the issue of whether Assad himself, an Alawite, could be said to be a Muslim, a question quickly resolved in Assad's favour (and at his behest) by a religious decree. A clause to the effect that the head of state should be Muslim was rapidly inserted, and Assad's constitution was endorsed by the population at large in a referendum in March 1973 – the fifth time Syrians were called to vote in three years, showing just how keen Assad was to legitimize his rule.

However, during the late 1970s, Assad's regime started to become increasingly unpopular: the government was increasingly regarded as corrupt and Alawite-dominated, Syria's military deployment in Lebanon was proving to be expensive and ill-considered, and the arrival of Lebanese refugees in Syria deepened a severe housing crisis. In the forefront of opposition were the **Muslim Brotherhood**, an extremist movement strongest in Aleppo and Hama, who advocated replacing the regime with an Islamic state. They assassinated several major Ba'ath Party figures during the late 1970s and early 1980s, and their city-centre bombings killed hundreds of civilians (more than three hundred in Aleppo alone between 1979 and 1981).

Opposition to the regime also encompassed many non-violent secular groups and Muslims who were not supporters of the Brotherhood. In March 1980 a one-day national **general strike** was organized by Damascene lawyers and supported by numerous professional associations calling for political reform. Many businesses, schools and universities shut down, while in some cities security forces attempted forcibly to ensure shops remained open, which led to violent clashes in the streets. In the days immediately following, the medical, engineers' and bar association councils were dissolved, and hundreds of activists were arrested. In the same month a hundred demonstrators who had set fire to the Ba'ath Party headquarters in Jish ash-Shughur were executed.

Due in large part to the growing influence Assad's brother Rifaat had within the government, an increasingly hard line was taken with the opposition, and from April 1980 to February 1981 Aleppo was virtually a battleground between the army and the Muslim Brotherhood; a special prison camp was even set up in the citadel for the insurgents. All in all between one and two thousand people were killed in the city by security forces in response to attacks on government troops or buildings; on several occasions it was reported that males over the age of 15 were simply rounded up, marched to an open space and shot – 83 died like this on August 11, 1980 after an attack on a patrol.

In June 1980 Assad himself was the victim of an **assassination attempt**; the following morning around five hundred inmates of Tadmor prison were shot dead by army troops, and then on July 7 membership of the Muslim Brotherhood was made punishable by death. In April 1981, following the ambush of a security checkpoint on the outskirts of Hama, government troops killed at least 350 men at random in the city, leaving their bodies in the streets.

On February 3, 1982 an army unit in **Hama** was attacked, with the deaths of around twenty soldiers; the government immediately sent in troops who were met by a fierce response that effectively became a **general uprising**. Within hours over seventy leading Ba'athists were killed and the city was effectively out of control. At the time, central Hama was a confusing maze of tiny streets, which would have been very difficult to fight in, so instead the government decided to subject the city centre to massive shelling before sending troops in to finish the job; at least five thousand fatalities are thought to have resulted.

In the aftermath of this unrest came the imposition of a **state of emergency** (still in force at time of writing), with widespread **human rights abuses**. Arrests took place on the mere suspicion of opposition sympathies or any kind of link to outlawed political organizations, principally the Muslim Brotherhood, the Communist Party and non-official wings of the Ba'ath Party. People were arrested without charge and often without a subsequent trial or any legal representation – even on occasions being held in prison long after the imposed sentence had been served.

Amnesty International has alleged that torture has been used frequently by the Syrian security forces, and that deaths in custody have occurred through torture, suicide or inadequate medical attention. The establishment of a widespread network of informers meant that Syrians became ultra-cautious about talking of domestic politics, and it was assumed, rightly or not, that phones were tapped and mail opened. The government rigidly suppressed books, films and other media which it deemed to contain anti-state (or pro-Israel) propaganda; foreign newspapers and magazines appeared with all articles relating to Syria carefully cut out and foreign books about contemporary Syrian or Middle Eastern history were banned.

In the later years of Hafez al-Assad's rule the government became much less paranoid; satellite TV and fax machines were legalized and there were **amnesties** – in 1992 over two thousand political prisoners were released, and in 1995 another 1200 were set free. Yet at the time of Hafez al-Assad's death an estimated two thousand political prisoners were still languishing in Syrian jails.

FOREIGN POLICY: ISRAEL AND LEBANON

From the start of his presidency, Hafez al-Assad was determined to avenge the losses of the Six-

Day War. On October 6, 1973 – the Jewish Day of Atonement, or **Yom Kippur** – at 2pm, Egypt and Syria launched a co-ordinated **attack** upon Israel. The offensive was spectacular and successful at first, and within the first 48 hours Israel had lost over 500 tanks. However, whereas Assad was committed to winning back all the territory lost in the 1967 war, Sadat was content with regaining enough territory in the Sinai to strengthen his bargaining hand. Once they'd crossed the Suez Canal and arrived in the Sinai, the Egyptian troops simply dug in, leaving the Syrians to face the full might of the Israeli air force. It was not until October 14 that the Egyptians finally continued their offensive, though by then it was too little too late. A ceasefire was agreed by Israel and Egypt on October 22, but the Syrians kept fighting until May 1974; relations between Sadat and Assad plummeted to an all-time low in January 1974 when Egypt signed a bilateral disengagement agreement with Israel; in May of that year a Syrian–Israeli agreement providing for the return of **Quneitra** in the Golan Heights was signed.

Armed attacks against the Israelis by Palestinian groups in Lebanon and the subsequent Israeli reprisals contributed to the outbreak of **civil war in Lebanon** in April 1975. As Syria regards it as vital that Lebanon be both stable and reasonably well disposed to Syrian interests, Assad was left in a difficult position: to intervene might provoke Israel to become embroiled, but there was a chance the Israelis would get directly involved anyway in view of the Palestinian challenge it was facing from within Lebanese territory. In the event, Assad sent Syrian troops into Lebanon, where they soon found themselves embroiled in small-scale clashes with the Palestinians who were supposedly, in the grander scheme of things, their allies. Indeed, Syria's intervention initially provoked great hostility in the Arab world, where many believed that Assad was simply carrying out a personal vendetta against the leader of the Palestine Liberation Organization (**PLO**), Yasser Arafat, a man he regarded as a dangerous loose cannon. In the wider scheme of things, however, the effect of Syrian and Israeli intervention in Lebanon was to transfer their own conflict to Lebanon.

In June 1982, in response to the attempted murder by Palestinian gunmen of the Israeli ambassador to the United Kingdom, Israel started advancing on PLO positions in Lebanon. Syrian soldiers fought doggedly to prevent the Israelis reaching the Beirut–Damascus road while Assad flew to Moscow to plead for help from the Soviet leadership. Brezhnev contacted Reagan who put pressure on the Israelis to agree to a ceasefire. This they did, only to ignore it immediately and advance on Beirut, bombarding it by air, land and sea until an evacuation plan was hatched by the Americans, allowing ten thousand Palestinian fighters – and stranded Syrian troops – to leave the city.

After the withdrawal of Israeli troops from Beirut following the arrival of a multinational force, Assad concentrated his efforts on providing assistance to Lebanese guerrilla fighters and the Lebanese Shiite militia **Hezbollah**. Violence continued in and around Beirut, and in 1985 the Israeli army pulled back to a self-styled "security zone" along the Lebanese border. Assad's support for Hezbollah led to Syria being labelled a sponsor of **terrorism** by the United States and loosely or otherwise implicated in a number of international incidents, including the 1988 bombing of an American airliner over Lockerbie in Scotland, and the attempt by a Jordanian to blow up an Israeli El-Al plane in London; the latter event led to Britain breaking off diplomatic relations with Syria in 1986.

Syria's rehabilitation only came with its participation in the Gulf War, in the aftermath of which Assad was able to consolidate his position in Lebanon and force the explusion of the pro-Israeli Maronite leader Michel Aoun. Within months of the end of the Gulf War, the first Bush administration moved to set the **Arab-Israeli peace negotiations** back in motion, leading to the **Madrid conference** of October 1991, at which Syrian and Israeli negotiators met face to face for the first time in forty years. Between August 1992 and March 1996, the Israeli governments of Yitzhak Rabin and Shimon Peres were involved in almost constant peace negotiations with Syria, but despite the agreements with Jordan and with the PLO at that time, no breakthrough was made with the Syrians. Assad, who never met with Israeli leaders himself, stated repeatedly that the price of peace was full Israeli withdrawal from the Golan Heights to the lines of June 4, 1967, and that any agreement with Syria should also encompass agreements with Lebanon and the Palestinians.

The assassination of Yitzhak Rabin in November 1995 and Peres' loss of power to hardliner Benjamin Netanyahu in Israel's May 1996 elections in effect put Israeli–Syrian negotiations on hold. Assad was either too tired or too ill to make much progress with Israel in the last few months before his death; however, just before he died, Assad did witness one of the primary objectives of his foreign policy, the **withdrawal** of Israeli troops from Lebanon.

BASHAR AL-ASSAD

Upon Hafez al-Assad's death, the Syrian parliament immediately met to change the constitution, lowering the minimum age for the president to 34 so that **Bashar**, his second son, could assume power. However, there was an immediate challenge to Bashar's succession, from his uncle, **Rifaat**, most notorious for his part in the 1982 destruction of Hama.

Following Hafez al-Assad's suspected heart attack in 1984, Rifaat had briefly attempted to seize power, and had been banished for his sins; within two days of his brother's passing, Rifaat announced that he wanted to return to Syria and bring democracy to the country. However, in the months before his death Hafez al-Assad had taken steps finally to remove Rifaat from the power equation – the military elite was purged of his suspected supporters, Rifaat was stripped of his nominal title of vice-president, and in October 1999 his marina in Latakia – which had been used as a virtual free port for the export of drugs and import of arms – was raided and closed by government forces, with the deaths of around twenty people. Rifaat's announcement of his desire to come home was greeted in Damascus with the response that Rifaat would be arrested if he attempted to attend his brother's funeral, and – having had his power base in the country disposed of – the new self-proclaimed champion of democracy wisely decided to stay away.

PROSPECTS FOR REFORM

Though Bashar had been groomed for power since the death of his elder brother Bassel in 1994, the new head of state was very much an unknown quantity not just to Western countries but also to many inside Syria; Bashar had hitherto remained largely in the background, although his face had been appearing alongside those of his brother and his father on posters around the country. Thus it was that Bashar's use of his inaugural address to speak of the need for **reform** and greater openness came as a surprise to many.

However, Bashar faces some real problems if he seriously intends to **modernize** Syria; the country lacks a sophisticated banking system and has no large-scale privately owned firms and very little foreign investment. Before coming to power, Bashar had been heavily involved in an **anti-corruption drive** which led to former intelligence chief Bashir Najjar being sentenced to twelve years for embezzlement and former prime minister Mahmoud Zohbi committing suicide while under a similar investigation. Yet it is not individuals but the system that is fundamentally at fault: state salaries are fixed at around US$100 a month, creating fertile conditions for bribery and corruption, while an elite core of officials seems to have been the main beneficiaries of the foreign aid Syria has received from its wealthy Arab neighbours. Effective reform in Syria requires tackling the drugs trade emanating from Lebanon, opening up the economy and radically reforming the way taxes are levied (presently, the black economy rules in Syria). What is uncertain is how far Bashar can go without upsetting the very elite upon whom his power rests, and how far he can liberalize the economy without prompting a desire for fundamental political change from the populace.

PROSPECTS FOR PEACE AND STABILITY

On the face of it, it's hard to see if and how there might be a **challenge** to Bashar's leadership. Following the repression that characterized his father's regime, there is now no organized opposition in Syria, and the Syrian business community does not appear to be greatly politicized – indeed it's not clear how widespread the desire for democratic change is within Syria as a whole. There is of course the danger of a military coup, the army having underpinned every Syrian government since the late 1940s, so Bashar cannot afford to be seen as a weak player on the Middle Eastern stage. On the other hand, Bashar is of a generation of Syrians too young to have personal memories of war with Israel, and it is thus possible that time will see a slightly more flexible approach from Syrian peace negotiators.

RELIGION

Unlike many Arab countries Syria, a socialist state, does not have an official state religion (though constitutionally the head of state must, in theory at least, be a Muslim); Syria's governing Ba'ath Party has made a conscious effort to keep separate the realms of religion and politics. The place of religion in the country today has largely been defined by the late President Hafez al-Assad, a member of the Alawite sect, who deliberately set out to create a cohesive state founded on modern notions of citizenship, emphasizing a pan-Arab stance, specifically in the face of the Israeli threat. His regime's perceived atheism has at times prompted protests, and even riots, from Islamists, most notoriously in the late 1970s and early 1980s, which were brutally put down (see p.307).

Around ninety percent of Syrians are **Muslim** or members of Muslim-derived groups (such as the **Alawites**, from which the Assad clan are drawn); **Christians** account for the remaining tenth or so of the population. Historically there has also been an important **Jewish** community in Damascus; however, only a tiny number of them remain today thanks to emigration (and to the restrictions they faced in Syria in the wake of the foundation of Israel; see p.316). Generally though, relations among Syria's religious groups are good; the mutual respect and tolerance shown by members of the different faiths towards one another is one of the most notable aspects of the country.

ISLAM

The Arabic word **Islam** means "submission to God". The central tenets of the faith are that there is only one God (in Arabic, **Allah**) and that **Mohammed** was the last in a line of prophets which includes Adam, Abraham, Moses, Joseph, David and Jesus. Muslims believe that all the monotheistic religions are essentially the same, but that the teachings of the earlier prophets were distorted by their followers; furthermore, they hold that Mohammed was chosen by God to purify His message and that the Koran is God's last word to mankind.

MOHAMMED

Mohammed was born in **Mecca** (in present-day Saudi Arabia) in 570. His father died before he was born, his mother when he was 6, and he was looked after first by his grandfather and then by an uncle. Mohammed first started to receive revelations from God – via the angel Gabriel – in around the year 610; these were subsequently set down in what became Islam's holy book, the **Koran**. After he had been receiving these revelations for two years, Mohammed began to preach from the top of Mt Safa in Mecca, instructing members of his tribe, the **Quraysh**, to give up the worship of idols. Initially he was assumed to have gone mad and was treated with much derision, but some important early converts were made, including Hamzah, a great warrior, and Abu Bakr, an important businessman. Mohammed then caused a real stir in Mecca when he instructed his followers to pray at the **Ka'ba** – venerated by the Quraysh as a temple of considerable antiquity. At the time many gods were worshipped at the Ka'ba, and Mohammed's insistence that the false idols be removed inflamed many tempers. The leaders of the Quraysh attempted to mediate by allowing Mohammed to pray to his deity alongside all the others, but Mohammed refused to compromise. The subsequent persecution of Mohammed and his followers resulted in the prophet leading his faithful to exile in **Medina** in 622.

Upon entering Medina, the Prophet agreed to a charter of peaceful coexistence with the predominantly Jewish tribes living there, but by the mid-620s the Muslims began to clash again with the Quraysh over issues of trade, and these disputes eventually escalated into a full-scale conflict. A succession of battles were fought against the Quraysh which resulted in the conquest of Mecca in 630, and after Mohammed's death in 632 Muslim-held territory expanded dramatically; in 636 Byzantine forces were routed by Muslim forces at the **Battle of Yarmouk River** in southern Syria (see box on p.135), and by 656 the whole of Persia was under Muslim control.

THE KORAN

The **Koran** is the holy book of Islam, as sporadically revealed to the Prophet Mohammed in a series of trances he experienced from around 610 until shortly before his death in 632. The word *qur'aan* means "recitation", and Muslims regard the book's contents not as Mohammed's words but as God's.

Mohammed remained illiterate all his life, and so after receiving a revelation he would tell his scribes where each particular verse should go. The Koran's 114 **surahs**, or chapters, were not revealed in the order presented; during his final year Mohammed recited the whole of the Koran in its final order all the way through. Those *surah*s revealed before the Prophet's flight to Mecca tend to be shorter and to deal with the essence of the faith, whereas those revealed subsequently tend to concern themselves with social, economic and political matters; this mirrors Mohammed's early role as a mystic and his later metamorphosis into the leader of a community of people.

It is not just the text of the Koran which is integral to the Muslim faith, but also everything that Mohammed said and did (as well as everything he allowed or permitted) – though Mohammed did not claim infallibility for himself, beyond his transmission of the Koran. For example, the injunction to pray and the times of prayer are mentioned in the Koran, but the postures adopted in prayer come from Mohammed's own practice. Any instructions that come from Mohammed rather than the Koran are referred to as **sunnah**, the sources of which are the **hadith** – basically collected sayings of the Prophet and reports of his behaviour. The *sunnah* and the Koran together are the basis for **shariah**, Islamic law.

The interpretation of both the Koran and the *hadith* has become quite involved. The former contains hidden meanings, allegory and symbolism, and so a vast literature of interpretation has been produced, as people struggle to adapt the words set down in the seventh century to an increasingly complicated modern world; the *hadith* are derived from contemporaneous accounts of Mohammed's life, a fact which led to the emergence of a rigorous science of *hadith* criticism, aimed at determining what was reliable information and what was made up (or exaggerated). Two collections of *hadith*s that survived this vetting (compiled by Ismail al-Bukhari and Muslim ibn al-Hajjaj, and published in the ninth century) are given almost the same weight and importance as the Koran itself.

THE FIVE PILLARS

The **five pillars** of Islam form the moral basis of a way of life for both the individual Muslim and the Islamic community as a whole. The first of these, **shahadah**, is to bear witness; for this, Muslims use a standard credo which translates as "There is no god but God and Mohammed is his messenger." Initially all that anyone has to do to become a Muslim is to say these words with sincerity.

Salah, meaning prayer, is usually performed in a **mosque**, the Muslim house of worship (though prayers can be performed outside too – in Muslim countries, it is not unusual to come

---

THE MOSQUE

The **mosque** (*masjid* or *jaami'*) is the Muslim house of worship, designed originally on the plan of Mohammed's house in Medina. The mosque interior tends usually to be quite bare so as not to distract the worshippers. All mosques are built so that one wall faces the direction of Mecca (*qiblah*). In the middle of the *qiblah* wall is a niche, the **mihrab**, marking the direction all are to pray in. Beside the *mihrab* is a raised platform, known as the **minbar**, where the **imam** stands when he is leading prayers or delivering his Friday sermon (*khutbah*). The precise origins of the **minaret** are unclear; some authorities suggest it was based on the lighthouse at Alexandria, others that the minaret emerged from the traditional Syrian architectural practice of placing a small tower at the corners of large buildings. Damascus's Umayyad Mosque is known to represent one of the earliest examples of the use of the minaret; indeed it wasn't for another couple of centuries that the practice of attaching a minaret to a mosque became standard.

Muslim architects also adapted the Roman/Byzantine use of the **dome** for a number of different buildings, and the Ayyubid period saw the start of the use of **muqarnas** – arrays of scallop-shaped recesses – to decorate the area where the dome met the corners of the interior walls; *muqarnas* decoration was then later adapted to beautify entrance portals. The use of **ablaq** stonework – alternating bands of different-coloured stone – in mosques and madrasas emerged in Syria in the thirteenth century, and became one of the architectural signatures of the Mameluke and Ottoman periods.

across someone prostrating themselves in worship by the side of a road or in a hotel lobby). Prayer involves specific rituals, the most important of which is the act of purification through ritual cleansing (*taharah*), a mental and physical preparation for worship. The mouth is rinsed out, water is sniffed into the nostrils, and then the face, head, ears, neck, feet and lastly the hands and forearms are washed; every mosque has an ablution fountain for this purpose. The faithful are summoned to prayer by the **muezzin**, whose call starts and ends with the words "God is great" and includes the *shahadah*; in times gone by the muezzin would have made his call from the top of the mosque's minaret at every prayer, but nowadays he is often replaced by a tape recording. Worshippers remove their shoes before entering the prayer hall; once inside they face towards Mecca and recite their prayers, which often include the first chapter of the Koran and take only take a few minutes to complete. Muslims pray five times a day – at dawn (the *fajr* prayer), midday (*zuhr*), afternoon (*'asr*), evening (*maghrib*) and night (*'isha*). At midday on Fridays, there is a congregational prayer together with a sermon by the **imam**, who often also acts as a spiritual advisor for the community. Anyone may lead prayers if they are able to recite from the Koran; whenever two or more people are gathered to pray, the one with the greater knowledge of the Koran will function as the *imam*. The term *imam* is also used by the Shiah to refer specifically to those who succeeded Mohammed as leader of the world's Islamic community.

Zakah refers to the giving of **alms** (though the word itself means "purity"); it is thought that alms-giving purifies the heart of greed and miserliness, while receiving donations purifies it of envy and hatred. Charity is also considered important in engendering a sense of responsibility to others, and so is both an act of worship and a service to the community. In Syria, *zakah* is not a tax collected by the state (though it was under the caliphs); rather it is down to the individual to give.

Sawm, meaning **fasting**, takes place during **Ramadan**, the ninth month of the lunar cycle when Mohammed first received his revelations. From dawn to sunset during Ramadan Muslims must refrain from consuming food and drink, smoking and sexual relations. Shops and offices tend to operate shorter hours during Ramadan; at sunset people hurry home to break the fast, when a substantial meal is served, often a major family occasion. Often families will also stay up all night and partake in a large breakfast before dawn.

The last of the pillars is the **hajj**, the **pilgrimage to Mecca** which occurs during the month of Dhul Hijja. All Muslims are expected to perform the pilgrimage at least once in their lifetime if they have sufficient means.

SUNNIS AND SHIITES

The cause of the divide between Islam's two great denominations, the **Sunnis** and **Shiites**, was essentially political rather than religious: Mohammed died leaving no male heir, and without naming a successor to lead the Muslim community. The two obvious candidates to fill the power vacuum were Ali, the husband of the Prophet's daughter Fatimah, and Abu Bakr, the father of one of Mohammed's wives; it was the latter who eventually took the title of **caliph**. Abu Bakr died in 634 and was succeeded by Umar, then Othman, a member of the Umayyad family. When Othman was murdered in 656 Ali became caliph, but immediately he faced a rebellion by the Umayyad governor of Syria, Moawiya. In 661, when Ali was assassinated, Moawiya declared himself caliph in his place. It is this political infighting which is essentially the source of the great schism between the majority Sunnis and the Shiites, as the latter regard Ali as their first legitimate **imam**. The martyrdom of Ali's son Hussein at Kerbala in Iraq, after an abortive rebellion he led against the Umayyads, only reinforced the Shiahs' view of themselves as an oppressed minority within Islam, loyal to the true succession of the Prophet and struggling to restore just rule – a state of mind that persists to this day.

Though Sunnis and Shiites do not differ greatly on fundamental religious issues, they do have differences of approach. Whereas Sunnis attach far more importance to the practice of *taqlid*, the strict following of the *sunnah* (whence the name "Sunni"), Shiites place great store by the teachings of certain key individuals to discover the Koran's hidden, esoteric meaning. Shiites also attach great importance to the visiting of saints' shrines and to the celebration of the anniversaries of their births and deaths.

SUFIS

Sufism is not a separate sect but rather a religious movement within both Sunni and Shiah Islam; while *shariah* represents the exterior way for the individual to order life so as to follow the will of God, Sufism represents the interior path by which an individual might come to know God. According to the early Sufis, the way to achieve this knowledge was to purify the mind and body by detaching oneself from the distractions of the material world, and then to dedicate one's life to prayer, fasting and meditating on the words of the Koran. The early Sufis became renowned for the simple garments they wore, and the word Sufi is thought to derive from *suf*, the Arabic term for wool.

Many of these early Sufis were outspoken critics of what they saw as the spiritual corruption of the Umayyads. This forthrightness led to some persecution of the Sufis and even some martyrdoms, the most famous being that of the mystic Mansur al-Hallaj in 922. Reconciliation was largely achieved through the works of **Abu Hamid al-Ghazali** (1058–1111), who managed to synthesize Sufi ideas concerning direct religious experience with traditional concepts of law and theology, and so establish a place for the Sufis firmly within the Islamic community. During the twelfth century Sufism became a mass movement, and by the following century the Sufis had become the great missionary force within Islam. They developed one very popular method of allowing believers to experience a form of ecstatic union with God – through the use of song and dance, most famously as practised by **whirling dervishes** (see p.105).

Yet over time the Sufi emphasis on the limitations of reason in the search for a direct experience of God led to the rejection of much Islamic learning, and the spiritual high ground claimed by the early Sufis became lost in a mire of secularism, superstition and ignorance. Their devotion to the arts of music and dance turned into excuses for sensualism and drunkenness, the spiritual heads of the Sufi Orders became feudal landlords in all but name, and Sufi excesses were ultimately blamed as one of the primary causes for the decline of the Islamic movement as a whole from the seventeenth century – so much so that modern reformist movements have done their best to suppress Sufism.

MUSLIM-DERIVED SECTS IN SYRIA

If members of Muslim-derived sects are counted among Syria's Muslims, then **Sunnis** make up around four-fifths of the country's Muslims,

with a small minority of **Shiites**; the rest consist of various sects that have sprung from Shiah Islam, of which the most significant in Syria are the **Alawites**.

ISMAILIS

Most Shiites are so-called Twelvers, because they recognize twelve legitimate successors to Mohammed, believing that the last one, who died in 878, will appear again just before the Day of Judgement. The **Ismailis**, a subsect of the Shiah, are followers of an alternative seventh imam and are thus known as Seveners. Today the Ismailis are mainly to be found in India and Pakistan, with only small pockets in Syria itself (mainly in and around the town of Salamiyeh to the southeast of Hama).

ALAWITES

The **Alawites**, of which the Assad family are members, are an offshoot of the Ismailis. Today the Alawites comprise thirteen percent of Syria's Muslims and make up around two-thirds of the population of the province of Latakia.

They are thought to have been founded in the late ninth century by **Mohammed ibn Nusayr** on the basis of a belief in the divinity of Ali, though the word Alawite (meaning followers of Ali) was not applied to them until the period of the French mandate; prior to this they were known as **Nusayris** after their founder (and the mountains of Syria where they settled consequently known as the Jebel Nusayriya or Ansariya). Centuries of persecution were dramatically reversed during the mandate era when the French created a separate mini-state for the Alawites around Latakia, and with the coming to power of Hafez al-Assad it suddenly became very fashionable to be an Alawite; many members of the community found themselves coming to favour under the regime, which prompted a certain amount of resentment from the population as a whole (as manifested during the great civil unrest of the late 1970s; see p.307). The death of Hafez al-Assad in 2000 prompted some Middle Eastern observers to predict an anti-Alawite backlash in Syria from the majority Sunni population, but at the time of writing, things have remained peaceful.

Historically, the Alawites have adopted the doctrine of **taqiyya** – the concealment of one's beliefs in order to survive and as protection against persecution. This, combined with the fact that few of their members even learn the tenets of their faith, has only served to heighten the confusion as to what they do believe; indeed the Alawites are considered heretics by many Sunnis, who have attributed a great number of strange and shocking beliefs to them over the centuries, largely out of ignorance. The Alawite faith is known to encompass teachings from a wide variety of sources, including Zoroastrianism and paganism, and adherents certainly use elements from Christianity, observing many of the Christian festivals.

DRUZE

The **Druze** are essentially another offshoot of the Ismailis. Their existence dates back to two missionaries called Darazi and Hamza ibn Ali, who were sent to southern Lebanon by the Fatimid Caliph Al-Hakim (996–1021) to spread the Ismaili word. Al-Hakim was something of an eccentric ruler, renowned for his persecution of Jews and Christians, who came to believe that he was the incarnation of God. When he disappeared (or more likely was murdered) Hamza developed a separate Druze religion whose central tenet was a belief in Al-Hakim's divinity; Hamza, too, later "disappeared", and Druze believe that he will return along with Al-Hakim at some later date to initiate a golden age. Conversion to or from the religion has not been permitted since 1043, and marriage outside the religion is also forbidden; as a result the Druze are very much a closed group within Syrian society.

The word "Druze" is thought to derive from the name of the preacher Darazi, though the term the Druze use to refer to themselves is *mowahhidoon* ("monotheists"). Although they consider themselves to be the true carriers of Islam, the Druze are regarded as heretics by most other Muslims as their beliefs diverge from Islam at many points. Druze don't pray in mosques but rather in a **khalwa** (usually an ordinary building located on the outskirts of the community), their holy day is Thursday, and they reject all the five pillars of Islam. Central to their doctrines is a belief in **reincarnation** – that all people are reborn as humans and how you act in this life affects your fortune in the next. They even have their own religious texts, and though they hold the Koran to be a sacred text (as indeed they do the Bible), they look upon it as an outer shell holding an inner esoteric meaning.

In the late nineteenth century many Druze retreated to the Hauran following clashes with the Maronite Christian population in Lebanon. During the mandate era French attempts to break down traditional Druze hierarchy and to impose their own administrative order provoked an uprising, assisted by Syrian nationalists, which spread to Damascus; it was only when the French resorted to bombarding both the capital and Sweida that the revolt was quelled. Estimates of how many Druze there are today worldwide vary from anything between 300,000 and 900,000 – most live in the Middle East (southern Lebanon, the Golan and the Hauran mainly), but there are also small communities in Europe and North America, and indeed the US and Canadian Druze even have their own Web sites (*www.druze.com* and *www.druze.net* respectively).

CHRISTIANITY IN SYRIA

The vast majority of Syria's Christians either are **Orthodox** or owe allegiance to Rome through being **Catholic** or **Maronite**. The Orthodox churches split with Rome in 1054, subsequently coming under the Patriarch of Constantinople, though over time some of its member churches again acknowledged the supremacy of the pope. In return, they were allowed to retain their own languages in their services rather than adopt a Latin liturgy, and were given a degree of independence from Rome.

A significant minority among Syrian Christians are the **Armenians** (indeed Armenia was the first Christian nation, the Armenian Orthodox Church having come into being in 301 following the conversion of King Tirdate). Communities of Armenians have lived in Syria for many centuries, though there was a major influx from Turkey following the two genocides in 1894–96 and 1915–21, when up to a million and a half people perished. Today, Syria's Armenians number over 200,000, most of whom are based in Aleppo, though there is also a significant community in Damascus.

THE ORTHODOX

Three branches of the **Eastern Orthodox** Church are represented in Syria: the **Greek Orthodox**, which uses an Arab liturgy; the **Armenian Orthodox**, which uses classical Armenian; and the **Syrian Orthodox**, which uses Syriac (closely related to Aramaic, the

SYRIA'S JEWISH COMMUNITY

The existence of the Dura Europos synagogue, and the fact that the Bible records that St Paul incurred the ire of Damascene Jews by preaching in the city's synagogues nearly two thousand years ago (Acts 9:23 in the New Testament), indicate that today's tiny **Jewish community** in Syria has roots which go back to ancient times. In 1948, when the State of Israel was carved out of land which many Arabs consider to be theirs, there were thirty thousand Jews living in Syria. During the early years of Syrian independence Jews were scapegoated for the perceived wrongs of Israel, a situation which continues today, albeit in a rather less virulent and vindictive manner. In the 1950s thousands of Jews left the country via Lebanon or Turkey, many finding their way to the United States where there is a big Syrian Jewish community. Those Jews who remained had their religion stamped on their ID cards in red and were not allowed to travel more than 4km from their homes without a permit; their rights to own property were also curtailed. This state-sponsored prejudice could not help but encourage armed attacks by Palestinian groups against Jewish homes, and the burning of synagogues in Damascus and Aleppo.

The status of Syrian Jews improved considerably in the 1970s. Encouraged to adopt a more lenient stance by former US Secretary of State Henry Kissinger and President Jimmy Carter, Hafez al-Assad allowed female Jewry to leave for the US to look for potential husbands, and relaxed laws on property ownership and rights of movement. The Syrian Chief Rabbi, Avraham Hamra, developed a close working relationship with Assad, and on one occasion persuaded him to release from imprisonment two Syrian Jews who had broken the law by visiting Israel. In 1992, Assad allowed all remaining Jews to **leave** the country, provided that they did not go to Israel; about 3500 emigrated, mainly for New York, leaving behind a community which now numbers fewer than one hundred.

language Jesus spoke). The last of these broke away from the main Orthodox family in 451 following a theological dispute over the nature of Christ's divinity. Syrian Orthodox claim to be the original church of Antioch, where the followers of Jesus were – according to the New Testament – first referred to as Christians; however, it is in Damascus that the Patriarch of Antioch, the head of the church, has resided since 1959.

CATHOLICS AND MARONITES

The patriarchate of Jerusalem is responsible for Syria's small communities of **Roman Catholics** in Aleppo and western Syria. **Greek Catholics** make up the largest single Catholic community in the country; they are still very much bound to Byzantine tradition and so their diocesan clergy must remain celibate (though priests responsible for rural parishes are allowed to marry). More than half Syria's **Armenian Catholics** live in Aleppo, though the patriarch now resides in Beirut; they use classical Armenian in their services.

Following the preaching of the Jesuits and Capuchins in Aleppo in the seventeenth century, a number of Syrian Orthodox communities were united with Rome and became known as **Syrian Catholics**. They were heavily persecuted by the Syrian Orthodox Church throughout the eighteenth century; it was not until 1782 that Syrian Catholics could function openly enough to appoint a continuous series of patriarchs. Like the Syrian Orthodox, the Syrian Catholics use Syriac in their liturgy, though some services are conducted in Arabic.

The **Maronite church** was founded in the seventh century, basing its doctrine on the teachings of St Maron, a monk who lived near Cyrrhus and died around 410. During the tenth century the Maronites were largely driven out of Syria by the Muslims, and settled in the valleys of Mount Lebanon. The arrival of the Crusaders in the region in the late eleventh century led to improved relations with Rome, and in 1180 the Maronites declared full **union with Rome**. Today the Maronites are still found mainly in Lebanon, though there is also a sizeable community in Aleppo.

ART, CINEMA AND MUSIC

Although Syria by no means has as lively a cultural scene as Lebanon or Egypt, the country – and in particular Damascus – does pride itself on standing at the heart of Arab culture. Here we explore briefly Syria's contributions to art and cinema, following which, in an extract from the *Rough Guide to World Music*, Bill Badley and Zein al-Jundi look at Syria's music scene.

MODERN ART

Surprisingly, Syria has quite a vibrant **modern art** scene; the Damascus and Aleppo Museums both have sizeable sections devoted to contemporary Syrian artists, and Damascus has a number of small private galleries; on the Internet, the work of a selection of Syrian artists can be found at *www.syria-online.com*

The most internationally successful Syrian painter has been expressionist **Fateh Moudarres** (b. 1922), whose canvases, characterized by sombre hues and by the naive – almost tragic – child-like faces that populate them, have been exhibited all over the Middle East, Europe and the United States. The only Syrian artist with a reputation to match his is **Louay Kayyali** (1934–78), who combined expressionism and realism; he derived the majority of his inspiration from the everyday scenes he saw around him. His depiction of the

fishermen of Arwad is one of the highlights of the modern art display in the Damascus Museum.

ORIGINS
Although sculpture, the decorative arts and calligraphy all have long histories in the Middle East, Western notions of painting onto canvas as a distinct artistic medium only arrived in the region in the nineteenth century. The origins of this go back to Napoleon's **invasion of Egypt** in 1798, after which a number of Western artists, writers and intellectuals were attracted to the East, leading to the spread of Western ideas, first to the political and intellectual elite of Cairo, then the region as a whole. The Arab elite soon became very keen to imitate Western lifestyles, and by the late nineteenth century portrait painting had become a flourishing craft in Beirut, Damascus and Aleppo. The most important Syrian painter working during the Ottoman period was **Tawfeek Tarek** (1875–1940), a Damascene who studied painting in Paris and became famed for his portraits, landscapes and use of epic historical subject matter.

During the mandate era, a number of French artists came to Syria to paint or teach, as a result of which Syrian painters became acquainted with the **impressionist** movement. The finest local exponent of impressionism was **Michel Kurche** (1900–73), the subject matter of whose paintings remained firmly within established impressionist parameters (essentially landscapes, portraits and still lifes); however, many other Syrian painters began to demonstrate their opposition to the French occupation of the country by recalling the glories of Arab history – the battles of Hittin and Yarmouk River becoming particular favourite themes.

POST-INDEPENDENCE
The period following the declaration of independence in 1946 saw a great **flourishing** of the artistic and cultural life of Damascus, and a number of talented young painters began to emerge. Three artists of this period are especially worthy of mention, their work being well represented in Damascus's National Museum: **Nasser Shoura** (1920–92), predominantly a painter of landscapes, who developed a daring abstract style through his interest in colour; **Mahmoud Jalal** (1911–75) who spent most of his time recording the day-to-day activities of

ordinary working people, endowing their endeavours with an almost heroic quality; and **Nazeem al-Jaafari** (b. 1918), who adopted a solidly impressionist style for his paintings (landscapes and portraits mainly), though today he is better known for his drawings of the Old City of Damascus.

During the 1950s, the growth of a new assertive Arab nationalism had a major effect on Syrian artists, who increasingly began to look back to the old **Arab traditions** of decorative arts in an effort to forge a distinctive new cultural identity. One of the most important pioneers in this quest was **Adham Ismail** (1923–63), whose *The Porter* (1952), combining Arabesque style with bold, expressionistic colouring, has been lauded as the first true example of a distinctly Syrian form of modern art. **Mamdouh Kashlan** (b. 1929) tackled subject matter from everyday Arab life, depicting musicians, fortune-tellers and merchants in a style which combined elements of expressionism and cubism. **Mahmoud Hammad** (1923–88) was an impressionist who arrived at abstraction when he began to explore the world of Arabic calligraphy; one of the founders of the **Arabic Lettrism** movement, Hammad combined calligraphy with abstraction and expressionism to produce a series of highly individualistic canvases.

THE SEARCH FOR NEW FORMS

As artists began freely to interpret and combine different artistic influences, the scene as a whole began to fragment. The most experimental artists have tended to be graduates of the Faculty of Fine Arts in Damascus, whose founding in 1960 is one of the landmark events in the history of contemporary Syrian painting. One of the first professors appointed to the Faculty was **Elias Zayyat** (b. 1935), whose own paintings combine many different styles, including realism, impressionism, abstraction and expressionism. Another teacher at the Faculty, **Khuzayma Elwani** (b. 1934) is one of the more directly accessible of the modern Syrian artists. His canvases are noted for their highly dramatic nature (he was originally trained in stage design), usually depicting in some form the struggle between man and the forces of evil; often his use of surrealism mutates this struggle onto a mythical – even nightmarish – level.

Foremost among the painters active at the moment is **Abdallah Murad** (b. 1944); his combination of abstraction and impressionism has produced a series of memorable canvases which express a raw, almost elemental, sense of energy and movement. Similar claims could be made for **Omar Hamdi** (b. 1951), though his tendency towards using garish colours tends to infuse his work with a more optimistic quality – a sense of energy whizzing out of control as opposed to the almost nightmarishly spasmodic fidgeting to be found in Murad's work.

CINEMA

The most commercially successful **Syrian films** have been those featuring the comics **Dureid Lahham** and **Nihad al-Qali**, a Syrian Laurel

---

CENSORSHIP

Rigorous government **censorship** has rendered freedom of expression on political, social and sexual issues highly problematic for film-makers during the last few decades. **Omar Amirally**'s full-length documentary *Daily Life in a Syrian Village* (1974), which depicted the failure of the Ba'ath agricultural programme, was banned, as were five out of the twenty documentary shorts produced by the Syrian Film Organization up to 1974, when President Hafez al-Assad replaced the organization's director. During the 1970s **film clubs** became important pockets of intellectual resistance to the regime, but they were closed in 1980 during the great crackdown against the civil disobedience of the time (see p.308). At this time many of the more talented film-makers went abroad, including Amirally, who went to work for French television.

In Syria, all film projects must go before a state committee for permission to start shooting, and once filming is completed an official licence must be obtained in order to legally distribute the film. A case in point is **Usama Muhammed**'s *Stars In Broad Daylight* (1988), depicting the moral crisis of a rural family whose members become involved in corrupt city life. The film won first prize at the Valencia film festival, and after impressing many at Cannes achieved commercial distribution in Spain, France, Germany and Switzerland – however, it was never distributed back in Syria, effectively amounting to a ban.

and Hardy whose films resemble the popular Egyptian farces that so characterize Syrian daytime TV. They made about a dozen films together in the 1960s, the most popular being *The Vagabonds* (1967), in which they play a pair of small-time crooks who are themselves taken for a ride by a wealthy Egyptian widow. Lahham has since gone on to star in his own vehicles, including *The Frontiers* (1984) and *Kafrun* (1990), which use musical sequences and verbal comedy in much the same way as their Egyptian precursors.

Dureid Lahham aside, Syria can claim the distinction of being one of the few Arab countries to have had an indigenous **film industry** since the early days of cinema. That said, its cinematic output has been sporadic; indeed Syria's film industry, run by the state, is presently in the doldrums. The first full-length feature produced and directed by Syrians inside the country was **Ayyub Badri**'s *The Innocent Accused* (1928), whose production was continually hampered by the French authorities; they eventually ordered the film to be completely reshot because the main character was a Muslim girl (which didn't square well with French attempts to suppress local culture). In the late 1940s and early 1950s a small number of musicals and light comedies were being produced every year, primarily with Lebanese finance and distribution, yet the vast majority of films Syrians were watching were Egyptian, American and European imports. Eventually critics and film-makers alike began to demand government support, and in 1969 the state took over all film distribution within the country via the **Syrian Film Organization**.

Though it was established in 1963, the Syrian Film Organization only made its first feature, *The Truck Driver*, in 1968. Its output during the early 1970s was essentially socialist in motivation and relied upon talent from across the Arab world; three of the five full-length features it produced between 1969 and 1972 dealt with the Palestinian plight, the most successful of which, *The Duped* (1972), based on a tale by Palestinian writer Ghassan Kanafani and directed by the Egyptian Taufik Salih, depicted an attempt by three Palestinians to enter Kuwait illegally from Iraq in the empty water tank of a truck, and their eventual death by suffocation while waiting at the border.

NEW ARAB CINEMA

Despite all the difficulties posed by government censorship, a number of talented film-makers have continued to emerge in Syria; Mohammed Malas, Nabil al-Maleh and Samir Zikra in particular are regarded as being in the forefront of New Arab Cinema, a term coined in France during the late 1970s following the appearance of a number of directors in the Arab world working within the aesthetics of European "art-house" cinema. Each has focused their attentions on the domestic social and political issues which, according to Malas, "express our inner disquiet and concern".

In **Mohammed Malas**'s semi-autobiographical *Dreams of the City* (1984) the political struggles and divisions of the 1950s are explored through the eyes of a small boy who witnesses the adults around him quarrelling, fighting and even killing each other. The debacle of the Six-Day War is the background for **Samir Zikra**'s *The Half-Meter Incident* (1981), which explores the moral bankruptcy of the petty bourgeoisie through the story of an ambitious white-collar worker who is put in charge of a civil defence unit during the mid-1960s. The 1967 war comes and goes, but rather than being the source of a great awakening, the defeat is met with indifference by the protagonist and its only effect is to land him a promotion; the Arab defeat is presented as the natural consequence of a society that has stagnated through the selfishness of its inhabitants.

Social themes are the subject of *The Extras* (1993), in which **Nabil al-Maleh** tells the touching story of a courtship between a young petrol-station attendant and a poor widow, conducted entirely under the oppressive gaze of the woman's overbearing brothers. The couple finally meet alone for the first time in a friend's apartment but they are plagued by feelings of awkwardness, shame and anxiety – the film's point being the oppressive nature of some customs in Muslim society.

MUSIC

Though members of the older generation of Syrians reminisce wistfully about **Damascus**'s classical tradition of music, visitors to the city are liable to be disappointed. Even though there are some fine players living in the city, there are few opportunities for them to perform. The old Andalusian repertoire with its complex rhythmic

Ensemble Al-Kindî

French-born Muslim Jalal Eddine heads up a brilliant ensemble in Syria, exploring classical Arabic music in collaboration with the region's top singers.

The Aleppian Music Room – The Art of Classical Arab Singing (Le Chant du Monde, France).
A lavish CD package, presented with photos that will make you want to jump on the next plane to Aleppo. Jalal Eddine and his ensemble accompany the dazzling Sabri Moudallal and Omar Sarmini in a selection of *wasla* (suites of songs and improvisations).

The Whirling Dervishes of Damascus (Le Chant du Monde, France).
A worthy successor to *The Aleppian Music Room*, these two CDs – featuring the powerful baritone voice of Sheikh Hamza Chakour, one of the outstanding Sufi singers of the near East – and thoughtfully written booklet offer an excellent overview of the ritual of the whirling dervishes (see p.105). The performances are poised, perfectly judged and deeply powerful.

Sabah Fakhri

The Syrian master of traditional Arab song, Sabah began singing on Damascus Radio in the 1940s. He has made hundreds of recordings and is also notable for his place in the *Guinness Book of Records* – he once sang non-stop for ten hours.

Au Palais des Congrès
(Club du Disque Arabe, France).
Recorded live in 1978, this gives a good account of Sabah's masterful control of melody, which has enchanted the Arab world for decades.

Mayada el-Hennawy

The woman singer Mayada is the toast of Damascus's flashy night clubs.

Bayent al-Hob Alaya (EMI Arabia, Dubai).
This album (its title translates as "I declared my love to him") is Mayada's most popular release, and widely available around the world.

Nur Mahana

Nur Mahama is Damascus's king of good-time pop. Though extremely popular in Syria, his cassettes can be tricky to find outside the country, and hard to identify if you don't read Arabic. Look out for the dapper, bank-manager-as-pop-star covers!

Hafla Amreeka (various cassette versions available).
This "American Concert" recording shows Nur on fine form and includes most of his hits. It gives a good idea of what you can expect in Damascus's more upmarket nightclubs.

Sabri Moudallal

The most respected religious singer in a city renowned for its musical tradition, Sabri Moudallal is the first *muezzin* at the Great Mosque in Aleppo. Despite his venerable age – he's in his late seventies – he still has one of the finest voices in the Eastern Mediterranean.

Songs from Aleppo (Institut du Monde Arabe, France).
What really stands out on this recording, on which Moudallal is accompanied by a deft ensemble of oud (lute), *qanun* (zither), *kamandja* (violin), *nay* (flute) and hand percussion, is how he imbues every note with an inspired, and inspiring, lust for life. The only let-down on this beautifully presented disc is the poor English translations of the sleeve notes.

George Wasoof

Having flirted with a rough-hewn, George Michael image, Wasoof has gone MOR and is now firmly entrenched in the Cairo hit factory. He is perhaps rather less interesting for it, though still a voice to be reckoned with.

Kalem al-Nas (Relax In, Kuwait).
A recent, Cairo-recorded album but one that still retains some charming Syrian touches.

---

and melodic patterns has largely given way to Egyptian style **al-jeel** dance music, played on mainly electric instruments. Long musical apprenticeships and vocal training have lost out to looks and charisma.

Aleppo, too, has a reputation for fine musicians; its soirées in the 1920s and 1930s were legendary, and it is still said that any singer who meets with approval in Aleppo is assured success elsewhere. The city has a tradition of singers specializing in the Andalous *muwashshah* (decorated) – sung poetry that draws on Levantine Sufi ideology. Its chief exponent is octogenarian **Sabri Moudallal**, a national treasure with an extraordinary vocal technique; any chance to see him in action should not be missed.

Aleppo is also home to **Sabah Fakhri** (born in 1933), considered Syria's pre-eminent singer – and the major Syrian musical export to the Arab world. He has also probably done more than anyone alive to keep the flame of traditional Andalusian music alive, with his abundant recordings of nagham al ams (melodies of the past), and his international tours. After Fakhri, the most active exponent of **Syrian classical music** in recent years has been Jalal Eddine, a Frenchman (born Julien Weiss) who converted to Islam and has studied the *qanun* (arab zither) to a very high standard. His discs and tours with Ensemble Al-Kindî, sometimes featuring the singers Sabri Moudallal or Sheikh Hamza Chakour, and **whirling dervishes**, are as fine a representation of Syrian art music as you are presently likely to find.

Out in the villages, both Syria and Lebanon share the muscular **dabka** dance-song tradition: an energetic communal celebration with strong Turkish overtones.

In **popular Arab song**, the biggest Syrian star in recent years is the singer **George Wasoof** – though he made his reputation in Beirut (in the early 1980s) and he has subsequently set up base in Cairo. He draws upon Syrian and Levantine folk melodies, however, mixing them with classic Egyptian song.

Two younger, Damascus-based performers are **Nur Mahana** and **Mayada el-Hennawy**. Nur's infectious pop sound, exemplified by his hit *Jameel al-Ruh* (Beautiful Soul), has made him a widely travelled star, entertaining Syrian communities all over the globe. Mayada's style is truly *shamee* (Syrian): shades of Egypt and Turkey combine with a homespun glamour that is instantly recognizable to anyone who has spent a few days in the country.

BOOKS

There are comparatively few books which relate solely to Syria; most of the time the country is included in books dealing with general Middle Eastern history, travel, politics or culture. That said, there are a number of excellent reads on the market, both about the country specifically or the Middle East as a whole.

There are two very good bookshops in London specializing in the Middle East, both of which have a worldwide mail order service: Al-Saqi, 26 Westbourne Grove, London W2 5RH (020/7221 9347, fax 7229 7492, *alsaqibooks@compuserve.com*) and Al-Hoda, 76 Charing Cross Road, London WC2H 0BB (020/7240 8381, fax 7497 0180, *www.alhoda.com*). In addition, Green Street Books, Yardley's, 12 Newbiggen Street, Thaxted, Essex CM6 2QR (01371/831449, fax 831599, *www.gsb.org.uk*) produces a catalogue of books on the Islamic world and also does worldwide mail order. Alternatively try the *amazon.com*, *borders.com* and *barnesandnoble.com* online bookshops.

In the list below, publishers' details for books in print are given in the form (UK publisher; US publisher) where they differ; if books are published in one country only, this follows the publisher's name; where a book is published by the same firm in both the UK and the US, only the name of the firm is given. If a book is listed as "o/p", it's out of print – you'll have to consult a library or specialist secondhand bookseller to get hold of it. We've made a point of listing the pick of English-language archeological guides **published in Syria**; despite their general shortcomings (including poor translation), these titles, available from Syrian museums and bookshops, often provide useful historical insights and illustrations not found in books published elsewhere.

TRAVELLERS AND TRAVEL WRITING

Accounts by early travellers to Syria and the Middle East are particularly worth trying to get hold of, providing fascinating insights into how Syria has – or in many cases hasn't – changed in the past hundred years.

EARLY TRAVELLERS

Baedeker, *Guide to Syria and Palestine* (o/p). Written when present-day Syria was simply part of a crumbling Turkish empire, with fascinating observations on the archeological sites in the days when people still lived in the Bel Temple at Palmyra and in the Crac des Chevaliers. The practical information focuses on how to hire horses and camels, and deal with demands for *baksheesh*.

Johann Burckhardt, *Travels in Syria and the Holy Land* (Darf, UK). Originally published in 1822, this fascinating account by one of the most important Middle Eastern travellers is most interesting for his descriptions of the ruined cities of the Hauran.

Sir John Mandeville, *The Travels of Sir John Mandeville* (Collins). Written in the fourteenth century, this was one of the first great commercial successes of the printing press – and it wasn't for about three hundred years that anyone realized that this is a work of fiction. Mandeville's fantastical descriptions of the places he never visited remain thoroughly readable to this day, especially in this abridged version which has been helpfully translated into modern English.

Frank McLynn, *Burton: Snow Upon the Desert* (John Murray, UK). Probably the best available biography of the famed traveller, linguist and one-time British consul in Damascus; fluently written and dodging none of the mucky stuff.

TWENTIETH-CENTURY TRAVELLERS

Agatha Christie, *Come, Tell Me How You Live* (Fontana, UK, o/p). Christie accompanied her husband, the archeologist Sir Max Mallowan, on excavations at many sites in northeastern Syria (most notably Tell Brak) in the 1930s. This entertaining, highly readable little book recounts her impressions of the landscape and people of Syria during the mandate era – but says nothing about the history he researched, which absorbed Max but largely bored his wife.

William Dalrymple, *From the Holy Mountain* (HarperCollins; Henry Holt & Co). Readable account of a journey across the Middle East loosely based upon one made by two Byzantine monks. As with most travel writing it's all a bit rudderless (and there's an annoying tendency towards facetiousness) but this is compensated for by the occasional neat turn of phrase.

Robin Fedden, *Syria and Lebanon* (John Murray, UK, o/p). First published in 1946, this is an interesting and readable historical survey covering all the major sights in a broad chronological order. By the same author is the stimulating and well-photographed *Crusader Castles* (John Murray, UK, o/p), written in 1950.

Lieve Joris, *The Gates of Damascus* (Lonely Planet Publications). Account by a Belgian author of a year spent living with a Damascus woman whose husband has been jailed for political crimes. Her depiction of the lives of ordinary Syrians from a woman's perspective is moving, provocative, funny and always perceptive.

T.E. Lawrence, *Seven Pillars Of Wisdom* (Penguin). Lawrence's classic account of the Arab revolt during World War I. See also the recently published *Seven Pillars Of Wisdom: Complete 1922 Text* (Castle Hill, UK) written in a far less "literary" style than the standard 1926 version, making it a much better read – it's also longer by about a third.

Robert Tewdwr Moss, *Cleopatra's Wedding Present* (Duckworth, UK). Witty and readable account of a gay journalist's travels in Syria during the summer of 1995, finished on the day that its author was murdered in his London flat by an Arab rent-boy. His comments on the landscape and individuals he encounters (particularly the Palestinian ex-commando with whom he falls in love) are wry but discerning.

Freya Stark, *Letters from Syria* (John Murray, UK, o/p). The letters of the title, written in the late 1920s, are most interesting for their description of the hostility of the locals to the ruling French, particularly in the Hauran which had recently seen a prolonged revolt. See also *Freya Stark in the Levant* (Garnet, UK) edited by

Malise Ruthven, a selection of the estimated fifty thousand photographs Stark took in the Middle East in the early part of the twentieth century.

Colin Thubron, *Mirror to Damascus* (Penguin). Packed with anecdotes, this classic piece of travel writing, written in 1966, is a loose guide to the Syrian capital, whose districts are covered in historical order. Entertaining and thought-provoking.

Jeremy Wilson, *Lawrence of Arabia: The Authorized Biography* (Heinemann; Sutton). Skilfully researched, fluently written and as near definitive as any biography of Lawrence is likely to get. The only thing that's likely to put you off is the sheer size of it. For something equally sensible but slightly more digestible try **Malcom Brown**, *A Touch of Genius: The Life of T.E. Lawrence* (J.M. Dent & Sons Ltd, UK).

ARCHEOLOGY AND ARCHITECTURE

Ali Abou Assaf, *The Archeology of Jebel Hauran* (Sidawi, Damascus). The Hauran is, after the Dead Cities, the most fascinating region in Syria for archeology enthusiasts, and this is the best locally published guide to travelling off the beaten track in the area.

Warwick Ball, *Syria: An Historical and Architectural Guide* (Melisende; Infolink). Good account, though the unbroken text makes it a bit of a slog.

Iain Browning, *Palmyra* (Chatto and Windus, UK, o/p). A thorough appraisal of the site, intelligently illustrated; still widely available within Syria.

Ross Burns, *Monuments of Syria* (I.B. Tauris; New York University Press). Essential reference book for those who want to explore the sites as thoroughly as they can. Not a travel guide but a hefty gazetteer of sites, so there's little practical information.

Richard Ettinghausen and Oleg Grabar, *The Art and Architecture of Islam 650–1250* (Penguin; Yale University Press). The fact that the best introduction to this vast subject is this one-volume work reveals the general paucity of the available literature. *Islamic Arts* by **Jonathan Bloom and Sheila Blair** (Phaidon; Yale University Press) covers the period up to 1800 and is a decent complementary work.

Zakieh Hanna, *The Castles and Archeological Sites in Tartous* (Sidawi, Damascus). Intelligently illustrated, this is useful for anybody wishing to explore the more obscure castles in the mountain region around Tartous.

Clark Hopkins, *The Discovery of Dura Europos* (Yale University Press, o/p). Fascinating, highly recommended account of the excavation of the site, produced by the American director of the effort during the 1930s.

Brigid Keenan, *Damascus: Hidden Treasures of the Old City* (Thames & Hudson). Pricey, beautifully photographed coffee-table book devoted to the neglected nooks and crannies of the capital.

T.E. Lawrence, *Crusader Castles* (Oxford University Press; Hippocrene). Lawrence's Oxford thesis expanded with a few letters to illustrate his pre-World War II journeys through East Anglia, Wales, France and the Middle East. It's a slight, overpriced, rather dry book, enlivened by some well-worn quotes and anecdotes and a scent of the man, but had it not been written by Lawrence it would never have seen the light of day.

Shawqi Sha'ath, *Qalaat Semaan and Other Sites* (Dar Al-Qalam Al-Arabi, Aleppo). The best Syrian-produced guide to the Church of St Simeon and surrounding Dead Cities; look for it in Aleppo.

RELIGION

A.J. Arberry (trans), The Koran (Oxford University Press). The best English-language version. The main alternative, N.J. Dawood's translation (Penguin), is also very impressive, and is available as a bilingual text.

Karen Armstrong, *Mohammed: A Western Attempt to Understand Islam* (Gollancz; Harper). An uncritical, uncontroversial work very much written with Western misconceptions in mind; readable and reasonable. For something less reverential, try **Maxime Rodinson**'s *Mohammed* (Penguin).

Robert Betts, *The Druze* (Yale University Press). Slightly pompous account of the Druze's origins and beliefs, with good sections on the bewilderment that the sect has engendered in the outside world.

John Esposito, *Islam: The Straight Path*

(Oxford University Press, UK). Pretty useful read covering everything from the history of Islam and its beliefs to its recent resurgence in the last few decades of the twentieth century. A loose, non-academic introduction for the general reader.

Idries Shah, *The Sufis* (Octagon, UK). Challenging and at times genuinely inspirational, this highly recommended book is the most definitive study of the history and practice of Sufism available. Good chapters on whirling dervishes.

Abdulkader Tayob, *Islam: A Short Introduction; Signs Symbols and Values* (One World, UK). A short introduction written by a professor of the University of Cape Town, which takes the form of a tour around a mosque from minaret to *minbar*, using the architecture as a jumping-off point to explain Islam to the novice. Slightly meandering but useful for the complete beginner.

HISTORY

O.R. Gurney, *The Hittites* (Penguin, UK). Everything you ever wanted to know about Hittite politics, culture and society – still the essential text, originally published way back in 1952.

Philip Hitti, *History of Syria* (o/p). The classic history, though a little dry and not the most accessible introduction for the general reader.

Albert Hourani, *A History of the Arab Peoples* (Faber; Warner). Heavy scholastic work (with little directly on Syria) covering the period from the seventh century to the present day. Especially good on the fragmentation of Arab Islamic society and culture, and the reassertion of Islamic identity in the late twentieth century.

Joinville and Villehardouin, *Chronicles of the Crusades* (Penguin). The best way to get under the skin of the Crusades is to get back to the original source material; here, Joinville's famous life of the saintly King Louis IX of France (whose actual crusading was a bit of a disaster) is combined with Villehardouin's memoir of the Fourth Crusade (which ironically ended up as a war against Christian Byzantium).

Philip Khoury, *Syria and the French Mandate* (I.B. Tauris; Princeton University Press). Valuable contribution to a period of history that French historians have shown little interest in, and Arab ones have been too emotive about.

Bernard Lewis, *The Assassins – A Radical Sect in Islam* (Al-Saqi; Oxford University Press). Sensible account of the sect which dispels a few myths – particularly of their drug-taking.

Amin Maalouf, *The Crusades Through Arab Eyes* (Al-Saqi; Shocken). A lively read by a Lebanese journalist, who here explores the writings of contemporaneous Arab chroniclers of the Crusaders.

Peter Mansfield, *A History of the Middle East* (Penguin). Broad general survey covering the period from 1800 to 1990, with little specifically on Syria, though very readable for all that. Written by the former Middle Eastern correspondent of the *Sunday Times*, who also penned *The Arabs* (Penguin).

John Julius Norwich, *Byzantium: The Early Centuries* (Viking). Part of a trilogy by the established master of Byzantine studies, this volume, covering 330–800 AD, has the greatest relevance to Syria.

Alan Palmer, *The Decline and Fall of the Ottoman Empire* (John Murray, UK). Examines the break-up of the Turkish empire in the late nineteenth century; it contains little that's specific to Syria, but is a good comprehensive overview.

Jonathan Riley-Smith (ed), *Oxford Illustrated History of the Crusades* (Oxford University Press; Getty Centre for Education). A series of stimulating essays rather than a straight chronology; available both as a bumper fun-sized illustrated version and as a more handily sized paperback.

Steven Runciman, *A History of the Crusades* (Penguin; Cambridge University Press). Simply a classic of history writing right up there with Gibbon and Macaulay; comprehensive three-volume work pulling no punches on the gossip and gore.

ARAB POLITICS AND SOCIETY

T.G. Fraser, *The Arab–Israeli Conflict* (Macmillan; St Martin's Press). A lucid, compact and even-handed skip through the major events of its subject, from the beginning of the twentieth century to the symbolic Arafat–Rabin handshake in 1993.

Thomas Friedman, *From Beirut to Jerusalem* (Fontana; Anchor). In which the *New York Times* journalist describes his work in Beirut and Jerusalem in the 1970s and 1980s. A thought-provoking read, chiefly interesting from a Syrian angle for his analysis of the Hama massacre.

Fatima Mernissi, *Islam and Democracy* (Virago; Addison-Wesley). Whimsical, erudite and, at times, delightfully quirky investigation into why democracy hasn't taken root in modern Islamic societies, written by one of the Arab world's leading feminist writers.

Edward Said, *Covering Islam* (Routledge & Kegan Paul). An important study whose main focus is not so much Islam as the shortcomings of a Western media governed by notions of crisis and newsworthiness rather than a desire to accurately record the world around it.

SYRIA

Daniel Pipes, *Greater Syria – The History of an Ambition* (Oxford University Press). Interesting history, covering 1920–88, of Syria's dissatisfaction with the borders imposed on it by the European powers.

Itamar Rabinovich, *The Brink of Peace* (Princeton University Press). Written by the head of the Israeli delegation, this is an account of the 1992–96 Israeli–Syrian negotiations which so nearly (or perhaps not, depending on your point of view) saw an historic breakthrough.

David Roberts, *The Ba'ath Party and the Creation of Modern Syria* (Croom Helm, UK, o/p). General work written as a basic introduction to the fluid nature of Ba'ath ideology, by the ex-British ambassador to Damascus.

Patrick Seale, *The Struggle for Syria* (I.B. Tauris; Yale University Press). Expert analysis of the political intrigues in between Syria's independence and the attempt to achieve Arab unity in 1958; most interesting on the Anglo-American-Iraqi attempt to overthrow the Syrian government in 1957.

Patrick Seale, *Assad: The Struggle for the Middle East* (I.B. Tauris; University of California Press). Based partly on interviews with the man himself and many of his most important ministers, this is a sympathetic, insightful portrait of the late president without being an apologia for the man. An essential read to understand the man largely responsible for shaping Syria as it is today.

WOMEN'S ISSUES

Richard Antoun (ed), *Syria: Society, Culture and Polity* (State University of New York Press). Series of stimulating essays, well worth a dip especially for its chapter on women's role in society through the eyes of its female writers.

Asghar Ali Engineer, *The Rights of Women in Islam* (Hurst & Co; St Martin's Press). Intelligent and tightly argued reassessment of women's role in Islam, examining the differences between what the Koran says and how it has been interpreted over the centuries. However, Engineer possibly spends too much time refuting arguments than creating them, and the examples from history could have been matched by some more contemporary ones.

Judy Mabro, *Veiled Half-Truths: Western Travellers' Perceptions of Middle Eastern Women* (I.B. Tauris). Interesting examination of the attitudes of eighteenth and nineteenth century orientalists to the women they found on their travels. Lays bare all the preconceptions and misconceptions.

Fatima Mernissi, *Beyond the Veil* (Al-Saqi). Fascinating and thought-provoking essay on the tensions between Muslim women's modern democratic rights and religious and familial pressures – most entertaining is the section based on letters to the Moroccan religious counselling service illustrating the confusions. See also Mernissi's *The Veil and the Male Elite* (Addison-Wesley, US), which focuses on the relationship between men and women as laid down in the Koran.

Bouthaina Shaaban, *Both Right and Left Handed* (The Women's Press; Indiana University Press). Account of the woman's role in modern-day Arab society (including a chapter on Syria), presented through a series of conversations with local women.

SYRIAN AND ARAB WRITING

Samar Attar, *The House on Arnus Square* (Passeggiata). A renowned linguist, essayist and poet, Attar here produces an evocative memoir about her childhood in Damascus, built around a return to her old family home after twenty years. See also her *Lina: Portrait of a Damascene Girl* (Three Continents Press).

Michel Azrak (trans), *Modern Syrian Short Stories* (Three Continents Press). Good cross-section of work illustrating the great diversity of styles and subject matter that modern Syrian writers have tackled.

Halim Barakat, *Six Days* (Three Continents Press). Born in Syria, raised in Beirut, Barakat now lives in America. This fictional depiction of a short-lived war was inspired by the plight of the Palestinians, though the title isn't a reference to the 1967 Arab–Israeli war, which this book predates.

Kamal Boullata (ed), *Women of the Fertile Crescent* (Three Continents Press). Anthology of women poets from Syria and neighbouring countries.

Ulfat Idilbi, *Grandfather's Tale* (Quartet; Interlink). Idilbi's second novel, written when she was at the ripe old age of 79, revolves around an old woman telling her grandchildren stories of her grandfather who was exiled to Damascus from his homeland. A moving and ultimately uplifting tale.

Salma Khadra Jayyusi (ed), *Modern Arabic Poetry, An Anthology* (Columbia University Press). Easily the best available English-language anthology of Arab poets, with a useful introductory essay and good short biographical sketches.

Hanna Mina, *Sun on a Cloudy Day* (Passeggiata). In this novel, a young Syrian is forced to begin to question the traditions of the landowning aristocracy and the power of the occupying French.

Nizar Qabbani, *Arabian Love Poems* (Three Continents Press). Syria's most popular modern poet, Qabbani wrote in a very direct, accessible way about love and politics, and his verses are known by heart by many in the Arab world through their use in popular songs. When Qabbani died while in exile in London in 1998, his body was flown back to Syria at the behest of President Hafez al-Assad and buried in the Bab al-Saghir cemetery in Damascus.

Ghada al-Samman, *Beirut Nightmares* (Quartet; Interlink). One of the Arab world's leading feminist writers, Damascus-born Al-Samman has spent most of her life in Beirut, where she now has her own publishing house. This novel is a harrowing, though at times very funny, account of the day-to-day terror inflicted upon ordinary citizens living in a war zone.

Siham Tergeman, *Daughter of Damascus* (University of Texas Press). Slightly disjointed homage to the life and times of the Old City in the early part of the twentieth century, originally printed by the author herself and distributed via a sweet-seller in the Damascus souks.

GENERAL

Lee Allane, *Oriental Carpets – A Buyer's Guide* (Thames & Hudson). The most easily digestible guide on the market, readily available in the more expensive hotels in Syria. See also his *Kilims – A Buyers Guide* (Thames & Hudson).

Mouni Atassi (ed), *Contemporary Art in Syria 1898–1998* (Atassi Gallery, Damascus). This large, copiously illustrated work is essential for anyone who wants to become familiar with modern Syrian art.

Miriam al-Hashimi, *Traditional Arabic Cooking* (Garnet). Enticing selection of Middle-Eastern eats, the majority of which you'll never have the chance to eat in a run-of-the-mill Syrian restaurant, so here's a good opportunity to learn how to do them yourself.

Johannes Kalter, *The Arts and Crafts of Syria* (Thames & Hudson). Well-illustrated general work; essential for anyone taking their souvenir-hunting seriously, or seeking a deeper appreciation of the local culture and the meaning of clothes and jewellery in Syrian – particularly Bedouin – society.

Voila Shafik, *Arab Cinema* (The American University in Cairo Press). Easily the most comprehensive survey available on Arab film in general and Syrian cinema in particular, charting both the history and the cultural context admirably. A fascinating read even if you haven't actually seen any of the films.

Coleman South, *Culture Shock! Syria* (Kuperard, UK). Well-informed and extremely useful guide to the country for those intending to live there, covering everything from how to get a phone line installed at home to points of etiquette and how to enrol your children at an international school. For visitors, its background information on Syrian politics, society, culture, history and economics also makes it an absorbing pre-visit read.

Walter Weiss, *The Bazaar: Markets and Merchants of the Islamic World* (Thames & Hudson). Remarkable primarily for its exquisite photography, though there are also short pieces of accompanying text and some reflections on the Aleppo and Damascus souks.

LANGUAGE

Spoken in over twenty countries from northwest Africa to the Arabian Gulf, Arabic is a Semitic language (others in this family are are modern Hebrew, Maltese and Aramaic). Like other Semitic languages, Arabic uses a consonantal root-system consisting of three (occasionally four) consonants, from which variations in shades of meaning are obtained either by using different vowels, or by adding or changing prefixes or suffixes.

For example, in Arabic the three consonants **k-t-b** connote the idea of writing. Thus we get:

kataba	he wrote
kitaab	book
ma**ktaba**	library
kaatib	clerk
mi**ktaab**	typewriter

The Arabic **alphabet** has 28 letters and is written cursively (the letters are usually joined up) from right to left – except numbers, which are from left to right. There are no capital letters, although the shapes of the letters vary depending on where in the word they occur and which letters precede or follow them.

There are three main categories of written and spoken Arabic. **Classical Arabic**, the language of the Koran, does not evolve, being the vehicle of God's Revelation. So-called **Modern Standard Arabic** (**MSA**) is used across the contemporary Arab world, being the written language of books and newspapers, and the spoken language of radio and TV. It differs slightly in idiom and vocabulary from the classical language, but nowhere near as much as, say, Kipling's English differs from Chaucer's. Lastly, **colloquial Arabic** comprises the spoken dialects of the different regions of the Arab world, which can differ from one another quite considerably. The most widely understood among these is Egyptian, due to the ubiquity of movies and TV soap operas from Cairo. The Arabic spoken in Syria is similar to that used elsewhere in the Levant – in Lebanon, Jordan and Israel and the Palestinian Territories.

TRANSLITERATION AND PRONUNCIATION

Transliteration of Arabic can be a complex affair, as several Arabic **consonants** do not have exact equivalents in the Roman alphabet. Particularly worth singling out among these are:

H an emphatic version of the usual h, pronounced with a stronger exhalation than its non-emphatic equivalent

kh like the **ch** in the Scottish **loch**

gh like the French **r**

q like *k*, but pronounced with the tongue at back of the mouth

r trilled, as in Spanish

' a brief grunt, which can sound like someone gargling or choking

The **'** sound does take a bit of practice for foreigners to get to grips with, and is best learnt by listening to native speakers. It's worth noting that **q** is sometimes replaced by a glottal stop, rather like the word "bottle" when pronounced without the "t" sound.

Arabic **vowels** present no special difficulties. They come in short and long versions; we've denoted the latter **aa**, **ee**, and **oo**. The short vowels are pronounced much as in English, while long vowels should be lingered on momentarily – a useful analogy is to compare the pronunciations of the English words "h**a**rry" and "h**ai**ry". Arabic also has two diphthongs, **ey** (pronounced as in h**ey**) and **ow** (as in bl**ow**).

Every letter written in transliterated Arabic must be pronounced; thus **ahlen** (*welcome*) is pronounced **a-h-len** and not *alan*. Where a consonant is repeated, both letters must be pronounced, as in the word for bathroom, which is **hammam**, pronounced **Ham-maam** (if you should ask for a **Hamam**, you are requesting a pigeon!).

BOOKS

Among a plethora of **books** on formal and dialect Arabic, the most relevant to Syria is the widely

PHRASES AND EXPRESSIONS

In what follows, (m), (f) and (pl) denote forms to be used when speaking to a man, woman or group respectively; (M) and (F) denote forms used by male or female speakers respectively.

Greetings and farewells

Welcome	*ahlen wa-sahlen*	(response)	*sabaaH en-noor*
(response)	*ahlen beek (m)/beekee (f)/*	Good evening	*masaa al-kheyr*
	bikum (pl)	(response)	*masaa an-noor*
Hello (formal)	*as-salaamu aleykum*	How are you?	*shlonak* (m)/*shlonik* (f)
(response)	*wa-aleykum as-salaam*	I am well	*ena bikheyr*
Hi!	*marHaba*	Thanks be to God	*el-Hamdu lillaah*
(response)	*marHabteyn*	Goodnight	*tisbaH* (m)/*tisbaHee* (f)
Nice to meet you	*fursa sa'eeda*		*'alaa kheyr*
Good morning	*sabaaH al-kheyr*	Goodbye	*ma'a as-salaama*

Basics

Yes	*ey*	Please	*min fadlak* (m)/	Sorry	*aasif* (M)/*aasifa* (F)
No	*laa*		*fadlik* (f)	No problem	*mish mushkileh*
Thank you	*shukran*	Excuse me	*ismaHlee* (m)/	God willing	*inshallaah*
You're welcome	*afwan*		*ismaHeeli* (f)	Nothing	*wala ishee*

Pronouns

I	*ena*	He	*huwa*	We	*eHna*	They	*homma*
You (sing.)	*enta* (m)/*enti* (f)	She	*hiya*	You (pl)	*entoo*		

Questions, directions, signs

What is your name?	*shoo ismak* (m)/*shoo ismik* (f)?	the pharmacy	*as-saydeliye*
My name is…	*ismee…*	the police	*ash-shurta*
I am…	*ena*	the post office	*maktab al-bareed*
American	*amreekee* (M)/*amreekiyya* (F)	the restaurant	*al-mat'am*
Australian	*ustraalee* (M)/*ustraaliyya* (F)	the telephone office	*maktab at-telifoon*
Canadian	*kanadee* (M)/*kanadiyya* (F)	the toilet	*at-twalet, al-Hammaam*
English	*ingleezee* (M)/	the tourist office	*maktab as-siyaaHa*
	ingleeziyya (F)	the market	*as-sooq*
I don't speak Arabic	*ena ma baHkee 'arabi*	Left/ right/ straight	*ash-shimaal/al-yemeen/*
I speak a little Arabic	*ena baHkee 'arabi shweiya*	ahead	*ala tool*
I don't understand	*ena ma bafhem*	Near/far	*qareeb/ba'eed*
Do you speak English?	*btaHkee ingleezi?*	How many?	*kem/qaddeysh?*
What's that in English?	*shoo haaza bil-ingleezee?*	Here/there	*hown/honaak*
Where is …	*weyn*	To/from	*ilaa/min*
the hotel	*al-funduk*	East/west	*sharq/gharb*
the airport	*al-mataar*	North/south	*shimaal/jenoob*
the bank	*al-bank*	When does the train/	*imta byetruk al-qitaar/*
the bus station	*maHattat al-baas*	bus leave?	*al-autobaas?*
the train station	*maHattat al-qitaar*	Ticket	*tezkara*
the church	*al-kaneesa*	What time is it?	*as-saa'a kem?*
the mosque	*al-masjid*	First/last/next	*al-awwel/al-akheer/*
the city centre	*wasat el-medina*		*al-qadeem*
the doctor	*al-doktoor*		
the hospital	*al-musteshfa*	Closed/open	*msakkir/maftooH*
the museum	*al-matHaf*	No entry	*mamnoo' ad-dokhool*
the passport and	*maktab al-jawazat*	No photography	*mamnoo' at-tasweer*
immigration office	*wa al-hijra*	No smoking	*mamnoo' at-tadkheen*

continues overleaf…

PHRASES AND EXPRESSIONS contd.

Shopping

Do you have ...?	*andak* (m)/*andik* (f) ...?	Too big	*kabeer jiddan*
cigarettes	*sajaayir*	Too small	*sagheer jiddan*
matches	*kibreet*	How much is it?	*bi-kam?*
newspapers	*jaraayid*	That's fine	*kweyis*
stamps	*tawaabi'*	I (don't) want	*ena (maa) biddee*
Too expensive	*ghaalee jiddan*	Money	*fuloos/masaaree*

Accommodation

Do you have a . . .?	*andak* (m)/*andik* (f) . . .?	air-conditioning	*takyeef al-hawa*
room	*ghurfa*	a telephone	*telifoon*
single room	*ghurfa mufrada*	a blanket	*battaneyya*
double room	*ghurfa bi sareerayn*	Breakfast	*al-futoor*
Is there . . .?	*fee . . .?*	Full	*malyaan*
hot water	*mayyi haarra*	Key	*miftaaH*
a shower	*doosh*	Manager	*mudeer*
a balcony	*balkona*	Lift	*mas'ad*

Reactions and small talk

I (don't) know	*ena (maa) ba'rif*	I am (not) married	*ena (mish) mutazawwij* (M)/
I am . . .			*mutazawwija* (F)
tired/unwell	*ena ta'baan* (M)/*ta'baana*	It's not your business	*haza leysa shoghlak*
	(F)	Don't touch me!	*la telmesnee!*
sick	*mareed* (M)/*mareeda* (F)	Go away	*imshee*
hungry	*jo'aan* (M)/*jo'aana* (F)	Let's go	*yalla*
thirsty	*'atshaan* (M)/*'ashaana* (F)	Help me!	*sa'idoonee!*
Are you married?	*enta mutazawwij* (m)/	Can I ...?	*mumkin ....?*
	enti mutazawwija (f)?	It's not possible	*mish mumkin*

Money

I have (not) any money	*(ma) andee fuloos*	US dollars	*dolar amreekee*
I want to change . . .	*biddee ughayyir . . .*	travellers' cheques	*shikaat siyaaHiyya*
British pounds	*jinayh isterling*		

Dates and times

January	*kaanoon ath-thaani*	Wednesday	*yawm al-arba'a*
February	*shoobaaT*	Thursday	*yawm al-khamees*
March	*athaar*	Friday	*yawm el-jum'ah*
April	*nisaan*	Saturday	*yawm as-sabt*
May	*ayyaar*		
June	*Huzeyran*	Minute	*daqeeqa*
July	*tammooz*	Hour	*saa'a*
August	*aab*	Day	*yawm*
September	*aylool*	Night	*layl*
October	*tishreen al-awwal*	Week	*isboo'*
November	*tishreen ath-thaanee*	Month	*shahar*
December	*kaanoon al-awwal*	Year	*sana*
		Today	*al-yawm*
Sunday	*yawm el-aHad*	Tomorrow	*bukra*
Monday	*yawm al-ithnayn*	Yesterday	*imbaariH*
Tuesday	*yawm ath-thalaatha*		

ARABIC PLACE NAMES

Aleppo	حلب	Qalaat Marqab	قلعة مرقب
Amrit	عمريت	Qalaat Salah al-Din	قلعة صلاح الدين
Apamea	افاميا	Qalaat Semaan	قلعة سمعان
Ath-Thawra	الثورة	Qamishli	القمشلي
Baalbak (Lebanon)	بعلبك	Qanawat	قناوات
Beirut (Lebanon)	بيروت	Quneitra	القنيطرة
Bloudane	بلودان	Raqqa	الرقة
Bosra	بصرة	Ras al-Bassit	رأس البسيط
Crac des Chevaliers	قلعة الحصن	Resafe	الرصافة
Damascus	دمشق	Safita	صافيتا
Deir ez-Zur	دير الزور	Salhiye (for Dura Europos)	الصلحية
Dera	درعا	Sednaya	صيدنايا
Hama	حماه	Shahba	شهبا
Hassakeh	الحسكة	Sweida	السويداء
Homs	حمص	Tadmor (Palmyra)	تدمر
Idleb	ادلب	Tartous	طرطوس
Latakia	اللاذقية	Tibne (for Halebiye)	تبني
Maalula	معلولا	Tripoli (Lebanon)	طرابلس
Maarat al-Numan	معرة النعمان	Ugarit	رأس شمرا
Misyaf	مصياف	Zabadani	زبداني
Qalaat Jaber	قلعة جعبر		

NUMBERS AND FRACTIONS

0	*sifir*	13	*thalatht'ashr*	60	*sitteen*
1	*waaHid*	14	*arba'ta'shr*	70	*sab'een*
2	*ithneyn*	15	*khamasta'shr*	80	*thamaaneen*
3	*thalaatha*	16	*sitta'shr*	90	*tis'een*
4	*arba'a*	17	*sab'at'ashr*	100	*mia*
5	*khamsa*	18	*thamant'ashr*	101	*mia wa waaHid ... etc*
6	*sitta*	19	*tis'at'ashr*	200	*miateyn*
7	*sab'a*	20	*'ishreen*	300	*thalaathet-mia ...etc*
8	*thamaanya*	21	*waaHid wa 'ishreen ...*	1000	*alf*
9	*tis'a*	etc		2000	*alfeyn*
10	*'ashara*	30	*thalatheen*	3000	*thalaathet aalaaf ...etc*
11	*iHda'ashr*	40	*arba'een*	1/2	*nos*
12	*ithna'ashr*	50	*khamseen*	1/4	*rub'*

Numerals

١	1	١٠	10	١٩	19	٨٠	80
٢	2	١١	11	٢٠	20	٩٠	90
٣	3	١٢	12	٢١	21	١٠٠	100
٤	4	١٣	13	٢٢	22	٢٠٠	200
٥	5	١٤	14	٣٠	30	٣٠٠	300
٦	6	١٥	15	٤٠	40	٤٠٠	400
٧	7	١٦	16	٥٠	50	١٠٠٠	1000
٨	8	١٧	17	٦٠	60		
٩	9	١٨	18	٧٠	70		

available *Colloquial Arabic (Levantine)* by Leslie McLoughlin (Routledge), which teaches the Levantine dialect using transliteration rather than Arabic script. There are no **phrasebooks** dedicated to Syrian Arabic, but a useful second best is *The Rough Guide to Egyptian Arabic*, which covers essential expressions in Arabic script with phonetic equivalents, as well as a little basic grammar and some useful tourist information.

You may feel like venturing into the Arabic **script**, in which case by far the best introduction is *The Arabic Alphabet* by Nicholas Awde and Putros Samo (Al-Saqi Books); this is an invaluable companion – it's a slim volume too – for reading a menu or a street sign, or understanding labels in a street market. Also highly recommended is *Arabic: The 100-Word Exercise Book*, by Mahmoud Gaafar (GW Publishing), which is billed as an ideal introduction to the script.

Very useful for further **self-study** is *Mastering Arabic*, by Jane Wightwick and Mahmoud Gaafar (Macmillan), a lively, imaginative textbook, accompanied by two audio cassettes. *Teach Yourself Arabic* by J.R. Smart (Hodder & Stoughton) also comes with an optional audio cassette.

GLOSSARY

Alternative spellings of Arabic terms are given in brackets where appropriate.

ABU Arabic for "father of"; a male parent is often referred to as "Abu" followed by the name of his eldest son.

AIN ('AYN, EIN) Spring.

BA'ATH Arabic for "renaissance", and the name of the Arab socialist party led in Syria by President Bashar al-Assad.

BAB Gateway, door.

BAHR Sea.

BAKSHEESH Tip or alms.

BEDOUIN The nomadic Arabs who inhabit desert areas.

BEIT (BAYT, BAIT) House.

BURJ Tower.

CALIPH (KHALIFA) The successors of the Prophet Mohammed; the position was formally abolished by the Turks in 1924.

CARAVANSERAI Inn and marketplace for caravans.

DEIR (DAYR) Monastery or convent.

DIN Religion.

FRANKS A term often used synonymously for the Crusaders.

HADITH The sayings of Mohammed, gathered together in the ninth century.

HAJJ (HADJ, HAJ) The pilgrimage to Mecca. Also used as a term of respect for someone who has made the pilgrimage, or as a polite way of addressing an old person assumed to have done it.

HAMMAM Public Turkish bath; also a regular bathroom or toilet.

HAURAN (HAWRAN) Black basalt desert region to the south of Damascus.

HIJAB Veil worn by women.

IMAM Someone who leads prayers in the mosque; Shiites also apply the word to the successors of Mohammed.

IWAN (LIWAN) Open reception area set off a courtyard.

JALABIYYEH Long traditional robe worn by Arab men.

JAWLAN Arab name for the Golan Heights.

JEBEL (DJEBEL, JABAL) Mountain.

JIHAD Usually equated with "holy war" but actually means "striving" or "effort".

JISR Bridge.

KANEESA Church.

KEFFIYEH Headscarf worn by males, often patterned.

KHAN Warehouse/hostel for merchants.

KHIRBET Ruin.

KUFIC Early form of Arabic script, often seen in decorative inscriptions.

MADRASA (MEDERSA, MERDRESSA) Islamic school.

MAMELUKE (MAMLUK) Used to describe a slave who had been trained as a soldier. Also the name of the dynasty founded in 1250 in Egypt and which fought the Crusaders.

MAR Saint.

MARISTAN Medieval hospital.

MASJID Mosque.

MAYDAN (MIDAN) Square.

MIHRAB Niche in mosque indicating the direction of Mecca.

MINARET Tower of a mosque from where the muezzin gives the call to prayer.

MINBAR Mosque pulpit from where the imam delivers the Friday sermon.

MUEZZIN The person who gives the call to prayer.

MUKHABARAT Secret police.

NAHR River.

NARGILEH (ARGILEH, NARJILEH, ARJILEH) Water pipe used to smoke tobacco; hubble-bubble.

NORIA Wooden wheel used to lift water from a river.

PASHA Governor of an Ottoman province.

PLAS Square.

QALAA (KALAA, QAL'AT) Castle; becomes *qalaat* when it precedes the name of a castle..

QASR (KASR) Palace – in practice often interchangeable with *qalaa*.

QIBLAH (QIBLA) The direction of Mecca, indicated by the *mihrab*.

RAMADAN The Muslim fasting month.

RAS Head; can mean the source of a river.

SHAM Local name for Damascus.

SHARIA Street.

SHEIKH (SHAYKH) Can refer to a chief, an elder or a religious leader.

SHIITE A member of the smaller of Islam's two main branches. Shiites regard Ali – Mohammed's son-in-law – and his descendants as the true imams, whom God has chosen to provide spiritual guidance for the world's Muslims.

SOUK (SUQ) Market.

SUFI Muslim mystic.

SUNNI A member of one of Islam's two main branches. Sunnis emphasize adherence to the *sunna*, the code of behaviour exemplified by the life of Mohammed.

TAQIYYA The hiding of one's beliefs for self-protection, a practice used by the Druze.

TAREQ Avenue.

TEKKE Dervish monastery.

UMM Arabic for "mother"; a female parent is often referred to as "Umm" followed by the name of her eldest son.

WADI A valley which is dry except during rain.

ARCHITECTURAL TERMS

ABLAQ Decorative effect created by using alternating bands of different stone – used particularly in the Mameluke and Ottoman periods.

AGORA Marketplace in a Greek or Roman city.

AISLE The parts of a church on either side of the central nave.

APSE Large semicircular recess with domed roof found at the eastern end of a church.

ATRIUM Courtyard of a Roman villa, or the courtyard in front of a Byzantine church.

BAPTISTRY Building designed for the baptism of converts.

BARBICAN An outer tower of a castle, not part of the main fortification.

BASILICA Rectangular Roman/Byzantine church with a nave, two aisles and apse.

CALDARIUM Hot room of a Roman public bath.

CARDO MAXIMUS Main road running usually north–south through a Roman city.

CELLA Sacred chamber, located in the centre of a Classical temple compound, housing the image of the deity worshipped there.

CHANCEL Section around the altar of a church.

CITADEL Fortress which commands a city.

COLONNADE Columns set in rows (usually supporting a roof).

CORNICE Ornamental moulding around the top of the wall of a room, or the horizontal moulding crowning a building.

CRYPT Chamber beneath a church floor.

CRYPTOPORTICUS Dark passage used for storage, often running beside a colonnaded street.

CUPOLA Dome.

DECUMANUS East–west street that would cross the cardo maximus in a Roman city.

DONJON A castle keep.

EXEDRA A recess, usually semicircular, for sitting in.

FLUTING The grooves along the surface of a column.

GLACIS Smooth, artificial slope beneath a castle.

HAREMLEK Private quarters of an Ottoman residence.

HYPOCAUST Hollow space under a Roman floor into which hot air would flow – basically creating a system of underfloor heating.

HYPOGEUM Underground tomb.

ICONOSTASIS A screen with icons separating the nave from the chancel in a church.

KALYBE Shrine with niches for the display of statues.

KHADAMLEK Servants' quarters of an Ottoman house.

MACHICOLATION A parapet of a castle with openings for dropping stones onto attackers.

MARTYRIUM A church built on the site of a martyrdom.

MUQARNAS Intricate arrays of scallop- or honeycomb-shaped hollows adorning recesses and doorways in mosques and madrasas.

MYTHRAEUM Temple devoted to the god Mithras.

NARTHEX Entrance porch at the western end of a church.

NAVE Central part of a church, usually with aisles either side.

NECROPOLIS Graveyard.

NYMPHAEUM Public water fountain in a Greek or Roman city with niches for statues.

ORCHESTRA The semicircular area in front of the stage of a Classical theatre.

PANDOCHEION Inn to house pilgrims.

PEDIMENT Triangular design over a door or window.

PERISTYLE A row of columns surrounding a court.

PORTAL Doorway.

PORTICO Porch.

PRAETORIUM Roman governor's residence.

PROPYLAEUM Entrance gateway to a temple.

QUBBA Dome – or a domed building.

SELAMLEK Entertaining area of an Ottoman house.

SERAIL Turkish governor's headquarters.

STELE Inscribed slab of stone.

TELL Mound or artificial hill concealing an archeological site.

TETRAPORTICUS Four-sided gateway.

TETRAPYLON Arrangement of columns and arches marking the intersection of two major Roman roads within a city.

TRANSEPT Either arm of that part of a cross-shaped church at right angles to the nave.

TRICLINIUM Dining room of a Roman house.

VIA SACRA Sacred way leading to a church or temple.

INDEX

This index omits the initial "al-" from place names and surnames that contain it.

Stay in touch with us!

ROUGHNEWS is Rough Guides' free newsletter.
In three issues a year we give you news, travel
issues, music reviews, readers' letters and the
latest dispatches from authors on the road.

ROUGH GUIDES: Travel

Alaska
Amsterdam
Andalucia
Argentina
Australia
Austria

Bali & Lombok
Barcelona
Belgium &
  Luxembourg
Belize
Berlin
Brazil
Britain
Brittany &
  Normandy
Bulgaria
California
Canada
Central America
Chile
China
Corsica
Costa Rica
Crete
Croatia
Cuba
Cyprus
Czech & Slovak
  Republics

Dodecanese &
  the East Aegean
Devon &
  Cornwall
Dominican
  Republic
Dordogne & the
  Lot
Ecuador
Egypt
England
Europe
Florida
France
French Hotels &
  Restaurants
  1999
Germany
Goa
Greece
Greek Islands
Guatemala
Hawaii
Holland
Hong Kong &
  Macau
Hungary

Iceland
India
Indonesia
Ionian Islands
Ireland

Israel & the
  Palestinian
  Territories
Italy
Jamaica
Japan
Jordan
Kenya
Lake District
Languedoc &
  Roussillon
Laos
London
Los Angeles
Malaysia,
  Singapore &
  Brunei
Mallorca &
  Menorca
Maya World
Mexico
Morocco
Moscow
Nepal
New England
New York
New Zealand
Norway
Pacific
  Northwest
Paris
Peru
Poland
Portugal
Prague
Provence & the
  Côte d'Azur
The Pyrenees
Romania
St Petersburg
San Francisco

Sardinia
Scandinavia
Scotland
Scottish
  highlands and
  Islands
Sicily
Singapore
South Africa
South India
Southeast Asia
Southwest USA
Spain
Sweden
Switzerland
Syria

Thailand
Trinidad &
  Tobago
Tunisia
Turkey
Tuscany &
  Umbria
USA
Venice
Vienna
Vietnam
Wales
Washington DC
West Africa
Zimbabwe &
  Botswana

AVAILABLE AT ALL GOOD BOOKSHOPS

ROUGH GUIDES: Mini Guides, Travel Specials and Phrasebooks

MINI GUIDES

Antigua
Bangkok
Barbados
Beijing
Big Island of Hawaii
Boston
Brussels
Budapest
Cape Town
Copenhagen
Dublin
Edinburgh

Florence
Honolulu
Ibiza & Formentera
Jerusalem
Las Vegas
Lisbon
London Restaurants
Madeira
Madrid
Malta & Gozo
Maui
Melbourne
Menorca

Montreal
New Orleans

Paris
Rome
Seattle
St Lucia
Sydney
Tenerife
Tokyo
Toronto
Vancouver

TRAVEL SPECIALS

First-Time Asia
First-Time Europe
Women Travel

PHRASEBOOKS

Czech
Dutch
Egyptian Arabic
European
French
German
Greek

Hindi & Urdu
Hungarian
Indonesian
Italian
Japanese
Mandarin
  Chinese
Mexican
  Spanish
Polish
Portuguese
Russian
Spanish
Swahili
Thai
Turkish
Vietnamese

ROUGH GUIDES:
Reference and Music CDs

REFERENCE

Blues:
   100 Essential CDs
Classical Music
Classical:
   100 Essential CDs
Country Music
Country:
   100 Essential CDs
Drum'n'bass
House Music
Hip Hop
Irish Music
Jazz

Music USA
Opera
Opera:
   100 Essential CDs
Reggae
Reggae:
   100 Essential CDs
Rock
Rock:
   100 Essential CDs

Soul:
   100 Essential CDs
Techno
World Music

World Music:
   100 Essential CDs
English Football
European Football
Internet
Money Online
Shopping Online
Travel Health

ROUGH GUIDE MUSIC CDs

Music of the Andes
Australian Aboriginal
Bluegrass
Brazilian Music
Cajun & Zydeco
Music of Cape Verde
Classic Jazz
Music of
   Colombia
Cuban Music
Eastern Europe

Music of Egypt
English Roots Music
Flamenco
Music of Greece
Hip Hop
India & Pakistan
Irish Music
Music of Jamaica
Music of Japan
Kenya & Tanzania
Marrabenta
   Mozambique
Native American
North African
Music of Portugal
Reggae
Salsa
Samba
Scottish Music
South African Music
Music of Spain
Sufi Music
Tango

Tex-Mex
West African Music
World Music
World Music Vol 2
Music of Zimbabwe

AVAILABLE AT ALL GOOD BOOKSHOPS